Portlets in Action

Portlets in Action

ASHISH SARIN

MANNING

SHELTER ISLAND

For online information and ordering of this and other Manning books, please visit
www.manning.com. The publisher offers discounts on this book when ordered in quantity.
For more information, please contact

    Special Sales Department
    Manning Publications Co.
    20 Baldwin Road
    PO Box 261
    Shelter Island, NY 11964
    Email: orders@manning.com

Manning Publications Co.	Development editors:	Emily Macel, Jeff Bleiel
20 Baldwin Road	Copyeditor:	Andy Carroll
PO Box 261	Proofreader:	Katie Tennant
Shelter Island, NY 11964	Typesetter:	Dennis Dalinnik
	Cover designer:	Marija Tudor

ISBN: 9781935182542
Printed in the United States of America
1 2 3 4 5 6 7 8 9 10 – MAL – 17 16 15 14 13 12 11

brief contents

v

        10 ■ Personalizing portlets   375
        11 ■ Communicating with other portlets   405
        12 ■ Ajaxing portlets   437
        13 ■ Reusable logic with portlet filters   494
        14 ■ Portlet bridges   510
        15 ■ Web Services for Remote Portlets (WSRP)   533

contents

vii

3 Portlet 2.0 API—portlet objects and container-runtime options   86

preface

I first came across the Java Portlet technology in 2006. I was working on a data warehousing project, and data from different sources was managed by a portal application. My first encounter with the technology wasn't a pleasant one—I faced issues with inter-portlet communication, Ajax, file downloading, and so on. After a lot of struggles and analysis, I was able to get past the limitations inherent in Portlet 1.0 by building ad hoc solutions involving Java servlets to address the business requirements. The design of these solutions resulted in a highly complex system that was hard to maintain and understand. It left me feeling that the Java Portlet technology wasn't ready for developing web portals in the real world.

But even though Portlet 1.0 (JSR-168) had limitations, it didn't stop businesses from taking advantage of the benefits web portals offered—personalization and content aggregation. The lack of support for some critical features in the Java Portlet technology meant that portlets had to rely on portal server–specific extensions, which resulted in portlets that were not portable across different portal servers and were not Portlet 1.0–compliant.

In 2008, Portlet 2.0 (JSR-286) was released, and it addressed the limitations that existed in Portlet 1.0. Portlet 2.0 was a major step forward in the adoption of Java Portlet technology. The portlet technology received a further boost when portlet bridges made it possible to develop applications using existing web frameworks like JSF, Wicket, Struts, and so on, without learning the Java Portlet technology.

Towards the beginning of 2009, I started working on a portal project using Portlet 2.0. Unlike the early days, I no longer had to worry about developing Ajax portlets or implement ad hoc approaches to perform inter-portlet communication. I felt

xix

that the Java Portlet technology had finally arrived. It now addresses all the features that were always expected of it.

During this time, I also evaluated and used Spring Portlet MVC—a subframework of Spring, specifically designed for developing Java portlets. The use of Spring Portlet MVC further simplified the development and testing of portlets, and it became my favorite framework for developing portlets. By early 2009, JSR-329 (Portlet 2.0 Bridge for JavaServer Faces 1.2 specification) was started to simplify the development of JSF portlets using Portlet 2.0; this further supported developing Java portlets using existing web frameworks.

Developing portlets requires not only a good understanding of portlet technology, but also an understanding of how portlet technology can be used with other technologies to develop real-world web portals, and that's the topic of this book. My goal was to open up the exciting world of Java Portlet technology to you and help you get started developing portlets and web portals.

acknowledgments

Writing *Portlets in Action* has been a grueling task because of its length and the diverse content it covers. When I began writing in July 2009, I was not sure if I would be able to consistently give the necessary time and energy to the project over a period of a year or so.

This book has largely been possible because of the readers who took time to post comments on Manning's Author Online forum. The forum has been a constant source of inspiration for me and has kept me motivated to complete the book. I would like to thank Bruce Phillips, Richard Palacios, Barbara Regan, John Joseph Ryan III, and Wayne Lund for taking the time to post their findings and suggestions in the forum, and also for participating in the technical reviews of the book. Doug Warren did an outstanding job of providing detailed comments on and improving the technical content of the book. Thanks also to the following reviewers who gave generously of their time: Joshua White, Lester Martin, Patrick Steger, Srini Penchikala, Prasad Chodavarapu, and Jakub Holy.

This book owes a great deal to Emily Macel at Manning for improving the presentation and structure of the book and helping me transition from a developer to an author. Special thanks to Jeff Bleiel for ensuring that the book met Manning's standards. Thanks as well to Christina Rudloff for getting this book started and to publisher Marjan Bace for giving me the opportunity to write for Manning Publications.

about this book

Portlets are web components, like servlets, that are responsible for accessing distinct applications, systems, or data sources and generating markup fragments to present the content to web portal users. The Java Portlet technology simplifies the process of developing web portals by providing personalization and content aggregation as an integral part of the technology.

Portlets in Action is a step-by-step guide to developing portlets using the Java Portlet technology. The text is complemented by numerous examples to demonstrate how different features of the Java Portlet technology are used in developing portlets. The book covers not only the core Portlet 2.0 API, but also goes beyond to cover leading frameworks that simplify portlet development.

Roadmap

The book is divided into three parts.

Part 1 introduces the Java Portlet technology and includes chapters 1–6. If you're new to portlets, you should read chapters in sequence.

Chapter 1 introduces you to the world of portlets and web portals. In this chapter, you'll learn what portlets and web portals are, and why they're so important in today's world. This chapter lays the foundation for learning the portlet concepts described in later chapters. We'll also look at how to install a Liferay Portal server, set up the Eclipse IDE and a portlet application's project structure, and develop a Hello World portlet.

Chapter 2 takes you an inch deep into the portlet world and presents a simple User Registration portlet. This chapter introduces the portlet lifecycle and some of the commonly used Portlet 2.0 classes and interfaces. It also introduces container-runtime options, which provide additional portlet container features to the portlets. This chapter sets the stage for diving deep into the Java Portlet technology.

Chapters 3 and 4 describe the Portlet 2.0 API in the context of a Book Catalog portlet. In these chapters, we'll look at the different request and response objects used in portlets and the specific features they provide. We'll see how JavaScript and CSS are programmatically added to portal pages, how portlet content is localized using resource bundles, how portlets are secured, and how portlet content is cached. We'll also look at the details of the different container-runtime options defined by the portlet specification.

Chapter 5 shows you how to develop an example Book Portal web portal using Liferay Portal. This chapter shows how a portal server's built-in portlets can help minimize the effort involved in building a web portal. This chapter also shows how the Liferay Plugins SDK can be used to develop a custom theme and layout for a web portal. Readers who are using the GateIn Portal with the examples in this book can refer to appendix A, which describes how to develop a web portal using GateIn Portal.

Chapter 6 introduces portlet tag library tags, which are used for developing portlets with JSP as the view technology. Different portlet tag library tags are introduced in the context of a Book Catalog portlet.

Part 2 of this book shows you how to develop portlets using Spring Portlet MVC, Spring JDBC, and Hibernate. This part includes chapters 7–9, and it's recommended that you read chapters 7 and 8 sequentially.

Chapter 7 introduces the Spring Framework and the classes and interfaces of Spring Portlet MVC. This chapter describes the Spring Portlet MVC architecture and lays the foundation for learning more advanced concepts in Spring Portlet MVC, and it uses a variety of examples to explain different Spring Portlet MVC concepts.

Chapter 8 takes a deep dive into the annotation-driven development support in Spring Portlet MVC and in Spring in general. This chapter covers Spring's form tag library, JSR 303 (Bean Validation), the Spring Validation API, dependency injection using JSR 330 and JSR 250, and Spring's TestContext framework for unit and integration testing. All the concepts are introduced in the context of the example Book Catalog portlet.

Chapter 9 looks at how you can write database-driven portlets using the Spring JDBC module and Hibernate. This chapter also provides a quick introduction to aspect-oriented programming and transaction support in Spring. The concepts described in this chapter are put to use while developing the example Book Catalog portlet.

Part 3 of the book covers advanced concepts in portlet development, including inter-portlet communication, WSRP, personalization, portlet bridges, Ajax/Comet, and portlet filters. This part of the book includes chapters 10–15, and there's no need to read the chapters in this part sequentially.

Chapter 10 looks at the personalization support available in portlets and how it can be used to personalize the content and behavior of a portlet. In the context of the Book Catalog portlet, this chapter shows how preferences are defined for a portlet, saved into a persistent store, and later retrieved to personalize the content and behavior of the portlet.

Chapter 11 looks at different techniques for inter-portlet communication, using sessions, public render parameters, and events. The examples in this chapter show how each communication technique is implemented.

Chapter 12 introduces Ajax and how it's used for developing highly responsive portlets. The chapter looks at different Ajax frameworks, like jQuery, DWR, and Dojo, to show how each one of them can be used to incorporate Ajax features in portlets. This chapter also looks at how Comet (or Reverse Ajax) is used for developing real-time portlets. The chapter makes use of numerous code examples to demonstrate these concepts.

Chapter 13 introduces you to the world of portlet bridges, which are used to expose existing web applications as portlets. The chapter shows how a JSF 2.0 web application and a Wicket web application can be exposed as portlets using portlet bridges.

Chapter 14 looks at developing portlets that make use of portlet filters for pre- and post-processing portlet requests and responses.

Chapter 15 looks at how Web Services for Remote Portlets (WSRP) can be used by a web portal to publish portlets to the external world, so that they can then be consumed by other web portals.

Appendix A introduces the GateIn Portal and describes the steps required to create an example Book Portal web portal.

Appendix B shows how to configure Liferay Portal to use a MySQL database.

How to use this book

This book contains numerous working examples that demonstrate how to develop portlets using Portlet 2.0 and other leading frameworks, like Spring Portlet MVC, Hibernate, DWR, Spring JDBC, Dojo, jQuery, and so on. The book contains CODE REFERENCE callouts to inform you when you should import an Eclipse project into your Eclipse IDE for reference. I recommend that you install the Liferay Portal or GateIn Portal and try out the examples while reading the book, and that you refer to the source code when it's suggested in the text. This approach will help you learn portal and portlet development more effectively.

Who should read this book?

In writing this book, I haven't assumed that you have any prior knowledge of the Java Portlet technology or the different frameworks referenced here. The concepts are described in such a way that readers who have prior knowledge of web application development using JSPs and servlets can easily understand the content.

The different frameworks covered in this book, like Spring Portlet MVC, Spring JDBC, Hibernate, Spring AOP, DWR, Dojo, jQuery, and so on, are gently introduced, so that the example portlets can be easily understood even if you're new to these frameworks.

If you have prior experience working with web portals using Portlet 1.0, you'll also find this book useful, because it explains the new features introduced in Portlet 2.0 and how to go about creating portlets that make use of frameworks like Spring Portlet MVC, Spring AOP, Spring JDBC, Spring Transaction, Hibernate, Dojo, jQuery, and DWR.

Because the book provides complete coverage of Portlet 2.0's features and integration with different frameworks, portal architects will also find this book useful for architecting solutions around Portlet 2.0.

Source code conventions

This book contains numerous examples that include portlet classes, XML configuration files for portlets and portal servers, JSP pages, build.xml files for the Ant build tool, and pom.xml files for the Maven build tool. The code explained in the book targets Liferay Portal server. GateIn Portal–specific Eclipse projects additionally contain a README.TXT file that specifies GateIn Portal–specific changes made to the portlets developed for Liferay Portal.

In the text, a `monospace typeface` is used to denote code (JSP, Java, and XML) as well as Java methods, JSP tag names, and other code elements.

Java, HTML, and XML can all be quite verbose, and in many cases the original source code (available online) has been reformatted, adding line breaks and reworking indentation, to accommodate the available page space in the book. In rare cases, even this was not enough, and listings include line continuation markers (➥).

Additionally, comments in the source code have been removed from the listings presented in the book. Code annotations accompany many of the source code listings, highlighting important concepts. In some cases, numbered bullets link to explanations in the text following the listing.

Software requirements

To deploy and run the example portlets in this book, you need to install GateIn Portal 3.1, Liferay Portal 6 CE GA3, or any Portlet 2.0–compliant portlet container. GateIn Portal 3.1 and Liferay Portal 6 CE GA3 are freely downloadable and have low memory footprints. The examples in this book make use of Liferay Portal and GateIn Portal, which come bundled with the Tomcat server.

Chapters 3 and 4 make use of Jetspeed and GlassFish Server with OpenPortal Portlet Container to show that support for some of the Portlet 2.0 features varies from one portal server to another. If you want to test the example Book Catalog portlet described in chapters 3 and 4, you'll need to install Jetspeed 2.2.1 and GlassFish Server 3.0.1 with OpenPortal Portlet Container 2.1.

To run the example portlets in chapter 9, you'll also need to install the MySQL database and HeidiSQL client, the details of which are provided in appendix B.

Source code downloads

The source code for all the examples in this book is available from Manning's web site: www.manning.com/PortletsinAction/. The examples have been provided for both GateIn Portal and Liferay Portal servers, and they've been tested on GateIn Portal 3.1 and Liferay Portal 6 CE GA3, but they'll work on any Portlet 2.0–compliant portlet container with little or no modification.

The source code explained in this book is for Liferay Portal. Because GateIn Portal required some minor changes to the source code, these changes have been recorded in the README.TXT file that you'll find in the Eclipse projects for GateIn Portal.

To run the examples, you can download the Tomcat bundle for GateIn Portal or Liferay Portal and deploy the example portlets as described in chapter 1 (for Liferay Portal) and in appendix A (for GateIn Portal).

The source code for the book is divided into separate Eclipse projects, and the names of the folders reflect the chapter to which the example belongs. For instance, if the folder name is ch7_Controllers, the source code is for chapter 7. Each example can be built by using either Ant or Maven, and the steps required are explained in chapter 1.

Author Online

Purchase of *Portlets in Action* includes free access to a private web forum run by Manning Publications where you can make comments about the book, ask technical questions, and receive help from the author and from other users. To access the forum and subscribe to it, point your web browser to www.manning.com/PortletsinAction. This page provides information on how to get on the forum once you're registered, what kind of help is available, and the rules of conduct on the forum.

Manning's commitment to our readers is to provide a venue where a meaningful dialog between individual readers and between readers and the author can take place. It is not a commitment to any specific amount of participation on the part of the author, whose contribution to the Author Online forum remains voluntary (and unpaid). We suggest you try asking the author some challenging questions lest his interest stray!

The Author Online forum and the archives of previous discussions will be accessible from the publisher's website as long as the book is in print.

about the cover illustration

The figure on the cover of *Portlets in Action* is captioned "Le petit fermier," which means smallholder or the owner of a small farm, just large enough to support one family. The illustration is taken from a nineteenth-century edition of Sylvain Maréchal's four-volume compendium of regional dress customs published in France. Each illustration is finely drawn and colored by hand. The rich variety of Maréchal's collection reminds us vividly of how culturally apart the world's towns and regions were just 200 years ago. Isolated from each other, people spoke different dialects and languages. In the streets or in the countryside, it was easy to identify where they lived and what their trade or station in life was just by their dress.

Dress codes have changed since then and the diversity by region, so rich at the time, has faded away. It is now hard to tell apart the inhabitants of different continents, let alone different towns or regions. Perhaps we have traded cultural diversity for a more varied personal life—certainly for a more varied and fast-paced technological life.

At a time when it is hard to tell one computer book from another, Manning celebrates the inventiveness and initiative of the computer business with book covers based on the rich diversity of regional life of two centuries ago, brought back to life by Maréchal's pictures.

Part 1

Getting started with portlet development

Developing a web portal requires understanding the challenges it addresses—challenges that can't be addressed by a group of distinct web applications. Also, web portals require certain distinctive features, and your choice of technology plays a crucial role in how easily you can develop a web portal.

In this part of the book, you'll learn the basics of web portals and Java portlet technology. As you progress through these chapters, you'll discover how portlet technology simplifies the development of web portals. Java portlets are deployed in a portlet container, which is similar to a servlet container, so a substantial portion of this part of the book focuses on the portlet container's features and how you can use them to implement your portlets. Toward the end of this part, you'll develop a real-world web portal example to get a feel for web portals.

Introducing portals and portlets

This chapter covers

- An overview of portals and the Java portlet technology
- Installing and using Liferay Portal
- Setting up the Eclipse IDE and creating the project structure
- Developing a Hello World portlet

When the internet first came about, "content" reigned supreme. Then the "user experience" took over. If you've been an internet user for the last couple of years, this transformation didn't go unnoticed. During this transformation, most websites got a facelift intended to enrich the user experience by providing user-customizable themes and features that allow users to control *what* content is presented and *how* it's presented.

The lack of a standard approach and technology to address user-experience requirements, such as personalization, customization, and content aggregation in web applications, led to ad hoc ways of implementing these features. The result was maintenance nightmares, lost developer productivity, and longer turnaround time for incorporating new features. With the arrival of the Java portlet technology, this has changed. The Java portlet technology provides a standard approach to incorporating user-experience features in web applications.

The Java portlet technology isn't a standalone technology, and using JSPs and servlets (along with portlets) in portal development is common. The Java portlet technology not only helps you quickly build a web portal but also provides service orchestration, in which distinct services can be integrated seamlessly at the user interface layer, allowing businesses to quickly adapt to changes.

This chapter will first introduce you to web portals and the portlet technology, and to the infrastructure you need to deploy a web portal that uses portlet technology. Most of the latter half of this chapter is dedicated to quickly getting started with Liferay Portal and setting up the Eclipse IDE. Towards the end of this chapter, you'll see how to deploy a Hello World portlet on Liferay Portal.

The concepts behind portlets can be best understood through deploying example portlets on a portal server and adding them to a portal page. We use Liferay Portal in this book because of its ease of installation, intuitive interface, low memory footprint, and more importantly, you can download and use the Community Edition of Liferay Portal for free. This book touches upon some of the features of Liferay Portal at a high level, but it shouldn't be considered a reference or user guide for Liferay Portal.

> **NOTE** Even though this book uses Liferay Portal for deploying and running portlets, the concepts covered in the book are generic and can be used for developing portlets for any Portlet 2.0–compliant portal server.

If you're already familiar with the concepts behind portals and portlet technology, you may want to skim or skip this chapter. If you're new to portlets, this chapter will give you a solid foundation for the rest of the book.

As portals and portlet technology go hand in hand, we'll first look at what a web portal is and how portlets can be used to develop a web portal.

1.1   What is a portal?

Everyone who's been using the internet knows something about portals. It's not a new concept, but there was no formal definition until recently.

A *portal* is a collection of mini web applications, called *portlets*. A portal supports features like personalization, content aggregation, authentication, and customization. Portlets act as windowed web applications within the portal, and each window in a portal web page (called a *portal page*) represents a portlet.

To get a feel for portals, you can visit the iGoogle portal (http://www.google.com/ig). Figure 1.1 shows the iGoogle portal home page after a user logs into it. You can see portlets showing emails from Gmail, headlines from CNN, content from YouTube, and so on. The portlets can be personalized by users to change the number of emails displayed in the portlet, the number of CNN headlines they want to view, the location they want to receive RSS feeds from, and so on. Users can drag and drop these portlet windows on the portal page to customize the way

Figure 1.1 The iGoogle home page containing portlets that show information from different sources: CNN, YouTube, Gmail, and so on. The portlets display the most relevant content and provide limited features to the user, in contrast to full-fledged web applications.

information is organized. They can also choose to add more portlets or remove one or more of them from the portal page.

The take-away from figure 1.1 is that the user gets a unified view of information from different sources. This is similar to a TV showing different channels in distinct windows on the screen.

> **NOTE** I've referred to portlets as *mini web applications* because they provide limited information and features to the user compared to the original web applications they represent. For example, in figure 1.1, the Gmail portlet displays email and provides options to compose or delete emails, but it doesn't provide an option to add emails to your tasks list, which is provided by the original Gmail web application.

The core business functionality provided by a portal is no different from what a set of distinct web applications would provide. In figure 1.1, the content (information or service) provided by the Gmail, YouTube, and CNN portlets is also provided by the Gmail, CNN, and YouTube applications.

But if the business functionality remains the same, what's the business value in creating a portal? In figure 1.1, the information displayed to the user comes from disparate data sources (as depicted in figure 1.2), and the portal aggregates the information to provide a consolidated view to the user.

The use of portals to aggregate content from different sources results in increased efficiency for the user, and an enriched user experience, because the user doesn't need to go to distinct web applications to access the content. In figure 1.2, the portlets

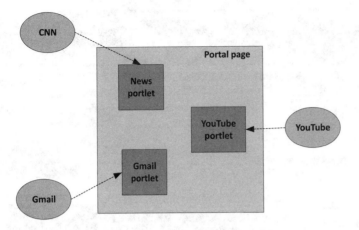

Figure 1.2   Portals aggregate content from different information sources.
The portlets on the iGoogle portal page generate content for the page by
retrieving information from the CNN, YouTube, and Gmail applications.

on the iGoogle portal page display the most frequently accessed information or features from the applications they represent.

> **NOTE**   Developing a web portal makes good business sense if you need to gather and present information from various data sources, applications, and systems to users based on their identity. It's expected that the user experience will be enhanced by a single point of entry to the information, and by the flexibility to customize and personalize the information that's provided.

Now that you know about portals, let's take a look at the benefits of using portals, compared to web applications, for content aggregation and personalization.

1.2   Benefits of web portals

Web portals provide benefits beyond those of a group of distinct web applications that serve content. In this section, we'll look at how end users access content from different information sources using distinct web applications, and how web portals and web applications can coexist to take the user experience to new heights.

For instance, a user might access content from different sources by directly accessing different web applications, or by accessing those web applications from an intranet website, or by using a combination of web portals and web applications.

1.2.1   Enriched user experience

Let's say that as an employee of an organization you need to frequently access organization-specific business-to-employee (B2E) applications (like time card, help desk, knowledge management, and service request applications) so you can keep track of missing time cards, recently published articles, closed help desk tickets, and so on. These different web applications have their own data sources, and you'd usually

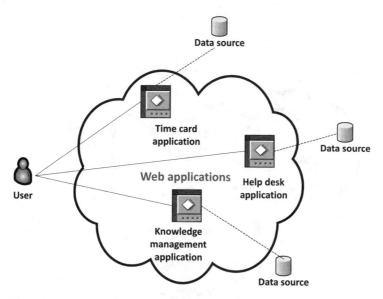

Figure 1.3 In this scenario, the user interacts with multiple web applications to access content. A separate web application exists to access content from each of the distinct sources of information.

need to go to each of these different applications to access this information. This interaction between employee and B2E applications is represented in figure 1.3.

This isn't an optimal way of accessing information and services, because you need to go to different web applications and authenticate each time. An intranet site that provides a single sign-on feature and access to all these different applications would be a better solution.

Suppose the organization takes a step ahead and provides a single sign-on solution and access to the different web applications from an intranet site, as represented in figure 1.4. By providing the single sign-on feature, the organization has provided easy access to the B2E applications, but you still need to filter the information that interests you. For example, if you're interested only in automobile-related articles, you'll have to search for the articles in the knowledge management application; if you're only interested in your open help desk tickets, you'll need to search for them in the help desk application; and so on.

These individual B2E applications may provide some level of personalization and customization based on your identity and preferences, but this approach still fails to provide a unified view of information and easy access to services offered by different B2E applications. For instance, you still need to go to the help desk application to access its information and services.

The ideal scenario for an employee is to view information and access the most commonly used services from distinct B2E applications in a single application. This scenario is represented in figure 1.5 and is achieved using intranet portals. Here, the

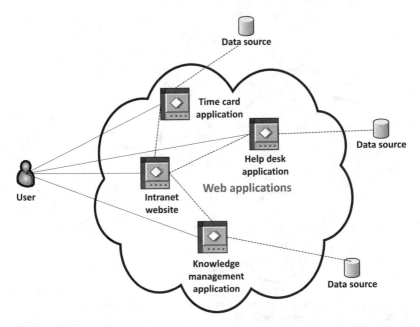

Figure 1.4 The organization's intranet makes it easy for users to access different web applications by redirecting users to the original web applications. In this scenario, the user is still interacting with individual web applications for information and services.

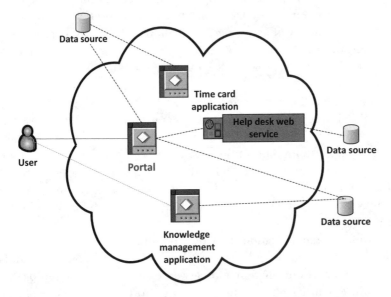

Figure 1.5 The organization's intranet portal gathers content from different data sources, which means that users don't need to access different web applications for information or services. In figure 1.4, the intranet website simply redirected users to the original web applications, but when using portals, the user is taken to the original web application only if little-accessed information or services are requested by the user.

user mostly interacts with the portal, and in some cases also with the original web application. For instance, the portal directs the user to the knowledge management web application if certain features or details are requested by the user.

Usually, portals provide users with the most-used features of the original web application, and when less-used features are requested, the portal redirects the user to the original application. The portal may not even display the least-used features but may instead provide an option to visit the original application.

Some of the web portal's functionality may be built into the portal itself, so that no external web applications or systems are involved. For instance, if you don't have a separate content management system available, you could develop it as part of your web portal.

> **NOTE** The design of existing systems greatly affects how quickly a business can start using portals. In figure 1.5, information for the knowledge management and time card applications comes from the databases that were used by these applications, which requires rewriting the business logic. In contrast, the help desk application's business logic is accessed using Web Services because the application was designed as a set of services that can be reused by other applications—a service-oriented architecture (SOA) approach. It's recommended that applications make use of SOA internally, because it allows you to expose business functionality as a service in the future, saving you the effort of redoing the business logic.

Portlets in a web portal provide limited content compared to the dedicated web applications they represent, which means portals have to be used along with web applications to provide content to the user.

> **Portals complement web applications**
>
> Portals aren't a replacement for web applications but are meant to extend the functionality of existing web applications. Portals gather relevant content from the existing information systems and display it to users based on their identity and preferences. When certain information or features are requested by the user, the portal redirects the users to the original web applications.

1.2.2 Unified information view

Web applications generally target a part of the business process and not the complete business. For example, there would be separate web applications for customer management, inventory, order processing, and so on. These web applications give a disjointed view of the business, because the inventory application doesn't know about orders placed, and the customer management application doesn't know about the inventory status.

These web applications don't need to know about information managed by other web applications, but a business user might need a unified view of the business. A web portal can bridge the information gap between these individual web applications by bringing information together from the different data sources used by these web applications, and presenting it to a business user, providing the unified view that's required.

The portlets in a web portal are dynamic, and they may interact with each other to show relevant information in response to user actions. For instance, in a Weather portal (which contains Location and Weather portlets), if a user selects a city from the Location portlet, the Weather portlet updates the content to display the weather forecast for the selected city. In contrast, web applications communicate with each other using databases or messaging middleware. The result of such communication isn't immediately visible and requires users to access the web applications separately to view the effects of the communicated information.

One size doesn't fit all

Portals aren't the answer to every business requirement; organizations should consider carefully whether there is a business case for developing a portal. If the business requirement doesn't require gathering content from distinct information systems to loosely integrate disparate systems, the business should consider developing independent web applications to meet the business requirement.

The personalization and customization features of portals are important from the user's perspective. From the business's perspective, the most important requirement to consider is content aggregation.

A portal consists of multiple portal pages, just as web applications consist of multiple web pages. The only way content can be added to a portal page is via portlets.

1.3   What is a portlet?

A *portlet* is a pluggable user interface component that provides specific content, which could be a service or information from existing information systems. Portlets provide the user interface of the portal by accessing distinct applications, systems, or data sources and generating markup fragments to present their content to portal users. Some examples of portlets are a Weather portlet that provides weather information for a city by accessing a Yahoo! Weather RSS feed, or a Help Desk portlet that displays the pending help desk tickets from a database.

The primary responsibility of a portlet is to generate a markup fragment (such as HTML, XML, or WML), which is then displayed on a portal page within a window, called a *portlet window.* A portal page usually displays multiple portlets in distinct portlet windows, each with its own title and set of buttons to change its look and feel, set its preferences, and maximize, minimize, or remove the window.

Figure 1.6 shows what a portlet window looks like when rendered on a portal page. The options available for a portlet, such as changing window state, preferences, and

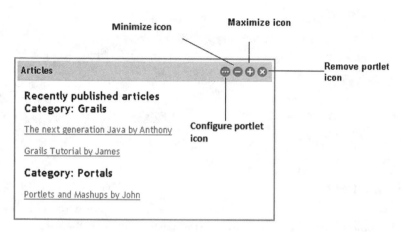

Figure 1.6 An Articles portlet with buttons to configure, minimize, maximize, and close the portlet window. The options shown for a portlet will vary depending upon its configuration and the user's access permissions.

configuration, may vary based on the user's permissions and the configuration of the portlet in the portal.

Portlets are *pluggable user interface components*, which means a portlet is responsible for generating the user interface specific to that component, unlike servlets, where the user interface isn't componentized. So what makes portlets pluggable user interface components?

A portlet generates a markup fragment, and not the complete portal page. The responsibility of displaying the complete portal page rests with the *portal server*, which aggregates fragments generated by portlets and displays them in the portlet windows on the portal page. This division of responsibility makes it possible for a portlet to focus on generating its own user interface.

Like any software component, portlets can be combined with other portlets to create a web portal, bringing pluggability to the user interface. For instance, a News portlet that shows news from the CNN website can be used in any web portal that intends to show news from CNN.

> **NOTE** A web application that contains portlets is referred as a *portlet application*. In the rest of the book, I'll use *web application* to refer to applications consisting of servlets and JSPs and *portlet application* to refer to a web application consisting of portlets (which may also contain servlets and JSPs). A portlet application usually also contains servlets and JSPs.

Portlets generate user interfaces and so do servlets. It's possible to create a web portal using Java servlet technology, but there are limitations. In the next section, we'll look at the reasons for choosing portlets over servlets and widgets or gadgets. We'll also look at why portlets are best suited for creating *mashups*.

> **The Portlet 1.0 vs. Portlet 2.0 specification**
> The two versions of the Java Portlet Specification that currently exist are 1.0 (described by JSR 168) and 2.0 (described by JSR 286). The 2.0 specification addresses most of the frequently required features of portlets that were missing from the 1.0 specification, such as resource serving (discussed in chapter 12), inter-portlet communication (chapter 11), and portlet filters (chapter 13). Most portlet containers support both specifications, and the 2.0 specification is backward compatible with the 1.0 specification.

1.4   Why use portlets?

In the service-oriented architecture (SOA), service orchestration (or collaboration) makes it possible to develop applications from existing services. As portlets represent services and are pluggable components, you can get plug and play behavior using portlets. Because portlets can interact with each other at the user interface layer (a process referred to as *inter-portlet communication*), they play a crucial role in developing SOA applications.

If the services represented by portlets in a portal need to interact with each other to orchestrate a service, the portlets need to communicate. The portlet specification enables this inter-portlet communication using *events* and *public render parameters*. The *portlet container* is responsible for handling the communication between portlets, keeping communicating portlets and the distinct services they represent independent of each other.

> **NOTE**   The integration between services is only at the presentation layer; services don't interact directly with each other, but through the presentation layer provided by the portlets.

One of the most important features of portlets is inter-portlet communication, which is built into the portlet architecture.

1.4.1   Inter-portlet communication vs. inter-servlet communication

Inter-portlet communication makes it possible to develop web portals in which portlets can update their content based on actions taken by users in other portlets.

Let's say there are three portlets:

- *Location portlet*—Allows users to search for and select a city
- *Weather portlet*—Provides weather information service for a city
- *Businesses portlet*—Provides information about businesses in a city

The location, weather, and businesses services are distinct services, and each of the portlets wrapping these services generates a user interface specific to the service, as shown in figure 1.7. For instance, the Location portlet will generate a user interface that allows users to search for and select a city, and the Businesses portlet will display information about a business based on predefined categories. The Location portlet

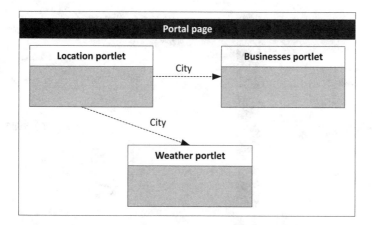

Figure 1.7   The Location, Businesses, and Weather portlets interact with each other. The city information is passed from the Location portlet to the other portlets using the inter-portlet communication mechanism, resulting in seamless integration of the services represented by the portlets.

can interact with the Weather and Businesses portlets via the inter-portlet communication mechanisms provided by the portlet container, resulting in seamless integration of the services.

Servlets generate complete web pages, not markup fragments, and they can't work in collaboration with other servlets to generate a complete web page. A servlet can be designed to encapsulate a service, but it will be a standalone service because the web container doesn't allow communication between servlets unless they're directly dependent upon each other.

Let's now look at how widgets compare to portlets.

1.4.2   Portlets vs. widgets

Widgets (commonly also called *gadgets*) are similar to Java portlets in the sense that they're used to aggregate content from distinct data sources on a web page, and they provide some level of personalization of content and behavior. You can quickly develop a widget if you know JavaScript and XML; there's a steeper learning curve involved with the Java portlet technology.

Portlets, in contrast, are well suited for medium to complex application requirements, which are often seen in enterprise portals. Portlets provide a sophisticated API to standardize inter-portlet communication, request processing, and server-side session management. The portal infrastructure, which includes a *portlet container* and *portal server*, provides portlet instance lifecycle management, instance pooling, content caching, security, a consistent look and feel, and single sign-on features to your web portal.

It is important to note that widgets in a web page typically interact directly with information systems to generate their content. The web page shows aggregated content because it contains different widgets, which interact with different information

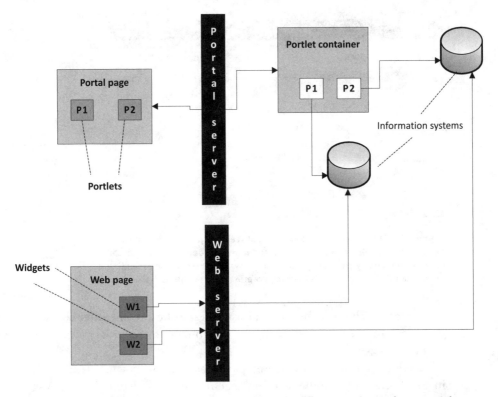

Figure 1.8   A portal server aggregates content generated by different portlets to form a portal page. Widgets in a web page interact with different information systems to obtain their content.

systems, so no special mechanism is employed by a web page containing widgets to show aggregated content. In contrast, a portal server aggregates content generated by portlets to form a portal page.

Figure 1.8 highlights the difference in how aggregated content is displayed using widgets and portlets. It shows a portal page containing portlets P1 and P2 and a web page containing widgets W1 and W2. The portal page is generated by the portal server after aggregating content generated by the portlets. The web page doesn't need any special mechanism to show aggregated content because W1 and W2 generate their content by directly interacting with their information systems.

If you're using portlets, that doesn't mean you can't use widgets in your web portal. Portal servers like Liferay Portal and WebSphere Portal, provide built-in portlets that integrate with Google gadgets to provide access to the services offered by the gadgets.

> **NOTE**   With the use of *portlet bridges*, which we'll discuss in chapter 14, you can also develop portlets as web applications, using well-established frameworks like Spring MVC, JSF, Wicket, and Struts, without learning portlet technology.

Let's now look at what a mashup is and how portlets can be used to create mashups.

1.4.3   Creating mashups

A *mashup* is an application that uses data or services from distinct sources and combines them to produce a new user service. Portlets can be used to create mashups by aggregating data from different data sources and combining it.

An important distinction between mashups and portals is that portals don't really combine information from different sources to provide a new user service; instead they show information from different sources in different portlets. Mashups, on the other hand, combine information to provide a new service. An application that searches several different shopping engines to find the lowest price for a product is an example of a mashup.

Because portlets are responsible for interacting with data sources to provide information to users, you can create portlets that interact with multiple data sources, and combine the data to provide a new service to the user. Additionally, users can specify preferences about the data source or the type of information they're interested in, resulting in a personalized mashup.

Now that you know what a portal is and how portlets provide content for a portal, let's see what's involved in deploying portals.

1.5   Portal infrastructure

When creating web applications using servlets, the web container provides the environment that manages the servlet and the web server is responsible for serving web pages to the web browser. Similarly, portlets are managed by the *portlet container,* and the *portal server* is responsible for serving portal pages to the web browser. The portlet container and portal server together form part of the portal infrastructure required for deploying web portals.

Let's look at the portal server and portlet container features in detail and at how they work together to deliver content.

1.5.1   The portlet container

A portlet on a portal page is represented by a portlet instance inside the portlet container. Figure 1.9 shows the portal infrastructure components and how they fit together.

A portlet container's responsibilities include managing portlet instances and sending the fragments generated by the portlets to the portal server for aggregation.

LIFECYCLE MANAGEMENT
The portlet container is responsible for invoking lifecycle methods on the portlet instances and providing them with the required runtime environment. A portlet container is an extension to a servlet container; it provides what a servlet container provides, and it additionally manages the portlet instances. The portlets access their runtime environment using the `PortletContext` object (similar to `ServletContext`), which allows portlets to share data with other portlets and with servlets in the same portlet application.

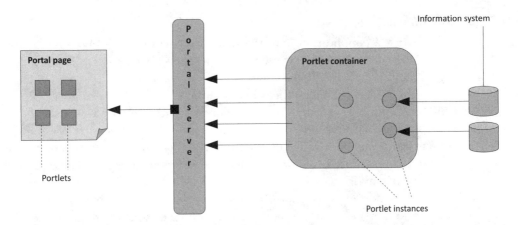

Figure 1.9 The portal infrastructure consists of a portal server and a portlet container. The portlet container manages the portlet instances and hands over the markup fragments generated by the portlets to the portal server. The portal server aggregates the markup fragments to create the portal page.

PORTLET PORTABILITY

A portlet container must follow the requirements laid down by the Portlet 2.0 specification in order for portlets to be portable across portlet containers. Most portlet containers provide extensions to the base set of requirements detailed in the specification, and it's the choice of the portlet developer whether to use such features or not. Using these extensions will make the portlets noncompliant with the specification, so they won't be portable across different portlet containers. If you're developing portlets targeted to a specific portlet container, and they don't need to be portable, you should consider using container-specific extensions.

1.5.2 *The portal server*

The portal server is responsible for submitting user requests received from the portal page to the portlet container, and for aggregating responses generated by portlets to form the portal page. A portal server is responsible for generating the portal page, so the responsibility of providing a consistent look and feel for the portal lies with the portal server.

> **NOTE** You can consider a portal server as a component that sits between the user requests from the portal page and the portlet container.

A portlet container isn't responsible for generating the portal page; it hands over the content generated by the portlets to the portal server, which aggregates the content and displays the portal page. Figure 1.10 shows the interaction between portal page, portal server, portlet container, and portlet instance when handling a portlet request.

There are many open source portal servers (such as Liferay Portal and GateIn Portal) and commercial ones (such as IBM's WebSphere Portal) that provide a wide range of features (administration, content management, search, single sign-on, and so on)

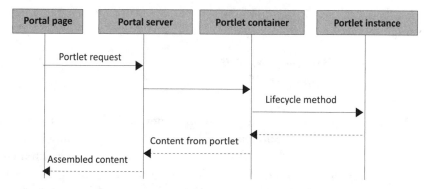

Figure 1.10   The portal server and portlet container roles in handling a portlet request. The portlet container is responsible for invoking lifecycle methods and handing over the portlet content to the portal server. The portal server assembles the content from different portlets to generate the portal page.

to portal developers, making it easy to quickly set up a fully functional portal. The choice of portal server plays an important role in portal projects, because it can help you reduce the development time by providing built-in portlets, integration with external systems (LDAP, SAP, and so on), and the ability to access portal server functionality from your custom portlets.

CHOOSING A PORTAL SERVER

A portal server's biggest assets are the built-in portlets that it provides. The choice of a portal server should be driven by comparing your portal requirements with the features that are provided out of the box by the various portal servers. For instance, if your portal requires a discussion forum, a document library, and announcements, you should evaluate portal servers based on whether they have built-in portlets for these functions.

   The requirements of a portal may change over a period of time as business requirements evolve, and it may be difficult to implement certain functions that weren't considered when selecting the portal server. To take care of such scenarios, you should also consider how easy it is to customize the behavior and information displayed by the built-in portlets, and whether portlets can access the portal server's features (document storage facility, workflow services, and so on) to address new business requirements.

   Now that you have some understanding of portals and portlet technology, let's install and use Liferay Portal.

> **NOTE**   If you prefer to use GateIn Portal for developing and deploying portlets, please refer to appendix A for details on how to install and use that portal server. Separate source directories have also been provided, containing examples tailored for deployment on GateIn Portal. You'll find that there's hardly any difference in the example code for GateIn and Liferay. The examples for GateIn Portal contain a README.TXT file that highlights the changes

that were made to the configuration or source code to adapt Liferay Portal examples to work on GateIn Portal.

1.6   Getting started with Liferay Portal

Regardless of which portal server you're using, the basic steps for creating a portlet and setting it into action are the same:

1 Install the portal server and portlet container. In most cases, the portlet container and portal server are packaged together as a single component.
2 Create portal pages, which you can think of as blank web pages with no content.
3 Set up your favorite IDE to create a portlet application project.
4 Write a portlet class that contains the logic to generate the markup fragment.
5 Create portlet configuration files to register the portlet with the portal server.
6 Create a portlet deployment descriptor.
7 Package portlets in a WAR file using a build tool like Ant or Maven.
8 Deploy the portlet WAR file on the portal server.
9 Add portlets to the portal page.

In this section, we'll cover steps 1 and 2. You'll see how to install Liferay Portal (Community Edition), and we'll cover some of the basic Liferay Portal features. You'll create a portal page called "My Home Page" (which you'll later add portlets to).

Step 3 is covered in section 1.7, and steps 4–9 are covered in section 1.8. If you already have a portal server installed and your favorite IDE configured, you can go directly to section 1.8 to learn how to create a simple Hello World portlet.

1.6.1   Installing Liferay Portal 6.x

Liferay Portal comes prepackaged with widely used application servers like Glassfish, JBoss, and Tomcat. In this book, we'll be using Liferay Portal with Apache Tomcat, which is a lightweight application server that's easy to install.

You can download the bundle containing Liferay Portal and Tomcat from the Liferay Portal website (http://www.liferay.com/downloads/liferay-portal/available-releases), which maintains a list of all the downloadable versions of Liferay Portal. Download the zip file with the name Liferay-portal-tomcat-6.x, which means Liferay Portal version 6.x bundled with Tomcat.

Installing the prepackaged bundle involves unzipping the downloaded file in a local directory. This will result in a single directory, liferay-portal-6.x (which we'll refer to as LIFERAY_HOME).

You should familiarize yourself with the two most important directories inside LIFERAY_HOME (both of which are shown in figure 1.11):

- *deploy*—This directory is used for hot deployment of portlets. If you copy your portlet WAR file into the deploy folder while the server's running, the server hot deploys the portlets, which saves you the time of restarting the server to deploy portlets.

- *tomcat-6.x*—This is the Tomcat application server directory, which contains startup and shutdown scripts for the application server. Because Liferay Portal runs on top of the application server, you need to run the Tomcat server's startup script to use Liferay Portal.

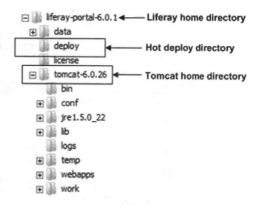

Figure 1.11   The directory structure for the Liferay-Tomcat prepackaged bundle. The deploy directory is the hot deployment directory, and tomcat-6.0.26 is the Tomcat home directory.

All portal servers (such as GateIn Portal, Liferay Portal, and WebSphere Portal) come with their own internal database, which contains the initial configuration data required by the portal server, the portal user information, the portlet preferences, and a lot more. As you add users, portlets, portlet preferences, and web content to your portal, the information is saved in the portal's database. By default, Liferay Portal comes with an embedded HSQLDB database, which is lightweight and has a small memory footprint. HSQLDB isn't meant to be used in production and is ideally suited for development purposes only. If you're planning to use HSQLDB for development purposes (where multiple developers need to access the same HSQLDB database instance), running the HSQLDB in *server* mode is recommended. For more information regarding HSQLDB, see the HSQLDB website (www.hsqldb.org).

Before running the portal server, check that Java SE 5 or later is installed on your system and that the JAVA_HOME environment variable is set to the installation directory of Java SE 5. Verify that the installation is correct by running the startup.bat (on Windows) or startup.sh (on UNIX) script in the LIFERAY_HOME/tomcat-6.0.26/bin directory.

It may take some time for the server to start the first time, because Liferay Portal creates its internal database and populates it with the setup data required to use the sample application that comes with it. This only happens the first time it's run; after this, the server startup is faster.

If the server startup is clean—without errors—the server will start up the system's default browser and open the Liferay Portal home page. You can also directly access the Liferay Portal home page at http://localhost:8080 using your favorite browser. If you see the Liferay Portal home page (shown in figure 1.12), it indicates that you have successfully installed Liferay Portal.

Once the server starts, you can start playing around with the sample application that comes with the Liferay Portal installation.

Liferay Portal provides a feature-rich, intuitive administrator user interface for adding users, organizations, and roles; associating roles to users; adding portlets;

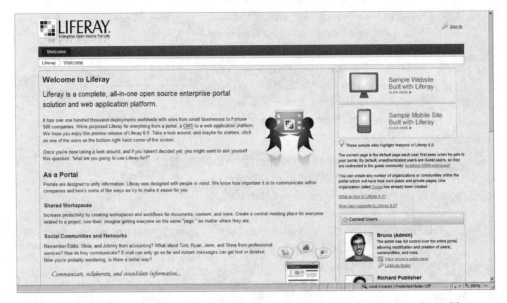

Figure 1.12 The Liferay Portal home page shows information about the portal server along with information about the sample website and the preconfigured users.

creating portal pages; and so on. The next few sections will familiarize you with some of these management capabilities.

1.6.2 Registering users with Liferay Portal

A guest user (an unauthenticated user) in Liferay Portal will see an option to sign in at the top-right corner of the home page, as shown in figure 1.13.

Clicking on the Sign In option will display a Sign In page. Because you don't have an account with Liferay Portal when you access it for the first time, you can select the Create Account option (as shown in figure 1.14).

You can create an account by entering all the information that's asked for. If the account

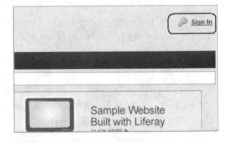

Figure 1.13   The Sign In option on the Liferay Portal home page

is created successfully, Liferay Portal displays a success message along with the initial password assigned to the newly created user. Use the newly created userid (which is your email ID) and password to log in to the portal.

Let's now look at how you can create a public portal page in Liferay Portal.

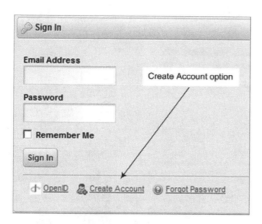

Figure 1.14 The Create Account option is for creating a user account with Liferay Portal

1.6.3 Creating a public portal page in Liferay Portal

Once you log in to Liferay Portal, it shows you a *dockbar*, which offers options available to an authenticated user, as shown in figure 1.15.

The Manage > Control Panel option allows authenticated users to manage their account and create public or private portal pages. A *public* page is accessible to all users (including anonymous users) of the portal, and a *private* page is accessible only to the logged-in user who created the private page.

A private page may be created by the user, or it may be set up for the user by the portal administrator. An example of a private page set up by an administrator is the iGoogle home page that a user sees after logging in, as shown in figure 1.16. (Figure 1.1, earlier in this chapter, showed a customized portal page with additional portlets.)

The content of a private page can be customized or personalized by the user. Similarly, a user who creates a public page can customize or personalize the page, and the changes will be visible to other users of the portal.

To view the public and private pages set up by an administrator or created by you, select Manage > Control Panel from the dockbar (see figure 1.15). The Control Panel page shows My Account, My Pages, and other options. Figure 1.17 shows the information displayed when the user selects the My Pages option.

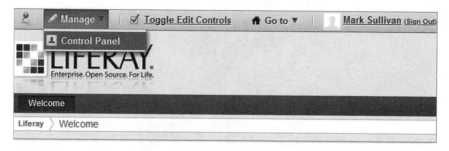

Figure 1.15 Authenticated users can do more things than unauthenticated users in Liferay Portal, such as changing their account settings and managing their public and private portal pages.

Figure 1.16   The iGoogle home page that users see when they log in. By default, the portal page has preconfigured portlets in it, which users can customize or personalize. A user-customized version of the iGoogle home page was shown in figure 1.1.

The Public Pages and Private Pages options provide information about the user's public and private pages. As you can see in figure 1.17, a public Welcome page already exists by default. By default, Liferay Portal creates public and private Welcome pages for each user.

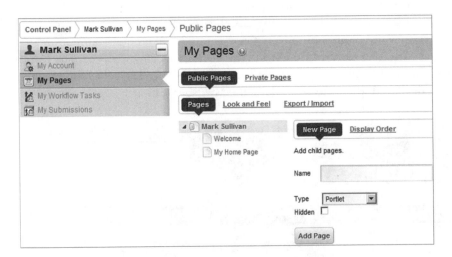

Figure 1.17   The My Pages option allows you to manage your public and private pages. The page information is displayed in a tree structure. You also have the option to create new pages for the portal.

To create a new public page named "My Home Page," enter My Home Page in the Name field of the form shown in figure 1.17. Keep the Type as Portlet and leave the Hidden check box unchecked. The newly created public page will appear in the list of public pages, as shown in figure 1.17. Now you're ready to look at your newly created portal page and add portlets to it.

The dockbar of Liferay Portal provides an option to visit your public and private pages, as shown in figure 1.18. To view public pages, select Go To > My Public Pages.

You'll see a My Home Page tab in the Liferay Portal header, along with a Welcome tab, when you first visit your public portal pages. My Home Page will appear completely blank at the beginning, because no content has been added to it.

Figure 1.18 The My Public Pages and My Private Pages options allow users to access the public and private portal pages associated with the organizations that the user has access to.

Let's now see how you can add a portlet to My Home Page.

1.6.4 Adding portlets to a Liferay Portal page

Liferay Portal comes with many built-in portlets that can help you quickly create your own portal pages. To add a portlet, use the dockbar menus and select Add > More under the Applications category, as shown in figure 1.19. Liferay Portal will display a list of portlets registered in Liferay Portal, organized by category (Collaboration, Community, Content Management, News, and so on). Portal administrators can create new portlet categories and add portlets to it, or add portlets to existing portlet categories.

Figure 1.19 The More option in the Applications category allows authenticated users to add portlets to a portal page. Users can add portlets to portal pages only if they have permission to do so. By default, users can add or remove portlets from portal pages they created.

Figure 1.20 **In most cases, portlets you add will have configure, minimize, maximize, and close options for customizing the portlet. The availability of these options depends upon the design of the portlet and the access permissions of the user.**

Adding a portlet to a portal page in Liferay Portal is easy: drag and drop a portlet from the list shown in figure 1.19, or click the Add link next to the portlet in the list. To see how this works, add the RSS portlet from the News category to the My Home Page portal page, which by default shows news from Yahoo.

Once you have added the RSS portlet to the My Home Page portal page, you'll see options to customize the portlet content (to change its look and feel, and to change the location of RSS feeds), to change permissions, and to minimize, maximize, or remove the portlet from the page. The portlet options available to a user depend upon the user's role and associated permissions. Figure 1.20 shows the options for the newly added RSS portlet.

Let's now look at some of the roles defined in Liferay Portal and their associated permissions.

1.6.5 *Roles and permissions in Liferay Portal*

In Liferay Portal, the default roles associated with authenticated users are User and Power User, and the default role associated with unauthenticated users is Guest. A Power User role simply indicates that the user has the privileges to create public and private portal pages.

Liferay Portal administrators can create new roles and manage permissions associated with these roles based on the business requirements of the web portal. Adding a portlet to a public portal page allows unauthenticated users—users with the Guest role—to view that page and its portlets, unless the permissions for the portlet don't allow unauthenticated users to view it. For example, if a guest user wants to view the public My Home Page, they could do so using the following URL:

```
http://<host-name>:<port-number>/web/<users-screen-name>/<portal-page-name>
```

For example, if you try to access My Home Page without authenticating with Liferay Portal, the URL will be

```
http://localhost:8080/web/mark123/my-home-page
```

Figure 1.21 The Configuration option for portlets in Liferay Portal allows you to set the access permissions for the portlet.

In this URL, *mark123* is the screen name of the user whose public portal page you want to view, and *my-home-page* is the name of the public portal page.

> **NOTE** To create portal page URLs, Liferay Portal converts the page names to lowercase and replaces spaces between words with hyphens, so the name of the My Home Page portal page becomes *my-home-page*.

When guest users view My Home Page, they don't by default have permission to customize the portlet, but they can view its contents. To prevent guest users from viewing the portlet, select the Configuration option for the portlet (as shown in figure 1.21) and select the Permissions option.

The Permissions table (shown in figure 1.22) shows that the Guest role has View permission but not Configuration permission for the RSS portlet, which means Guest users can view the content of the portlet but can't customize the portlet's content, look and feel, permissions, and so on. Uncheck the View permission for the Guest user, and click the Save button. If you now go to My Home Page (http://localhost:8080/web/ mark123/my-home-page) as a Guest user, you'll receive a message indicating that you don't have the role required to access the portlet.

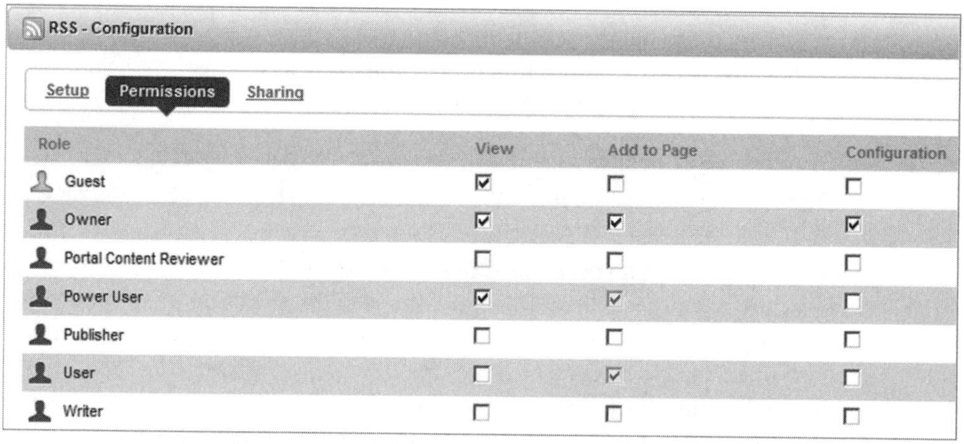

Role	View	Add to Page	Configuration
Guest	☑	☐	☐
Owner	☑	☑	☑
Portal Content Reviewer	☐	☐	☐
Power User	☑	☑	☐
Publisher	☐	☐	☐
User	☐	☑	☐
Writer	☐	☐	☐

Figure 1.22 Permissions assigned to the RSS portlet. View permission allows the user to view the content generated by the portlet, and Configuration permission allows the user to configure the portlet's look and feel and permissions.

Now that you've installed Liferay Portal and created a portal page, it's time to set up the development environment for creating portlets.

1.7   *Setting up the development environment*

In this section, you'll learn how to set up the development environment and see the structure of the ch1_HelloWorld Eclipse project in the book's source code. The configuration steps described in this section will help you quickly build, deploy, and debug the example portlets that accompany this book. If you're using Eclipse IDE, the setup described here should be sufficient to quickly get you started with developing your own portal project.

1.7.1   *Configuring Eclipse IDE*

First you need to download the Eclipse IDE for Java EE Developers from www .eclipse.org. Installing the Eclipse IDE is a simple matter of unzipping the contents of the downloaded zip file to a directory.

> **NOTE**   Eclipse Galileo was used during the writing of this book, but the steps described in this section are also applicable to the Eclipse Helios IDE.

Now import the ch1_HelloWorld Eclipse project, which accompanies this book. To import an existing Eclipse project, select the File > Import menu option and select the Existing Projects into Workspace option under the General category.

The ch1_HelloWorld project contains the Hello World portlet class, the configuration files, and the Ant buildfile. An Ant build tool comes bundled with Eclipse IDE, so you don't need to separately download and install it.

To configure the Eclipse IDE to work with Liferay Portal (which you installed in section 1.6.1), you need to do the following:

1 Create a new server profile in Eclipse.
2 Specify the installation directory of the Tomcat server.
3 Configure the server.

You should also configure the Eclipse IDE to use JDK 5.0 or later and to check the source code for Java 5 compatibility, in order to work with the examples in this book. We'll look at each of these steps in turn.

CREATING A NEW SERVER PROFILE IN ECLIPSE

Start by opening the Eclipse IDE's Servers view by selecting Window > Show View > Servers. Right-click in the Servers view and choose the option to create a new server; this will open the New Server dialog box.

In the Define a New Server dialog box, shown in figure 1.23, select the version of Tomcat that your Liferay Portal bundle is using (the Tomcat version is 6.0.26 if you're using Liferay Portal 6.x). Then click Next.

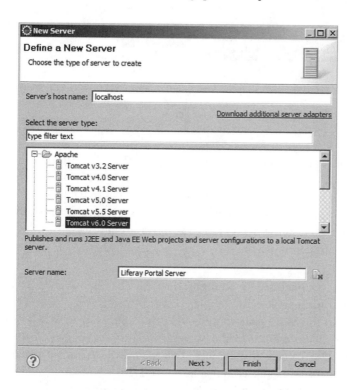

Figure 1.23 In the New Server dialog box, select the Tomcat version used by your Liferay Portal installation. If you're using Liferay Portal 6.x, Tomcat v6.0 Server should be selected.

SPECIFYING THE INSTALLATION DIRECTORY OF THE TOMCAT SERVER

The next step is to specify the installation directory of the Tomcat server, which I'll refer to as TOMCAT_HOME in the rest of this chapter. In the Tomcat Server page of the New Server dialog box, shown in figure 1.24, specify the Tomcat installation directory and the JDK that you want to use for running the Tomcat server.

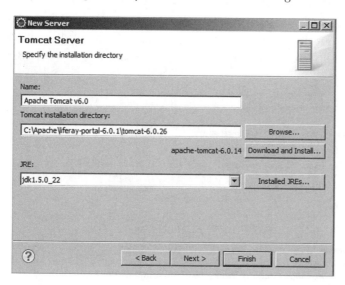

Figure 1.24 Specify the Tomcat home directory and the JDK for the server. The Tomcat home directory is located inside the Liferay Portal home directory.

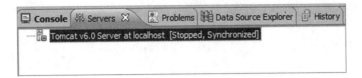

**Figure 1.25   The Servers view shows the newly created server
definition in Eclipse.**

It's important to select an installed JDK as the value for the JRE option, to help with
compilation of Java sources, debugging, and so on. To select JDK 1.5 or later, click the
Installed JREs button and configure a JDK to use with the Eclipse IDE.

Click Finish to complete the server definition in Eclipse. If the server is successfully
created, it will be displayed in the Servers view, as shown in figure 1.25.

Now, you're ready to configure the server.

CONFIGURING THE SERVER

The newly created server needs to be configured so the ch1_HelloWorld project can
be deployed on the Tomcat server and debugged at runtime.

Select the server in the Servers view, right-click, and select Open, which shows the
server configuration information. On the server configuration page, on the Server
Locations tab, select Use Tomcat Installation (Takes Control of Tomcat Installation),
and set Deploy Path to be webapps, as shown in figure 1.26.

To ensure that enough memory is available to the server at runtime, click the
Open Launch Configuration hyperlink in the General Information tab of the server
configuration page to open the Edit Configuration dialog box, where you can edit the
server launch configuration properties, and on the Arguments tab, add the following
virtual memory arguments, as shown in figure 1.27:

```
-Xms128m -Xmx512m -XX:MaxPermSize=256m
```

Next, select the Classpath tab, and add servlet-api.jar, el-api.jar, and jsp-api.jar to the
Bootstrap Entries from the TOMCAT_HOME\lib directory. Add all the JAR files from
the TOMCAT_HOME\lib\ext directory to User Entries, as shown in figure 1.28.

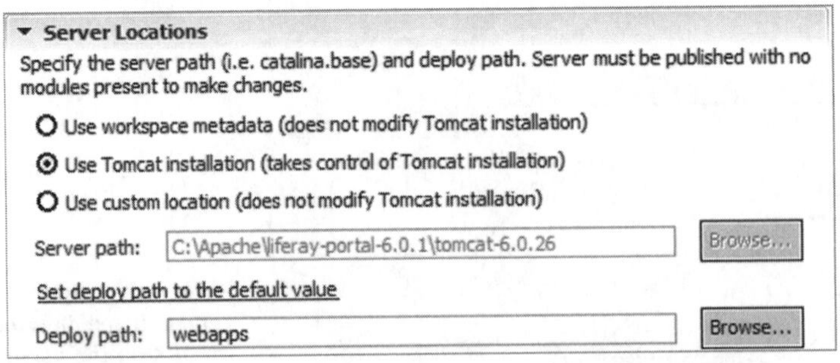

▼ **Server Locations**

Specify the server path (i.e. catalina.base) and deploy path. Server must be published with no
modules present to make changes.

○ Use workspace metadata (does not modify Tomcat installation)

⊙ Use Tomcat installation (takes control of Tomcat installation)

○ Use custom location (does not modify Tomcat installation)

Server path: C:\Apache\liferay-portal-6.0.1\tomcat-6.0.26   Browse...

Set deploy path to the default value

Deploy path: webapps   Browse...

**Figure 1.26   On the Server Locations tab, the Use Tomcat Installation
option must be selected, and the Deploy Path setting must be webapps,
which corresponds to the webapps directory inside the Tomcat installation.**

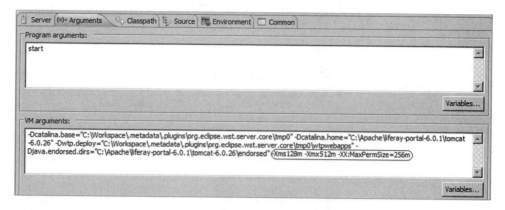

Figure 1.27   Specifying additional virtual memory arguments in the launch configuration properties. If these additional arguments aren't set, chances are good that you'll get an out-of-memory error when you start Liferay Portal.

Select the Source tab and add the ch1_HelloWorld Java project that you imported into the Eclipse IDE at the beginning of this section (as shown in figure 1.29). You need to add the source so that you can debug the source code during development.

If you start the server now, you'll probably receive a timeout error because, by default, the server configuration in Eclipse expects the server to start within 45 seconds. Depending on your machine's configuration, it may be possible for Tomcat to

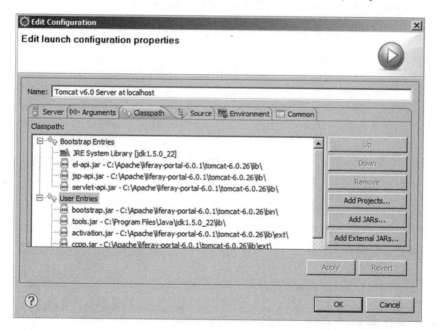

Figure 1.28   Adding libraries in the Edit Launch Configuration Properties page of the Edit Configuration dialog box. The libraries added here are used by Eclipse IDE to launch the server.

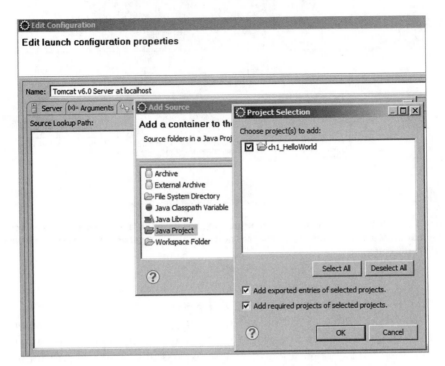

Figure 1.29   Adding the ch1_HelloWorld source in the Edit Launch Configuration Properties page of the Edit Configuration dialog box. This ensures that you can debug the source code.

start within 45 seconds, but it's safer to increase the startup and shutdown times for Tomcat server to around 180 seconds and 120 seconds respectively.

To increase the startup and shutdown times of the server, select the server in the Servers view, right-click, and select Open. This will show the server configuration page. Now, go to the server configuration and select the Timeouts tab, as shown in figure 1.30.

To verify the setup, start the server and check if it starts cleanly and opens the home page of Liferay Portal.

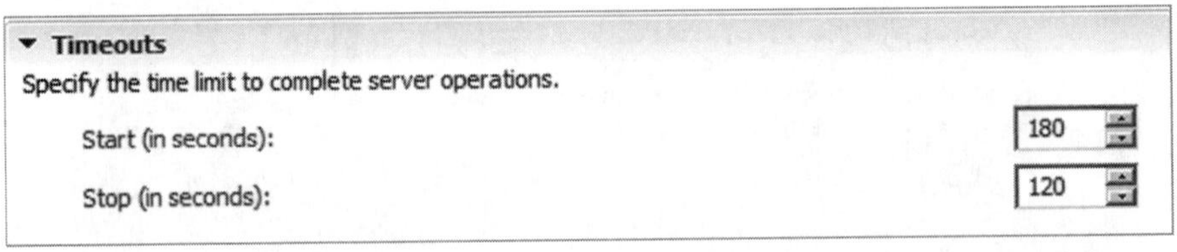

▼ **Timeouts**	
Specify the time limit to complete server operations.	
Start (in seconds):	180
Stop (in seconds):	120

Figure 1.30   Specifying timeouts for the server. If the timeout has a lower time limit than it takes to start the portal server, an exception will be thrown during server startup.

CONFIGURING ECLIPSE FOR JDK 5 OR LATER

The examples in this book make use of Java SE 5 features like annotations and generics, so your Eclipse IDE should be configured to use JDK 5.0 or later, and the source code compliance should be set to 5.0.

To configure the JDK that should be used by Eclipse IDE, select the Window > Preferences menu option. In the Preferences dialog box, select the Java > Installed JREs option from the list, as shown in figure 1.31.

Figure 1.31 shows the JREs that are available to the Eclipse IDE. If JDK 5 or later is available in the list, make sure that it's checked. If JDK 5 or later isn't in the list, click the Add button to start the wizard for adding a new JDK.

Figure 1.32 shows the JRE Type page of the Add JRE wizard. Select the Standard VM option and click Next.

In the JRE Definition wizard page, select the home directory of the JDK that you want to add, as shown in figure 1.33. Click Finish to complete the process of adding a new JDK.

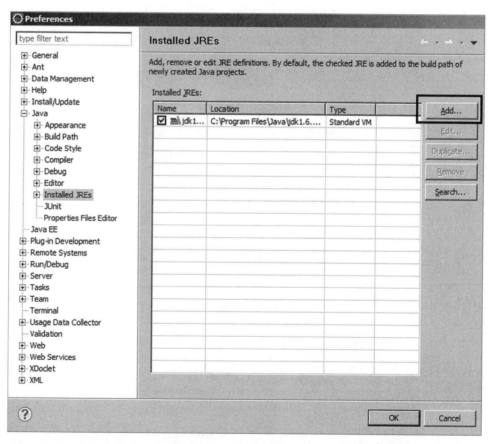

Figure 1.31 The Installed JREs preference allows you to set the JDK that will be used by the Eclipse IDE for all projects. The Add button allows you to add a new JDK to the Eclipse IDE.

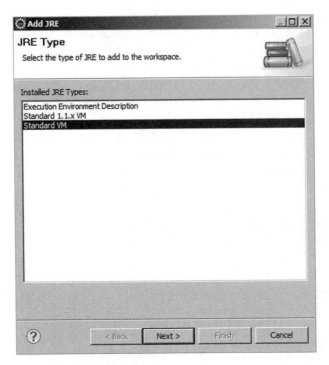

Figure 1.32   The Add JRE wizard will help you add a new JDK to the Eclipse IDE.

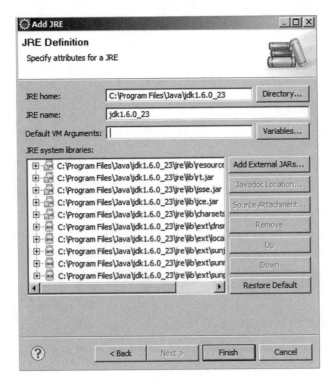

Figure 1.33   The Compiler preferences let you specify compliance level for source code and generated class files.

The newly added JDK will now be available in the list of installed JREs shown earlier in figure 1.31.

The examples in this book make use of Java SE 5 features, so you also need to instruct the Eclipse IDE to check the source code for compatibility with Java 5, and that the generated class files are compatible with Java 5.

SETTING SOURCE AND GENERATED CLASS FILE COMPLIANCE

To set the compliance level for all the projects to Java 5, select the Window > Preferences menu option in the Eclipse IDE, and select the Compiler option, as shown in figure 1.34.

In figure 1.34, select 1.5 as the value for the Compiler Compliance Level, and select the Use Default Compliance Settings check box. Click OK to save the changes. This instructs Eclipse to ensure that the source code of Eclipse projects and their class files are Java 5 compatible.

Now it's time to create a project structure in Eclipse, which will help organize your portlet project files.

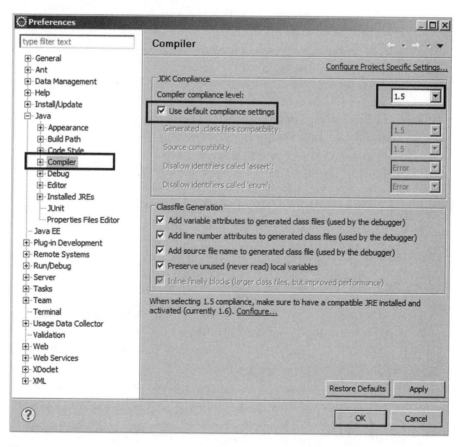

Figure 1.34   Specifying the home directory of the JDK you want to add to the Eclipse IDE

1.7.2   *Setting up the project structure*

The project structure that we'll discuss in this section is for the Hello World portlet application, but the structure is generic, and we'll use the same structure in the rest of the book for other examples. You've already imported the ch1_HelloWorld Eclipse project in section 1.7.1. Figure 1.35 shows the project structure and some of the files that form the Hello World portlet application.

The project structure presented here is generic and can be used in most portal projects with little or no modification. Let's go through the directories in the project:

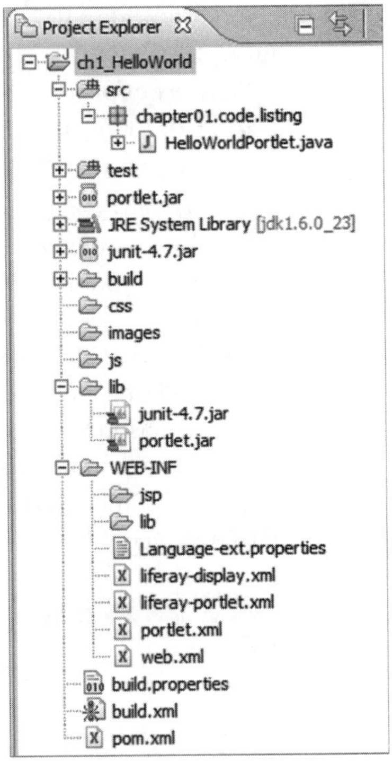

Figure 1.35   The ch1_HelloWorld project structure is a generic project structure that we'll use consistently in this book for creating portlet applications.

- *src*—Contains the source code of the project, which includes portlet and utility classes.

- *test*—An empty directory in which you can create your test classes for the project.

- *build*—The build directory is created when you first run the Ant build for the project. It contains the WAR file that's generated when the project is built using Ant.

- *css*—Contains CSS files for the project to define the look and feel for the portlets. You can also use the look and feel feature provided by the portal server to change the look and feel of the portlet.

- *images*—Contains the images that are used by the portlets in the project.

- *js*—Contains the JavaScript files used by the portlet. Portlets may also make use of JavaScript libraries like DWR, Dojo, and jQuery, which are normally packaged in a JAR file and accessed directly by the portlets. In most cases, portlets consist of multiple pages of information, and the JavaScript may be required for creating HTML widgets on the fly or using Ajax.

- *lib*—Contains the JAR files required at build time but that don't need to be packaged with the generated WAR file, such as JUnit and portlet JAR files. The JUnit JAR file is required to run unit tests at build time, and a portlet JAR file is required for compiling the portlet classes.

- *WEB-INF/jsp*—Contains the JSP files used in the project. We'll be using JSP as the view technology in this book, but you can use other view technologies like Velocity and Facelets to create portlet pages.

- *WEB-INF/lib*—Contains JAR files required by the portlets at build time and at runtime.

With the development environment set up, it's time to look at the different files in the Hello World portlet example.

1.8   The Hello World portlet example

We're now ready to look at our first portlet application, which consists of a simple Hello World portlet, as shown in figure 1.36. This section will familiarize you with the Java source files and configuration files that are involved in a typical portlet application, how to deploy and undeploy a portlet, and how to use the Ant and Maven build tools.

Figure 1.36   A simple Hello World portlet that displays the message "Hello World" when added to a portal page

In the context of the Hello World portlet, you'll learn how to perform the following activities:

- Create the necessary portlet files
- Build the portlet project using either Ant or Maven, and deploy the portlet application WAR file on the portal server
- Add the deployed portlet to a portal page
- Undeploy a portlet from the portal server

We'll look at each of these in turn.

1.8.1   Creating a Hello World portlet

To create the Hello World portlet, you need the following files:

- `HelloWorldPortlet` *class*—This is the portlet class.
- *portlet.xml file*—This is the configuration file that defines settings for the portlet, like the portlet request handler (the portlet class), supported modes, supported locales, supported MIME types, and the resource bundle.
- *Language-ext.properties file*—This is the properties file used by the portlet to support localization. In the Hello World example, this file is used to specify the portlet title and to assign a category under which the Hello World portlet should be displayed in Liferay Portal (refer to figure 1.19).
- *liferay-display.xml and liferay-portlet.xml files*—These are Liferay Portal–specific configuration files for configuring the portlet. These files are optional and you aren't required to provide them with your project's WAR file. In this example, we'll create these configuration files to keep things simple.
- *web.xml file*—This is a deployment descriptor for the web resources (like servlets), except for portlets.

If you've imported the ch1_HelloWorld project into your Eclipse workspace, these files will already exist; otherwise you'll need to create them. But even if you imported the ch1_HelloWorld project and don't need to create the files, it's important that you understand their contents.

> **NOTE** If you want to develop the Hello World portlet using the Spring Portlet MVC framework, you can jump directly to section 7.3 in chapter 7 to create the portlet files, and then return to this section to create the Liferay Portal–specific configuration files and build and deploy the portlet.

THE PORTLET CLASS

A portlet class must implement the `javax.portlet.Portlet` interface, directly or indirectly. The portlet API has a `GenericPortlet` abstract class that implements the `Portlet` interface and provides a default implementation for its methods. Developers will usually subclass the `GenericPortlet` class and override one or more methods to provide a specific implementation. The `HelloWorldPortlet` class is an example of a portlet class.

The portlet class requires Portlet 2.0 API classes and interfaces, so you should add the portlet.jar file, located in TOMCAT_HOME\lib\ext, to the project's classpath.

This listing shows the `HelloWorldPortlet` class.

Listing 1.1   The `HelloWorldPortlet` class

```
package chapter01.code.listing;

import java.io.IOException;           ❶ Imported classes
import java.io.PrintWriter;
import javax.portlet.*;
                                       ❷ HelloWorldPortlet
public class HelloWorldPortlet extends GenericPortlet      class
{
    @RenderMode(name = "VIEW")        ❸ Annotation for
    public void sayHello(RenderRequest request,      sayHello method
            RenderResponse response) throws
                PortletException, IOException {
            PrintWriter out = response.getWriter();   ❹ sayHello
            out.println("Hello World");                   method
    }
}
```

At ❶, you import the classes needed to create the `HelloWorldPortlet` class. The `HelloWorldPortlet` class extends the `GenericPortlet` abstract class of the Portlet 2.0 API ❷.

The `HelloWorldPortlet` class defines the `sayHello` method ❹, which accepts `javax.portlet.RenderRequest` and `javax.portlet.RenderResponse` objects as parameters. The `sayHello` method writes the "Hello World" message to the output stream. The `getWriter()` method of `RenderResponse` is similar to the `getWriter()` method of `HttpServletResponse`, which returns a `PrintWriter` object. The `PrintWriter` object is used by the `sayHello` method to write the "Hello World" character data to the response.

At ❸, the @RenderMode annotation for the sayHello method informs the Java run-time that the sayHello method is the portlet's *render* method in VIEW mode (we'll come back to this in chapter 2).

PORTLET SETTINGS

The portlet.xml file contains portlet settings including portlet name, portlet class, supported locales, initialization parameters, and so on. The following listing shows the portlet.xml file for the Hello World portlet.

Listing 1.2   The portlet.xml file

```
<portlet-app
xmlns="http://java.sun.com/xml/ns/portlet/portlet-app_2_0.xsd"
xmlns:xsi="http://www.w3.org/2001/XMLSchema-instance" version="2.0"
xsi:schemaLocation="http://java.sun.com/xml/ns/portlet/portlet-app_2_0.xsd
http://java.sun.com/xml/ns/portlet/portlet-app_2_0.xsd">
  <portlet>
    <portlet-name>HelloWorldPortlet</portlet-name>
    <display-name>Hello world</display-name>
    <portlet-class>chapter01.code.listing.HelloWorldPortlet</portlet-class>
    <supports>
      <mime-type>text/html</mime-type>
      <portlet-mode>view</portlet-mode>
     </supports>
     <resource-bundle>content.Language-ext</resource-bundle>
  </portlet>
</portlet-app>
```

Here are some of the important elements of the portlet.xml file in listing 1.2:

- <portlet-app>—The root element of the portlet.xml file
- <portlet>—The element that defines a single portlet in the portlet application
- <portlet-class>—The fully qualified name of the portlet class
- <portlet-mode>—The supported portlet mode; possible values include VIEW, EDIT, and HELP (the value is case insensitive)
- <resource-bundle>—The resource bundle for the portlet

THE RESOURCE BUNDLE

The Language-ext.properties file is the resource bundle used by the Hello World port-let. The properties defined in the file include the following:

```
category.chapter01.helloWorld=Chapter 01 Portlets
javax.portlet.title=My Hello World portlet
```

Let's look at these properties:

- category.chapter01.helloWorld—This specifies the name of the category under which the portlet is displayed by Liferay Portal (as illustrated in figure 1.19).
- javax.portlet.title—This specifies the title of the portlet. It's important to note that only a property named javax.portlet.title in the portlet resource bundle is considered by the portlet container as a candidate for the portlet title.

Liferay Portal has a Language.properties file, located under the content directory in the portal-impl.jar file (which can be found in the {TOMCAT_HOME}\webapps\ROOT\WEB-INF\lib directory), that defines the names of predefined categories in Liferay Portal (apart from labels, messages, and portlet titles). But if you don't want to use the predefined categories or override the names of predefined categories, you can create a Language-ext.properties file and place it in the portlet's classpath. To localize the category name, you can create other Language-ext files with a naming convention similar to the resource bundles. For example, the Language-ext_pt_BR.properties file would be used for the Portuguese language in Brazil.

LIFERAY PORTAL CATEGORY

The liferay-display.xml file allows you to specify the category under which you want the portlet to be displayed. The content of liferay-display.xml file is as follows:

```
<display>
    <category name="category.chapter01.helloWorld">
        <portlet id="HelloWorldPortlet" />
    </category>
 </display>
```

These are the most important elements of the liferay-display.xml file:

- <category>—The name attribute refers to a key in the Language-ext.properties file that identifies the category under which the portlet needs to be displayed (as illustrated in figure 1.19).
- <portlet>—The id attribute must be the name of a portlet, defined by the <portlet-name> element in the portlet.xml file.

LIFERAY PORTAL–SPECIFIC FEATURES

The liferay-portlet.xml file allows you to configure Liferay Portal–specific features for the portlet. In Hello World, this file contains a liferay-portlet-app element, as follows:

```
<liferay-portlet-app>
    <portlet>
        <portlet-name>HelloWorldPortlet</portlet-name>
        <instanceable>true</instanceable>
        <remoteable>true</remoteable>
    </portlet>
 </liferay-portlet-app>
```

These are the important elements of the liferay-portlet.xml file:

- <portlet-name>—The name of the portlet as defined by the <portlet-name> element in the portlet.xml file.
- <instanceable>—If true, the same portlet can appear on a portal page more than once. The default value is false.
- <remoteable>true</remoteable>—If true, the portlet can be exposed as a remote portlet by a *WSRP producer*. We'll discuss WSRP (Web Services for Remote Portlets) in detail in chapter 15.

Those are all the necessary files for the ch1_HelloWorld project. You're now ready to build the project.

1.8.2 *Building the Hello World project with Ant*

The source code of this book can be built using either Ant or Maven. If you want to use Maven to build the examples, jump ahead to section 1.8.3.

THE ANT BUILD TOOL

Ant is an open source Java tool that provides a flexible and cross-platform build utility for Java projects. Ant makes use of an XML configuration file (called a *buildfile*), containing instructions about tasks to be performed while building the project.

The tasks in the buildfile may include cleaning output directories, compiling Java sources, copying files to appropriate directories, and creating a WAR file. These tasks are logically grouped into *targets*, which may depend on other targets. For instance, there can be a build target (which takes the Java classes and configuration files as inputs and creates a WAR file), and it is dependent upon the clean (which removes the class files from the output folder of the project) and compile (which compiles the Java source files and creates the corresponding class files in the output folder of the project) targets.

The following XML fragment shows how the build target is defined in an Ant buildfile:

```
<target name="compile">
    ...tasks to compile the source code
</target>
<target name="clean">
    ...tasks to remove the class files from the output folder
</target>
<target name="build" depends="clean,compile">
    ...tasks to create the WAR file
</target>
```

The depends attribute of a target element specifies the dependent targets. The execution order of targets in the depends attribute is important when creating a build file. In the preceding code fragment, the build target depends on the clean and compile targets, which instruct Ant to execute the clean target first, and then the compile target, before executing the build target.

A buildfile contains one project element and at least one target element. There are other useful elements like fileset (for defining a group of files), property (for defining properties, which may be read from an external properties file), and so on.

Ant targets contain tasks, which are like instructions in a program. The targets represent a program, and tasks represent programming instructions in that program. Examples of tasks are war (for creating a WAR file), delete (for deleting files), and copy (for copying files).

THE ANT BUILD SCRIPT

The build.xml file is the Ant buildfile in our ch1_HelloWorld project, and it contains information on how to compile and build a WAR file from Java sources and other resources in the ch1_HelloWorld project. This listing shows the `build` target in ch1_HelloWorld's build.xml file.

Listing 1.3   The build.xml file for Hello World

```
<project name = "ch1_HelloWorld"                  ❶  Defines project
        default="build" basedir=".">                  and default target
...
<property file="build.properties" />               ❷  Loads properties from
<property name="build.dir" value="build"/>             build.properties file
<target name="build" depends="clean,compile">      ❸  Defines
<mkdir dir="${build.dir}"/>                            property
<war destfile="${build.dir}/ch1_HelloWorld.war"    ❹  Creates
        webxml="${web.xml}">                           WAR file
<fileset refid="war.files"/>
</war>
<copy todir="${liferay.portal.home}/deploy">
        <fileset dir="${build.dir}">               ❺  Copies generated
            <include name="**/*.war" />                WAR file
        </fileset>
</copy>
</target>
```

At ❶, you define the project name and the default target to be used when no target is specified for running the build script.

In build.xml, it's possible to define properties directly or to load properties from an external properties file. The build.xml file defines a property with the name `build.dir` and value `build` ❸. Line ❷ instructs the Ant build tool to load the build.properties file and use the properties defined in the file if the build.xml file references them.

The build script specifies the creation of a WAR file named ch1_HelloWorld.war ❹, and it specifies that the generated WAR file should be copied to {liferay.portal.home}/deploy ❺, which refers to Liferay Portal's hot deploy directory.

The build.properties file in the Hello World project contains a single property that refers to the home directory of the Liferay Portal installation (LIFERAY_HOME):

```
liferay.portal.home=C:/liferay-portal-6.0.1
```

> **NOTE**   Make sure that you edit the `liferay.portal.home` property in the build.properties file to point to the Liferay Portal installation directory or the build won't work as expected.

Building the Hello World project requires you to add the necessary JAR files to the project's lib directory and then to run the `build` Ant target in the build.xml file.

ADDING JARS

The ch1_HelloWorld project's build.xml file requires the portlet API classes to be available when the `HelloWorldPortlet` class is compiled. As discussed in section 1.7.2, the JAR files that are required at compilation time are copied to the lib directory (and not to the WEB-INF\lib directory). You can copy portlet.jar from TOMCAT_HOME\lib\ext to the project's lib directory.

BUILDING THE PROJECT

Before you initiate the build process for ch1_HelloWorld, check that all the necessary JAR files are available in the project's lib and WEB-INF/lib directories and that the liferay.portal.home property in the build.properties file refers to the Liferay Portal installation directory on your system.

To build the ch1_HelloWorld project, right-click on the build.xml file, choose Run As > Ant Build, and select the build target from the list of available targets, as shown in figure 1.37.

The Ant build tool takes the following actions when the build target is executed:

1 It removes the generated WAR file from the build directory by executing the clean target.
2 It compiles the Java source to the WEB-INF/classes directory, creates a content directory, and copies the Language-ext.properties file to it. This is all done by executing the compile target.

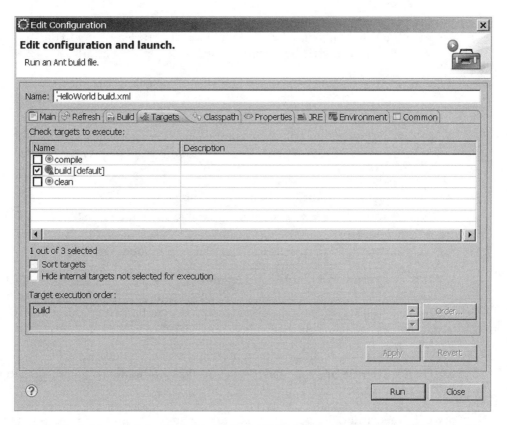

Figure 1.37   Ant targets defined in build.xml. The build target is selected by default. The compile and clean targets can also be executed separately, if you want to compile or clean the project.

3   It creates the WAR file in the build directory and copies the generated WAR file to LIFERAY_HOME/deploy (which is Liferay Portal's hot deploy directory). This is done by executing the `build` target.

4   If your Liferay Portal is already running, the `build` target will hot deploy the Hello World portlet. If the server isn't running, the portlet will be deployed when the server is started. At deployment time, the information from liferay-display.xml is used to register the portlet with Liferay Portal.

1.8.3   *Building the Hello World project with Maven*

The source code for each chapter also comes with a pom.xml file, which is meant for readers who want to build the source code using the Maven build tool. In this section, you'll learn how to build source code using the Maven distribution. Keep in mind that when you're using Maven, you need to ensure that you're connected to the internet so you can download any JAR dependencies of projects and the Maven build tool.

> **NOTE**   If you want to use the Maven Eclipse Plugin, please refer to the Apache Maven Project (http://maven.apache.org/eclipse-plugin.html).

If you don't already have Maven installed, the first thing you need to do is download Maven from the Apache Maven Project website (http://maven.apache.org/download.html). The current version of Maven is 3.x, and we'll use it as the reference for developing the Hello World portlet and other portlet examples in this book.

Once you've downloaded Maven, follow these steps to prepare for building the example source code:

1   Unzip the downloaded zip file into a directory.

2   Set the `JAVA_HOME` environment variable to point to your Java SE 5 installation directory.

3   Add Maven's bin directory to the `PATH` environment variable.

You're now ready to build the ch1_HelloWorld source code using Maven. You can either use the Maven Eclipse Plugin to build your project from within the Eclipse IDE, or you can use Maven from the command prompt to build the project. If you're using Maven from command prompt, follow these steps:

1   Open a command prompt and go to the ch1_HelloWorld folder in your local filesystem. Make sure that the ch1_HelloWorld folder contains a pom.xml file.

2   Run the following command: `mvn clean install`.

When you execute the `mvn clean install` command, Maven looks for a pom.xml file in the current directory and kicks off the build process. During the build process, many artifacts are downloaded from the internet, including dependencies specified in the pom.xml file. If the build is successful, you'll see a "BUILD SUCCESSFUL" message at the command prompt.

Successful execution of the Maven build process will generate a file named ch1_HelloWorld.war in the portlets-in-action subdirectory of the local Maven repository. The *local Maven repository* is a directory in your local file system where all the relevant artifacts and dependencies are downloaded by the Maven build tool. It's identified as <user-home>/.m2/repository, where user-home is the home directory of the user. On UNIX this refers to the ~/.m2/repository directory and on a Windows machine this is usually C:\Documents and Settings\<*yourUserName*>\.m2\repository.

To learn more about the Maven build tool, please refer to the Apache Maven Project website at http://maven.apache.org.

Let's now add the Hello World portlet to a portal page.

1.8.4 Adding the Hello World portlet to a portal page

When a portlet is deployed in Liferay Portal 6.x, it isn't immediately available to users. To make the newly added Hello World portlet available to authenticated users of Liferay Portal so that they can add it to their portal page, you must log in as administrator and grant Add to Page permission to the user. Let's go step by step and grant Add to Page permission to the User role.

The Liferay Portal administrator can access all the portlets that are deployed in Liferay Portal. If you want to test the Hello World portlet without granting Add to Page permission to authenticated users, then log in as administrator, and add the Hello World portlet by going directly to the Add > More option under the Applications category (as shown earlier in figure 1.19).

Liferay Portal comes preconfigured with an administrator user, Bruno, as shown in figure 1.38.

Figure 1.38   Bruno is the default administrator of Liferay Portal. Click the Login as Bruno link to log in to Liferay Portal as the portal administrator.

Click the Login as Bruno link, as shown in figure 1.38, to access features that are only available to the Liferay Portal administrator. Once you're logged in, the dockbar will show additional options that are available to the portal administrator. Select the Manage > Control Panel option from the dockbar, as shown in figure 1.39, to view the administrative features available.

Figure 1.39   The Control Panel provides administrative options, which include granting access to portlets to roles defined in Liferay Portal.

In the control panel, select the Roles option from the left navigation bar, as shown in figure 1.40. The Roles option lets you view existing roles in Liferay Portal, create roles, edit role permissions, and so on.

Because the User role is associated with authenticated users, you should provide the User role with permission to add the Hello World portlet to a portal page. To do so, select the Actions > Define Permissions option corresponding to the User role, as shown in figure 1.41.

Selecting the Define Permissions option displays the list of portlets currently deployed in Liferay Portal for which you can define permissions. Select the My Hello World Portlet from the Add Permissions dropdown list (under the Applications category), as shown in figure 1.42.

Selecting My Hello World Portlet in figure 1.42 displays the permissions that can be specified for the portlet, as shown in figure 1.43.

In figure 1.43, check the Add to Page check box to allow users with the User role to add My Hello World Portlet to a portal page. Save the permissions, and log out from Liferay Portal.

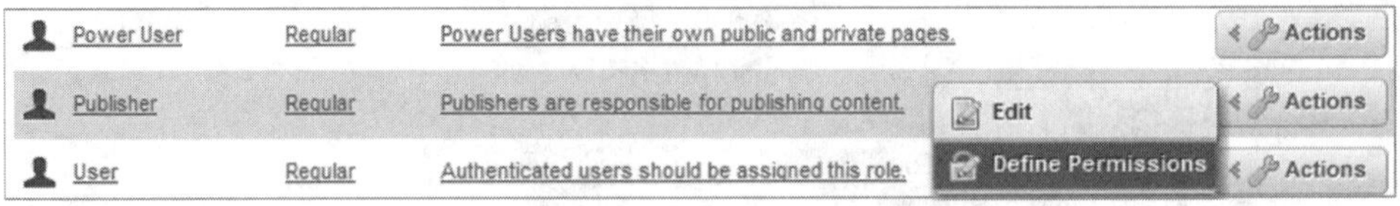

Figure 1.40   The Roles option lets the administrator view, edit, and create roles. The administrator can also modify permissions associated with different roles in the portal.

Figure 1.41   The Define Permissions option lets a portal administrator define permissions for a role, including permission to add a portlet to a portal page.

Figure 1.42 The Add Permissions drop-down list shows the portlets currently deployed in Liferay Portal under the Applications category. You can select the portlet for which you want to modify permissions.

Now, if you log in with the account you created in section 1.6.2 and go to the My Home Page portal page, you'll be able to view and add the My Hello World portlet, as shown in figure 1.44.

In figure 1.44, you can see that a new Chapter 01 Portlets category was added to the list of available categories. The title assigned to the Hello World portlet is shown under that category. When the Hello World portlet is added to the portal page, it shows the message "Hello World."

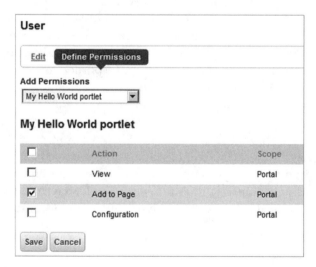

Figure 1.43 Permissions defined for the My Hello World portlet. Add to Page permission allows a user to view and add portlets from the Add > More option (under the Applications category).

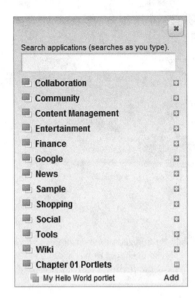

Figure 1.44   **The My Hello World Portlet listed under the Chapter 01 Portlets category, and the Hello World portlet on the portal page**

The files that you created as part of this Hello World portlet are required for creating most portlets in real projects.

1.8.5 *Undeploying a portlet application*

In a typical web application scenario, removing the WAR file from the filesystem undeploys the web application. In the case of portlet applications, when you add a portlet to a portal page, the portlet instance information is saved to the portal's internal database, which also needs to be cleaned up when undeploying.

To undeploy a portlet, you must first remove all the portlet instances from all portal pages by using the remove icon, as you saw in figure 1.6. In the case of Liferay Portal, when you remove the portlet from the portal page, the portlet instance information is also removed from the internal database. After removing the portlet instance from all the portal pages, you can delete the portlet application's WAR file from the {TOMCAT_HOME}/webapps directory to undeploy the portlet application.

In this section, you saw how a typical portlet application is developed, built using Maven or Ant, deployed on a portal server, and added to a portal page. We also touched upon some Liferay Portal–specific configurations that you need to provide in order to add a deployed portlet to a portal page. If you're using a different portal server than Liferay Portal, all you need to do is to replace the Liferay Portal–specific configuration and steps described in this section with the configuration and steps that apply to your portal server.

1.9 *Summary*

The portlet technology is promising in terms of its reach and impact. The focus on portals has increased in recent years, and has gained momentum with the release of the Portlet 2.0 specification. It's important to understand the unique features of a portal (personalization, content aggregation, customization, and authentication) to get a feel for how Java portlet technology makes it easy to develop portals.

In this chapter, you were introduced to portals and Java portlet technology using a simple Hello World example. The information covered in sections 1.6 ("Getting started with Liferay Portal") and 1.7 ("Setting up the development environment") provide the foundation for developing and deploying example portlets in the rest of this book.

Now that you have some understanding of portals and portlets, the next chapter introduces the portlet lifecycle and the foundation concepts of portlet technology.

The portlet lifecycle 2

This chapter covers

- Creating portlet URLs
- Portlet lifecycle management
- Portlet content generation using JSPs and servlets
- Commonly used Portlet API classes and interfaces

In chapter 1 you saw the steps required to develop, build, and deploy a simple Hello World portlet. Understanding the portlet lifecycle is important for effectively using portlets in your portlet applications.

This chapter introduces the portlet lifecycle and some of the core concepts of Java portlet technology. We'll first look at the requirements for an example User Registration portlet that you'll develop using the concepts discussed in this chapter. The concept of *portlet URLs* is at the heart of portlet technology, so before discussing the lifecycle of a portlet, we'll take a quick look at what portlet URLs are and what they're used for. The rest of this chapter focuses on the portlet lifecycle, initialization parameters, portlet URLs, portlet modes, portlet context, portlet configuration, localization, container-runtime options, and how to use JSP pages to render portlet content. We'll conclude this chapter by discussing how the User Registration portlet is implemented.

> **CODE REFERENCE**   The source code for this chapter is located in the ch2_ UserRegistration folder. Before you build the User Registration project, set the `liferay.portal.home` property in the build.properties file to point to your Liferay Portal installation directory.

Let's begin by looking at the requirements of the example User Registration portlet that you'll build later in this chapter.

2.1   *Requirements for the User Registration portlet*

The User Registration portlet, which you'll build later in this chapter, allows users to register with a web portal. To keep the requirements of the User Registration portlet simple, we won't save the registration information to a database. The User Registration portlet displays a user registration form, as shown in figure 2.1.

Figure 2.1 shows the User Registration form, shown in VIEW portlet mode, which accepts the first name, last name, and email address of the user. The first and last name fields are optional, but the email address field is mandatory, and it shows @liferay.com as its default value. The default value of the email address needs to be easily customizable for use in different web portals.

The Reset hyperlink lets the user reset the entered information in the registration form. Later in this chapter, you'll see that the Reset hyperlink is associated with a *portlet URL*, which invokes a method of the User Registration portlet class to reset the form. The user clicks the Submit button to register with the portal after entering the necessary information in figure 2.1. If the user is successfully registered, a success page is displayed, as shown in figure 2.2.

The Home hyperlink shown in figure 2.2 directs the user to the home page of the User Registration portlet. Like the Reset link, the Home hyperlink uses a portlet URL to invoke a method of the User Registration portlet class to perform its function. If the user doesn't enter any value for the Email field and clicks the Submit button, an error message is displayed, as shown in figure 2.3. The first and last name entries are preserved on the form.

Figure 2.1   The form displayed by User Registration portlet

Figure 2.2   The User Registration success page shows the information that was entered during registration. The Home link takes the user back to the portlet's user registration form.

Figure 2.3   An error message is displayed if the user doesn't enter a value for the required Email field. The entered values for first and last name are redisplayed.

You may have noticed that the User Registration portlet doesn't show any hyperlinks or buttons to let users access the personalization options for the portlet. Later in this chapter, you'll see how a portlet specifies support for the personalization feature, which in turn instructs the portal server to generate a hyperlink or button that allows users to access the personalization page. For now, you can assume that the User Registration portlet does support the personalization feature, but that the personalization page shows nothing but a message, as shown in figure 2.4.

As with the personalization option, if a portlet specifies that it supports showing help information, the portal server is responsible for generating a hyperlink or button that allows users to access that help information. A portlet's help information should describe how the portlet should be used, how to personalize it, and so on. Figure 2.5 shows the help page for the User Registration portlet.

Now that you've seen what you have to develop, we'll cover some portlet concepts that will help you meet these requirements. In most of this chapter, we'll focus on the foundation concepts in portlet technology, and in section 2.7 we'll dive into the details of implementing the User Registration portlet.

The first thing we'll look at is how portlet technology compares to servlets. This comparison will set the tone for the rest of the chapter.

Figure 2.4   The message displayed when a user selects the option to personalize the User Registration portlet

Figure 2.5   The User Registration portlet's help information page, displayed when the user selects the option to view help information about the portlet

2.2   *Portlets vs. servlets—an in-depth look*

In chapter 1, we touched upon some of the functional differences between servlets and portlets. In this section, we'll take an in-depth look at the differences between the two technologies, and particularly at their container support for developing web portals and their lifecycles.

2.2.1   *Portlet and servlet containers*

Like servlets, portlets are web components, and their lifecycles are managed by their portlet container. The portlet container is responsible for loading, instantiating, initializing, and routing requests to the portlet instance, and finally for destroying the portlet instance.

   If you've worked with servlets, you can easily correlate the responsibilities of a portlet container to that of a web container. So what differentiates a portlet from a servlet component when both are web components? It's the container. Let's take a quick look at some of the main shortcomings of servlets, which can be attributed to the servlet container.

- *Servlets aren't appropriate for content aggregation.*
  If you want to use a servlet to aggregate content on a web page, the responsibility for aggregating and presenting content in separate windows rests with the servlet itself. If you use portlets, the portal server is responsible for aggregating the content generated by different portlets and for displaying it in portlet windows on the portal page.

- *Servlets require more effort to personalize content.*
  If you want to personalize content in your servlet application, you have to create appropriate data structures for saving and retrieving the user's personalization data. Also, you have to write code to save and retrieve personalization data. In the case of portlets, the portlet container is responsible for saving and retrieving preference data; the portlet developer doesn't need to know how or where personalization options are saved. You'll find more detailed information about portlet personalization support in chapter 10.

- *Servlets have no built-in support for event-based inter-servlet communication.*
  To enable inter-servlet communication, your only option is to use the Servlet API to directly invoke a servlet. The portlet container, on the other hand, supports inter-portlet communication using *events*. This use of events keeps the communicating portlets loosely coupled, and you can easily add or remove portlets that

receive these events. We'll discuss inter-portlet communication in detail in chapter 11.

Now that you know the high-level differences between portlets and servlets, let's look at how request processing in portlets is different from in servlets.

2.2.2 Portlets—web components with multiple request-processing phases

The advantage of portlets over servlets is their unique request-processing lifecycle. A servlet request invokes the servlet's `service` method, which performs certain actions and generates the complete web page. Request processing in portlets is a more involved process, because each portlet request goes through multiple request-processing phases: *render, event, resource,* and *action.* Each request-processing phase has a well-defined role, as outlined in table 2.1.

Table 2.1   Request-processing phases in portlet

Request-processing phase	Purpose
Render	The portlet generates content—HTML or WML markup.
Action	The portlet performs state-changing functions, like database updates.
Resource	The portlet serves resources, like PDF files.
Event	The portlet responds to the events received by the portlet.

If you compare the request-processing phases of portlets, defined in table 2.1, with those of servlets, you'll find that the *action* and *render* phases of portlets are similar to how servlets perform request processing. Like portlets, servlets also perform actions and generate markup, the only difference being that a servlet does it in a single phase, whereas portlets have better-defined phases for markup generation and action processing.

It's important to note that not all request-processing phases apply to a request received by the portlet. For instance, if a request is received for processing an action (also referred to as an *action request*), only the action and render phases apply to the request; similarly, if a request is received for generating content (a *render request*), only the render phase applies. This effectively means that portlets not only have the concept of multiple request-processing phases but also the concept of multiple *request types.* We'll discuss how to send different request types to a portlet in section 2.3.

Each portlet request-processing phase maps to a method in the portlet class that processes the requests received in that phase. For example, the render phase maps to the portlet class's `render` method, and the action phase maps to the `processAction` method. We'll discuss these methods in detail later in this chapter, but for now you can safely assume that each request-processing phase is represented by a method in the portlet, and the action request phase is *always* followed by the render request phase.

NOTE In chapter 1, we used the @RenderMode annotation to specify that the sayHello method in the Hello World portlet is a render method.

Let's now look at how the multiple request-processing phases in portlets make them ideal for developing web portals that aggregate content from different sources. Figure 2.6 shows how a web portal with two portlets (A and B) on a portal page works.

A request for portlet A is received from a user of the web portal ❶. The request may be generated because a user clicked a hyperlink or submitted a form. The request is found to be a render request for portlet A ❷, so the portal server sends it to the portlet container. Because the request is a *render request* for portlet A, only the render request-processing phase applies. As I mentioned earlier, the render request-processing phase maps to the portlet's render method, so portlet A's render method is invoked ❸. The content is generated for portlet A, and it's returned to the portlet container. Even though the render request was for portlet A, the portlet container invokes portlet B's render method too ❹. The portlet container returns the contents of both portlets A and B to the portal server ❺, which combines the content from the

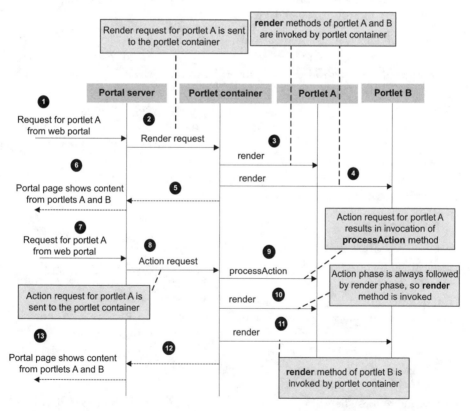

Figure 2.6 A portlet's request-processing phases apply to incoming requests based on the request type (action or render). The portlet's render method is always called to ensure that the updated portlet content is displayed by the web portal.

portlets, puts window decoration around it, composes a new portal page, and sends the page to the browser **6**.

At **7**, a request for portlet A is received from the web portal. The request is an *action request*, and it's sent by the portal server to the portlet container **8**. The action request-processing phase applies to the request, which in turn maps to the process-Action method of portlet. This results in portlet A's processAction method being invoked **9**. Even though the *action request* was for portlet A, the portlet container invokes the render method of portlets A *and* B (**10** and **11**). The order in which the render methods of the portlets are invoked is undefined; portlet A's render method may be called before portlet B's, or vice versa. The portlet container returns the content generated by both portlets' render methods to the portal server **12**. The portal server aggregates the content from the portlets, puts window decoration around it, composes a new portal page, and sends it to the browser **13**.

> **NOTE**   Figure 2.6 is a simplified version of the portlet request-processing life-cycle, because it only covers the render and action phases. We'll look at how event and resource phases form part of the request-processing lifecycle in chapters 11 and 12 respectively.

Figure 2.6 shows the benefit of having different phases for content generation and action processing. When an *action request* is sent to portlet A, it results in a processAction method call on portlet A, followed by render method calls on portlets A and B. The processAction call is followed by a render method call on portlet A because the processAction method invocation might have resulted in a change of the state of portlet A, thus giving an opportunity to portlet A to generate fresh content. The render method call on portlet B gives portlet B an opportunity to regenerate its content.

Now that you know how portlets work, we can discuss how different request types are sent to the portlets using portlet URLs.

2.3   *Portlet URLs*

In our User Registration example portlet, you might wonder how a request of a particular type (action or render) is sent to a portlet when the user submits the registration form (see figure 2.1) or when a user clicks the Home hyperlink (see figure 2.2). In portlets, *portlet URLs* are used to send requests of particular request types to portlet instances. In this section, we'll look at how portlet URLs are different from servlet URLs and at the different types of portlet URLs there are in portlets.

Let's begin by looking at how portlet URLs are different from servlet URLs.

2.3.1   *Portlet URLs vs. servlet URLs*

During request handling in servlets, the servlet's service method is invoked. The HTTP method (identified by the method attribute of the HTML form tag) is used to determine the specific method (like doGet or doPost) of the servlet to be invoked.

The `action` attribute of the HTML `form` tag identifies the servlet that needs to be invoked when the form is submitted.

Here's an example `form` tag in an HTML page:

```
<form id="myId" name="myForm" method="POST" action="/myapp/myservlet.do">
```

In this `form` tag, the servlet mapped to the URL `/myapp/myservlet.do` is called when `myForm` is submitted.

In the case of portlets, you don't have the option to specify the URL to which a portlet maps. In the case of servlets, you create a servlet-to-URL mapping in the `web.xml` deployment descriptor using the `<servlet-mapping>` element. As you saw in the Hello World portlet example in chapter 1, we didn't create any portlet-to-URL mapping. In portlet applications, the portlet container provides objects that can be used by portlets to create self-referencing URLs. These URLs refer to the portlet that created them, and they're called *portlet URLs*. Figure 2.7 shows how portlet URLs work.

A request for a portlet is received by the portlet container ❶. The portlet container invokes the portlet, which in turn generates content in its render phase. In the case of the User Registration portlet, the content can be the registration form (see figure 2.1) or the registration information that's shown after registration is successful (see figure 2.2).

When the user clicks the Submit button (see figure 2.1) or the Home hyperlink (see figure 2.2), the request should be sent to the User Registration portlet instance for processing. The portlet sets portlet URL A as part of its generated content ❷. As

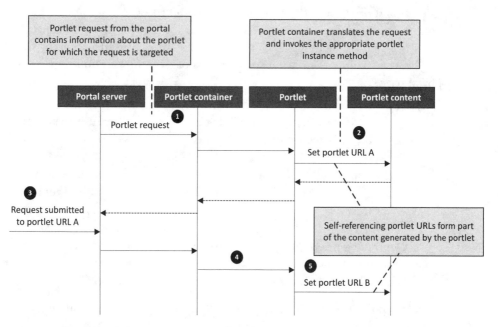

Figure 2.7 The portlet URL is interpreted by the container to generate the portlet request. During request processing, the portlet sets self-referencing portlet URLs as part of its content.

requests can only be sent to a portlet using self-referencing portlet URLs, the portlet instance is responsible for setting portlet URLs as part of it generated content. In the context of the User Registration portlet, this means that, while generating the user registration form, the User Registration portlet must set the value of the `action` attribute (of the `form` tag) to a portlet URL. That way, when a user clicks the Submit button on the user registration form, a request is submitted to the portlet URL, which results in the User Registration portlet instance being invoked. A user action results in a request being sent to portlet URL A ❸, which causes the portlet to be invoked ❹. The portlet creates fresh content and sets portlet URL B as part of its content ❺.

> **NOTE**   It isn't possible for a portlet to generate URLs referring to other portlets in the portal.

You may have noticed that figure 2.7 doesn't show how the request was received by the portlet the first time. How does a portlet first receive a request to generate content? You saw in chapter 1, when the Hello World portlet was added to the portal page, that the portlet displayed the "Hello World" message without you having to explicitly send a request to the portlet. This happens because the content generation request (called a *render request*) is sent to the portlet by the portal server when a user adds a portlet to a portal page or visits a portal page containing portlets.

Let's now look at the different types of URLs in portlets.

2.3.2   *Portlet URL types*

The request-processing cycle for a portlet is kicked off when the user clicks a hyperlink or submits a form, which in turn submits a request to the portlet URL. Portlet URLs are related to the portlet request types we discussed earlier in this chapter; they're classified by the portlet specification based on the action requested from the portal page.

There are three different types of portlet URLs:

- *Render URL*—Used to ask a portlet instance to generate markup (like HTML, XML, WML) based on its current state. The request sent to the portlet by a render URL is referred to as a *render request.*
- *Action URL*—Used for action processing, which results in a state change on the server. The request sent to the portlet by an action URL is referred to as an *action request.*
- *Resource URL*—Used to render content or retrieve resources (like image files). Depending upon the application requirement, a resource URL may be used for updating application state. The request sent to the portlet by a resource URL is referred to as a *resource request.*

> **NOTE**   Portlets don't have an *event URL* type for sending event requests. In chapter 11, we'll discuss portlet events in detail.

A portlet URL is like any other URL, but it's generated by the portlet container for internal use only. When a request is submitted from the portal (by a user clicking a link or a button), the portlet container interprets the portlet URL associated with the link or button to identify the target portlet instance and the type of request (action, render or resource). For example, the following `form` tag from HTML rendered by a portlet shows a portlet URL in the `action` attribute:

```
<form id="search" name="... " action="http://localhost:8080/web/guest/home?
p_p_id=HelloWorldPortlet_WAR_helloWorld_INSTANCE_MrP9
&amp;p_p_lifecycle=1&amp;p_p_state=normal&amp;p_p_mode=view&amp;
p_p_col_id=column-1&amp;p_p_col_count=1&amp;
_HelloWorldPortlet_WAR_helloWorld_INSTANCE_MrP9_action=someAction"
method="post">
```

It's important to understand the purpose of different portlet URLs because the URL type determines the lifecycle method(s) (like `render` and `processAction`) that are invoked on the portlet instance.

The next section covers the `Portlet` interface and `GenericPortlet` class, which are used to create portlets.

2.4   *Creating portlets*

In servlets, there's only one lifecycle interface, the `Servlet` interface. In portlets, the lifecycle contract exists between the portlet container and the portlet through the `javax.portlet.Portlet`, `javax.portlet.EventPortlet`, and `javax.portlet.ResourceServingPortlet` interfaces. These interfaces define the lifecycle methods of a portlet. Portlets must implement the `Portlet` interface, and they can optionally implement `EventPortlet` and `ResourceServingPortlet`. The `EventPortlet` interface is discussed in detail in chapter 11, and the `ResourceServingPortlet` interface is discussed in chapter 12.

2.4.1   *Creating portlets with the Portlet interface*

The `Portlet` interface is at the heart of Java's portlet technology, and it's mandatory for portlets to implement it, either directly or indirectly. The `Portlet` interface methods are invoked by the portlet container to manage the lifecycle of a portlet instance. In this section, we'll discuss the lifecycle methods defined by the `Portlet` interface and how some of the lifecycle methods relate to the portlet URLs (the portlet request types).

The lifecycle methods defined by the `Portlet` interface are `init`, `processAction`, `render`, and `destroy`. The Portlet 2.0 specification also introduced some optional lifecycle interfaces, `EventPortlet` and `ResourceServingPortlet`, which are covered in chapters 11 and 12.

Figure 2.8 shows the invocation of lifecycle methods on a portlet instance. The dotted lines represent methods that are invoked by the portlet container at an appropriate time, depending on the container implementation. The solid lines represent

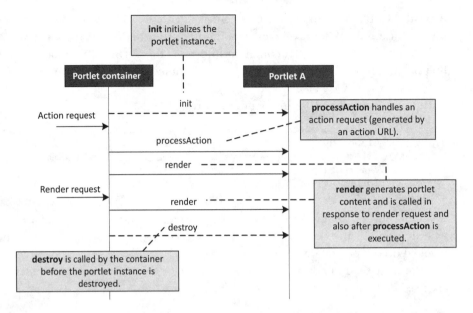

Figure 2.8   Portlet lifecycle methods defined in the `Portlet` interface. An action request invokes the `processAction` method, followed by the `render` method. A render request invokes the `render` method. The timing of the `init` and `destroy` invocations depends on the portlet container implementation.

portlet methods that are invoked directly or indirectly in response to actions taken by the user on the displayed portlet.

THE INIT METHOD

The `init` method is invoked by the portlet container after it has loaded and instantiated the portlet. The method gives the portlet instance an opportunity to initialize itself before processing any request. In the `init` method, the portlet instance initializes the costly resources (such as setting up a database connection or reading configuration data from an external file) that it will require for request processing. The resources initialized in the `init` method usually remain unchanged during the lifetime of the portlet instance.

The signature of the `init` method is as follows:

```
void init(PortletConfig config) throws PortletException
```

The `javax.portlet.PortletConfig` object is provided by the portlet container. The `PortletConfig` object provides portlet instances with access to their runtime environment and to the information that's configured in the portlet deployment descriptor (portlet.xml).

THE RENDER METHOD

The `render` method is invoked by the portlet container when a render request is received for the portlet instance. The `render` method is responsible for generating portlet content; for example, a News portlet generates the latest news information as part of its content when a render request is sent to it.

This is the signature of the `render` method:

```
void render(RenderRequest request, RenderResponse response)
    throws PortletException, IOException
```

The `RenderRequest` and `RenderResponse` objects are created by the portlet container at request-processing time. The `RenderRequest` object provides the portlet instance with access to data sent as part of the render request. In the `render` method, a portlet typically reads information from a data source and uses the `RenderResponse` object to write content.

> **NOTE** The responsibility for generating content in portlets lies completely with the `render` method.

THE PROCESSACTION METHOD

The `processAction` method is invoked in response to an action request. This method represents a user action that results in a state change, such as submitting an order request form.

This is the signature of the `processAction` method:

```
void processAction(ActionRequest request, ActionResponse response)
    throws PortletException, IOException
```

The `ActionRequest` and `ActionResponse` objects are provided by the portlet container at request-processing time. `ActionRequest` provides the action request data to the portlet instance, and `ActionResponse` is used by the portlet to respond to the action request. The response from an action request may include changing the portlet window state or portlet mode, redirecting to a different URL, or persisting action request data into a persistent store.

> **NOTE** The `processAction` method isn't meant to generate content for the portlet, and any attempt to do so is ignored by the portlet container.

THE DESTROY METHOD

The `destroy` method is invoked by the portlet container *before* removing the portlet instance from memory. This is the portlet cleanup method, where the instance may release any held resources (like database connections or EJB references) or save its state to persistent storage (like a database or file).

This is the signature of the `destroy` method:

```
void destroy()
```

A portlet's `destroy` method can be invoked by the portlet container at any time, depending upon the container implementation. The portlet container ensures that all the requests currently being processed by the portlet instance are completed before destroying the instance.

NOTE   In chapter 1, you saw an <instanceable> element used in liferay-portlet.xml. The instanceable element has nothing to do with the number of portlet object instances maintained by the portlet container; instead, <instanceable> instructs the portal to allow or deny users from adding the same portlet more than once on a portal page. If the same portlet appears more than once on the same or different portal pages, it's possible that user actions on the portlets might be directed to the same portlet instance.

THE PORTLET LIFECYCLE—IMPORTANT POINTS

A portlet may be initialized by the portlet container as soon as it's deployed or when the first request for the portlet is received. In either case, the init method of the portlet instance is invoked before making the instance available for request handling.

As figure 2.8 indicates, the init and destroy methods don't form part of the portlet request-processing cycle and are meant to be called by the portlet container at a time determined by the container implementation. The following inferences can be drawn from figure 2.8:

- *Action request*—Invokes the processAction method, followed by a call to the portlet's render method. If there are more portlets on the portal page, the render methods of all portlets are invoked by the container.
- *Render request*—Invokes the render method only. If there are more portlets on the portal page, the render methods of all portlets are invoked by the container.

Portlets are multithreaded; each request received by the portlet container is executed in a different thread, and at a given time it's possible that multiple threads are accessing a portlet instance. It's the portlet developer's responsibility to design portlets that can handle concurrent requests.

NOTE   When designing portlets, you should synchronize access to shared mutable resources, like mutable instance variables, to address multithreading issues.

To create your own portlet class, you can either directly implement the Portlet interface or you can extend the GenericPortlet abstract class.

2.4.2   *Creating portlets with the GenericPortlet class*

The GenericPortlet class provides a default implementation for all the methods defined in the different lifecycle interfaces (Portlet, ResourceServingPortlet, and EventPortlet), along with convenience methods, making it easy for developers to write their own portlets. There are several benefits of extending the GenericPortlet class to create your own portlet:

- You only need to override the methods for which you want to provide a portlet-specific implementation. This saves you the effort of providing empty implementations for all the methods in the lifecycle interfaces.

- Your portlet class isn't directly dependent upon the portlet lifecycle interfaces. If the portlet lifecycle interfaces undergo any changes in future versions of the Java Portlet specification, those changes can be absorbed by the `Generic-Portlet` class, making your portlets forward compatible.

- `GenericPortlet` provides convenience methods that make it easy for you to handle requests. For example, the default implementation of the `render` method in `GenericPortlet` attempts to dispatch a render request to a `doView`, `doEdit`, or `doHelp` method, depending upon the *portlet mode*. We'll discuss portlet modes and the `doView`, `doEdit`, and `doHelp` methods later in this chapter.

- `GenericPortlet` makes use of the Java *annotation* facility to dispatch requests to the appropriate method. This allows you to give developer-friendly names to your methods so you can recognize them easily. We'll discuss the annotations available in the `GenericPortlet` class later in this chapter.

Figure 2.9 shows that the `GenericPortlet` class implements lifecycle interfaces and provides convenience methods. For brevity, not all methods of the `GenericPortlet` class are shown in the figure.

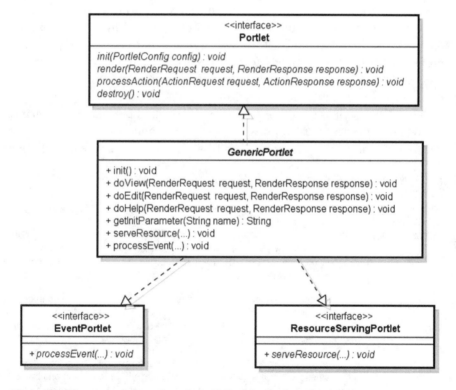

Figure 2.9 **The `GenericPortlet` abstract class implements the `Portlet`, `EventPortlet`, and `ResourceServingPortlet` interfaces. It provides default implementations of the `Portlet` interface's `render` method, and it dispatches render requests to the `doView`, `doHelp`, and `doEdit` methods, depending upon the portlet's mode.**

To gain the benefits offered by the `GenericPortlet` class, the User Registration example portlet extends the `GenericPortlet` class.

> **CODE REFERENCE**   If you haven't done so already, you should now import the ch2_UserRegistration Eclipse project from the book's source code, and refer to the `UserRegistrationPortlet` class, which extends `GenericPortlet`.

Now that you know the various lifecycle methods defined in the `Portlet` interface and the role that the `GenericPortlet` class plays in creating portlets, it's time to dive deeper into the default implementation of the `render` method provided by the `GenericPortlet` class. This requires an understanding of portlet modes.

2.5   *Generating portlet content based on portlet mode*

Portlet modes allow portlets to generate different content (different markup fragments) depending upon the *functionality requested* by the user.

We saw earlier in this chapter that the `render` method of a portlet is responsible for generating content. For instance, the `render` method of a Weather portlet will generate weather information. So far, we've talked about the content and behavior of portlets from the business perspective. In reality, a portlet needs to generate different content depending upon the functionality requested by the user, as indicated by the *portlet mode*. For example, if the user wants to personalize the portlet by setting preferences, the portlet needs to generate content that allows the user to enter their preferences; if the user wants to view information on how to use the portlet, the portlet needs to generate help information.

Table 2.2 describes the three portlet modes defined by the portlet specification.

When a portlet that supports `EDIT` or `HELP` mode, or both, is rendered by a web portal, additional options are available to the user for viewing the help infor-

Table 2.2   Portlet modes and the content generated in those modes

Portlet mode	Generated content
VIEW	A portlet generates content that reflects the current state of the portlet instance. This content carries business value. The `GenericPortlet` class provides the `doView` method, which is the `render` method in `VIEW` mode. It's mandatory for portlets to support `VIEW` mode.
EDIT	A portlet generates content that allows users to personalize the content and behavior of the portlet. This content doesn't carry any business value; it's meant for users to specify their preferences. The `GenericPortlet` class provides the `doEdit` method, which is the `render` method in `EDIT` mode.
HELP	A portlet generates content that shows help information. This content doesn't carry any business value; it's meant to provide users with information on how to use the portlet. The `GenericPortlet` class provides the `doHelp` method, which is the `render` method in `HELP` mode.

Figure 2.10 Additional options are available when the portlet supports additional portlet modes. The Preferences option is available when the portlet supports EDIT portlet mode, and the Help option is available when the portlet supports HELP portlet mode.

mation and personalizing the portlet. Figure 2.10 shows these additional options for a News portlet.

In figure 2.10, the Preferences and Help options are shown to the user because the News portlet supports both EDIT and HELP modes.

> **NOTE** The way these additional options are shown to the user varies from one portal server to another. For example, Liferay Portal displays additional options in a pop-up menu, and in Jetspeed they're displayed as icons in the portlet window's title bar.

Figure 2.11 shows the personalization options available for the News portlet.

Figure 2.11 These personalization options for the News portlet are displayed when you select the Preferences option.

Figure 2.12 displays the help information for the News portlet.

> **NOTE** The User Registration portlet also shows help information and a personalization page to users, so it must support EDIT and HELP portlet modes.

Now that you've seen what the standard portlet modes and their purposes are, let's look at each of the doXXXX methods defined in the GenericPortlet class.

Figure 2.12 Help information for the News portlet is displayed when you select the Help option.

2.5.1   *Writing content generation methods for each portlet mode*

In the context of the News portlet (see figures 2.11, and 2.12), you saw that different markup is generated by the portlet depending upon the portlet mode, but how can the Portlet interface's render method generate this different content? You can achieve this in two ways, depending on whether your portlet class directly implements the Portlet interface or extends the GenericPortlet class.

PORTLET CLASS IMPLEMENTS THE PORTLET INTERFACE

If the portlet class directly implements the Portlet interface, the render method will check for the current portlet mode and, based on the portlet mode, will generate appropriate markup. The next listing shows the ExamplePortlet class, which implements the Portlet interface's render method in this way.

> **Listing 2.1   Portlet class implements `Portlet` interface**

```
import javax.portlet.*;

public class ExamplePortlet implements Portlet {
  public void render(RenderRequest request,
    RenderResponse response)                                ❶ Checks if
      throws PortletException, IOException {                  portlet mode
    if(request.getPortletMode() == PortletMode.VIEW) {       is VIEW
      ...                                                    ❷ Generates content
    }                                                           for VIEW mode
    if(request.getPortletMode() == PortletMode.EDIT) {       ❸ Checks if portlet
      ...                                                       mode is EDIT
    }
    if(request.getPortletMode() == PortletMode.HELP) {       ❹ Checks if portlet
      ...                                                       mode is HELP
    }
  }
  ...
}
```

The render method checks if the portlet mode is VIEW ❶. If so, the render method generates content ❷ for the VIEW mode. Similarly, the render method checks the portlet mode and generates content appropriate for the mode ❸ and ❹.

In this listing, you can also see that the portlet mode is obtained from the Render-Request object using the getPortletMode method. The PortletMode class of the Portlet API defines VIEW, EDIT, and HELP constants, which have also been used in listing 2.1 to identify the portlet mode. We'll discuss the RenderRequest object in chapter 3 and the PortletMode class in chapter 4.

PORTLET CLASS EXTENDS THE GENERICPORTLET CLASS

The GenericPortlet class provides a default implementation of the render method that delegates calls to the doView, doEdit, and doHelp methods, depending upon the portlet mode. You can override these methods to generate markup fragments for each portlet mode. For instance, this is what the methods do in the News portlet:

- doView—Generates a markup fragment for displaying news
- doEdit—Generates a markup fragment for displaying the personalization options, like number of news items to display and the preferred news category
- doHelp—Generates a markup fragment for displaying information regarding what the News portlet does, how to use it, and how to personalize the news content

The signatures of doEdit, doView, and doHelp are the same as for the Portlet interface's render method. The GenericPortlet class not only provides separate methods for rendering content in different portlet modes, it allows you to have developer-friendly render method names. This is achieved using the @RenderMode annotation for render methods. This is the syntax:

```
@RenderMode(name=<portlet mode name>)
```

where <portlet mode name> is the name of the portlet mode (VIEW, EDIT, or HELP).

You can annotate a method with @RenderMode if it has the following signature:

```
void <method_name> (RenderRequest, RenderResponse) throws
    PortletException, IOException.
```

where <method_name> is a developer-friendly method name for the render method.

The following code snippet shows an @RenderMode annotation indicating that the method is a render method for the VIEW portlet mode:

```
@RenderMode(name = "VIEW")
public void sayHello(RenderRequest request, RenderResponse response)
   throws PortletException, IOException {
  ...
}
```

This is the same method we used in chapter 1 when we created the Hello World portlet.

If you're using the GenericPortlet class to create your own portlet, you can choose to override the doXXXX methods (doView, doEdit, and doHelp) of the GenericPortlet class to handle render requests, or you can create your own render methods and annotate them with the @RenderMode annotation. The sequence diagram in figure 2.13 shows how the default implementation of the GenericPortlet class's render method handles render requests.

In figure 2.13, when a render request comes from the web portal, the GenericPortlet class's render method dispatches the request to the doDispatch method, which attempts to find the @RenderMode annotated method for the current portlet mode. If a method is found, it's invoked. If an @RenderMode annotated method for the portlet mode isn't found, the GenericPortlet's doXXXX method corresponding to the current portlet mode is invoked.

CODE REFERENCE   Refer to the UserRegistrationPortlet class in the ch2_UserRegistration folder to see the @RenderMode annotation in use.

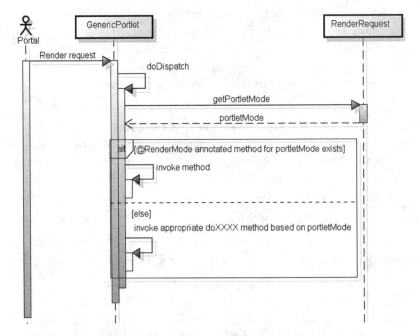

**Figure 2.13 A sequence diagram depicting the default implementation of the
`GenericPortlet` class's `render` method. Based on the portlet mode, either the method
with the `@RenderMode` annotation or the corresponding `doXXXX` method is invoked.**

The next listing shows the `UserRegistrationPortlet` class written using the `@Render-Mode` annotation.

Listing 2.2   The `UserRegistrationPortlet` class extends `GenericPortlet`

```
import javax.portlet.*;

public class UserRegistrationPortlet extends GenericPortlet {

  @RenderMode(name="VIEW")
  public void renderForm(RenderRequest request,
    RenderResponse response) throws ...{
  ...
  }
  @RenderMode(name="EDIT")
  public void renderPrefs(RenderRequest request,
    RenderResponse response) throws ...{
  ...
  }
  @RenderMode(name="HELP")
  public void renderHelp(RenderRequest request,
    RenderResponse response) throws ...{
  ...
  }
  ...
  }
```

❶ **renderForm is render method for VIEW mode**

❷ **renderPrefs is render method for EDIT mode**

❸ **renderHelp is render method for HELP mode**

First, the `renderForm` method is defined ❶. It's annotated with the `@RenderMode` annotation and the mode name is specified as `VIEW`. This means the `renderForm` method is a render method if the portlet mode is `VIEW`.

Next, the `renderPrefs` method is defined ❷. It's annotated with the `@RenderMode` annotation and the mode name is specified as `EDIT`. The `renderPrefs` method is a render method if the portlet mode is `EDIT`.

Using the `@RenderMode` annotation, `renderHelp` is defined as the render method for `HELP` mode ❸.

> **NOTE** The access modifier for methods annotated with the `@RenderMode` annotation must be `public`.

The `GenericPortlet` class also provides a default implementation of the `process-Action` method, which attempts to dispatch an action request to a method annotated with `@ProcessAction`. The following code shows an `@ProcessAction` annotation in use:

```
@ProcessAction(name = "registerUserAction")
public void registerUser(ActionRequest request,
  ActionResponse response) throws PortletException, IOException {
  ...
}
```

Here the `@ProcessAction` annotation marks the `registerUser` method as an action method. Note that the signature of the `registerUser` action method is same as that of the `Portlet` interface's `processAction` method, except for the name of the method. The `name` attribute specifies the value of a request parameter named `javax.portlet` `.action` in the `ActionRequest`. If the `ActionRequest` contains a `javax.portlet.action` parameter whose value matches the value specified for the `name` attribute of an `@ProcessAction` annotation of an action method, that action method is invoked. For instance, in the preceding code, if the value of the `javax.portlet.action` request parameter in `ActionRequest` is `registerUserAction`, then the `registerUser` method of the portlet class is invoked. The `ActionRequest` object also defines an `ACTION_NAME` constant that has the value `javax.portlet.action`, so you can use the `ACTION_NAME` constant when you're creating an action URL to specify the value of the `javax.portlet.action` request parameter, as described in section 2.6.7.

Providing an implementation of the `GenericPortlet`'s `doXXXX` methods or annotating custom render methods with `@RenderMode` in your portlet class isn't enough to make your portlets support a portlet mode. Support for a portlet mode must be specified in the portlet deployment descriptor.

2.5.2 *Defining support for portlet modes*

A portlet defines the portlet modes it supports in the portlet deployment descriptor: portlet.xml. The supported modes are defined with the `<portlet-mode>` element, which is a subelement of the `<portlet>` element's `<supports>` subelement.

The User Registration portlet must support EDIT and HELP portlet modes, and the following XML fragment shows how this is specified in its portlet.xml file.

```
<portlet>
    <portlet-name>UserRegistrationPortlet</portlet-name>
    <display-name>User Registration Portlet</display-name>
    <portlet-class>chapter02.code.listing.
      ➥UserRegistrationPortlet</portlet-class>
    <supports>
      <mime-type>text/html</mime-type>
      <portlet-mode>VIEW</portlet-mode>
      <portlet-mode>EDIT</portlet-mode>
      <portlet-mode>HELP</portlet-mode>
    </supports>
    <resource-bundle>content.Language-ext</resource-bundle>
    ...
</portlet>
```

You aren't required to specify that a portlet supports VIEW mode, because the portlet container assumes that all portlets must support VIEW mode.

That's all you need to know about portlet modes for now. We'll discuss custom portlet modes and changing the portlet mode programmatically in chapter 4.

You now know about the portlet lifecycle and how portlet URLs result in the invocation of render and processAction lifecycle methods. The rest of this chapter will introduce some of the foundation concepts for portlets, so you'll be ready to build the User Registration portlet.

2.6   *Portlet development in depth*

So far in this chapter, you've learned the basic concepts behind portlets, portlet URLs, portlet request types, the Portlet interface, the GenericPortlet class, portlet modes, and so on. In this section, we'll focus on some of the core concepts in detail. This section focuses on the following topics:

- Portlet API objects
- Creating JSPs to display portlet content
- The portlet deployment descriptor
- Dispatching portlet requests using the PortletRequestDispatcher
- Internationalization and localization using resource bundles
- Portlet initialization parameters
- Creating self-referencing render and action URLs
- Container-runtime options

Let's first look at the objects that the User Registration portlet will be using.

> **CODE REFERENCE** This section frequently refers to source code in the ch2_UserRegistration folder. To get the maximum out of this section, you should have the source code from that folder imported into your Eclipse IDE.

2.6.1 *The Portlet API objects*

Figure 2.14 shows some of the important Portlet API objects that the User Registration portlet uses, along with their intended purpose.

The User Registration portlet class's `init` method makes use of the `PortletConfig` object **1** to access portlet settings, such as the supported portlet modes, supported locales, resource bundle information, and so on. The portlet class uses `Portlet-Context` to obtain the `PortletRequestDispatcher` object **2**. The portlet class uses `PortletRequestDispatcher` to dispatch requests to JSPs or servlets in the same portlet application **3**, and a request is dispatched to a JSP or servlet **4** via the `Portlet-RequestDispatcher`. At **5**, it uses the `RenderResponse` object to create action and render URLs, which are then passed to the JSP page using request attributes **6**. These action and render URLs form part of the content generated by the JSP page, which can be a hyperlink (as in the case of the Reset link in figure 2.1 or the Home link in

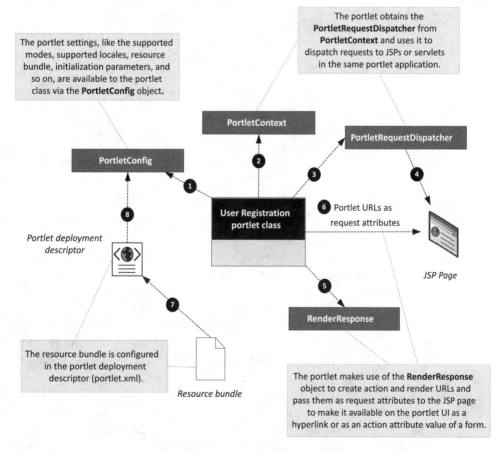

Figure 2.14 **The User Registration portlet makes use of several objects, including `PortletConfig`, `PortletContext`, and `RenderResponse`, to accomplish its task.**

figure 2.2) or they can be the value of an HTML `form` tag's action attribute (as in the case of the user registration form shown in figure 2.1). At ❼, the portlet deployment descriptor (portlet.xml) specifies the resource bundle that will be used for the portlet. At ❽, the User Registration portlet class's `registerUser` method uses `PortletConfig` object to read the resource bundle information identified in the portlet deployment descriptor.

Let's now look at the JSPs that you need to create to implement the User Registration portlet.

2.6.2 Creating JSPs to display portlet content

The User Registration portlet uses JSPs to show portlet content. Table 2.3 lists the JSPs used by the portlet and the content they display.

Table 2.3   JSPs used by the User Registration portlet

JSP page name	Content displayed
registrationForm.jsp	Shows the user registration form (see figure 2.1). The same form is redisplayed by the portlet if a validation error occurs during the saving of the registration information (see figure 2.3).
preferences.jsp	Shows the personalization message (see figure 2.4).
help.jsp	Shows help information about the portlet (see figure 2.5).
success.jsp	Shows the success message if the registration information is successfully saved, along with the registration information that was saved (see figure 2.2).

Now that you know which Portlet API objects you need to work with, and the JSPs used by the User Registration portlet, let's see how the User Registration portlet should behave internally in response to actions taken by a user. Figure 2.15 shows the various methods that should be provided by the User Registration portlet class, when these methods should be invoked, what JSP pages should be used to generate portlet content, and so on.

The portlet container receives a render request for the User Registration portlet ❶. If the mode of the portlet is VIEW, the `UserRegistrationPortlet` class's `renderForm` method ❷ is invoked. This method uses registrationForm.jsp to display its content. If the mode of the portlet is EDIT, the `renderPrefs` method ❸ is invoked; it uses preferences.jsp to display its content. If the mode of the portlet is HELP, the `renderHelp` method ❹ is invoked; it uses help.jsp to display its content.

The portlet container receives an action request for the User Registration portlet ❺. An action request is sent for the User Registration portlet when the user clicks the Submit button, because the registration action is a state-changing action. At ❻, the `registerUser` action method is invoked. As discussed earlier, an action method is always followed by a render method, and `registerUser` must communicate

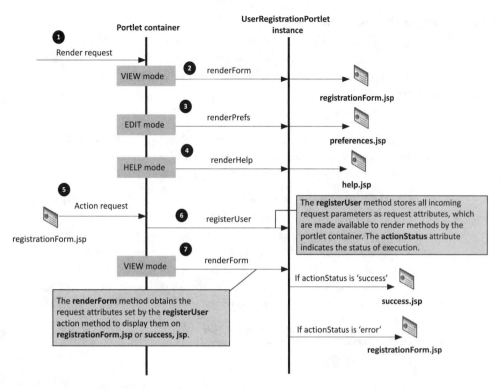

Figure 2.15 The User Registration portlet page flow. The portlet defines the `renderForm` method for rendering the registration form and the `registerUser` method for processing the form submission.

the success or failure of the registration action to the following render method so it can show the appropriate view. The `registerUser` method communicates registration success or failure using the `actionStatus` request attribute. The portlet container invokes the `renderForm` method ❼ to render the content of the portlet. If the `actionStatus` value is `success`, success.jsp is used to generate the portlet content; if its value is `error`, registrationForm.jsp is used to display the portlet content.

An important thing to notice in figure 2.15 is that the `registerUser` action method needs to communicate with the following `renderForm` render method. This communication is vital for the portlet to show appropriate content depending on whether the registration succeeds or fails. You'll see later in this chapter how portlets pass information from their action methods to their following render methods.

You might be wondering why figure 2.15 shows the `UserRegistrationPortlet`'s `renderForm` method being invoked by the portlet container after the `registerUser` action method. This is because portlet container invokes the render method in the same portlet mode as the preceding action method, unless the action method changes the portlet mode.

Now let's look at the portlet deployment descriptor.

2.6.3 *The portlet deployment descriptor*

A *web application* contains JSPs, servlets, Java classes, and a web application deployment descriptor, web.xml. A *portlet application* is a web application with portlets and a portlet deployment descriptor added to it. The portlet.xml file acts as a portlet application deployment descriptor, containing information and settings for portlets that form part of the portlet application.

> **TIP** Another way of saying this is that a portlet application is a web application (consisting of JSPs, servlets, classes, and web.xml) in which you have portlets, and for these portlets you create a separate deployment descriptor file, portlet.xml.

The <portlet-app> element is the root element of portlet.xml, and a portlet declaration is enclosed within the <portlet> subelement of the <portlet-app> element. In most cases, a single portlet.xml file contains multiple portlet declarations (because a portlet application usually consists of more than one portlet), and all the portlets defined in a single portlet.xml file form part of a single portlet application.

This next listing shows the portlet deployment descriptor of a portlet application that contains the User Registration portlet.

Listing 2.3 A portlet.xml file

```
<portlet-app ... >
  <portlet>
    <portlet-name>UserRegistrationPortlet</portlet-name>        ❶ Unique portlet
    <display-name>User Registration Portlet</display-name>          name in portlet
    <portlet-class>                                                 application
        chapter02.code.listing.UserRegistrationPortlet          ❷ Fully qualified
    </portlet-class>                                               class name of
                                                                   portlet
    <init-param>
      <name>defaultEmail</name>                                 ❸ Portlet initialization
      <value>@liferay.com</value>                                 parameter
    </init-param>

    <supports>
      <mime-type>text/html</mime-type>
      <portlet-mode>VIEW</portlet-mode>                         ❹ Supported mime
      <portlet-mode>EDIT</portlet-mode>                           type and modes
      <portlet-mode>HELP</portlet-mode>
    </supports>

    <resource-bundle>                                          ❺ Portlet resource
      content.Language-ext                                       bundle
    </resource-bundle>
  </portlet>
  <container-runtime-option>
    <name>
      javax.portlet.actionScopedRequestAttributes             ❻ Container-runtime
    </name>                                                      options
    <value>true</value>
  </container-runtime-option>
</portlet-app>
```

The <portlet-name> element ❶ specifies the portlet name. The name of a portlet must be unique within the scope of a portlet application; you must not have multiple portlets with the same name in a portlet.xml file. The <portlet-class> element ❷ defines the fully qualified class name of the portlet that implements the Portlet interface directly or indirectly.

The <init-param> element ❸ defines a portlet initialization parameter that's passed to the portlet instance when its init method is invoked by the portlet container. You can pass multiple initialization parameters to the portlet using the <init-param> element.

The <supports> element ❹ defines the portlet modes and MIME types supported by the portlet. The <resource-bundle> element ❺ defines the resource bundle the portlet will use to show labels, messages, and so on.

The portlet deployment descriptor ❻ instructs the portlet container to allow *action-scoped request attributes*. In section 2.6.8 of this chapter, we'll discuss what these attributes are and why they're useful in the context of the User Registration portlet.

When you make use of JSP pages to render content for the User Registration portlet, you need some mechanism to dispatch requests to the appropriate JSP pages from the UserRegistrationPortlet class's render methods. In figure 2.14, you saw that portlets make use of the PortletRequestDispatcher object to dispatch requests to JSP pages, and you can obtain that object by using the PortletContext object.

2.6.4 *Dispatching portlet requests using the PortletRequestDispatcher*

Before we get into the details of portlet request dispatching, let's first take a quick look at the PortletContext object.

The concept of a portlet context is similar to a servlet context: it provides access to the environment in which the portlet is running. In the case of portlets, the environment is the portlet application to which the portlet belongs, and the portlet container in which the portlet is running.

Portlet applications are extensions of web applications, so in portlet applications the PortletContext and ServletContext objects coexist. A single PortletContext instance is associated with a portlet application, and it's used by portlets to access resources in that application (which could be a JSP, servlet, or other portlet). We'll discuss the PortletContext object in detail in chapter 3.

> **NOTE** The GenericPortlet class provides a getPortletContext convenience method that returns the PortletContext object associated with the current portlet application. The PortletContext object can also be obtained using the PortletSession or PortletConfig objects, both of which are discussed in chapter 4.

Portlet content can be generated by writing directly to the PrintWriter object, as you did in the Hello World example in chapter 1, or by dispatching a request to a JSP, servlet, or HTML page. But if the markup fragment generated by the portlet is complex, it's better to pass on the responsibility of content generation to a JSP page, using the `PortletRequestDispatcher` object.

You can obtain the `PortletRequestDispatcher` object from the `PortletContext` object with either of these methods:

- `getRequestDispatcher(String path)`—The `path` parameter is the path to the JSP, servlet, or HTML page within the portlet application. The `path` is relative to the portlet application's context root and must begin with a slash (/).
- `getNamedDispatcher(String name)`—The `name` parameter is the name of a servlet (defined in web.xml) within the portlet application.

NOTE It isn't possible to use the `PortletContext` object to obtain the `PortletRequestDispatcher` object, which refers to resources (like JSPs, servlets, and HTML) outside the portlet application. A container implementation may provide special objects to dispatch requests to servlets or JSPs in other portlet applications, but these should be used carefully because they'll make your portlet noncompliant with the Portlet 2.0 specification.

The `PortletRequestDispatcher` defines the following methods to include content generated by a resource or forward request to a resource:

- `include`—This method includes the content generated from the resource in the portlet response. There are two versions of the `include` method, one of which is meant purely for backward compatibility with the Portlet 1.0 specification; it accepts the `RenderRequest` and `RenderResponse` objects as method parameters.
- `forward`—This method forwards the request for generating content to another resource.

The following code snippet shows how the User Registration portlet's `renderHelp` method uses `PortletRequestDispatcher` to include content generated by the help.jsp page:

```
@RenderMode(name="HELP")
public void renderHelp(RenderRequest request,
      RenderResponse response)throws PortletException, IOException {
  getPortletContext().getRequestDispatcher("/WEB-INF/jsp/help.jsp").
    include(request,response);
}
```

In the preceding code, the request and response objects are passed to the included JSP page, allowing the JSP page to access the attributes associated with the request.

In most scenarios, it's expected that the portlets can provide localized content based on user locale, a requirement that's addressed by *resource bundles*. The User Registration portlet makes use of resource bundles to externalize labels and messages, as you saw in the portlet.xml file (listing 2.3).

2.6.5 *Internationalization and localization using resource bundles*

A portlet in a portlet application has its own resource bundle, which is specified in the portlet deployment descriptor using the `<resource-bundle>` element (see listing 2.3). The `PortletRequest` interface's `getLocale` method returns the `java.util.Locale` object identifying the user's locale.

`ActionRequest` and `RenderRequest` are subinterfaces of the `PortletRequest` interface, so both the `processAction` and `render` methods (or `@ProcessAction` and `@RenderMode` annotated methods) of a portlet class have access to the user locale.

You can access the resource bundle configured for a portlet by using the `Portlet-Config` object, as you saw in figure 2.14. The `PortletConfig` object is meant to provide portlets with the configuration information specified in the portlet deployment descriptor, and a distinct `PortletConfig` object exists for each portlet in the portlet application. It can be used to access supported locales, resource bundles, portlet initialization parameters, and container-runtime option information from the portlet deployment descriptor.

The `PortletConfig` object's `getResourceBundle(java.util.Locale)` method provides access to the resource bundle configured for the portlet. The following code snippet shows how the User Registration portlet's `registerUser` action method uses the `PortletConfig` object to obtain error messages corresponding to the key `email.errorMsg.missing` from its resource bundle:

```
ResourceBundle bundle =
    getPortletConfig().getResourceBundle(request.getLocale());
String message = bundle.getString("email.errorMsg.missing");
```

In the preceding code, `getPortletConfig` is a convenience method, available in the `GenericPortlet` class, which returns a `PortletConfig` object for the portlet. In the User Registration portlet, the messages and labels for the portlet are defined in the resource bundle for easier internationalization and maintenance.

JSPs used by the User Registration portlet make use of JavaServer Pages Standard Tag Library (JSTL) formatting tags to allow JSP pages to obtain labels and messages from the resource bundle, as shown here:

```
<%@ taglib prefix="fmt" uri="http://java.sun.com/jstl/fmt" %>
<fmt:setBundle basename="content.Language-ext"/>
<fmt:message key="help.message"/>
```

The `<setBundle>` tag in this code loads the resource bundle named `Language-ext.properties` (see listing 2.3), which is inside the `content` package. The `<message>` tag displays the text from the resource bundle that has `help.message` as its key.

Portlet resource bundles contain static labels and messages for the portlet—they don't change when the same portlet is used across different web portals. In the User Registration portlet, the default email address (the one displayed on the registration form) is expected to change when the portlet is deployed as part of different web portals, so that makes it an ideal candidate to be configured as a portlet initialization parameter.

2.6.6   *Portlet initialization parameters*

Portlet initialization parameters allow you to move portlet configuration information outside of the portlet class. This approach allows the same portlet to be reused in different web portals by changing the configuration parameter values. We'll use this technique in the User Registration portlet to change the default value of the email address when the portlet is used in different web portals.

The initialization parameter for a portlet is defined by an <init-param> element in the portlet deployment descriptor; <init-param> has two mandatory subelements: <name> and <value>. The portlet initialization parameters are passed to the portlet's init method by the portlet container, and they're used by the portlet instance to initialize the instance.

The following fragment of the User Registration portlet's portlet.xml file shows the defaultEmail initialization parameter being used to pass the value @liferay.com to the init method:

```
<init-param>
  <name>defaultEmail</name>
  <value>@liferay.com</value>
</init-param>
```

> **NOTE**   The value of the <name> element must be unique within the scope of a portlet definition, which means within a <portlet> element.

If your portlet class extends from the GenericPortlet class, you can use its get-InitParameter convenience method to obtain the initialization parameter value. If you're directly implementing the Portlet interface, you can make use of the getInitParameter method of the PortletConfig object, which is passed as an argument to its init method.

The scope of a portlet initialization parameter is the portlet for which it's specified, but if you need to create an initialization parameter that's accessible to all portlets (and servlets) in a portlet application, you must use a *servlet context initialization parameter.* You can define servlet context initialization parameters in web.xml using <context-param> elements.

In the User Registration portlet, the user interacts with the portlet by clicking the Reset hyperlink or Submit button, and these actions must translate into action or render requests. To do this, the User Registration portlet, or any other portlet, creates portlet URLs (also referred to as *self-referencing URLs,* as discussed in section 2.3) and embeds them as the value of an href attribute (of the anchor tag) or action attribute (of the form tag).

Let's see how portlets create these self-referencing URLs.

2.6.7   *Creating portlet URLs*

Portlet URLs are created programmatically using the RenderResponse object, or by using the *portlet tag library* (which will be explained in chapter 6). Portlet URLs are container-specific, so if you deploy the same portlet on two different portlet containers, you'll find that the portlet URLs are entirely different.

CREATING A RENDER URL

A portlet instance can make use of the `RenderResponse` object to create render URLs. The `RenderResponse` object is available to a portlet's `render` method, making it possible to create a render URL within the `render` method.

The following code fragment shows how the `UserRegistrationPortlet` class creates a render URL for the Reset link:

```
@RenderMode(name="VIEW")
public void renderForm(RenderRequest request, RenderResponse response)
    throws PortletException, IOException {
  ...
  PortletURL resetRenderUrl = response.createRenderURL();
  ...
}
```

The `RenderResponse` object's `createRenderURL` method returns a `PortletURL` object that allows you to add parameters, set window state (maximized, minimized, or normal), and set the portlet mode.

CREATING AN ACTION URL

The `RenderResponse` object provides a `createActionURL` method to create action URLs. This method returns an object of type `PortletURL`, which defines methods to add parameters, set window state, and set portlet mode. The parameters in the action URL can be used by the `processAction` method (or by the `@ProcessAction` annotated method) to determine the action to be taken.

The following code snippet shows the `UserRegistrationPortlet` class's render-Form render method creating an action URL and adding an `action` parameter to it:

```
@RenderMode(name="VIEW")
public void renderForm(RenderRequest request, RenderResponse response)
    throws PortletException, IOException {
  ...
  PortletURL registerUserActionUrl = response.createActionURL();
  registerUserActionUrl.setParameter(ActionRequest.ACTION_NAME,
    "registerUserAction");
  ...
}
```

In the preceding code, the `ACTION_NAME` constant of the `ActionRequest` object has the value `javax.portlet.action`.

In general, you can add a parameter to the action URL with any name. If your portlet class extends from the `GenericPortlet` class, the value of the `javax.portlet.action` request parameter is useful in invoking the appropriate `@ProcessAction` annotated method. When `registerUserActionUrl` is rendered as a hyperlink or as the value of an `action` attribute of an HTML form, clicking the link or submitting the form will result in the execution of the `processAction` method (or the @ProcessAction annotated action method that specifies its name attribute value as registerUserAction).

For example, the following registerUser method of the UserRegistration-Portlet class is invoked when the value of the ActionRequest.ACTION_NAME request parameter is registerUserAction:

```
@ProcessAction(name="registerUserAction")
public void registerUser(ActionRequest request, ActionResponse response)
  throws PortletException, IOException {
  ...
}
```

> **NOTE**   The access modifier for methods annotated with the @ProcessAction annotation must be public.

The portlet container features that we've discussed so far in this book are available to portlets by default. For instance, you don't need to instruct the portlet container that your portlet needs a PortletConfig object to have it available at runtime. But in some cases you may need to instruct the portlet container to provide additional features to the portlet at runtime. These additional features are referred to as *container-runtime options*, and they're specified in the portlet deployment descriptor. For example, the User Registration portlet makes use of the javax.portlet.actionScoped-Request-DAttributes container-runtime option to share request attributes set in the registerUser action method with the renderForm method (see figure 2.15).

2.6.8   *Container-runtime options*

Container-runtime options are specified in the portlet deployment descriptor to provide additional features to portlets at runtime. In listing 2.3, the <container-runtime-option> element specified the value of the javax.portlet.actionScoped-RequestAttributes runtime option as true, which allows attributes set in the ActionRequest object (during action processing) to be available to the Render-Request object (during content rendering).

> **NOTE**   The runtime option is called *action-scoped request attributes* because the attributes set in the action request are available until another action request is executed. After the action method is executed, the request attributes set in the action method are available in subsequent render method invocations, until another action request is sent to the portlet.

In figure 2.8 you saw that the execution of the processAction method is followed by an invocation of the render method by the portlet container. In portlets, the render and processAction lifecycle methods aren't designed to communicate with each other, resulting in a clear separation of responsibility between action processing and content generation. But in some cases, you may need to send data from the process-Action method to a subsequent render method; you can do this either by using the javax.portlet.actionScopedRequestAttributes container-runtime option or by setting *render parameters* in the ActionResponse.

Render parameters are set using either of these two methods of Action-Response object:

```
setRenderParameter(String key, String value)
setRenderParameters(String key, String[] values)
```

Render parameters set using ActionResponse objects are available to the subsequent render method via the RenderRequest object. As the signatures of setRender-Parameter and setRenderParameters suggest, you can only pass String or String[] parameters to the subsequent render method. If you want to pass complex objects, you should use the javax.portlet.actionScopedRequestAttributes container-runtime option. The container-runtime options are specified in the portlet deployment descriptor using the <container-runtime> element.

The User Registration portlet uses the javax.portlet.actionScopedRequest-Attributes container-runtime option to display the registration success message, which includes name and email address information. When the user clicks the Submit button (see figure 2.1), the information in the form is sent to the registerUser action method as request parameters, which then need to be sent to the renderForm method so it can render the success.jsp page. This transfer is achieved with the help of the javax.portlet.actionScopedRequestAttributes container-runtime option. Figure 2.16 illustrates how this container-runtime option is used by the portlet container to allow request attributes stored in ActionRequest to be accessible (through the RenderRequest object) to the subsequent render method.

First, the user submits a request to register with the web portal ❶. The form's values, like first name, last name, and email, are sent as request parameters to the registerUser action method. The processAction method ❷ does the action processing and stores the request parameters as request attributes in the ActionRequest object. The portlet container ❸ checks whether the value of the javax.portlet.actionScopedRequestAttributes container-runtime option is true or false. If it's true, the container retrieves the attributes from the ActionRequest object and stores them in memory. The portlet container invokes the User Registration portlet's renderForm method ❹ and passes the request attributes it stored previously to the render method, which can retrieve them from the RenderRequest object.

NOTE Liferay Portal 5.2.3/6.x supports forwarding request attributes from ActionRequest to RenderRequest, even if you don't specify the use of the javax.portlet.actionScopedRequestAttributes container-runtime option in the portlet deployment descriptor. This out-of-the-box feature shouldn't be relied upon if you're creating a portlet that will be deployed across different portlet containers.

The Portlet 2.0 specification defines a couple of container-runtime options, one of which is the javax.portlet.actionScopedRequestAttributes runtime option. It's

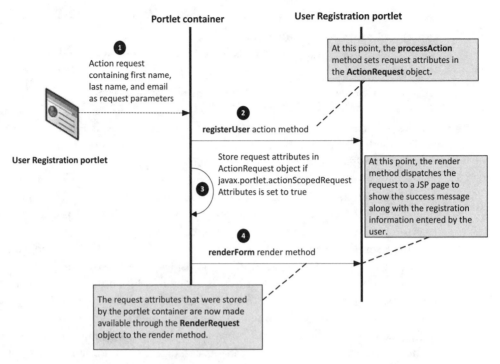

Figure 2.16   Registration information sent by the User Registration portlet is rendered again by the portlet using the `javax.portlet.actionScopedRequestAttributes` container-runtime option. The portlet container retains the request attributes stored in the `ActionRequest` object and makes them available to the render method through the `RenderRequest` object.

the only container-runtime option that must be supported by portlet containers. We'll discuss container-runtime options in detail in chapter 3.

Now that we've covered all the basics required to build the User Registration portlet, let's go through its implementation details. You may want to look back to section 2.1 to review the User Registration portlet's requirements before looking at its implementation in the next section.

2.7   *Implementing the User Registration portlet*

The concepts that you've learned so far in this chapter will be put to test in this section. You'll look specifically at the portlet class and the JSP pages used in the User Registration portlet.

> **NOTE**   The User Registration portlet makes use of JSTL to output values and to read labels and messages from the resource bundle, so it requires the standard.jar and jstl.jar files at runtime. The ch2_UserRegistration Eclipse project already contains these jar files in the WEB-INF/lib directory.

Let's discuss the methods defined in the UserRegistrationPortlet class.

2.7.1 The UserRegistrationPortlet class

The UserRegistrationPortlet class extends the GenericPortlet class and makes use of @RenderMode and @ProcessAction annotations to specify the portlet's render and action methods. The following code snippet shows the init method:

```
private String defaultEmail;
public void init() {
   defaultEmail = getPortletConfig().getInitParameter("defaultEmail");
}
```

The init method makes use of the GenericPortlet class's getInitParameter convenience method to obtain the defaultEmail portlet initialization parameter from the portlet deployment descriptor.

RENDER METHODS

The next listing shows the render method, for VIEW mode, of the UserRegistrationPortlet class.

Listing 2.4 The `UserRegistrationPortlet` class's render method

```
@RenderMode(name="VIEW")                                    ❶ Specifies @RenderMode
public void renderForm(RenderRequest request,                 annotation for render method
➥RenderResponse response)
   throws PortletException, IOException {
   if ("success".equalsIgnoreCase((String) request
      .getAttribute("actionStatus"))) {
    PortletURL homeUrl = response.createRenderURL();
    request.setAttribute("homeUrl", homeUrl);              ❷ Shows success.jsp page
    getPortletContext().getRequestDispatcher                after registration
      ("/WEB-INF/jsp/success.jsp").include(
    request, response);
    return;
   }

   PortletURL registerUserActionUrl =                      ❸ Creates action URL
         response.createActionURL();
   registerUserActionUrl.setParameter(                     ❹ Adds javax.portlet.action
     ActionRequest.ACTION_NAME,"registerUserAction");        parameter to action URL

   PortletURL resetRenderUrl =                             ❺ Creates render URL
         response.createRenderURL();
   request.setAttribute("registerUserActionUrl",
     registerUserActionUrl);
   request.setAttribute("resetRenderUrl",
     resetRenderUrl);

   if (!"error".equalsIgnoreCase((String) request          ❻ Sets attributes in
    .getAttribute("actionStatus"))) {                        RenderRequest
     request.setAttribute("email", defaultEmail);
   }

   getPortletContext().getRequestDispatcher(               ❼ Dispatches
      "/WEB-INF/jsp/registrationForm.jsp").                  request to JSP
      include(request, response);
}
```

The @RenderMode annotation ❶ is used to mark the renderForm method as the portlet's render method in VIEW mode. The renderForm method ❷ checks the value of actionStatus request attribute (set by the registerUser action method) to decide whether the request needs to be sent to success.jsp to show the success message. The action URL named registerUserActionUrl is created ❸ using RenderResponse object's createActionUrl method.

A parameter named ActionRequest.ACTION_NAME (which has the value javax.portlet.action) is added to the registerUserActionUrl ❹. The parameter is used by the default implementation of the GenericPortlet class's processAction method to identify which action method to invoke. The value of this parameter has been set to registerUserAction, so the default implementation of the process-Action method in the GenericPortlet class will invoke the UserRegistration-Portlet class's registerUser method (see listing 2.6), because it's annotated with @ProcessAction(name="registerUserAction").

The render URL named resetRenderUrl is created ❺ using the Render-Response object's createRenderUrl method. The resetRenderUrl URL is used by the Reset hyperlink on the user registration form (see figure 2.1). Because you aren't setting any portlet mode as part of the resetRenderUrl, clicking the Reset hyperlink of the user registration page will always result in the invocation of the renderForm method.

At ❻, registerUserActionUrl, resetRenderUrl, and defaultEmail are stored as request attributes so that when the request is dispatched (using the Request-Dispatcher object) to registrationForm.jsp ❼. These request attributes can be used by success.jsp to show the registered user's information.

The next listing shows the render methods of the UserRegistrationPortlet class for EDIT and HELP portlet modes.

Listing 2.5   Render methods in HELP and EDIT modes

```
@RenderMode(name="EDIT")
public void renderPrefs(RenderRequest request, RenderResponse response)
    throws PortletException, IOException {
  getPortletContext().getRequestDispatcher("/WEB-INF/jsp/preferences.jsp").
    include(request,response);
}

@RenderMode(name="HELP")
public void renderHelp(RenderRequest request, RenderResponse response)
    throws PortletException, IOException {
  getPortletContext().getRequestDispatcher("/WEB-INF/jsp/help.jsp").
    include(request,response);
}
```

In listing 2.5, the renderPrefs and renderHelp methods are the render methods in EDIT and HELP modes respectively. These methods obtain the PortletRequest-Dispatcher object using PortletContext and then dispatch requests to the appropriate JSP pages.

The `UserRegistrationPortlet` class provides an action method that processes registration form submissions, as described next.

ACTION METHODS

The `UserRegistrationPortlet` class defines a single action method, `register-User`, which is invoked when the registration form is submitted. The `registerUser` method is responsible for validating the form and setting the first name, last name, and email as `ActionRequest` attributes to make them available to the `renderForm` render method.

The listing below shows the `registerUser` action method.

Listing 2.6 The `UserRegistrationPortlet` class's `registerUser` method

```
@ProcessAction(name="registerUserAction")          ◁─┐  Specifies @ProcessAction
public void registerUser(ActionRequest request,    ❶    annotation for method
➥ActionResponse response)
    throws PortletException, IOException {
  String email = request.getParameter("email");
  request.setAttribute("user",                       ❷   Sets User object as
     new User(request.getParameter("firstName"),         request attribute
  request.getParameter("lastName"), email));
  ...                                                ❸   Checks if email
  if(email == null || email.trim().equals("")) {     ◁─      was entered
    ResourceBundle bundle = getPortletConfig().
    getResourceBundle(request.getLocale());          ❹   Obtains
    request.setAttribute("errorMsg",                     message from
    bundle.getString("email.errorMsg.missing"));         resource bundle
    request.setAttribute("actionStatus", "error");  ◁─
  } else {                                           ❺   Sets actionStatus
    ...                                                   request attribute
    request.setAttribute("actionStatus", "success");
  }
}
```

The `@ProcessAction(name="registerUserAction")` annotation ❶ marks the `registerUser` method as an action method that's invoked by the default implementation of the `GenericPortlet` class's `processAction` method when the incoming action request has a request parameter with the name `ActionRequest.ACTION_NAME` and value `registerUserAction`. The `User` object is created (using the first name, last name, and email request parameters) and set as a request attribute ❷. The form submission is validated ❸ to verify whether the user has entered a value for the email mandatory field. The error message, "Please enter Email", is obtained from the resource bundle ❹ and set as a request attribute. User information is saved into the database ❺ and the `actionStatus` (`success` or `error`) is set in the request attribute to allow the `render-Form` method to take appropriate action based on the `actionStatus`.

2.7.2   *JSP pages*

The User Registration portlet consists of multiple JSP pages, and all of them are created along similar lines. We'll cover the details of registrationForm.jsp in this section. To view all the JSP pages, please refer to the book's source code.

Our next listing shows the content of the registrationForm.jsp page, which displays the registration form to the user.

Listing 2.7   The registrationForm.jsp page

```jsp
<%@ taglib prefix="c"
   uri="http://java.sun.com/jsp/jstl/core"%>
<%@ taglib prefix="fmt"
    uri="http://java.sun.com/jstl/fmt"%>

<%@ page contentType="text/html" isELIgnored="false" %>

<fmt:setBundle basename="content.Language-ext"/>

<form action="<c:out
   value='${requestScope.registerUserActionUrl}'/>"
     method="POST">
  <tr>
     <td colspan="2">
       <font color="#FF0000">
          <c:out value="${requestScope.errorMsg}"/>
       </font>
       </td>
  </tr>
  <tr>
     <td><fmt:message key="label.firstName"/></td>
     <td><input type="text" name="firstName"
          value="${requestScope.user.firstName}">
     </input></td>
  </tr>
  ...
  <input type="submit" value="Submit">
        
     <a href="<c:out
       value='${requestScope.resetUrl}'/>">
       <b><fmt:message key="label.reset"/></b>
     </a>
</form>
```

1 Declare Formatting and Core tag library

2 Enable EL expression evaluation

3 Set resource bundle and form action

4 Display error message from request

5 Retrieve label and firstName value

6 Display reset render URL as hyperlink

The `taglib` directive **1** declares that the JSP is using the core and formatting tags of JSTL. At **2**, you enable the EL expression evaluation for the JSP page.

The `<setBundle>` tag is used to set up the resource bundle that will be used for labels and messages **3**. Then the `<form>` tag is defined with `registerUserActionUrl` as the `action` attribute's value. The `registerUserActionUrl` is an action URL, and when you submit the user registration form, `UserRegistrationPortlet`'s `register-User` method will be executed. The form data is available to the `registerUser` method as request parameters.

If any error message is found in the request, it's displayed in red **❹**; an error message is displayed if you don't enter a value for the Email field on the registration form (see figure 2.3). The `registerUser` method is responsible for validating the form. It puts a request attribute named `errorMsg` in `ActionRequest` if the email field value is found blank in the submitted request.

The label for the first name field is obtained from the resource bundle **❺**, and the value of `firstName` field is obtained from the request. The `registerUser` method is responsible for obtaining form field values and putting them as request attributes in `ActionRequest`. A hyperlink referring to `resetUrl` (which is a render URL) is created **❻** to allow a render request to be sent to the portlet when the Reset link is clicked on the registration form.

That covers all the files required for developing the User Registration portlet. The next steps are to build the project, deploy the corresponding WAR file to the Liferay Portal server, and add the portlet to a portal page as described in section 1.8 of chapter 1. If everything goes well, adding a User Registration portlet to a portal page will display the registration form, as shown in figure 2.1.

2.8   Summary

In this chapter we discussed the portlet lifecycle and you learned about some of the basic portlet concepts. The different lifecycle interfaces in a portlet help separate the responsibilities for generating content, processing actions, handling received events, and serving resources.

A clear understanding of the purpose of the different lifecycle interfaces and methods will help you segregate your logic appropriately in your portlet class. For instance, the `processAction` method is meant for processing actions and not for generating content. If you attempt to generate content by dispatching a request to a JSP page (using `PortletRequestDispatcher`) or by directly writing to the response output stream, this effort to generate content will be ignored by the portlet container. Similarly, the `render` method is for generating content and not for processing user actions. If you write action-processing logic in the `render` method, instead of in the `processAction` method, action processing will take place every time the portlet's `render` method is invoked (regardless of whether the user refreshed the portal page or an action request was sent to another portlet on the same portal page), which is undesirable.

In the next chapter, we'll go deeper into the Portlet 2.0 API, discuss various request and response objects and container-runtime options, and take a more in-depth look at some of the features provided by the Portlet 2.0 specification.

Portlet 2.0 API— portlet objects and container-runtime options

This chapter covers

- Using the portlet container's request and response objects
- Adding external JavaScript and CSS files to a portal page
- Accessing a logged-in user's information via user attributes
- Understanding `PortletContext`, `PortletConfig`, and `PortletSession`
- Using container-runtime options

In the context of the example User Registration portlet, chapter 2 introduced you to some of the classes and interfaces of the Portlet 2.0 specification. This chapter and the next will provide comprehensive coverage of the Portlet 2.0 API using an example Book Catalog portlet.

In this chapter, we'll look at portlet objects, methods, and features that you'll come across often while developing portlets. Chapter 4 will cover advanced portlet features that let you cache portlet content, localize portlet content, define custom portlet modes and window states, and secure portlets from unauthorized access.

NOTE　We'll cover classes and interfaces specific to serving resources, inter-portlet communication, portlet filters, and personalization in chapters dedicated to these topics.

In this and the next chapter, you'll learn the importance of knowing your portal server before you start developing portlets for it. This will remain important even as new versions of various portal servers are introduced, with more features and fewer limitations. The example Book Catalog portlet in this chapter looks at using portlets with servlets, and will serve as a basis for learning the concepts discussed in this and the next chapter.

The intent of these chapters is to show you that it isn't difficult to develop portlets that are portable across different portal servers, irrespective of portal server limitations or the dependence of portlets on portal server–specific APIs.

3.1　*Requirements for the Book Catalog portlet*

If you tried running the User Registration portlet (developed in chapter 2) on portal servers other than Liferay Portal, there's a good chance that it didn't work at all, or that it behaved differently. The reason for this is that the other portal server is missing support for an optional feature, or there's an existing bug in the portlet container or portal server software, or there are portal server–specific configuration requirements for a portlet.

In this chapter, you'll look at a Book Catalog portlet that allows users to manage a book catalog. With the Book Catalog portlet, you can add, remove, search for, and list books in the catalog. This example portlet will help you learn and allow you to implement the concepts described in this chapter.

The rest of the chapters in this book will follow a similar pattern. We'll begin with a subset of Book Catalog portlet requirements to implement, and the chapter will discuss and explain the concepts needed to implement the changes in the Book Catalog portlet.

The Book Catalog portlet that we'll discuss in this chapter is expected to work on Liferay Portal 5.2.3/6.x as well as the following portal servers:

- Jetspeed-2.2.1, available from Apache at http://portals.apache.org/jetspeed-2/; Jetspeed internally uses the Pluto portlet container. Refer to the Apache Pluto web page for more information about the Pluto portlet container (http://portals.apache.org/pluto/).
- GlassFish Server 3.0.1 (available from http://glassfish.java.net/) with OpenPortal Portlet Container 2.1.2 (available from https://portlet-container.dev.java.net/). OpenPortal Portlet Container 2.1.2 can be installed on Tomcat, Jetty, JBoss AS, GlassFish, and so on.

The portlet class in the User Registration portlet (in chapter 2) was responsible for generating content and processing actions. In this chapter there's a servlet component, `BookServlet`, that generates content and does the action processing. The

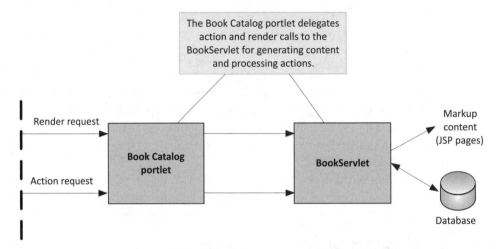

Figure 3.1   The Book Catalog portlet makes use of the BookServlet to generate content and process actions. The BookServlet generates HTML markup using JSP pages, and it interacts with the database to obtain or store book information.

Book Catalog portlet class delegates action and render requests to BookServlet to generate content for the portlet and to add books to or remove them from the catalog. Figure 3.1 illustrates the interaction between the Book Catalog portlet class and BookServlet.

In figure 3.1, the Book Catalog portlet receives action and render requests from the portal, which in turn delegates them to the BookServlet for further processing. The content generated by the BookServlet is included in the response generated by the Book Catalog portlet.

> **WARNING**   In fresh development projects, you shouldn't use servlets to process actions or generate content for your portlet. Only if you have an existing servlet that contains the processing logic you want to use should you consider using servlets with your portlets.

In the Book Catalog portlet, the user action information is sent by the JSP pages to the portlet class using the myaction *request parameter*. The BookServlet uses a *request attribute* named myaction to determine which action needs to be taken by BookServlet. The Book Catalog portlet is responsible for setting the myaction attribute in the request before dispatching the request to the BookServlet.

In this chapter, the Book Catalog portlet requirements focus on the following Portlet 2.0 concepts:

- Using servlets for content generation and action processing.
- Programmatically changing the portlet title.
- Using the actionScopedRequestAttributes container-runtime option. In chapter 2, you used this option to share request attributes set in the action

method with the render method of the portlet. This chapter discusses the pros and cons of using the option.

- Using optional container-runtime options.
- Sharing session information between portlet and servlet components in the same portlet application.
- Including CSS and JavaScript in portlets. This is where we'll discuss restrictions on the content generated by portlets.

Figure 3.2 shows the home page (also referred to as the *initial content*) of the Book Catalog portlet.

At ❶, you can specify search criteria for the book. The table below the search criteria displays matching books. You can use the Refresh Search Results hyperlink ❷ to refresh your search results; if a book was deleted or added and it matches your search criteria, the results will be updated accordingly.

You can download or upload the table of contents (TOC) for a book using Download and Upload ❸ hyperlinks. The implementation of this feature will be discussed in chapter 12, which discusses resource serving.

You can use the FULL SCREEN hyperlink ❹ to view the Book Catalog portlet in maximized window state. The Book Catalog portlet ❺ displays information about the portal server on which the portlet is currently deployed.

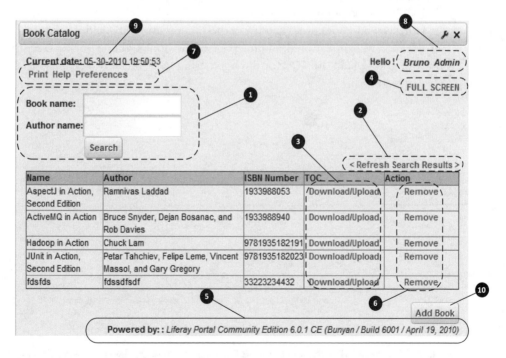

Figure 3.2 The Book Catalog portlet's home page. The portlet provides features to search for books, run the portlet in full-screen mode, upload and download book TOCs, and display the current portal server information.

The Remove hyperlink ❻ allows you to remove a book from the catalog. Clicking Remove displays a JavaScript popup message to confirm the removal.

Links are provided ❼ to print the book catalog, set preferences, and view help information about the portlet. The Print option shows the Book Catalog portlet in *print* portlet mode, to allow users to print the complete list of books in the catalog. In print mode, the Book Catalog portlet shows all books in the catalog with no hyperlinks, text fields, or buttons on the page. If you're using a portal server that doesn't support print portlet mode, clicking the Print option will have no effect.

The first and last names of the user are displayed ❽. The current system date and time is displayed ❾ in MM-dd-yyyy HH:mm:ss format. Clicking the Add Book button ❿ opens the form for adding a new book to the book catalog.

You may have noticed that the hyperlinks in figure 3.2 aren't underlined and their colors are also different. We'll be using CSS to specify the color and effects for hyperlinks in our portlet.

Figure 3.3 shows the Add Book page, where you enter information about new books.

The Home link ❶ takes you back to the home page of the Book Catalog portlet, shown in figure 3.2. Clicking the Add Book button ❷ saves the book information into the catalog if no validation errors are found in the entered book information. The portlet's title bar ❸ has changed from Book Catalog (refer to figure 3.2) to Book Catalog: Add Book to identify the page.

Once you add book information to the catalog using the Add Book form, the book information will appear on the home page of the Book Catalog portlet (see figure 3.2). You can now upload the TOC for the book using the Upload link. Figure 3.4 shows the TOC upload form.

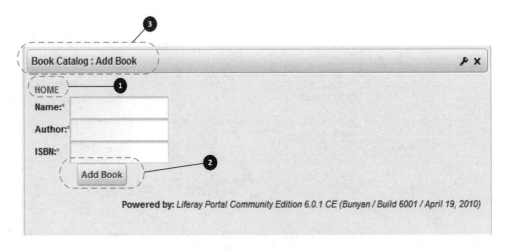

Figure 3.3   The Add Book form of the Book Catalog portlet lets you add new book information to the book catalog.

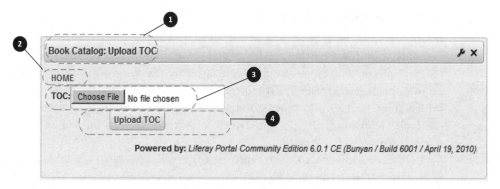

Figure 3.4   The Upload TOC form used to upload a TOC for a book

The title of the portlet ❶ has changed to Book Catalog: Upload TOC. The Home link ❷ takes you back to the portlet's home page. You can upload the TOC by choosing a file ❸ from your local filesystem. The maximum file size that can be uploaded is 1 MB. Clicking the Upload TOC button ❹ uploads the file to the local filesystem of the portal server, if the size of the selected TOC file is less than or equal to 1 MB. If the TOC file is bigger than 1 MB, an error page is displayed.

The Book Catalog portlet must additionally support the following features:

- *Localization*—Like most real-world portlets, the Book Catalog portlet must support localization of text, labels, and messages. For now, it should support the fr_FR locale.

- *Caching*—If the portlet container supports a *validation-based* caching strategy, the Book Catalog portlet must cache content based on that strategy. If validation-based caching isn't supported, the portlet will retrieve data from the data source every time it receives a render request. We'll discuss the validation-based caching strategy in detail in chapter 4.

CODE REFERENCE   The source code for the example Book Catalog portlet is located in the ch3_BookCatalog folder. Before you build or deploy the portlet, make sure you change the value of the uploadFolder initialization parameter in the portlet deployment descriptor. Also, before you build the project, set the liferay.portal.home property in the build.properties file to point to your Liferay Portal installation directory.

That's it for the requirements of the Book Catalog portlet that we'll develop in this chapter and chapter 4. The rest of this chapter will look at the various portlet concepts mentioned at the beginning of the chapter, and along the way you'll learn how to use them to implement the Book Catalog portlet.

Let's now dive into the details of the Portlet 2.0 API, beginning with portlet request objects.

3.2   *Portlet request objects*

In this section, we'll look at the different portlet request objects that are made available to portlets by the portlet container, depending upon the portlet's current lifecycle phase. The request objects are used by the Book Catalog portlet to obtain request parameters, user information, window states, portlet mode, portal server information, and so on. As we go along this section, you'll learn details about how particular features of the portlet request object are used in implementing the Book Catalog portlet.

Let's take a quick look at the different lifecycle interfaces available in Portlet 2.0 before we dive into the details of the various request object types.

3.2.1   *Portlet request objects and lifecycle interfaces*

Which portlet request object is available to a portlet instance depends on the lifecycle phase of the portlet. The different lifecycle phases that a portlet can have depend on the lifecycle interfaces implemented by the portlet class.

Table 3.1 describes the three lifecycle interfaces in portlets: `Portlet`, `Event-Portlet`, and `ResourceServingPortlet`.

Table 3.1   Portlet lifecycle interfaces

Lifecycle interface	Description
`Portlet`	Mandatory interface that defines `init`, `destroy`, `processAction`, and `render` lifecycle methods.
`ResourceServingPortlet`	Optional interface implemented by portlets if they serve resources (such as binary content) to the client. It defines the `serveResource` method, which accepts `ResourceRequest` and `ResourceResponse` objects as arguments.
`EventPortlet`	Optional interface implemented by portlets if they want to receive events from other portlets or the portlet container. It defines the `processEvent` method, which accepts `EventRequest` and `EventResponse` objects as arguments.

The `ResourceServingPortlet` and `EventPortlet` interfaces were introduced in the Portlet 2.0 specification to allow portlets to serve resources to clients and to process events generated by other portlets, respectively. We'll discuss these interfaces in detail in chapters dedicated to serving resources (chapter 12) and inter-portlet communication (chapter 11).

Portlet request objects provide request information such as window state, portlet mode, request parameters, request attributes, and so on, to the portlet instance during request processing. In previous chapters, we saw two different portlet request objects: `RenderRequest` and `ActionRequest`. They were made available to the portlet instance depending upon whether the portlet container received a render or action

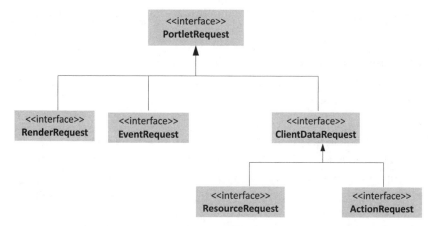

Figure 3.5 `PortletRequest` is the superinterface of the `RenderRequest`, `ActionRequest`, `ResourceRequest`, and `EventRequest` interfaces. The subinterfaces define methods and fields specific to the request type.

request for the portlet. If your portlet serves *resources* and handles *events*, you'll come across two more request objects: `ResourceRequest` and `EventRequest`.

All request objects implement a common interface, `PortletRequest`, as shown in figure 3.5.

In figure 3.5, specialized interfaces define methods and fields that are specific to particular request types. For example, `RenderRequest` defines an `ETAG` field, which is used in validation-based caching (discussed in chapter 4); `ClientDataRequest` defines methods to help you upload files; `ActionRequest` defines an `ACTION_NAME` field, which is used to identify the name of the action associated with an `ActionRequest`; and so on. This means that specific request types provide additional request information and methods to allow your portlet class to process these specific request types.

> **TIP** As you can see in figure 3.5, the file upload feature is available to both the `ActionRequest` and `ResourceRequest` interfaces because of their common superinterface. You'll usually use `ActionRequest` to upload a file and `ResourceRequest` when downloading a file because the action method invocation is followed by a call to a render method, which generates appropriate content (like a success or validation error message) in response to the upload file action.

The request information that's sent to a portlet instance by *all* request types consists of the portlet mode, window state, portal context, portlet session, and portlet preferences. The additional information that's passed as part of the request is specific to that request type (event, resource, action, or render).

> **NOTE** The portlet container is responsible for providing the portlet with objects implementing the `RenderRequest`, `ActionRequest`, `ResourceRequest`, and `EventRequest` interfaces, depending upon the lifecycle phase of the portlet.

We'll now take a look at some of the interesting constants that are defined in `PortletRequest`.

3.2.2 *PortletRequest constants*

`PortletRequest` defines many constants. In this chapter we'll discuss the following ones:

- `LIFECYCLE_PHASE`, `ACTION_PHASE`, `RENDER_PHASE`, `RESOURCE_PHASE`, `EVENT_PHASE`—Constants for identifying the current portlet lifecycle phase
- `ACTION_SCOPE_ID`—Constant used by the portlet container for locating action-scoped request attributes
- `RENDER_PART`, `RENDER_HEADER`, `RENDER_MARKUP`—Constants for use by streaming- (and not buffering-) based portals
- `USER_INFO`—Constant that identifies the name of the request attribute that contains user attributes information

Let's now look at what these constants are and how they're used.

USING THE LIFECYCLE_PHASE CONSTANT

The value of the `LIFECYCLE_PHASE` constant in `PortletRequest` is the name of the request attribute that identifies the current request-processing phase.

Portlets have four lifecycle phases (action, render, resource, and event phases) identified by `PortletRequest` interface constants: `ACTION_PHASE`, `RENDER_PHASE`, `RESOURCE_PHASE`, and `EVENT_PHASE`. The values of these constants are the same as their names. The value of the `LIFECYCLE_PHASE` constant is the name of the request attribute that contains the current request-processing phase of the portlet. The valid *values* (we're not talking about constants now) are `ACTION_PHASE`, `RENDER_PHASE`, `RESOURCE_PHASE`, and `EVENT_PHASE`.

You'll probably never need to use the `LIFECYCLE_PHASE` constant directly in your portlets, unless you're writing a framework on top of portlets. The `LIFECYCLE_PHASE` is used by frameworks to cast request and response objects to the appropriate type based on the lifecycle phase.

The following code fragment shows how the `LIFECYCLE_PHASE` constant is used by frameworks:

```
if(portletRequest.getAttribute(PortletRequest.LIFECYCLE_PHASE).equals(
    PortletRequest.RENDER_PHASE)) {
  RenderRequest request = (RenderRequest)portletRequest;
  RenderResponse response = (RenderResponse)portletResponse;
  ...
}
```

In real-world portlets, you'll probably use a portlet framework, like Spring Portlet MVC (discussed in chapter 7 and 8), to build your portlets. A portlet framework is ideally suited for developing multipage portlets; it's responsible for casting portlet requests to appropriate request types based on the request lifecycle phase. For instance, in the

Spring Portlet MVC framework, if the lifecycle phase is RENDER_PHASE, the preceding code would cast the PortletRequest object to RenderRequest and the Portlet-Response object to RenderResponse and then send them to the render method of the handler object.

Portlet bridges

If you want to expose an existing web application as a portlet, you'll need to use a *portlet bridge*. A portlet bridge is responsible for making your existing web application compatible with the portlet specification. For instance, if you want to expose an existing JavaServer Faces (JSF) application as a portlet, you could do so by using the reference implementation for JSR 301 (Portlet 1.0 Bridge for JSF 1.2) or JSR 329 (Portlet 2.0 Bridge for JSF 1.2) from the MyFaces Portlet Bridge project (http://myfaces.apache.org/portlet-bridge/index.html). Chapter 15 discusses portlet bridges in detail.

USING THE ACTION_SCOPE_ID CONSTANT

As you saw earlier, action-scoped request attributes (specified using the javax .portlet.actionScopedRequestAttributes container-runtime option) are available in the subsequent render method invocations. The portlet container internally stores the action-scoped request attributes at the end of the action or event lifecycle phase and sets a render parameter with the name javax.portlet.as (which is the value of the PortletRequest interface's ACTION_SCOPE_ID constant). (Render parameters were discussed more fully in section 2.6.8 of chapter 2.) The value of the javax .portlet.as render parameter is used by the portlet container to obtain the internally stored request attributes and make them available when calling subsequent render methods. In a way, the javax.portlet.as render parameter has container-specific semantics and is used to send a pointer to the internally stored request attributes from the action method to the render method.

You don't need to work directly with the ACTION_SCOPE_ID constant; I explain it here only so you can understand how the actionScopedRequestAttributes container-runtime option works in portlet containers.

USING THE RENDER_PART, RENDER_HEADER, AND RENDER_MARKUP CONSTANTS

You only need to know about these constants if you're using a *streaming-based* portal (Jetspeed, Liferay Portal, and GateIn Portal are buffering portals). Streaming-based portals directly stream portlet content from data sources.

In streaming-based portals, portlet rendering is divided into two different phases, represented by the RENDER_HEADER and RENDER_MARKUP constants. In such portals, a request attribute whose name is the value of the RENDER_PART constant is set by the portal server, and this value identifies the rendering phase (RENDER_HEADER or RENDER_MARKUP). In the RENDER_HEADER render phase, the header and title of the portlet are set, and in the RENDER_MARKUP render phase, the markup of the portlet is set. This rendering behavior of streaming-based portals is like watching a video on a website, where the title and window (in which the video will appear) are rendered before the video.

USING THE USER_INFO CONSTANT

There could be many portlet requirements where you need to show user information for the logged-in user. For instance, the Book Catalog portlet shows a greeting, "Hello! *<first-name> <last-name>*," inserting the first and last names of the logged-in user, as shown in figure 3.2.

Portal user information is maintained by portal servers in the portal server–specific database, and you probably won't find enough documentation about the database structure to directly retrieve the user information. You could consider using the portal server APIs to extract the user information from the database, but that would have the downside of making your portlet dependent on the current portal server. If you managed to get the user information by directly accessing the database or using your portal server APIs, your portlet would be unlikely to work if it were migrated from one portal server to another, because it would be tied to that specific portal server API or database. The Portlet 2.0 specification defines a way of retrieving user information in a portal server–agnostic way with *user attributes*.

User attributes are defined in portlet.xml (using the `<user-attribute>` elements) and are made available as a request attribute by the portlet container to the portlets. The name of the request attribute is the value of the `PortletRequest` interface's `USER_INFO` constant. Portlets can obtain user attributes from the request and display them in the portlet or use it in processing the request. Chapter 9 (which discusses integration with databases) shows how the Book Catalog portlet uses user attributes to associate a book with the user who added (or updated) it.

> **CODE REFERENCE** At this point, you should import the ch3_BookCatalog source code into your Eclipse workspace. That will allow you to follow along with the code referenced in the rest of this chapter.

The following listing shows the portlet.xml file for the Book Catalog portlet and demonstrates how user attributes are defined.

Listing 3.1   Defining user attributes in the Book Catalog's portlet.xml file

```
<portlet-app ...>
   <portlet>
    <portlet-name>bookCatalog</portlet-name>
         ...
   </portlet>
     ...
   <user-attribute>
           <description>user first name</description>
           <name>user.name.given</name>
   </user-attribute>
   <user-attribute>
       <description>user last name</description>
```

❶ User attribute element

```
        <name>user.name.family</name>
    </user-attribute>
</portlet-app>
```

The `<user-attribute>` element **①** is used to define a user attribute. The `<user-attribute>` element is a subelement of the `<portlet-app>` element, which implies that user attributes defined in the portlet.xml file are available to all the portlets that form part of the portlet application. The `<description>` subelement provides a description of the user attribute, and `<name>` identifies the name of the user attribute that should be made available to the portlet application.

The user attributes defined in the portlet.xml file are available to a portlet as a request attribute; the name of the request attribute is the value of the `Portlet-Request.USER_INFO` constant, and the attribute value is of type `java.util.Map`. The attribute value contains a map of user attribute name to user attribute value. The following code fragment shows how the `BookCatalogPortlet` class (from the Book Catalog portlet) obtains the user attribute map from a request:

```
Map<String, Object> userAttributeMap =
   (Map<String, Object>)request.getAttribute(PortletRequest.USER_INFO)
String firstName = (String)userAttributeMap.get("user.name.given");
```

CODE REFERENCE   Refer to the `BookCatalogPortlet` class's `showBooks` render method in ch3_BookCatalog to see how the Book Catalog portlet makes use of user attributes.

The question that you might be asking at this point is how the values of the `user.name.given` and `user.name.family` attributes were set in the request. A portal server usually has *predefined* user attributes, the values of which are made available if they are referred to by the `<user-attribute>` elements of a portlet deployment descriptor. The Portlet 2.0 specification recommends that the names of commonly used user attributes should be made available by portal servers to portlets that have defined them in their portlet deployment descriptors. These recommended user attribute names are defined in the `PortletRequest` interface's `P3PUserInfos` nested class.

NOTE   A portal server (like Liferay Portal or Jetspeed) may also allow you to create custom user attributes. If a portal server allows this and if you migrate a portlet application to another portal server, the portlet application deployer needs to map these custom user attributes to the user attributes available in the new portal server environment.

Now let's take a look at some of the important methods of the `PortletRequest` interface.

3.2.3   *PortletRequest methods*

`PortletRequest` defines methods that are useful for obtaining request parameters, cookies, request attributes, and so on. Most of the methods defined in `PortletRequest` have similar semantics to the methods defined in the `HttpServletRequest` interface. Table 3.2 lists some of the interesting methods of the `PortletRequest` interface.

Table 3.2 Methods defined in the `PortletRequest` interface

Method	Description
getParameterMap getPrivateParameterMap getPublicParameterMap	Portlets make use of *public render parameters* (explained in chapter 11) that are shared between portlets. `Portlet-Request` provides the `getPublicParameterMap` method, which returns a Map of the public render parameters, and the `getPrivateParameterMap`, which returns a Map of the parameters that aren't shared between portlets. If you want to obtain a Map of all the request parameters, irrespective of whether they're public or private, you should use the `getParameterMap` method.
getPortalContext	Returns a `PortalContext` object (discussed later in this chapter) that contains information about the portal server in which the portlet is deployed.
getPreferences	Returns a `PortletPreferences` object (discussed in chapter 10) that contains the user preferences associated with the portlet.
getProperties getProperty	Obtain any properties associated with the portlet request. You can add a property to a request using the `<property>` tag, as described in chapter 6.
getPortletSession	Returns the `PortletSession` associated with the current request (discussed later in this chapter).
getWindowState	Returns the `WindowState` object representing the current window state of the portlet sending the request. (`WindowState` is discussed in chapter 4.)
isPortletModeAllowed	Checks whether a portlet mode is allowed for the current portlet request.
isWindowStateAllowed	Checks whether a window state is allowed for the current portlet request.
getPortletMode	Returns the `PortletMode` object (discussed in chapter 4) representing the portlet mode associated with the current request.

The `PortletRequest` methods defined in table 3.2 are available to specific request types (action, render, event, and resource requests) and will be used extensively in the Book Catalog portlet example. For instance, when the user enters search criteria, the `getParameter` method is used to retrieve it, the `getPortletSession` method is used to obtain the `PortletSession` object to store the search results, and so on.

Table 3.2 mentions that the `PortalContext` object provides portal server information to the portlet instance. We'll now see how portlets can use the `PortalContext` object to customize their request-handling logic for a particular portal server.

3.2.4 *Handling portal server–specific requests using PortalContext*

The `PortalContext` object provides portal server information, such as the portal server name, version number, supported window states, supported portlet modes, and any other properties that are set by the portal server. You should use the `Portal-Context` object in the following cases:

- To customize the portlet's request-handling logic based on the portal server in which the portlet is deployed. This is similar to customizing the presentation logic in HTML pages, using JavaScript, based on the browser type and version.
- To check whether the portlet can add custom JavaScript and CSS DOM elements to the `head` section of a portal page (discussed later in this chapter).
- To obtain a list of portlet modes supported by the portal server.
- To obtain a list of window states supported by the portal server.

You can retrieve a `PortalContext` object using the `PortletRequest` object's `get-PortalContext` method. Listing 3.2 shows how the Book Catalog portlet makes use of the `PortalContext` object (refer to figures 3.2 and 3.3) to customize request-handling logic for the Jetspeed portal server.

> **Listing 3.2 Using `PortalContext` to customize request-handling logic**

```
import chapter03.code.listing.utils.Constants;

public class BookCatalogPortlet extends GenericPortlet {
  protected void doHeaders(RenderRequest request,                    ❶ Overrides
     RenderResponse response) {                                         GenericPortlet's
    super.doHeaders(request, response);                                 doHeaders method
    PortalContext portalContext =
        request.getPortalContext();
    String portalInfo = portalContext.getPortalInfo();               ❷ Customizes
    if(portalInfo.contains(Constants.JETSPEED)) {                       request handling
      ...                                                               for Jetspeed
    }
  }
}
```

`BookCatalogPortlet` overrides ❶ the `GenericPortlet` class's `doHeaders` method. The `doHeaders` method is invoked internally by the default implementation of the `GenericPortlet` class's `render` method; you should override `doHeaders` in your portlet class if you want to set response headers before the content is rendered.

Request handling is customized ❷ if the portal server is Jetspeed. The `Portlet-Request` object's `getPortalContext` method is used to obtain the `PortalContext` object, and that object's `getPortalInfo` method is used to retrieve the portal server name and version information. The portal server information retrieved via `getPortal-Info` is then checked to determine whether the portlet is deployed on the Jetspeed portal server. (The value of the `Constants.JETSPEED` constant used in the code is `Jetspeed`.) If the portal server is Jetspeed, you can set Jetspeed-specific response headers in the `doHeaders` method.

The PortalContext object defines getSupportedWindowStates and getSupported-PortletModes methods, which you can use to obtain information about the window states and portlet modes supported by your portal server. You'll probably never use these methods directly in your portlets, except in situations where you want to discover window states and portlet modes supported by your portal server. For instance, if you retrieve the list of window states supported by Liferay Portal, you'll find that there are two custom window states: exclusive and pop_up. If you want to use these custom window states, you can explicitly set them in the action response, as shown here:

```
actionResponse.setWindowState(new WindowState("exclusive"));
```

You've now seen the constants and methods defined by the PortletRequest object and how they can be used by a portlet. You also saw how you can use the Portal-Context object to perform portal server–specific request handling.

Once the request is received by the portlet, the portlet is responsible for responding by generating content or performing some action, like updating database tables. Portlets respond to requests by using response objects whose type depends on the life-cycle phase of the portlet. Let's look at the portlet response objects and how they're used by the Book Catalog portlet.

3.3   *Portlet response objects*

The Book Catalog portlet responds to user actions by generating content or updating the data store that contains the catalog. For instance, when you enter search criteria in the Book Catalog portlet, the portlet accesses the data store to find matching books and generates markup showing the books found.

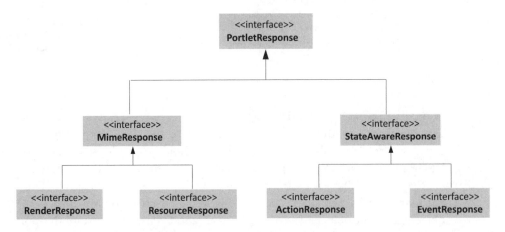

Figure 3.6 The RenderResponse, ResourceResponse, ActionResponse, and EventResponse interfaces have a common superinterface, PortletResponse. The subinterfaces define additional fields and methods specific to the response types.

To respond to portlet requests, portlets use response objects. For instance, the Hello World portlet in chapter 1 wrote a "Hello World" response using the `PrintWriter` object obtained from the `RenderResponse` object, and the User Registration portlet in chapter 2 generated a response using JSP pages.

The different lifecycle methods in portlets are designed to accept different portlet request and response objects, because each method requires some additional request information and response generation functionality. Like portlet requests, portlet response objects implement a common interface, `PortletResponse`, as shown in figure 3.6.

In figure 3.6, `PortletResponse` represents the base interface for all the response objects used by portlets. Table 3.3 describes the purposes of the various response interfaces in the figure.

Table 3.3 Portlet response types

Response interface	Description
PortletResponse	Defines methods that add DOM element properties to the response (see section 3.3.5 of this chapter for example usage), and retrieve the portlet *namespace* (see chapter 12, which is on creating highly interactive portlets, and the discussion of the <namespace> tag in chapter 6 for examples).
MimeResponse	Extends the PortletResponse interface and defines additional methods that create action, resource, and render URLs and that set the content type of the response. MimeResponse also defines constants that are used in expiration-based and validation-based caching (discussed in chapter 4).
RenderResponse	Extends the MimeResponse interface and defines additional methods that set the title of the portlet window and that set the possible portlet modes that the portlet can have next.
ResourceResponse	Extends the MimeResponse interface and allows portlets to serve resources (such as binary content) to the client. The ResourceResponse interface is different from RenderResponse in the sense that the portal server doesn't add any additional markup (like window decoration) to the content served by ResourceResponse (see chapter 12 for details).
StateAwareResponse	Extends the PortletResponse interface and defines additional methods that set render parameters, events to be published, portlet mode, and window state.
ActionResponse	Extends the StateAwareResponse interface and defines additional methods that redirect users to different URLs.
EventResponse	Extends the StateAwareResponse interface and defines an additional method that sets the same render parameters in the response that were received by the portlet in the event request (refer to chapter 11 for details).

Table 3.3 describes the various response types in portlets. In portlet methods you'll only work directly with objects implementing the `RenderResponse`, `ActionResponse`, `ResourceResponse`, and `EventResponse` interfaces. These objects are made available to portlets by the portlet container.

The `PortletResponse` interface's `encodeURL` method plays an important role in addressing portlet portability issues, and we'll discuss it next.

3.3.1   Encoding URLs with the encodeURL method

The `PortletResponse` interface provides an `encodeURL` method to let portlets encode portal server or portlet container–specific data (like session ID) in the URL. Such URLs can refer to resources like JSPs, servlets, images, and static files (like JavaScript and CSS) in the portlet application.

> **TIP**   URLs referring to resources within the portlet application must be encoded to ensure that the portlet application is portable across different portal servers and portlet containers. You don't need to encode URLs that refer to resources outside the portlet application.

The following code snippet shows the `encodeURL` method in the Book Catalog portlet encoding a URL referring to `BookServlet`:

```
PortletRequestDispatcher dispatcher = request.getPortletSession().
    getPortletContext().getRequestDispatcher(
    response.encodeURL("/myservlet/bookServlet")
);
```

In this case, the /myservlet/bookServlet URL refers to the `BookServlet` servlet.

In the preceding code, the /myservlet/bookServlet URL is encoded using the `PortletResponse` interface's `encodeURL` method. The following listing shows how the `BookCatalogPortlet` class encodes URLs referring to the `BookServlet` servlet and JavaScript and CSS files.

Listing 3.3   Using `encodeURL` in the `BookCatalogPortlet` class

```
public class BookCatalogPortlet extends GenericPortlet {

   protected void doHeaders(RenderRequest request,
     RenderResponse response) {
    ...
 Element cssElement = response.createElement("link");
  cssElement.setAttribute("href",
  response.encodeURL((request.getContextPath() +          ❶ Encodes URL to
    "/css/bookCatalog.css")));                                bookCatalog.css file
    ...
  Element jsElement = response.createElement("script");
  jsElement.setAttribute("src",
    response.encodeURL((request.getContextPath()          ❷ Encodes URL to
      + "/js/bookCatalog.js")));                              bookCatalog.js file
    ...
  }
```

```
@RenderMode(name = "VIEW")
public void showBooks(RenderRequest request,
RenderResponse response)throws ... {
...
PortletRequestDispatcher dispatcher =
request.getPortletSession().
  getPortletContext().getRequestDispatcher(
    response.encodeURL("/myservlet/bookServlet")
  );
dispatcher.include(request, response);
...
  }
...
}
```

❸ Encodes URL to
access BookServlet

The encodeURL method **❶** is used to encode a URL to the bookCatalog.css CSS file. It's used to encode a URL to the bookCatalog.js JavaScript file **❷**. Finally, it's used to encode a URL to the BookServlet servlet **❸**, which resides in the same portlet application as the Book Catalog portlet.

NOTE Listing 3.3 shows that the BookCatalogPortlet class creates URLs to JavaScript and CSS files. In section 3.3.5, you'll see the rationale for doing so.

Next, let's look at some of the specific PortletResponse types that help portlets generate content and respond to actions.

3.3.2 Generating content using RenderResponse

Portlets use RenderResponse to write content. It can also be used to set the title of a portlet and the next possible portlet modes.

In the examples that we've covered so far, portlet titles were either specified in the portlet deployment descriptor or the portlet resource bundle, but the Book Catalog portlet requires the portlet title to change when the Add Book form is shown to the user (see figure 3.3). This can be done by using the RenderResponse object's set-Title method, as shown here:

```
response.setTitle("Book Catalog: Add Book");
```

If you want to localize the messages based on locale, you can use portlet resource bundles to store the portlet titles and retrieve them programmatically, as shown here:

```
ResourceBundle bundle = ResourceBundle.getBundle("content.messages",
    request.getLocale());
response.setTitle(bundle.getString("portlet.title.books"));
```

In this code, content.messages identifies the location of the messages properties file containing the portlet title, response refers to the RenderResponse object, and bundle refers to the resource bundle used by the portlet.

You can programmatically load the portlet resource bundle using the java.util .ResourceBundle class, or you can use the getResourceBundle convenience method of the GenericPortlet class to retrieve the resource bundle configured for the portlet in the portlet deployment descriptor.

NOTE The setTitle method is defined only in the RenderResponse interface; you can only change the portlet title in the render request-processing phase.

The RenderResponse object not only allows you to generate content; its setNext-PossiblePortletModes method allows you to set the next possible portlet modes that a portlet can have. Here's an example:

```
response.setNextPossiblePortletModes(portletModeList);
```

In this code line, portletModeList is a list of the next possible portlet modes in which the portlet can be invoked.

The BookCatalogPortlet class retrieves the portlet title from the resource bundle based on the value of the myaction session attribute, as shown in here.

Listing 3.4 Dynamically setting the portlet title in the BookCatalogPortlet class

```
public class BookCatalogPortlet extends GenericPortlet {
    ...
  @RenderMode(name = "VIEW")
  public void showBooks(RenderRequest request,
    RenderResponse response) ... {
    ...
    String titleKey = "portlet.title."         ❶ Creates portlet
        + (String) request.getPortletSession().      title key
        getAttribute("myaction");
                                                 ❷ Sets title of portlet
    response.setTitle(                              window
      getResourceBundle(request.getLocale()).
        getString(titleKey));
    ...
  }
    ...
  }
```

portlet.title ❶ is prepended to the value of the myaction session attribute to create the title key used to store the title in the resource bundle. The value of the myaction session attribute is same as the value of the myaction request parameter received by the BookCatalogPortlet class. The RenderResponse object's setTitle method is invoked ❷ to set the title of the portlet window. The GenericPortlet class's get-ResourceBundle convenience method is used to obtain the resource bundle for the Book Catalog portlet.

Let's now look at how you can respond to an action request by using the Action-Response object.

3.3.3 Responding to an action using ActionResponse

The ActionResponse object allows portlets to respond to action requests. This response may include redirecting the user to another URL, setting render parameters, or setting the portlet mode or window state.

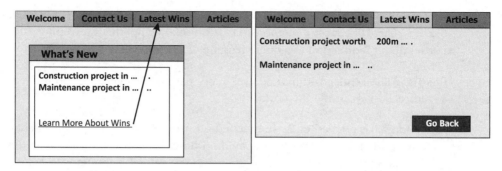

Figure 3.7   The What's New portlet shows two major project wins. The Learn More About Wins link takes you to the Latest Wins portal page.

Let's say an organization's portal consists of multiple pages: Welcome, Contact Us, Latest Wins, and Articles, as shown in figure 3.7. The Welcome portal page provides a What's New portlet that shows a summary of two major projects won by the organization. It also shows a Learn More About Wins link that takes you to the Latest Wins page, which provides detailed descriptions about the projects recently won by the organization. The Latest Wins page can be accessed by several other pages in the portal, so its Go Back button should always take the user back to the page they came from.

So far we've only looked at creating links with URLs that invoke a portlet's render and action methods. Because `ActionResponse` is the only portlet response object with redirection capability, we'll create the Learn More About Wins link referring to the What's New portlet's action URL. When the Learn More About Wins link is clicked, the action method of the What's New portlet is invoked, allowing the portlet to redirect the user to the Latest Wins page, as shown here:

```
actionResponse.sendRedirect("/myportal/latestWins?referrer=
➥http://orgportal.com/myportal/welcome");
```

In this code, /myportal/latestWins is the full URI to the Latest Wins portal page, and the `referrer` query parameter refers to the page from which the user came to the Latest Wins portal page.

The http://orgportal.com/myportal/welcome URL in the preceding code line is the absolute URL for the Welcome portal page, and it's used by the Go Back button to return the user to the referrer (the Welcome page in this case).

That code line also uses the `ActionResponse` object's `sendRedirect(String location)` method to redirect the user to the Latest Wins page. The `location` argument specifies the full URI or absolute URL to which the user should be redirected.

> **WARNING**   If you call the `ActionResponse` object's `setPortletMode`, `setWindowState`, `removePublicParameter`, `setRenderParameter`, or `setRenderParameters` methods before invoking the `sendRedirect(String location)` method, it will result in an `IllegalStateException`.

ActionResponse also defines a less frequently used sendRedirect(String location, String renderUrlparam) method that additionally appends the render URL of the portlet doing redirection as a query parameter named renderUrlParam.

> **NOTE**   The render URL passed as a query parameter may be of no use if the redirection is outside the portal.

In section 2.6.8 of chapter 2, we touched on using render parameters to share information between a portlet's action method and the following render method. The Book Catalog portlet makes use of the myaction render parameter to communicate view information to the render method, which internally uses BookServlet to render content.

The next listing show the use of render parameters in the Book Catalog portlet.

Listing 3.5   Setting render parameter in the Book Catalog portlet

```
@RenderMode(name = "VIEW")
public void showBooks(RenderRequest request,       ❶ showBooks render
  RenderResponse response)throws ...{                  method
  ...
  PortletRequestDispatcher dispatcher =
     request.getPortletSession().
       getPortletContext().getRequestDispatcher(
          response.encodeURL("/myservlet/bookServlet"));
  dispatcher.include(request, response);
}

@ProcessAction(name = "removeBookAction")
public void removeBook(ActionRequest request,       ❷ removeBook
  ActionResponse response)throws ...{                  action method
  ...
  response.setRenderParameter("myaction", "showCatalog");
}

@ProcessAction(name = "uploadTocAction")
public void uploadToc(ActionRequest request,        ❸ uploadToc
  ActionResponse response)throws ... {                 action method
  try {
    ...
    response.setRenderParameter("myaction", "showCatalog");   myaction and ❹
  } catch(Exception ex) {                                     exceptionMsg
    response.setRenderParameter("myaction", "error");     render parameters
    response.setRenderParameter("exceptionMsg",
      "Exception occurred while uploading the file.
      ➥Please check the file size is <= 1MB");
  }
}
```

The showBooks render method ❶ is used for VIEW mode in the Book Catalog portlet. The dispatcher.include (request, response) statement in the showBooks method dispatches a render request to the BookServlet servlet to generate content. Though it's not shown in the above code, the showBooks method retrieves the myaction request parameter and sets it as a request attribute with the same name before dispatching the request to the BookServlet. The BookServlet makes use of the myaction request attribute to determine which JSP page to use for generating content.

The removeBook action method ❷ is used to remove a book from the book catalog. The response.setRenderParameter("myaction", "showCatalog") statement sets showCatalog as the value of the myaction render parameter.

The uploadToc action method ❸ is used to upload the TOC file for a book. If the TOC file is uploaded successfully, the response.setRenderParameter("myaction", "showCatalog") statement sets the value of the myaction render parameter to show-Catalog.

If the TOC file upload fails, the myaction render parameter ❹ is set to error, and the exceptionMsg render parameter represents an error message.

In listing 3.5, the showBooks method receives render parameters set by the removeBook and uploadToc action methods as request parameters. As the value of the myaction render parameter is used indirectly by the BookServlet to render the appropriate JSP page, each action method is able to control the view that needs to be rendered after the action request is processed.

3.3.4 Choosing an appropriate phase for an action

Each request-processing phase of a portlet has access to different request and response objects, which lets you perform certain functions in one phase that can't be performed in other phases. Table 3.4 lists which functions should be performed in which request-processing phases.

Table 3.4 Request-processing phases suited for handling a particular portlet action

Function	Request-processing phase
Set window state and portlet mode	Action
Set render parameters	Action
Redirect user to a different page	Action
Programmatically create render, action, and resource URLs	Render
Change window title	Action
Add JavaScript and CSS to the portal page	Render
Dispatch events to portlets	Action
Generate markup content	Render
Submit forms	Action
Set expiration timestamp	Render
Upload files	Action

Table 3.4   Request-processing phases suited for handling a particular portlet action *(continued)*

Function	Request-processing phase
Download files	Resource
Send events to other portlets	Action or event
Process events	Event

> **TIP**   As a general rule, you should avoid doing computationally intensive or resource-intensive tasks in the render method (or in the render phase) because it's called every time a portal page is rendered. Such tasks should be performed in the action method (or in the action phase), because it's called only when a user interacts with the portlet.

A portlet's content may change in response to a render request if there's change in the data displayed by the portlet and the expiration time has been reached or a validation token has become invalid. Actions performed by a portlet that are *repeatable* (with no side effects) and *idempotent* should be performed in the render phase. The *non-repeatable* and *non-idempotent* actions should be performed in the action phase. Examples of *non-repeatable* or *non-idempotent* actions are uploading a file, storing data in a PortletSession, and saving data in a data store.

The RenderResponse object can also be used to add <script> and <link> elements (for including JavaScript and CSS respectively) to the HEAD element of the generated markup. We'll now look at some approaches you can follow to add custom JavaScript and CSS to your portal page, which, in turn, will apply to your portlets on the portal page.

3.3.5   *Adding custom JavaScript and CSS files to a portal page*

How you add custom JavaScript and CSS to a portal page varies from one portal server to another. You can either use a portal server–specific approach to add them, or you can use the RenderResponse object's MARKUP_HEAD_ELEMENT, as suggested by the portlet specification.

Let's first look at how you can use the RenderResponse object's MARKUP_HEAD_ELEMENT to add custom JavaScript and CSS to your portal page.

USING MARKUP_HEAD_ELEMENT

PortalContext defines a single constant, MARKUP_HEAD_ELEMENT_SUPPORT, that refers to the name of a property in the PortalContext object. A non-null value for the MARKUP_HEAD_ELEMENT_SUPPORT property indicates that the portal server supports adding DOM elements to the head section of the HTML markup that's sent by the portal server to the browser for rendering. This element is useful when you want to add portlet-specific JavaScript and CSS to the head section of the generated markup so that your portlets can make use of custom CSS and JavaScript functions.

Support for adding DOM elements to the head section of the markup is optional for portal servers. If your portlet application requires JavaScript and CSS, make sure that your portal server provides documentation on how you can introduce your custom JavaScript and CSS files as part of the markup.

Table 3.5 compares MARKUP_HEAD_ELEMENT support in different portal servers on which the Book Catalog portlet will be deployed.

Table 3.5   Comparing MARKUP_HEAD_ELEMENT support in different portal servers

Portal server	Portlet container	MARKUP_HEAD_ELEMENT support	Alternate approaches
Liferay Portal 5.2.3/6.x	Default portlet container	Not supported	You can configure your JavaScript and CSS files in the liferay-portlet.xml file of your portlet.
Jetspeed 2.2	Pluto 2.0.0	Supported	
GlassFish Server v3.0.1	OpenPortal Portlet Container 2.1.2	Supported	

You may be wondering if it's important to worry about which portal servers allow you to include JavaScript and CSS when you can easily incorporate that content in the <HEAD> tag of the JSPs used by the portlet. It turns out that there's a restriction on the content generated by portlets; portlets must not generate the following tags as part of their markup content: <head>, <html>, <body>, <title>, <base>, <frame>, and <frameset>. If you use these tags in your markup, there's no guarantee that your portal page won't break. You can use the <iframe> tag in portlet markup, but the portal and portlet context isn't available to content displayed by the <iframe> tag. As you'll see in chapter 14, the <iframe> tag may be used by a portlet to expose an external web application as a portlet.

Let's say that you define a <HEAD> tag in your JSP page and include <link> and <script> tags to include custom CSS and JavaScript files. If you have two <HEAD> tags in your HTML markup, it's not valid HTML markup, and it may not be rendered correctly by some browsers. Some portal servers don't put any restrictions on these tags in the markup, and others simply ignore them.

You should add <link>, <script>, <meta>, and so on, tags either by adding DOM elements to the head section of the markup, or by using portal server–specific configuration files to configure your JavaScript and CSS files for the portal page. If none of these approaches are supported by your portal server, your last option is to modify the CSS and JavaScript files that are included by the base portal pages of your portal server.

NOTE   The <link> and <meta> tags must be inside the <head> element of the HTML document. The <script> element can also appear in the body of an HTML document, which means it's possible to use the <script> tag in your JSP page to write JavaScript code specific to your portlet. Using the <script> tag in the JSP page helps you with *namespacing* JavaScript variables and functions, which we'll discuss in chapter 6.

The following listing shows how the Book Catalog portlet adds <link> and <script> tags to the head section of the markup to include the bookCatalog.css and bookCatalog.js files in the portal page.

Listing 3.6 Adding a `<link>` element to the `head` section

```java
public class BookCatalogPortlet extends GenericPortlet {

 protected void doHeaders(RenderRequest request,
   RenderResponse response) {                          ❶ Obtains PortalContext
  PortalContext portalContext =                           from request
        request.getPortalContext();
  ...                                                   ❷ Checks support for
  if(portalContext.getProperty(PortalContext.             adding elements
  ↪MARKUP_HEAD_ELEMENT_SUPPORT) != null)
  {
    Element cssElement = response.createElement("link");
    cssElement.setAttribute("href",
       response.encodeURL(request.getContextPath() +   ❸ Creates and
       "/css/bookCatalog.css"));                          adds link
    cssElement.setAttribute("rel", "stylesheet");         element
    cssElement.setAttribute("type", "text/css");
    response.addProperty
     (MimeResponse.MARKUP_HEAD_ELEMENT,
        cssElement);

    Element jsElement = response.createElement("script");
    jsElement.setAttribute("src", response.encodeURL(
      (request.getContextPath() + "/js/bookCatalog.js"))
    );                                                  ❹ Creates and
    jsElement.setAttribute("type", "text/javascript");    adds script
    response.addProperty(MimeResponse.MARKUP_HEAD_ELEMENT,  element
      jsElement);
  }
 }
}
```

The `PortalContext` object ❶ is obtained using the `RenderRequest` object's `getPortalContext` method. The value of the `PortalContext.MARKUP_HEAD_ELEMENT_SUPPORT` property ❷ in `PortalContext` is checked for a non-`null` value.

The `link` DOM element is created using the `RenderResponse` object's `createElement` method ❸ and is added to the response. The `href`, `rel`, and `type` attributes of the `link` element are set using the `Element` object's `setAttribute` method, and the `link` element is added to the response using the `addProperty` method. The name of the property must be `MimeResponse.MARKUP_HEAD_ELEMENT`.

The `script` DOM element is created and added to the response ❹. The `src` and `type` attributes of the `script` element are set using the `Element` object's `setAttribute` method. The `script` element is added as a response property using the

addProperty method, and the name of the property must be MimeResponse
.MARKUP_HEAD_ELEMENT.

The code in listing 3.6 adds <link> and <script> tags to the head section of the
markup sent by the portal server to the browser, as shown here:

```
<head>
  ...
  <link href="/ch3_BookCatalog/css/bookCatalog.css"
    rel="stylesheet" type="text/css">
  <script src="/ch3_BookCatalog/css/bookCatalog.js"
    type="text/javascript">
  ...
</head>
```

Now that you know how to programmatically create and add DOM elements to the
response, the next question is, where should this code that adds these elements be
written? If your portlet class extends from GenericPortlet, you should set the
response properties in the doHeaders method. The default implementation of
doHeaders in the GenericPortlet class does nothing.

> **NOTE** If you're using a portlet framework, instead of directly extending
> GenericPortlet class, you are required to extend the portlet framework's
> portlet class. For instance, if you're using Spring Portlet MVC to develop port-
> lets, you need to extend the DispatcherPortlet class (which in turn extends
> the GenericPortlet class) and override the doHeaders method, as described
> in chapter 8.

As of Jetspeed 2.2, a call to portalContext.getProperty(PortalContext.MARKUP_
HEAD_ELEMENT_SUPPORT) returns null, even though it supports adding DOM elements
to the markup's head section. In this case, you need to make use of the server information returned by getPortalInfo to determine whether the portlet is deployed on
Jetspeed or not. If it is, you should create and add DOM elements to the response even
if the value of the MARKUP_HEAD_ELEMENT_SUPPORT property is null.

USING PORTAL SERVER–SPECIFIC CONFIGURATION
As table 3.5 indicates, Liferay Portal 5.2.3/6.x doesn't support adding DOM elements
to the head section, but it provides a much simpler alternative. You can use the liferay-
portlet.xml file, as shown here:

```
<liferay-portlet-app>
 <portlet>
  <portlet-name>bookCatalog</portlet-name>
  <instanceable>true</instanceable>
  <header-portlet-css>/css/bookCatalog.css</header-portlet-css>
  <header-portlet-javascript>/js/bookCatalog.js</header-portlet-javascript>
 </portlet>
</liferay-portlet-app>
```

The liferay-portlet.xml file shown here makes use of <header-portlet-css> and
<header-portlet-javascript> to add <link> and <script> tags to the generated
markup; those tags in turn include the bookCatalog.css and bookCatalog.js files.

TIP   If several of your portlets on the same or different portal pages need to use the same JavaScript file, you can consider including the JavaScript file as part of the portal theme. Because the portal theme applies to all of your portal pages, the JavaScript file will be included by default in all of your portal pages. See section 5.5.2 of chapter 5 for an example Liferay Portal theme that includes a JavaScript file.

The lifetime of a portlet request object is limited to the lifecycle method of a portlet. That means that if you store user-specific information in a portlet request, it won't be available in the next request. If you want to maintain user-specific information across multiple requests, you should use a portlet session.

3.4   *Storing user-specific data in a portlet session*

Portlet containers provide the `PortletSession` object so you can store user-specific data across portlet requests. `PortletSession` is similar to `HttpSession`, and it provides methods to maintain session attributes, get and set the maximum interval of time for which the session can remain inactive, get `PortletContext`, and so on. Just as each web application has a unique `HttpSession` per user, each portlet application has a unique `PortletSession` per user.

In this section, we'll look at `PortletSession` scopes, `PortletSession` methods, and when to use which scope when developing portlets. We'll also look at how the Book Catalog portlet makes use of `PortletSession` scopes and methods to achieve its intended functionality.

3.4.1   *PortletSession object and methods*

`PortletSession` is different from `HttpSession` because `PortletSession` provides you with two different scopes to store session attributes, identified by the constants `APPLICATION_SCOPE` and `PORTLET_SCOPE` in the `PortletSession` interface. `HttpSession` doesn't have the concept of scoped attributes. You should choose an appropriate scope for your session attributes based on your application's requirements.

If a portlet stores session attributes in `PORTLET_SCOPE`, the attributes are only available to the same portlet instance (an *instance* in this paragraph and the following refers to a single occurrence of a portlet in a portal page) and are not shared with other web components (portlets, servlets, and JSPs) in the same portlet application. `PORTLET_SCOPE` session attributes aren't even shared between portlet instances if you're using the same portlet multiple times on the same or different portal pages.

If a portlet stores session attributes in `APPLICATION_SCOPE`, the attributes are accessible to other web components (portlets, servlets, and JSPs) in the same portlet application and to *instances* of the same portlet on the same or different portal pages.

The `PortletSession` interface defines the following methods to set session attributes:

- setAttribute(String name, Object attribute)—Stores attribute in PORTLET_ SCOPE with the name specified.
- setAttribute(String name, Object attribute, int scope)—Stores attribute in the specified scope with the name specified. The possible values of scope are the PortletSession interface's APPLICATION_SCOPE and PORTLET_SCOPE constants.

You can retrieve session attributes from PortletSession using following methods:

- getAttribute(String name)—Retrieves session attribute with the specified name from PORTLET_SCOPE.
- getAttribute(String name, int scope)—Retrieves session attribute with the specified name from the specified scope.

Now that you know the methods provided by the PortletSession object and the different scopes it supports, let's look at how the Book Catalog portlet makes use of them.

3.4.2 *PortletSession usage in the Book Catalog portlet*

In the Book Catalog portlet, the BookCatalogPortlet class stores search criteria in APPLICATION_SCOPE when the user enters the search criteria and clicks the Search button (see figure 3.2). When the user clicks the Refresh Search Results hyperlink, the BookServlet servlet uses HttpSession to retrieve the search criteria stored in APPLICATION_SCOPE.

Listing 3.7 shows code snippets from the BookCatalogPortlet and BookServlet classes to show how the search criteria is stored in PortletSession (by the Book-CatalogPortlet class) and retrieved from HttpSession (by the BookServlet class).

Listing 3.7 Sharing session data using PortletSession's APPLICATION_SCOPE

```
public class BookCatalogPortlet extends GenericPortlet {
  ...
  @ProcessAction(name = "searchBookAction")
  public void searchBook(ActionRequest request,            ❶ Action method
    ActionResponse response) throws ... {                      to search books
    ...
    request.getPortletSession().setAttribute(
      "authorNameSearchField",request.getParameter
        ("authorNameSearchField"),
          PortletSession.APPLICATION_SCOPE);              ❷ Obtains search
    request.getPortletSession().setAttribute(                criteria from
      "bookNameSearchField",request.getParameter             request
        ("bookNameSearchField"),
          PortletSession.APPLICATION_SCOPE);
  }
  ...
}

public class BookServlet extends HttpServlet {

  public void doGet(...)throws ...{
    BookService bookService = new                         ❸ Creates BookService
      BookServiceImpl(this.getServletContext());             instance
```

```
String action = (String) request.getAttribute
    ("myaction");
...
if (action != null &&
  action.equalsIgnoreCase("refreshResults")) {
String bookNameSearchField = (String)
request.getSession().getAttribute(
  "bookNameSearchField");

String authorNameSearchField = (String)
  request.getSession().getAttribute(
    "authorNameSearchField");
...
bookService.searchBooks(bookNameSearchField,
  authorNameSearchField);
}
...
}
...
}
```

④ Obtains search criteria and invokes BookService

The `BookCatalogPortlet` class's `searchBook` action method **①** is responsible for searching for books when the user clicks the Search button. The search criteria is saved to the `PortletSession`'s `APPLICATION_SCOPE` **②** for later use by the `BookServlet` servlet. The `BookServlet`'s `doGet` method creates an instance of `BookServiceImpl` **③**, passing `ServletContext` to the constructor, and it obtains the `myaction` request attribute from the request. The search criteria that was stored in the `Portlet-Session`'s `APPLICATION_SCOPE` at **②** is retrieved using the `HttpSession` object **④**, and the `BookService`'s `searchBooks` method is responsible for finding books matching the search criteria.

Listing 3.7 illustrates a couple of interesting points in the design of the Book Catalog portlet:

- `BookCatalogPortlet` portlet class delegates most method calls to the `Book-Servlet` servlet, including render and action requests.
- The `myaction` request attribute is used by `BookServlet` to identify the action to be performed, which may be rendering a JSP page or processing an action (like searching for books).
- The `ServletContext` object is passed to the `BookService` object at creation time because `ServletContext` holds the book catalog information.

In some scenarios, you may want to access attributes stored in `PORTLET_SESSION` scope from other web components, such as servlets and JSPs. To do this, you can use the `PortletSessionUtil` class.

3.4.3   *Obtaining session attributes using PortletSessionUtil*

In the Book Catalog portlet, `BookServlet` accesses the search criteria stored in the `PortletSession`'s `APPLICATION_SCOPE` using `HttpSession`.

In scenarios where servlets and JSPs included by your portlet need to access the PORTLET_SCOPE session attributes, you should use the PortletSessionUtil class, because, behind the scenes, the session attributes added to PORTLET_SCOPE are added to APPLICATION_SCOPE with a *fabricated* (or *encoded*) name, which makes them accessible to included JSPs and servlets.

The use of PORTLET_SCOPE and APPLICATION_SCOPE gives the impression that the session attributes are stored in two differently scoped containers, with the APPLICATION_SCOPE scoped container being accessible to other web components in the portlet application. In reality, when you add a session attribute to PORTLET_SCOPE, what happens is that the portlet container stores the attribute in APPLICATION_SCOPE with a *fabricated* (or *encoded*) name. The fabricated name for the PORTLET_SCOPE session attributes follows this format:

```
javax.portlet.p.<window_id>?<attribute_name>
```

Here, window_id is the window ID (an identifier assigned to a portlet instance by the portal server to uniquely identify it in the web portal) obtained by using the PortletRequest's getWindowID method. attribute_name is the name of the attribute specified in the PortletSession's setAttribute method.

Let's say you set your PORTLET_SCOPE session attribute using the following code:

```
portletSession.setAttribute("myAttr", myAttr);
```

Assuming that the PortletRequest's getWindowID method returns the window ID as XX, the session attribute would be stored in the APPLICATION_SCOPE with this name:

```
javax.portlet.p.XX?myAttr
```

If you want to retrieve the PORTLET_SCOPE session attributes stored by a portlet in other portlets, servlets, or JSPs of the same portlet application, you need to programmatically construct the name used to store the PORTLET_SCOPE session attribute in the APPLICATION_SCOPE. This is where PortletSessionUtil class comes into the picture. It lets you *decode* the name and scope of an attribute based on its encoded (or fabricated) name.

For instance, the following piece of code can be used in a servlet that's part of the same portlet application to obtain a PORTLET_SCOPE session attribute:

```
session.getAttribute(
  PortletSessionUtil.decodeAttributeName(<encoded_attr_name>)
);
```

Here, encoded_attr_name refers to the encoded (fabricated) name of the attribute (which has the format javax.portlet.p.XX?myAttr, with XX being the window ID) in the APPLICATION_SCOPE.

In the preceding code, you need to know the encoded attribute name to obtain it using the PortletSessionUtil class, but you won't know the encoded name in a JSP or servlet component. To obtain a PORTLET_SCOPE portlet session attribute in your JSP or servlet, you need to iterate over the session attribute names, which are obtained by calling the `HttpSession`'s `getAttributeNames()` method and decoding each attribute name to find a match for the attribute. For instance, the following listing shows a servlet that looks for the `myAttr` attribute in `PORTLET_SCOPE`.

Listing 3.8   An example of using `PortletSessionUtil`

```
String myAttrValue = "";
Enumeration names = request.getSession().getAttributeNames();
while(names.hasMoreElements()) {
  String attributeName = (String)names.nextElement();
  String decodedName =
    PortletSessionUtil.decodeAttributeName(attributeName);
  if(decodedName.equals("myAttr")
      && PortletSessionUtil.decodeScope(attributeName)
      == PortletSession.PORTLET_SCOPE) {
    myAttrValue = session.getAttribute(attributeName);
    break;
  }
}
```

❶ Decodes attribute name

❷ Checks decoded attribute name and scope

The `PortletSessionUtil`'s `decodeAttributeName` method is used **❶** on the attribute name obtained from `HttpSession`. You check whether the decoded name of the attribute is `myAttr` **❷**. If it is, you use the `PortletSessionUtil`'s `decodeScope` method to check whether the attribute belongs to `PORTLET_SCOPE` or not.

If the decoded name of the attribute is `myAttr` and it belongs to `PORTLET_SCOPE`, it's the `myAttr` attribute you want. It's important to check whether the attribute belongs to `PORTLET_SCOPE` because the `decodeAttributeName` method in listing 3.8 checks both `PORTLET_SCOPE` and `APPLICATION_SCOPE` `PortletSession` attributes. If you have an attribute named `myAttr` in `APPLICATION_SCOPE`, the `PortletSession-Util`'s `decodeAttributeName` method will return `myAttr` as its decoded name because `decodeAttributeName` returns the name of an `APPLICATION_SCOPE` attribute unchanged. If you don't check the scope, you could end up with a wrong match.

You've seen how different portlet session scopes are used, so let's take an in-depth look at their differences and the things that you need to take care of while storing data in a portlet session.

3.4.4   *An in-depth look at portlet session scopes*

Figure 3.8 summarizes the concept of `PORTLET_SCOPE` and `APPLICATION_SCOPE` in the `PortletSession`.

The portlet sets a session attribute named `portletAttr` **❶** in `PORTLET_SCOPE`. The attribute is stored in the `APPLICATION_SCOPE` with a fabricated name. The included or forwarded servlet or JSP component **❷** tries to retrieve the `portletAttr` attribute from the `HttpSession` (which looks for session attributes stored in `APPLICATION_SCOPE`), but it can't retrieve the session attribute because `portletAttr` is stored with a fabricated name. The portlet stores a session attribute named `appAttr` in `APPLICATION_SCOPE` **❸**, so it's stored with the same name as was specified by the

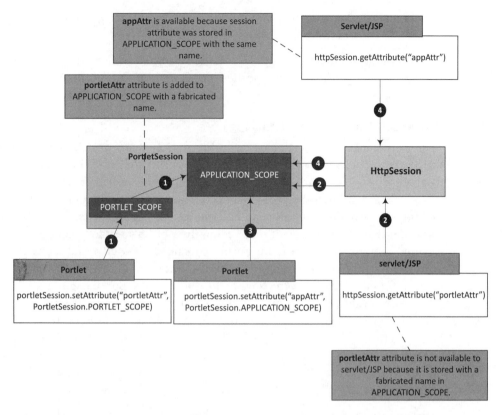

Figure 3.8 The `HttpSession` can access `PortletSession` attributes, which are stored with fabricated names in `PORTLET_SCOPE`. It can also access `PortletSession` attributes stored in `APPLICATION_SCOPE` using the names under which they were stored.

portlet. The included or forwarded servlet or JSP component ❹ successfully retrieves the `appAttr` attribute from `HttpSession`.

The use of the window ID in the fabricated name of the `PORTLET_SCOPE` session attribute plays an important role in ensuring that `PORTLET_SCOPE` session attributes are *easily* accessible only to included or forwarded servlets or JSPs, and not to every servlet or JSP in the portlet application. The included or forwarded JSPs or servlets have access to the window ID of the portlet invoking them, making it easy for the JSP or servlet to access `PORTLET_SCOPE` attributes using the `PortletSessionUtil` class. If you have two instances of the same portlet on a portal page, the unique window IDs of the two portlets help differentiate between `PORTLET_SCOPE` session attributes set by those portlets.

WARNING Because both `PORTLET_SCOPE` and `APPLICATION_SCOPE` session attributes are accessible to other web components in a portlet application, you should synchronize access to session attributes by methods that intend to modify them. It's best to avoid setting session attributes during the portlet's render phase because the render phase isn't meant to modify the state of the application, and it should be *repeatable* with no side effects.

Let's now look at how the portlet session comes in handy if you don't want to use the caching strategy provided by the portlet container, or if your portlet container doesn't support caching.

3.4.5   *Portlet session and content caching*

In some situations, you may have no other option than to set session attributes in the render phase. Suppose you've developed a portlet that reads information from the database during its render phase. If the information retrieved from the database rarely changes, it might be preferable to use an expiration-based or validation-based caching strategy (discussed in chapter 4) to let the portlet container cache the portlet content and redisplay it without calling the portlet's render method. Support for caching is an optional feature for portlet containers; if your portal server *doesn't* support caching, the portlet's render method will be called every time to retrieve information from the database, affecting the load time of the portal page.

If your target portlet container doesn't support content caching, and you still want to use a caching mechanism to reduce the load time of the portal page, you can load data from the database and store it in a `PortletSession` to avoid round trips to the database in the render phase. If you don't want to overload your sessions by storing application data in them, you can consider caching data using a caching library like Ehcache.

> **WARNING**   You shouldn't store huge amounts of application data in the `PortletSession` because if your portlet application is deployed in a clustered environment, the session replication requires your sessions to have small memory footprints.

You've now seen the differences between `PortletSession` and `HttpSession`. There are also many similarities between the two session types that make it possible for portlets to reuse some `HttpSession` listeners for `PortletSession`.

3.4.6   *Similarities between HttpSession and PortletSession*

The portlet specification mandates that if you store an attribute in `PortletSession`, it must be accessible to `HttpSession`, and vice versa. The specification also requires that the portlet container must invalidate the `PortletSession` if `HttpSession` is invalidated by the web container, and vice versa.

Because both `HttpSession` and `PortletSession` mirror stored attributes and follow the same lifecycle, you can use the following `HttpSession`-related listeners for `PortletSession` too: `HttpSessionAttributeListener`, `HttpSessionBindingListener`, and `HttpSessionActivationListener`.

`PortletSession` attributes aren't shared by all the portlets deployed on a portal server. The `PortletSession` attributes are accessible only to portlets (and to included or forwarded JSPs and servlets) that form part of the same portlet application, as described next.

3.4.7 *Sharing session data across portlet applications*

We briefly discussed portlet applications in chapter 1, but we didn't cover the impact of having portlets in different portlet applications. A portlet application is packaged like any other web application; you create a WAR file consisting of portlets, servlets, and JSPs. If portlets belong to different WAR files, they're parts of *different* portlet applications and they won't share `PortletSession` attributes. This is true even for two portlets on a single portal page.

> **NOTE** In chapter 11, you'll see how `PortletSession` can also be used to achieve inter-portlet communication.

You saw the `PortletContext` and `PortletConfig` objects used in the User Registration example in chapter 2. Let's take a more comprehensive look at these objects.

3.5 *Discovering the portlet environment using PortletContext*

`PortletContext` provides portlets with access to its environment, which includes the portlet application and the portlet container. Each portlet application has its own unique `PortletContext`; if you have portlets in different portlet applications, they don't share attributes set in the `PortletContext`. You saw earlier that you can use `PortletContext` to obtain a `PortletRequestDispatcher` to generate portlet content by including or forwarding portlet requests to a JSP page using the `PortletRequest-Dispatcher` object's `getRequestDispatcher` method. In this section, we'll look at some of the important methods of the `PortletContext` interface.

Table 3.6 describes some of the important `PortletContext` methods.

Table 3.6   Important `PortletContext` methods

Method	Description
`getAttribute, setAttribute, removeAttribute`	Get, set, and remove context attributes. The context attributes that are available to portlets through `PortletContext` are also accessible to JSPs and servlets (that form part of the same portlet application) through `ServletContext`, and vice versa.
`getInitParameter`	Obtains the context initialization parameters. Context initialization parameters are different from portlet initialization parameters in the sense that they're available to all portlets in the same portlet application. Context initialization parameters are specified in web.xml using the `context-param` element.

Table 3.6   Important `PortletContext` methods *(continued)*

Method	Description
`getContainerRuntimeOptions`	Returns an enumeration of portlet container-runtime options supported by the portlet container. The return type is `Enumeration<String>`.
`getNamedDispatcher`	Accepts the servlet name to which the returned `RequestDispatcher` refers.
`getMimeType`	Accepts a filename as an argument and returns its MIME type (such as `text/html` and `application/pdf`).

A portlet application is also a web application, and like any web application it has a `ServletContext`. Like `HttpSession` and `PortletSession`, `PortletContext` and `ServletContext` mirror attributes stored in the context and they follow the same lifecycle. If you store an attribute in `PortletContext`, it's available to `Servlet-Context`, and vice versa. If the `ServletContext` is destroyed by the servlet container, the `PortletContext` is also destroyed by the portlet container. Because `Portlet-Context` mirrors the `ServletContext` attributes and follows the same lifecycle, you can use the following `ServletContext` listeners for your `PortletContext`: `Servlet-ContextListener` and `ServletContextAttributeListener`.

> **CODE REFERENCE**   The book catalog data is accessed by the `BookCatalog-Portlet` class as well as the `BookService` class. Because any attribute stored in `ServletContext` is accessible to portlets using `PortletContext`, the Book Catalog portlet uses `BookCatalogContextListener` (a `ServletContextListener` configured in the web.xml file) to store book catalog data in `ServletContext` with an attribute named `bookCatalog`. The `BookCatalogPortlet` class's show-Books method obtains the `bookCatalog` attribute using the `PortletContext` object, and `BookService` obtains it using `ServletContext`.

`PortletContext` provides information at the portlet application level. If you want to obtain portlet information for a specific portlet, you should use the `Portlet-Config` object.

3.6   *Retrieving portlet configuration using PortletConfig*

The `PortletConfig` object provides portlets with the portlet configuration information specified within its `<portlet>` element in the portlet deployment descriptor. This portlet configuration information includes the supported container-runtime options, initialization parameters, resource bundles, public render parameter names, and so on.

Table 3.7 lists some of the important methods defined by the `PortletConfig` interface.

Table 3.7   Important `PortletConfig` **methods**

Method	Description
`getContainerRuntimeOptions`	Returns the portlet container-runtime options supported by the container and their corresponding settings for the portlet. Return type is `Map<String[]>`.
`getSupportedLocales`	Returns the locales supported by the portlet. You specify supported locales using the `<supported-locale>` element.
`getInitParameter(String name)`	Returns the value of the initialization parameter.
`getPortletContext`	Returns the `PortletContext` object of the portlet application that contains the portlet.
`getPortletName`	Returns the name of the portlet.

Table 3.7 shows that `PortletConfig` defines the `getContainerRuntimeOptions` method, which isn't the same as the `PortletContext`'s `getContainerRuntime-Options` method, as is evident from the difference in the return types of the two methods. In chapter 11, we'll discuss additional `PortletConfig` methods related to obtaining supported public render parameters, events that a portlet can dispatch, and events that a portlet can receive or process.

> **CODE REFERENCE**   The `BookCatalogPortlet` uses the `GenericPortlet` class's `getInitParameter` method to obtain the `uploadFolder` initialization parameter (which identifies the folder on the portal server where the uploaded book TOCs are stored). If you create your portlet class by directly implementing the `Portlet` interface, you'll need to use the `PortletConfig` object in your code to obtain the portlet initialization parameter.

Now let's look at the container-runtime options that can ease your development efforts by providing additional runtime features to your portlets. We'll also look at how the Book Catalog portlet can make use of the `actionScopedRequestAttributes`' container-runtime option to simplify portlet development.

3.7   *Container-runtime options*

You saw the `javax.portlet.actionScopedRequestAttributes` (`actionScoped-RequestAttributes`, for short) option in chapter 2, in the context of the User Registration portlet. This section covers that option in more detail, and also the remaining container-runtime options that may be supported by your portlet container. We'll spend a little more time discussing `actionScopedRequestAttributes` because it's the most often used container-runtime option, and it's more complex to understand than the others. Because container-runtime options can be defined for a portlet or for the complete portlet application, we'll wrap this section up by looking at configuring portlet- and portlet application–level container-runtime options in the portlet deployment descriptor.

The container-runtime options defined by the Portlet 2.0 specification are outlined in table 3.8.

Table 3.8   Portlet container-runtime options

Container-runtime option	Description
`actionScopedRequestAttributes`	If set to `true`, the request attributes set in the action, event, or resource requests are available until the next action request is sent to the portlet. The default is `false`.
`escapeXml`	If set to `true`, the URL generated by the tag library is XML-escaped. If set to `false`, the URL isn't XML-escaped. The default is `true`.
`renderHeaders`	If set to `true`, portlets can write headers in the render phase.
`servletDefaultSessionScope`	If set to `true`, the session attributes stored by portlets in their `PORTLET_SCOPE` are available to included or forwarded JSPs or servlets. The default is `false`.

Before we discuss the portlet container-runtime options defined in table 3.8, let's take a look at what the `PortletContext`'s `getContainerRuntimeOptions` method returns for the portal servers on which we want to deploy the Book Catalog example portlet. Table 3.9 shows the container-runtime options supported by different portal servers.

Table 3.9   Container-runtime options support in different portal servers

Portal server	Supported container-runtime options (obtained by using the `PortletContext`'s `getContainerRuntimeOptions` method)
Liferay Portal 6.x/5.2.3	Returns `null`, which means Liferay Portal 6.x/5.2.3 doesn't support any container-runtime options, including `actionScopedRequestAttributes`. We'll see shortly that Liferay Portal 5.2.3/6.x does provide a feature similar to `actionScopedRequestAttributes`.
Jetspeed 2.2	Returns `escapeXML` and `javax.portlet.servletDefaultSessionScope`.
GlassFish Server (with Open-Portal portlet container 2.1.2)	Returns `javax.portlet.actionScopedRequest-Attributes` and `javax.portlet.escapeXml`.

TIP While developing your portlet applications, if you plan to use any of the portlet container-runtime options, make sure either that the options are supported by all the target portlet containers or that there is some workaround available to ensure that the portlet application works as expected. There are normally workarounds available for portlet container-runtime options to help you develop portlets with or without container-runtime options.

Let's look at the various container-runtime options in detail.

3.7.1 Using actionScopedRequestAttributes

The `javax.portlet.actionScopedRequestAttributes` is the most important container-runtime option and supporting it is mandatory for Portlet 2.0 containers. It ensures that the request attributes set in the action request are available to the subsequent render, resource, and event requests, until a new action request is sent to the portlet instance. In the User Registration portlet in chapter 2, you used `actionScopedRequestAttributes` to allow request attributes set in the `ActionRequest` to be available in the subsequent `RenderRequest`.

Table 3.9 shows that Liferay Portal 6.x doesn't support the `actionScopedRequestAttributes` option, so you might wonder why the `actionScopedRequestAttributes` container-runtime option was specified for the User Registration portlet. The reason was to ensure that the portlet works on other portlet containers that do support the `actionScopedRequestAttributes` container option.

You might also wonder how the User Registration portlet retrieved request attributes set in `ActionRequest` from `RenderRequest`, given that Liferay Portal 6.x doesn't support the `actionScopedRequestAttributes` option. The portlet container in Liferay Portal 5.2.3/6.x allows request attributes set in `ActionRequest` to be available to the *following* `RenderRequest` *only*, and then they're gone; it's a one-time thing. Also note that the request attributes aren't available to *subsequent* render, event, and resource requests. Subsequent requests aren't part of the current portlet request.

Figure 3.9 shows a sequence diagram with multiple requests being dispatched to a portlet. Let's compare the behavior of a portlet when it's deployed on Liferay Portal 6.x, Jetspeed 2.2, and GlassFish Server 3.0.1 (with OpenPortal Portlet Container 2.1.2).

An action request ❶ is sent to the portlet. The portlet sets a request attribute named "x" in the `ActionRequest` object ❷. The render request is called on the portlet ❸ by the portlet container because, in the portlet lifecycle, an action request is always followed by a render request. The portlet attempts to get the value of the "x" attribute ❹ from `RenderRequest`. A render request ❺ is sent to the portlet, which attempts to get the value of the "x" attribute from `RenderRequest` ❻. An action request is sent to the portlet ❼, which attempts to get the value of attribute "x" from `RenderRequest` ❽.

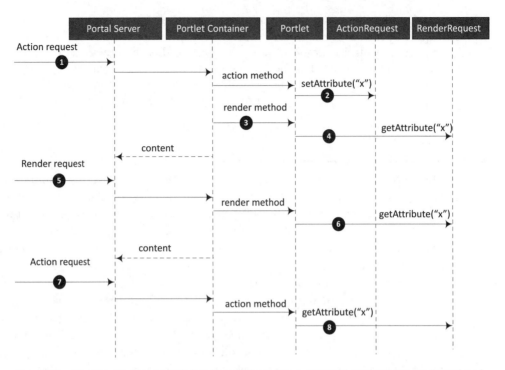

Figure 3.9   A series of action and render requests is sent to a portlet to demonstrate the behavior of the portlet on different portal servers: Liferay Portal 5.2.3/6.x, Jetspeed 2.2, and GlassFish Server (with OpenPortal Portlet Container 2.1.2).

Table 3.10 shows what happens when you try to retrieve the value of request attribute "x" at **4**, **6**, and **8** for different portal servers. We'll assume that the `actionScoped-RequestAttributes` container-runtime option is enabled for the portlet in the portlet deployment descriptor.

Table 3.10   Availability of request attribute "x" (from figure 3.9) on different portal servers

Portal server	Request attribute "x" available?
Liferay Portal 5.2.3/6.x	At **4**: Yes At **6**: No At **8**: No
Jetspeed 2.2	At **4**: No At **6**: No At **8**: No
GlassFish Server v3.0.1 (with OpenPortal Portlet Container 2.1.2)	At **4**: Yes At **6**: Yes At **8**: No

From table 3.10, we can conclude the following about the behavior of the portal servers:

- Jetspeed doesn't support the `actionScopedRequestAttributes` option, so request attributes set in the `ActionRequest` aren't available in the *following* `RenderRequest`.
- GlassFish Server v3.0.1 (with OpenPortal Portlet Container 2.1.2) supports the `actionScopedRequestAttributes` option, so request attributes set in `Action-Request` are available in the *following* and *subsequent* `RenderRequest`s.
- Liferay Portal 5.2.3/6.x doesn't support the `actionScopedRequestAttributes` option, but it allows request attributes set in `ActionRequest` to be available in the *following* `RenderRequest`, but not in *subsequent* `RenderRequest`s.

If you're only looking to make your `ActionRequest`'s attributes available to the following `RenderRequest`, you can consider setting the request attribute as a render parameter in the `ActionResponse`. As was mentioned in chapter 2, render parameters only allow you to pass `String` objects and can't be used for passing complex objects to the following render request. If your container doesn't support the `actionScoped-RequestAttributes` option (as in the case of Jetspeed 2.2), and you need to pass complex objects to the following render method, you should consider using the `PortletSession` to hold the attributes.

If your application requirement is to share the request attributes (`String` type or complex objects) with subsequent render, event, and resource requests, and your portlet container doesn't support the `actionScopedRequestAttributes` option (as in the case of Liferay Portal 5.2.3/6.x and Jetspeed 2.2), you should consider storing the attributes in the `PortletSession`.

> **WARNING** Attributes stored in the `PortletSession` are accessible to other web components, and you could have problems if they're modified accidentally. Also, if the user opens the portal page that contains the portlet in multiple browser windows, any change in `PortletSession` is reflected in the portlet in all browser windows.

SCOPE OF ACTION-SCOPED REQUEST ATTRIBUTES

The scope of action-scoped request attributes lies between two subsequent action requests. The starting point of the scope is when an action request is received for a portlet by the portlet container, and the scope ends when another action request is received by the portlet container for the same portlet. The attributes added to the portlet request (`ActionRequest`, `EventRequest`, `ResourceRequest`, and `Render-Request`) from the beginning of scope, until it ends, are available to all of the lifecycle methods of the portlet.

You may also specify a `numberOfCachedScopes` value for `actionScopedRequest-Attributes`, which specifies that the portlet container should cache action-scoped request attributes. Caching action-scoped request attributes is useful when users navigate in a portal using the Back and Forward browser buttons. The action-scoped attributes in the cache additionally record whether the render method *following* the action method was invoked or not. That means that if the user presses the browser's Back button and then attempts to invoke the action method (for example, by submitting a form) the portlet container checks whether the render method following the action method was previously invoked or not. If it was, the portlet container simply invokes the render method. If the render method wasn't invoked previously, the action method is invoked, followed by the render method. This results in a consistent user experience even when the user moves backward and forward using the browser buttons.

USE CASE FOR ACTIONSCOPEDREQUESTATTRIBUTES

In the Book Catalog portlet, the Refresh Search Results hyperlink refreshes the search results. Let's look at how this feature is usually implemented in web applications: Usually, the search criterion is cached in the session when the search is first made by clicking the Search button. When the user clicks the Refresh Search Results link, the search is executed again to get fresh results from the database.

This approach can also be used by the Book Catalog portlet for searching, as follows:

1 The user clicks the Search button, and the book and author name search criteria is sent to an action method of the portlet. The action method stores the book and author name criteria in the `PortletSession`.

2 The portlet's render method retrieves the search criteria from `PortletSession` and executes the search function to obtain the results from the database. The render method then generates the necessary markup by dispatching the request to a JSP page or servlet.

3 When the user clicks the Refresh Search Results link, it sends a render request to the Book Catalog portlet. The render method obtains the search criteria from the `PortletSession` and executes the search function, as in step 2.

The problem with the preceding approach is storing data in the `PortletSession`— the portlet developer is responsible for removing the search criteria from the `PortletSession` when it's no longer required. For instance, when the user clicks the Add Book button and goes to the Add Book form, the search criteria doesn't need to be maintained in the `PortletSession`. If the preceding approach is followed for a multipage portlet, the `PortletSession` becomes heavy as the user accesses portlet functionality on different portlet pages. A heavy portlet session can cause problems when it comes to migrating or replicating sessions in a clustered environment, impacting the performance of your web portal.

In contrast, the `actionScopedRequestAttributes` option makes it easy to share data between an action request and the subsequent render, resource, and event requests by letting the portlet container take care of making request attributes available to subsequent requests, and cleaning them up when a new action request is received for the portlet. The following steps show how the Book Catalog portlet will function if the `actionScopedRequestAttributes` option is used:

1 The user clicks the Search button, and the book and author name search criteria are sent to an action method of the portlet. The action method stores the book and author name criteria in `ActionRequest`.

2 The portlet's render method retrieves the search criteria from `RenderRequest` and executes the search function to obtain results from the database. The render method then generates the necessary markup by dispatching the request to a JSP page or servlet.

3 When the user clicks the Refresh Search Results link, it sends a render request to the Book Catalog portlet. The render method obtains the search criteria from `RenderRequest` and executes the search function, as in step 2.

In the preceding steps, you're no longer dealing with the `PortletSession` because the portlet container takes care of making request attributes (set in the action request) available to subsequent render requests.

Using the `actionScopedRequestAttributes` container-runtime option isn't a silver bullet solution for sharing data between portlet requests. You may find yourself in situations where using this approach may cause problems. For instance, in the Book Catalog portlet, the FULL SCREEN link (see figure 3.2) sends an action request to the portlet to show the portlet in maximized window state. In the preceding steps, if a user clicks the FULL SCREEN link after step 2, it will wipe out the search criteria set in the `ActionRequest` in step 1. Then, if the user clicks the Refresh Search Results link, the previous search criteria won't be available to the render request.

> **TIP** Consider using `actionScopedRequestAttribute` in your portlet in combination with `PortletSession` to hold data that's required across portlet requests. `PortletSession` keeps data that spans multiple action requests, and `actionScopedRequestAttribute` mandates that the portlet container keep data between two consecutive action requests. For instance, the search criteria in the Book Catalog portlet spans multiple action requests, so it should be stored in `PortletSession`. You should, by default, enable the `actionScoped-RequestAttributes` option for your portlets and specify an appropriate default value for `numberOfCachedScopes` for it. Don't set a high value for `numberOfCachedScopes`, because caching action-scoped request attributes will require the portlet container to use more memory and resources to maintain the cache.

3.7.2 *Using servletDefaultSessionScope*

You saw in figure 3.8 and listing 3.7 that, by default, `HttpSession` retrieves and stores attributes in the `PortletSession`'s `APPLICATION_SCOPE`. If you want your included or forwarded JSPs and servlets to retrieve and set attributes in the `Portlet-Session`'s `PORTLET_SCOPE`, you should use the `servletDefaultSessionScope` container-runtime option.

The following XML fragment shows how you can specify the `servletDefault-SessionScope` container-runtime option in the portlet deployment descriptor:

```
<container-runtime-option>
  <name>javax.portlet.servletDefaultSessionScope</name>
  <value>PORTLET_SCOPE</value>
</container-runtime-option>
```

In the preceding definition, the value of the `<value>` element specifies the `Portlet-Session`'s `PORTLET_SCOPE` scope within which the included or forwarded JSP or servlet should look for or store session attributes. The default value of the `<value>` element is `APPLICATION_SCOPE`, which means that the included or forwarded JSP or servlet should look for or store session attributes in the `PortletSession`'s `APPLICATION_SCOPE`.

Table 3.9 shows that the `servletDefaultSessionScope` option is supported by Jetspeed and not by Liferay Portal 5.2.3/6.x and GlassFish Server (with OpenPortal Portlet Container 2.1.2). If you want to test this container-runtime option, you can do it on the Jetspeed portal server. Figure 3.10 is a modified version of figure 3.8, showing what happens when your portlet or portlet application makes use of the `servletDefaultSessionScope` portlet container-runtime option.

The portlet sets an attribute named `portletAttr` **❶** in the `PortletSession`'s `PORTLET_SCOPE`. The portlet sets an attribute named `appAttr` **❷** in the `Portlet-Session`'s `APPLICATION_SCOPE`. The included or forwarded servlet or JSP **❸** fails to retrieve the `appAttr` session attribute because `HttpSession` looks for attributes in `PORTLET_SCOPE` and not in `APPLICATION_SCOPE` when the `servletDefaultSessionScope` container-runtime option is set to `PORTLET_SCOPE`. The included or forwarded servlet or JSP **❹** successfully retrieves the `portletAttr` session attribute from `HttpSession`.

Figure 3.10 shows that the `HttpSession` looks for session attributes in `PORTLET_SCOPE` when the `servletDefaultSessionScope` container-runtime option is set to `PORTLET_SCOPE`. So how can you retrieve an `APPLICATION_SCOPE` session attribute from `HttpSession`? Well, you can't access `APPLICATION_SCOPE` session attributes any longer, because the `HttpSession` is now completely focused on the session attributes in the `PortletSession`'s `PORTLET_SCOPE`. This means that if you want to share session attributes stored in the `PortletSession`'s `APPLICATION_SCOPE` with included or forwarded servlets and JSPs, you must *not* set the value of the `servletDefaultSessionScope` container-runtime option to `PORTLET_SCOPE`.

3.7.3   *Using escapeXml*

Escaping XML refers to converting special characters, like &, >, <, and so on, into character entity codes, like &, >, <, and so on. If a portlet relies on a URL generated by the portlet tag library (discussed in chapter 6) that isn't XML-escaped, you should set this container-runtime option to `false`. In the Portlet 2.0 specification, all URLs generated by the portlet tag library are XML-escaped by default.

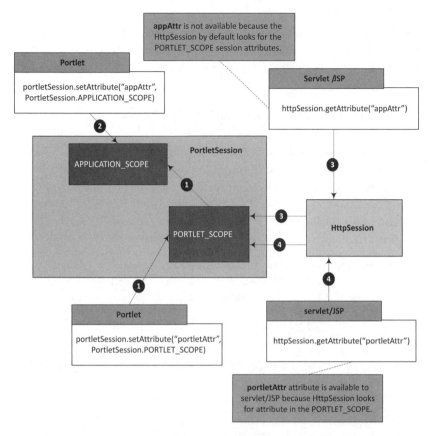

Figure 3.10 The servletDefaultSessionScope container-runtime option allows included or forwarded JSPs or servlets to set or retrieve attributes directly to and from the PortletSession's PORTLET_SCOPE. The APPLICATION_SCOPE session attributes are no longer accessible to included or forwarded servlets and JSPs.

Escaping XML in Portlet 1.0

Portlet 1.0 didn't specify whether the portlet URLs generated by the portlet tag library tags (actionURL and renderURL) are XML-escaped or not. This lack of clarity resulted in mixed implementations of this feature: some portlet containers escaped XML and some didn't. Because some portlet developers assumed in their implementations that portlet URLs aren't XML-escaped, the escapeXml attribute and javax.portlet.escapeXml container-runtime option were introduced in Portlet 2.0 to clarify that the portlet container must generate XML-escaped portlet URLs or not, depending upon the values of escapeXml and javax.portlet.escapeXml. If you have a portlet that was developed assuming that portlet URLs aren't XML-escaped (during the Portlet 1.0 days), you can still use the portlet with Portlet 2.0–compliant portlet containers by setting the javax.portlet.escapeXml container-runtime option to false.

3.7.4   *Using renderHeaders*

The `renderHeaders` container-runtime option is meant for streaming portals, where content is streamed, and not for buffering portals, where content is buffered. We're mainly talking about buffering portals in this book, so this container-runtime option isn't covered.

3.7.5   *Specifying Portlet and Portlet application container-runtime options*

Portlet container-runtime options can be specified at the portlet- or portlet application–level or both. Keep your portlet requirements in mind as you decide whether the container-runtime option should apply to all portlets in the portlet application or only to specific portlets. For instance, if one of your portlets has form functionality, you'll probably want to implement the portlet with the `actionScopedRequestAttribute` container-runtime option enabled, to simplify development.

> **TIP**   Portlet runtime options add overhead on the portlet container, which can result in reduced performance. If a portlet can function without a container-runtime option, it's better not to enable the option for that portlet.

This listing shows how you can specify container-runtime options at portlet and portlet application levels.

Listing 3.9   Container-runtime options in the portlet.xml file

```
<portlet-app>
    <portlet>
        <name>userRegistration</name>            ❶ User Registration
        ...                                          portlet
    </portlet>
    <portlet>
        <name>bookCatalog</name>                 ❷ Book Catalog
        ...                                          portlet
        <container-runtime-option>
            <name>...actionScopedRequestAttributes</name>    ❸ Portlet-level
            <value>false</value>                                container-runtime
        </container-runtime-option>                             option
    </portlet>
    <container-runtime-option>
        <name>...actionScopedRequestAttributes</name>    ❹ Portlet application–
        <value>true</value>                                 level container-
    </container-runtime-option>                             runtime option
</portlet-app>
```

The `userRegistration` portlet is defined ❶, and it doesn't specify any portlet-specific container-runtime options. The `bookCatalog` portlet is defined ❷, specifying the portlet-specific `actionScopedRequestAttributes` container-runtime option. The `actionScopedRequestAttributes` container-runtime option is set to `false` ❸ for the `bookCatalog` portlet. The `actionScopedRequestAttributes` container-runtime option is specified ❹ for the portlet application (for all the portlets in the portlet application).

CODE REFERENCE   Refer to the Book Catalog portlet's portlet.xml file, which specifies the `actionScopedRequestAttributes` container-runtime option at the portlet application level.

Portlets that don't define container-runtime options inherit any such options defined at the portlet application level. For instance, the `userRegistration` portlet in listing 3.9 inherits the `actionScopedRequestAttributes` option defined at the portlet application level, so the value of the `actionScopedRequestAttributes` option is `true` for the `userRegistration` portlet.

A portlet may also override the container-runtime options set for the portlet application by redefining the container-runtime options in its definition. The `bookCatalog` portlet in listing 3.9 overrides the `actionScopedRequestAttributes` option by redefining it and setting its value to `false`.

3.8   *Summary*

This chapter discussed the Portlet 2.0 API in the context of the Book Catalog portlet. We'll continue building the Book Catalog portlet in the next chapter and use it to create a sample Book Portal in chapter 5.

In this chapter, you saw the importance of having a detailed understanding of the portal servers on which your portlet application will be deployed. Portal servers are currently moving to the Portlet 2.0 API, and it's important to consider their limitations, their specific features, and also their open bugs when you decide on an approach to make your portlets work across different portal servers.

In the next chapter, we'll continue to explore the Portlet 2.0 API, and we'll discuss an approach to designing portlets that use portal server–specific APIs and still need to be portable across different portal servers.

Portlet 2.0 API— caching, security, and localization

In chapter 3, we discussed some of the common Portlet 2.0 API concepts and applied them to the example Book Catalog portlet. But we haven't yet looked at how portlets can show localized content to users in different locales, cache content for better performance, make use of a custom portlet mode or window state for showing content, upload files, and so on. In this chapter you'll see how Portlet 2.0 API concepts are applied to the Book Catalog portlet to use caching, show content in fr_FR locale, upload TOC files, and use custom portlet modes and window states. Portlets may also depend on portal server–specific APIs to achieve some of their features, so we'll conclude this chapter by discussing how to design portlets so that they can easily be adapted to different Portlet 2.0–compliant portal servers.

> **CODE REFERENCE**   The Book Catalog example in chapters 3 and 4 share the same code base, so you'll find the source code references in this chapter in the ch3_BookCatalog folder. Before you build or deploy the portlet, make sure you change the value of the uploadFolder initialization parameter in the portlet deployment descriptor. Also, before you build the project, set the liferay.portal.home property in the build.properties file to point to your Liferay Portal installation directory.

4.1　*Caching generated content*

Content generated by a portlet may be cached by the portlet container to allow the web portal faster access to it. There are two main approaches to improve portal performance: caching portlet data and caching portlet content.

You've seen in earlier examples that a portlet generates content when it services a render request. In most cases, portlets retrieve data from one or more databases, web services, or other data sources, and then display it using JSPs (or any other view technology). In some cases, portlets delegate the generation of content to a servlet, which is then responsible for retrieving data from data sources. In either case, the portlet or servlet component is responsible for retrieving data every time a render request is sent to the portlet. One way to reduce this performance overhead is by caching the data using caching libraries like Ehcache. If you were using an actual database in the Book Catalog portlet, you could cache the catalog data to reduce the portlet's rendering time.

When using data caching to improve portal performance, the portlet retrieves data from the cache instead of firing a query to the database or invoking web services. But while caching data improves performance, the data still needs to be retrieved from the cache, transformed, and displayed by the portlet. If the request processing is computationally or resource intensive, you may still not achieve the desired performance benchmarks for your web portal.

Data caching can also have a negative impact on performance if there are many portlets on your portal page and each portlet retrieves data from the cache every time a render request is received. For instance, consider a portal page with five portlets: A, B, C, D, and E. Suppose a user sends an action request to portlet A, and while rendering the portal page the render methods of portlets B, C, D, and E are invoked. Even if each portlet has its data cached, the cumulative effect of rendering five portlets could have a substantial effect on the performance of the portal.

> **NOTE**   Portlets that show real-time data should get their data from the data sources every time the render request is received by the portlet container. It would be bad design to use data caching in such scenarios, unless the data

cache is *actively* synched with the data source holding the real-time data. Chapter 12 shows how *Comet* (or Reverse Ajax) can be used to push data from the server to create a portlet which shows real-time data.

If you're convinced that data caching isn't good enough to boost your portal's performance, you can use *content caching*. Content caching involves caching the *markup* generated by the portlet. If the markup is cached, your portlet doesn't even need to access the data cache to generate content. Portlet containers are responsible for caching the markup generated by the portlet and sending it to the portal server when a render request is received for the portlet.

A portlet is responsible for specifying whether it wants to use content caching or not. You can't specify at the portlet application level that the content of all the portlets must be cached by the portlet container.

> **NOTE**   Portlet containers cache *portlet* content and not portal *page* content.

You may have multiple portlets on your portal page, where some portlets show fresh content and some cached content. Portlets that are meant to show real-time data shouldn't use content caching and should generate fresh content every time they receive a render request.

A portlet may also specify whether its cached content can be shared by the portlet container with different users of the portal, or whether the content should be cached on a per-user basis. If a portlet shows content that isn't specific to a user, such as public announcements, the cached content of the portlet could be shared with different portal users.

The portlet specification defines two types of content caching strategies: *expiration-based* and *validation-based*.

4.1.1   *Expiration-based content caching*

In the expiration-based caching strategy, the cached content of the portlet is valid only for a *predefined* period of time. Once the time expires, the portlet is asked to generate fresh content, which is again cached by the portlet container for a period of time.

> **NOTE**   The expiration-based caching strategy must not be used in portlets that show content based on real-time data. It's ideally suited for portlets that generate content based on computationally or resource-intensive request-processing operations.

As long as the portlet content is cached, the portlet container doesn't invoke the portlet's render method (with exceptions we'll discuss shortly). Instead, the portlet container returns the cached content when it receives a render request for the portlet. After the content expires, if the portlet container receives a render request for the portlet, it invokes the portlet's render method. If at any time the portlet container receives an action or event request for the portlet, the portlet container immediately expires the portlet's cached content and sends the action or event request to the portlet instance.

> **CODE REFERENCE** At this time, it's recommended that you import ch3_Book-Catalog Eclipse project into your Eclipse workspace so you can follow the code references in the rest of this chapter.

You can specify expiration-based caching in the portlet deployment descriptor or set it programmatically. The following XML fragment shows how the Book Catalog portlet defines expiration-based caching in portlet.xml:

```
<portlet>
  ...
  <expiration-cache>60</expiration-cache>
  <cache-scope>private</cache-scope>
  <supports>
   ...
  </supports>
  ...
</portlet>
```

In this code, the `<expiration-cache>` element defines how long (in seconds) the portlet content is cached by the portlet container. The value `60` indicates that the Book Catalog portlet defines 60 seconds as its cache expiration time. The `<cache-scope>` element defines the scope of the cache—whether it's shared across all portal users (`public`) or it's user-specific (`private`). The value `private` indicates that the Book Catalog portlet's cache is user-specific.

You can also set the cache expiration time and scope programmatically in one of the following ways:

- Use the `CacheControl` object's `setExpirationTime` and `setScope` methods (`CacheControl` is obtained from `MimeResponse`).
- Set the `EXPIRATION_CACHE` and `CACHE_SCOPE` properties in `RenderResponse`. The `MimeResponse` interface defines `EXPIRATION_CACHE` and `CACHE_SCOPE` constants. It also defines `PRIVATE_SCOPE` and `PUBLIC_SCOPE` constants, which can be specified as values for the `CACHE_SCOPE` property.

You can override the cache expiration settings in the portlet deployment descriptor by setting the cache expiration information programmatically.

UNDERSTANDING PORTLET BEHAVIOR

Figure 4.1 highlights some of the important elements of the Book Catalog portlet that we'll discuss in this section.

The current system date and time is displayed ❶ in MM-dd-yyyy HH:mm:ss format. If a user clicks the Refresh Search Results hyperlink ❷, a render request is sent to the portlet. If a user clicks the Search button ❸, an action request is sent to the portlet. If a user clicks the Print, Help, or Preferences hyperlink ❹, a render request is sent to the portlet.

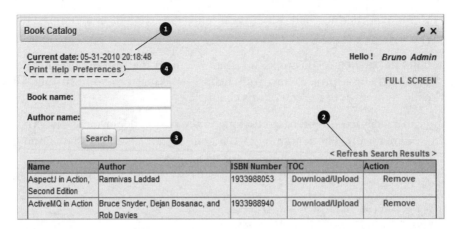

Figure 4.1   Initial content of the Book Catalog portlet, showing current date and time, books in the catalog, and the options to search for books in and add books to the catalog

A render request is dispatched to the Book Catalog portlet in a couple of scenarios:

- When the user refreshes the portal page containing the Book Catalog portlet by using the browser's Refresh button.
- When user interaction with the Book Catalog portlet results in a render request being sent to the portlet. For instance, clicking the Refresh Search Results or Print hyperlink sends a render request to the portlet.
- When the user interacts with some other portlet on the same portal page. In this case, a render request is sent to all portlets on the portal page, including the Book Catalog portlet.

Because the Book Catalog portlet defines 60 seconds as its cache expiration time, render requests received within 60 seconds of content generation will always result in showing the cached content. The current date and time displayed by the Book Catalog portlet can be used to identify whether the content is fresh or cached.

Table 4.1 shows the behavior of the Book Catalog portlet when it's deployed on Jetspeed 2.2 and Liferay Portal 5.2.3/6.x. A user who isn't logged in to the Liferay Portal will see the current date and time change even when actions are taken on other portlets or when the page is refreshed using the browser's Refresh button. This is because Liferay Portal currently supports private caching scope only.

> **WARNING** In Jetspeed 2.2, some of the Book Catalog portlet's functionality won't work because Jetspeed 2.2 caches content based on the render URL that generated the content. Re-invoking the portlet using the same render URL won't have any effect until the content expires. To use the Book Catalog portlet on Jetspeed 2.2, set the expiration time for the cache to 0 so that the content is always considered expired.

Table 4.1 Effect of expiration caching on the behavior of the Book Catalog portlet

User action	Jetspeed 2.2	Liferay Portal 5.2.3/6.x
User clicks the browser's Refresh button	Current date and time displayed by the Book Catalog don't change.	Current date and time displayed by the Book Catalog don't change.
User clicks the Refresh Search Results or Print hyperlink, or any other hyperlink that sends a render request to the portlet	Current date and time displayed by the Book Catalog change if the render URL isn't the one that generated the content; to generate fresh content, there should be a difference in the render parameters or portlet mode of the URLs.	Current date and time displayed by the Book Catalog change to reflect that the content is freshly generated.
User takes any action on another portlet on the same portal page as the Book Catalog portlet	Current date and time displayed by the Book Catalog change to reflect that the content is freshly generated.	Current date and time displayed by the Book Catalog don't change.

CONFIGURING EXPIRATION CACHING SUPPORT

The expiration caching support is optional for portlet containers. The portlet container can disable portlet content caching at any time to reclaim the memory held by the cached content.

GlassFish Server 3.0.1 (with OpenPortal Portlet Container 2.1.2), Liferay Portal 5.2.3/6.x, and Jetspeed 2.2 support expiration-based caching strategy.

NOTE In multipage portlets, like the Book Catalog portlet, it's sometimes preferable to cache content for specific pages, instead of caching content for all the portlet's pages. Some portal servers, like WebSphere, allow the caching of content for specific portlet pages.

Let's now look at the validation-based caching strategy, which is an extension of the expiration-based caching strategy.

4.1.2 Validation-based content caching

The validation-based caching strategy extends the expiration-based caching strategy by allowing portlets to *validate* the cached content after the expiration time has passed. If the portlet finds that the cached content is still valid, it instructs the portlet container to use the cached content for another expiration period. If the cache has become invalid, the portlet generates fresh content.

In validation-based caching, a validation token is used to validate the cached content; the value of the validation token is *unique* to the cached content. The token is set by the portlet and stored by the portlet container when the content is cached, and it's made available to the portlet once the cached content expires. The portlet then compares the value of the token with that of the current state of the system to determine whether the cached content is still valid or not. If the cached content is still valid, the portlet instructs the portlet container to continue using it. Otherwise, the portlet generates fresh content.

Figure 4.2 illustrates the steps that are followed in validation-based caching for the Book Catalog portlet. The portlet uses the number of books in the data store as the value of the validation token. If the number of books in the data store changes, the Book Catalog portlet generates a fresh list of books.

A render request is sent to the Book Catalog portlet ❶, and the portlet container checks whether the cached content's expiration time has passed or not. If the expiration time has passed, the portlet's render method is invoked ❷.

In the Book Catalog portlet, the number of books stored in the data source is used as a validation token value. In the `isMarkupValid` method ❸, the portlet uses the

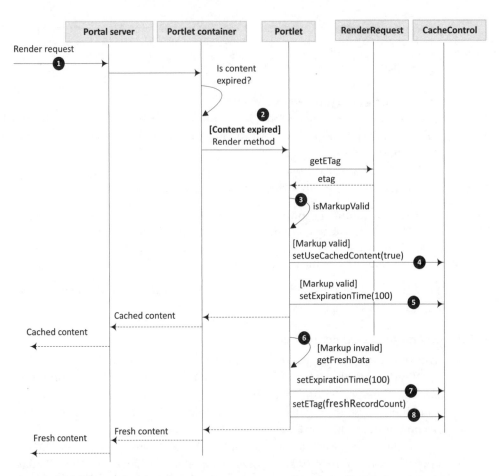

Figure 4.2 Validation caching in the Book Catalog portlet. The portlet obtains the value of the validation token (which represents the record count value when the portlet content was last cached) from `RenderRequest` using the `getETag` method. The portlet then compares that value with the current record count in the database or data store.

RenderRequest's getETag method to obtain the validation token's value, which is the number of books when the content was cached. The portlet checks how many books are currently in the data store and compares that with the validation token's value.

If the validation token's value is the same as the number of books currently stored in the database, the portlet instructs the portlet container to use the already cached content by calling the CacheControl object's setUseCachedContent method ❹. The Portlet 2.0 CacheControl object allows you to programmatically set scope, expiration time, and validation token value, and also to instruct the portlet container to use cached content. If the expiration time isn't set ❺, the content will be considered *always* expired, which means that the portlet container will invoke the portlet's render method when it receives a render request.

If the validation token's value and the current number of books in the data store don't match, that means the cached content is no longer valid, so the portlet retrieves fresh data ❻ from the data source and generates fresh content for the portlet.

The portlet uses the CacheControl object's setETag method ❼ to set the current number of books in the data store as the new value of the validation token. The Book Catalog portlet ❽ sets the expiration time to 100 for the newly generated content.

Listing 4.1 shows how the Book Catalog portlet implements the isMarkupValid method shown in figure 4.2. The BookCatalogPortlet class's isMarkupValid method is responsible for checking whether the content cached by the portlet container is still valid.

Listing 4.1 The BookCatalogPortlet class's isMarkupValid method

```
private boolean isMarkupValid(RenderRequest request,
    RenderResponse response) {
  boolean isMarkupValid = false;
  BookDataObject catalog = (BookDataObject)
    getPortletContext().getAttribute("bookCatalog");       ❶ Gets count of
  int currentCountInDatastore =                               books in catalog
      catalog.getBooks().size();

  String earlierCount =
    response.getCacheControl().getETag();
                                                           ❷ Compares current
  if (String.valueOf(currentCountInDatastore).               count with
          equals(earlierCount)) {                            validation token
    isMarkupValid = true;
  }
  return isMarkupValid;
}
```

The isMarkupValid method ❶ gets the number of books that are currently in the catalog. The validation token's value ❷ is obtained from the request and is compared with the current book count. If the values match, it's assumed that the book catalog hasn't changed since the last time content was cached.

The following listing shows how the isMarkupValid method is used by the Book-CatalogPortlet class's render method.

Listing 4.2   **The `BookCatalogPortlet` class's `showBooks` render method**

```
@RenderMode(name = "VIEW")
public void showBooks(RenderRequest request,
   RenderResponse response) throws ...{
 if(isMarkupValid(request, response)) {
   response.getCacheControl().
    setUseCachedContent(true);                        ① Instructs portlet
   response.getCacheControl().                            to use cached
    setExpirationTime(100);                               content
   return;
 } else {
   BookDataObject catalog = (BookDataObject)
     getPortletContext().getAttribute("bookCatalog");
   int currentCountInDatastore = catalog.getBooks().size();    ② Sets validation
   response.getCacheControl().setETag("" +                         token value to
    currentCountInDatastore);                                      book count
 }
 ...
}
```

If the cached content is found valid (if the `isMarkupValid` method returns `true`), the Book Catalog portlet's `showBooks` render method ① instructs the portlet container to use the cached content, via the `CacheControl` object's `setUseCachedContent` method. A new expiration time is also set for the cached content. If the expiration time isn't set for the cached content, the content is treated as always expired.

If the cached content isn't valid, the current book count is obtained from the data store ②, and the validation token value is set to the current book count.

> **TIP**   The Book Catalog portlet makes use of the record count as a validation token value to introduce you to the concept of validation tokens. In real-world portlets, you'll need to choose an appropriate validation token value for the portlet's cached content. Some examples of values you could use are the last modified timestamp of a record, or the hash code value of an object. The `setETag` method accepts `String` as the value of the validation token, which may not be sufficient for your portlets to identify whether the cached content is valid or not. To address scenarios where a `String` value doesn't meet your requirements, you can store your actual validation token value (a complex object) in the `PortletSession` and store a dummy validation token value using the `setETag` method. When the portlet's render method is invoked, you could then obtain the actual validation token from `PortletSession` and validate the cached content.

CONFIGURING VALIDATION CACHING SUPPORT
Validation caching support is optional for portlet containers. None of the servers I discuss in this book—GlassFish Server 3.0.1 (with OpenPortal Portlet Container 2.1.2), Jetspeed 2.2, and Liferay Portal 5.2.3/6.x—support validation caching; the `Cache-Control` object's `getETag` method always returns `null`.

In some scenarios, you may need a portlet to display content in different languages depending upon the locale associated with the web portal user. Let's look now at how portlets support localization.

4.2   *Localizing portlet content*

The Book Catalog portlet described in chapter 3 requires that the messages and labels displayed as part of the portlet content should also be displayed in the French locale, fr_FR. In this section, we'll look at how the Book Catalog portlet can be localized using localization support available in the Java portlet technology, and we'll also see how a web portal user can change their locale.

You can localize portlets based on the user's locale either by using the xml:lang attribute in the deployment descriptor or by using portlet resource bundles.

The xml:lang attribute isn't supported for portlet window titles, so you can define localized portlet window titles in the portlet resource bundles using the javax.portlet.title key, as you saw in the Hello World portlet in chapter 1.

If you aren't using a portlet framework, you can use the JavaServer Pages Standard Tag Library (JSTL) formatting tags to localize texts and labels. To localize messages displayed by the portlet, you can programmatically load resource bundles and retrieve messages, as you'll see later in this chapters. If your portlet class extends the Generic-Portlet class, you can get access to the resource bundle configured in the deployment descriptor (using the <resource-bundle> tag) by calling the GenericPortlet class's getResourceBundle method. The recommended approach to localizing your portlets is to use resource bundles.

Figure 4.3 shows the Book Catalog portlet content in the fr_FR locale. In this figure, labels and buttons are shown in the French locale. The data itself isn't localized because we aren't storing localized data in the data store. If you want to show localized data along with labels and messages, you must also save localized data in the data store.

Livre Catalogue				🔧 ✕
Current date: 02-17-2011 13:20:47			Bonjour ! *Bruno Admin*	
Imprimer Aide Préférences			**PLEIN ECRAN**	
Titre du livre:				
Nom de l'auteur:				
Rechercher				
			< Rafraîchir les résultats de recherche >	
Titre	**Auteur**	**Numéro ISBN**	**TdM**	**Action**
AspectJ in Action, Second Edition	Ramnivas Laddad	1933988053	Télécharger/téléverser	Supprimer
ActiveMQ in Action	Bruce Snyder, Dejan Bosanac, and Rob Davies	1933988940	Télécharger/téléverser	Supprimer

Figure 4.3   The Book Catalog portlet displays labels in French when the locale is fr_FR.

4.2.1   *Implementing portlets to support localization*

If your portlet needs to be localized, you need to create locale-specific resource bundles. The locale-specific resource bundle has the following naming convention:

```
<resource-bundle-name>_<language>_<country>.properties
```

Here, <resource-bundle-name> is the name of the resource bundle, as specified by the <resource-bundle> element of the portlet.xml file, <language> is the ISO language code, and <country> is the ISO country code. For the Book Catalog portlet, you'd need to create a resource bundle with the name Language-ext_fr_FR.properties.

The following entry in the Book Catalog portlet's portlet.xml file shows how you would configure a resource bundle for a portlet:

```
<resource-bundle>content.Language-ext</resource-bundle>
```

The resource bundle configured in the portlet definition can either be retrieved programmatically or by using JSTL formatting tags. You can programmatically retrieve a resource bundle in your portlet class by using the PortletConfig object's get-ResourceBundle method, as shown here:

```
ResourceBundle bundle =
    getPortletConfig().getResourceBundle(request.getLocale());
```

In this code, the GenericPortlet class's getPortletConfig() method returns the PortletConfig object whose getResourceBundle method returns a java.util.ResourceBundle object referring to the locale-specific resource bundle. The Portlet-Request's getLocale method returns the current locale used for the request. Once you obtain the ResourceBundle for the specific locale, you can programmatically retrieve messages for that locale using the ResourceBundle object's getString methods.

The following code shows how a portlet can set the window title by retrieving it from the resource bundle based on the current locale:

```
response.setTitle(getResourceBundle(request.getLocale()).
    getString("portlet.title.books"));
```

That's all there is to programmatically retrieving messages from the resource bundle and using them in a portlet to show locale-specific titles and messages.

To localize the labels used in JSP pages, you can make use of JSTL formatting tags to load locale-specific resource bundles. In chapter 2, the JSPs in the User Registration portlet used the JSTL setBundle tag to load labels from the Language-ext.properties resource bundle. The setBundle tag lets JSP pages load the resource bundle, but it always loads the default resource bundle identified by the basename attribute of the setBundle tag. To load a locale-specific resource bundle, you must set the locale for which the setBundle tag should load the resource bundle, as shown here:

```
<fmt:setLocale value="<%=request.getLocale()%>"/>
<fmt:setBundle basename="content.Language-ext"/>
```

The setLocale tag is used to set the locale used by the setBundle tag.

CODE REFERENCE Refer to `Language-ext_fr_FR.properties` (the resource bundle for the `fr_FR` locale), portlet.xml (which defines support for the `fr_FR` locale for the Book Catalog portlet), and the home.jsp file to see how localization is implemented in the Book Catalog portlet.

4.2.2 Changing locales using built-in portlets

The locale for a web portal is associated with the complete web portal and not with a single portlet on a portal page. Most portal servers provide built-in portlets that allow you to easily change the locale of the web portal.

Figure 4.4 shows the Liferay Portal's built-in Language portlet and Jetspeed's built-in Locale Selector portlet, both of which can be used to change the locale of the portal.

NOTE If you're using a portlet framework to develop portlets, you can use the framework's built-in localization strategy. Chapter 8 describes how you can use the Spring Portlet MVC framework's localization strategy by using the `MessageSource` bean.

In previous chapters, we touched on portlet modes. Let's now look at portlet modes in detail.

4.3 Portlet modes in depth

In chapter 2, we discussed the basics of portlet modes. In this section, we'll look at

- Custom portlet modes
- Portal-managed and portlet-managed portlet modes

The `PortletMode` class defines three constants—`VIEW`, `EDIT`, and `HELP`—corresponding to the `VIEW`, `EDIT`, and `HELP` portlet modes, which we discussed in chapter 2. It's mandatory for portlets to support `VIEW` mode; the other two are optional. Support for optional portlet modes must be specified in the portlet deployment descriptor, as mentioned in chapter 2.

Apart from those three standard portlet modes, you can also use custom portlet modes supported by your portal server. The portlet specification allows portal server vendors to provide additional portlet modes, like `config`, `print`, and so on.

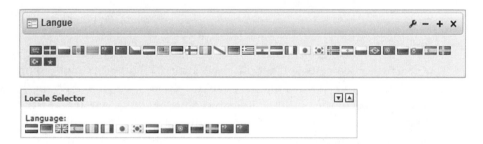

Figure 4.4 The Language and Locale Selector portlets built into Liferay Portal and Jetspeed, respectively. You can select the locale by selecting one of the locale icons displayed in the portlets.

In the context of the Book Catalog portlet, we'll look at how Liferay Portal's custom `print` portal-managed portlet mode can be used to display a printable (with no form elements) book catalog.

4.3.1   *Custom portlet modes*

A portal may define support for additional portlet modes supported by the portal server or by the portlet. For instance, Liferay Portal 5.2.3/6.x provides `config`, `edit_defaults`, `preview`, and `print` custom portlet modes.

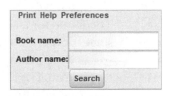

Figure 4.5   The Book Catalog portlet shows Help and Preferences links to view the portlet in HELP and EDIT portlet modes. The Print hyperlink displays the portlet in `print` custom portlet mode supported by Liferay Portal.

You can use a custom portlet mode in a portlet by defining its support in the portlet deployment descriptor and providing an implementation for that mode in your portlet class. For instance, the Book Catalog portlet (see figure 4.5) provides links to view portlet preferences, help information, and a printable catalog.

The Help and Preferences links change the portlet mode to HELP and EDIT, respectively. The Print link displays the Book Catalog portlet in `print` portlet mode, which allows users to view a list of all the books on a single page without any form elements, like text fields and buttons. This display is suitable for printing a list of books in the catalog.

DEFINING SUPPORT FOR CUSTOM PORTLET MODES IN PORTLET.XML

If your portlet is going to use a custom portlet mode (or any portlet mode other than VIEW mode), you *must* specify it in the portlet deployment descriptor using the `<portlet-mode>` subelement of the `<supports>` element. The following snippet shows this for the Book Catalog portlet:

```
<portlet>
  <portlet-name>bookCatalog</portlet-name>
  <portlet-class>
    chapter03.code.listing.base.BookCatalogPortlet</portlet-class>
  <supports>
    <mime-type>text/html</mime-type>
    <portlet-mode>print</portlet-mode>
    ...
  </supports>
  ...
</portlet>
```

The `<portlet-mode>` element specifies the name of the portlet mode supported by the portlet. You can specify multiple `<portlet-mode>` elements to list all the portlet modes supported by the portlet. In the preceding XML fragment, the `<portlet-mode>` element informs the portlet container that the `print` portlet mode is supported by the `bookCatalog` portlet.

A custom portlet mode must also be defined at the portlet application level, as shown here for the Book Catalog portlet:

```
<portlet-app ...>
  <portlet>
    <portlet-name>bookCatalog</portlet-name>
    <portlet-class>
      chapter03.code.listing.base.BookCatalogPortlet</portlet-class>
    <supports>
      <mime-type>text/html</mime-type>
      <portlet-mode>print</portlet-mode>
      ...
    </supports>
    ...
  </portlet>
  <custom-portlet-mode>
    <portlet-mode>print</portlet-mode>
  </custom-portlet-mode>
</portlet-app>
```

The `<custom-portlet-mode>` subelement of `<portlet-app>` specifies the custom portlet modes that are available to portlets in the portlet application. The portlets that want to use these custom portlet modes can specify them in their definition (using the `<portlet-mode>` subelement of `<supports>`, as shown previously).

If you define a custom portlet mode for your portlet application, it must be supported by the portal server on which the portlet is deployed. You can find out which portlet modes are supported by your portal server by using the `PortalContext`'s `getSupportedPortletModes` method. If a custom portlet mode isn't supported by the portal server, any attempt to use the portlet in that mode will result in an exception.

SETTING THE PORTLET MODE PROGRAMMATICALLY

The Book Catalog portlet uses `print` portlet mode, which isn't supported by GlassFish Server. If you intend to set custom portlet modes (or predefined portlet modes) programmatically in your action (or event) methods, you should have your code check whether the portlet mode is allowed, by using the `PortletRequest` object's `isPortletModeAllowed` method. The `isPortletModeAllowed` method not only checks whether a particular portlet mode is supported by the portal server, but also whether the portlet mode is supported by the portlet and the user is allowed to switch to that portlet mode.

The following code fragment shows how to use the `isPortletModeAllowed` method:

```
if(PortletRequest.isPortletModeAllowed(new PortletMode("print"))) {
    actionResponse.setPortletMode(new PortletMode("print"));
}
```

The preceding code checks whether the `print` portlet mode is allowed for the request. If it's allowed, it uses the `StateAwareResponse` interface's `setPortletMode` method to set the `print` portlet mode. `StateAwareResponse` is the interface implemented by the `ActionResponse` and `EventResponse` objects. If the portlet mode is set in the action method, the following render method is invoked in the changed portlet mode.

> **WARNING** There's no guarantee that the following render request received by the portlet will be in the same portlet mode that you set in the action

method. A portlet container or portal server may override the portlet mode and invoke the portlet in a different mode.

If a portlet mode isn't applicable for the portlet because it's not supported by the portlet or by the portal server or the user doesn't have access to the mode, a `Portlet-ModeException` will be thrown. You should use the `isPortletModeAllowed` method before setting the portlet mode to ensure that exceptions won't be thrown because the portlet mode isn't allowed.

IMPLEMENTING A CUSTOM PORTLET MODE

If a custom portlet mode is supported by your chosen portal server, and you've specified in portlet.xml that the custom portlet mode is supported by your portlet, the next step is to provide an implementation of the portlet's behavior in the custom portlet mode. Just as you implement action and render methods to perform appropriate tasks for the standard portlet modes (for example, `EDIT` mode should allow users to set preferences for the portlet), your custom portlet mode needs to be implemented to perform tasks that match the purpose of the portlet mode.

In the Book Catalog portlet, clicking the Print hyperlink shows the list of books in the catalog without any form elements, making it easy for users to print the list of books in the catalog. This display is shown in figure 4.6.

> **NOTE** The printout of the web page shown in figure 4.6 won't look pretty because of the window decoration and possible presence of other portlets on the portal page. We'll address this issue in section 4.4, where we'll discuss portlet window states.

How do you go about generating the content for the `print` portlet mode, as shown in figure 4.6? You saw in chapter 2 that you can associate a portlet's render method to a particular portlet mode using the `@RenderMode` annotation. In the same way, you can write a render method for the `print` portlet mode, as shown here:

```
@RenderMode(name="print")
public void showPrint(RenderRequest request,
    RenderResponse response) throws IOException, PortletException {
        showPrintableCatalog(request, response);
}
```

Book Catalog		⇐ Return to Full Page
Name	**Author**	**ISBN Number**
AspectJ in Action, Second Edition	Ramnivas Laddad	1933988053
ActiveMQ in Action	Bruce Snyder, Dejan Bosanac, and Rob Davies	1933988940
Hadoop in Action	Chuck Lam	9781935182191
JUnit in Action, Second Edition	Petar Tahchiev, Felipe Leme, Vincent Massol, and Gary Gregory	9781935182023

Figure 4.6 The Book Catalog portlet in `print` mode shows no form elements, making it easier for users to print out the book catalog.

The `@RenderMode(name="print")` annotation identifies the `showPrint` method as the render method for the `print` portlet mode. The `showPrintableCatalog` method generates the list of books without form elements.

> **CODE REFERENCE** The Book Catalog portlet uses the `print` *portal-managed* portlet mode, which is supported both by Liferay Portal 5.2.3/6.x and Jetspeed 2.2. Refer to the portlet.xml file for the configuration of the `print` portlet mode, and see the `BookCatalogPortlet` class's `showPrint` render method for the `print` portlet mode implementation.

SETTING THE PORTLET MODE IN THE URL

You can set the portlet mode in the action (or event) request and not in the render request. If the Print hyperlink in the Book Catalog portlet refers to the portlet's action URL, the corresponding action method can set the portlet mode to `print`, and the following render method for the `print` portlet mode will generate the necessary content.

It may be unnecessary to use an action method just to change the portlet mode. A simpler way to do this is to create a render URL that requires the portlet mode to be changed to `print` when the user submits the request to the render URL. In chapter 2, we created render URLs using the `RenderResponse` object's `createRenderURL` method, which returned a `PortletURL` object. In the same way, you can create a render URL and set the portlet mode to `print`, as shown here:

```
PortletURL printModeUrl = response.createRenderURL();
if(PortletRequest.isPortletModeAllowed(new PortletMode("print"))) {
  printModeUrl.setPortletMode(new PortletMode("print"));
}
request.setAttribute("printModeUrl", printModeUrl);
```

The `setPortletMode` method accepts a `PortletMode` argument, which you can create by passing the name of the portlet mode (print, in this case) to the `PortletMode` constructor. As you can see, the `isPortletModeAllowed` method checks whether the `print` portlet mode is allowed or not, before setting it on the `PortletURL` object.

In the Book Catalog portlet, most portlet URLs are created programmatically and then set as request attributes. The JSP pages of the Book Catalog portlet retrieve portlet URLs from the request and use them in hyperlinks and in `action` attributes of `form` tags. For instance, the `printModeUrl` that was set in the request is used by the home.jsp page of the Book Catalog portlet to show the Print hyperlink:

```
<a class="anchor" href="${printModeUrl}"><b> Print </b></td>
```

> **CODE REFERENCE** Refer to the `BookCatalogPortlet` class's `generateUrls` method for more examples of setting the portlet mode programmatically in a portlet URL.

There are two types of portlet modes: *portal-managed* and *portlet-managed* portlet modes. We'll discuss them next.

4.3.2 *Portal-managed and portlet-managed portlet modes*

Portlet modes can either be managed by a portal server or by the portlet itself. If the portal server is responsible for managing the portlet mode, the portlet mode is referred to as *portal-managed*. If the portlet is responsible for managing the portlet mode, it's referred to as *portlet-managed*. The list of portlet modes that you get by calling the `PortalContext`'s `getSupportedPortletModes` method contains portal-managed portlet modes.

As a developer, you can use the existing portal-managed portlet modes, but you can also create your own portlet-managed portlet modes. (You can't create a portal-managed portlet mode because the portal server is responsible for providing them.) Portlet-managed portlet modes are useful when you want to split the portlet `VIEW` mode's rendering functionality along the lines of custom portlet modes.

In most portlets (if not all), most of the content generation responsibility is coded in the `VIEW` portlet mode, because it encloses the main business functionality of the portlet. For instance, in the Book Catalog portlet, you could split the business functionality of the portlet into the following:

- *Search*—User searches book catalog based on author and book name
- *Show catalog*—User is shown the list of books in the catalog
- *Add book*—User adds book to the catalog

The action processing methods are easier to split up because the `@ProcessAction` annotation allows you to specify the name of the action for which the method is defined. The preceding three functions can be written in three different action methods, as shown here:

```
@ProcessAction(name="search")
public void search(...) { ... }

@ProcessAction(name="showCatalog")
public void showBooks(...) { ... }

@ProcessAction(name="addBook")
public void addBook(...) { ... }
...
```

The render requests that follow the execution of the action methods invoke the same render method: `doView`. The portlet specification doesn't provide any mechanism to define a one-to-one relationship between action and render methods, so the complete content generation logic needs to be written in a single method: `doView` or a method annotated with the `@RenderMode(name="VIEW")` annotation.

Writing complete content generation logic in a single method will not only significantly affect the readability and maintainability of the code; it will also affect the testability of the portlet class. A simpler approach is to make your `doView` method be the first point of contact for the render request, after which control is transferred to more specific methods that know how to handle the content generation, as shown in figure 4.7.

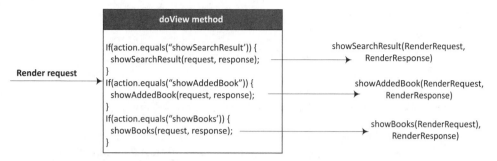

Figure 4.7 The portlet's `doView` or `@RenderMode(name="VIEW")` annotated method delegates render requests to more specific methods for content generation.

In figure 4.7, the `doView` method checks what content needs to be generated, and delegates the content generation responsibility to specific methods, such as `showSearchResult`, `showAddedBook`, and `showBooks`.

Your code would be much cleaner if you could directly invoke the content generation methods, rather than indirectly invoking them via `doView`. You can easily achieve this if you define custom portlet-managed portlet modes for your portlet application. Let's say you define a custom portlet-managed portlet mode named `search` in the portlet deployment descriptor of your portlet application, as shown here:

```
<custom-portlet-mode>
  <portlet-mode>search</portlet-mode>
  <portal-managed>false</portal-managed>
</custom-portlet-mode>
```

In this code, `<portlet-mode>` is the name of the custom portlet mode and `<portal-managed>` identifies whether the custom portlet mode is portlet- or portal-managed.

The preceding `search` portlet mode is portlet-managed because the value of the `<portal-managed>` element is `false`. If you don't specify the `<portal-managed>` element, the portlet container assumes that the custom portlet mode is portal-managed.

If you define a custom portlet mode that's *portal-managed*, your portal server must support that portlet mode, like the `print` portlet mode we discussed earlier in this section. A *portlet-managed* portlet mode isn't required to be supported by the portal server because it's meant to be used internally by the portlet.

As for portal-managed portlet modes, a portlet *must* define its support for the portlet-managed portlet mode, as shown here:

```
<portlet-app ...>
 <portlet>
   <portlet-name>bookCatalog</portlet-name>
   <portlet-class>
     chapter03.code.listing.base.BookCatalogPortlet</portlet-class>
   <supports>
     <mime-type>text/html</mime-type>
     <portlet-mode>search</portlet-mode>
     ...
```

```
  </supports>
  ...
 </portlet>
 ...
</portlet-app>
```

In the preceding portlet deployment descriptor, the `bookCatalog` portlet specifies that it supports the `search` portlet-managed portlet mode.

CODE REFERENCE Refer to the Book Catalog portlet's portlet.xml file for examples on configuring portlet-managed and portal-managed portlet modes.

This is all you need to do to make your portlet support a custom portlet-managed portlet mode. After that, all you need to do is use the newly introduced `search` portlet mode in your portlet class, as shown here:

```
@RenderMode(name="search")
public void showSearchResult(RenderRequest request,
  RenderResponse response) throws IOException, PortletException {
    //-- generate search results content
  }
```

The `@RenderMode(name="search")` annotation identifies the `showSearchResult` method as the render method for the `search` portlet mode. If the action method responsible for performing the book search changes the portlet mode of the current portlet request to `search` (by calling the `ActionResponse`'s `setPortletMode` method), the following render method will be in `search` portlet mode. That means the method annotated with `@RenderMode(name="search")` will be called; in the method shown above, that's the `showSearchResult` method.

NOTE Check your portal server to determine whether or not it honors the custom portlet-managed portlet mode set programmatically in action requests (or set in the `PortletURL` using the `setPortletMode` method) before using this approach to create your portlets. As of Liferay Portal 5.2.3/6.x, custom portlet-managed portlet modes are ignored. Jetspeed 2.2 allows you to use custom portlet-managed portlet modes.

A portlet must define the portlet mode supported for a particular markup type (HTML, WML, and so on) generated by the portlet. Next, we'll look at how portlets define this support in the portlet deployment descriptor.

4.3.3 *Portlet modes and markup types*

A portlet can generate different markup types, like HTML for regular browsers and WML for mobile devices. The portlet specification provides the option to define portlet modes for a particular markup type. For instance, when displaying a portlet on a mobile device, you may prefer not to allow the predefined `EDIT` portlet mode.

You define supported portlet modes for a particular markup type by using the `<supports>` element in the portlet definition. Earlier in this chapter, you saw how you can use <supports> to define support for a portlet mode in portlets. You'll also notice that every <supports> element has a mandatory <mime-type> element that identifies the markup type generated by the portlet. Because the <supports> element allows only one <mime-type> subelement, you need to define multiple <supports> elements to indicate that the portlet supports multiple markup types, as shown here:

```
<portlet>
  <portlet-name>bookCatalog</portlet-name>
  <portlet-class>
    chapter03.code.listing.base.BookCatalogPortlet</portlet-class>
  <supports>
    <mime-type>text/html</mime-type>
    <portlet-mode>edit</portlet-mode>
    <portlet-mode>help</portlet-mode>
    <portlet-mode>print</portlet-mode>
  </supports>
  <supports>
    <mime-type>text/vnd.wap.xhtml+xml</mime-type>
  </supports>
  ...
</portlet>
```

The preceding bookCatalog definition shows that it supports two different markup types: text/html and text/vnd.wap.xhtml+xml. The text/html markup (used for regular browsers) supports all the predefined portlet modes and the print custom portlet mode. The text/vnd.wap.xhtml+xml markup (used by mobile devices) only supports the VIEW portlet mode.

Let's now look at the WindowState class of the Portlet API and see how you can use a custom window state.

4.4   *Portlet window states in depth*

In this section, we'll look at the WindowState class and how to define support for custom window states. We'll also look at how the Book Catalog portlet makes use of Liferay Portal's custom pop_up window state to show a printable book catalog with no window decoration.

The window state of a portlet is represented by the Portlet API's WindowState class. This class defines (as constants) the three standard window states that portlets support: NORMAL, MINIMIZED, and MAXIMIZED.

> **NOTE**   If the portlet is in MINIMIZED state, the default behavior of Generic-Portlet is to ignore render request calls on the portlet; the render methods (doView, doEdit, doHelp, or the @RenderMode annotated methods) aren't invoked.

A portlet's window state can be useful in customizing the *content* of the portlet; if a portlet's window state is maximized, the portlet can show additional information to the user that it didn't display when the portlet was in the normal window state. For instance, in the Book Catalog portlet, you can show the last-modified date for the book when the window state is maximized. You can also consider showing rich user interface components (like the components offered by the Dojo toolkit) when the window is maximized.

> **NOTE**   The standard window states *must* be supported by portlets, unlike portlet modes. You can't limit which standard window states a portlet supports.

Let's look at how custom window states can be used by a portlet.

4.4.1   *Custom window states*

If your portal server defines additional window states, you can discover them by using the `PortalContext` object's `getSupportedWindowStates` method. For instance, Liferay Portal 5.2.3/6.x supports two custom window states, one of which is `pop_up`.

The `pop_up` window state is used to represent a browser window that contains *only* the content generated by the portlet, with no window decorations or portal page headers. The `pop_up` window state is ideal when you want to print out the portlet's content, as in the case of the Book Catalog portlet.

If your portlet uses custom window states, your portlet definition *must* include support for them, as shown here for the Book Catalog portlet:

```
<portlet>
  <portlet-name>bookCatalog</portlet-name>
  <portlet-class>
    chapter03.code.listing.base.BookCatalogPortlet</portlet-class>
  <supports>
    <mime-type>text/html</mime-type>
    <window-state>pop_up</window-state>
    ...
  </supports>
  ...
</portlet>
```

The `<window-state>` element specifies the name of the window state supported by the portlet. You can specify multiple `<window-state>` elements to list all the window states supported by the portlet. In the preceding XML fragment, the `<window-state>` element informs the portlet container that the `pop_up` window state is supported by the `bookCatalog` portlet.

As in the case of custom portlet modes, you *must* define the custom window states that apply to your portlet application, as shown here for the portlet application to which the Book Catalog portlet belongs:

```
<portlet-app ...>
  <portlet>
    <portlet-name>bookCatalog</portlet-name>
    <portlet-class>
      chapter03.code.listing.base.BookCatalogPortlet</portlet-class>
    <supports>
      <mime-type>text/html</mime-type>
```

```
      <window-state>pop_up</window-state>
      ...
    </supports>
    ...
  </portlet>
  <custom-window-state>
    <window-state>pop_up</window-state>
  </custom-window-state>
  ...
</portlet-app>
```

The <custom-window-state> subelement of <portlet-app> defines the custom window states that are available to the portlets in the portlet application. The portlets that want to use these custom window states can specify them in their definitions using the <window-state> subelement of <supports>, as shown previously.

If you define a custom window state for your portlet application, it must be supported by the portal server on which the portlet is deployed. If a custom window state isn't supported by the portal server, attempting to use the portlet in that window state will result in a WindowStateException. If you're programmatically setting the window state, you should first check whether the window state is allowed by calling the PortletRequest object's isWindowStateAllowed method. A window state may not be allowed for a request for three reasons: the portlet definition doesn't define support for the window state, the portal server doesn't support the window state, or the user isn't allowed to access the portlet in the window state.

Unlike custom portlet modes, there are no portlet-managed window states.

CODE REFERENCE   Refer to the portlet.xml file and the BookCatalogPortlet class's generateUrls method to see how the Book Catalog portlet makes use of the pop_up custom window state supported by Liferay Portal 5.2.3/6.x.

Like portlet modes, a portlet must define which window states are supported for a particular markup type. Let's look at how portlets define this in the portlet deployment descriptor.

4.4.2   Portlet window states and markup types

The Book Catalog portlet's portlet.xml file shows that the pop_up window state is supported only if the markup type is text/html:

```
<portlet>
  <portlet-name>bookCatalog</portlet-name>
  <portlet-class>
    chapter03.code.listing.base.BookCatalogPortlet</portlet-class>
  <supports>
    <mime-type>text/html</mime-type>
    <portlet-mode>edit</portlet-mode>
    <portlet-mode>help</portlet-mode>
    <portlet-mode>print</portlet-mode>
    <window-state>pop_up</window-state>
  </supports>
```

```
<supports>
  <mime-type>text/vnd.wap.xhtml+xml</mime-type>
</supports>
...
</portlet>
```

The preceding `bookCatalog` definition supports two different markup types: `text/html` and `text/vnd.wap.xhtml+xml`. The `text/html` markup (used for regular browsers) supports the predefined window states and the `pop_up` custom window state. The `text/vnd.wap.xhtml+xml` markup (used by mobile devices) supports only the predefined window states.

As in any web application, programmatic security plays an important role in securing portlets from unauthorized access. Let's take a look at the programmatic security in portlet applications and how it affects how you write your portlets.

4.5   *Programmatic security*

Securing portlets from unauthorized access in a web portal is important, and it must be considered for any portlet application. In this section, we'll only discuss the programmatic approach to securing portlets. In chapter 5, you'll see how the portal server can help address security concerns without requiring you to write a single line of code.

The `PortletRequest` interface defines the following methods that can be used to programmatically secure your portlets:

- `getRemoteUser`—This method can be used to check whether the user is authenticated or not. For an authenticated user, this method returns a non-`null` value that is the login name of the user.
- `getUserPrincipal`—This method can be used to obtain the name of the authenticated user. It returns a `java.security.Principal` object that defines the `getName` method which you can use to obtain the name of the authenticated user.
- `isUserInRole`—This method is used to implement role-based security in your portlets. It accepts a role name (specified using the `<role-name>` subelement of the `<security-role-ref>` element in the portlet deployment descriptor), and it checks whether the authenticated user belongs to that role.

The `getRemoteUser` and `getUserPrincipal` methods return values that usually have portal server–specific semantics. The `isUserInRole` method is the most useful in the real portlet world, because you'll generally group portal users based on their roles and define access rights for those roles in the system.

Suppose the Book Catalog portlet has the following security requirements:

- Users belonging to the `User` role must not be able to download the table of contents (TOC) of the book. Also, a `User` isn't allowed to add books to the catalog.
- Users belonging to the `Administrator` role can download the TOC and add books to the catalog.

To address the preceding requirements, you can use the `PortletRequest`'s `isUserIn-Role` method to restrict users from accessing or allow them to access different features of the portlet.

The first step in using role-based security is to define the roles in the portlet deployment descriptor file using the `<security-role-ref>` element, as shown here:

```
<security-role-ref>
  <role-name>administrator</role-name>
  <role-link>Administrator</role-link>
</security-role-ref>
```

Here, the `<role-name>` element is the name of the user role that will be used by the `isUserInRole` method to check whether the authenticated user belongs to the `Administrator` role. The `<role-link>` element links the role name specified in the `<role-name>` element with the role that exists in the deployment environment.

Your portlet code depends on the `<role-name>` element and not on the `<role-link>` element. That's advantageous, because if the portlet is deployed in a different environment, the roles available in the deployment environment may change, but your portlet code won't be impacted. If you move to a different deployment environment, you only need to change the `<role-link>` element to map to the roles available in the new environment.

In Liferay Portal, liferay-portlet.xml does the mapping of the `<role-name>` specified in the portlet.xml file to the roles available in the Liferay Portal deployment environment:

```
<role-mapper>
  <role-name>administrator</role-name>
  <role-link>Administrator</role-link>
</role-mapper>
<role-mapper>
  <role-name>user</role-name>
  <role-link>User</role-link>
</role-mapper>
```

The `<role-mapper>` element maps the `administrator` role name to the `Administrator` role in Liferay Portal, and the `user` role name to the `User` role in Liferay Portal.

> **NOTE** If you define your own roles in Liferay Portal, you can provide their mapping in liferay-portlet.xml and use the roles in your portlets for programmatically performing role-based security.

The next step is to use the `<role-name>` specified in portlet.xml to programmatically check the user role, as shown here:

```
if(request.isUserInRole("administrator")) {
    //-- allow user to add book
} else {
    //-- throw security exception
}
```

In the preceding code, if the user's role is `Administrator`, the `isUserInRole` method returns `true`; otherwise it returns `false`.

In chapter 5 we'll discuss Liferay Portal security in more detail, and you'll see how you can use Liferay Portal's security features to secure portlets.

> **CODE REFERENCE**   Refer to the Book Catalog portlet's portlet.xml and liferay-portlet.xml files for examples of how to define roles that are used to restrict access to features.

Let's now look at how you can upload files using portlets, how you can wrap request and response objects to modify the default behavior of their methods, and how you can use `PortletURLGenerationListener` to customize all the render, action, and resource URLs generated by the portlet container.

4.6   *Uploading files, wrapping requests and responses, and creating portlet URL generation listeners*

In this section, we'll look at how you can upload TOC files in the Book Catalog portlet using the Apache Commons `FileUpload` library. We'll also look at portlet request and response *wrapper* objects and how they can be used to modify the behavior of the underlying portlet request and response objects. We'll conclude this section by taking a look at the `PortletURLGenerationListener`, which you can use to universally set properties on all portlet URLs generated by the portlet container.

> **NOTE**   In this chapter, the Book Catalog portlet doesn't make use of request and response wrappers, but you'll find a more detailed example of them in chapter 13. The Book Catalog portlet does use the `PortletURLGeneration-Listener` to set the window state to `MAXIMIZED` for all its action and render portlet URLs.

Let's first see how to go about uploading files in portlets.

4.6.1   *Uploading files*

The Book Catalog portlet in chapter 3 requires that a user should be able to upload the TOC of a book, and that the size of the uploaded TOC file must not be more than 1 MB. You can upload files using the `ClientDataRequest` object or by using a file upload library, like Apache Commons `FileUpload`. In this section, we'll look at uploading files using the Apache Commons `FileUpload` library.

> **TIP**   If you want to upload files using the `ClientDataRequest` object, some of the tasks you'll have to perform in your code include checking whether the request is a multipart request or not, obtaining the name of the file to be uploaded from the portlet request, extracting the content type from the request (if you want to restrict uploads to certain content types), and so on. Using a file upload library like Apache Commons `FileUpload` saves you the effort of writing logic to perform these tasks.

UPLOADING FILES USING APACHE COMMONS FILEUPLOAD

The Apache Commons `FileUpload` library provides convenience classes that provide easy access to a variety of information, such as whether the portlet request is a multipart request or not and what the name of the file to be uploaded is, and it also provides access to the input stream where the file can be uploaded. Listing 4.3 shows how the `BookCatalogPortlet` makes use of the Apache Commons `FileUpload` classes to read an uploaded file and write it to disk.

NOTE The `PortletFileUpload` class was introduced in the Apache Commons `FileUpload` library in version 1.1. If you want to use this library in your portlets, you need to use `FileUpload` version 1.1 or later.

Listing 4.3   Uploading files using Apache Commons `FileUpload`

```
PortletFileUpload pfu = new PortletFileUpload();          ❶ Creates
pfu.setFileSizeMax(MAX_UPLOAD_FILE_SIZE);                   PortletFileUpload

if(PortletFileUpload.isMultipartContent(request)) {

  FileItemIterator iter = pfu.getItemIterator(request);

  while (iter.hasNext()) {
    FileItemStream item = iter.next();
    InputStream stream = item.openStream();
    byte[] buffer = new byte[1024];
    while (true) {
      if (!item.isFormField()) {
        byte[] bytes = new byte[buffer];          ❷ Gets uploaded
        stream.read(bytes);                          file as byte[ ]

      }
    }
  }
}
```

You create an instance of the `PortletFileUpload` class ❶ and set the maximum size of the file that can be uploaded. The `PortletFileUpload` class is the central class in the Apache Commons `FileUpload` library, and it returns a `FileItemIterator` from `ActionRequest` and allows you to set the maximum size of the file that can be uploaded.

A `FileItem` object represents a *form field* or *file field* in your HTML form. A *file* field represents an HTML form element of type *file*, as shown here:

```
<input type="file" name="tocFile"/>
```

The `PortletFileUpload` class's `isMultipartContent(ActionRequest)` method is used to verify that the portlet request is a file upload request. The `isMultipartContent` method returns `true` if the content type header for the `ActionRequest` is `multipart/form-data`. The HTML form that you use to upload files must specify the content type as `multipart/form-data` using the `enctype` attribute of the HTML `form` tag, as shown here:

```
<form name="uploadTocForm" method="post"
    action="${uploadTocActionUrl}" enctype="multipart/form-data">
```

It may seem trivial to check whether the request contains multipart content, but it's important. If a request isn't a multipart request, it'll result in an exception when parsing `ActionRequest` using the `getItemIterator` method to obtain file fields in the submitted form. If you're directly using `ClientDataRequest` to upload the file, the `getPortletInputStream` and `getReader` methods will throw an `IllegalState-Exception` if the request isn't a multipart request.

The `PortletFileUpload` class's `getItemIterator(ActionRequest)` method returns a `FileItemIterator`, which lets you iterate over the `FileItems` present in the action request. The `FileItemStream` object provides access to the content of the `File-Item` instance using the `openStream` method. The `isFormField` method is used to check whether the `FileItem` represents a form field or a file field. The contents of a file field represents the uploaded file. As you're only interested in file fields in this example, you read the contents of the `FileItem` representing a file field into a byte array ❷.

> **CODE REFERENCE** See the `BookCatalogPortlet` class's `uploadToc` action method to see the Apache Commons `FileUpload` library being used to upload a file in the Book Catalog portlet. The sample code uploads a file to a folder in the portal server's local filesystem, the location of which is specified by the `uploadFolder` portlet initialization parameter in portlet.xml. The TOC file is saved with the name *<ISBN number>.<extension>*, where *ISBN Number* is the ISBN number of the book for which you're uploading the TOC, and *extension* is the file extension of the TOC file uploaded.

Next, we'll look at the request and response wrapper classes.

4.6.2   *Using wrapper classes*

Like the servlet API, the Portlet 2.0 API introduced the concept of wrapper classes for portlet requests and responses. These wrapper classes hold references to the request or response object and implement all the methods of the request or response. The wrapper class is an example of a *decorator pattern*, where the decorating or wrapping class delegates all method calls to the wrapped request or response object.

> **TIP** Use wrapper classes when you want to override the default functionality of a request or response object's methods. This is particularly useful when working with portlet filters. Chapter 13 discusses how `RenderResponseWrapper` can be used to modify the response generated by the Book Catalog portlet.

The Portlet 2.0 API provides request and response wrappers for each request and response type, such as `PortletRequestWrapper`, `ActionRequestWrapper`, `Resource-ResponseWrapper`, `RenderRequestWrapper`, and so on.

> **WARNING** In Liferay Portal 5.2.3, the support for request and response wrapper objects is broken, and it results in a `ClassCastException`.

The following code fragment shows how you can override the `RenderRequest` object's `getAttribute` method to return the value of the `myparam` request parameter:

```
public class MyRenderRequestWrapper extends RenderRequestWrapper {
  public MyRenderRequestWrapper(RenderRequest request) {
    super(request);
  }
  public Object getAttribute(String attributeName) {
    Object attribute;
    if("myparam".equalsIgnoreCase(attributeName)) {
      attribute = getRequest().getParameter(attributeName);
    } else {
      attribute = getRequest().getAttribute(attributeName);
    }
    return attribute;
  }
}
```

In the preceding code, the `RenderRequestWrapper`'s `getAttribute` method is overridden to get the value of the `myparam` attribute from the request parameters, instead of the request attributes. The `getRequest` method in the preceding code returns the wrapped `RenderRequest` instance.

> **CODE REFERENCE**   See the `MyRenderRequestWrapper` and `MyActionRequest-Wrapper` classes in the ch3_BookCatalog folder for examples of how to create your own wrapper classes. For a working example of wrapper objects, see chapter 13.

Listeners in a web application allow applications to listen to events that indicate when a context is initialized, when an attribute is added or removed from a session, and so on. Portlet applications can use some of the listeners defined by the Servlet specification, like `ServletContextListener`, `HttpSessionListener`, and others (see chapter 3). Let's look at the `PortletURLGenerationListener` listener, which is specific to portlet applications.

4.6.3 *Using the PortletURLGenerationListener interface*

The concept of listeners isn't limited to web applications. The Portlet 2.0 API added `PortletURLGenerationListener`, which is specific to portlets. In portlets, you can create a portlet URL either by using portlet tag library tags (described in chapter 6) or programmatically by using the create URL methods (`createActionURL`, `create-RenderURL`, and `createResourceURL`) defined in the `MimeResponse` interface. The `PortletURLGenerationListener` allows you to intercept the portlet URL generation and take specific actions before it's written out as part of the content, helping you centralize actions that you want to perform on all the portlet URLs generated in a portlet application.

> **NOTE**   The `PortletURLGenerationListener` is supported in Liferay Portal 6.x and OpenPortal Portlet Container 2.1.2 with GlassFish Server.

The `PortletURLGenerationListener` defines methods that you can implement to take specific actions on portlet URLs. Listing 4.4 shows an example `PortletURL-GenerationListener` that modifies the action and render URLs so that they send the action or render requests over a *secure* connection (that is, `HTTPS`) and the portlet is displayed in `MAXIMIZED` window state. If these settings are applied to all portlet URLs, the portlet will always be accessed over a secure connection and the portlet will always be in a maximized state when the render and action requests are sent to a portlet.

Listing 4.4   `PortletURLGenerationListener` example

```
public class MyUrlGenerationListener
    implements PortletURLGenerationListener
{
  public void filterActionURL(PortletURL actionUrl) {          ❶ filterActionURL
    try {                                                         method
      actionUrl.setWindowState(WindowState.MAXIMIZED);
      actionUrl.setSecure(true);
    } catch (Exception e) {
      ...
    }
  }
  public void filterRenderURL(PortletURL renderUrl) {
    try {                                                       ❷ filterRenderURL
        renderUrl.setWindowState(WindowState.MAXIMIZED);          method
      renderUrl.setSecure(true);
    } catch (Exception e) {
      ...
    }
  }
  public void filterResourceURL                               ❸ filterResourceURL
    ➥(ResourceURL resourceURL) {                                method
    ...
  }
}
```

The `MyUrlGenerationListener` class implements `PortletURLGenerationListener`. The `PortletURLGenerationListener`'s `filterActionURL` method is implemented ❶. It sets the window state to `MAXIMIZED` for portlets receiving the action request, and it uses the `PortletURL`'s `setSecure` method to instruct the portlet container that all action request invocations must be transferred over a secure connection (`HTTPS`). At ❷ and ❸, the `MyUrlGenerationListener` implements the `PortletURLGenera-tionListener`'s `filterRenderURL` and `filterResourceURL` methods.

> **WARNING**   In Liferay Portal 6.x, the portal server doesn't honor the window
> state set on the `PortletURL` object by `PortletURLGenerationListener`.

The `PortletURLGenerationListener` defines methods that take specific actions on the render, action, and resource URLs of portlets, as shown in listing 4.4. The `MyUrl-GenerationListener` must be registered in the portlet deployment descriptor to instruct the portlet container to invoke the listener before the URLs are written out.

The following XML fragment shows how you can configure listeners in the portlet deployment descriptor:

```
<portlet-app ...>
  <portlet>
    ...
  </portlet>
  <listener>
    <listener-class>
      chapter03.code.listing.utils.MyUrlGenerationListener
    </listener-class>
  </listener>
</portlet-app>
```

> **NOTE**   In Portlet 2.0, the render and action URLs belong to the same type, `PortletURL`. The resource URL belongs to the `ResourceURL` type.

The `<listener>` element is a subelement of `<portlet-app>`, so the listeners are applied to all portlets in the portlet application.

> **CODE REFERENCE**   Refer to the `MyUrlGenerationListener` class and the portlet deployment descriptor in the source code's ch3_BookCatalog folder to see an example of the `PortletURLGenerationListener` in use. In this case, it sets the window state to `MAXIMIZED` for all action and render URLs.

In this chapter and the previous one, we've seen that there could be many reasons why a portlet might work differently on different portal servers; different servers have varying features, different limitations and bugs, and differing support for optional features. In most cases, you'll be able to find an intermediate solution that works on all platforms. For instance, if expiration- and validation-based content caching isn't supported, you can use data caching to boost portal performance, and if adding JavaScript or CSS files isn't supported using the `RenderResponse` object's `MARKUP_HEAD_ELEMENT`, you can check for its support in the portlet code before injecting JavaScript and CSS in the portal page.

But in some scenarios, using portal server–specific APIs and databases is the only way to address a particular business requirement. Even if you don't plan to deploy the portlet across different portal servers, you should design it so that it can be easily adapted for different portal servers, in case it becomes necessary to migrate portlets from one portal server to another. The downside of this is that it requires an additional initial effort to create the portlet.

4.7   *Designing portable portlets*

In order to design portlets that are portable across different portal servers, the following points should be taken into account during development:

- Portal server features and limitations
- Portal server–specific code should be separated out from common code

Let's discuss these two points in detail.

4.7.1   *Portal server features and limitations*

The key to developing portable portlets is to know your target portal servers.

Suppose you have been assigned to develop the Book Catalog portlet for the Jetspeed 2.2 and Liferay Portal 6.x portal servers. You start developing the portlet using Jetspeed, and you use custom portlet-managed portlet modes. If you deploy that portlet on Liferay Portal, it would be bound to behave differently, because Liferay Portal's support for custom portlet-managed portal modes is broken. If you discover a problem with your portal server at a later stage in development, the code may require a major rewrite, and the overall design of the portlet may need to be changed. You can minimize the effort required to develop portable portlets if you invest some time up front in learning the features and limitations of your portal servers.

Knowing your target portal servers isn't only important for developing portable portlets; it's also helpful in deciding what portlets you should build, and which of the built-in portlets offered by your portal server you should reuse or customize. For instance, if your target portal server provides a built-in Discussion Forum portlet, it may be better to reuse that portlet, because the effort required to create a discussion forum portlet is significant.

REUSING BUILT-IN SERVICES

In many scenarios, you may want to reuse the portal server services used by the built-in portlets, but not the user interface offered by the portlets. For instance, Liferay Portal offers a Document Library portlet that you can use to store your documents. If users of your portlet have to upload and retrieve documents (like the book TOC in the Book Catalog portlet), you can reuse the Document Library portlet's service classes to upload or download files.

Figure 4.8 shows the built-in Document Library portlet in Liferay Portal, which allows you to organize your documents. You can create folders (and subfolders) to

Figure 4.8   Liferay Portal's built-in Document Library portlet allows you to manage documents. You can create folder structures and search for documents maintained by the library.

define categories under which you want to keep your documents. The Search option allows you to search for documents within the document library.

Reusing built-in services tightly couples your portlet with the portal server, which affects the portability of your portlets across portal servers. Nevertheless, you can still design your portlets to adapt to new portal server environments by using *service adapters*.

DIRECTLY USING PORTAL DATABASES

If the documentation for your portal server provides details about the internal database used by the portal server, you could use the database tables directly to retrieve or store data, but this isn't recommended. Accessing database tables that are used internally by your portal server may result in data inconsistency if the documentation doesn't provide sufficient details about the links between various tables.

Directly using the portal database also affects the portability of your portlets, because each portal server has its own specific database for storing portal information like user roles, user groups, and more. But you can still design your portlets to be portable by using *data access adapters*.

4.7.2 Designing for change

If you want to use your portlets across different portal servers, you need to customize the code at three levels, depending upon what you're trying to customize. In this section, we'll look at these three levels and at what type of customization is performed in each.

CUSTOMIZING REQUEST-HANDLING LOGIC

Your request-handling logic may need some customization to address limitations or bugs specific to the portal server your portlet uses. For instance, you'll need to add JavaScript and CSS to the `head` section of the markup if you have Jetspeed 2.2 using `MimeResponse`'s `MARKUP_HEAD_ELEMENT` property. Liferay Portal 5.2.3/6.x doesn't support adding JavaScript and CSS using the `MARKUP_HEAD_ELEMENT` property; to address this, you'll need to customize your request-handling logic so that JavaScript and CSS elements are added to the `head` section of the markup only if the portal server is Jetspeed.

To customize request-handling logic, you can use the `PortalContext`'s `getPortal-Info` method to determine which portal server the portlet is deployed on.

CUSTOMIZING THE SERVICE LAYER

If you're using an existing portal service while developing your portlets, the service implementation needs be customized for different portal server environments. For instance, if you're using Liferay Portal's Document Library service in the Book Catalog portlet to manage the book TOCs, you need to provide a replacement service that can be used when the Book Catalog portlet is deployed on Jetspeed.

CUSTOMIZING THE DATA ACCESS LAYER

If you're using portal server–specific database tables to store and retrieve information, you need to customize the data access logic when the portlet is deployed on a different portal server. For instance, if you're directly using the *announcement* tables in the Liferay Portal database to store or retrieve announcement details in your Announcement portlet, the logic for storing and retrieving data needs to be altered when the Announcement portlet is deployed on Jetspeed or some other portal server.

The request-handling logic specific to a portal server can't be easily separated out, because it's tightly coupled with the portlet request and response. Service and data access logic can easily be separated out from the portlet code because it's not tightly coupled with the web tier.

To design portlets that are dependent on a portal's internal database tables or portal server–specific services, you should use *adapters* for the data access and service. Figure 4.9 shows how you can implement a service adapter for each portal server.

In figure 4.9, the `PortalService` interface defines the methods that use portal server–specific services. `LiferayPortalService` and `JetspeedPortalService` represent `PortalService` implementations specific to Liferay Portal and Jetspeed, respectively. Similarly, you'll need data access implementations specific to each portal server, if your portlets directly interact with portal server–specific databases.

The signatures of the portal server–specific methods defined in the `Portal-Service` interface are as follows:

```
Map <method_name>(Map parameters)
```

Here, method_name is the name of the method in the portal server–specific service interface.

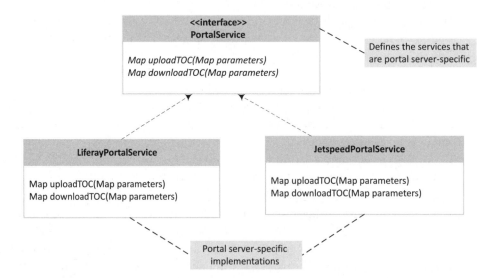

Figure 4.9   The PortalService interface defines methods that invoke portal server–specific methods. LiferayPortalService and JetspeedPortalService are concrete implementations of PortalService and provide service implementations specific to Liferay Portal and Jetspeed.

One of the important things to notice in the service method signatures is that the argument and return types of the method are of type `java.util.Map`. The use of the `Map` type argument makes the service interface methods generic in nature, so you can pass any arguments, regardless of what the portal service–specific services might need for processing. Similarly, the `Map` return type ensures that you can return multiple types as the return value. The use of `Map` as the argument and return type also means you can change the parameters without affecting the method signature.

Figure 4.10 shows how you can use portal server–specific services and data access objects from portlet-specific services. In this figure, `MyBookCatalogPortlet` represents the portlet class for the Book Catalog portlet. `BookCatalogService` provides the implementation of services required by the Book Catalog portlet. `Portal-ServiceFactory` and `DataAccessObjectFactory` are factories for creating portal server–specific services and data access objects.

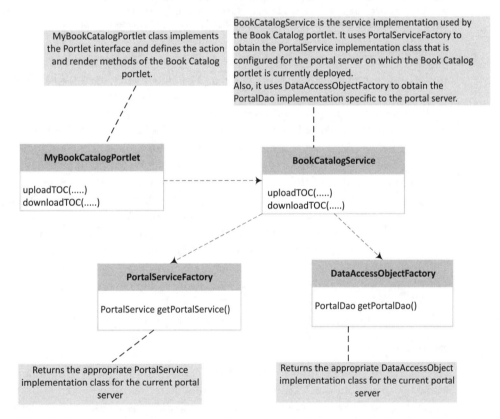

Figure 4.10 The `BookCatalogService` class implements the business functionality of the Book Catalog portlet. The `BookCatalogService` uses factory classes to obtain portal server–specific DAOs and services.

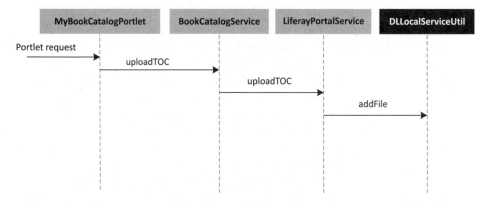

Figure 4.11   A sequence diagram showing how `MyBookCatalogPortlet` accesses the Liferay Portal–specific services. `BookCatalogService` has a reference to the appropriate implementation of the `PortalService` interface (`LiferayPortalService`, in this case), which invokes the `addFile` method of the `DLLocalServiceUtil` Liferay Portal service class.

`MyBookCatalogPortlet` is directly dependent upon `BookCatalogService` and not on portal server–specific services, so if the portal server–specific services change over time, the impact of that change can be addressed in the service layer.

The sequence diagram shown in figure 4.11 shows how a portal server–specific method invocation takes place in the design described in figures 4.9 and 4.10.

In figure 4.11, `MyBookCatalogPortlet` invokes the `BookCatalogService`'s upload-TOC method. `BookCatalogService` contains a reference to the appropriate `Portal-Service` instance that needs to be used for the current portal server, which it obtained using a service factory (refer to figures 4.9 and 4.10). If the portal server is Liferay Portal, the `uploadTOC` method of `LiferayPortalService` is called. Next, `LiferayPortal-Service` is responsible for invoking the Liferay Portal–specific portal service, which is `DLLocalServiceUtil`'s `addFile` method. The `DLLocalServiceUtil` class represents a utility class in Liferay Portal that implements services used by Liferay Portal's built-in Document Library portlet. So, in a way, by invoking the `DLLocalServiceUtil`'s methods, you're reusing the services offered by Liferay Portal.

This completes our two-chapter discussion of the Portlet 2.0 API.

4.8   Summary

In this chapter, you saw how to create portlets that show localized content and how to make use of custom portlet modes and window states. We also looked at how you can programmatically secure portlets, and how you can design portlets that can easily be adapted to different portal servers.

In the next chapter, we'll look at how to create a portal in Liferay Portal using the Book Catalog portlet and Liferay Portal's built-in portlets. We'll also look at how knowledge of the target portal server can help reduce the effort involved in creating custom portlets, like the Book Catalog portlet.

Building your own portal

5

This chapter covers

- Creating organization, roles, and users in Liferay Portal
- Creating portal pages and adding portlets
- Setting permissions for portal pages and portlets
- Configuring Liferay Portal
- Developing portal themes and layouts with the Liferay Plugins SDK

Chapters 3 and 4 introduced the Portlet 2.0 API with an example Book Catalog portlet. Now that you know the nuts and bolts of portal development, it's time to build your own web portal. In this chapter, you'll develop a web portal, named Book Portal, with Liferay Portal.

You'll see firsthand the importance of knowing your portal server and how built-in features of the portal server can reduce your development effort for custom portlets. How quickly you can develop and deploy a functional web portal should be one of the criteria you use in selecting a portal server. In some cases, depending on your portal server's features, you may consider adjusting the design of your custom portlets so they're easier to develop quickly (you'll see this in the context of the Book Catalog portlet, later in this chapter).

> **NOTE** This chapter is specific to Liferay Portal. If you're not using Liferay Portal, you might want to skip or skim through this chapter. If you're new to portlet development, you should read this chapter to get a feel for web portal development. If you're using GateIn Portal, refer to appendix A for details on how to create a web portal with GateIn.

In this chapter, you'll develop Book Portal using Liferay Portal as your portal server. The development approach followed in this chapter is common in developing web portals. As we go through the process of developing Book Portal, we'll touch upon some of the features offered by Liferay Portal. You'll also see how the Book Catalog portlet (developed in chapters 3 and 4) uses Liferay Portal's document storage feature to store e-books.

Let's first look at the requirements of the Book Portal web portal.

5.1   *Requirements for Book Portal*

Book Portal allows its registered users to search for and download e-books. The following are the main requirements for Book Portal:

- Book Portal allows the portal administrator to publish announcements on the portal's home page, and these should be visible to both anonymous and registered users. The published announcements should be made available either immediately or at the date and time the administrator specifies for their publication.
- Book Portal displays the most popular products available at www.amazon.com that are tagged with "Java."
- Book Portal shows books in the catalog that are currently available to registered users of the portal. The book catalog can only be updated by the portal administrator. For each book in the catalog, the following information should be displayed to the registered user: title, author, ISBN, and a download link for the book. Registered users should be able to take a printout of the catalog if they choose. They should also be able to set their preference regarding the number of books they want to view on the page. The book catalog provides a search facility so users can easily locate books.
- Book Portal provides discussion forums for each book in the catalog to allow registered users to discuss the books.
- The portal administrator can additionally perform the following actions on the book catalog: update book information, add new book information, and remove book information.
- Book Portal has a message board for each of the books in the book catalog. The administrator is responsible for creating the message board for a book.

Registered users can post comments on the message board and subscribe to posts or message boards for books. Anonymous users of the portal can view the message boards, but they can't post messages.

- It should be easy for the Book Portal administrator to change the look and feel of the portal or the layout of the pages.
- The company developing Book Portal has an internal application, In-Demand Book Apps, which the company staff uses to store information about the books that are most frequently sought after on the internet. The company plans to make this application available via Book Portal to a few select users, to allow them to submit information about the books that they would like to be made available by Book Portal.

Book Portal's requirements are typical of web portals. In a web portal, there are often different types of users (such as registered users, anonymous users, administrators, and so on), and each user type has a different set of access permissions. A web portal may also act as the single point of entry to other web applications, like the In-Demand Book Apps web application, which is accessed via Book Portal. In a web portal, themes let you easily change the look and feel of the portal, and page layouts let you easily organize portlets on portal pages.

It's important to know the different types of users of your web portal, because each user type has access to a different set of operations and information. Book Portal has three different types of users: portal administrator, registered users, and anonymous users.

- *Portal administrator*—The Book Portal administrator is responsible for creating the portal pages, adding portlets to the portal pages, and configuring portlets so that only authorized individuals can access portlets and perform restricted actions. The portal administrator also handles the tasks related to maintaining the book catalog, like adding, removing, and editing books in the catalog. You can think of the portal administrator as the superuser of the portal who can perform all the actions available in the portal server.
- *Registered users*—Registered users of Book Portal can view the book catalog and download books. They also can post messages on message boards.
- *Anonymous users*—Anonymous users of the system can only view published announcements and RSS feeds from Amazon. They don't have access to the book catalog or to post messages on message boards.

NOTE Both Jetspeed and Liferay Portal provide administration features to define access rights for a portlet based on the user role. You could use either of these portal servers to address the security requirements of Book Portal.

Now let's look at how you can create Book Portal and its users in Liferay Portal.

5.2   *Getting started developing Book Portal*

To get started with developing Book Portal in Liferay Portal, you need to perform the following activities:

- Create an *organization*—Liferay Portal's way of identifying a web portal
- Create users and roles, and map users to roles

Liferay Portal lets you identify users belonging to an organization. You can think of Book Portal as an organization whose user base consists of registered users and a portal administrator. The registered users in the Book Portal organization have the BookUser custom role, and the Book Portal administrator has the Portal-Administrator custom role.

Initially, you need to set up the following for Book Portal:

1 *Create the Book Portal organization in Liferay Portal*—The starting point for developing Book Portal is to create an organization in Liferay Portal with which users of the portal are associated.

2 *Create roles that are applicable to the Book Portal organization*—This includes Portal-Administrator and BookUser. Liferay Portal treats anonymous users as users having the Guest role, which is a predefined role in Liferay Portal, so you don't need to create it.

3 *Create users*—You need to create users who are predefined in the portal. For instance, a registered user is created in Book Portal when a user registers with the web portal, but the Book Portal administrator (who has the Portal-Administrator role) needs to be created.

4 *Map users to roles*—When a user registers with Book Portal, they should automatically be assigned the BookUser role. Anonymous users are by default mapped to the Guest role by Liferay Portal.

5 *Assign users to the organization*—Registered users should be automatically assigned to the Book Portal organization.

Figure 5.1 shows the process for setting up the web portal.

NOTE   The concept of an *organization* is specific to Liferay Portal, but in most portal servers you'll find features for creating roles and users and for assigning roles to users.

Let's begin by creating the organization with which Book Portal is associated.

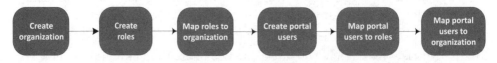

Figure 5.1   The process described in this chapter for setting up a portal in Liferay Portal

5.2.1 Creating an organization for Book Portal

To create an organization for Book Portal, you need to log in as the Liferay Portal administrator. Once you do that, you'll have full control over the portal, and you'll be able to create organizations, roles, users, portal pages, and a lot more. In this chapter, you're interested in creating an organization for Book Portal and a user whose role is `PortalAdministrator`. Once you have a user with the `Portal-Administrator` role, the job of creating portal pages, adding portlets to portal pages, and defining additional roles for the Book Portal organization will lie with the `PortalAdministrator`.

To log in as the Liferay Portal administrator, go to the home page of Liferay Portal 6.x and select the Login as Bruno option, as described in chapter 1. Once you are logged in as administrator (Bruno), you can create an organization for Book Portal. Follow these steps:

1　Select Manage > Control Panel from the dockbar.

2　In the control panel screen, select the Organizations option, which lets you manage organizations in the portal.

3　In the Organizations window, as shown in figure 5.2, you'll see that the 7Cogs, Inc. organization already exists—it comes by default with Liferay Portal to give you the feel of how a portal created using Liferay Portal works. Click Add to add a new organization to the portal.

4　A form will be displayed where you can enter the *name* of organization you want to create and its *type*, as shown in figure 5.3. Enter `MySamplePortal, Inc` as the Name of organization, and select Regular Organization as its Type. Click Save to save the organization information.

5　Once the organization information is saved successfully, you'll see more information that can be entered for your newly created organization, as shown in figure 5.4. You can upload a logo for the organization, and you can specify miscellaneous details such as phone numbers, email addresses, and so on. Enter any information you wish for the organization, and click Save.

Figure 5.2　Click the Add button to add a new organization to the portal.

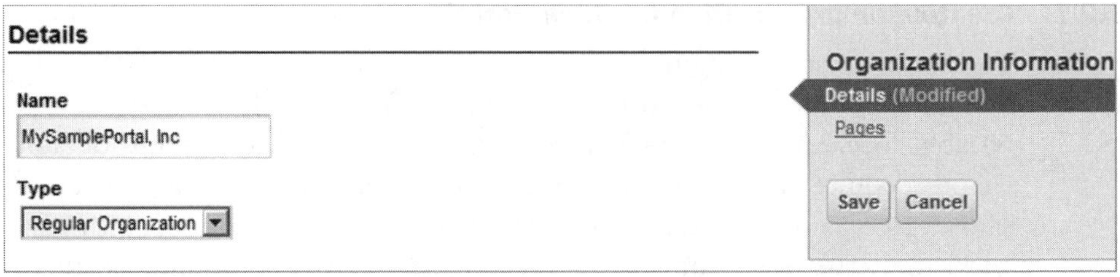

Details

Name

MySamplePortal, Inc

Type
Regular Organization ▾

Organization Information

Details (Modified)

Pages

Save   Cancel

Figure 5.3   Create an organization by entering a name and type for it. Clicking the Save button will save the organization information in the database used by Liferay Portal internally. The Modified message is displayed at the top right whenever a modification is made to the organization's information.

The newly created MySamplePortal, Inc organization will now be displayed in the list of organizations defined in Liferay Portal. The Group ID shown in figure 5.4 uniquely identifies the organization in Liferay Portal.

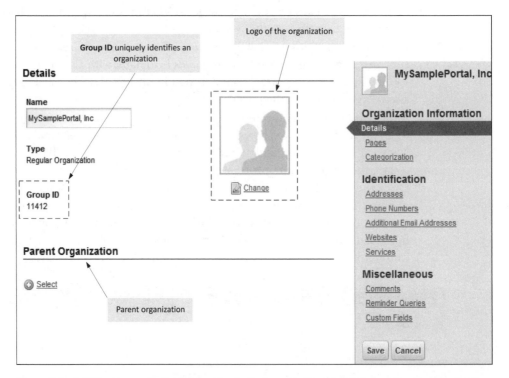

Figure 5.4   Additional organization information is displayed to the administrator after the organization information is saved the first time. The administrator can upload a logo for the organization and specify its parent organization (if any). The Group ID uniquely identifies an organization in Liferay Portal.

NOTE The Group ID is useful in implementing custom portlets that interact with Liferay Portal's services or database.

You have successfully created the Book Portal organization in Liferay Portal. You're now ready to create the `PortalAdministrator` and `BookUser` roles.

5.2.2 Creating roles for Book Portal users

Roles in Liferay Portal are independent of organizations; you can create a role and associate any user, of any organization, with that role. For instance, you can create a `BookUser` role and associate it with a user of organization X and also with a user of organization Y.

To create a role, select Manage > Control Panel from the dockbar, and in the control panel screen select the Roles option, which allows you to add, remove, or edit role information. On the Roles page, click Add to add the `BookUser` custom role.

Figure 5.5 shows the information that you need to enter to create a role in Liferay Portal. Enter `BookUser` as the role Name, add a description for the role, and click Save. Once the role is saved, it will show up among the other roles defined in Liferay Portal.

Now that you have created the `BookUser` role, you're ready to create the `Portal-Administrator` role. But consider for a moment whether you really need a `PortalAdministrator` role. The predefined `Administrator` role in Liferay Portal is for a user who has full control over Liferay Portal. This is similar to the `Portal-Administrator` role for Book Portal, so you don't need to create a new role. Liferay Portal's built-in `Administrator` role meets your requirements for Book Portal.

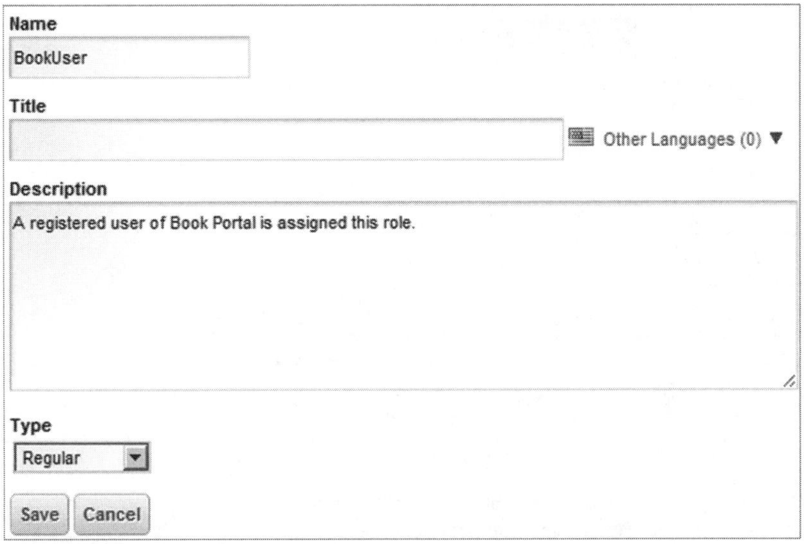

Name

BookUser

Title

                                                             Other Languages (0) ▼

Description

A registered user of Book Portal is assigned this role.

Type

Regular ▼

Save Cancel

Figure 5.5 Role information that needs to be added to Liferay Portal

NOTE   It's recommended that you check the predefined roles in your portal server before creating a new role, to avoid creating duplicate roles with the same permissions.

You're now ready to associate the BookUser role with the MySamplePortal, Inc organization, because the BookUser role is specific to MySamplePortal, Inc.

5.2.3   *Mapping roles to the Book Portal organization*

Look at the list of roles defined in Liferay Portal, and click the Action button for the BookUser role. Click the Assign Members option to associate the BookUser role with the MySamplePortal, Inc organization. Figure 5.6 illustrates how you can do this.

In figure 5.6, select Assign Members > Organizations > Available to view the organizations defined in Liferay Portal. Click the check box beside the MySamplePortal, Inc organization, and click the Update Associations button to associate the BookUser role with MySamplePortal, Inc.

THE IMPORTANCE OF ASSOCIATING A CUSTOM ROLE WITH AN ORGANIZATION

In Book Portal, you have associated the custom BookUser role with the MySamplePortal, Inc organization, which means that any user having the BookUser role is implicitly associated with the MySamplePortal, Inc organization. The reason for making this association is so that it's explicit that the BookUser role is meaningful *only* in the context of MySamplePortal, Inc. In Liferay Portal, you may have multiple organizations,

Figure 5.6   Assigning a Liferay Portal role to an organization. The Update Associations button lets you associate a particular role with an organization.

and explicitly associating a custom role with an organization can help clarify that the role is meaningful only in the context of a particular organization.

You're now ready to create a user who will act as the portal administrator for the MySamplePortal, Inc organization.

5.2.4 Creating Book Portal users and assigning them to the organization

If your portal has predefined users, you need to create them for the portal. Registered users are created when users register with Book Portal, so you don't need to create them. The Book Portal administrator is the only predefined user of Book Portal, so that's the only user you need to create.

What you need to do is create a user in the MySamplePortal, Inc organization, and then assign that user the built-in Liferay Portal role of Administrator.

You can create a user by selecting Manage > Control Panel from the dockbar, and selecting the Users option. Click Add to create new users in Liferay Portal. Figure 5.7 shows the form for adding a user to Liferay Portal.

For this example, keep the email address of the Book Portal administrator as admin@sampleportal.com. You'll use this email address to log in as the Book Portal administrator. Enter the user information, and click Save to save the user information.

Once the basic information about the portal administrator user is saved, additional information can be entered for the user, as shown in figure 5.8.

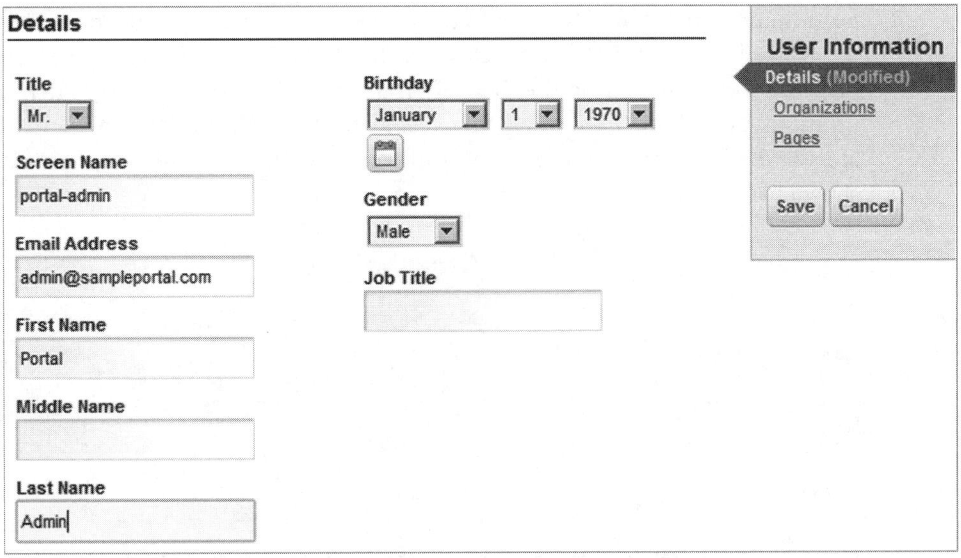

Figure 5.7   Enter information about the user to be created in Liferay Portal.

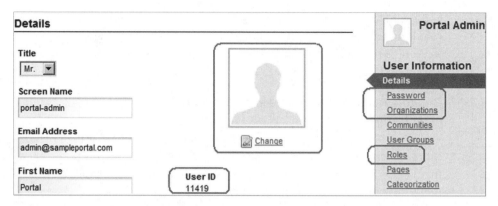

Figure 5.8 Additional user information can be entered after the basic information is saved. The User ID uniquely identifies a user in Liferay Portal, the Password option is used to set the user's password, the Organizations option is used to assign the user to an organization, and the Roles option is used to assign roles to the user.

In figure 5.8, the additional information displayed after the basic user information is saved lets you assign the user to an organization and set a password. You can also upload the user's photograph at this time. The User ID shown in figure 5.8 is a unique identifier for the user, generated by Liferay Portal, and it's useful in developing custom portlets that interact with the Liferay Portal services or database.

In figure 5.8, click the Password option to set the password for the Book Portal administrator. You also need to associate the Book Portal administrator with the MySamplePortal, Inc organization so that MySamplePortal, Inc is reflected as the organization managed by the Book Portal administrator. To do so, click the Organizations option in figure 5.8. Now, click the Select hyperlink to view and associate the Book Portal administrator with the MySamplePortal, Inc organization, as shown in figure 5.9.

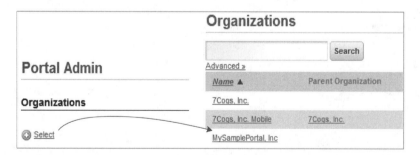

Figure 5.9 Clicking the Select hyperlink opens the list of organizations in Liferay Portal. To associate the Book Portal administrator with MySamplePortal, Inc, click MySamplePortal, Inc organization from the list.

Once you have selected MySamplePortal, Inc, save the Book Portal administrator details by clicking Save (shown in figure 5.7).

The next step is to associate the Book Portal administrator user with the predefined `Administrator` role.

5.2.5 *Mapping users to roles*

Registered users of Book Portal need to be mapped to the `BookUser` role. You'll see later in this chapter how registered users are automatically mapped to the `BookUser` role when they register. In this section, you'll see how the Book Portal administrator is mapped to Liferay Portal's built-in `Administrator` role.

Click the Roles option in figure 5.8 to view or edit the roles the Book Portal administrator is associated with. Figure 5.10 shows the form that's used to select appropriate roles for the Book Portal administrator.

In figure 5.10, click the Select option under the Regular Roles heading. Choose the `Administrator` role for the Book Portal administrator, because you want the portal administrator to have full control over Liferay Portal.

So far, you have completed the following steps:

1 Created the MySamplePortal, Inc organization.
2 Created the `BookUser` role for users who will register with Book Portal. Note that you didn't create any users with `BookUser` role. The users who register themselves with Book Portal will be associated with the `BookUser` role.
3 Associated the `BookUser` role with the MySamplePortal, Inc organization.
4 Created a user, with email address admin@sampleportal.com, who acts as the Book Portal administrator.
5 Assigned the `Administrator` role to the user you created to act as the Book Portal administrator.

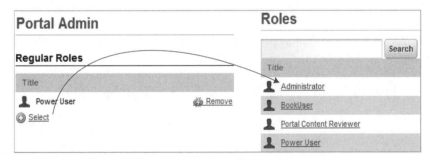

Figure 5.10   The Select option under Regular Roles lets you select regular roles like Administrator, Power User, BookUser, and so on. Select Administrator as the role for the Book Portal administrator.

The next step is to log in as the Book Portal administrator and create *public* portal pages for the MySamplePortal, Inc organization, and to add portlets to those portal pages.

5.3 *Creating portal pages and adding portlets*

A web portal consists of portal pages containing portlets that display content. Regardless of which portal server you're using, you'll be required to create portal pages and to add portlets to them. Depending upon the requirements of your web portal, you'll also need to define permissions for the portal pages and portlets. For instance, registered users in Book Portal shouldn't have access to add, update, and remove books from the book catalog, and anonymous users shouldn't be able to view portal pages that are accessible only to registered users.

In this section, you'll create portal pages for Book Portal, add required portlets to the portal pages, and learn how to restrict unauthorized access to portal pages and portlets as specified by the Book Portal requirements. In this section, you'll also see how the Book Portal requirements determine whether a built-in or a custom portlet should be used.

Let's first go through the steps required to create the Book Portal Home page, which will also show you how to create portal pages in Liferay Portal in general.

5.3.1 *Creating a Home portal page*

To create portal pages for the MySamplePortal, Inc organization, log in as the Book Portal administrator (the userid is the email of the Book Portal administrator: admin@sampleportal.com). Select the Manage > Control Panel option from the dockbar, and select the Organizations option in the control panel. You'll see the list of organizations that have been created in Liferay Portal, as shown in figure 5.11.

In figure 5.11, if you click the Actions button, it will show you the actions you can perform on the organization (which will vary depending on your role). Figure 5.12 shows the actions that you can perform as an `Administrator`.

Select the Manage Pages option to create public portal pages for MySamplePortal, Inc. Figure 5.13 shows the options that you'll see.

	Name ▲	Parent Organization	Type	City	Region	Country	
☐	7Cogs, Inc.		Regular Organization				◀ 🔧 Actions
☐	7Cogs, Inc. Mobile	7Cogs, Inc.	Regular Organization				◀ 🔧 Actions
☐	MySamplePortal, Inc		Regular Organization				◀ 🔧 Actions

Figure 5.11 MySamplePortal, Inc is shown as an organization that has been created in Liferay Portal.

Figure 5.12   Options available to the Book Portal administrator on the MySamplePortal, Inc organization

Figure 5.13 shows all the options related to managing an organization's portal pages. At the top are three tabs: Public Pages, Private Pages, and Settings. The Public Pages tab has three subtabs: Pages, Look and Feel, and Export/Import. In this section, we'll focus on the Pages subtab, which is where you create Book Portal pages. The Look and Feel subtab is discussed in section 5.5.2.

The Pages subtab allows you to create and edit your public portal pages. Under the New Page tab, enter Home as the Name of the portal page, and keep the Type of page

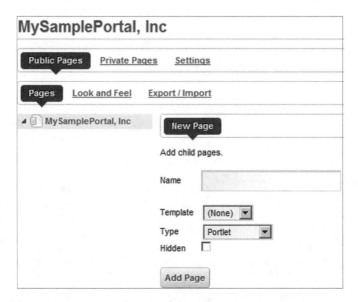

Figure 5.13   The Public Pages top-level tab shows three subtabs for managing the public portal pages of the MySamplePortal, Inc organization. You can add a new page here, edit an existing page's title, or change the order in which they're displayed in the portal.

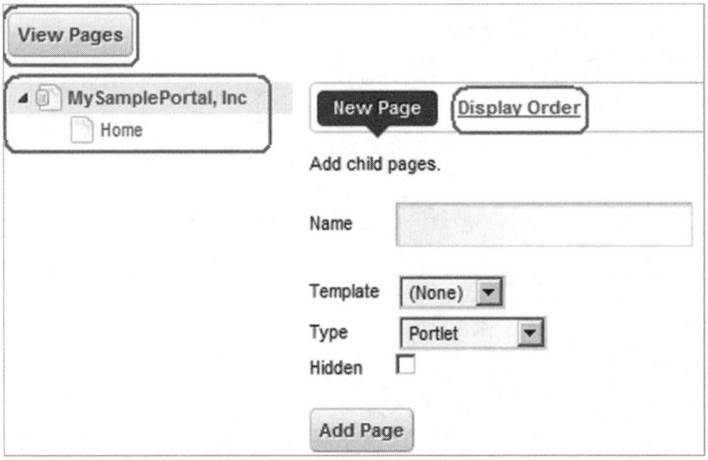

View Pages

◢ ▣ MySamplePortal, Inc
    📄 Home

New Page   Display Order

Add child pages.

Name   [   ]

Template   (None) ▼
Type   Portlet ▼
Hidden   ☐

Add Page

Figure 5.14   The newly added Home page is shown in the page hierarchy displayed on the left side of the form. The View Pages button lets you view the pages of the MySamplePortal, Inc organization. The Display Order option lets you change the order in which the pages are displayed in the web portal.

as `Portlet`. Click Add Page to save the Home page. When the page information is successfully saved, the newly added page is shown in the page hierarchy on the left side of the form, as shown in figure 5.14.

Now that the MySamplePortal, Inc Home page has been created, let's add portlets to it. To view the MySamplePortal, Inc pages, select Go To > MySamplePortal, Inc from the dockbar.

Once you're on the Home page of the MySamplePortal, Inc organization, you can add appropriate portlets to create the home page of your Book Portal, as shown in figure 5.15.

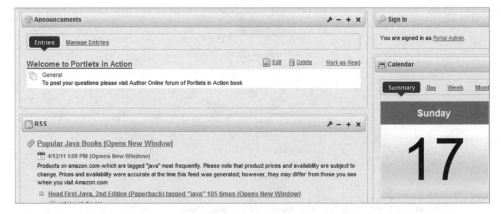

Figure 5.15   Book Portal's Home page, consisting of built-in Announcements, RSS, Sign In, and Calendar portlets

Figure 5.15 shows how the Home page of Book Portal looks to the Book Portal administrator. The Home page includes the following built-in portlets:

- *Sign In*—Located under the Tools application category that shows up when you select the Add > More option from the dockbar. It allows users to log in to Book Portal.
- *Calendar*—Located under the Collaboration application category that shows up when you select the Add > More option from the dockbar. It shows important upcoming events.
- *Announcements*—Located under the News application category that shows up when you select the Add > More option from the dockbar. It shows announcements.
- *RSS*—Located under the News application category that shows up when you select the Add > More option from the dockbar. It displays the most popular products tagged with Java that are available at www.amazon.com.

By default, the page layout of the Home page is set to 2 Columns (30/70)—the page is partitioned into two columns with the first column taking 30 percent of the page width and the second column taking the remaining 70 percent. You may want to change the page layout so that all the portlets are displayed appropriately on the page. To change the layout, select the Manage > Page Layout option from the dockbar and choose the 2 Columns (70/30) page layout, as shown in figure 5.16.

After selecting 2 Columns (70/30) as the page layout of the Home page, save changes by clicking Save. You'll now see that the portlets in the Home page of Book Portal are resized to the new page layout.

Let's take a look at the Announcements and RSS portlets in detail.

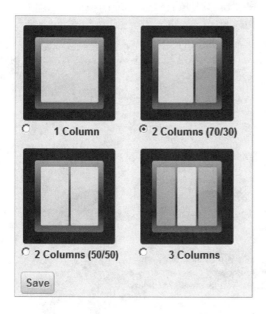

Figure 5.16 The 2 Columns (70/30) page layout partitions the page into two columns where the first column takes 70 percent of the page width and the second column takes 30 percent of the page width.

5.3.2   *Adding an Announcements portlet*

The announcement feature in Book Portal is *not* simple, because each announcement can either be published immediately or at a scheduled date and time. Neither Jetspeed nor GlassFish (with OpenPortal Portlet Container 2.1.2) provide any built-in portlets for publishing announcements, but Liferay Portal does have a built-in Announcements portlet that exactly matches the requirements of Book Portal's publish announcement feature. You can find the Announcements portlet under the News category when you select the Add > More option from the dockbar.

Figure 5.17 shows the Announcements portlet, which allows you to publish announcements immediately or at a scheduled date and time. The Manage Entries tab allows you to add, edit, and delete announcements.

> **NOTE**   If you don't see the Manage Entries tab, make sure that you're logged in as the portal administrator.

The Distribution Scope drop-down list in the Announcements portlet allows you to choose the roles for which the announcement is meant. There are many predefined roles in Liferay Portal, such as `Administrator`, `User`, `Guest`, `Power User`, and so on, that you can select. It also shows any custom roles you have created in Liferay Portal. For instance, the Distribution Scope drop-down list also shows the `BookUser` role, which you created earlier in this chapter.

To add a new announcement, click Add Entry shown in figure 5.17. An Entry announcement form will be displayed, in which you can enter the announcement information, as shown in figure 5.18.

Figure 5.18 shows that while adding an announcement you can select a Distribution Scope, which means you can select the user roles to which the published announcement is visible. If you choose General as the Distribution Scope of an announcement, it's visible to all users of the system, including anonymous users. The Book Portal requirement in section 5.1 specifies that the announcements must be visible to *anonymous* users, so you should choose General as the Distribution Scope for the announcement.

Figure 5.17   The Manage Entries tab allows you to add, edit, and delete announcements. The Distribution Scope drop-down list allows you to select the role for which you want to view, add, modify, or delete announcements.

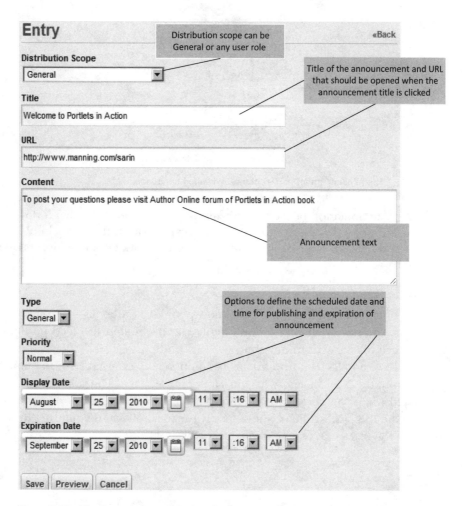

Figure 5.18 The Announcement portlet allows you to specify the date and time when the announcement will be published and expired. The Distribution Scope lets you choose the user roles for which the announcement is being published.

The Display Date and Expiration Date options allow you to specify the date and time when the announcement is published (when it's made visible to users) and removed from Book Portal's Home page.

As you can see, the features offered by the built-in Announcement portlet match the requirements for Book Portal. Figure 5.19 shows how the announcement portlet will appear to a registered user.

Figure 5.19 shows the announcement that was published using the built-in Announcements portlet. If an announcement's Display Date is after the current date, or its Expiration Date is before the current date, the announcement isn't shown by the portlet.

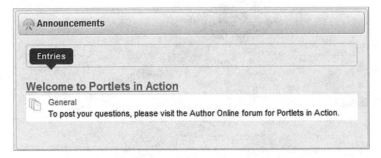

Figure 5.19   The announcement portlet shows published announcements.

NOTE   The limitation of the built-in Announcement portlet is that it doesn't allow you to localize the announcement's text based on the user's locale. As there is no localization requirement specified for Book Portal, we don't need to worry about this.

5.3.3   *Adding an RSS feed portlet*

You can obtain information about the most popular Java books from Amazon using RSS feeds. You saw in chapter 1 that Liferay Portal's built-in RSS feed portlet can be used to receive RSS feeds from websites.

To receive an RSS feed from Amazon, you first add an instance of the built-in RSS portlet from the News category to your Home portal page. The Configuration option (displayed when you click the configure portlet icon from the portlet window's title bar) for the RSS portlet allows you to specify the locations on the internet from which to obtain the RSS feeds, as shown in figure 5.20.

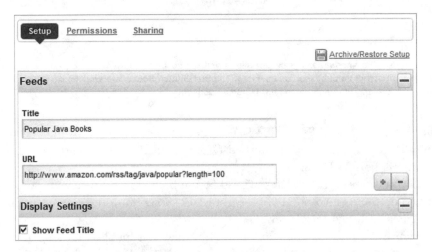

Figure 5.20   The Configuration option for the RSS portlet lets you specify the URL from which to receive the RSS feeds.

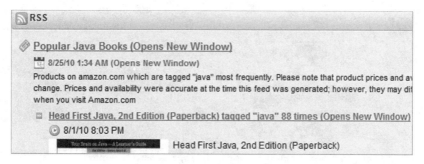

Figure 5.21 The RSS portlet showing the most popular products from Amazon tagged with "Java"

In figure 5.20, you specify the title for the RSS feed and its location. In the Title field, enter `Popular Java Books`, and in the URL field enter the following URL: `http://www.amazon.com/rss/tag/java/popular?length=100`.

> **TIP** For more information about how to retrieve RSS feeds for tagged products from Amazon, see Amazon's RSS help: http://www.amazon.com/gp/tagging/rss-help.html.

Figure 5.21 shows the RSS portlet showing the most popular products from Amazon tagged with "Java."

As you can see, the features offered by Liferay Portal's built-in RSS portlet meet the Book Portal requirements.

Next we'll look at how you can define permissions for portal pages, portlets, and roles.

5.3.4 Setting permissions for portal pages and portlets

An `Administrator` user can define permissions for the portal pages and portlets that form part of an organization.

Select Go To > MySamplePortal, Inc from the dockbar. To specify permissions for a portal page, select the Manage > Page option from the dockbar. Select the Home page from the hierarchy, to specify permissions for it. The Page tab has a Permissions button (shown in figure 5.22), and clicking it allows you to set the permissions for the page.

Once you click the Permissions button, you'll be presented with options to view and edit the permissions for the Home portal page, as shown in figure 5.23. This figure shows the various roles in Liferay Portal and their access permissions for the Home portal page. These are some of the permissions you can configure:

- *Add Discussion*—Allows a user to post a comment. This permission is useful when you want users to post comments regarding the web content published on the portal page.

Figure 5.22   You can define permissions for a portal page by selecting the Manage > Page option from the dockbar. The Permissions button lets you modify permissions for the selected portal page.

- *Update*—Allows a user to remove portlets from a portal page and to move them around on the portal page.
- *View*—Allows a user to view the portal page.

Figure 5.23 shows that BookUser doesn't have view, update, or add discussion permissions for the Home portal page.

To allow BookUser to view the Home portal page, select the View permission for BookUser and save the changes. Custom roles (and other roles in Liferay Portal) inherit their permissions from the Guest role, so this change isn't required, but it's good to make it explicit that BookUser can view the Home portal page. Now users with Guest (also referred to as *anonymous*) or BookUser roles can view the Home portal page.

> **NOTE** You shouldn't give users Update permission for public portal pages (except for the portal administrator), because it will allow them to change the page structure, remove portlets from the portal page, and change settings for the portlets.

Like portal pages, portlets can also have permissions for different users. To view the permissions for a portlet, log in as the Book Portal administrator and select the Configuration option (displayed when you click the configure portlet icon from the portlet window's title bar) for any of the portlets you have added to the Home portal page.

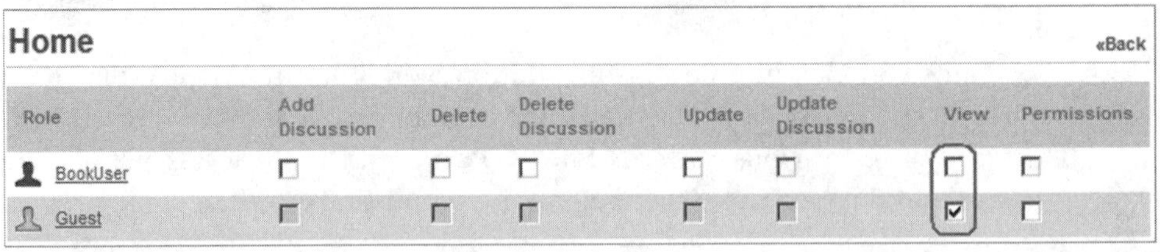

Home							«Back
Role	Add Discussion	Delete	Delete Discussion	Update	Update Discussion	View	Permissions
👤 BookUser	☐	☐	☐	☐	☐	☐	☐
👥 Guest	☐	☐	☐	☐	☐	☑	☐

Figure 5.23   Home page permissions for different roles. The BookUser role isn't even allowed to view the portal page, and the Guest user can view the portal page but can't update it.

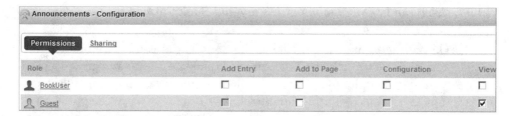

Figure 5.24   The Permissions tab shows the permissions for the portlet. On this screen, you can modify the permissions for a portlet.

The Configuration option shows the configuration options available for the portlet, as shown in figure 5.24 for the Announcements portlet.

In figure 5.24, the Permissions tab shows the portlet permissions that are defined for different roles. This is what the permissions do:

- *View*—Allows a user to see the portlet.
- *Configuration*—Allows a user to configure the portlet with the portlet's Configuration option.
- *Add to Page*—Allows a user to add the portlet to a portal page. You saw this permission in chapter 1.
- *Add Entry*—Allows a user to add new announcements to the Announcements portlet.

As mentioned earlier, roles in Liferay Portal inherit their permissions from the Guest role; any user can view the portlet if the Guest role has the permission to view the portlet.

In figure 5.24, only the View, Configuration, Add Entry, and Add to Page options can have permissions defined. If the portlet supports additional *portal-managed* portlet modes (as discussed in chapter 4), you'll see additional options, as in the case of the Book Catalog portlet. The Book Catalog portlet supports print, help, and edit portlet modes, which will also show up in the Permissions tab.

> **NOTE**   You'll usually give only View permissions to users, as well as Preferences permissions if the portlet allows users to personalize the portlet content (which means it supports EDIT portlet mode). If you give Configuration permissions, users can change the look and feel of the portlet and define permissions for it, which is usually not allowed.

Now let's look at the custom Book Catalog portlet from chapter 4 and see how it can use the built-in Document Library portlet to meet its requirements.

> **CODE REFERENCE**   You should now import the code from the ch5_Book-Catalog project into your Eclipse workspace, and build and deploy the portlet in your Liferay Portal server.

5.3.5   Using the built-in Document Library and Book Catalog portlets together

One of the primary requirements for Book Portal is that it should allow the portal administrator to manage books in the catalog and allow registered users to view, search for, and download e-books. The most important point to consider is where to store the e-book. You can store the book in a database or in the portal server's filesystem. Liferay Portal provides a Document Library portlet, which we discussed in chapter 4, and you can consider using it to store your e-books. Let's see how the Document Library portlet can be used in collaboration with the Book Catalog portlet.

To start, log in as the Book Portal administrator and create a Catalog portal page and set page layout to 2 Columns (50/50), as explained in section 5.3.1. Add the Book Catalog and Document Library portlets to the Catalog portal page, as shown in figure 5.25.

To organize documents stored by the Document Library portlet, create a folder named Java Books using the portlet's Add Folder option, as shown in figure 5.26.

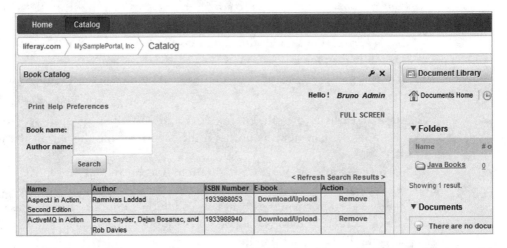

Figure 5.25   The Catalog portal page shows the Book Catalog and Document Library portlets to a portal administrator. The Document Library portlet isn't visible to registered users of the portal.

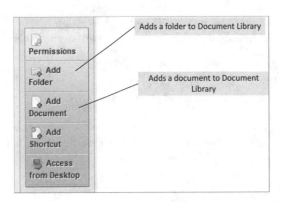

Figure 5.26   The Add Folder option enables you to add a folder to the Document Library portlet. The Add Document option is for uploading a document to be stored by the portlet.

Figure 5.27 The Document Library portlet is used to store documents. You can view the download URL for a document by selecting the document in the portlet.

Figure 5.26 shows that you can use the Add Folder option to add a folder, and Add Document to store a document using the Document Library portlet.

The Document Library portlet provides the download URL for each document that's stored in the document library. Just select the document in the Document Library portlet, and the portlet will display the URL, as shown in figure 5.27.

In figure 5.27, we want to view the download URL for the *AspectJ in Action* e-book. Selecting the AspectJ in Action.doc hyperlink displays its download URL, as shown in figure 5.28.

The download URL of a document in the Document Library portlet refers to a servlet in Liferay Portal that's responsible for downloading the document or file identified by the URL. The same URL can be used by the Book Catalog portlet to allow the downloading of e-books. By using the Document Library portlet to store the e-books, the Book Catalog portlet isn't responsible for uploading e-books or storing them in a filesystem or database.

Figure 5.29 shows the Book Catalog portlet, which uses the download URL provided by the Document Library portlet to allow the downloading of e-books. In this figure, the Download link for each of the books refers to the download URL provided by the Document Library portlet for the corresponding e-book. The Book Catalog portlet's Upload Book form (which is shown when the Book Portal administrator clicks the Upload hyperlink for a book) only requires the download URL for the e-book and not the e-book itself, as shown in figure 5.30.

Figure 5.28 The Document Library portlet provides the download URL for a document, which can be used by other portlets to download a document directly without needing to go to the Document Library portlet.

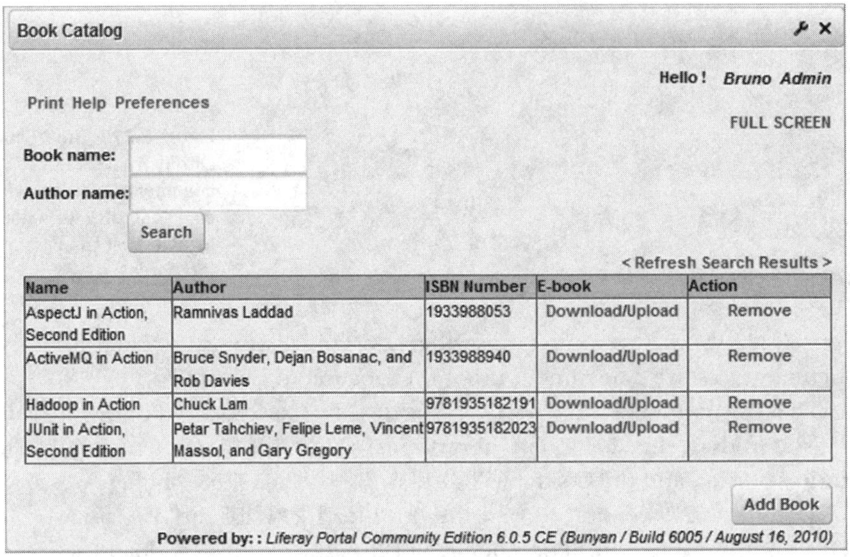

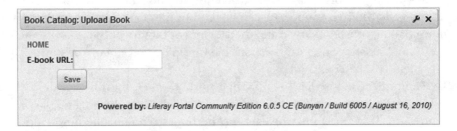

Figure 5.29   The Download link in the Book Catalog portlet refers to the download URL obtained for the e-book from the Document Library portlet.

Book Catalog: Upload Book   🔧 ✕

HOME

E-book URL:

Save

Powered by: *Liferay Portal Community Edition 6.0.5 CE (Bunyan / Build 6005 / August 16, 2010)*

Figure 5.30   The Book Catalog portlet's Upload Book form. You don't upload the e-book; instead, you enter the download URL of the e-book, which is then used by the Book Catalog portlet's Download link.

In figure 5.30, you don't upload the e-book. Instead, you provide the download URL of the corresponding e-book that was stored in the Document Library portlet. The download URL is later used by the Book Catalog portlet's Download link to allow users to download e-books.

THE IMPACT OF USING BUILT-IN PORTLETS

The use of the Book Catalog portlet in combination with the Document Library portlet demonstrates the impact that a portal server's built-in portlets can have on the design of custom portlets. Using the Document Library portlet to store e-books reduces the time and effort required to implement the Book Catalog portlet, making it possible to quickly develop your Book Portal. As a general rule, if you're creating portlets targeted for a particular portal server, consider reusing the functionality offered by built-in portlets before finalizing the design of custom portlets.

Now that you've created the Catalog portal page and added the Document Library and Book Catalog portlets, it's time to set permissions for the Catalog portal page and its portlets.

5.3.6 *Setting permissions for displaying the book catalog*

Book Portal requires that the registered users of the portal can view the catalog and download e-books. The portal administrator is responsible for managing the catalog. A registered user only needs to interact with the Book Catalog portlet, but a portal administrator needs to use both the Book Catalog (for managing book information) and the Document Library (to upload e-books) portlets.

When defining permissions for the Catalog portal page and its portlets, you need to take care of the following requirements:

- The Catalog portal page isn't accessible to `Guest` (or anonymous) users.
- The Catalog portal page shows both the Book Catalog and Document Library portlets to the portal administrator so that it's easy for the administrator to move between the two portlets when the upload URL for a book needs to be specified in the Book Catalog portlet.
- The Catalog portal page shows *only* the Book Catalog portlet to registered users. As registered users of Book Portal are represented by the `BookUser` role, a user with the `BookUser` role can view the Book Catalog portlet. Registered users aren't allowed to add, remove, or update book information, so if they click Add Book or the Remove and Upload hyperlinks in the Book Catalog portlet, they should see an "access denied" message.

Let's see how you can address these requirements.

RESTRICTING GUEST USERS

The `Guest` (or *anonymous*) users of the portal *must not* have access to the Catalog portal page. The registered users—those users with the `BookUser` role—should be able to access the Catalog portal page.

In section 5.3.4 you saw how to set permissions for a portal page. For the Catalog portal page you need to provide View permission for the `BookUser` role and remove it for `Guest` users. This is shown in figure 5.31.

Catalog

Role	Add Discussion	Delete	Delete Discussion	Update	Update Discussion	View
👤 BookUser	☐	☐	☐	☐	☐	☑
👤 Guest	☐	☐	☐	☐	☐	☐

Figure 5.31   Giving View permission to the `BookUser` role and removing it from the `Guest` role

Figure 5.32 View permission for `Guest` is removed to restrict `BookUser` from accessing the Document Library portlet.

In figure 5.31, View permission is assigned to the `BookUser` role, so registered users of the application can access the Catalog portal page. The `Guest` role doesn't have View permission, so those users can't access the Catalog portal page.

RESTRICTING REGISTERED USERS

The registered Book Portal users shouldn't have access to the Document Library portlet, so you need to remove the View permission for the `Guest` role, as shown in figure 5.32. Because all roles in Liferay Portal inherit from the `Guest` role's permissions, removing View permission for `Guest` removes the View permission that was implicitly available to `BookUser`.

The registered users of Book Portal aren't allowed to add or remove books from the catalog. Also, registered users aren't allowed to specify the download URL of an e-book using the Upload hyperlink. This requirement is addressed in the Book Catalog portlet using *programmatic security*; it uses the `PortletRequest`'s `isUserInRole` method to check the user role before allowing access to functionality for adding, removing, or specifying the download URL for books. Chapter 4 goes into detail on how to use the `isUserInRole` method in portlets. If the user's role is `BookUser`, the add, remove, and upload book functionality isn't allowed; if the user's role is `Administrator`, that functionality is enabled.

5.3.7 *Setting permissions for displaying discussion forums*

The last portal page that you need to create is for the discussion forums, where registered Book Portal users can discuss the book with other registered users.

To create the forums, log in as the Book Portal administrator and create a portal page named Forums (as described in section 5.3.1) and add the built-in Message Boards portlet (found under the Collaboration category), as shown in figure 5.33. Also, set page layout to 1 Column, as explained in section 5.3.1.

Figure 5.33 shows the Forums portal page of Book Portal, which contains the built-in Message Boards portlet. With this portlet, a portal administrator can create forums for various books, and registered users can discuss the books in the forum. You create forums in the Message Boards portlet by clicking the Add Category button, shown in figure 5.33, and creating a Category.

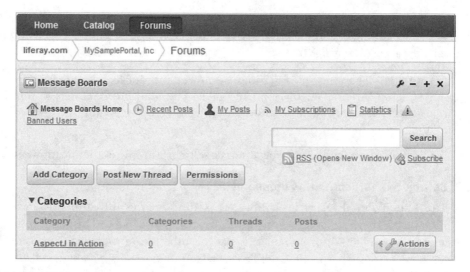

Figure 5.33 The Forums portal page contains the Message Boards portlet, which shows the message boards for various books.

In the case of the Message Boards portlet, permissions need to be defined at the Category (forum) level and at the portlet level. Portlet-level permission for the Message Boards portlet is specified using the Configuration option (displayed when you click the configure portlet icon from the portlet window's title bar) to allow or restrict users from viewing the portlet. Category-level permissions (displayed when you click Permissions button) are specified to control the functions offered by the message board, such as adding messages, subscribing to threads, deleting messages, and so on.

You should define portlet-level permissions to allow the `Guest` and `BookUser` roles to view the portlet. Define Category-level permissions to allow the `BookUser` role to view messages, add messages, reply to messages, and subscribe to threads.

This completes the development of Book Portal, but there are still a few settings that need to be defined for Liferay Portal server before Book Portal is ready for use. In the next section we'll discuss these settings.

5.4 *Configuring Liferay Portal server settings*

Liferay Portal server settings are meant for providing global settings for all portals created on the same portal server instance. By using Liferay Portal server settings, you can define the authentication settings for users, default roles with which a newly registered user is associated, the email server that's used to send emails to users, events for which emails are sent out, the default display settings to be used by web portals, and so on.

Book Portal was created in Liferay Portal, and it's possible that multiple portals are supported by the same instance of Liferay Portal server. The portal server settings apply to all the portals on the server instance.

To view the portal server settings, log in as the Book Portal administrator and select the Settings option from the control panel. It lets the Liferay Portal administrator view and edit settings that apply to the portal server instance.

WARNING   The Manage > Settings option in the dockbar is different from the Settings option in the control panel. The Manage > Settings option is for specifying virtual host information, setting up a staging environment, and so on.

We'll begin our discussion of portal server settings with the authentication setting.

5.4.1 *Setting the authentication mechanism*

The Liferay Portal server authentication setting defines the authentication mechanism used by the portal server, as shown in figure 5.34. This figure shows the authentication settings that you can use to authenticate users with the Liferay Portal server. You can specify whether users authenticate using an email address or userid, whether people can sign up with the portal or retrieve their password, and so on. You can also choose an appropriate authentication provider like LDAP, CAS, OpenSSO, and so on.

Figure 5.35 shows how Liferay Portal makes use of OpenSSO to implement single sign-on functionality so that the In-Demand Book Apps and Book Portal can be accessed without requiring users to re-authenticate with the In-Demand Book Apps application.

OpenSSO authenticates a user against its User Repository, and on successful login it allows the user to access the Book Portal and In-Demand Book Apps application. A User Repository contains user credentials in addition to other information about the users.

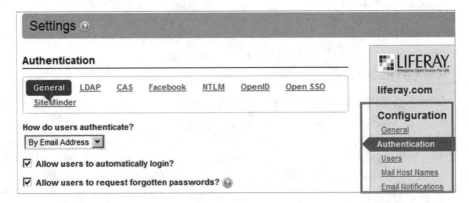

Figure 5.34 Authentication settings allow you to set the authentication mechanism used to authenticate users with the portal server. You can choose LDAP, OpenSSO, or any other appropriate authentication provider supported by Liferay Portal.

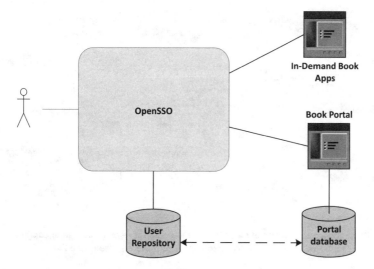

Figure 5.35   OpenSSO authenticates the user against the User Repository, and if the authentication is successful, it allows access to the Book Portal and In-Demand Book Apps. The User Repository contains user credentials, and it's in sync with the user information stored in the Liferay Portal database.

You can create a user in the User Repository either by manually creating users using the OpenSSO user interface or by using an LDAP service to authenticate users. When using OpenSSO with Liferay Portal, if you create a user in the User Repository, the user's information is persisted in Liferay Portal after authentication, if it doesn't already exist.

> **NOTE** The Liferay Portal wiki (http://www.liferay.com/community/wiki) provides information on how to integrate Liferay Portal with OpenSSO and other SSO products. Integrating OpenSSO with Liferay Portal is accomplished in a few simple steps, which include dropping an OpenSSO WAR file in Liferay Portal and performing configuration in Liferay Portal.

Now let's look at how you can associate the default user role of BookUser with registered users of Book Portal.

5.4.2   *Specifying the default user associations*

Liferay Portal, by default, assigns User and PowerUser roles to all users who register with the portal. In Book Portal, the registered users should get the default role of BookUser.

To assign the default role of BookUser to registered users, select the Users option from the list of configuration options displayed on the Settings page, as shown in

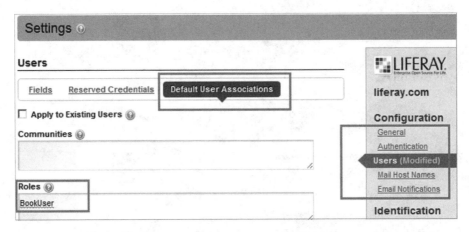

Figure 5.36   The `BookUser` **role is specified as the default role for users. You can associate multiple default roles with a registered user by specifying each role on a separate line.**

figure 5.36. Go to the Default User Associations configuration option, and specify `BookUser` as the default role of the user.

This completes our discussion of how to develop a portal using Liferay Portal server's built-in portlets and the custom Book Catalog portlet.

One of the Book Portal requirements is to allow administrators to easily change the look and feel of the web portal, and also the layout of portal pages. This requirement is typical in web portal development projects. Most portal servers provide some mechanism to simplify the creation of new layouts and portal themes. In the next section, we'll look at how Liferay Portal lets you do this with the help of the Liferay Plugins SDK.

5.5   *Developing with the Liferay Plugins SDK*

The Liferay Plugins SDK (software development kit) is a Liferay Portal–specific SDK that provides a development environment for themes, layouts, and portlets. In this section we'll discuss how to develop themes and layouts using the Liferay Plugins SDK.

You can download the Liferay Plugins SDK from the Additional Files page of the Liferay Portal website (http://www.liferay.com/downloads/liferay-portal/additional-files) and extract the zip file to a location in your local filesystem. Because we're using Liferay Portal 6.0.5 Community Edition, download Liferay Plugins SDK CE GA3 (which corresponds to Liferay Portal 6.0.5) under the Files for Developers section of the web page.

> **NOTE**   Every release of Liferay Portal server has a corresponding Plugins SDK, specific to that release. It's recommended that you use the Plugins SDK specific to the Liferay Portal release for which you're creating your custom portlets, layouts, and themes. For instance, if you're using Liferay Portal Server 6.0.5, you should use Plugins SDK 6.0.5.

The directories in the Plugins SDK that are important for developing layouts and themes include the following:

- *themes*—The themes folder contains custom themes. It provides scripts to create your own custom theme folder structure, to create a WAR file for the theme, and to hot deploy it on the portal server.
- *layouttpl*—The layout template folder contains the custom page layout templates. It provides scripts to create your own custom layout folder structure, to create a WAR file for the layout, and to hot deploy it on the portal server.

Before you begin creating custom themes and layouts, you must configure the Plugins SDK to work with your Liferay Portal installation.

5.5.1 *Configuring the Plugins SDK*

It's important to configure the Plugins SDK because it works in the context of the Liferay Portal server you're using.

You configure the Plugins SDK by creating a properties file that has a name following this convention:

```
build.<user-id>.properties
```

In this name, `<user-id>` is the userid with which you're logged into your computer. For instance, if you log in to your laptop with the userid of `peters`, your properties file should have the name build.peters.properties.

You create this properties file in the home directory of your Plugins SDK installation, as shown in figure 5.37. This figure shows the Plugins SDK directory structure for Liferay Portal 6.x. The portlets directory is used when you want to create plugin portlets for Liferay Portal. The build.asarin .properties file is a custom properties file that overrides the properties defined in the build.properties file. Because Plugins SDK works in combination with the Liferay Portal server, the properties that you'll usually override in the custom properties file are those that identify directories of the Liferay Portal installation.

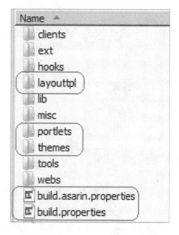

Figure 5.37 The Plugins SDK directory structure. The build.asarin.properties file represents a custom properties file that overrides the configuration in the build.properties file.

Once you've created your custom properties file, you can define the following properties in it:

```
app.server.dir=C:\\liferay-portal-6.0.5\\tomcat-6.0.26
app.server.lib.portal.dir=C:\\liferay-portal-6.0.5\\tomcat-
➥6.0.26\\webapps\\ROOT\\WEB-INF\\lib
auto.deploy.dir=C:\\liferay-portal-6.0.5\\deploy
app.server.portal.dir=C:\\liferay-portal-6.0.5\\
➥tomcat-6.0.26\\webapps\\ROOT
```

The preceding properties file is specific to Windows. If you're using a Linux or Mac OS X system, your properties file should look something like this:

```
app.server.dir=/liferay-portal-6.0.5/tomcat-6.0.26
app.server.lib.portal.dir=/liferay-portal-6.0.5/tomcat-
⇒6.0.26/webapps/ROOT/WEB-INF/lib
auto.deploy.dir=/liferay-portal-6.0.5/deploy
app.server.portal.dir=/liferay-portal-6.0.5/
⇒tomcat-6.0.26/webapps/ROOT
```

Table 5.1 describes the properties defined in the preceding code.

Table 5.1   Properties defined in the custom properties file

Property	Description
app.server.dir	The installation directory of the Liferay Portal server. If you're using a Liferay-Tomcat bundle, this property refers to the Tomcat installation directory.
app.server.lib.portal.dir	The location of the libraries used by Liferay Portal server. If you're using a Liferay-Tomcat bundle, this property refers to the ${app.server.dir}/ROOT/WEB-INF/lib directory.
auto.deploy.dir	The hot deploy directory for Liferay Portal. This is the deploy directory of Liferay Portal, as mentioned in chapter 1.
app.server.portal.dir	The web application directory of the Liferay Portal installation. If you're using a Liferay-Tomcat bundle, this property refers to the ${app.server.dir}/ROOT directory.

To create themes and layouts using the Plugins SDK, you also need to install an Ant build tool and add its bin directory to the PATH variable, as shown here:

```
set ANT_HOME=C:\apache-ant-1.7.1
set PATH=%PATH%;%ANT_HOME%\bin
```

If you're using a Linux or Mac OS X system, export the $PATH as shown here:

```
export ANT_HOME=/apache-ant-1.7.1
export PATH=$PATH:$ANT_HOME/bin
```

Now that you've configured the Plugins SDK, you're ready to create a theme for Book Portal.

5.5.2   *Developing portal themes*

Portal themes let you customize the look and feel of a portal, and every portal server provides a mechanism to allow portal developers to create custom themes. For instance, Liferay Portal provides the Plugins SDK, and Jetspeed provides a similar directory structure that you can use to create custom themes. The portlet specification doesn't define a standard way to develop portal themes, so any themes you develop will be portal server–specific.

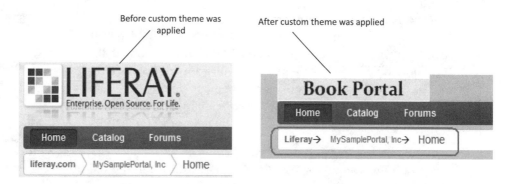

Figure 5.38   A Book Portal page that uses a custom theme. The background color is grey, the company logo is no longer the default Liferay Portal logo, and the breadcrumbs image looks like an arrow and not like an angle bracket (>) character.

In this section, we'll look at

- How to change the background color of the portal page in Liferay Portal
- How to change the default breadcrumbs image in Liferay Portal
- How to add JavaScript files as part of the portal theme so that there's a single copy of the JavaScript file included in a portal page

We'll also look at how to deploy a theme and set it for a portal. In this section, your customized portal page will end up looking like what you see in figure 5.38.

To modify the company logo, all you need to do is upload a new logo using the control panel. Earlier in this chapter, figure 5.4 showed where you could upload a logo for the organization when it was created in Liferay Portal.

> **CODE REFERENCE**   The Book Portal theme described in this section is available in the ch5_book-portal-theme.zip file in the book's source code. Extracting the contents of the zip file creates a book-portal-theme folder. Copy the book-portal-theme folder into the themes folder of your Liferay Plugins SDK folder, and execute the `ant deploy` command from the book-portal-theme folder to deploy the theme in your Liferay Portal server.

The default Liferay Portal themes are located in the classic folder of the Liferay Portal installation:

```
${app.server.dir}\webapps\ROOT\html\themes\classic
```

Figure 5.39 shows the directory structure of this classic directory. This figure shows that the classic folder contains five subdirectories: _diffs, css, images, js, and templates. The _diffs directory mirrors the structure of the classic folder and overrides theme files. The _diffs directory contains *only* the folders and files that need to be overridden. For instance, if you want to override the CSS elements defined in the custom.css file in the css folder, you should first create a css folder in the _diffs directory, and then create a custom.css file inside it.

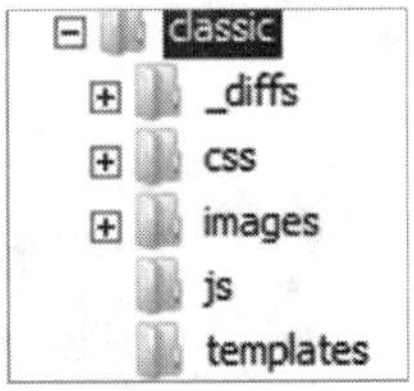

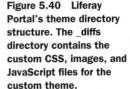

Now that you have an understanding of Liferay Portal themes, let's look at how the custom theme in the ch5_book-portal-theme.zip file was created for Book Portal. If you copied the book-portal-theme folder to the themes directory of Liferay Plugins SDK, then remove the book-portal-theme folder.

Figure 5.39 Subdirectories of the classic folder, which contains the default Liferay Portal themes

To create themes for Liferay Portal server, go to the themes directory in the Plugins SDK, and issue the following command:

```
create book-portal "Book Portal Theme"
```

If you're using a Linux or Mac OS X system, to execute the create.sh shell script located in themes folder, you first need to execute the chmod command, as shown here:

```
chmod +x create.sh
```

Now, execute create.sh shell script from themes folder, as shown here:

```
./create.sh book-portal "Book Portal Theme"
```

The create command creates a book-portal-theme project for the new theme with the title Book Portal Theme. Figure 5.40 shows the book-portal-theme project's directory structure.

The docroot directory of the book-portal-theme project contains _diffs and WEB-INF directories. The _diffs subdirectory of docroot is where you'll put your CSS and image files.

Initially all the directories are empty, except the WEB-INF directory, which contains the liferay-plugin-package.properties file, which contains theme information that can be changed, such as name, author, and so on.

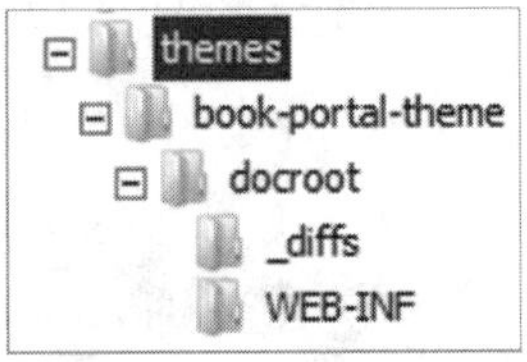

Figure 5.40 Liferay Portal's theme directory structure. The _diffs directory contains the custom CSS, images, and JavaScript files for the custom theme.

You can add custom theme files in the _diffs directory to create a theme for Book Portal. The _diffs directory of the book-portal-theme project must be a mirror image of the classic directory of the Liferay Portal installation, which contains the default Liferay Portal themes.

Let's now look at how you can go about changing the default background color of portal pages and change the breadcrumbs image.

CHANGING THE BACKGROUND COLOR OF A PORTAL PAGE

Let's say the custom theme of the Book Portal changes the background color of the pages to grey. The custom.css file in the css subdirectory of the classic folder contains the CSS element that defines the background color of a portal page, as shown here:

```
body {
    background: #EEF0F2;
    font-size: 11px;
}
```

You need to change the value of background attribute to #CCCCCC, as shown here:

```
body {
    background: #CCCCCC;
    font-size: 11px;
}
```

To change the background color, you first need to create a css subfolder in the _diffs directory of the book-portal-theme project. That's because you need to mirror the folder structure of the classic folder that contains the default Liferay Portal themes.

Create a css folder inside the _diffs directory of the book-portal-theme project, and copy the custom.css file from ${app.server.dir}\webapps\ROOT\html\themes\classic\css to book-portal-theme_diffs\css. You *copy* the file because you only want to change the body element of custom.css and keep the other CSS elements. After you've copied the file, change the body CSS element as previously described.

CHANGING THE DEFAULT BREADCRUMBS IMAGE

The default breadcrumbs image used in Liferay Portal is specified in the custom_common.css file (inside the css directory of the classics folder). To change the image, copy the custom_common.css file to the _diffs directory of your custom theme folder, and change the url element of the following CSS class to point to your custom breadcrumbs image:

```
.site-breadcrumbs li span {
    background: url(../images/common/breadcrumbs.png) no-repeat 100% 50%;
    display: block;
    padding: 0.5em 15px 0.5em 0;
}
```

In the case of the custom Book Portal theme, the new breadcrumbs image represents a right arrow and is located in the _diffs/images directory of your theme project, with the name my_breadcrumbs.png. You need to change the url element of the preceding CSS class to reflect the new breadcrumbs image, as shown here:

```
.site-breadcrumbs li span {
    background: url(../images/common/
    ➥my_breadcrumbs.png) no-repeat 100% 50%;
    display: block;
    padding: 0.5em 15px 0.5em 0;
}
```

Now you can create an images directory inside the _diffs directory of your theme project, and copy the my_breadcrumbs.png file.

The last, optional, step in creating the theme is to provide a thumbnail image for the theme. The image is displayed, along with the name of the theme, on the theme-selection Liferay Portal page.

> **NOTE** The name of the theme's thumbnail image must be thumbnail.png and it must be located in the images directory, and not one of its subdirectories.

ADDING JAVASCRIPT FILES AS PART OF THE PORTAL THEME

To add JavaScript files as part of the portal theme in Liferay, you need to do the following:

1 Create a js subfolder in the _diffs directory of the book-portal-theme project. Again, this is because you need to mirror the folder structure of the classic folder that contains the default Liferay Portal themes.

2 Add your custom JavaScript files to the js folder. Let's say you want to use jQuery in your portlets and you want only a single copy of jquery-1.5.2.min.js in your portal page. To do so, download jquery-1.5.2.min.js (http://code.jquery.com/jquery-1.5.2.min.js) and copy it to the js subfolder of _diffs.

3 Create a templates subfolder in the _diffs directory of the book-portal-theme project, and copy the portal_normal.vm file from ${app.server.dir}\webapps\ROOT\html\themes\classic\templates to book-portal-theme_diffs\templates. You *copy* the file because portal_normal.vm defines the overall structure of the portal page and specifies the JavaScript files that are included in the portal page. After you've copied the file, add a <script> element to the <head> section, as shown here:

```
<head>
    <title>$the_title - $company_name</title>
    <script type="text/javascript"
        src="$javascript_folder/jquery-1.5.2.min.js"></script>
    $theme.include($top_head_include)
</head>
```

In the preceding code, the <script> element adds the jquery-1.5.2.min.js JavaScript file to the portal page. The $javascript_folder variable refers to the directory containing the JavaScript files.

If the JavaScript files that you want to add to your portal page are hosted externally, you don't need to create the js subfolder in the _diffs directory. You only need to change the portal_normal.vm file to refer to the externally hosted JavaScript files. For instance, you could use the following <script> element in portal_normal.vm to refer to the jquery-1.5.2.min.js file from Google CDN:

```
<script type="text/javascript"
    src="http://ajax.googleapis.com/ajax/libs/
    ➥jquery/1.5.2/jquery.min.js">
</script>
```

DEPLOYING AND SETTING A PORTAL THEME

Now you're ready to deploy your custom theme using the following command:

```
ant deploy
```

When you issue the ant deploy command from within the themes folder of the Plugins SDK, it builds all the custom themes projects you've created and copies the generated WAR files to the hot deploy directory of your Liferay Portal installation. If you execute the ant deploy command from a particular folder inside the themes folder, only the theme represented by that folder is deployed.

The deployed theme can be viewed: log in as the Book Portal administrator, select the Manage > Page option from the dock-bar, and select the Look and Feel tab. If the theme was successfully deployed, you'll see the newly added theme, as shown in figure 5.41.

Figure 5.41   The custom Book Portal theme is displayed along with other themes.

To use the Book Portal theme, select the Manage > Page option from the dockbar. You'll see the Look and Feel tab for the entire MySamplePortal, Inc portal and for individual pages, as shown in figure 5.42.

Select the Look and Feel tab to view available themes in the portal, and select Book Portal Theme to modify the look and feel of the portal. (Figure 5.42 shows that the Look and Feel tab is also displayed for individual portal pages, which means you can set the theme of an individual portal page.)

Next, we'll look at how you can change the layout of your portlets on a portal page by creating a custom layout template.

5.5.3   Developing page layout templates

Portals use layout templates to define the layout of a portal page. Portal servers come with their own predefined layout templates, but they also allow you to create custom layouts. Like themes, layouts are portal-specific and can't be reused across different portal servers.

In this section, you'll see how to create a custom layout for the Book Portal using the Liferay Plugins SDK. The custom layout splits the horizontal space on a page into 80/20 size, where the left side gets 80 percent of the horizontal space and the right side gets 20 percent.

Figure 5.42   The Look and Feel tab allows you to change the theme for the portal or for an individual portal page.

CODE REFERENCE   The two-column layout described in this section is available in the ch5_2-column-layouttpl.zip file of the source code that accompanies this book. Extracting the contents of the zip file creates a 2-column-layouttpl folder. Copy this 2-column-layouttpl folder into the layouttpl folder of your Liferay Plugins SDK folder. Then, execute the `ant deploy` command from the 2-column-layouttpl folder to deploy the layout in your Liferay Portal server.

Let's now look at how to create the layout defined in the ch5_2-column-layouttpl.zip file. If you copied the 2-column-layouttpl folder to the layouttpl directory of Liferay Plugins SDK, remove the 2-column-layouttpl folder.

To create a layout template, go to the layouttpl folder of the Plugins SDK, and execute the following command:

```
create 2-column "2 columns (80/20)"
```

The `create` command creates a layout template project named 2-column-layouttpl and titled "2 columns (80/20)". Figure 5.43 shows the contents of the docroot directory of the 2-column-layouttpl project.

The following files are shown in figure 5.43:

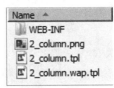

- 2_column.png—The image that's shown when Liferay Portal displays the list of available layouts. You can replace this default image if you want to.

Figure 5.43   Contents of the 2-column-layouttpl project's docroot directory

- 2_column.tpl—The layout template file, which contains the layout of the template.
- 2_column.wap.tpl—The layout template file for WAP.

NOTE   Portal servers provide support for mobile devices, which is why there's a WAP version of the layout template.

The next step is to write the 80/20 layout logic in the 2_column.tpl file. The content of the 2_column.tpl file that creates a 80/20 layout template is as follows:

```
<div class="columns-3" id="content-wrapper">
 <table class="portlet-layout">
 <tr>
 <td class="aui-w80 portlet-column portlet-column-first" id="column-1">
   $processor.processColumn("column-1",
        ➥"portlet-column-content portlet-column-content-first")
 </td>
   <td class="aui-w20 portlet-column portlet-column-last" id="column-2">
   $processor.processColumn("column-2","portlet-column-content
        ➥portlet-column-content-last")
 </td>
 </tr>
 </table>
</div>
```

The layout template contains HTML and processing instructions. Notice the use of the `aui-w20` and `aui-w80` classes to represent the space taken up by each `<td>` tag. The `id` and `class` elements must be used as shown in the preceding template code. The `portlet-column-first` CSS class is represents the first column in the layout, and the `portlet-column-last` CSS class represents the last column.

Similarly, you could create a three-column 20/60/20 template as shown here:

```
<div class="columns-3" id="content-wrapper">
 <table class="portlet-layout">
  <tr>
   <td class="aui-w20 portlet-column portlet-column-first" id="column-1">
    $processor.processColumn("column-1",
       ➥"portlet-column-content portlet-column-content-first")
   </td>
   <td class="aui-w60 portlet-column portlet-column-first" id="column-2">
    $processor.processColumn("column-2", "portlet-column-content")
   </td>
   <td class="aui-w20 portlet-column portlet-column-last" id="column-3">
    $processor.processColumn("column-3","portlet-column-content
       ➥portlet-column-content-last")
   </td>
  </tr>
 </table>
</div>
```

You can see that creating a new layout template in Liferay Portal is very intuitive.

You're now ready to deploy your layout template on Liferay Portal. To do so, execute the following command from the layouttpl directory:

```
ant deploy
```

This will generate a WAR file for the layout template project and copy it to the hot deploy folder of Liferay Portal.

If the layout is successfully deployed, you can verify that the template is available by going to dockbar and selecting Manage > Page Layout. This will display the list of all available layout templates, as shown in figure 5.44.

Selecting a layout template from the list of available templates changes the layout of the current portal page, and the portlets are rearranged on the page.

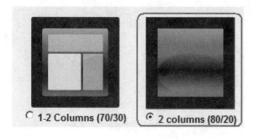

○ 1-2 Columns (70/30)   ◉ 2 columns (80/20)

Figure 5.44   The newly created "2 columns (80/20)" layout template is available in the list of layout templates.

5.6   *Summary*

In this chapter, you saw how the choice of a portal server can impact the time and effort required to develop and deploy a web portal. The key to quickly developing a web portal is having a good understanding of the target portal server's features. You saw (in the Book Catalog portlet) that you can use the features offered by built-in portlets to build your custom portlets, and in some scenarios you can simply use built-in portlets to address business requirements.

In the next chapter, we'll look at the portlet tag library, which can help you perform some basic tasks in the JSP page itself, like creating portlet URLs.

Using the portlet tag library

This chapter covers

- Accessing portlet objects in JSPs
- Creating portlet URLs in JSPs
- Creating portlet-specific HTML elements

Having read the past five chapters and learned the basics of working with portlets, you may be wondering if there's an easy way to create portlet URLs or to access portlet API objects in JSP. Well, you're about to find out.

In previous chapters, you used JSP as the view technology for displaying portlet content. In servlet-based web applications, JSPs included or forwarded by servlets have access to certain implicit variables like request, session, and so on. You used these in the Book Catalog portlet to display user information (like the name of the logged-in user) and the book catalog. You also created render and action URLs programmatically in the portlet's render method by using the RenderResponse object.

The portlet tag library is a set of tags that provide included and forwarded JSPs with access to portlet-specific objects (such as RenderRequest, RenderResponse, and PortletSession) and it also makes it simpler for JSPs to create portlet URLs. In this chapter, we'll discuss the portlet tag library tags, their attributes, and their usage in developing portlets. You'll rebuild the Book Catalog portlet so that it uses portlet tag library tags.

We'll look at the following tags and their attributes:

- `<defineObjects>`—Used to make portlet objects available to the JSP page
- `<renderURL>`, `<actionURL>`, and `<resourceURL>`—Used to create render, action, and resource portlet URLs, respectively
- `<param>`—Used to add parameters to portlet URLs
- `<namespace>`—Used to create HTML elements that are specific to the portlet instance
- `<property>`—Used to add properties to portlet URLs

WARNING   Portlet 2.0 supports the JSP 2.0 specification, so if you're using JSP tags that use new features of JSP 2.1 (like the `@Resource` annotation to inject a database connection in your tag implementation class), the tags may not work.

Let's first look at the requirements of the Book Catalog portlet, which we'll use as a reference for understanding the different portlet tag library tags.

6.1   *Using the tag library to build a Book Catalog portlet*

Let's redefine the requirements for the Book Catalog portlet, developed in chapters 3 and 4, to make use of portlet tag library tags. Figure 6.1 shows the modified Home page of the Book Catalog portlet, which you'll create in this chapter. You'll be coming back to this figure every so often in this chapter.

The Book Catalog portlet shows hyperlinks ❶ to print the book catalog, view help information, and set preferences. The Print, Help, and Preferences hyperlinks must be created using the portlet tag library.

The Book Name and Author Name fields ❷ are used to enter the book search criteria. The scope of these fields must be restricted to the Book Catalog portlet; other portlets in the same portal page must not be able to access the Book Name and Author Name fields using JavaScript.

Clicking the Search button ❸ submits the search HTML form (which consists of the Book Name and Author Name fields) whose `action` attribute refers to the action URL of the Book Catalog portlet. The action URL to which the search form is submitted must be created using portlet tag library tags.

Hyperlinks must be created (❹ through ❽) using portlet tag library tags. Clicking the Add Book button ❾ submits the book catalog form whose `action` attribute refers to the render URL of the Book Catalog portlet. The render URL to which the book catalog form is submitted must be created using portlet tag library tags.

Finally, the debugging information is printed ❿ by the Book Catalog portlet to show the value of the `myaction` request attribute, the current portlet mode, the

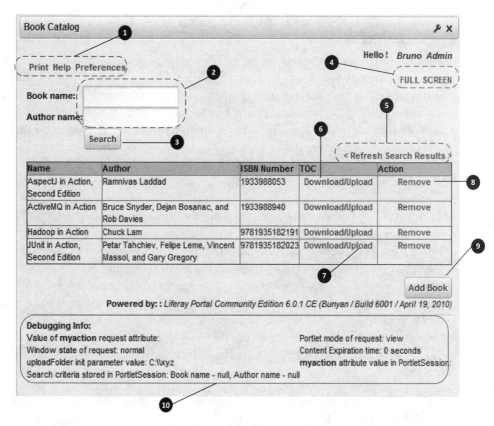

Figure 6.1　The Book Catalog portlet's Home page showing debugging information, including the values of the `myaction` request attribute, the `myaction` session attribute, and the `uploadFolder` portlet initialization parameter, along with the current portlet mode, the window state, and so on

current window state, the value of the `uploadFolder` portlet initialization parameter, and so on. All the debugging information printed by the Book Catalog portlet must be generated exclusively in the JSP page itself.

CODE REFERENCE　The source code for the Book Catalog portlet discussed in this chapter is located in the ch6_TagLibrary folder. Before you build or deploy the portlet, make sure you change the value of the `uploadFolder` initialization parameter in the portlet deployment descriptor. Also, before you build the project, set the `liferay.portal.home` property in the build.properties file to point to your Liferay Portal installation directory.

Now that you know what you're going to create in this chapter, let's begin our discussion of the portlet tag library with one of the most important tags, `<defineObjects>`.

6.2   Accessing portlet-specific objects using <defineObjects>

JSPs in previous chapters relied on JSP implicit objects to achieve their functionality. It's perfectly fine to use them in your JSP pages, but your JSP will be dealing with servlet-specific objects (like `HttpServletRequest` and `HttpSession`) and not portlet-specific objects (like `RenderRequest` and `PortletSession`).

You saw in chapter 3 that if you add an attribute to `RenderRequest`, it's mirrored by `HttpServletRequest` and vice versa, and the same applies to `HttpSession` and `PortletSession`. So what difference does it makes if you use portlet-specific objects in JSPs? There are subtle but important differences between the servlet and portlet APIs. For instance, in your JSP page, you can't use `HttpServletResponse` to create a portlet URL; only the `RenderResponse` object provides methods to create portlet URLs. Similarly, `HttpServletRequest` can't provide information about the portlet mode and window state; the `PortletRequest` provides methods to obtain window state and portlet mode. The objects look similar, but they offer slightly different functionality.

In general, your JSP pages will use a combination of portlet and servlet objects to generate content. For instance, if you want to set the expiration time for the content in the JSP page, you'll use the `RenderResponse` portlet object. If you need to obtain the value of an `APPLICATION_SCOPE` portlet session attribute, you may prefer to use `session` (which refers to the `HttpSession` object) or the `sessionScope` JSP implicit object (which is a `java.util.Map` of session attributes stored in the `HttpSession` object).

> **NOTE**   JSPs included by portlets have access to JSP implicit objects because a portlet application is also a web application.

Let's look at the different portlet objects that are made available to included and forwarded JSP pages using the `<defineObjects>` tag.

6.2.1   Making portlet objects available with <defineObjects>

The `<defineObjects>` name suggests that it can be used by JSP developers to define custom objects in their JSP pages, but that's not the case. The portlet tag library's `<defineObjects>` tag provides JSPs with access to portlet objects like `RenderRequest`, `RenderResponse`, `PortletSession`, and so on.

Table 6.1 lists the scripting variables (and their types) that are available to JSP pages that use the `<defineObjects>` tag.

Table 6.1   Scripting variables defined by the `<defineObjects>` tag

Variable name	Variable type	Description
renderRequest, renderResponse	RenderRequest, RenderResponse	The renderRequest and renderResponse variables are available to JSP only if the JSP was included during the render request phase.

Table 6.1   Scripting variables defined by the `<defineObjects>` tag *(continued)*

Variable name	Variable type	Description
actionRequest, actionResponse	ActionRequest, ActionResponse	The `actionRequest` and `actionResponse` variables are available to JSP only if the JSP was included during the action-processing phase.
resourceRequest, resourceResponse	ResourceRequest, ResourceResponse	The `resourceRequest` and `resourceResponse` variables are available to JSP only if the JSP was included during the resource-serving phase. The `ResourceRequest` and `ResourceResponse` objects are discussed in detail in chapter 12.
eventRequest, eventResponse	EventRequest, EventResponse	The `eventRequest` and `eventResponse` variables are available to JSP only if the JSP was included during the event-processing phase. The `EventRequest` and `EventResponse` objects are discussed in detail in chapter 11.
portletConfig	PortletConfig	The `portletConfig` variable is available to JSP regardless of the request-processing phase in which it was included.
portletSession	PortletSession	The `portletSession` variable is available to JSP regardless of the request-processing phase in which it was included.
portletSession- Scope	Map<String, Object>	The `portletSessionScope` variable is used to obtain attributes stored in the `PortletSession`'s `PORTLET_SCOPE`.
portletPreferences	PortletPreferences	The `portletPreferences` variable is used to obtain portlet preferences defined for the portlet. `PortletPreferences` is discussed in detail in chapter 10.
portletPreferences Values	Map<String, String[]>	The `portletPreferencesValues` variable is used to obtain portlet preference values.

As you can see, `<defineObjects>` provides JSP pages with all the Portlet 2.0 API objects they'll ever need to use portlet-specific features. In JSP pages, you'll usually use a combination of JSP implicit objects and the implicit objects made available by the `<defineObjects>` tag. You'll probably never use the `actionRequest`, `actionResponse`, `eventRequest`, or `eventResponse` objects in your JSP pages because portlet containers ignore content written out to the response in the action- and event-processing phases.

NOTE The `<defineObjects>` tag doesn't define any attributes.

The version of the Book Catalog portlet in this chapter makes use of scripting variables introduced by the <defineObjects> tag to show the debugging information, as shown earlier in figure 6.1.

> **CODE REFERENCE** If you haven't already, you should now import the ch6_TagLibrary source code into your Eclipse workspace so you can follow along with the code references in the rest of this chapter.

Let's look at how the Book Catalog portlet uses the <defineObjects> tag to show debugging information to users.

6.2.2   *Using <defineObjects> in the Book Catalog portlet*

Listing 6.1 shows the debug.jsp page, which is included by all the JSP pages in the Book Catalog portlet. This page prints information about the portlet mode, the window state, the value of the myaction attribute from the request, the content expiration time, and so on, most of which is obtained by using scripting variables introduced by the <defineObjects> tag.

Listing 6.1   The debug.jsp page uses variables introduced by <defineObjects>.

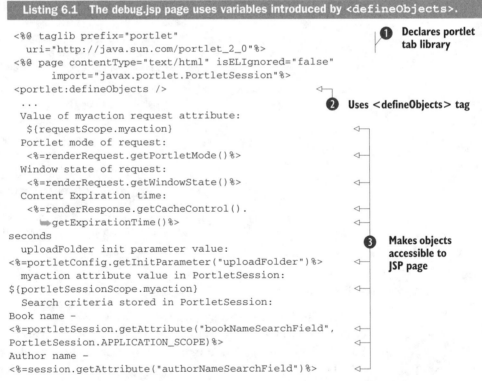

```
<%@ taglib prefix="portlet"                             ❶ Declares portlet
   uri="http://java.sun.com/portlet_2_0"%>                 tab library
<%@ page contentType="text/html" isELIgnored="false"
      import="javax.portlet.PortletSession"%>
<portlet:defineObjects />
   ...                                                  ❷ Uses <defineObjects> tag
  Value of myaction request attribute:
   ${requestScope.myaction}
  Portlet mode of request:
   <%=renderRequest.getPortletMode()%>
  Window state of request:
   <%=renderRequest.getWindowState()%>
  Content Expiration time:
   <%=renderResponse.getCacheControl().
     getExpirationTime()%>
seconds
  uploadFolder init parameter value:                   ❸ Makes objects
<%=portletConfig.getInitParameter("uploadFolder")%>       accessible to
  myaction attribute value in PortletSession:             JSP page
${portletSessionScope.myaction}
   Search criteria stored in PortletSession:
Book name -
<%=portletSession.getAttribute("bookNameSearchField",
PortletSession.APPLICATION_SCOPE)%>
Author name -
<%=session.getAttribute("authorNameSearchField")%>
```

The JSP page declares the portlet tag library using the taglib directive ❶. The value of the uri attribute is http://java.sun.com/portlet_2_0 if you want to use the Portlet 2.0 tag library. If you're using the Portlet 1.0 tag library, you should specify the value of uri as http://java.sun.com/portlet. The <defineObjects> tag in Portlet 2.0 introduced additional variables, such as `portletSessionScope`, `portletSession`, and so on, which makes it easy to develop portlets using JSP as the view technology.

The `<defineObjects>` tag ❷ is used to introduce scripting variables in the JSP page.

You can see the use of implicit JSP objects as well as objects made available to JSP ❸ by the `<defineObjects>` tag:

- The `requestScope` JSP implicit variable is used to obtain the value of the `myaction` attribute.
- The `renderRequest` variable is used to obtain the current portlet mode and window state information.
- The `renderResponse` variable is used to obtain the `CacheControl` object, which is in turn used to obtain the expiration time for the generated content.
- The `portletConfig` object is used to obtain the `uploadFolder` portlet initialization parameter.
- The `portletSessionScope` variable is used to obtain the value of the `myaction` attribute from `PortletSession`.
- The `portletSession` variable is used to obtain the value of the `book-NameSearchField` value from the `PortletSession`'s `APPLICATION_SCOPE`.
- The `session` JSP implicit variable is used to obtain the value of the `author-NameSearchField` attribute from `HttpSession`. Using the `session` JSP implicit variable makes it easy to retrieve an `APPLICATION_SCOPE` attribute stored in `PortletSession`.

Listing 6.1 demonstrates how you can make use of JSP implicit variables and variables introduced by the `<defineObjects>` tag to create JSP pages. If you browse through the pages of the Book Catalog portlet, the debugging information will change to reflect the current value of various attributes.

In earlier chapters, you created self-referencing portlet URLs using create methods defined in the `RenderResponse` interface. The portlet tag library provides `<action-URL>`, `<renderURL>`, and `<resourceURL>` tags for creating URLs in the JSP page. Let's look at these tags next.

6.3 *Using <actionURL>, <renderURL>, and <resourceURL>*

This time, what the tag names suggest is true—the `<actionURL>`, `<renderURL>`, and `<resourceURL>` tags let you create portlet URLs in the JSP page included by your portlet. These tags share some common attributes and have the same semantics, so we'll look at these common attributes in the context of the `<actionURL>` tag. In our discussions of the `<resourceURL>` and `<renderURL>` tags, we'll merely mention the common attributes that apply to these tags.

6.3.1 *Using the <actionURL> tag*

The action URL created with the `<actionURL>` tag can be used in hyperlinks or in the form tag's `action` attribute to send an action request to a portlet when a user clicks a hyperlink or submits a form. In this section, we'll take a look at the how and why of action URLs, and look at a few examples you can try yourself.

The <actionURL> tag defines attributes that let you specify additional options for the generated action URL, such as portlet mode, window state, and so on. Let's take a look at each of the <actionURL> attributes in detail.

SPECIFYING THE DESIRED WINDOW STATE

The <actionURL> tag's windowState attribute is optional, and it specifies the desired window state when the action request is received by the portlet. The windowState attribute is useful if a certain action on a portlet UI must be invoked in a particular portlet window state.

The value for the windowState attribute is case insensitive; the values MAXIMIZED and maximized are treated the same way. You can specify either a standard window state or a custom window state as the value. If the specified window state isn't supported or allowed by the portlet, an exception will be thrown.

The following <actionURL> tag shows how you can use the windowState attribute to set the portlet's window state to MAXIMIZED:

```
<portlet:actionURL windowState="maximized"/>
```

SPECIFYING THE DESIRED PORTLET MODE

The <actionURL> tag's portletMode attribute is optional, and it specifies the desired portlet mode when the action request is received by the portlet. This attribute is useful when a certain action on a portlet UI must be invoked in a particular portlet mode, such as if the portlet mode must be EDIT when setting portlet preferences (as discussed in chapter 10).

The value for the portletMode attribute is case insensitive; the values EDIT and edit are treated the same way. You can specify either a standard portlet mode or a custom portlet mode as the value. If the portletMode isn't supported or allowed, it'll result in an exception.

The following <actionURL> tag shows how you can use the portletMode attribute to set the portlet mode to EDIT:

```
<portlet:actionURL portletMode="edit"/>
```

STORING AN ACTION URL IN A VARIABLE

If you want to keep the <actionURL> tag separate from your HTML code, you should use the var attribute of the <actionURL> tag. The var attribute specifies the name of a variable (of type String) that contains the action URL generated by the <actionURL> tag. The var attribute is then used in the HTML code to refer to the action URL, as shown here:

```
<portlet:actionURL portletMode="edit" windowState="maximized" var="myUrl"/>
<form name="myForm" action="${myUrl}">
  ...
</form>
```

In the preceding code, the action URL generated by the <actionURL> tag is stored in the myUrl variable, which is later used in myForm's action attribute. If myForm is submitted, an action request is dispatched to the portlet.

It isn't always possible to use the <actionURL> tag's var attribute to store an action URL for later use in the HTML code. For instance, in figure 6.1, the Remove link is dynamic and makes use of the portlet tag library's <param> tag (discussed later in this chapter) to send the ISBN number of the book as a parameter in the action request. This means the action URL referenced by the Remove link must be created during the generation of the book catalog information in the HTML code, as shown in listing 6.2 for the Book Catalog portlet.

> **CODE REFERENCE** Refer to the home.jsp page in the ch6_TagLibrary folder to see how the <actionURL> tag is used to create dynamic links for the Upload, Download, and Remove hyperlinks.

Listing 6.2 Using `<actionURL>` to create dynamic links

```
<c:forEach var="book" items="${books}">          Iterates over       Creates
 <td>                                       ❶    books in catalog  ❷ <actionURL>
  <a class="anchor" href=                                            tag
    "<portlet:actionURL name="removeBookAction">
      <portlet:param name="isbnNumber"
        value="${book.isbnNumber}" />          ❸ Obtains ISBN
    </portlet:actionURL>"
      onclick="javascript: return confirmRemove()">
    <b><fmt:message key="label.remove" /></b>
  </a>
 </td>
 ...
</c:forEach>
```

The forEach JSTL tag ❶ iterates over books (represented by the books variable) and generates the book information, such as title, author, and ISBN number, along with the Upload, Download, and Remove hyperlinks. The <actionURL> tag ❷ is used to create the action URL referenced by the Remove hyperlink. The <param> tag ❸ is used to define a request parameter named isbnNumber, with the ISBN number of the book as its value. The isbnNumber request parameter defined for the action URL is sent to the portlet when the Remove link is clicked.

In the Book Catalog portlet, the ISBN number of a book uniquely identifies a book in the catalog. If you want to remove a book from the catalog, clicking the Remove link must send the book's ISBN number to the portlet's action method. Because you won't know the ISBN number that should be associated with the Remove link until the forEach JSTL tag starts generating the book catalog information, you must place the <actionURL> tag within the forEach JSTL tag. The var attribute isn't required in this case because the URL generated by the <actionURL> tag is used at the same place (inside the HTML anchor element) where it's defined.

SECURING AN ACTION URL

The `secure` attribute is an *optional* attribute of the `<actionURL>` tag that indicates whether the generated action URL is a secured URL (meaning it uses the HTTPS protocol) or an unsecured URL (one that uses the HTTP protocol). If the value of the `secure` attribute is `true`, the generated URL is an HTTPS URL; if the value is `false` (which is the default value), the generated URL is an HTTP URL.

The following `<actionURL>` tag shows how the `secure` attribute is used to instruct the tag implementation to generate an HTTPS URL:

```
<portlet:actionURL secure="true"/>
```

If the security setting specified by the `secure` attribute isn't supported by the portal server's current runtime environment, an exception will be thrown.

ADDING PRIVATE RENDER PARAMETERS TO AN ACTION URL

A render parameter, in general, is a request parameter that's available in the render lifecycle phase of a portlet. Public render parameters (discussed in chapter 11) are used in inter-portlet communication, and private render parameters are used by the action (or event) phase of a portlet to communicate with its render phase. For instance, the action methods of the Book Catalog portlet in chapter 4 (see the ch3_BookCatalog folder of the source code) use the `myaction` private render parameter to communicate information about the content that should be displayed in the render phase.

The `<actionURL>` tag's `copyCurrentRenderParameters` attribute is optional, and it instructs the tag implementation to add all the *private* render parameters from the request to the generated action URL as request parameters. For instance, if a private render parameter named `myparameter` exists in the request, it's added to the generated action URL as a request parameter.

This attribute is particularly useful when the render parameters set in the action or event phase need to be automatically added as *action* parameters to action URLs generated using the `<actionURL>` tag. Action parameters are request parameters that are sent to the action method, and they can be obtained in the action method using the `getParameter`, `getParameterMap`, and other such methods of the `ActionRequest` object.

> **NOTE** Private render parameters can be set in the action or event phase of a portlet using the `setRenderParameter` or `setRenderParameters` methods of `StateAwareResponse`. The private render parameters can be obtained in the render lifecycle phase using the `PortletRequest`'s `getParameter`, `getPrivateParameterMap`, `getParameterMap`, and `getParameterValues` methods.

You can set render parameters in a variety of different ways:

- By using the `setRenderParameter` or `setRenderParameters` methods of the `ActionResponse` or `EventResponse` objects in the action or event phase
- By using `<param>` tags to add a request parameter to the render URL generated with the `<renderURL>` tag (discussed later in this chapter)

- By using the `PortletURL` object's `setParameter` method (when the PortletURL represents a render URL)

If an HTML form's `action` attribute refers to the render URL of the portlet, submitting the form will also send the HTML form elements (such as text fields) as render parameters.

In the Book Catalog portlet in chapter 4, when a user clicks the Upload hyperlink to upload the TOC for a book, the ISBN number of the book is sent as a render parameter (named `isbnNumber`). The `BookCatalogPortlet` then saves the ISBN number in `PortletSession`. When the TOC is uploaded, the corresponding action method in the Book Catalog portlet retrieves the ISBN number from `Portlet-Session` and uses it to name the uploaded TOC file. The sequence diagram in figure 6.2 illustrates this process.

The user clicks the Upload link ❶ to upload the TOC of the book (see figure 6.1). The Upload link sends a render request to the Book Catalog portlet, and the `isbn-Number` render parameter is sent as part of that request.

The Book Catalog portlet implementation class (the `BookCatalogPortlet` class in the ch3_BookCatalog folder) retrieves the render parameter from the render request (using the `RenderRequest` object's `getParameter` method) and stores it ❷

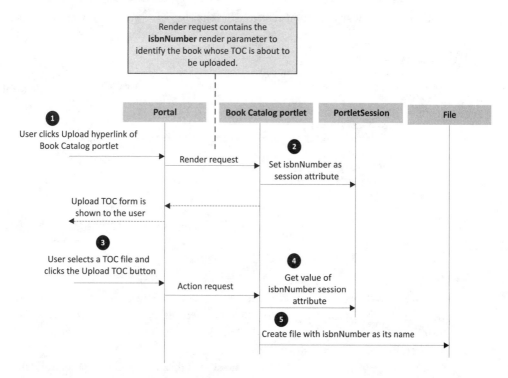

Figure 6.2 The Book Catalog portlet implementation (from chapter 4), where the `PortletSession` stores the ISBN of the book for which the user wants to upload a TOC. The book's ISBN is used to name the uploaded TOC file.

in the `PortletSession` (using the `PortletSession` object's `setAttribute` method). The Book Catalog portlet then displays a form so the user can upload the selected book's TOC.

The user selects the TOC file on the upload TOC form ❸ and clicks the Upload TOC button to upload the file. When the upload TOC form is submitted, it sends an action request to the Book Catalog portlet.

The Book Catalog portlet implementation class ❹ retrieves the ISBN from `PortletSession`, and ❺ it creates a file with the ISBN as the name and writes the uploaded TOC file content to it.

As you can see, the book's ISBN is only required when you're uploading the TOC file. You'll now learn how you can save the effort of explicitly managing the ISBN information in `PortletSession` by using the `<actionURL>` tag's `copyCurrentRender-Parameters` attribute.

Listing 6.3 shows the uploadForm.jsp page that generates the HTML form for uploading the TOC. It uses the `<actionURL>` tag (with the `copyCurrentRender-Parameters` attribute set to true) to create an action URL to which the form is submitted when the user clicks the Upload TOC button.

Listing 6.3   The uploadForm.jsp file

```
<portlet:actionURL name="uploadTocAction"              ❶ Creates
  var="uploadTocActionUrl"                                 action URL
  copyCurrentRenderParameters="true"/>
<form name="uploadTocForm" method="post"
  action="${uploadTocActionUrl}"                         ❷ Sets action URL as
  enctype="multipart/form-data">                            action attribute value
  <table>
   <tr>
     <td><b>TOC:</b></td>
     <td><input type="file" name="tocFile" /></td>
   </tr>
   <tr align="center">
     <td colspan="2">
       <input type="submit" value="Upload TOC" />
     </td>
   </tr>
  </table>
  ...
</form>
```

The `<actionURL>` tag is used ❶ to create an action URL with the `copyCurrent-RenderParameters` attribute's value set to true. When the uploadForm.jsp file is included by the Book Catalog portlet, the render parameters from the request are added to the generated action URL as action parameters. The generated action URL is stored in the `uploadTocActionUrl` variable.

The value of the `uploadTocActionUrl` variable is specified ❷ as the value of the form tag's `action` attribute. When the user clicks the Upload TOC button, the form is submitted to the action URL identified by the `uploadTocActionUrl` variable.

In figure 6.2, you saw that the render request sent to the Book Catalog portlet contains the `isbnNumber` render parameter. If you're using the uploadForm.jsp shown in listing 6.3, the `isbnNumber` render parameter is added to `uploadTocAction-Url` as an action parameter (because the `<actionURL>` tag specifies the value of the `copyCurrentRenderParameters` attribute as `true`). Now, if the upload TOC form is submitted, the corresponding action method will be able to receive the book's ISBN as an action parameter.

The sequence diagram in figure 6.3 shows how the `<actionURL>` tag's `copyCurrent-RenderParameters` attribute can be used instead of `PortletSession` to provide the book's ISBN to the action method responsible for uploading the TOC.

The Book Catalog portlet renders the `uploadForm` JSP page ❶. The `<actionURL>` tag (identified by the `uploadTocActionUrl` variable) in the uploadForm.jsp page copies the render parameters from the request as action parameters in the generated action URL, including `isbnNumber`. Then, when the upload TOC form is submitted, the action request sent to the Book Catalog portlet ❷ contains `isbnNumber`.

The action method responsible for uploading the book's TOC ❸ retrieves the `isbnNumber` action parameter from the action request (by using the `ActionRequest`'s `getParameter` method). The action method responsible for uploading the book's

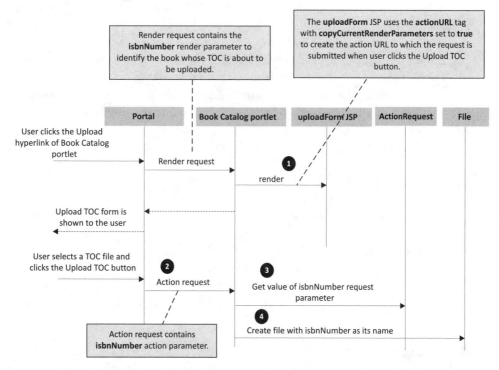

Figure 6.3 This Book Catalog portlet implementation makes use of the `<actionURL>` tag's `copyCurrentRenderParameters` attribute to send the book's ISBN to the action method responsible for uploading the book's TOC. The book's ISBN is used to name the uploaded TOC file.

TOC ❹ uses the ISBN obtained from the `isbnNumber` action parameter to create a file with the same name.

The `copyCurrentRenderParameters` attribute is an effective way to add render parameters to a JSP page's action *and* render URLs. The downside to using `copy-CurrentRenderParameters` is that you can't specify which render parameters should be added to the generated action URL.

ESCAPING XML IN A GENERATED ACTION URL

The `<actionURL>` tag's `escapeXML` attribute indicates whether characters like &, >, <, and so on, are converted into their corresponding character entity codes, like `&amp;`, `&gt;`, `&lt;`, and so on. If a portlet relies on a URL generated by the `<actionURL>` tag that isn't XML-escaped, you should set this attribute's value to `false`. The default value for the `escapeXML` attribute is `true`. Refer to section 3.7.3 of chapter 3 for more about escaping XML in portlet URLs.

SPECIFYING AN ACTION NAME

The `<actionURL>` tag's `name` attribute lets you specify the name of the action to which the generated action URL corresponds. The default implementation of the `Generic-Portlet` class's `processAction` method uses the value of the `javax.portlet.Action` request parameter to identify the action method that needs to be invoked. If you specify the `name` attribute of the `<actionURL>` tag, it effectively adds a parameter named `javax.action.Action` to the generated action URL.

For instance, if the value of the `name` attribute is `myAction`, the default implementation of the `GenericPortlet` class's `processAction` method dispatches the request to a method annotated with `@ProcessAction(name="myAction")`.

In figure 6.1, the Full Screen and Remove hyperlinks refer to action URLs created using the `<actionURL>` tag. When you click the Search button, the form is submitted to an action URL created using the `<actionURL>` tag.

Let's now look at the `<renderURL>` tag, which is used to create render URLs.

6.3.2   *Using the <renderURL> tag*

The `<renderURL>` tag is used to create render URLs in JSP pages included by portlets. You can specify the following attributes in the `<renderURL>` tag: `windowState`, `portlet-Mode`, `var`, `secure`, `copyCurrentRenderParameters`, and `escapeXML`. The semantics of these attributes is same for the `<actionURL>` tag.

In figure 6.1, the Print, Help, Preferences, Refresh Search Results, and Upload hyperlinks refer to render URLs created using the `<renderURL>` tag. When you click the Add Book button, the form is submitted to a render URL created using the `<renderURL>` tag.

6.3.3   *Using the <resourceURL> tag*

A portlet that implements the `ResourceServingPortlet` interface (which will be discussed in chapter 12) can make use of resource URLs to serve static resources, such as binary files. A portlet class's `serveResource` method (defined in the

ResourceServingPortlet interface) is invoked when a request is sent to the portlet using its resource URL. Like action and render URLs, you can use resource URLs in hyperlinks or in a form tag's action attribute, depending upon your application's requirements.

The <resourceURL> tag accepts the following *optional* attributes: var, secure, escapeXML, id, and cacheability. The semantics of the var, secure, and escapeXML attributes is same as in the <renderURL> and <actionURL> tags.

Let's look at the <resourceURL> tag's id and cacheability attributes.

IDENTIFYING RESOURCES

The id attribute is used to identify the resource that should be served by the portlet. For instance, if you want to download a file named samples.doc from folder myfolder, you could specify this in the <resourceURL> tag as shown here:

```
<portlet:resourceURL id="myfolder/samples.doc "/>
```

The id provided in the <resourceURL> tag can be accessed by the portlet in the serveResource method to read the samples.doc file and write it to the portlet response.

CACHING RESOURCES

The cacheability attribute is used to specify the cache level for the resource URL. The attribute can take the following possible values: FULL, PORTLET, or PAGE; the default value is PAGE.

In figure 6.1, the Download link is used to download a book's table of contents, so it refers to a resource URL. In chapter 12, we'll discuss in detail how the <resourceURL> tag can be used to download a book's TOC.

6.4   *Adding parameters to portlet URLs using <param>*

Request parameters play an important role in sending information to the portlet class for request handling. For instance, in figure 6.1, when a user clicks the Search button, the book title and author name information must be sent to the Book Catalog portlet class as search criteria. When a user clicks the Remove link, the book's ISBN must be sent to the Book Catalog portlet class so the book can be removed.

By using <param> tags, you can add request parameters to portlet URLs that are referenced by buttons or hyperlinks and created using <renderURL>, <actionURL>, or <resourceURL> tags.

6.4.1   *Using the <param> tag*

The HTML form elements (like text fields) are available to a portlet class as request parameters when a form is submitted to the portlet's render, action, or resource URL. If you want to pass extra request parameters to the portlet class, you can use the <param> tag with <renderURL>, <actionURL>, or <resourceURL> tags, as shown here:

```
<a class="anchor" href="
 <portlet:actionURL name="removeBookAction">
     <portlet:param name="isbnNumber" value="${book.isbnNumber}" />
```

```
</portlet:actionURL>"
>
  Remove
</a>
```

In the preceding `<actionURL>` tag, the `<param>` tag has been used to add a request parameter named `isbnNumber` to the generated action URL.

A portlet class can retrieve the values of a request parameter by using the `Portlet-Request`'s `getParameter` or `getParameterValues` method. For instance, the following action method retrieves the ISBN from the `ActionRequest`:

```
@ProcessAction(name="removeBookAction")
public void removeBook(ActionRequest request, ...) {
  request.getParameter("isbnNumber");
  ...
```

The `<param>` tag can exist multiple times within the same `<renderURL>`, `<actionURL>`, or `<resourceURL>` tag. If multiple `<param>` tags are defined for the same parameter, the portlet receives an array as the value of the request parameter. For instance, consider the following `<actionURL>` tag, which contains two `<param>` tags for the same parameter named `category`.

```
<a href="
 <portlet:actionURL name="doSomething">
    <portlet:param name="category" value="Java" />
    <portlet:param name="category" value="Portlets" />
 </portlet:actionURL>"
>
 Do Something
</a>
```

The `<actionURL>` tag in the preceding code contains two `<param>` tags for the `category` parameter values `Java` and `Portlets`. A portlet class can retrieve both values by using the `PortletRequest`'s `getParameterValues` method (which returns a `String[]`), as shown here:

```
@ProcessAction(name="doSomething")
public void doingSomething(ActionRequest request, ...) {
  String[] categories = request.getParameterValues("category");
  ...
}
```

The `categories` variable will contain the request parameter values in the same sequence as they were defined in the corresponding `<actionURL>` tag; the value of `categories[0]` is `Java` and `categories[1]` is `Portlets`.

Let's now explore the attributes that can be specified for the `<param>` tag.

NOTE   You can set parameters on a portlet URL programmatically (using the `setParameter` method of `PortletURL` or `ResourceURL`) or declaratively (using the `<param>` tag of the portlet tag library). In either case, request parameters set on render, action, and resource URLs are referred to as render, action, and resource parameters, respectively.

USING <PARAM> TAG ATTRIBUTES

The <param> tag defines two *required* attributes:

- name—Specifies the name of the request parameter that you want to add to the URL
- value—Specifies the value of the request parameter

NOTE If you want a particular parameter to be added to or removed from all portlet URLs, you should consider using the PortletURLGenerationListener (discussed in section 4.6.3 of chapter 4). To remove a parameter from a URL, you can set the parameter value to null.

6.4.2 *Adding parameters using string concatenation*

In servlet-based web applications, you'll sometimes add parameters to a URL using string concatenation, as shown here:

```
someUrl = someUrl + "&category=Java";
```

In this example, someUrl represents a URL to which you're adding a parameter named category with a value of Java.

You might expect that you could add request parameters to portlet URLs using string concatenation as follows (but you can't):

- Call the toString method of PortletURL or ResourceURL and then add request parameters.
- Use the var attribute value (which refers to a string representation of the portlet URL) of the <renderURL>, <actionURL>, or <resourceURL> tag, and then add request parameters.

These approaches *must not* be followed for adding request parameters to a portlet URL.

We mentioned in chapter 2 that portlet URLs are created by the portlet container, and they're implementation-dependent. If request parameters are added using param tags or the setParameter method, the portlet container assigns internal names or encodes these parameters while generating the portlet URL. If you add request parameters using string concatenation, you're adding parameters to an already-generated portlet URL. Because the request parameters are internally managed, the newly added request parameters won't be accessible to the portlet instance.

Let's now look at the <namespace> tag, which is used to uniquely identify HTML elements and JavaScript functions in a portlet.

6.5 *Creating portlet-specific HTML elements using <namespace>*

In previous chapters, you saw that a portlet can use HTML forms (like the Search and Add Book forms of the Book Catalog portlet), JavaScript, and CSS (like the book-Catalog.js and bookCatalog.css files for the Book Catalog portlet) to render its content. The <namespace> tag generates a unique string value specific to the portlet, and you can *append* or *prepend* it to the name of a form field, JavaScript function or variable, and ID attributes of HTML elements (like HTML DIV elements) to ensure that these elements don't conflict with other page elements in the portal page.

Let's now look at some scenarios that require you to use the <namespace> tag.

6.5.1   *When to use the <namespace> tag*

Consider a scenario in which you have two portlets, the Book Catalog portlet (which you developed in chapters 3 and 4) and the User Registration portlet (developed in chapter 2), on the *same* portal page. Let's suppose that these two portlets include different JavaScript files (bookCatalog.js and userRegistration.js) containing a function with the same name, confirmSave.

The confirmSave function is defined in bookCatalog.js as shown here:

```
function confirmSave() {
  return confirm("Do you want to save Book information?");
}
```

The confirmSave function in userRegistration.js is defined as shown here:

```
function confirmSave() {
  return confirm("Do you want to save User details?");
}
```

When a user clicks a button that's supposed to invoke the confirmSave function specific to the Book Catalog portlet, either the User Registration or the Book Catalog portlet's confirmSave function will be invoked. It may happen that clicking the button of the Book Catalog portlet invokes the confirmSave function specific to the User Registration portlet or vice versa.

> **NOTE** A JavaScript global variable is a variable that's defined outside a JavaScript function and that's available to all functions defined on the HTML page. A JavaScript local variable is defined within a JavaScript function and has a local scope, which means it isn't accessible to other JavaScript functions.

To resolve the issue with duplicate JavaScript functions or global variables, you can include your JavaScript code inside an HTML <script> tag in your JSP page, and use the <namespace> portlet tag library tag to make the name of the function or global variable unique to the portlet, as shown here:

```
<script type='text/javascript'>
  var <portlet:namespace/>someVar = 10;
  function <portlet:namespace/>confirmSave() {
    return confirm("Do you want to save Book information?");
  }
</script>
```

In the preceding code, the <namespace> tag is *prefixed* to the name of the someVar global variable and to the name of the confirmSave function, making their names unique on the portal page.

NOTE   You can't add <namespace> tags to the functions and global variables defined in external JavaScript files included by your portlet. When using the HTML `<script>` tag within a JSP page included by a portlet, the <namespace> tag is processed by the JSP engine, making it available to the inline JavaScript functions and global variables.

If you now want to use the function or the global variable in your JSP, you must also use the <namespace> tag to identify the function or global variable, as shown here:

```
<a href="<portlet:actionURL name="save"/>"
onclick="javascript: return <portlet:namespace/>confirmRemove()">Save</a>
```

In the preceding code, the <namespace> tag is added to the `confirmRemove` JavaScript function call, which ensures that the JavaScript function of the same portlet is invoked.

NOTE   Even if you include multiple instances of the same portlet on a portal page, the <namespace> tag will generate a unique value for each portlet.

Because you can't use the <namespace> tag in the external JavaScript file, the only option is to make the JavaScript functions part of your JSP page. But sometimes you may not be able to include all the JavaScript functions as part of the JSP page, in which case there's no simple way to address the namespace issue. For instance, if you're using a JavaScript library like the Dojo toolkit in your JSP page, you can't copy all the functions defined by Dojo into your JSP page and add the <namespace> tag to them. The issue with externally loaded JavaScript is further compounded if portlets on a portal page use different versions of the same JavaScript library. For example, you could have two different portlets on a portal page using different versions of the Prototype JavaScript framework.

The namespace issue isn't limited to JavaScript. It's possible that external CSS files used by different portlets on the same portal page have conflicting style definitions, resulting in the wrong styles being applied to the wrong elements. In chapter 3, the Book Catalog portlet defined an `anchor` CSS class in bookCatalog.css that's used to render a hyperlink in red:

```
.anchor { text-decoration: none; color: red; }
```

A hyperlink in the Book Catalog portlet makes use of the `anchor` CSS class using the `class` attribute, as shown here:

```
<a class="anchor" href="${fullScreenUrl}">
  <b><fmt:message key="label.fullScreen" /></b>
```

It's possible that the User Registration portlet (or any other portlet on the same portal page) defines a conflicting `anchor` class. For instance, the User Registration portlet might define an `anchor` CSS class in its userRegistration.css file to show hyperlinks in green, as shown here:

```
.anchor { text-decoration: none; color: green; }
```

If conflicting CSS class definitions exist, the Book Catalog portlet may show hyperlinks in *green* or User Registration may show hyperlinks in *red*. To ensure that the correct CSS class definitions are applied to the correct portlets, you should name your CSS classes to uniquely identify the portlet they're defined for or use CSS *selectors* to confine the scope of the CSS classes to the portlet.

The following entry in bookCatalog.css shows the use of a CSS selector:

```
div.bookCatalogPortlet_ch6 .anchor { text-decoration: none; color: red; }
```

The preceding CSS entry applies to elements with the class attribute anchor and that are inside a div tag with a class attribute of bookCatalogPortlet_ch6.

You can enclose your JSP page fragment inside a div tag with a class attribute of bookCatalogPortlet_ch6 to ensure that the preceding CSS applies only to the Book Catalog portlet:

```
<div class="bookCatalogPortlet_ch6">
  <table align="left">
    <tr>
      <td><a class="anchor" href="${printModeUrl}"><b> <fmt:message
        key="label.print" /> </b></td>
        ...
    </tr>
</table>
</div>
```

In the preceding JSP code, the div tag's class attribute value of bookCatalog-Portlet_ch6 matches the CSS entry defined in bookCatalog.css, so the CSS entry will apply to the hyperlink (with class anchor) shown previously.

> **NOTE** A simpler way to avoid conflicts between CSS elements on portal pages is to use the style attribute of HTML elements to style your portlets.

If you're using Ajax (which we'll discuss in chapter 12), you may also need to uniquely identify the IDs of HTML elements and the names of HTML forms and form fields. You can easily do this by adding a <namespace> tag to an HTML element ID and to the names of form fields, as shown here:

```
<form name="<portlet:namespace/>addBookForm">
  <tr>
    <td>
      <input type="text" name="<portlet:namespace/>book"/>
    </td>
    <td>
      <div id="<portlet:namespace/>bookErrorMessage"></div>
    </td>
  </tr>
  ...
</form>
```

In chapter 14, you'll see how the div tag (shown here) will act as a placeholder for all the error messages that occur for the book text field.

Let's now look at how to retrieve form fields that use <namespace> tags in the portlet class.

6.5.2   *Obtaining form field values in the portlet class*

If you're using <namespace> tags in form fields, you must append or prepend a tag (depending upon whether you appended or prepended the <namespace> tag to the name of the form fields) to the name of the field when retrieving them in your portlet class.

Consider the following JSP fragment, which defines a text field with the name bookTitle and prepends it with the <namespace> tag:

```
<input type="text" name="<portlet:namespace/>bookTitle"/>
```

When the form containing the preceding text field is submitted, the request will contain the bookTitle field with a name that you don't know (because the <namespace> tag will generate a unique value that is prepended to the name bookTitle). To retrieve the value of the bookTitle form field in the portlet class, you need to add the namespace value (obtained using the PortletResponse's getNamespace method) to the name of the form field, as shown here:

```
@ProcessAction(name = "addBookAction")
public void addBook(ActionRequest request, ActionResponse response)
  throws PortletException, IOException {
    String bookTitle =
      request.getParameter(response.getNamespace() + "bookTitle");
    ...
}
```

In the preceding code, the value returned by the getNamespace method is added to bookTitle before retrieving the value of the bookTitle form field from the request.

You may encounter differences in how different portal servers allow you to access namespaced request parameters. Suppose you define the bookTitle text field in your JSP page as shown here:

```
<input type="text" name="<portlet:namespace/>bookTitle"/>
```

Let's see how different portal servers allow you to access this bookTitle text field in the portlet class.

LIFERAY PORTAL: ACCESSING NAMESPACED REQUEST PARAMETERS
WITHOUT THE NAMESPACE VALUE

Liferay Portal 5.2.3/6.x removes the namespace value from the form fields (or any other request parameter) before making them available to your portlet class. You access namespaced form fields in Liferay Portal without adding the namespace value to their names.

If you want to access the bookTitle text field in your code, you *must* access it *without* adding the namespace value to its name, as shown here:

```
String bookTitle = request.getParameter("bookTitle");
```

If you add the namespace value to the name of the form field, the portlet class in Liferay Portal will return `null`, as shown here:

```
String bookTitle =
  request.getParameter(response.getNamespace() + "bookTitle");
```

JETSPEED: ACCESSING NAMESPACED REQUEST PARAMETERS BY ADDING A NAMESPACE VALUE
If you're using Jetspeed 2.2 (which uses the Pluto portlet container), you must access a namespaced form field (or any other request parameter) by adding the namespace value to the form field's name, as shown here:

```
String bookTitle =
  request.getParameter(response.getNamespace() + "bookTitle");
```

You'll get a `null` return value if you access the `bookTitle` text field without adding the namespace value to its name. As you can see, this is the opposite of the behavior in Liferay Portal 5.2.3/6.x.

GLASSFISH: ACCESSING REQUEST PARAMETERS WITH OR WITHOUT NAMESPACE VALUES
GlassFish (with OpenPortal Portlet Container 2.1.2) provides a much simpler way to access namespaced form fields. In GlassFish, you can access a form field (or any other request parameter) *with* or *without* adding the namespace value to its name. For instance, to access the `bookTitle` text field, you can use either of the following code lines:

```
String bookTitle = request.getParameter("bookTitle");
```

or

```
String bookTitle =
  request.getParameter(response.getNamespace() + "bookTitle");
```

In GlassFish (with OpenPortal Portlet Container 2.1.2), when you access a request parameter, the portlet container checks for the existence of the parameter in the request. If the request parameter is found in the portlet request, then it returns its value (which is why you can access form fields in GlassFish by adding the namespace value to the form field name). If the request parameter isn't found in the portlet request, the portlet container prepends the namespace value to the request parameter name and again attempts to access the parameter in the request (which is why you can access form fields in GlassFish *without* adding the namespace value to the form field name).

Let's now look at the `<property>` tag of the portlet tag library.

6.6   *Adding properties to URLs using `<property>`*

Properties contain portal- or portlet container–specific information that's used by the portlet. You can add properties to a portlet URL with the `<property>` tag. This tag serves the same purpose as the `PortletURL`'s `addProperty` method, and it can be used only inside `<renderURL>`, `<actionURL>`, and `<resourceURL>` tags.

The <property> tag defines two *required* attributes:

- name—Specifies the name of the property that you want to add to the URL
- value—Specifies the value of the property

NOTE If you want to add a property to all portlet URLs, you should consider using the PortletURLGenerationListener (refer section 4.6.3 of chapter 4).

If you're using Liferay Portal 5.2.3 or Jetspeed 2.2, the <property> tag won't work because Liferay Portal and Jetspeed ignore properties set in the portlet URL. If in Liferay Portal or Jetspeed you set a custom property using the <property> tag and retrieve it in the portlet class by using the PortletRequest's getProperty method, it will return null.

NOTE If you're using Glassfish with OpenPortal Portlet Container 2.1.2, you'll see that the OpenPortal Portlet Container translates properties into request parameters—properties added to a portlet URL are added as request parameters to the URL.

The <property> tag is one of the least used tags in JSPs, but it could be useful if a more consistent implementation of it were available across different portal servers.

That covers all the portlet tag library tags that are available as part of Portlet 2.0.

6.7 Summary

In this chapter, you saw how the portlet tag library tags can be used to simplify the development of JSP pages used by portlets. In chapter 4, you created render and action URLs in the portlet class—a task that should lie with the JSP page. Using portlet tags results in the content responsibility being contained completely within the JSP page.

If you're using any other view technology, it's up to your portal server to provide the necessary portlet objects and tag library features to your view technology.

Take a deep breath now, because we're going to dive headfirst into Spring Portlet MVC next. It's not simple, but we'll walk through it step by step.

Part 2

Developing portlets using Spring and Hibernate

Java portlet development is simple if you're using frameworks like Spring and Hibernate. This part of the book begins with a quick introduction to the Spring Framework and quickly progresses to show how you can develop portlets using Spring Portlet MVC, Spring JDBC, Spring AOP, and Hibernate. You'll also see how to use JSR 330 and JSR 250 annotations for dependency injection, JSR 303 annotations for validating domain objects, the Spring Validation API, Spring's form tag library, and unit and integration testing using Spring's Test-Context framework.

7

Getting started with Spring Portlet MVC

This chapter covers

- Spring Framework basics
- Handlers or controllers
- Handler mappings
- Handler interceptors
- Exception handling

In earlier chapters, you learned about the portlet lifecycle and core concepts of the Java portlet technology. You developed the Book Catalog portlet by extending the `GenericPortlet` class and writing action and render methods containing navigation and validation logic, along with action processing and content generation logic. The portlet class acted as a *controller*, responsible for data validation, dispatching requests to appropriate JSPs, preparing data for the JSP pages, and encapsulating calls to business services.

As more and more features are added to a portlet, the portlet class becomes bloated with extra responsibilities, resulting in unfocused and unmanageable code. To deal with a bloated controller class, you can split the request-processing responsibilities into more focused components or classes by using a portlet framework.

Web or portlet frameworks make use of best design practices and patterns to simplify development. Some of the widely used web frameworks, like Struts, JSF, and Wicket, currently let you develop portlets by bridging the differences between portlet and servlet technologies.

This chapter focuses on Spring's *Portlet MVC framework*, which can be used to build real-world portlets. Spring Portlet MVC is the *only* framework designed specifically to develop portlets. You could alternatively use a web framework like JSF or Wicket (coupled with a portlet bridge) to create portlets, but that approach hides the multiple lifecycle phases of portlets, and in some scenarios you might find it difficult to take full advantage of the portlet technology. For instance, if you're using the Wicket portlet bridge, you won't be able to use Portlet 2.0's inter-portlet communication feature. For more details on how you can use JSF or Wicket along with a portlet bridge, refer to chapter 14.

This chapter will begin with a gentle introduction to Spring Framework, and then we'll move on and implement a simple Hello World portlet using the Portlet MVC framework. We'll then cover the fundamentals of the Spring 3.0 Portlet MVC framework, which includes controllers or handlers, handler mappings, web application contexts, handler interceptors, and so on. You'll find that handlers and controllers are discussed in great detail in this chapter because Spring Portlet MVC provides many built-in controllers or handlers to simplify portlet development. You'll also find many code examples to demonstrate how the various pieces of the framework work together to handle portlet requests and generate content.

> **NOTE**   Advanced concepts, like annotation-driven development support in Spring Portlet MVC, and unit testing portlets using mock objects, are covered in chapter 8.

7.1   *Why use Spring Portlet MVC?*

Spring (http://www.springsource.org/) is a non-intrusive framework that has gained prominence in recent years with its POJO (plain old Java object) approach to developing enterprise applications, which has resulted in increased productivity and ease of testing. In this chapter, we'll discuss the basics of Spring's Portlet MVC framework, which is Spring's MVC framework for developing portlets. The Portlet MVC framework is designed around the same concepts as, and mirrors the classes and interfaces of, Spring's *Web MVC framework*, which is used to develop servlet-based web applications. Developers who have prior experience in developing web applications using the Web MVC framework will find it easy to use.

The Spring Portlet MVC framework differs from other frameworks because it's exclusively designed for developing portlets; it avoids the limitations that come with developing portlets in an existing web framework. Web frameworks are based on servlet technology, which doesn't have the concept of lifecycle phases, so they end up hiding the different lifecycle phases of a portlet. With the Spring Portlet MVC framework you get not only a full-featured portlet framework that preserves the lifecycle phases of portlets, but also features like dependency injection, POJO-based development, and ease of testing, which are the cornerstones of the Spring Framework.

If you have prior experience working with Spring Framework or the Spring Web MVC framework, this chapter will get you started with portlet development using the Portlet MVC framework. This chapter attempts to provide a brief introduction to Spring Framework, but for a more comprehensive introduction to Spring, I recommend you refer to Spring's tutorials, available at http://www.springsource.org, which cover the foundation concepts of Spring Framework. You may also want to refer to *Spring in Action, Third Edition,* by Craig Walls, also from Manning, to get a solid Spring Framework foundation.

Let's now look at dependency injection and the application context in Spring.

7.2 *Dependency injection and the application context*

Dependency injection (DI) is at the core of Spring Framework. You'll need a good understanding of DI to understand the rest of the topics discussed in this chapter. In this section, we'll take a quick look at what DI is and how Spring uses it to allow developers to quickly configure and develop applications. We'll also look at the concept of the *application context* in Spring, which provides access to the objects that form part of Spring-based applications.

7.2.1 *An e-commerce example*

Let's consider an e-commerce application that involves a few application objects, as defined here:

- OrderHandler—A presentation-tier component that's responsible for handling orders submitted by customers. It depends upon OrderService to save the submitted orders.
- OrderService—A component that contains the business logic for saving an order in the database. It depends upon OrderDAO to save the order information in the database.
- OrderDAO—A data access object that's responsible for interacting with the database to save the order information submitted by the customer.

Figure 7.1 shows the dependency between the OrderHandler, OrderService, and OrderDAO application objects.

The dependency of application objects, as shown in figure 7.1, can be fulfilled by manually creating these objects in the dependent objects, as shown next.

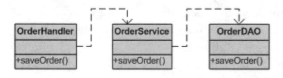

Figure 7.1 OrderHandler **depends upon** OrderService, **which in turn depends upon** OrderDAO.

```
public class OrderHandler {
    private OrderService orderService = new OrderService();
    public void saveOrder(...) {
        orderService.saveOrder(...);
    }
}
public class OrderService {
    private OrderDAO orderDAO = new OrderDAO();
    public void saveOrder(...) {
        orderDAO.saveOrder(...);
    }
}
```

In the preceding code, the OrderHandler object is tightly coupled with OrderService, and OrderService is tightly coupled with OrderDAO.

Let's now assume that you want to use the OrderService object in a different application that requires the business functionality of OrderService but that saves data differently than the way it is implemented in OrderDAO. The tight coupling of OrderService and OrderDAO makes it difficult to reuse the OrderService object in other applications.

The logical step is to factor out the dependency logic from OrderService and use a factory object, as shown here:

```
public class OrderService {
    public void saveOrder(...) {
        DaoFactory.getOrderDao().saveOrder(...);
    }
}
public class DaoFactory {
    public static OrderDAOIntf getOrderDao(...) {
        return new OrderDAO();
    }
}
public interface OrderDAOIntf {
    void saveOrder(...);
}
public class OrderDAO implements OrderDAOIntf {
    void saveOrder(...);
}
```

In the preceding code, OrderDAOIntf is an interface that's implemented by OrderDAO. The DaoFactory is a factory class responsible for creating the OrderDAO object and returning it as OrderDAOIntf to the OrderService class.

The use of a factory class removes the direct dependency of OrderService on OrderDAO. With the introduction of the OrderDAOIntf interface, OrderService now depends on OrderDAOIntf, instead of OrderDAO. This is a better design, because direct dependency on the implementation was removed.

Now, if you want to use OrderService in a different e-commerce application, you only need to add the logic to create a different OrderDAOIntf implementation, specific to that e-commerce application. This means you still need to write code in the DaoFactory class, and at compile time, OrderDAO must be in the classpath.

A much cleaner approach is to use dependency injection (DI) to create and inject object dependencies.

7.2.2 *Dependency injection and application contexts*

When using DI, dependencies are specified in an external configuration file (like an XML file) or within the source code (using annotations), and these dependencies are injected into the dependent objects by an *IoC* (Inversion of Control) container. An IoC container is responsible for creating and managing application objects, and for injecting dependencies based on the configuration information. This relieves developers of the responsibility of managing application objects and injecting dependencies; it *inverts the control* of managing application objects and injecting dependencies.

Spring Framework consists of an IoC container that's responsible for reading configuration information from an *application context* XML file, creating and managing application objects and injecting dependencies.

> **NOTE** Spring's IoC container provides many features, but for the sake of simplicity I'll focus only on the DI feature in this section.

To use Spring's IoC container for DI in the e-commerce application, you'd first need to explicitly specify dependencies in the source code of the application objects. In Spring, dependencies are specified in the source code of an application object using constructors and setter methods.

> **NOTE** Spring offers many ways to inject dependencies into an application object. For the purposes of this book, I'll just discuss DI using setter methods and constructors. Refer to Spring 3.0 reference documentation for a detailed discussion of different approaches for injecting dependencies.

The following listing shows how the `OrderHandler` and `OrderService` classes define their dependencies.

Listing 7.1   Defining dependencies in application objects

```
package mypackage;

public class OrderHandler {                         ❶ OrderService
    private OrderService orderService;                 dependency
    public void setOrderService(OrderService
    ➥orderService) {                                ❷ Setter for
        this.orderService = orderService;              OrderService
    }                                                  dependency
    public void saveOrder(...) {
        orderService.saveOrder(...);
    }
}

package mypackage;
public class OrderService {                         ❸ OrderDAOIntf
    private OrderDAOIntf orderDaoIntf;                  dependency
```

```
   public void setOrderDAOIntf(OrderDAOIntf
   ➥orderDaoIntf) {
      this.orderDaoIntf = orderDaoIntf;
   }
   public void saveOrder(...) {
      orderDaoIntf.saveOrder(...);
   }
}
```

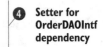 ❹ Setter for OrderDAOIntf dependency

OrderHandler defines OrderService ❶ as an attribute of the class, and ❷ a setter method is defined for the OrderService attribute. OrderService defines OrderDAO-Intf ❸ as an attribute of the class, and ❹ a setter method is defined for the Order-DAOIntf attribute.

In listing 7.1, setter methods define dependencies of the application objects, and they leave it up to Spring's IoC container to inject the dependencies when the container initializes the application objects.

Now that the application objects have defined their dependencies using setter methods, you need to tell Spring's IoC container about the existence of these objects in the application. The application context XML file is used to define the application objects and their dependencies, and it's then read by the IoC container to create objects and wire dependencies.

You can define an object in Spring's application context XML as follows:

```
<bean id="<beanId>" class="<beanClass>"/>
```

Here, beanId is the unique ID for the bean in the application context, and beanClass is the fully qualified name of the bean class.

NOTE Application objects defined in the application context XML are referred to as *beans*, but that doesn't mean that you can't define non-bean objects in the application context XML.

The following application context XML shows how you can define the e-commerce application objects:

```
<beans ...>
  <bean id="handler" class="mypackage.OrderHandler"/>
  <bean id="service" class="mypackage.OrderService"/>
  <bean id="dao" class="mypackage.OrderDAO"/>
</beans>
```

In the preceding application context XML, beans is the root element of the XML, and each bean element represents an application object. You can assign any value as an id of the object, as long as it's unique within the application context. The preceding XML simply defines the application objects, without any details about how the wiring happens between the application objects.

NOTE The value of the id attribute is also referred to as the *bean name*.

You saw earlier that using setter methods for dependencies effectively makes the dependencies look like bean properties. If you want to call an application object's setter method, you can use the `property` subelement of the `bean` and pass a value, which could be another bean, a simple `String` value, or any other value type. The next listing shows how the e-commerce application objects will be represented in Spring's application context XML file.

Listing 7.2   Spring's application context XML file

```
<beans ...>
  <bean id="handler" class="mypackage.OrderHandler">          ❶ OrderHandler
    <property name="orderService">                              definition
      <ref bean="service"/>
    </property>
  </bean>                                                     ❷ OrderService
  <bean id="service" class="mypackage.OrderService">            definition
    <property name="orderDaoIntf">                            ❸ OrderService's
      <ref bean="dao"/>                                         orderDaoIntf
    </property>                                                  property
  </bean>
  <bean id="dao" class="mypackage.OrderDAO">
    <property name="dburl"
        value="jdbc:mysql://localhost/mydb?
          ➥useUnicode=true&">                                ❹ OrderDAO
    <property name="driverClassName"                            object's
        value="com.mysql.jdbc.Driver">                          properties
    <property name="username" value="asarin">
    <property name="password" value="password">
  </bean>
</beans>
```

The `handler` definition ❶ refers to the `OrderHandler` class. The `name` attribute of the `property` element identifies the property of the `OrderHandler` class that's set by Spring's IoC container when the `OrderHandler` object is initialized. Because the `name` attribute refers to the `OrderHandler` class's `orderService` property, the container will call the `OrderHandler` class's `setOrderService` method.

The `setOrderService` method is defined to accept an instance of the `Order-Service` object as an argument (see listing 7.1), so you need to set a value of type `OrderService` for the property. This is accomplished by using the `ref` element. In the application context XML, the `ref` element is used to cross-reference the application object defined in the application context XML file. The `ref` element's `bean` attribute uniquely identifies an application object defined in the application context XML; it has a value of `service`, which instructs the container to find an application object whose `id` attribute value is `service`.

`OrderService` is defined ❷ with an `id` attribute value of `service`, so the container invokes the `OrderHandler`'s `setOrderService` method and passes it an instance of the `OrderService` application object. `OrderService` defines how the `OrderService`'s orderDAOIntf property ❸ is to be resolved by the container. The OrderDAO properties are set to String values ❹ using the property element's value attribute.

Listing 7.2 shows how the configuration information regarding the initialization of and dependency between application objects is specified using Spring's application context XML file. If you look at the OrderService class, it's dependent on the Order-DAOIntf interface and not on the OrderDAO concrete implementation class.

As defined in the XML file, OrderService depends on OrderDAO in the current configuration. If you need to change the dependency from OrderDAO to a new XyzDAO implementation, all you need to do is create a new XyzDAO class that implements the OrderDAOIntf interface and change the configuration in the application context XML, as shown here:

```
<bean id="service" class="mypackage.OrderService">
    <property name="orderDaoIntf">
        <ref bean="dao"/>
    </property>
</bean>
<bean id="dao" class="somePackage.XyzDAO">
    <property ...>
        ...
    </property>
    ...
</bean>
```

The preceding XML fragment shows that as long as OrderService isn't directly dependent on OrderDAO, you can easily replace the dependency with a different implementation.

The Spring IoC container uses the application context XML file to instantiate and initialize application objects and inject dependencies, which effectively saves you the effort of writing boilerplate code in the factory class. Because the Spring IoC container only takes the application context XML file as input, you can configure Spring Framework features in the application context XML. For instance, you can define transactional methods in the application context XML, and the Spring container takes care of invoking the methods within a transaction. For a detailed set of features offered by Spring Framework, refer to the Spring 3.0 reference documentation.

Let's now look at the web application context XML, which is a variation on the application context XML file.

7.2.3   *Web application contexts*

You now know how to define beans in the Spring application context XML, and how to initialize their properties and resolve dependencies. Defining beans and their dependencies is fundamental to any Spring application.

If you're using Spring Portlet MVC, *each* portlet in your portlet application is associated with its own *web application context* XML file. Note that even though we're using the term "web application context XML," the file isn't associated with the web application but with an individual portlet. The *portlet application* (which is also a web application) is also associated with a web application context XML file, which is referred to as the *root web application context* XML file.

A portlet's web application context XML file defines the controllers, services, DAOs, and other application objects that form part of that portlet. You may also define Spring's *special* beans in your web application context XML; they provide functionality suitable for implementing most portlets. For instance, the Spring Portlet MVC framework's `PortletModeHandlerMapping` bean is useful in mapping portlet requests to appropriate handlers based on the current portlet mode.

In the case of Spring Portlet MVC–based portlets, the beans defined in the web application context XML files are instantiated and initialized when the framework is initialized. The scope of the beans defined in the web application context XML file is the portlet for which they're defined. If the portlet application also defines a *root* web application context XML file, the beans defined in that file are available to the web application contexts of the portlets in the portlet application. You can think of the *root* web application context as the parent of all the web application contexts associated with portlets in the portlet application.

With this basic understanding of Spring IoC containers and how you can define beans in an application context XML file, you're now ready to create a portlet that uses the Spring Portlet MVC framework.

7.3   *A Hello World portlet, the Spring way*

The Hello World portlet that we'll discuss in this section is same as the one in chapter 1, except that this version will use Spring Portlet MVC and will demonstrate what you need to do to create a portlet using Spring Portlet MVC.

Because the Hello World portlet uses Spring-specific JAR files, you can either download the Spring 3.0 release JAR files from the SpringSource website (http://www.springsource.org/download) or you can import the ch7_HelloWorld Eclipse project from the source code that accompanies this book.

> **CODE REFERENCE** You should import the ch7_HelloWorld project so that you can follow along with the code references and discussions in the rest of this section.

The following JAR files must be present in the WEB-INF/lib directory of the project structure described in chapter 1:

- org.springframework.asm-3.0.0.RELEASE
- org.springframework.beans-3.0.0.RELEASE (add this file to your project's build path)
- org.springframework.context-3.0.0.RELEASE (add this file to your project's build path)
- org.springframework.core-3.0.0.RELEASE
- org.springframework.expression-3.0.0.RELEASE

- org.springframework.web-3.0.0.RELEASE (add this file to your project's build path)
- org.springframework.web.portlet-3.0.0.RELEASE (add this file to your project's build path)
- org.springframework.web.servlet-3.0.0.RELEASE

The rest of this section shows the configuration files and classes for the version of the Hello World portlet that uses Spring Portlet MVC.

7.3.1 The Hello World portlet's controller class

In Spring Portlet MVC, the controller class (and *not* the portlet class) contains the actual request-handling logic for the portlet. The next listing shows the HelloWorldController controller class.

Listing 7.3   The HelloWorldController class

```
import javax.portlet.*;
import org.springframework.web.portlet.ModelAndView;
import org.springframework.web.portlet.mvc.Controller;

public class HelloWorldController implements Controller{
  public void handleActionRequest(ActionRequest request,
    ActionResponse response)throws Exception {
  }

  public ModelAndView handleRenderRequest
     (RenderRequest request, RenderResponse response)
       throws Exception {
    Map<String, Object> model =
      new HashMap<String, Object>();
    model.put("helloWorldMessage", "Hello World");
    return new ModelAndView("helloWorld", model);
  }
}
```

❶ Request handler implements Controller interface

❷ handleRenderRequest returns ModelAndView

The HelloWorldController portlet request handler implements the org.springframework.web.portlet.mvc.Controller interface ❶, which defines two methods:

- handleActionRequest—This is the same as portlet's action method
- handleRenderRequest—This is the same as portlet's render method

The HelloWorldController's handleRenderRequest method returns a ModelAndView object ❷ that contains the *model* data and *view* information. You've seen in earlier chapters that a render method creates content by dispatching a render request to a JSP page, and the data that needs to be rendered by the JSP page is passed as request attributes. In Spring Portlet MVC, the ModelAndView object holds the model data (the data to be rendered) and the view information (the JSP page), and it's used by the Spring Portlet MVC framework to dispatch the render request to the view and to pass the model data.

NOTE Because the Spring Portlet MVC framework takes care of dispatching requests and passing data to the JSP page, you don't use the Portlet-RequestDispatcher in the handleRenderRequest method, nor do you set any request attributes.

The ModelAndView object in the HelloWorldController class contains a model (the model variable in the handleRenderRequest method in listing 7.3) as a Map object and a view name (the helloWorld string argument passed to the ModelAndView constructor in listing 7.3) as a String object. The "Hello World" message that you want to display using the JSP page is passed as a model attribute with the name hello-WorldMessage.

7.3.2 The Hello World portlet's JSP page

Listing 7.3 included a helloWorldMessage model attribute with a value of "Hello World". The Spring Portlet MVC framework converts model attributes (like the hello-WorldMessage attribute) to *request attributes* so that JSP pages can easily access them.

The helloWorld.jsp page in the Hello World portlet shows the "Hello World" message as shown here:

```
<%@ taglib prefix="c" uri="http://java.sun.com/jsp/jstl/core" %>
<%@ page contentType="text/html" isELIgnored="false" %>
<c:out value="${helloWorldMessage}"/>
```

In the preceding JSP page, the <c:out value="${helloWorldMessage}"/> code writes the "Hello World" message to the response stream because that's the value of the helloWorldMessage request attribute.

7.3.3 The Hello World portlet's portlet deployment descriptor

If you're using the Spring Portlet MVC framework to create your portlet, you'll use the org.springframework.web.portlet.DispatcherPortlet class as the portlet class. It extends the javax.portlet.GenericPortlet class and is responsible for dispatching portlet requests to the appropriate handler. The following listing shows the portlet.xml file for the Hello World portlet example.

Listing 7.4 The portlet.xml file

```
<portlet>
  <portlet-name>helloWorld</portlet-name>
  <portlet-class>
    org.springframework.web.portlet.DispatcherPortlet
  </portlet-class>
  <supports>
    <mime-type>text/html</mime-type>
    <portlet-mode>view</portlet-mode>
  </supports>
  <resource-bundle>content.Language-ext</resource-bundle>
  <portlet-info>
```

❶ Spring Portlet MVC's DispatcherPortlet class

❷ <portlet-info> element for portlet title

```
    <title>Hello World</title>
  </portlet-info>
</portlet>
```

The Spring Portlet MVC framework's `DispatcherPortlet` class ❶ is specified as the portlet class. The `<portlet-info>` element ❷ is used to specify the portlet title.

> **NOTE** If you specify the title both in the resource bundle using the `javax` `.portlet.title` key and in the portlet.xml file, the title specified in the resource bundle takes precedence.

7.3.4 *The Hello World portlet's web application context*

As discussed earlier, the core of a Spring Framework application is the *application context*, which identifies the objects that form part of the application, and their interdependencies.

Listing 7.5 shows the objects defined in the Hello World portlet's web application context XML file. The name of the web application context file must be

```
<portlet_name>-portlet.xml
```

where `<portlet_name>` is the name of the portlet, as defined by the `<portlet-name>` element in the portlet.xml file. This file must reside in the WEB-INF folder of your project.

Listing 7.5   The helloWorld-portlet.xml file

```xml
<?xml version="1.0" encoding="UTF-8"?>
<beans ... >
 <bean id="helloWorldController"                                    ❶ Handler
  class="chapter07.code.listing.HelloWorldController"/>                definition

 <bean id="portletModeHandlerMapping"                               ❷ Portlet mode to
  class="org.springframework.web.portlet.handler.                     handler mapping
    ➥PortletModeHandlerMapping">

 <property name="portletModeMap">
  <map>
   <entry key="view">                                               ❸ VIEW mode mapped to
    <ref bean="helloWorldController" />                               HelloWorldController
   </entry>
  </map>
 </property>
 </bean>

 <bean id="viewResolver"                                            ❹ View resolver
  class="org.springframework.web.servlet.view.
    ➥InternalResourceViewResolver">
 <property name="viewClass"
  value="org.springframework.web.servlet.view.JstlView"/>
 <property name="prefix" value="/WEB-INF/jsp/" />
 <property name="suffix" value=".jsp" />
 </bean>
</beans>
```

The `HelloWorldController` handler is defined ❶. The `PortletModeHandlerMapping` bean ❷ maps the portlet mode to the handler responsible for handling portlet requests in that mode. The `VIEW` portlet mode of the Hello World portlet ❸ is mapped to `HelloWorldController`, which means that any portlet request (render or action) sent by the portlet in `VIEW` mode will be handled by `HelloWorldController`.

The `InternalResourceViewResolver` is Spring Framework's built-in bean ❹, which is used to map view names (see listing 7.3) to the actual view (which could be a servlet or a JSP). It makes use of the `viewClass` property to define the class responsible for generating the view. If you're using JSPs that contain JSTL, you should specify the value of the `viewClass` property as `JstlView`. The `prefix` property value is prepended, and the `suffix` property value is appended, to the view name to create the URL referring to the actual view.

In the Hello World portlet, the `HelloWorldController`'s handleRenderRequest method returns a `ModelAndView` object containing the `helloWorld` view name (see listing 7.3). That view name is resolved to an actual view by `InternalResourceView-Resolver`, by prepending `/WEB-INF/jsp/` and appending `.jsp` to the `helloWorld` view name. This makes the URL of the actual view `/WEB-INF/jsp/helloWorld.jsp`. This means that the helloWorld.jsp page shown in section 7.3.2 must reside in the `/WEB-INF/jsp/` folder.

7.3.5 *The Hello World portlet's web application deployment descriptor*

The `InternalResourceViewResolver` bean resolves a view name to an actual view, and the rendering of the view is done by Spring's built-in `ViewRendererServlet` servlet. The `ViewRendererServlet` acts as a bridge between the portlet and the actual view.

The following listing shows the `ViewRendererServlet` configuration in the web.xml file.

Listing 7.6 The web.xml file

```
<web-app ...>
  ...
  <servlet>
    <servlet-name>ViewRendererServlet</servlet-name>
    <servlet-class>
      org.springframework.web.servlet.ViewRendererServlet
    </servlet-class>
  </servlet>
  <servlet-mapping>
    <servlet-name>ViewRendererServlet</servlet-name>
    <url-pattern>/WEB-INF/servlet/view</url-pattern>
  </servlet-mapping>
  ...
</web-app>
```

❶ **ViewRendererServlet definition**

❷ **ViewRendererServlet mapping**

Spring's `ViewRendererServlet` ❶ is defined. The `ViewRendererServlet` ❷ is mapped to the URL `/WEB-INF/servlet/view`. This URL is used internally by `Dispatcher-Portlet` to dispatch a request to `ViewRendererServlet` for view rendering. The

URL can be modified by using the `DispatcherPortlet`'s `viewRendererUrl` initialization parameter.

That's all you need to do to create a Hello World portlet using Spring Portlet MVC. You're now ready to build and deploy the portlet, as explained in chapter 1.

The Hello World example in this section was a bit more involved than the Hello World portlet example in chapter 1 because of the new configuration file (the web application context XML file) and some new classes and interfaces (`ViewRenderer-Servlet`, `Controller`, and so on). Spring Portlet MVC is most useful when creating multipage portlets that provide multiple functionalities, as you'll see later in this chapter.

If this section has left you wondering exactly how Spring Portlet MVC works, the next section will show you how the different special beans of Spring Portlet MVC work together to handle portlet requests and generate responses.

7.4 *How Spring Portlet MVC works*

You saw in the previous section that the `DispatcherPortlet` acts as the portlet class for Spring Portlet MVC portlets. So what does `DispatcherPortlet` do?

If you have prior experience working with the Struts framework, you can closely relate the `DispatcherPortlet` here to the `RequestProcessor` class in the Struts framework. The `DispatcherPortlet` is at the heart of the Spring Portlet MVC framework and, like the `RequestProcessor` of the Struts framework, it's responsible for coordinating all the request handling activities on receipt of a portlet request. It works with the other Spring Portlet MVC classes and interfaces that you saw in the Hello World portlet; figure 7.2 illustrates how they all interact.

When a portlet request is received by the `DispatcherPortlet` (which is the portlet class) ❶, it first attempts to find an appropriate handler for the request, and Spring Portlet MVC's `HandlerMapping` type bean helps with this. Depending upon how you want to select a handler based on the portlet request, you'll select an appropriate built-in `HandlerMapping` bean implementation. The Hello World portlet uses the `PortletModeHandlerMapping` bean which implements `HandlerMapping` and which selects an appropriate handler based on the current portlet mode ❷. In the Hello World portlet, the `PortletModeHandlerMapping` maps the `VIEW` portlet mode to the `HelloWorldController` (see listing 7.5), so `HelloWorldController` is the handler for the render request received ❶ by `DispatcherPortlet`.

 Once the handler is selected for request processing, the `DispatcherPortlet` invokes the appropriate handler method to do the actual request processing. In listing 7.3, the handler's `handleRenderRequest` method is responsible for handling render requests, and the `handleActionRequest` method handles action requests. The request received at ❶ is a render request, so the request is handled by the `HelloWorldController`'s `handleRenderRequest` method ❸. That method returns a `ModelAndView` object. The `DispatcherPortlet` uses the view information in the `ModelAndView` object to obtain a reference to the actual view, which, in the case of the Hello World portlet, is a JSP page.

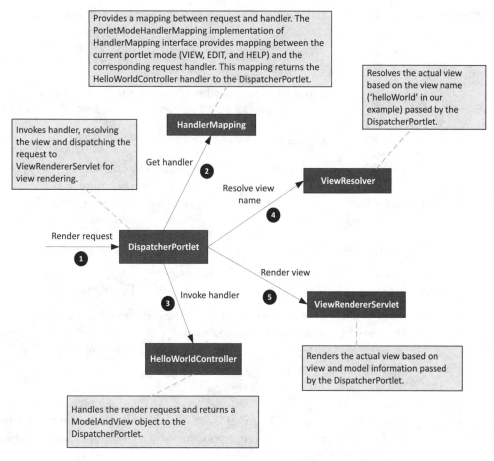

Figure 7.2   Request processing in Spring Portlet MVC. The `DispatcherPortlet` acts as the front controller for each portlet and finds the handler mapped to the request using `HandlerMapping`. The result of executing a handler, `ModelAndView`, is used to resolve the actual view to be rendered, and the request is dispatched to `ViewRendererServlet` for rendering.

Spring Portlet MVC's built-in `ViewResolver` type bean helps with resolving the view; it finds the actual view corresponding to the logical view name. The Hello World portlet makes use of the `InternalResourceViewResolver` bean (which implements `View-Resolver`) to resolve the view name to the actual JSP page ❹. Once the actual view is resolved, the `DispatcherPortlet` dispatches the request to the built-in `ViewRender-Servlet` servlet (see listing 7.6) and sends the reference to the actual view along with the model data for rendering the view ❺.

Spring Portlet MVC provides many built-in `ViewResolvers` that you can use, depending on the view technology you're using. The built-in view resolvers include `XmlViewResolver`, `VelocityViewResolver`, `FreeMarkerViewResolver`, and `Resource-BundleViewResolver`. Later in this chapter, you'll see how `HandlerMapping` and

`ExceptionResolver` chains are created. Similarly, you can also create a `ViewResolver` chain to resolve views.

> **NOTE** The `DispatcherPortlet` auto-detects view resolvers based on the type of bean defined in the portlet's web application context or in the root web application context, and applies them during view resolution. For example, if a bean that's defined in the portlet's web application context implements the `ViewResolver` interface, `DispatcherPortlet` makes use of that bean for resolving views for the portlet.

Now that you've a seen a simple Hello World example using Spring Portlet MVC, and you have a basic idea of what classes, interfaces, and configurations are involved while processing portlet requests in Spring Portlet MVC, we'll look at each of them in detail, starting with `DispatcherPortlet`.

7.5   *Using DispatcherPortlet*

The `DispatcherPortlet` acts as the *front controller* in the Spring Portlet MVC framework (as shown in figure 7.2). It's responsible for the following:

- Sending portlet requests to the appropriate handler (explained in section 7.7). The mapping of the portlet request to an appropriate handler is specified using `HandlerMapping` beans (explained in section 7.8). In the Hello World portlet, this mapping is specified by the `PortletModeHandlerMapping` bean in the hello-World-portlet.xml file (see listing 7.5).
- Resolving the view using `ViewResolver`. The `InternalResourceViewResolver` in listing 7.5 supports JSPs and servlets as view technologies. You can use different `ViewResolvers` depending upon the view technologies you're using (such as JSP, Velocity, and FreeMarker).
- Dispatching requests to the `ViewRendererServlet` to render views. The `ViewRendererServlet` is configured in the web application deployment descriptor (see listing 7.6), and by default it's mapped to the URL /WEB-INF/servlet/view. The `DispatcherPortlet` includes the content generated by the `ViewRendererServlet` using the `PortletRequestDispatcher` object:

```
getPortletContext().getRequestDispatcher(viewRendererUrl).
   include(request, response)
```

In this code, `viewRendererUrl` is the URL to which the `ViewRendererServlet` is mapped.

> **NOTE** The model and view information is passed to the `ViewRenderer-Servlet` using request attributes. The model information is passed as a `java.util.Map` object, which can be transformed into any format (depending upon the view technology being used) by `ViewRendererServlet`, making it possible for `ViewRendererServlet` to render views in any view technology.

In most application scenarios, the features offered by the `DispatcherPortlet` are sufficient, and you don't need to extend the `DispatcherPortlet` class to create a custom portlet class. `DispatcherPortlet` comes with certain built-in initialization parameters that you can use to customize its behavior. For instance, you can use the `viewRendererUrl` initialization parameter to change the default URL to which `DispatcherPortlet` sends requests for view rendering. Similarly, you can use the `contextConfigLocation` initialization parameter to provide a custom name and location for your web application context XML file, and so on.

Let's now take an in-depth look at the concept of the web application context in Spring Portlet MVC.

7.6 *Using the web application context*

`DispatcherPortlet` is central to portlet request processing, and the web application context is central to configuring your portlet in Spring Portlet MVC.

In Spring Portlet MVC, the web application context XML file contains configuration information about the portlet; the file defines beans that form part of the portlet (see listing 7.5). Beans and their interdependencies are defined declaratively in the web application context XML file, and the Spring Framework is responsible for injecting these dependencies while creating them.

> **NOTE** In chapter 8, you'll see how annotations can be used to specify bean dependencies.

The beans defined in a web application context XML file include application-specific beans (like services and DAOs) and Spring's special beans, which implement framework-specific interfaces (like handlers and interceptors, handler mappings, view resolvers, and so on). In a portlet application, each portlet is associated with its web application context XML file, and the file is represented by the `WebApplication-Context` object in Spring. This effectively means that each `DispatcherPortlet` is associated with a `WebApplicationContext` of its own. The portlet application also has its own `WebApplicationContext` object. The `WebApplicationContext` object associated with the `DispatcherPortlet` inherits the beans defined in the `WebApplication-Context` associated with the portlet application.

Let now look at how web application context XML files are named.

7.6.1 *Naming web application context XML files*

As you saw in the Hello World example, developing a portlet using the Spring Portlet MVC framework requires at least a handler, a handler mapping, and a view resolver bean—all of which are defined in the web application context XML file. In the Hello World portlet, the helloWorld-portlet.xml file is the web application context XML file for the `helloWorld` portlet (see the `<portlet-name>` element in listing 7.4) in portlet.xml. Also, the helloWorld-portlet.xml file represents the `WebApplicationContext` associated with the `helloWorld` portlet's `DispatcherPortlet`.

The name of the web application context XML file for a portlet must have the following format:

```
<portlet_name>-portlet.xml
```

Here, <portlet_name> is the name of the portlet as defined by the <portlet-name> element in the portlet.xml file. The web application context XML file must reside in the WEB-INF directory of your project, as shown in figure 7.3.

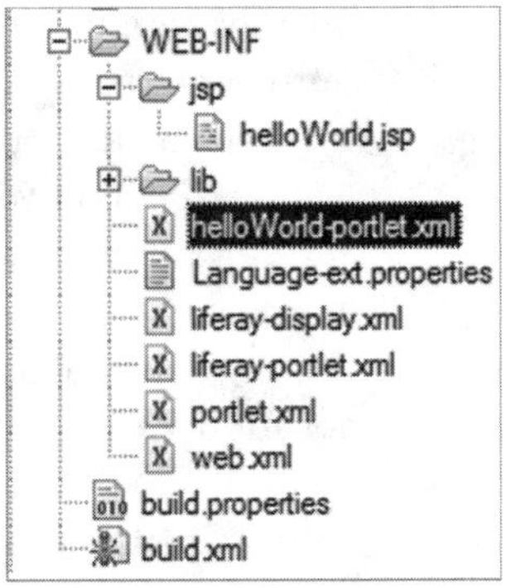

If you want to name your web application context XML files differently or store them in a different location, you can do so by using the Dispatcher-Portlet's contextConfigLocation initialization parameter, as shown here:

Figure 7.3   The web application context XML file is located in the WEB-INF directory and is named following the *portletName*-portlet.xml convention.

```
<portlet>
  <portlet-name>helloWorld</portlet-name>
  <portlet-class>
    org.springframework.web.portlet.DispatcherPortlet
  </portlet-class>
  <init-param>
   <name>contextConfigLocation</name>
   <value>/WEB-INF/context/portlet/myContext.xml</value>
  </init-param>
  ...
</portlet>
```

You can also specify multiple locations for the web application context XML files as comma-separated values in the contextConfigLocation parameter.

Let's now look at the scope of beans defined in the web application context XML file.

7.6.2   Scope of beans defined in the web application context XML

As mentioned earlier, DispatcherPortlet is associated with a WebApplication-Context of its own, defined by the portlet's web application context XML file. Beans defined in this file aren't accessible to other portlets in the same portlet application, which makes the bean definitions portlet-specific.

If you want to share beans across different portlets, you must define them in the *root* web application context associated with the portlet application. For instance, if you're using JSP with JSTL in your portlet application, you'd need to specify the following ViewResolver bean in all your portlet-specific web application contexts:

```
<bean id="viewResolver"
  class="org.springframework.web.servlet.view.
    ➥InternalResourceViewResolver">
  <property name="viewClass"
    value="org.springframework.web.servlet.view.JstlView"/>
```

```
    <property name="prefix" value="/WEB-INF/jsp/" />
    <property name="suffix" value=".jsp" />
</bean>
```

You can save the effort of writing this bean definition in all the portlet-specific web application contexts by defining it in the root web application context.

ROOT WEB APPLICATION CONTEXT XML

The root web application context XML file is associated with the *portlet application*. The web application context XML file for a *portlet* contains portlet-specific beans, whereas the root web application context XML file contains beans that are accessible to all portlets in the portlet application. A bean defined in the root web application context XML can be overridden by the portlet-specific application context XML file by defining a bean with the same bean ID.

The portlet-specific web application context will *implicitly* inherit beans from the root web application context. By default, the root web application context XML file is defined with the name applicationContext.xml, and it must be located in the WEB-INF directory. The root web application context XML file is loaded by the ContextLoader-Listener object, which is configured in the portlet application's web.xml file, as shown here:

```
<listener>
  <listener-class>
    org.springframework.web.context.ContextLoaderListener
  </listener-class>
</listener>
```

If you want to name your root web application context XML file differently or store it in a different location than the WEB-INF directory, you can specify the location of the root web application context XML file by using the contextConfigLocation context initialization parameter:

```
<context-param>
  <param-name>contextConfigLocation</param-name>
  <param-value>/WEB-INF/context/applicationContext.xml</param-value>
</context-param>
```

> **NOTE** The contextConfigLocation portlet-initialization parameter is used to specify a custom name or location for the web application context XML file used by DispatcherPortlet. The contextConfigLocation context-initialization parameter is used to specify a custom name or location for the root web application context XML file.

If you don't define a root web application context XML file, your portlets aren't associated with a root web application context.

As in the case of portlets, the root web application context is represented by the WebApplicationContext object. Spring stores the root WebApplicationContext as an attribute in ServletContext and the portlet's WebApplicationContext as an attribute in PortletContext. You saw earlier that PortletContext and ServletContext mirror each other's attributes, so Spring is responsible for naming each `WebApplication-Context` attribute with a unique name.

The web application context XML file used by `DispatcherPortlet` defines controller beans that contain the render and action request processing functionality of the portlet. It's possible that a controller contains only render or action request processing functionality of the portlet. Let's now look at the built-in controllers that you can use to develop your portlets.

7.7   *Using built-in controllers*

I've generally used the terms *controller* and *handler* interchangeably in this book. A *controller* is a specialized form of handler that implements the `Controller` interface directly or indirectly. A *handler* in Spring is any object that's responsible for handling any type of request (not necessarily web requests); a handler doesn't need to extend or implement any Spring-specific class or interface.

Controllers are special beans in Spring Portlet MVC that implement the request-handling functionality of the portlet. The `HelloWorldController` controller is an example of a handler that directly implements the `Controller` interface.

> **NOTE**   Spring Portlet MVC also supports annotations that allow you to use any Java class as a portlet request handler. This means that if you're using Spring Portlet MVC annotations, the portlet request handler isn't dependent on any Spring-specific interface or class. The use of annotations to create controllers is discussed in chapter 8.

Spring Portlet MVC provides many controller implementations, allowing you to use the controller implementation that best suits your application's requirements. In this section, we'll discuss the various types of controllers available in Spring Portlet MVC and see how they can be used in different scenarios.

The controller hierarchy in Spring Portlet MVC is similar to that of Spring MVC, as shown in figure 7.4. In this figure, the controllers that offer features for creating and validating command objects and for handling forms are deprecated as of Spring 3.0, in favor of annotated controllers. Annotated controllers are discussed in detail in chapter 8.

Let's first look at the `Controller` interface, which all other Spring Portlet MVC controllers implement, directly or indirectly.

> **CODE REFERENCE**   You should now import the ch7_Controllers Eclipse project that accompanies this book if you want to follow along with the code references in the rest of this section. You'll find that Spring's `Internal-ResourceViewResolver` is now defined in the root web application context (the applicationContext.xml file in the WEB-INF directory), and Spring's `ContextLoaderListener` has been added to web.xml to load the root web application context.

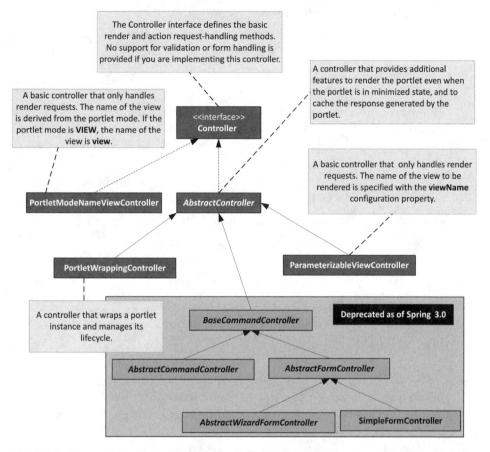

The Controller interface defines the basic render and action request-handling methods. No support for validation or form handling is provided if you are implementing this controller.

A controller that provides additional features to render the portlet even when the portlet is in minimized state, and to cache the response generated by the portlet.

A basic controller that only handles render requests. The name of the view is derived from the portlet mode. If the portlet mode is **VIEW**, the name of the view is **view**.

<<interface>>
Controller

A basic controller that only handles render requests. The name of the view to be rendered is specified with the **viewName** configuration property.

PortletModeNameViewController

AbstractController

PortletWrappingController

ParameterizableViewController

A controller that wraps a portlet instance and manages its lifecycle.

BaseCommandController

Deprecated as of Spring 3.0

AbstractCommandController

AbstractFormController

AbstractWizardFormController

SimpleFormController

Figure 7.4   The controller hierarchies in Spring Portlet MVC. The command and form controllers are deprecated in Spring 3.0 in favor of annotated controllers.

7.7.1   *Using the Controller interface*

The `Controller` interface is at the root of the Spring Portlet MVC controller hierarchy, and it provides the basic methods for handling action and render requests. It doesn't provide any request validation or form submission support. If you aren't comfortable with using annotations, you can still make use of the deprecated command and form controllers, which provide support for form submission and validation.

> **NOTE**   In this book, I won't cover the use of controllers deprecated in Spring 3.0. Instead, this book will focus on the use of annotated controllers.

The `HelloWorldController` in listing 7.3 showed how the `Controller` interface is used to implement portlet request handlers. `AbstractController` implements the `Controller` interface (refer to figure 7.4) and provides a base set of features to all built-in controllers (except `PortletModeNameViewController`) in Spring Portlet MVC.

7.7.2   *Using the AbstractController*

The `AbstractController` abstract class defines the following two render and action methods, which are meant to be overridden by the subclasses:

```
void handleActionRequestInternal(ActionRequest, ActionResponse)
ModelAndView handlerRenderRequestInternal(RenderRequest, RenderResponse)
```

The first of these two methods is meant to handle action requests, and the second is intended to handle render requests. The default implementation of these methods throws a `PortletException`, so you must override these methods if your controller class extends the `AbstractController` class.

AbstractController provides additional features that can be specified in the web application context XML file. Let's look at each of these properties in detail.

SPECIFYING WHETHER PORTLETSESSION IS REQUIRED

The `requireSession` property specifies whether the `PortletSession` is required to process the portlet request or not. This feature translates into the following piece of code:

```
if(requireSession){
  if(request.getPortletSession(false) == null) {
      throw new SomeException(...);
  } else {
      handleRenderRequestInternal(...);
  }
}
```

In this code, `getPortletSession(false)` returns the current `PortletSession`. If the request isn't associated with a session, it returns `null` and the code can throw an exception. If `getPortletSession(false)` returns the current portlet session, the `handleRenderRequestInternal` or `handleActionRequestInternal` method of the subclass is invoked, depending upon whether the portlet request is an action or render request.

> **TIP**   Instead of directly implementing the `Controller` interface to create your controller, it may be convenient to extend the `AbstractController` abstract class because it provides additional properties that simplify controller implementation.

CACHING PORTLET CONTENT

In chapter 4, you learned that expiration caching can be achieved by setting the `MimeResponse.EXPIRATION_CACHE` property in the response. The `cacheSeconds` property of `AbstractController` does exactly the same thing behind the scenes. It specifies the time (in seconds) for which the content generated by the portlet should be cached.

This property translates into the following piece of code:

```
response.setProperty(MimeResponse.EXPIRATION_CACHE, cacheSeconds);
```

Here, the `EXPIRATION_CACHE` constant defined in the `MimeResponse` object is set as a property in the `RenderResponse`, which instructs the portlet container to cache the portlet content for the number of seconds specified by `cacheSeconds`.

RENDERING A PORTLET EVEN WHEN IT'S MINIMIZED

The `renderWhenMinimized` property specifies whether or not a portlet is rendered (whether or not its render method is invoked) when the portlet window is in minimized state. The default implementation of the `GenericPortlet` class's render method doesn't invoke the render method if the portlet's window state is minimized.

This property translates into the following code:

```
if(renderWhenMinimized) {
  if(WindowState.MINIMIZED.equals(request.getWindowState())) {
    //do nothing
  } else {
    //invoke handleRenderRequestInternal method
  }
}
```

In this code, the `WindowState` object defines the standard portlet window states: `MINIMIZED`, `MAXIMIZED`, and `NORMAL`.

SYNCHRONIZING REQUEST PROCESSING

The `synchronizeOnSession` property specifies whether the invocation of the `AbstractConstoller`'s `handleRenderRequestInternal` and `handleActionRequest-Internal` methods are synchronized around the `PortletSession`. This property ensures that the invocation of the `handleRenderRequestInternal` and `handle-ActionRequestInternal` methods by the same client is serialized.

This property translates into the following code:

```
if(synchronizeOnSession) {
  synchronized(mutex) {
    //invoke render or action method
  }
}
```

In this code, `mutex` is the session mutex object, which serves as a safe reference to synchronize while calling the `handleRenderRequestInternal` and `handleAction-RequestInternal` methods.

The following listing shows how you can write a controller using the `Abstract-Controller` abstract class, instead of the `Controller` interface, to create a Hello World portlet.

Listing 7.7 An `AbstractController` example

```
public class MyAbstractHelloWorldController extends       Handler extends
         AbstractController{                               AbstractController

  public ModelAndView handleRenderRequestInternal
    (RenderRequest request, RenderResponse response)throws Exception {
    Map<String, Object> model = new HashMap<String, Object>();
    model.put("helloWorldMessage", "Hello World");
    return new ModelAndView("helloWorld", model);         Method returns
  }                                                       ModelAndView
}
```

In listing 7.7, you don't need to override the `handleActionRequestInternal` method because the Hello World portlet never sends an action request.

> **CODE REFERENCE** The `MyAbstractHelloWorldController` class in the ch7_Controllers folder shows how to use the `AbstractController` class to create your controllers in Spring Portlet MVC. Refer to the myAbstract-Controller-portlet.xml file to view the configuration of `MyAbstractHelloWorldController`.

The Spring Portlet MVC framework provides many out-of-the-box implementations of controllers that can be directly configured in your application context. The built-in controllers in Spring Portlet MVC include `ParameterizableViewController`, `PortletModeNameViewController`, and `PortletWrappingController`.

7.7.3 *Using the ParameterizableViewController*

The `ParameterizableViewController` is a basic controller that returns the name of the view to be rendered. The view name is configured as a property, named `viewName`, in the definition of the `ParameterizableViewController` bean in the application context.

> **NOTE** The `ParameterizableViewController` isn't designed to handle action requests.

The Hello World portlet developed in section 7.3 doesn't require action request processing, so we can make use of `ParameterizableViewController` to write a Hello World portlet.

Listing 7.8 shows the web application context XML file of a Hello World portlet that uses the `ParameterizableViewController` controller.

Listing 7.8 A `ParameterizableViewController` example

```xml
<?xml version="1.0" encoding="UTF-8"?>
<beans ...>
  <bean id="myParameterizableViewContoller"                        ❶ Defines the controller
    class="org.springframework.web.portlet.mvc.
      ParameterizableViewController">
    <property name="viewName" value="parameterizedView"/>          ❷ Sets viewName
  </bean>                                                              property to JSP
                                                                       name
  <bean id="portletModeHandlerMapping"
    class="org.springframework.web.portlet.handler.               ❸ Defines PortletMode-
      PortletModeHandlerMapping">                                    HandlerMapping bean
    <property name="portletModeMap">
      <map>
        <entry key="view">                                         ❹ Maps view portlet
          <ref bean="myParameterizableViewContoller"/>               mode to controller
        </entry>
      </map>
    </property>
  </bean>
</beans>
```

The `ParameterizableViewController` controller is defined ❶ with a `myParame-terizableViewController` id. The `ParameterizableViewController`'s `viewName` property is set to `parameterizedView` ❷, so the `viewResolver` bean resolves the `viewName` to the /WEB-INF/jsp/parameterizedView.jsp page (see the application-Context.xml file in the WEB-INF folder for the `ViewResolver` definition).

The `PortletModeHandlerMapping` bean is defined ❸; it's responsible for mapping the portlet request to an appropriate handler based on the portlet mode of the incoming request. The `PortletModeHandlerMapping` bean's `portletModeMap` property maps portlet modes to the controller responsible for handling requests in that portlet mode.

The `portletModeMap` property ❹ sets the `myParameterizableViewController` handler as the handler for all requests that are received by the portlet in `VIEW` portlet mode. The `map` subelement of the property element indicates that the type of the `portletModeMap` property is `java.util.Map`. Because `Map` type objects contain key-value pairs, the `entry` element is used to identify the key in the `Map`. The name of the key is specified by the `key` attribute of the `entry` element. The value corresponding to the key is defined using the `ref` subelement of the `entry` element. Because the value of the `entry` element's `key` attribute is `view`, and the `ref` subelement refers to the `myParameterizableViewController` controller, this controller is responsible for handling requests in `VIEW` portlet mode.

Listing 7.8 shows that `ParameterizableViewController` is responsible for handling requests received in `VIEW` portlet mode for the Hello World portlet. If your portlet supports multiple portlet modes, the `ParameterizableViewController`'s `portletModeMap` property will contain `entry` elements corresponding to all the supported portlet modes.

> **NOTE** The `ParameterizableViewController` example in the ch7_Controllers folder uses a separate parameterizedView.jsp JSP page to show the hardcoded "Hello World" message, because `ParameterizableViewController` doesn't provide the option to pass model data to the JSP page. In the case of the `Hello-WorldController` (see listing 7.3), the `handleRenderRequest` method sends the "Hello World" message as model data to the target JSP page.

If you want to use the current portlet mode as the name of the view, the `Portlet-ModeNameViewController` is the right option for you.

7.7.4 *Using the PortletModeNameViewController*

The `PortletModeNameViewController` is a basic controller that returns the portlet mode name as the name of the view to be rendered. For instance, if the current portlet mode is `VIEW`, `PortletModeNameViewController` returns `view` as the view name to be rendered. Like the `ParameterizableViewController`, the `PortletModeNameViewController` is not designed to handle action requests.

Listing 7.9 shows the web application context XML file of a Hello World portlet that uses Spring's built-in `PortletModeNameViewController` handler.

Listing 7.9   A `PortletModeNameViewController` example

```xml
<?xml version="1.0" encoding="UTF-8"?>
<beans ...>
  <bean id="myPortletModeNameViewController"
    class="org.springframework.web.portlet.mvc.
      PortletModeNameViewController">
  </bean>

  <bean id="portletModeHandlerMapping"
    class="org.springframework.web.portlet.handler.
      PortletModeHandlerMapping">
    <property name="portletModeMap">
      <map>
        <entry key="view">
          <ref bean="myPortletModeNameViewController" />
        </entry>
        <entry key="edit">
          <ref bean="myPortletModeNameViewController" />
        </entry>
        <entry key="help">
          <ref bean="myPortletModeNameViewController" />
        </entry>
      </map>
    </property>
  </bean>
</beans>
```

❶ PortletModeName-ViewController definition

❷ Handler mapping definition

❸ View portlet mode mapping

❹ Edit portlet mode mapping

❺ Help portlet mode mapping

The `PortletModeNameViewController` is defined ❶ with an id of `myPortletMode-NameViewController`. The `PortletModeHandlerMapping` bean is defined ❷; it's responsible for mapping the portlet request to an appropriate handler based on the portlet mode of the incoming request. At ❸, ❹, and ❺, the VIEW, EDIT, and HELP portlet modes are each mapped to `myPortletModeNameViewController`.

In listing 7.9, `PortletModeHandlerMapping` maps all portlet requests to the `PortletModeNameViewController`. Let's say a request comes in EDIT portlet mode to the Hello World portlet whose application context is shown in listing 7.9. As the portlet mode of the incoming request is EDIT, `PortletModeHandlerMapping` selects `PortletModeNameViewController` as the handler of the request, because EDIT mode maps to `PortletModeNameViewController`. The `PortletModeNameViewController` returns EDIT as the name of the view that needs to be rendered by the Spring Portlet MVC framework. The `ViewResolver`, defined in the root web application context XML file (see the applicationContext.xml file in the WEB-INF directory of the ch7_Controllers Eclipse project), resolves the EDIT view name to the /WEB-INF/jsp/edit.jsp JSP page.

If you want to invoke an existing portlet using Spring's dispatching mechanism, you should use `PortletWrappingController`.

7.7.5 *Using the PortletWrappingController*

The `PortletWrappingController` internally manages the complete lifecycle of a portlet instance, instead of allowing the lifecycle to be managed by the portlet container. This controller type is most appropriate when you want to invoke an existing portlet with Spring's request-dispatching mechanism.

The following listing shows an application context that uses the `PortletWrapping-Controller` to manage the Hello World portlet created in chapter 1.

Listing 7.10 A `PortletWrappingController` example

```xml
<?xml version="1.0" encoding="UTF-8"?>
<beans ...>
  <bean id="myPortletWrappingController"
    class="org.springframework.web.portlet.mvc.
      PortletWrappingController">                          ① Defines
                                                              PortletWrappingController
    <property name="portletClass">
      <value>chapter07.code.listing.wrapping.             ② Specifies class of
        controller.HelloWorldPortlet</value>                 wrapped portlet
    </property>
    <property name="portletName">
      <value>
        helloWorldPortletWrappingController               ③ Specifies name of
      </value>                                               wrapped portlet
    </property>
  </bean>
  <bean id="portletModeHandlerMapping"
    class="org.springframework.web.portlet.handler.
      PortletModeHandlerMapping">
    <property name="portletModeMap">
      <map>
        <entry key="view">                                ④ Maps VIEW mode
          <ref bean="myPortletWrappingController" />         to controller
        </entry>
      </map>
    </property>
  </bean>
</beans>
```

The `PortletWrappingController` ① is defined. The fully qualified name of the portlet class ② that the `PortletWrappingController` manages is specified. A name is assigned to the portlet managed by the controller ③. If you don't specify a name for the portlet, the name of the controller bean is set as the portlet name. `VIEW` portlet mode ④ is mapped to the `PortletWrappingController`.

> **WARNING** The `PortletWrappingController` internally manages the lifecycle of the wrapped portlet, so you should not declare your wrapped portlet in the portlet.xml file.

`PortletWrappingController` is most useful when Spring's request-dispatching mechanism is used to add features to the wrapped portlet. For instance, you could use

Spring's `HandlerInterceptors` (discussed later in this chapter) to pre- or post-process portlet requests.

> **NOTE** As you saw earlier, methods defined in the `Controller` interface cater to portlet action and render requests. The Spring Portlet MVC framework also provides additional controller interfaces that allow you to handle resource requests (`ResourceAwareController`, covered in chapter 12) and event requests (`EventAwareController`, covered in chapter 11). This shows that controllers in Spring Portlet MVC preserve the different lifecycle phases of a portlet request (action, render, resource, and event), which is a unique feature of Spring Portlet MVC, compared to other web frameworks that support portlet development.

In Spring Portlet MVC, a portlet request needs to be mapped to an appropriate handler. This is achieved by specifying handler mappings in the application context.

7.8   *Using built-in handler mappings*

Handler mapping beans in the Spring Portlet MVC framework are used to map portlet requests to a handler. The mapping can be based on the portlet mode, the value of a request parameter, a combination of both, or any other custom approach. A handler mapping bean must implement the `HandlerMapping` interface either directly or indirectly.

In all the portlet examples that we've covered so far, we've used `PortletModeHandlerMapping` to map incoming portlet requests to an appropriate handler. In this section, we'll discuss the role of handler mappings in portlet request processing and discuss the handler mappings that are available out of the box in the Spring Portlet MVC framework.

> **NOTE** A handler mapping maps a portlet request to exactly one handler; you can't have a portlet request mapped to more than one handler. If you want to add additional functionality to a handler, you can either modify the handler or use *handler interceptors* (discussed in section 7.9).

As shown in figure 7.2, the `DispatcherPortlet` requests that the `HandlerMapping` bean return an appropriate handler for the incoming portlet request. The `HandlerMapping` bean analyzes the portlet request and returns an object of type `HandlerExecutionChain`, which contains a single handler that matches the portlet request and handler interceptors, which are executed before or after the execution of the handler, or both.

Figure 7.5 is an extension to figure 7.2, showing the role played by `HandlerMapping` in processing a portlet request.

In figure 7.5, the `DispatcherPortlet` invokes the handler and handler interceptors of the `HandlerExecutionChain` returned by `HandlerMapping`.

Spring Portlet MVC comes with three `HandlerMapping` implementations: `PortletModeHandlerMapping`, `ParameterHandlerMapping`, and `PortletModeParameterHandlerMapping`, as shown in figure 7.6.

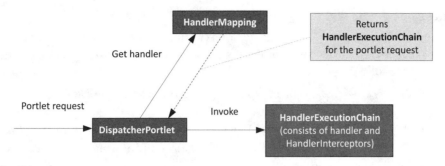

Figure 7.5 The role played by `HandlerMapping` in fulfilling the portlet request. `DispatcherPortlet` obtains a `HandlerExecutionChain` from the `HandlerMapping` bean and invokes the `HandlerExecutionChain`'s handler and interceptors (if any).

If you have special requirements, you can also create your own handler mapping implementation. In the rest of this section, we'll look at how these handler mapping implementations can be used in developing portlets.

Let's look first at the Book Catalog portlet that we'll develop in this section using the built-in handler mappings.

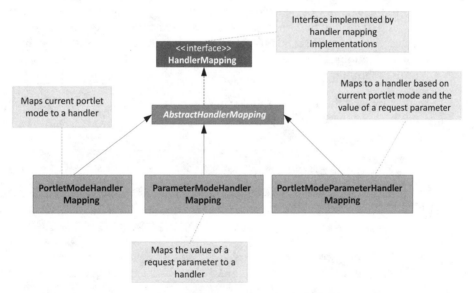

Figure 7.6 The `HandlerMapping` interface is implemented by the `AbstractHandlerMapping` class, which is in turn subclassed by the `PortletModeHandlerMapping`, `ParameterModeHandlerMapping`, and `PortletModeParameterHandlerMapping` classes.

7.8.1   *Developing a Book Catalog portlet with Spring Portlet MVC*

The Book Catalog portlet for this section is a trimmed-down version of the Book Catalog portlet we discussed in previous chapters. This section's Book Catalog portlet consists of the following pages:

- *Home page*—A page that displays all of the books in the catalog (shown in figure 7.7)
- *Add book page*—A page that allows users to add a new book to the catalog
- *Edit book page*—A page that allows users to edit information about an existing book in the catalog

NOTE   Because we're focusing on the Spring Portlet MVC framework features, the requirements for the Book Catalog portlet in this chapter exclude some of the features implemented in previous examples of the Book Catalog portlet.

Figure 7.7 shows the simplified Book Catalog portlet's home page with the option to add, edit, and remove books.

CODE REFERENCE   If you haven't done so already, you should now import the ch7_HandlerMappings Eclipse project into your Eclipse workspace so you can refer to the examples discussed in this section. That project contains example portlets that use the built-in `PortletModeHandlerMapping`, `ParameterHandlerMapping`, and `PortletModeParameterHandlerMapping` handler mapping implementations. It also contains an example portlet that shows how to create handler mapping chains.

Let's now look at the `PortletModeHandlerMapping` built-in handler mapping implementation in Spring Portlet MVC.

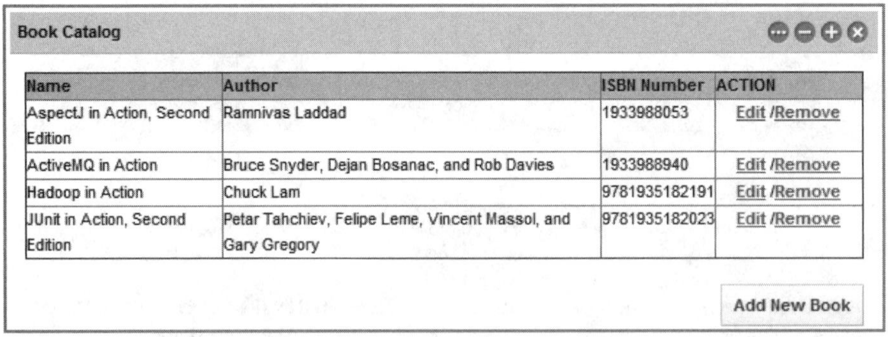

Name	Author	ISBN Number	ACTION
AspectJ in Action, Second Edition	Ramnivas Laddad	1933988053	Edit /Remove
ActiveMQ in Action	Bruce Snyder, Dejan Bosanac, and Rob Davies	1933988940	Edit /Remove
Hadoop in Action	Chuck Lam	9781935182191	Edit /Remove
JUnit in Action, Second Edition	Petar Tahchiev, Felipe Leme, Vincent Massol, and Gary Gregory	9781935182023	Edit /Remove

Add New Book

Figure 7.7   The Book Catalog portlet page that shows the list of books in the catalog. The portlet allows users to add books to the catalog, edit books already in the catalog, and remove books from the catalog.

7.8.2 Using PortletModeHandlerMapping

As you've seen in earlier examples, `PortletModeHandlerMapping` maps an incoming portlet request to a handler based on the current portlet mode, which can be obtained using the `PortletRequest` object's `getPortletMode` method. Our next listing shows the application context for a portlet that uses `PortletModeHandlerMapping`.

Listing 7.11 A `PortletModeHandlerMapping` example

```
<beans ...>
  <bean id="editModeController" class="chapter07.code.
      ➥listing.controller.EditModeController"/>

  <bean id="viewModeController" class="chapter07.code.
      ➥listing.controller.ViewModeController"/>
    <property name="bookService">
      <ref bean="bookService"/>
    </property>
  </bean>

  <bean id="helpModeController" class="chapter07.code.
      ➥listing.controller.HelpModeController"/>

  <bean id="portletModeHandlerMapping"
    class="org.springframework.web.portlet.handler.
    ➥PortletModeHandlerMapping">                        portletModeMap
    <property name="portletModeMap">                 ◁┘ property
      <map>
        <entry key="view">
            <ref bean="viewModeController" />          VIEW mode mapped to
        </entry>                                       ViewModeController
        <entry key="edit">
          <ref bean="editModeController" />              EDIT mode mapped to
        </entry>                                         EditModeController
        <entry key="help">
          <ref bean="helpModeController" />                HELP mode mapped to
        </entry>                                           HelpModeController
      </map>
    </property>
  </bean>
  ...
</beans>
```

As discussed earlier, the `PortletModeHandlerMapping` object's `portletModeMap` property provides the portlet mode to handler mapping information. For instance, `VIEW` mode is mapped to the `ViewModeController` handler, and `EDIT` mode is mapped to the `EditModeController` handler.

    If you want to use a properties file to maintain the portlet mode to handler mapping information, you can use the `PortletModeHandlerMapping` bean's `mappings` property instead of the `portletModeMap` property. The next listing shows how listing 7.11 can be rewritten using the `mappings` property.

Listing 7.12   A `PortletModeHandlerMapping` example

```
<beans...
xmlns:util="http://www.springframework.org/schema/util"          ◁─┐  Includes Spring's
xsi:schemaLocation="                                              ❶   util schema
...
http://www.springframework.org/schema/util
http://www.springframework.org/schema/util/spring-util-3.0.xsd
">
  <util:properties  id="modemappings"                        ❷  Loads modemapping.
      location="WEB-INF/modemappings.properties"/>               properties file
  ...
  <bean id="portletModeHandlerMapping"
    class="org.springframework.web.portlet.handler.
    ➥PortletModeHandlerMapping">                             ❸  References mappings
    <property name="mappings" ref="modemappings"/>    ◁─┘        defined in properties file
  </bean>
  ...
</beans>
```

Spring's `util` schema ❶ is referenced. The `util` schema's `properties` element ❷ loads the WEB-INF/modemappings.properties file and creates a bean of type `java.util.Properties` with a bean id of `modemappings`. The `PortletModeHandlerBean`'s mappings property ❸ is set to the `modemappings` bean.

The modemappings.properties file contains the portlet mode to handler mapping, as shown here:

```
view=viewModeController
edit=editModeController
help=helpModeController
```

> **CODE REFERENCE**   Refer to the portletModeHandlerMappingExample-portlet.xml and modemappings.properties files in ch7_HandlerMappings.

The `PortletModeHandlerMapping` is useful only if you want to use the current portlet mode to identify the appropriate handler for the portlet request. If you want to use a request parameter value to identify the appropriate handler for the portlet request, you should use the `ParameterHandlerMapping` bean.

7.8.3   Using ParameterHandlerMapping

One of the shortcomings of `PortletModeHandlerMapping` is that it requires you to have only one controller for each supported portlet mode. If you don't define any custom portlet modes for your portlet, you'll have exactly three controllers for your portlet: one for each portlet mode (`VIEW`, `EDIT`, and `HELP`).

If you use `PortletModeHandlerMapping` for the Book Catalog portlet, a single handler is responsible for all the business functions that the portlet needs to perform. In most multipage portlets, like the Book Catalog portlet, it's preferable to split the functionality of the portlet across different handlers, so that they're each more manageable and focused.

To split portlet functionality across different handlers, you need a `HandlerMapping` implementation that maps portlet requests to different controllers based on the values of request parameters, session attributes, a combination of the two, or on any other custom handler mapping approach. The `ParameterHandlerMapping` implementation provides mapping of portlet requests to a handler based on the value of a request parameter.

The next listing shows the `ParameterHandlerMapping` definition in a web application context XML file.

Listing 7.13 A `ParameterHandlerMapping` example

```
<bean id="parameterHandlerMapping"
  class="org.springframework.web.portlet.handler.
    ParameterHandlerMapping">
  <property name="defaultHandler"
    ref="showBooksController"/>

  <property name="parameterName" value="myaction"/>

  <property name="parameterMap">
    <map>
      <entry key="books"
        value-ref="showBooksController"/>
      <entry key="addBook"
        value-ref="addBookController" />
      <entry key="addBookForm"
        value-ref="addBookController" />
      <entry key="editBook"
        value-ref="editBookController" />
      <entry key="editBookForm"
        value-ref="editBookController" />
      <entry key="removeBook"
        value-ref="removeBookController" /> </map>
  </property>
</bean>
```

1 Default handler for mapping

2 Name of request parameter

3 Parameter value to handler mapping

The `defaultHandler` property **1** defines the default handler for the mapping, if no matching handler is found. The `parameterName` property **2** identifies the request parameter name whose value will be used by the handler mapping to find an appropriate handler. Because the value of `parameterName` is specified as `myaction`, the value of the `myaction` request parameter is used to find an appropriate handler for the portlet request. The `ParameterHandlerMapping` bean's `parameterMap` property **3** specifies the handler corresponding to the value of the request parameter named `myaction`.

CODE REFERENCE Refer to the parameterHandlerMappingExample-portlet.xml web application context XML file in ch7_HandlerMappings to see how the `ParameterHandlerMapping` bean is configured.

Figure 7.8 shows how the `ParameterHandlerMapping` bean defined in listing 7.13 selects an appropriate handler for the portlet request.

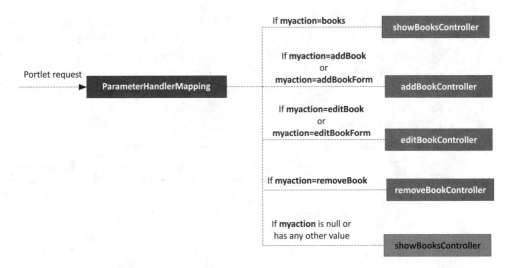

Figure 7.8 `ParameterHandlerMapping` **maps portlet requests to appropriate handlers based on the value of the** `myaction` **request parameter. If the request parameter is missing from the request, or if its value isn't mapped to any handler, the handler specified using the** `defaultHandler` **mapping is executed.**

> **NOTE** If you don't specify the `parameterName` property, `ParameterHandler-Mapping` considers `action` to be the name of the parameter for finding an appropriate handler.

From figure 7.8, you can draw following inferences:

- If the value of the `myaction` request parameter is `books`, the portlet request is handled by the `showBooksController` handler. If the value of the `myaction` request parameter is `addBook` or `addBookForm`, the portlet request is handled by the `addBookController` handler, and so on.

- If no matching handler is found in the `parameterMap` properties, the default `showBooksController` handler handles the portlet request. For instance, in listing 7.13, if the `myaction` parameter isn't in the request or its value is blank or anything but `books`, `addBook`, `addBookForm`, `removeBook`, `editBook`, or `edit-BookForm`, the `showBooksController` handles the portlet request.

> **NOTE** The `defaultHandler` property is defined in the `AbstractHandler-Mapping` class and is available to all built-in `HandlerMappings` in the Spring Portlet MVC framework.

You saw that the `ParameterHandlerMapping` implementation checks the value of a request parameter to determine the appropriate handler for the request. So how can you send a request parameter to the portlet? You do that by using hidden form fields or by adding the request parameter to the portlet URL with the `setParameter(...)`

method or the <param> portlet tag. The portlet URLs are discussed in chapter 2 and the <param> portlet tag is discussed in chapter 6. We'll look at hidden form fields here.

CREATING HIDDEN FORM FIELDS

To send a request parameter to a portlet, you can create a hidden field on the HTML form, and give the field the same name as the request parameter your handler mapping inspects to find a matching handler. The value of the hidden field is set depending on the user action.

Suppose in the Book Catalog portlet (shown in figure 7.7) that when a user clicks the Add Book button, the addBookController handles the request and renders a form in which the user can enter details for a new book. The handler mapping in listing 7.13 suggests that if the value of the myaction request parameter is addBookForm, the addBookController handler is responsible for handling the request. You can pass the myaction request parameter with a value of addBookForm to the Book Catalog portlet by creating a hidden field named myaction and setting its value to addBook-Form, as shown here:

```
<form name="booksForm" action="${myPortletUrl}"... >
     ...
   <input type="hidden" name="myaction" value="addBookForm"/>
   <input type="submit" value="Add Book"/>
</form>
```

When the Add Book button is clicked, the form is submitted to the myPortletUrl portlet URL, which sends the myaction form field as a request parameter.

Let's now look at Spring's built-in PortletModeParameterHandlerMapping handler mapping implementation.

7.8.4 Using PortletModeParameterHandlerMapping

The PortletModeHandlerMapping and ParameterHandlerMapping approaches either restrict the use of a handler to a single portlet mode or to a particular value of a request parameter. The PortletModeParameterHandlerMapping approach allows you to use a single handler for different portlet modes and for different values of a request parameter. For instance, you could define the following handler mapping: if the myaction request parameter has a value of addBookForm or addBook *and* the current portlet mode is VIEW, the handler for the request is addBookController.

The following listing shows an example of using PortletModeParameter-HandlerMapping to resolve handlers based on portlet mode and the value of a request parameter.

Listing 7.14 A PortletModeParameterHandlerMapping example

```
<bean id="portletModeParameterHandlerMapping"
  class="org.springframework.web.portlet.handler.
    ➡PortletModeParameterHandlerMapping">
```

```
<property name="defaultHandler"
    ref="showBooksController"/>
<property name="parameterName" value="myaction"/>
<property name="portletModeParameterMap">
  <map>
    <entry key="view">
      <map>
        <entry key="books"
          value-ref="showBooksController"/>
        <entry key="addBook"
          value-ref="addBookController" />
        <entry key="addBookForm"
          value-ref="addBookController" />
        <entry key="editBook"
          value-ref="editBookController" />
        <entry key="editBookForm"
          value-ref="editBookController" />
        <entry key="removeBook"
          value-ref="removeBookController" />
      </map>
    </entry>
    <entry key="edit">
      <map>
        <entry key="prefs" value-ref="editModeController"/>
      </map>
    </entry>
    <entry key="help">
      <map>
        <entry key="help" value-ref="helpModeController"/>
      </map>
    </entry>
  </map>
</property>
</bean>
```

❶ Handler mapping properties

❷ VIEW portlet mode–level mapping

❸ Parameter-level mapping

The `PortletModeParameterHandlerMapping` handler mapping properties ❶ are specified. The `defaultHandler` property defines the default handler for the mapping if no match is found. The `parameterName` property identifies the request parameter name (`myaction`, in this case) whose value will be used by the handler mapping to find an appropriate handler. The `PortletModeParameterHandlerMapping`'s `portletMode-ParameterMap` property specifies the handler corresponding to a portlet mode and the value of the `myaction` request parameter.

The first level of mapping is defined for the portlet request ❷ using portlet mode. If the portlet mode of the portlet request is VIEW, the portlet request is matched to a handler ❸, using the value of the `myaction` request parameter. Similarly, mappings for EDIT and HELP portlet modes are defined.

CODE REFERENCE Refer to the portletModeParameterHandlerMapping-Example-portlet.xml web application context XML file in ch7_HandlerMappings to see an example configuration for the `PortletModeParameterHandler-Mapping` bean.

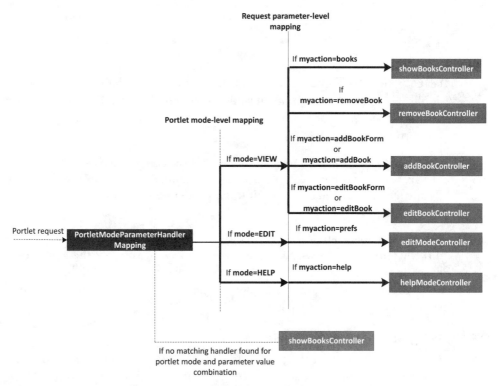

Figure 7.9   A portlet request is mapped to a handler by matching the current portlet mode and the value of the `myaction` request parameter. The default handler is executed if no matching handler is found for the combination of portlet mode and request parameter value.

Figure 7.9 shows how portlet requests map to controllers, as defined by the Portlet-ModeParameterHandlerMapping in listing 7.14. PortletModeParameterHandlerMapping takes into account the current portlet mode and value of myaction request parameter to find an appropriate handler for the request.

When using PortletModeParameterHandlerMapping, the default behavior of the handler mapping is to restrict you from specifying duplicate entries for the parameter value in different portlet modes. For example, the following handler mapping will result in an exception:

```
<entry key="view">
  <map>
    <entry key="books" value-ref="showBooksController"/>
    <entry key="addBook" value-ref="addBookController"/>
    <entry key="editBook" value-ref="editBookController"/>
  </map>
</entry>
<entry key="edit">
  <map>
    <entry key="prefs" value-ref="editModeController"/>
```

```
        <entry key="editBook" value-ref="editPrefsController"/>
    </map>
</entry>
```

In this handler mapping definition, duplicate entries exist for the parameter value editBook in VIEW and EDIT modes of the portlet. The default behavior of disallowing duplicate entries for the parameter value in different portlet modes can be overridden by setting the PortletModeParameterHandlerMapping's allowDuplicateParameters property to true.

> **NOTE**   Setting the PortletModeParameterHandlerMapping's allowDuplicate-Parameters property to true isn't recommended because of the unexpected portlet behavior that may result if the portlet mode is overridden by the portal or portlet container.

If you want to create your own handler mapping implementation, you can either directly implement the HandlerMapping interface or subclass the AbstractHandler-Mapping class. The AbstractHandlerMapping class provides additional properties that allow you to specify a default handler for the mapping, add handler interceptors, and create handler mapping chains.

7.8.5   *Using AbstractHandlerMapping*

AbstractHandlerMapping is an abstract class that implements the HandlerMapping interface (see figure 7.6) and does the following:

- Specifies a default handler if no matching handler for the portlet request is found
- Creates handler mapping chains
- Specifies handler interceptors for pre- and post-processing of portlet requests

The built-in handler mappings we've discussed so far are subclasses of Abstract-HandlerMapping, so the preceding features are also available to them. Let's look at each of these features in turn.

DEFAULT HANDLERS

AbstractHandlerMapping's defaultHandler property specifies the default handler for the mapping if no matching handler is found. You saw earlier in this section how this property is used in handler mappings.

HANDLER MAPPING CHAINS

A handler mapping chain is created when multiple handler mappings map to a particular request; the highest priority handler mapping is the first handler mapping in the chain. AbstractHandlerMapping's order property supports the creation of handler mapping chains. The order property has an integer value that specifies the priority of the handler mapping.

If you specify more than one handler mapping in your application context, the handler mapping with the *lowest* order value has the *highest* priority and is matched first against the portlet request. The matching handler returned by the highest priority handler mapping is responsible for handling the request. If a matching handler isn't found by the first handler mapping, the handler mapping with the next lowest priority is given the opportunity to find a matching handler. It's because of the `order` property that you can create handler mapping chains for your portlet.

The next listing shows a handler mapping chain consisting of `PortletMode-HandlerMapping` and `PortletModeParameterHandlerMapping`.

Listing 7.15 A handler mapping chain example

```
<beans ...>
  <util:properties id="modemappings_" location="WEB-
    INF/modemappings_.properties" />
  ...
  <bean id="portletModeHandlerMapping"
  class="org.springframework.web.portlet.handler.       ❶ PortletModeHandler-
       ⇒PortletModeHandlerMapping">                        Mapping definition
    <property name="mappings" ref="modemappings_"/>
    <property name="order" value="0"/>
    ...
  </bean>
  <bean id="parameterHandlerMapping"
    class="org.springframework.web.portlet.handler.       ❷ PortletModeParame-
         ⇒PortletModeParameterHandlerMapping">               terHandlerMapping
    <property name="parameterName" value="myaction"/>        definition
    <property name="order" value="1"/>
    ...
    <property name="portletModeParameterMap">
      <map>
        ...
      </map>
    </property>
  </bean>
  ...
</beans>
```

The `PortletModeHandlerMapping` is defined ❶, which maps a portlet request based on the current portlet mode of the portlet request. The `order` property of the handler mapping is set to 0. The `PortletModeParameterHandlerMapping` is defined ❷, which maps a portlet request based on the combination of current portlet mode and the value of the `myaction` request parameter. The `order` property of this handler mapping is set to 1.

> **CODE REFERENCE** Refer to the handlerMappingChainExample-portlet.xml web application context XML file in ch7_HandlerMappings to view the complete handler mapping chain shown in listing 7.15.

In listing 7.15, the value of the `order` property for `PortletModeHandlerMapping` is lower than the `order` value for `PortletModeParameterHandlerMapping`, so the portlet request is first matched against `PortletModeHandlerMapping` to find an appropriate handler. If no matching handler is found, `PortletModeParameterHandlerMapping` is consulted to find a matching handler for the portlet request.

> **NOTE** You should only specify `defaultHandler` for the lowest-priority handler mapping (the mapping with the highest value for the `order` property) in the handler chain. If you specify `defaultHandler` for higher-priority handler mappings, the `defaultHandler` would always result in a match for the incoming portlet request.

HANDLER INTERCEPTORS

The `AbstractHandlerMapping`'s `interceptors` property defines handler interceptors, which allow you to pre- and post-process the portlet request. You can specify any number of interceptors for a mapping by using this property.

Let's now look at handler interceptors and how to configure them in the application context.

7.9   *Using handler interceptors*

In some scenarios, you may need to pre- or post-process a portlet request, or both, for various reasons, such as logging, security, or tracing. Spring Portlet MVC provides *handler interceptors* to allow you to pre- and post-process portlet requests.

Handler interceptors are special beans in the Portlet MVC framework that implement the `HandlerInterceptor` interface. They're similar to servlet filters in servlet technology; they intercept portlet requests targeted to a handler and pre- or post-process the request. Handler interceptors help remove cross-cutting concerns from the handler code, such as logging, security checks, and so on.

In this section, we'll look at the role played by handler interceptors and how they're implemented and configured in Spring's web application context XML file.

Let's first look at how handler interceptors are implemented and configured.

7.9.1   *Implementing and configuring a handler interceptor*

Handler interceptor beans must implement the `HandlerInterceptor` interface directly or indirectly. You can create your own handler interceptor by implementing the `HandlerInterceptor` interface or subclassing the `HandlerInterceptorAdapter` abstract class.

> **NOTE** Like Spring Portlet MVC controllers, handler interceptors also preserve the lifecycle semantics of a portlet request by providing specific methods for intercepting the different lifecycle methods.

Handler interceptors are referenced by the `interceptor` property of the handler mapping. This listing shows a handler mapping that uses handler interceptors.

Listing 7.16   A handler interceptor example

```
<bean id="loggingInterceptor" class="..."/>
<bean id="securityInterceptor" class="..."/>
```

```
<bean id="portletModeHandlerMapping"
    class="org.springframework.web.portlet.handler.
        ➥PortletModeHandlerMapping">
    ...
    <property name="interceptors">
        <list>
            <ref bean="loggingInterceptor"/>
            <ref bean="securityInterceptor"/>
        </list>
    </property>
</bean>
```

In listing 7.16, `PortletModeHandlerMapping` specifies two interceptors, `logging-Interceptor` and `securityInterceptor`, which pre- and post-process portlet requests before and after the processing of the handler.

> **NOTE** If you're using Portlet 2.0, you can use portlet filters to pre- and post-process portlet requests. The difference lies in the scope: portlet filters do pre- and post-processing at the portlet level, and handler interceptors do pre- and post-processing at the handler level.

Let's now look at how handler interceptors do the pre- and post-processing of portlet requests and responses.

7.9.2 *Processing requests using handler interceptors*

Figure 7.10 shows the role played by handler interceptors in processing a render request.

The sequence diagram in figure 7.10 shows the order in which `HandlerInterceptor` methods are executed by `DispatcherPortlet` during the portlet request processing. The interceptor's `preHandle` method is invoked before the execution of the handler; `postHandle` is invoked after the execution of the handler; `afterCompletion` is invoked at the end to do any cleanup, if required.

Spring Portlet MVC provides a built-in `HandlerInterceptor` implementation, `ParameterMappingInterceptor`, which is useful when using the `ParameterHandler-Mapping` and `PortletModeParameterHandlerMapping` implementations. `Parameter-MappingInterceptor` ensures that the value of the request parameter (used for finding an appropriate handler in `ParameterHandlerMapping` and `PortletModeParameter-HandlerMapping`) is forwarded from the action request to the following render request; this can help in ensuring that the render and action methods of the same handler are invoked.

> **CODE REFERENCE** Refer to the handlerMappingChainExample-portlet.xml web application context XML file in ch7_HandlerMappings to see how `ParameterMappingInterceptor` is configured.

Our next listing shows `PortletModeParameterHandlerMapping`, which uses the `ParameterMappingInterceptor`.

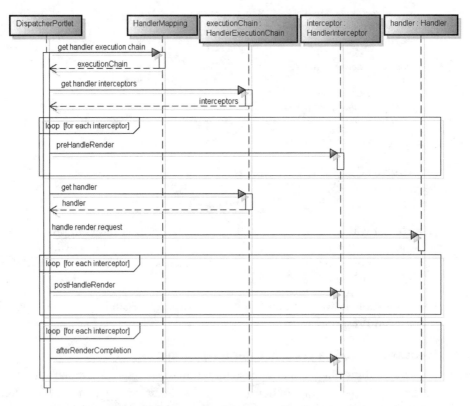

Figure 7.10 Handler interceptors are invoked before and after the execution of the handler. The preRenderHandle method is invoked before the handler execution, and the postRenderHandle method is invoked after the handler execution. The afterRenderCompletion method is invoked after the postRenderHandle method of all the interceptors is executed.

Listing 7.17   A handler interceptor example

```
  <beans ...>
    ...
<bean id="parameterInterceptor"
  class="org.springframework.web.portlet.handler.
  ➥ParameterMappingInterceptor">
  <property name="parameterName" value="myaction" />
</bean>
...
<bean id="portletModeParameterHandlerMapping"
  class="org.springframework.web.portlet.handler.
  ➥PortletModeParameterHandlerMapping">
  <property name="parameterName"
      value="myaction" />
  <property name="order" value="1" />
  <property name="interceptors">
    <list>
      <ref bean="parameterInterceptor" />
    </list>
```

❶ **Definition of Parameter-MappingInterceptor**

❷ **Parameter name used in handler mapping**

❸ **Interceptors for handler mapping**

```
      </property>
      <property name="defaultHandler" ref="showBooksController" />
      <property name="portletModeParameterMap">
       <map>
         <entry key="view">
           <map>
            <entry key="addBook"
                value-ref="addBookController" />
            <entry key="editBook"
                value-ref="editBookController" />
            ...
           </map>
         </entry>
       </map>
      </property>
    </bean>
    ...
</beans>
```

❹ **Mapping of handlers to mode and parameter**

The `ParameterMappingInterceptor`'s `parameterName` property ❶ is set to `myaction`. This property specifies the name of the request parameter whose value must be maintained in the render request that follows the action request processing.

The `PortletModeParameterHandlerMapping`'s `parameterName` property ❷ is set to `myaction`. It identifies the request parameter name used by `PortletModeParameter-HandlerMapping`.

The `PortletModeParameterHandlerMapping`'s `interceptors` property ❸ specifies the list of interceptors that apply to the handler mapping. `ParameterMapping-Interceptor` is the only interceptor that applies to `PortletModeParameter-HandlerMapping`.

`addBookController` and `editBookController` handle incoming portlet requests ❹ if the portlet mode is `VIEW` and the value of the `myaction` request parameter is `addBook` or `editBook`, respectively.

Figure 7.11 shows the request flow for a Book Catalog portlet that uses the application context defined in listing 7.17.

The value of the `myaction` request parameter ❶ is `addBook`, which means that `addBookController` is responsible for handling this action request (see listing 7.17). The `ParameterMappingInterceptor`'s `preHandleAction` method ❷ is invoked, which sets a render parameter with the same name and value as the incoming `myaction` parameter. The handler method for the action request ❸ is invoked. `DispatcherPortlet` again consults the `HandlerMapping` ❹ to obtain the handler execution chain.

In figure 7.11, the `ParameterMappingInterceptor`'s `preHandleAction` method is responsible for calling the `ActionResponse`'s `setRenderParameter` method to set the `myaction` request parameter as a render parameter. Because render parameters are available to the portlet in the following render request, `PortletMode-ParameterHandlerMapping` again returns `addBookController` as the handler for the render request.

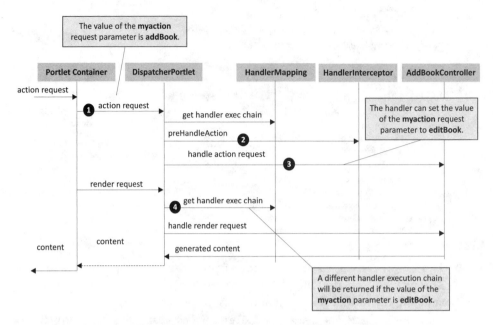

Figure 7.11   The request flow when an action request is received by `DispatcherPortlet`. The `AddBookController` is the handler for the action request because the value of the `myaction` parameter is `addBook`. If `AddBookController` changes the `myaction` parameter's value to `editBook`, the render request would be handled by `EditBookController` instead.

So far in this chapter, we've discussed scenarios in which exceptions don't occur during request processing. In real applications, this is rarely the case. Spring Portlet MVC provides a sophisticated exception-handling mechanism that allows you to gracefully handle exceptions that occur during request handling.

7.10   *Handling exceptions*

In Spring Portlet MVC, `DispatcherPortlet` catches exceptions thrown during request handling and uses registered *handler exception resolvers* to find the error view corresponding to the exception thrown. A handler exception resolver is a special bean that implements the `HandlerExceptionResolver` interface and is configured in the web application context XML like any other Spring bean.

The handler exception resolver defines `resolveException` methods that return `ModelAndView` objects. The returned `ModelAndView` object contains an error view and model information. `DispatcherPortlet` then uses `ViewResolver` to resolve the error view information and dispatches a request to `ViewRendererServlet` to render the error view.

Let's look at how a request is handled when an exception is thrown during request processing.

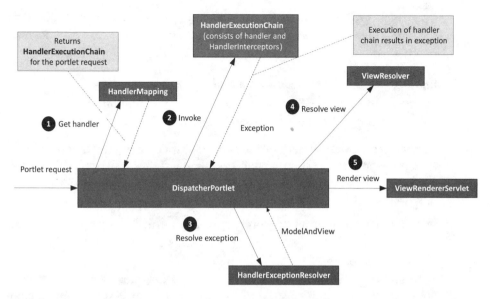

Figure 7.12 `DispatcherPortlet` uses `HandlerExceptionResolver` to resolve exceptions that occur during the execution of the handler. `HandlerExceptionResolver` returns a `ModelAndView` object that is then forwarded by `DispatcherPortlet` to `ViewRendererServlet` to render the view.

7.10.1 *Request handling with exceptions*

Figure 7.12 is an extension of figure 7.5, showing how `HandlerExceptionResolver` is used in the Spring Portlet MVC framework.

`DispatcherPortlet` obtains the `HandlerExecutionChain` **1** from `Handler-Mapping`. `DispatcherPortlet` invokes the `HandlerExecutionChain` **2**, which results in an exception being thrown.

`DispatcherPortlet` uses `HandlerExceptionResolver` **3** to resolve the exception thrown by `HandlerExecutionChain`. The `HandlerExceptionResolver` returns a `ModelAndView` object, which contains information about the view to be rendered for the thrown exception along with the corresponding model data.

`ViewResolver` is used to resolve the view to be rendered **4**. `DispatcherPortlet` dispatches a request to the `ViewRendererServlet` **5** and sends the model data as request attributes for rendering the view.

> **NOTE** `HandlerExceptionResolvers` are detected by type; `Dispatcher-Portlet` autodetects handler exception resolvers based on the type of bean defined in the application context of the portlet, or in the root web application context, and applies them when an exception occurs.

You can create your own exception resolver either by directly implementing the `HandlerExceptionResolver` interface or by extending the `AbstractHandlerException-Resolver` subclass, which allows you to control the handlers to which the `HandlerExceptionResolver` applies and to create a `HandlerExceptionResolver` chain.

Spring provides a concrete implementation of `AbstractHandlerException-Resolver`—the `SimpleMappingExceptionResolver`—that allows you to map exception class names to view names.

7.10.2 *Mapping exceptions to a view based on the exception class*

The `SimpleMappingExceptionResolver` maps an exception class name to the view that is to be rendered when the exception occurs.

> **CODE REFERENCE** Refer to the portletModeParameterHandlerMapping-Example-portlet.xml web application context XML file in ch7_Handler-Mappings to see a sample configuration for the `SimpleMappingException-Resolver` bean.

Let's take a close look at the properties supported by `SimpleMappingException-Resolver`.

EXCEPTION MAPPINGS

Exception mappings are specified with the `exceptionMappings` property, which defines the mapping of exception class names (not necessarily fully qualified class names) to view names. You can specify complete or partial exception class names using this property.

If you specify partial exception class names, the exception resolver maps all exception classes containing the partial class name to the same view name. For instance, consider the following definition of a `SimpleMappingExceptionResolver` bean in an application context:

```
<bean id="exceptionResolver"
  class="org.springframework.web.portlet.handler.
    ➥SimpleMappingExceptionResolver">
  <property name="exceptionMappings">
   <map>
      <entry key="StateException" value="myExceptionView"/>
   </map>
  </property>
</bean>
```

In the preceding `SimpleMappingExceptionResolver` definition, the `exception-Mappings` property defines a single mapping from the `StateException` exception class to the `myExceptionView` view name. The preceding exception mapping maps all exception classes that contain `StateException` in their name to `myException-View`. For example, if your portlet class throws `IllegalComponentStateException`, `IllegalMonitorStateException`, `IllegalPathStateException`, `IllegalState-Exception`, `IllegalThreadStateException` (which are all built-in exceptions in Java), or `MyUnknownStateException` (which is a custom exception), all these exceptions are mapped to the `myExceptionView` view name.

If you want to specify exception mappings in a properties file, you can do so as shown here:

```
<util:properties  id="exceptionmappings"
    location="WEB-INF/exceptionmappings.properties"/>

<bean id="exceptionResolver"
  class="org.springframework.web.portlet.handler.
    ➥SimpleMappingExceptionResolver">
  <property name="exceptionMappings" ref="exceptionMappings"/>
</bean>
```

If the `mappedHandlers` or `mappedHandlerClasses` property isn't set, the exception resolver applies to all the handlers in the application context, as in the previous case.

HANDLER MAPPINGS

You can specify the handlers to which the exception resolver applies by using the `mappedHandlers` and `mappedHandlerClasses` properties, as shown here:

```
<bean id="exceptionResolver"
  class="org.springframework.web.portlet.handler.
    ➥SimpleMappingExceptionResolver">
  <property name="exceptionMappings">
   <map>
     <entry key="StateException" value="myExceptionView"/>
   </map>
   </property>
  <property name="mappedHandlers">
    <set>
      <ref bean="showBooksController"/>
    </set>
   </property>
</bean>
```

The `mappedHandlers` property specifies that `showBooksController` is the only handler to which the exception resolver applies; an exception thrown by any other handler won't be resolved by this exception resolver.

DISPLAYING A VIEW WHEN AN EXCEPTION MAPPING ISN'T FOUND

If you want a particular view to be rendered if no exception mapping is found for the exception name or class, you can specify it with the `defaultErrorView` property. If the `mappedHandlers` or `mappedHandlerClasses` property is defined, the `defaultError-View` name applies only to the mapped handlers.

The following bean definition shows how you can use the `defaultErrorView` property:

```
<bean id="exceptionResolver"
    class="org.springframework.web.portlet.handler.
      ➥SimpleMappingExceptionResolver">
    <property name="exceptionMappings">
     <map>
       <entry key="StateException" value="myExceptionView"/>
     </map>
    </property>
    <property name="mappedHandlers">
```

```
      <set>
        <ref bean="showBooksController"/>
      </set>
    </property>
    <property name="defaultErrorView" value="defaultViewName"/>
</bean>
```

In the preceding definition of an exception resolver, if an exception that doesn't contain `StateException` in its name is thrown by the `showBooksController` handler, the `defaultViewName` view is rendered.

THE HANDLER-EXCEPTION-RESOLVER CHAIN

The `order` property defines the priority of the handler exception resolver. As with handler mappings, the `order` property is used for chaining handler exception resolvers. The exception resolver with the *lowest* order value is applied *first* for resolving the thrown exception. If the exception is resolved by an exception resolver in the chain, the execution of the chain is aborted and the `ModelAndView` object is returned to the `DispatcherPortlet`.

ACCESSING THE EXCEPTION AS A MODEL ATTRIBUTE

The `exceptionAttribute` property specifies the name of the model attribute with which the exception is available as a request attribute. You can use this exception attribute in your JSP pages to show the message contained in the exception.

7.11   *Summary*

In this chapter, you saw how Spring Portlet MVC simplifies the development of multi-page portlets by abstracting complex activities like exception handling, view resolution, and request dispatching. You learned that when using Spring Portlet MVC, request-handling code is moved to controllers or request handlers. You saw that `DispatcherPortlet` is responsible for analyzing the portlet request and delegating request handling to an appropriate controller based on the handler mapping strategy defined in the application context. You saw how `HandlerInterceptors` can be used to pre- and post-process requests. If an exception occurs during request processing, the configured `HandlerExceptionResolver` is used to resolve the exception to a customized error view. In normal request processing or in the case of exception processing, `ViewResolvers` configured in the application context are used to resolve logical views to actual views, which are then rendered by `ViewRenderServlet`.

In the next chapter, we'll discuss annotation support in Spring Portlet MVC, and you'll see how to test Spring Portlet MVC portlets using mock objects and Spring's `TestContext` framework.

Annotation-driven
development with Spring

8

This chapter covers

- Spring Portlet MVC annotations
- Dependency injection using JSR 330 and JSR 250
- Validation using Spring Validation API and JSR 303
- Using Spring's form tag library
- Localization and file upload support
- Unit testing with Spring's TestContext framework

In the previous chapter, you created Spring controllers and provided a `Handler-Mapping` bean definition in the web application context XML file to map portlet requests to appropriate controllers. But wouldn't it be easier if you could specify which portlet request is handled by a controller in the controller class itself? In this chapter, we'll expand on the core concepts covered in the previous chapter and see how Spring's annotation support helps you reduce the amount of configuration information in the application context XML files and simplify application development.

The annotations covered in this chapter span multiple aspects of portlet development using Spring, from writing request handlers, to dependency injection, to validation and testing. This chapter demonstrates these aspects in the development of the Book Catalog portlet, to show how Spring simplifies portlet development using annotations.

In the first half of this chapter, we'll look at Spring Portlet MVC annotations and discuss dependency injection using Spring's `@Autowired` annotation, JSR 330's `@Inject` annotation, and JSR 250's `@Resource` annotation. As we go through the implementation of the Book Catalog portlet, you'll see how Spring Portlet MVC annotations reduce the direct dependency of portlet request handlers on the Portlet API.

Most of the second half of this chapter focuses on the Spring Validation API, JSR 303's bean validation features, Spring's form tag library, and how you can test Spring Portlet MVC controllers. Because testing controllers is an important aspect of developing portlets, we'll look at how Spring simplifies testing using mock objects and the TestContext framework. Toward the end of this chapter, we'll look at how you can localize content using Spring Portlet MVC, upload files from a portlet, and add JavaScript and CSS to the portal page that contains the portlet.

The version of the Book Catalog portlet that we'll develop in this chapter is a multipage portlet that does the following:

- Uses Spring Portlet MVC annotations to develop controllers
- Uses dependency injection annotations to wire services
- Uses the Spring form tag library to create portlet pages
- Uses JSR 303 to validate domain objects
- Uses the Spring TestContext framework to unit test and integration test controllers

If you're new to Java annotations, you may be wondering what they are, how they're used, and what benefits they offer. The next section will provide a brief overview of annotations to set the stage for the rest of the chapter.

8.1   An overview of annotations

Annotations define metadata (data about data) that's specified in the application source code. You can think of annotations as instructions to the compiler and runtime environment about tasks that should be performed during compilation or at runtime.

Support for annotations was added to Java in Java 5. Annotations are represented by the @ symbol followed by the name of the annotation (like `@Controller` or `@Resource`).

Annotations can be used by tools to do any of the following:

- Generate boilerplate code
- Write configuration information in configuration files

- Provide information about application code to tools
- Modify program behavior at runtime

In most application development scenarios, metadata about the application is specified in external configuration files:

- *Web application deployment descriptor*—Contains information about servlets and the URL they map to
- *Web application context XML file*—In Spring Portlet MVC (discussed in the previous chapter), contains bean definitions

Annotations may have compile-time or runtime semantics, depending upon their definitions; when you create an annotation, you specify whether it's applied at runtime or during the compilation of the application's source code. For instance, the @Deprecated built-in Java annotation is a compile-time annotation that informs the Java compiler that a Java element, such as a method, field, interface, or class, is deprecated. If an @Deprecated Java element is used anywhere in the application, the Java compiler issues a warning specifying that the application source code makes use of a deprecated Java element.

Annotations with runtime semantics are meant to be read at runtime, using reflection, to change program behavior. For instance, the @RequestMapping annotation in Spring Portlet MVC has runtime semantics. It's used by Spring Portlet MVC controllers to specify the portlet request that's handled by the controller. At runtime, the Spring Portlet MVC framework makes use of the information provided by the @RequestMapping annotation to identify the controllers that will handle the incoming portlet requests.

Let's take a look at the requirements of this chapter's version of the Book Catalog portlet.

8.2   Developing the Book Catalog portlet using annotations

Figure 8.1 shows the Book Catalog portlet's home page, which displays the list of books in the catalog.

Book Catalog			
Title	**Author**	**ISBN Number**	**ACTION**
AspectJ in Action, Second Edition	Ramnivas Laddad	1933988053	Edit / Remove
ActiveMQ in Action	Bruce Snyder, Dejan Bosanac, and Rob Davies	1933988940	Edit / Remove
Hadoop in Action	Chuck Lam	9781935182191	Edit / Remove
JUnit in Action, Second Edition	Petar Tahchiev, Felipe Leme, Vincent Massol, and Gary Gregory	9781935182023	Edit / Remove
			Add Book

Figure 8.1   The Book Catalog portlet's home page listing the books in the catalog. The page gives the option to edit or remove an existing book's information or to add a new book to the catalog.

Figure 8.2   The form for adding a new book to the catalog. Book title, author, and ISBN information must be supplied to add a new book to the catalog. The Home link takes the user back to the home page of the portlet.

In figure 8.1, the Edit and Remove hyperlinks allow the user to edit or remove the selected book. If the user clicks Add Book, the Book Catalog portlet displays a form where the user can enter details about the book to be added, as shown in figure 8.2. This figure shows that book title, author, and ISBN fields are mandatory. If a user attempts to save the book information without completing any of the mandatory fields, or if the entered value for the ISBN isn't numeric, an error message is displayed, as shown in figure 8.3.

Because each book in the catalog has a unique ISBN, an attempt to add a book with an existing ISBN will display the following error message: "A book with the same ISBN number already exists. Please enter a different ISBN number." If the book information is successfully added, the user is taken to the portlet's home page (shown in figure 8.1).

The Book Catalog portlet represents a real-world portlet consisting of multiple pages and requiring form submission functionality. In the rest of this chapter, we'll develop this portlet using Spring Portlet MVC concepts, focusing primarily on using Spring annotations to reduce boilerplate code and configuration.

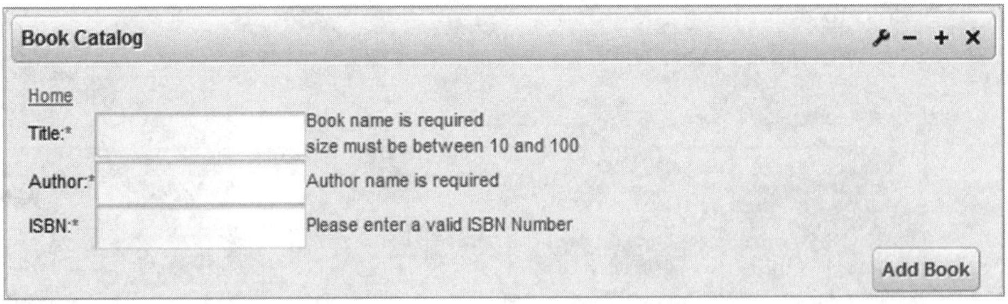

Figure 8.3   When editing an existing book's information or adding a new book to the catalog, error messages are shown if the required fields aren't completed or the ISBN value is non-numeric.

8.3 Spring Portlet MVC annotations

In Spring 2.5, annotations were introduced to create controllers that support form handling and command object functionality without requiring controllers to extend or implement framework-specific classes or interfaces. This new breed of controllers (referred to as *annotated controllers*) makes use of annotations at the *type* level (which is the class or interface level), *method* level, and *method parameter* level to provide the controller functionality.

> **NOTE** A *command object* acts as a placeholder for HTTP request parameters that can be entered in a portlet page. Storing request parameters in a command object makes the information independent of the HTTP protocol.

In this section we'll look at a variety of things you'll need to develop portlets using annotations:

- An annotation that identifies a class as a Spring Portlet MVC controller
- Spring's classpath-scanning feature for autoregistering Spring components
- Spring's annotations for autowiring dependencies by name or type
- JSR 250 and JSR 330 annotations for dependency injection
- Annotations for mapping requests to handlers and handler methods
- An annotation that binds request parameters to handler method arguments
- An annotation that identifies a model attribute
- An annotation that stores model attributes in a handler's conversational state
- An annotation that identifies a method as an exception handler
- An annotation that initializes `WebDataBinder`, setting the property editor and validator

Take a deep breath. We'll start with the `@Controller` Spring Portlet MVC annotation.

> **CODE REFERENCE** If you haven't yet done so, you should now import the ch8_BookCatalog Eclipse project from the source code that accompanies this book. This will allow you to follow along with the code references in the rest of this chapter. The `SomeController` handler, shown later in this chapter, isn't available as part of the source code and is only used to explain the concepts.

8.3.1 Identifying controllers with @Controller

The `@Controller` annotation is a type-level annotation, which indicates that the annotated class is a Spring component of type `controller`. The following listing shows the `@Controller` annotation in use in `AddBookController`.

Listing 8.1 An `@Controller` annotation

```
package chapter08.code.listing;
import org.springframework.stereotype.Controller;
```

```
@Controller(value="addBookController")
public class AddBookController {
  public String showAddBookForm(...) {
  }
  public void addBook(...) {
  }
}
```

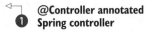

❶ @Controller annotated Spring controller

The @Controller type-level annotation ❶ accepts an *optional* value element, which specifies the logical name of the controller component. The value element is the same as the id attribute of a bean element, which you used in chapter 7 to define objects in the web application context XML file. As you can see, AddBookController doesn't extend or implement a Spring-specific class or interface. The showAddBook-Form method is a render method of the controller. The addBook method represents an action method of the controller.

Annotating a handler with the @Controller annotation doesn't automatically register it with the portlet's web application context. You'll need to use Spring's *classpath-scanning* feature to register your controllers. The key point in listing 8.1 is that if you're using the @Controller annotation, your controller class doesn't need to implement or extend any framework-specific class or interface.

> **NOTE** In listing 8.1, annotations for identifying action and render methods in the controller class have been intentionally omitted. Later in this chapter, you'll see how the action and render methods of Spring Portlet MVC controllers are identified using annotations.

Let's look at the Spring's *classpath scanning* and *autodetection*, which make the use of Spring annotations worthwhile.

8.3.2 *Classpath scanning and autoregistration*

The @Controller annotation is typically used along with Spring's *classpath-scanning* feature to allow *automatic registration* of controller classes. The classpath-scanning feature scans for Spring components in the classpath—components that are annotated with @Component, @Service, @Controller, or @Repository annotations—and automatically registers them with the web application context. This effectively means that if you're using classpath scanning along with Spring's component annotations, you don't need to explicitly declare beans in the web application context XML file.

> **NOTE** The @Component annotation is used to annotate a class as a *component*. The @Controller, @Service, and @Repository annotations are more specialized forms of @Component and are meant to annotate controllers, services, and DAOs (data access objects), respectively. In this chapter, we'll make use of the @Controller and @Service annotations. Refer to chapter 9 for examples of using the @Repository annotation.

To enable Spring's classpath-scanning feature for your portlet, you need to use the `component-scan` element of Spring's `spring-context` schema. The following element in the Book Catalog portlet's web application context XML file shows how the `component-scan` element is used:

```
<context:component-scan base-package="chapter08.code.listing"/>
```

Here, `context` is the namespace with which elements of the `spring-context.xsd` schema are available in the web application context XML file. The `base-package` attribute lists comma-separated names of packages under which the Spring container will look for Spring components. This `component-scan` element will scan all the classes inside the chapter08.code.listing package and its subpackages, and autoregister any `@Component`, `@Repository`, `@Controller`, or `@Service` annotated classes with the web application context. For example, the controller in listing 8.1 is annotated with the `@Controller` annotation and resides in the chapter08.code.listing.controller package, so it will be autoregistered with the web application context.

> **NOTE** You can also use the `include-filter` and `exclude-filter` subelements of `component-scan` to include or exclude components from scanning.

When you use classpath scanning to autoregister Spring components, the name with which a component is registered in the web application context is defined by the `value` element of the annotation. In listing 8.1, the `@Controller` annotation's `value` element is set to `addBookController`, so the `AddBookController` controller is registered with the name `addBookController` in the web application context. This is same as defining `AddBookController` in the web application context XML with the `id` attribute's value set to `addBookController`, as shown here:

```
<bean id="addBookController"
    class="chapter08.code.listing.controller.AddBookController"/>
```

You can also specify the value of the `value` element without explicitly mentioning the element in the annotation, as shown here:

```
@Controller("addBookController")
```

The `@Controller("addBookController")` and `@Controller(value = "addBook-Controller")` declarations are same.

> **NOTE** If a Spring component doesn't specify the `value` element, Spring registers it with the web application context as a bean whose name is the same as of that of the component class, but it begins with a lowercase letter. It's recommended that you use the `value` element to specify a custom name for Spring components because it's useful when injecting components "by name" into other beans using Spring's dependency injection facility. (We'll discuss this dependency injection feature and the benefits of specifying a custom name for the components in the next section.)

As you've seen, if you're using the classpath-scanning feature, controller beans aren't explicitly declared in the web application context XML file. So how are the dependencies of the controller beans defined? Let's look at how dependencies are injected in autoregistered Spring components using the @Autowired, @Resource (from JSR 250), and @Inject (from JSR 330) annotations.

8.3.3   *Dependency injection using @Autowired and @Qualifier*

The @Autowired annotation is used with a field, setter method, or constructor to instruct the Spring container to inject the dependency. For instance, the AddBook-Controller handler uses the @Autowired annotation to instruct the Spring container to inject the BookService bean, as shown here:

```
import org.springframework.beans.factory.annotation.Autowired;

@Controller(value="addBookController")
public class AddBookController {
    @Autowired
    private BookService bookService;
    ...
}
```

This code assumes that a class of type BookService is registered in the web application context. The BookService may be registered either by defining BookService in the web application context XML file or by being autoregistered by the classpath-scanning feature.

The @Autowired annotation resolves dependencies *by type* and not *by name*. If multiple implementations of BookService beans are available in the web application context, the preceding code would result in an exception because the Spring container would be unable to find a unique implementation of the Book-Service interface.

When multiple implementations of a bean are available in the web application context, you need to resolve dependencies by name, by using the @Autowired annotation along with the @Qualifier annotation. The @Qualifier annotation, in its simplest form, accepts the id of the bean to be injected. The following code snippet demonstrates how to resolve dependencies by name:

```
import org.springframework.beans.factory.annotation.Autowired;
import org.springframework.beans.factory.annotation.Qualifier;

@Controller(value="addBookController")
public class AddBookController {
    @Autowired
    @Qualifier("myBookService")
    private BookService bookService;
    ...
}
```

In the preceding code, @Qualifier accepts a String element that corresponds to the name of the BookService bean that is to be injected into AddBookController.

The `BookService` bean may be defined in the web application context XML file with the `myBookService id` or it may be defined as a Spring component using an `@Service` annotation whose `value` element's value is `myBookService`.

You can also inject dependencies in Spring components using the `@Resource` and `@Inject` annotations.

8.3.4 *Dependency injection using @Resource and @Inject*

You can also autowire dependencies *by name* by simply using the `@Resource` annotation from JSR 250 (Common Annotations). The `@Resource` annotation can *only* be applied to a class, field, and setter method (as compared with the `@Autowired` annotation, which can also be used with a constructor).

The following code shows the `@Resource` annotation in use:

```
import javax.annotation.Resource;

@Controller(value="addBookController")
public class AddBookController {
    @Resource(name="myBookService")
    private BookService bookService;
    ...
}
```

You can also use the `@Inject` annotation from JSR 330 (Dependency Injection for Java), instead of the `@Autowired` Spring annotation, as shown here:

```
import javax.inject.Inject;

@Controller(value="addBookController")
public class AddBookController {
    @Inject
    private BookService bookService;
    ...
}
```

The `@Inject` annotation can be applied to constructors, methods, and fields, just like `@Autowired`. The `@Inject` annotation exhibits the same behavior as `@Autowired`; both throw an exception if a unique bean implementation isn't found.

> **NOTE** To use the `@Resource` and `@Inject` annotations, you must include the JSR 250 (http://jcp.org/en/jsr/detail?id=250) and JSR 330 (http://jcp.org/en/jsr/detail?id=330) JAR files in the project's build path and in the classpath of the deployed WAR file. In the ch8_BookCatalog example folder, these JAR files are located in the WEB-INF/lib directory.

Once your controller is ready, the next step is to map portlet requests to your controller using the `@RequestMapping`, `@ActionMapping`, `@RenderMapping`, `@ResourceMapping`, and `@EventMapping` annotations.

Spring in pre-annotation days

A few years back, when I was working for the first time on a Spring-based project, doing anything in Spring involved two steps: *coding* and *configuring*. If I wrote a controller, I had to define that controller in the web application context XML. If I wrote a setter method for a service used by my controller, I had to go back to the web application context XML and define the dependency of the controller on the service. If I wrote a property editor, I had to configure it in the web application context XML.

Annotations let you focus on one thing: the *code*. The configuration information is captured as part of the source code, so you don't need to keep going back and forth between your code and XML configuration files.

8.3.5   *Mapping requests to handlers and methods using @RequestMapping*

The @RequestMapping annotation maps portlet requests to appropriate handlers and handler methods. @RequestMapping at type level maps portlet requests to handlers based on the current portlet mode and request parameters.

The following listing shows how you can use the @RequestMapping annotation to map all portlet requests received in VIEW mode to the AddBookController handler.

Listing 8.2   A type-level @RequestMapping annotation

```
import org.springframework.stereotype.Controller;
import org.springframework.web.bind.annotation.RequestMapping;

@RequestMapping(value = "VIEW")                    ⟵  @RequestMapping
@Controller(value="addBookController")                annotation
public class AddBookController {
  @Autowired
  @Qualifier("myBookService")
  private BookService bookService;

  public String showAddBookForm(...) {
  }
  public void addBook(...) {
  }
}
```

In listing 8.2, the @RequestMapping annotation is used at the type level to indicate that the AddBookController handler is responsible for handling portlet requests that are received in VIEW mode.

Let's now discuss the @RequestMapping annotation in detail and look at the different ways it can be used in controllers.

@REQUESTMAPPING ANNOTATION OPTIONS

In the previous example you saw that the @RequestMapping annotation is used to map portlet requests to a handler based on portlet mode. The @RequestMapping annotation can also be used to map requests to a handler based on the value of a request parameter. Let's say you want to map the `SomeController` handler to all portlet requests that are received in `VIEW` mode and that contain a request parameter named `action` with a value of `showSomething`. Here's how you can use the `@RequestMapping` annotation to achieve this behavior.

> **Listing 8.3   A type-level `@RequestMapping` annotation using the `params` element**

```
import org.springframework.stereotype.Controller;
import org.springframework.web.bind.annotation.RequestMapping;

@Controller(value="someController")
@RequestMapping(value="VIEW",                              @RequestMapping
        params="action=showSomething")                    annotation
public class SomeController {
  public String showSomething(...) {
    return "addBookForm";
  }
  public void doSomething(...) {
  }
}
```

In listing 8.3, the `value` element of the `@RequestMapping` annotation specifies the portlet mode that's supported by the `SomeController` handler. The `params` element specifies the request parameter name-value pairs, which must be present in the portlet request for `SomeController` to handle the request. As you may have guessed, the `@RequestMapping` annotation is doing what the `PortletModeParameterHandler-Mapping` handler mapping was responsible for doing in chapter 7.

Method-level `@RequestMapping` annotations are meant to narrow down the `@RequestMapping` specified at the type level to a particular method in the handler class. It's not mandatory that your controller has a type-level `@RequestMapping`; if it doesn't, the method-level `@RequestMapping` annotations must specify the portlet mode to which the method is mapped.

> **WARNING**   The sample code in the ch8_BookCatalog Eclipse project makes use of `@RenderMapping` and `@ActionMapping` method-level annotations instead of `@RequestMapping` method-level annotations. The `@RenderMapping`, `@ActionMapping`, `@EventMapping`, and `@ResourceMapping` annotations were introduced in Spring 3.0 and are the preferred means of mapping requests to methods in handlers.

The following listing shows a modified `SomeController` class that uses `@Request-Mapping` annotations at the method level.

> **Listing 8.4   Correct and incorrect method-level `@RequestMapping` annotations**

```
import org.springframework.stereotype.Controller;
import org.springframework.web.bind.annotation.RequestMapping;

@Controller(value="someController")
public class SomeController {
```

```
@RequestMapping(value="VIEW",
    params="action=showSomething")
public String showSomething(...) {
}
@RequestMapping(params="action=doSomeWork")
public void doSomething(...) {
}
}
```

@RequestMapping
for VIEW mode

@RequestMapping
without portlet

In listing 8.4, the SomeController handler contains @RequestMapping annotations only at the method level. The @RequestMapping annotation for the doSomething method doesn't specify the portlet mode in which the method is invoked. This is an exception condition, because every handler method *must* map to VIEW, EDIT, or HELP portlet mode.

In a typical scenario, the type-level @RequestMapping annotation defines the portlet mode and (if required) the request parameter combination to specify portlet requests mapped to the handler, and the @RequestMapping annotations at the method level define request parameters to further narrow down the portlet request to a particular method in the handler. It's an exception condition if the method-level @Request-Mapping defines a portlet mode that's different from the one defined at the type level.

The next listing shows another incorrect usage of @RequestMapping at the method level.

Listing 8.5   Correct and incorrect method-level @RequestMapping annotations

```
import org.springframework.stereotype.Controller;
import org.springframework.web.bind.annotation.RequestMapping;

@Controller(value="someController")
@RequestMapping(value="VIEW")
public class SomeController {
    ...
    @RequestMapping(value="EDIT",
        params="action=showSomething")
    public String showSomething(...) {
    }

    @RequestMapping(params="action=doSomeWork")
    public void doSomething(...) {
    }
}
```

@RequestMapping
for VIEW mode

@RequestMapping
for EDIT mode

@RequestMapping
without portlet mode

In listing 8.5, the type-level @RequestMapping annotation specifies that Some-Controller handles requests in VIEW portlet mode. But the @RequestMapping for the showSomething method specifies that it's meant to handle requests in EDIT portlet mode, which is contradictory to what is specified by the type-level @RequestMapping annotation. This difference in portlet mode definitions for the @RequestMapping annotation at type and method levels results in an exception condition.

WARNING   Spring 3.0 Portlet MVC doesn't treat it as an error if a portlet request ends up mapping to different methods of the same or different controllers. If you get a response that isn't expected, verify that the portlet request doesn't map simultaneously to different methods of the same or different controllers.

If a method-level `@RequestMapping` annotation doesn't specify the portlet mode and request parameter to which the method maps, the method is the *default* action or render method of the controller. For instance, the following method-level `@Request-Mapping` annotation indicates that the `doSomething` method is the default render or action method of the handler class:

```
@RequestMapping
public void doSomething(...) {
    ...
}
```

One of the advantages evident from looking at the `@RequestMapping` annotation is its flexibility in defining multiple render and action methods in the controller class. If you implement the `Controller` interface or extend the `AbstractController` class to create your controllers, you're restricted to having only one render and one action method. Refer to chapter 7 to see examples that make use of the `Controller` interface and `AbstractController` class to create handlers.

IDENTIFYING RENDER AND ACTION METHODS USING @REQUESTMAPPING

You saw earlier that the `@RequestMapping` annotation is used to map requests to a handler method. You also saw that the method-level `@RequestMapping` annotation doesn't specify whether the annotated method is an action or render method. So when it comes to invoking a controller's render or action method, how does Spring Framework know which method is a render method and which is an action method?

Spring identifies a method as an action, render, resource, or event method based on method arguments and return type. The following listing shows the `Some-Controller` handler, in which the method arguments are specified.

Listing 8.6   Method-level `@RequestMapping` annotations

```
import org.springframework.stereotype.Controller;
import org.springframework.web.bind.annotation.RequestMapping;

@Controller(value="someController")
@RequestMapping(value="VIEW")
public class SomeController {
    ...
    @RequestMapping(params="action=showSomething")        Render
    public String showSomething(Model model) {         ⊲┘ method
    }

    @RequestMapping(params="action=doSomeWork")           Action
    public void doSomething(ActionRequest request) {   ⊲┘ method
    }
}
```

In listing 8.6, the showSomething method is a *render* method, but it hasn't been defined to accept RenderRequest and RenderResponse objects; the doSomething method is an *action* method that only accepts an ActionRequest parameter. You can define action and render methods with such signatures because annotated controllers allow you to have flexible method signatures; you can pass arguments and define return types appropriate for your request-handling method.

In listing 8.6, the showSomething method is a render method because it defines its return type as String, which is a logical name of the view to be rendered by the portlet. An action method in annotated controllers can't have a non-void return type.

The doSomething method is an action method because it accepts an Action-Request as a method argument.

> **NOTE**   In chapter 7, you saw how the ViewResolver bean is used to resolve a logical view name to an actual view. Similarly, in annotated controllers, the ViewResolver configured in the application context XML is responsible for resolving the String value returned by the render method to an actual view name. There are other return types possible for render methods in annotated controllers, but we'll only be using render methods that return String values.

The possible arguments that you can pass to a method annotated with the @Request-Mapping annotation include ActionRequest, ActionResponse, RenderRequest, Render-Response, Model, command objects, and request parameters annotated with @RequestParam (discussed later in this chapter). The possible return types a method annotated with @RequestMapping can have include ModelAndView, View, String, and void. For a more detailed list of possible arguments and return types, refer to the Spring 3.0 API documentation.

> **TIP**   If the @RequestMapping annotated handler methods provide flexibility with method arguments and return types, they also add a little bit of confusion to the process of distinguishing a handler class's render methods from its action methods. The simplest way to distinguish your render and action methods from each other is by passing RenderRequest or RenderResponse arguments to your render method, and ActionRequest or ActionResponse arguments to your action method, and keeping the return type of the action method as void.

Your action method must be defined to return void. Any other return type will result in an error. A common misconception is that an @RequestMapping annotated method that returns void is an action method, but that's incorrect because you may have a render method that returns void and yet accepts a RenderResponse object as an argument to write directly to the output stream. For example, the following method is a render method, not an action method:

```
@RequestMapping(params="action=doSomeWork")
public void doSomething(RenderResponse response) {
```

```
    PrintWriter writer = response.getWriter();
    writer.println("Hello World");
}
```

In the preceding code, the `RenderResponse` object is passed to the `doSomething` method, which writes directly to the output stream and so acts as a render method.

@REQUESTMAPPING ANNOTATION AND PORTLET LIFECYCLE PHASES

In Portlet 1.0, a portlet had only two lifecycle phases: `RENDER_PHASE` and `ACTION_ PHASE` (refer to the Portlet API's `PortletRequest` interface). Portlet 2.0 introduced two additional lifecycle phases: `RESOURCE_PHASE` (a phase in which a resource is served by the portlet, like a binary file) and `EVENT_PHASE` (a phase in which an event received by other portlets or the portlet container is processed by the portlet; this is useful in inter-portlet communication). These latter two lifecycle phases aren't addressed by method-level `@RequestMapping` annotations.

Spring 3.0 introduced additional annotations to help clearly distinguish the action and render methods of a portlet and to address new portlet lifecycle phases. In this chapter, we'll only discuss the newly introduced annotations for render and action methods (`@RenderMapping` and `@ActionMapping`). The event and resource phases in the portlet lifecycle are discussed in detail in chapters 11 and 12 respectively.

8.3.6 *Identifying render methods with @RenderMapping*

You earlier saw that the `@RequestMapping` annotation makes it a bit difficult to distinguish render methods from action methods in annotated controllers. Spring 3.0 introduced the `@RenderMapping` annotation, which is used to specify a handler method as a render method. `@RenderMapping` is a method-level annotation that maps render requests to a handler class's render methods. You can still use the `@RequestMapping` annotation to annotate your render methods, but using the `@RenderMapping` annotation is recommended.

> **TIP** In an annotated controller, you can also use a combination of `@Render- Mapping` and `@RequestMapping` to annotate different render methods of the same handler, but it's not recommended.

The following listing shows the `@RenderMapping` annotation used in the `AddBook- Controller` controller.

Listing 8.7 An `@RenderMapping` annotation

```
import org.springframework.stereotype.Controller;
import org.springframework.web.bind.annotation.RequestMapping;
import org.springframework.beans.factory.annotation.*;
import org.springframework.web.portlet.bind.annotation.RenderMapping;

@RequestMapping(value = "VIEW")
@Controller(value="addBookController")
public class AddBookController {
  @Autowired
```

```
@Qualifier("myBookService")
private BookService bookService;

@RenderMapping(params="myaction=addBookForm")
public String showAddBookForm(RenderResponse response) {
 return "addBookForm";
}
public void addBook(...) {
}
}
```

@RenderMapping annotation

In listing 8.7, the @RenderMapping annotation marks the showAddBookForm method as a render method of the AddBookController handler. The optional params element specifies request parameter name-value pairs, which should be present in the portlet request to invoke the handler method. For instance, the showAddBookForm method is invoked when the current portlet mode is VIEW (see the AddBookController's @RequestMapping type-level annotation in the above listing) and the value of the myaction request parameter is addBookForm.

Let's now discuss the @RenderMapping annotation in detail and look at the different ways it can be used in controllers.

@RENDERMAPPING ANNOTATION OPTIONS

@RenderMapping additionally provides the value element, which is used to map the window state that applies to the method, as shown here.

Listing 8.8   An @RenderMapping annotation

```
import org.springframework.stereotype.Controller;
import org.springframework.web.bind.annotation.RequestMapping;
import org.springframework.web.portlet.bind.annotation.RenderMapping;

@Controller(value="someController")
@RequestMapping(value="VIEW")
public class SomeController {

  @RenderMapping(value="NORMAL",
      params="action=showSomething")
  public String showSomething(Model model) {
  }
}
```

@RenderMapping annotation

In listing 8.8, the @RenderMapping annotation marks the showSomething method as the SomeController handler's render method. The optional value element of @RenderMapping specifies the portlet window state to which the render method applies. The value element takes standard window states (like NORMAL, MAXIMIZED, and MINIMIZED) or custom window states (discussed in chapter 4) supported by the portal as values. If you don't specify the value element, the render method applies to all window states.

The showSomething method in listing 8.8 is invoked when the current portlet mode is VIEW (see the @RequestMapping type-level annotation of SomeController), the window state is NORMAL, and the value of the action request parameter is showSomething.

Because both `value` and `params` elements are optional in the `@RenderMapping` annotation, if neither is specified, the handler method becomes the handler's default render method for the portlet mode specified by the type-level `@RequestMapping` annotation. For instance, if the `params` and `value` elements were removed from the `@RenderMapping` annotation in listing 8.8, the `showSomething` method would become the render method for all render requests received in `VIEW` mode.

@RENDERMAPPING AND METHOD SIGNATURES

Methods annotated with the `@RenderMapping` annotation enjoy the same flexibility in terms of their signature as the `@RequestMapping`–annotated render methods. If you're using the `@RenderMapping` annotation in your handler class, the class must have an `@RequestMapping` annotation at the type level because `@RenderMapping` *doesn't* have the option to specify the portlet mode with which the method is associated.

As mentioned earlier, render and action methods in a portlet must be associated with a portlet mode, and if you define the `@RequestMapping` annotation at the type level for your handler class, all the methods (action and render) in the handler class are by default associated with the portlet mode specified by the type level `@Request-Mapping` annotation.

The following listing shows the `SomeController` handler, which doesn't use an `@RequestMapping` annotation at the type level.

Listing 8.9 An @RenderMapping annotation

```
import org.springframework.stereotype.Controller;
import org.springframework.web.bind.annotation.RequestMapping;

@Controller(value="someController")
public class SomeController {

  @RenderMapping(value="NORMAL",                    │ @RenderMapping
      params="action=showSomething")               │ annotation
  public String showSomething(Model model) {
    ...
  }
  ...
}
```

In listing 8.9, the `SomeController` handler doesn't have a `@RequestMapping` annotation at the type level, so the `showSomething` render method isn't associated with any portlet mode (`@RenderMapping` doesn't have the option to specify a portlet mode for the method). This results in an exception condition.

Let's now look at how we can specify a handler method as an action method using the `@ActionMapping` annotation.

8.3.7 *Identifying action methods with @ActionMapping*

`@ActionMapping` is a method-level annotation that maps action requests to handler methods. This annotation was introduced in Spring 3.0 and is the preferred way to annotate action handler methods.

The following listing shows how AddBookController makes use of the @Action-Mapping annotation.

Listing 8.10   An @ActionMapping annotation

```
import org.springframework.stereotype.Controller;
import org.springframework.web.bind.annotation.RequestMapping;
import org.springframework.beans.factory.annotation.*;
import org.springframework.web.portlet.bind.annotation.*;

@Controller(value="addBookController")
@RequestMapping(value = "VIEW")
public class AddBookController {
  @Autowired
  @Qualifier("myBookService")
  private BookService bookService;

  @RenderMapping(params = "myaction=addBookForm")
  public String showAddBookForm(RenderResponse response) {
   return "addBookForm";
  }

  @ActionMapping(params = "myaction=addBook")        ◁── @ActionMapping
  public void addBook(...) {                              annotation
    ...
  }
}
```

In listing 8.10, the @ActionMapping annotation marks the addBook method as an action method of AddBookController. The optional params element specifies request parameter name-value pairs, which must be present in the portlet request to invoke the addBook method. The addBook method is invoked if the portlet mode is VIEW and the value of the myaction request parameter is addBook.

Let's now discuss the @ActionMapping annotation in detail and look at different ways it can be used in controllers.

@ACTIONMAPPING ANNOTATION OPTIONS
In addition to the params element, @ActionMapping accepts an optional value element, which refers to the value of the javax.portlet.action request parameter.

The following listing shows the SomeController handler, which uses the value element of the @ActionMapping annotation.

Listing 8.11   An @ActionMapping annotation with a value element

```
import org.springframework.stereotype.Controller;
import org.springframework.web.bind.annotation.RequestMapping;
import org.springframework.web.portlet.bind.annotation.ActionMapping;

@Controller(value="someController")
@RequestMapping("VIEW")
public class SomeController {

  @ActionMapping(value="doSomeWork",                  @ActionMapping
    params={"work=laundry","time=enough"})            annotation
```

```
public String doSomething(ActionRequest request) {
    ...
}
    ...
}
```

In listing 8.11, the @ActionMapping annotation marks the doSomething method as an action method of SomeController. The value element specifies the value of the javax.portlet.action request parameter.

In the listing, the doSomething method is invoked when a portlet request meets the following requirements:

- The value of the javax.portlet.action request parameter is doSomeWork
- The value of the work request parameter is laundry, and the value of time is enough

TIP In your handler class, you can use a combination of @ActionMapping and @RequestMapping to annotate different action methods, but the use of @ActionMapping is recommended.

Methods annotated with the @ActionMapping annotation enjoy the same flexibility in terms of their signature as the @RequestMapping annotated action methods. As with @RenderMapping, the handler class that uses the @ActionMapping annotation must have a type-level @RequestMapping annotation. If value and params elements aren't specified for the @ActionMapping annotation, the corresponding method becomes the default action method of the handler.

The annotations that we've discussed so far are meant to map portlet requests to handler classes or methods. If you use these annotations, you don't need to specify the handler mapping configurations in the web application context XML file. The remaining annotations discussed in this chapter help in implementing controller functionality by providing access to form-backing or command objects, request parameters, and so on.

8.3.8 *Passing request parameters using @RequestParam*

@RequestParam is a method-parameter-level annotation meant for binding a request parameter to a method argument. It's useful when you want to pass a request parameter value as an argument to your handler method. If your handler method is annotated with @RequestMapping or any other annotation (like @ActionMapping, @RenderMapping, or @ModelAttribute), you can use the @RequestParam annotation; if your handler method isn't annotated, you can't use @RequestParam.

The following listing shows the EditBookController handler, which makes use of an @RequestParam annotation to obtain the ISBN of a book from a portlet request.

Listing 8.12 An @RequestParam annotation

```
import org.springframework.stereotype.Controller;
import org.springframework.web.bind.annotation.RequestMapping;
import org.springframework.web.bind.annotation.RequestParam;
```

```
@Controller(value="editBookController")
@RequestMapping("VIEW")
public class EditBookController {
  @Autowired
  @Qualifier("myBookService")
  private BookService bookService;
  ...
  @ModelAttribute("book")
  public Book getBook(@RequestParam Long isbnNumber) {
    return bookService.getBook(isbnNumber);
  }
  ...
}
```

@RequestParam annotation

In listing 8.12, the @RequestParam annotation binds the value of the isbnNumber request parameter to the getBook method's isbnNumber argument. The name of the method argument is used implicitly by @RequestParam to find a request parameter with the same name; if the isbnNumber request parameter is found in the request, its value is assigned to the getBook method's isbnNumber argument.

The @RequestParam annotation precedes the method argument whose value comes from the request parameter. In listing 8.12, @RequestParam is also responsible for the *type conversion* of the request parameter value from String to the method argument's java.lang.Long type.

One of the mains benefits of using @RequestParam is that your method isn't directly dependent on the Portlet API. For instance, in listing 8.12, you don't directly use the RenderRequest object to obtain the value of the isbnNumber request parameter.

Let's now discuss the @RequestParam annotation in detail and see how it can be used in controllers.

@REQUESTPARAM ANNOTATION OPTIONS

The @RequestParam annotation defines the required, value, and defaultValue elements, which you can use to customize its behavior. The following code snippet shows how you can use the required and value elements:

```
@RenderMapping(params="action=showPart")
public String showPart(@RequestParam(required=true,value="partNumber")
        long partNumber) {
  ...
}
```

In the preceding code fragment, the required element indicates whether the request parameter specified using the value element is mandatory or not. The value element specifies the name of the request parameter whose value needs to be assigned to the method argument. If the required element's value is true and the request parameter is missing from the portlet request, an exception is thrown.

To take care of such situations, you can specify a default value for the method argument, which is passed to the method if the request parameter is missing from the portlet request. For instance, in the following code snippet, 1234567 is passed as the value of the partNumber request parameter if it's missing from the portlet request:

```
@RenderMapping(params="action=showPart")
public String showPart(@RequestParam(required=true,
        value="partNumber", defaultValue="1234567")
        long partNumber) {
    ...
}
```

In this code, the `defaultValue` element specifies the default value of the request parameter.

> **CODE REFERENCE** To see an example of the use of the `@RequestParam` annotation, refer to `EditBookController` and `RemoveBookController` in the ch8_BookCatalog folder.

You saw in chapter 7 that data is stored as model attributes in the `Model` object, and it's used by views like JSP pages to show portlet content. We'll now look at how you can obtain or set model attributes using the `@ModelAttribute` annotation.

8.3.9 *Identifying model attributes using @ModelAttribute*

In chapter 7, you programmatically added model attributes to Spring's `Model` object, which is then used by JSP pages to show content. You can achieve the same functionality in annotated controllers using the `@ModelAttribute` annotation. (See sections 7.3.1 and 7.3.2 for more on model attributes.)

The `@ModelAttribute` annotation is responsible for adding and retrieving model attributes to and from the `Model` object. `@ModelAttribute` is a method-level, as well as a method-parameter-level, annotation. If used at the method level, it binds the return value of the method to a model attribute, that is, it stores the value returned by the method into the `Model` object. If used at the method-parameter level, it retrieves the model attribute from the `Model` object and binds it to the method argument.

Model attributes in Spring consist of command objects and *reference data* (if any). Reference data is the additional information that's required by the portlet to display the page. For instance, if you add a book category to each book in the Book Catalog portlet, the Book Catalog portlet's Add Book form would need to display a combo box displaying a list of categories. The list of book categories would be reference data required to display the Add Book form.

Views (like JSP pages) in Spring Portlet MVC usually get their data from model attributes, so to show the Book Catalog portlet's page (see figure 8.1), you need to obtain the list of books from the data source and store it as a model attribute. The following listing shows how `BookController` stores the list of books as a model attribute using the `@ModelAttribute` method-level annotation.

Listing 8.13   A method-level `@ModelAttribute` annotation

```
import org.springframework.stereotype.Controller;
import org.springframework.web.bind.annotation.*;
```

```
@Controller(value="bookController")
@RequestMapping("VIEW")
public class BookController {
  @Autowired
  @Qualifier("myBookService")
  private BookService bookService;
  ...
  @ModelAttribute(value="books")
  public List<Book> getBooks() {
    return bookService.getBooks(isbnNumber);
  }
  ...
}
```

◁──┘ **@ModelAttribute annotation**

In listing 8.13, the `@ModelAttribute` annotation instructs the Spring container to store the object returned by the `getBooks` method in a model attribute named `books`. The `value` element specifies the name of the model attribute used to store the method's returned value in the `Model`. The `@ModelAttribute(value="books")` annotation can be shortened to `@ModelAttribute("books")`.

> **NOTE**   If a handler class contains `@ModelAttribute` annotated methods, these methods are always called before the render or action method of the handler.

CREATING COMMAND OBJECTS USING @MODELATTRIBUTE

You saw in chapter 7 that Spring controllers that deal with command and form-backing objects are deprecated as of Spring 3.0 Portlet MVC, in favor of annotated controllers. In annotated controllers, the `@ModelAttribute` annotation allows you to create command or form-backing object.

Figure 8.2 shows the Add Book form, which is used to add a book to the catalog. What we'll do is create an empty command object when the Add Book form is displayed by the portlet, and bind the user-entered values to this command object when the form is submitted. The command object will then be used by the action method of a handler to perform validation and save the book information in the data store. Let's see how we can do this using the `@ModelAttribute` annotation.

> **NOTE**   Depending upon the approach you follow, you may be using domain objects as command objects in your application. In the Book Catalog portlet, `Book` is a domain object that's being used as a command object.

The following listing shows how the `AddBookController` creates a `Book` command object using the `@ModelAttribute` annotated method.

> **Listing 8.14   A method-level `@ModelAttribute` annotation for creating command object**

```
import org.springframework.stereotype.Controller;
import org.springframework.web.bind.annotation.*;

@RequestMapping(value = "VIEW")
@Controller(value="addBookController")
```

```
public class AddBookController {
  @Autowired
  @Qualifier("myBookService")
  private BookService bookService;
  ...
  @RenderMapping(params = "myaction=addBookForm")
  public String showAddBookForm(RenderResponse response) {
    return "addBookForm";
  }
  @ModelAttribute("book")                          ⟵  @ModelAttribute
  public Book getCommandObject() {                     annotation
    return new Book();
  }
  ...
}
```

In listing 8.14, the `showAddBookForm` method is the render method that's invoked when the user clicks the Add Book button on the home page of the Book Catalog portlet. The `getCommandObject` method is annotated with `@ModelAttribute`, so it will be invoked before the handler invokes an action or render method. The `getCommand-Object` creates a new `Book` object that's stored in the `Model` object with an attribute named `book`, which means a new command object is created before the render request is received by the `AddBookController` class.

> **NOTE** Methods annotated with the `@ModelAttribute` annotation have the same flexibility in their signature as methods with the `@RequestMapping` annotation. The `@ModelAttribute` method-level annotation is supported for handler classes that use the `@RequestMapping` type-level annotation.

In listing 8.14, an empty `Book` command object was created and bound to the `Model` object with the name `book`. When a user submits the Add Book form, you need to bind the user-entered values in the form to the `book` model attribute and make it available to the `AddBookController`'s action method, which is responsible for saving the book information. The binding of user-entered values to the `book` model attribute is handled by the Spring form tag library tags, which we'll discuss later in this chapter. For now, you can assume that when the Add Book form is submitted, the values entered by the user are bound to the `book` model attribute.

The `@ModelAttribute` annotation at the method-parameter level is used to bind a model attribute to a method argument. The following listing shows how `@Model-Attribute` is used by `AddBookController` to bind the `book` model attribute to the `addBook` action method's `book` argument.

Listing 8.15 An `@ModelAttribute` annotation

```
import org.springframework.stereotype.Controller;
import org.springframework.web.bind.annotation.*;

@RequestMapping(value = "VIEW")
@Controller(value="addBookController")
```

```
public class AddBookController {
  @Autowired
  @Qualifier("myBookService")
  private BookService bookService;
  ...

  @ActionMapping(params = "myaction=addBook")
  public void addBook(@ModelAttribute(value="book")          @ModelAttribute
    Book book, ...) {                                        annotation
    ...
    bookService.addBook(book);
  }
}
```

In listing 8.15, the @ModelAttribute method-parameter-level annotation binds the model attribute named book to the book argument of the addBook method. If you don't specify the value element of the @ModelAttribute annotation, the name of the model attribute to be bound is derived from the *nonqualified* name of the method parameter *type*. For instance, if you exclude the value element of the @ModelAttribute method-parameter-level annotation in listing 8.15, the model attribute named book (derived from the nonqualified name of the chapter08.code.listing.domain.Book argument type by changing the nonqualified name to lowercase) is bound to the book argument. This means that using @ModelAttribute(value="book") has the same effect as using the @ModelAttribute annotation without the value element in listing 8.15.

As mentioned earlier, a method annotated with @ModelAttribute is invoked every time a handler's action or render method is called. In some situations, this isn't desirable, because the command object may be created from data retrieved from a database. In such cases, command object creation is expensive, and creating the object at every render and action request would adversely impact the performance of the portal. To address such scenarios, the @SessionAttributes annotation is used.

8.3.10 *Reusing model attributes using @SessionAttributes*

The @SessionAttributes type-level annotation is used to store model attributes in a handler's *conversational state*. If a model attribute, specified using the @Model-Attribute method-level annotation, is found in a handler's conversational state, it's reused. A handler's conversational state is maintained in the PortletSession, and when the conversational session ends, the model attributes stored in it are removed from PortletSession.

> **TIP** If your model attribute is created based on information retrieved from a database or any other computation-intensive source, you should store the model attribute in the handler's conversational state.

In the following listing, the EditBookController handler uses the @SessionAttributes annotation to store book information, retrieved from the data store, in the handler's conversational state.

Listing 8.16 An @SessionAttributes annotation

```
import org.springframework.web.bind.annotation.SessionAttributes;

@Controller
@RequestMapping(value="VIEW")
@SessionAttributes(value="book")                         ❶ @SessionAttributes
public class EditBookController {                            annotation
  @Autowired
  @Qualifier("myBookService")
  private BookService bookService;                       ❷ Method-level
                                                            @ModelAttribute
  @ModelAttribute("book")                                   annotation
  public Book getBook(@RequestParam Long isbnNumber) {
    return bookService.getBook(isbnNumber);
  }

  @ActionMapping(params="myaction=editBook")
  public void editBook                                   ❸ Method-parameter-level
     (@ModelAttribute("book")Book book,...){                @ModelAttribute
    ...
    bookService.editBook(book);
    ...
    }
  }

  @RenderMapping(params="myaction=editBookForm")         ❹ Render method to
  public String showEditBookForm(){                         show Edit Book form
    return "editBookForm";
  }
}
```

The @SessionAttributes annotation ❶ lists the book model attribute as an attribute that should be stored as part of the handler's conversational state. The method-level @ModelAttribute ❷ specifies that the Book command object returned by the getBook method should be bound to a model attribute named book. The book model attribute ❸ is passed as a method argument to the editBook action method. The showEditBookForm method ❹ is the render method responsible for showing the Edit Book form of the Book Catalog portlet.

In listing 8.16, the EditBookController's methods are invoked in the following sequence, depending upon whether the request received by the handler is a render or action request:

- *The handler receives a render request*—The getBook method is called, followed by the showEditBookForm method. The getBook method accepts an ISBN as an argument and returns the Book object corresponding to the ISBN. The getBook method is annotated with @ModelAttribute("book"), which means that the returned Book is bound to the Model with the name book. The @Session-Attributes(value="book") attribute at type level specifies that the book model attribute is preserved as part of the conversational state (maintained in the PortletSession) of the EditBookController handler.

- *The handler receives an action request*—The editBook method is invoked. The get-Book method isn't invoked this time, because the book model attribute is available in the conversational state (maintained in the PortletSession) of the handler. The book model attribute is retrieved from the handler's conversational state and is passed to the editBook action method.

NOTE It's important to note that the model attributes stored in the Portlet-Session when using @SessionAttributes are removed from the Portlet-Session when the conversational session with the handler completes, which you have to explicitly do using the SessionStatus object. The Session-Status object's setComplete method clears all model attributes that were stored in the PortletSession by the @SessionAttributes annotation. As of Spring Framework 3.1 M1, the setComplete method only works if it's called from the render method of the portlet. It's expected that in a future Spring Portlet MVC release, the setComplete method will also work when called from an action method.

STORING MULTIPLE MODEL ATTRIBUTES OF THE SAME TYPE

In listing 8.16, the @SessionAttributes annotation uses the value element to specify the model attributes that need to be stored as part of the handler's conversational state. If there are multiple model attributes of the same *type*, it may be cumbersome to specify the name of each attribute as part of the @SessionAttributes annotation. To address such situations, @SessionAttributes also provides the types element, which defines model attribute types that should be stored as part of the handler's conversational state.

The @SessionAttributes annotation shown in listing 8.16 can alternatively be written to store all Book type model attributes in the handler's conversational state, as shown here:

```
@SessionAttributes(types=Book.class)
```

In this line, the types element specifies an *array* of model attribute types to be stored in the handler's conversational state.

If you use the @SessionAttributes(value="book") annotation, *only* the model attribute named book is stored in the handler's conversational state. If you use @SessionAttributes(types=Book.class), *all* model attributes of type Book will be stored.

CODE REFERENCE To see examples of the @SessionAttributes annotation in use, refer to EditBookController and AddBookController in the ch8_Book-Catalog folder.

In any application, exception handling plays an important role. The @Exception-Handler annotation is used in annotated controllers to handle exceptions gracefully.

8.3.11 Handling exceptions with @ExceptionHandler

In chapter 7, you used `HandlerExceptionResolver` to resolve exceptions to the appropriate model and view. When using annotated controllers, exception handling is done within the handler itself by the `@ExceptionHandler` annotated method.

`@ExceptionHandler` is a method-level annotation that handles exceptions thrown by handlers. The following code snippet shows how `@ExceptionHandler` is used:

```
@ExceptionHandler({MyException.class,
   IllegalStateException.class})
public String handleException() {
  return "errorPage";
}
```

In this code, `@ExceptionHandler` specifies an array of exception types that it handles. The `handleException` method returns a `String` that represents the logical name of a view. It's resolved to an actual view by `ViewResolver`, and it's rendered by `ViewRendererServlet`.

> **NOTE** You can also return a `ModelAndView` object from an `@Exception-Handler` annotated method. As with most annotated methods, `@Exception-Handler` annotated methods can have flexible signatures. Refer to the Spring 3.0 API for complete details about `@ExceptionHandler` annotated method signatures.

If the `@ExceptionHandler` annotation doesn't define the exception types handled by the annotated method, the method is assumed to handle the exception types defined as method arguments, as shown here:

```
@ExceptionHandler
public String handleException(MyException myException,
   IllegalStateException illegalStateException) {
  return "errorPage";
}
```

In the preceding code, the `@ExceptionHandler` annotation is empty, but the `handle-Exception` method accepts arguments of `MyException` and `IllegalStateException` types, so it will handle both these exceptions.

Let's now look at the `@InitBinder` annotation, which is used to initialize `Web-DataBinder`.

8.3.12 Initializing WebDataBinder using @InitBinder

The `WebDataBinder` object in Spring Framework is used to control how the binding of request parameters to model attributes happens. `WebDataBinder` controls binding by specifying which `PropertyEditor` to use for binding request parameters to a particular property type. `WebDataBinder` may also specify the validator to be used to validate model attributes or command objects. If binding or validation errors occur during request processing, they're stored in Spring Framework's `Errors` object, which is then used by the JSP page to display appropriate binding or validation error messages. The error messages displayed in figure 8.3, earlier in this chapter, are generated this way.

Because the request parameters are of type `String`, `WebDataBinder` is usually initialized with custom property editors that are responsible for transforming `String` type request parameters to the type defined for that parameter in the model attribute or command object. You may also want to validate the populated command object or model attribute before the handler method is executed. `WebDataBinder` can be initialized with custom validators that validate the populated model attribute or command object before the handler method is invoked. The `@InitBinder` method-level annotation is used to initialize the `WebDataBinder` instance.

The `WebDataBinder` gives you control over how request parameters are bound to model attributes. For instance, you can specify request parameter fields that are allowed to be bound, request parameters that must be present in the request during binding, custom property editors, custom formatters and validators to be used during binding, and so on.

The following code snippet uses the `@InitBinder` annotation in the `EditBook-Controller`:

```
@InitBinder("book")
public void initBinder(WebDataBinder binder) {
    binder.registerCustomEditor(Long.class,
      new LongNumberPropertyEditor());
    binder.setDisallowedFields(new String[]{"isbnNumber"});
}
```

The `@InitBinder("book")` annotation means that the `initBinder` method will initialize the `WebDataBinder` instance for the `book` command object or model attribute. The `setDisallowedFields` method instructs `WebDataBinder` not to bind the `isbnNumber` request parameter to the `book` model attribute (because the book's ISBN must not be changed when the book is edited by a user). The `registerCustomEditor` method registers the `LongNumberPropertyEditor` custom property editor for `Long` type properties in the `book` model attribute.

> **NOTE** You can have multiple `@InitBinder` annotated methods in your controller if you want to configure distinct `WebDataBinder` instances for different model attributes. This can be useful when request parameters are meant to be bound to different model attributes or command objects. Also, if you don't specify the model attribute in the `@InitBinder` annotation, the `WebData-Binder` instance configured by the `@InitBinder` annotated method applies to all model attributes of the handler.

`@InitBinder` methods have the same flexibility in terms of method arguments as `@RequestMapping` methods, except that they can't be defined to accept model attributes and the corresponding `BindingResult` object (discussed in section 8.5). The return type of an `@InitBinder` annotated method must be `void`.

GLOBALLY INITIALIZING WEBDATABINDER INSTANCES

An @InitBinder annotated method initializes the WebDataBinder for the handler in which it's defined. In some cases, WebDataBinder may need to be initialized globally so that the WebDataBinder configuration applies to all the handlers of the portlet. You can achieve this by defining the WebDataBinder initialization in the portlet's web application context XML file.

In the Book Catalog portlet, the ISBN is numeric, and it's defined as a Long type in the Book command object. The WebDataBinder should be initialized with a custom PropertyEditor (LongNumberPropertyEditor) that converts String to Long and vice versa, to support the ISBN property of Book. If LongNumberPropertyEditor is to be used by all the WebDataBinder instances in different handlers, you'll need to define an @InitBinder annotated method in all the handlers of the portlet and set the Long-NumberPropertyEditor property editor in WebDataBinder using its registerCustom-Editor method. In this situation, it's more appropriate to define a WebDataBinder that applies to all the handlers in the portlet.

You can set a custom property editor by using the WebDataBinder's register-CustomEditor method or by using a PropertyEditorRegistrar object. The Property-EditorRegistrar is useful when you have multiple property editors and you want to apply all those editors to a WebDataBinder. This saves you the effort of individually setting custom property editors on a WebDataBinder instance, and it also helps in reusing the same set of custom property editors in other scenarios.

Listing 8.17 shows how the Book Catalog portlet configures the WebDataBinder in the web application context XML file, and how it makes use of the PropertyEditor-Registrar to set the LongNumberPropertyEditor on the WebDataBinder instance. Because this defines the WebDataBinder in the web application context XML file, it applies to all the handlers in the Book Catalog portlet.

Listing 8.17 The WebDataBinder initialization

```
<bean class="org.springframework.web.portlet.mvc.
➥ annotation.AnnotationMethodHandlerAdapter">
  <property name="webBindingInitializer">
    <bean class="org.springframework.web.bind.support.
    ➥ConfigurableWebBindingInitializer">
      <property name="propertyEditorRegistrars">
        <list>
          <ref bean="myPropertyEditorRegistrar" />
        </list>
      </property>
    </bean>
  </property>
</bean>

<bean id="myPropertyEditorRegistrar"
  class="chapter08.code.listing.utils.
    ➥MyPropertyEditorRegistrar"/>
```

① HandlerAdapter for annotated controllers

② WebDataBinder initialization

③ Registrar for PropertyEditors

④ PropertyEditorRegistrar

You saw earlier that using the @Controller annotation along with the classpath-scanning feature autoregisters a handler with the web application context. In listing 8.17 the AnnotationMethodHandlerAdapter ❶ is responsible for providing access to annotated handlers that are autoregistered or manually registered with the portlet's web application context. The webBindingInitializer property ❷ represents a WebBindingInitializer object that initializes a WebDataBinder. An implementation of the WebBindingInitializer interface ❸, ConfigurableWebBindingInitializer, is used to initialize the WebDataBinder. Alternatively, you could create a custom implementation of the WebBindingInitializer interface to configure WebDataBinder. The propertyEditorRegistrars property ❹ of the WebBindingInitializer is used to set the list of PropertyEditorRegistrar objects that apply to the WebDataBinder.

Spring's PropertyEditorRegistrars are used to register custom property editors (like LongNumberPropertyEditor in the Book Catalog portlet) with the property editor registry maintained by the WebDataBinder. The following code shows the implementation of MyPropertyEditorRegistrar, which registers LongNumberPropertyEditor with the WebDataBinder:

```
public class MyPropertyEditorRegistrar implements PropertyEditorRegistrar {
  public void registerCustomEditors(PropertyEditorRegistry registry) {
    registry.registerCustomEditor(Long.class,
                    new LongNumberPropertyEditor());
  }
}
```

In the preceding code fragment, MyPropertyEditorRegistrar implements Spring's PropertyEditorRegistrar interface and its registerCustomEditors method to register LongNumberPropertyEditor with WebDataBinder's property editor registry.

> **CODE REFERENCE**   To see an example of the @InitBinder annotation in use, refer to the AddBookController and EditBookController handlers in the ch8_BookCatalog folder.

Phew! That was a lot to take in. So far we've covered the annotations that you need to know to develop Spring Portlet MVC portlets. If you want to see these concepts in practice, refer to the source code of the ch8_BookCatalog project that accompanies this book.

The Spring Portlet MVC framework uses built-in beans to support annotated handlers in portlets. In some cases, you may need to change the default behavior of these built-in beans to meet your portlet application's requirements. Let's take a look at these built-in beans and how you can customize them.

8.4   *Configuring beans that provide annotation support*

In chapter 7, you configured the HandlerMapping bean in the web application context to enable the mapping of portlet requests to appropriate handlers and handler methods. You also configured the HandlerExceptionResolver bean to resolve exceptions thrown by handlers during request processing. When using annotated controllers in this chapter, you didn't need to configure the `HandlerMapping` or `HandlerException-Resolver` beans because that's taken care of by default when `DispatcherPortlet` is initialized by the Spring container. In this section, we'll look at the special beans in Spring that are autoregistered when using annotated controllers, and you'll see how you can modify their default configuration. (Chapter 7 didn't focus on using annotated controllers, so I didn't cover these special beans in that chapter.)

Table 8.1 describes the built-in beans that are registered, by default, in the web application context of `DispatcherPortlet` to support annotated controllers.

Table 8.1   Default beans registered for annotated controllers

Implementation class	Description
`DefaultAnnotationHandlerMapping`	Implementation of the `HandlerMapping` interface that defines the handler mapping strategy for annotated controllers. This class maps portlet requests to the appropriate handler based on the portlet mode defined in the `@RequestMapping` annotation at the type or method level.
`AnnotationMethodHandlerAdapter`	Implementation of the `HandlerAdapter` interface that maps portlet requests to the appropriate handler method based on the portlet mode, any request parameters, and the portlet's lifecycle phase. As a result of this handler adapter, `DispatcherPortlet` is able to invoke annotated methods in handler classes.
`AnnotationMethodHandler-ExceptionResolver`	Implementation of the `HandlerExceptionResolver` interface that uses `@ExceptionHandler` annotated methods for handling exceptions.

In some scenarios, you may have to explicitly configure `DefaultAnnotation-HandlerMapping`, `AnnotationMethodHandlerAdapter`, and `AnnotationMethodHandler-ExceptionResolver` in the web application context because the default configuration doesn't meet your application's requirements.

For instance, as of Spring 3.0, there's no annotation that specifies that a class is a `HandlerInterceptor` and/or identifies which handlers it applies to. The following `@HandlerInterceptor` dummy annotation shows what such an annotation would look like:

```
@HandlerInterceptor(handlers="{bookController, editController}")
public class MyHandlerInterceptor {
    @AfterRenderCompletion
    public void afterRenderRequestComplete(RenderRequest request,
        RenderResponse response, Object handler) {
        ...
    }
}
```

In the preceding code, the `@HandlerInterceptor` annotation identifies the `MyHandler-Interceptor` class as being of type `HandlerInterceptor`, and its `handlers` element identifies the handlers to which the handler interceptor applies. The `@AfterRender-Completion` annotation identifies the `afterRenderRequestComplete` method as the method that's called after the render request is complete.

Unfortunately, the `@HandlerInterceptor` and `@AfterRenderCompletion` annotations don't exist as of Spring 3.0. But this doesn't mean that you can't configure handler interceptors when using annotated controllers.

You can configure handler interceptors by explicitly overriding the default configuration of `DefaultAnnotationHandlerMapping` in the web application context XML, as shown here.

Listing 8.18 Configuring a handler interceptor

```
<bean id="parameterInterceptor"                              Handler interceptor
    class="org.springframework.web.portlet.handler.          definition
        ParameterMappingInterceptor">
  <property name="parameterName" value="myaction" />
</bean>
<bean class="org.springframework.web.portlet.mvc.            DefaultAnnotationHandler-
        annotation.DefaultAnnotationHandlerMapping">         Mapping definition
  <property name="interceptors">
    <list>                                                   Interceptors
      <ref bean="parameterInterceptor"/>                     property
    </list>
  </property>
</bean>
```

Listing 8.18 shows how the `ParameterMappingInterceptor` handler interceptor class (discussed in chapter 7) can be configured with the `DefaultAnnotationHandlerMapping` handler mapping class to intercept portlet requests targeted towards annotated controllers. Similarly, you can configure a default handler for the mapping by using `DefaultAnnotationHandlerMapping`'s `defaultHandler` property, which is invoked when no matching handler is found for the portlet request.

You can also configure `AnnotationMethodHandlerAdapter` and `AnnotationMethodHandlerExceptionResolver` (as you can `DefaultAnnotationHandlerMapping`) to customize the default configuration provided by these classes. Listing 8.17 showed an example where `AnnotationMethodHandlerAdapter` was explicitly defined in the web application context to configure the `WebDataBinder` instance.

CODE REFERENCE For an example configuration of the `AnnotationMethodHandlerAdapter`, see the bookCatalog-portlet.xml application context XML file in the ch8_BookCatalog folder.

Now that we've covered the Spring annotations required to create annotated controllers, it's time to look at validation support in Spring Portlet MVC. The Book Catalog portlet uses this validation support to validate the book details entered by the user.

8.5   *Validating forms using Spring and JSR 303*

Validating user-entered data helps maintain data consistency. In the Book Catalog portlet, the Add Book form is validated to ensure that the book title, author name, and ISBN are provided by the user. If any of this information is missing, or if the ISBN entered already exists in the catalog or it isn't a valid number, an error message is shown to the user, as shown in figure 8.3. In this section, you'll see how you can use Spring Validation API and JSR 303 (Bean Validation) to validate form-backing and command objects.

The Spring Validation API is part of Spring Framework and provides validation for form-backing and command objects. JSR 303 defines a standard approach for validating objects, irrespective of the application layer.

Let's look first at the Spring Validation API.

8.5.1   *The Spring Validation API*

Spring Framework comes with its own Validation API, which is used for validating form-backing and command objects. The `org.springframework.validation.Validator` interface is central to the Spring Validation API, and it allows you to create custom validators for your applications.

Prior to Spring 3.0, annotated controllers were responsible for explicitly validating command objects, as shown here.

> **Listing 8.19   A Spring Validation API example**

```
import org.springframework.validation.Validator;
import org.springframework.validation.BindingResult;

...
@ActionMapping(params="action=doSomething")
public void doSomething(@ModelAttribute SomeObject someObject,
        BindingResult bindingResult) {                          ❶ Spring
  Validator validator = new SomeValidator();                       Validator
  validator.validate(someObject, bindingResult);
  if(!bindingResult.hasErrors()) {                               ❷ Validate SomeObject
    ...                                                            command object
  } else {
    ...
  }
}
```

The `SomeValidator` object is created ❶; it implements Spring's `Validator` interface and is responsible for validating the `SomeObject` model attribute. `SomeValidator`'s `validate` method is invoked ❷, and the validation results are stored in the `BindingResult` (a subinterface of the `Errors` interface) object, which is passed to the `validate` method.

> **CODE REFERENCE**   To view an example of the Spring `Validator`, see the `MyValidator` class in the ch8_BookCatalog folder.

In listing 8.19, the doSomething method is defined to accept a BindingResult object that provides the method with data binding results. If an error occurs during data binding, you can check for it by calling the BindingResult object's hasErrors method. If the data binding phase results in errors, you can skip validating the SomeObject model attribute. It is important to note that annotated handler methods can be defined to accept arguments of type BindingResult or Errors.

WARNING In the handler method signature, the Errors or BindingResult type argument must be preceded by the model attribute corresponding to which binding results are needed in the handler method implementation code.

In Spring 3.0, you don't need to programmatically validate your model attributes. Instead, you can use the @Valid annotation to validate the arguments of handler methods. The following listing shows the modified doSomething method, which makes use of the @Valid annotation.

Listing 8.20   The `SomeController` handler using the `@Valid` annotation

```
import org.springframework.validation.Validator;
import org.springframework.validation.BindingResult;
import javax.validation.Valid;

@ActionMapping(params="action=doSomething")
public void doSomething(
    @Valid @ModelAttribute SomeObject someObject,          ⟵  @Valid
    BindingResult bindingResult) {                             annotation
  if(!bindingResult.hasErrors()) {
    ...
  } else {
    ...
  }
}
```

In listing 8.20, the @Valid annotation instructs Spring to validate the SomeObject model attribute. The validation and binding results are available to the doSomething method through the BindingResult object.

NOTE The @Valid annotation is part of JSR 303 (Bean Validation) and is not Spring-specific.

When using the @Valid annotation to validate a handler method argument, the validator is specified in the @InitBinder method or in the WebDataBinder initialization configuration in the web application context XML file. The following listing shows how a portlet can set a validator as part of the WebDataBinder initialization configuration in the web application context XML.

```
Listing 8.21   The WebDataBinder configuration in the web application context XML
<beans...>
  ...
  <bean class="org.springframework.web.portlet.mvc.annotation.
  ➥AnnotationMethodHandlerAdapter">
    <property name="webBindingInitializer">
      <bean class="org.springframework.web.bind.support.
        ➥ConfigurableWebBindingInitializer">
        <property name="validator" ref="myValidator" />          ◁─┐ validator
      </bean>                                                          property
    </bean>
  </bean>

  <bean id="myValidator" class="..." />
  ...
</beans>
```

Listing 8.21 shows that `ConfigurableWebBindingInitializer`'s validator property accepts an object of type `org.springframework.validation.Validator`. It's here that you need to set the validator that should be applied to all the `WebDataBinder` instances in the portlet. The `Validator` injected in the `WebDataBinder` initialization definition applies to all the handlers in the portlet.

The approach used in listing 8.21 works well when you need a validator to apply to all `WebDataBinder` instances. To restrict the `validator` to a single controller, inject the validator bean into your controller and set it on the `WebDataBinder` instance inside the `@InitBinder` annotated method, as shown here.

```
Listing 8.22   Setting the validator in the @InitBinder method
public class SomeController {
  ...
  @Autowired
  @Qualifier("myValidator")
  private Validator myValidator;
  ...
  @InitBinder("someObject")
  public void initBinder(WebDataBinder binder) {         Setting validator for
    binder.setValidator(myValidator);               ◁─┘ someObject attribute
  }
  ...
}
```

To use the `@Autowired` annotation, as shown in listing 8.22, you need `myValidator` to be available in the web application context. You can either define `myValidator` in the web application context XML file, or you can annotate the corresponding `Validator` class with the `@Component` annotation.

> **CODE REFERENCE** To see an example of the Spring Validation API in use, refer to the `MyValidator` and `EditBookController` classes in the ch8_Book-Catalog folder.

Now that you have an understanding of the Spring Validation API it's time to look at JSR 303 (Bean Validation).

8.5.2 *Validating beans with JSR 303*

JSR 303 defines the Bean Validation API, which allows you to validate JavaBeans components in your application, irrespective of the application layer to which these components belong. In this section, we'll look at how you can use Spring with JSR 303 to validate model attributes. These model attributes can be form-backing or command objects (which could be domain objects).

The JSR 303 Bean Validation framework allows you to use annotations to define constraints on the properties of your beans, making validation constraints that apply on bean properties more informative and natural compared to the Spring Validation API. When using the Spring Validation API, you apply constraints on your application objects in the validator class.

The following listing shows an example `AddBookValidator` class that makes use of the Spring Validation API to validate a `Book` domain object. We'll later look at how `AddBookValidator` can be replaced with annotations defined in JSR 303.

Listing 8.23 Validating `Book` domain object using Spring Validation API

```
import org.springframework.validation.Validator;
import org.springframework.validation.BindingResult;

public class AddBookValidator implements Validator {
  @Autowired
  @Qualifier("myBookService")              ❶ Autowires
  private BookService bookService;           BookService
  public boolean supports(Class<?> klass) {      ❷ Identifies supported
    return Book.class.isAssignableFrom(klass);       class instances
  }

  public void validate(Object target, Errors errors) {   ❸ Validates
    Book book = (Book)target;                            target object
    ValidationUtils.rejectIfEmptyOrWhitespace(errors,
        "name", "name.field.required");
    ValidationUtils.rejectIfEmptyOrWhitespace(errors,
        "author", "author.field.required");
    String name = book.getName();
    if(name.length() >10 || name.length() < 3) {
      errors.reject("name", "name.field.max.min.size");
    }                                               ❹ Validates
    if(bookService.isUnique(book.getIsbnNumber())) {    ISBN
      errors.reject("isbnNumber", "isbnNumber.field.unique.constraint");
    }
  }
}
```

The `BookService` bean is autowired by name into the `AddBookValidator` object ❶. The `BookService` is used by `AddBookValidator` to validate that the ISBN doesn't already exist in the catalog. The `supports` method ❷ checks whether the object to be validated belongs to the `Book` class or its superclass. The `validate` method ❸ does the actual validation of the target object (the `Book` object). The `BookService`'s `isUnique` method is called ❹ to validate the uniqueness of the ISBN.

As you can see, the Spring Validation API constraints that apply to the `Book` domain object aren't defined in the `Book` class but in the `AddBookValidator` class. If you use JSR 303, the constraints are specified on the domain object itself, using annotations, as shown next.

Listing 8.24 Using JSR 303 with the `Book` domain object

```
import org.hibernate.validator.constraints.NotEmpty;
import javax.validation.constraints.Size;
import chapter08.code.listing.catalog.constraints.Unique;
...
public class Book {
    @NotEmpty
    @Size(max=100, min=10)
    private String name;

    @NotEmpty
    private String author;

    @Unique
    private Long isbnNumber;

    public Book(String name, String author, long isbnNumber) {
        this.name = name;
        this.author = author;
        this.isbnNumber = isbnNumber;
    }
    ...
}
```

In this code, the annotations check a variety of things:

- `@NotEmpty`—Checks that title of the book isn't `null` and that its length is greater than `0`
- `@Size`—Checks that length of the book title is at least `10` and no more than `100`
- `@NotEmpty`—Checks that author name isn't `null` and that its length is greater than `0`
- `@Unique`—Checks that the book's ISBN is unique—that no book already exists in the catalog with that ISBN

In listing 8.24, one of the interesting things to notice is the source of the annotations used in the `Book` class:

- The `@NotEmpty` annotation comes from the Hibernate Validator framework, which implements the Bean Validation API and provides additional annotations, like `@NotEmpty`, to put constraints on bean properties.
- The `@Size` annotation is defined as part of JSR 303.
- `@Unique` is a custom annotation defined as part of the Book Catalog portlet.

NOTE   To use JSR 303, the Book Catalog portlet uses Hibernate Validator's (http://hibernate.org/subprojects/validator) hibernate-validator-4.x.x.jar and validation-api-1.x.x.jar JAR files.

CONFIGURING JSR 303 WITH SPRING

Once you have defined constraints that apply to the properties of your command object or model attribute, the next step is to configure JSR 303 to work with Spring Framework. To allow easy access to JSR 303 validation, Spring provides the `Local-ValidatorFactoryBean`, which is responsible for bootstrapping the JSR 303 framework.

The `LocalValidatorFactoryBean` implements both the `javax.validation.Validator` and `org.springframework.validation.Validator` interfaces, giving you the flexibility to use Spring Validation API or JSR 303 to perform validation.

You can declare `LocalValidatorFactoryBean` in your web application context XML, as shown here:

```
<bean id="validator" class="org.springframework.validation.beanvalidation.
    ➥LocalValidatorFactoryBean" />
```

As described earlier, you can inject the `org.springframework.validation.Validator` bean into the `WebDataBinder` definition in the application context XML (if the validator applies to all the handlers of the portlet—see listing 8.21) or you can set the `WebDataBinder`'s `validator` property in the `@InitBinder` method of your handler (see listing 8.22). The `LocalValidatorFactoryBean` implements Spring's `Validator` interface, making it possible to set the `WebDataBinder`'s `validator` property with an instance of `LocalValidatorFactoryBean`.

NOTE   In most cases, you'll use the JSR 303 Bean Validation API to apply to all your application's objects. You'll generally configure `WebDataBinder` with `LocalValidatorFactoryBean` in the web application context XML so that it's available to all the handlers of the portlet.

The following listing configures JSR 303's `LocalValidatorFactoryBean` in the Book Catalog portlet's web application context XML file and injects it into the `WebData-Binder` instance.

Listing 8.25   Configuring `LocalValidatorFactoryBean` in application context XML

```
<bean id="validator" class="org.springframework.                    ❶ Defines bean for
    ➥validation.beanvalidation.LocalValidatorFactoryBean"/>            bootstrapping
                                                                       JSR 303
<bean class="org.springframework.web.portlet.mvc.annotation.
  ➥AnnotationMethodHandlerAdapter">
  <property name="webBindingInitializer">
    <bean class="org.springframework.web.bind.support.
      ➥ConfigurableWebBindingInitializer">                          ❷ Sets validator for
    <property name="validator" ref="validator" />                      WebDataBinder
    ...
  </bean>
</bean>
```

The `LocalValidatorFactoryBean` is defined ❶; it's responsible for bootstrapping the JSR 303 Bean Validation API. The `WebBindingIntializer` object's `validator` property is used ❷ to set the `LocalValidatorFactoryBean` as the validator for the `WebData-Binder` instance.

To perform validation using JSR 303, a validator class that implement's JSR 303's `javax.validation.Validator` interface must be created. Spring's `LocalValidator-FactoryBean` implements JSR 303's `Validator` interface, so it can be used for validating model attributes.

You saw in listing 8.21 that the `validator` property accepts objects of type `org.springframework.validation.Validator`. You can set the `validator` property to `LocalValidatorFactoryBean`, and it will work because `LocalValidatorFactory-Bean` implements Spring's `Validator` interface, as well as the `javax.validation.Validator` interface.

The validator set in listing 8.25 applies to all the model attributes of the portlet. The validation of a model attribute, which makes use of JSR 303 constraints, won't happen unless the `@Valid` annotation is specified for the handler argument representing the model attribute. This next listing shows how `AddBookController` makes use of the `@Valid` annotation to validate the `Book` model attribute.

Listing 8.26 Using the `@Valid` annotation in the `AddBookController`

```
@ActionMapping(params="myaction=addBook")
public void addBook(                                         @Valid
  @Valid @ModelAttribute(value="book")Book book,         ◁─  annotation
  BindingResult bindingResult,...) {
 if(!bindingResult.hasErrors()) {
   bookService.addBook(book);
   response.setRenderParameter("myaction", "books");
   sessionStatus.setComplete();
 } else {
   response.setRenderParameter("myaction", "addBook");
 }
}
```

In listing 8.26, the `@Valid` annotation validates the `Book` model attribute when the `AddBookController`'s `addBook` handler method is invoked. The validation results are stored in the `BindingResult` object, like when you use the Spring Validation API. If you're looking to programmatically validate your application objects using JSR 303, then you'll have to deal directly with the JSR 303 API.

Listing 8.27 shows how `AddBookController` can be rewritten to programmatically perform validation. It's important to note that when you're using programmatic validation, you don't need to configure the `LocalValidatorFactoryBean` for `WebData-Binder` (as was done in listing 8.25) or use the `@Valid` annotation in your handler method (as in listing 8.26). The `LocalValidatorFactoryBean` only needs to be defined in the web application context XML so that it's available to the `AddBook-Controller` handler.

Listing 8.27   Programmatic validation using the JSR 303 `Validator`

```
import javax.validation.Validator;
...
public class AddBookController {
 @Autowired                                              ❶ Autowires JSR 303
 private Validator validator;                               Validator interface
   ...
 @ActionMapping(params="myaction=addBook")
 public void addBook(@ModelAttribute(value="book") Book book,
     BindingResult bindingResult, ActionResponse response,...) {
   Set<ConstraintViolation<Book>> violations =              Validates Book
     validator.validate(book);                          ❷ domain object

   Iterator itr = violations.iterator();
   while(itr.hasNext()) {                                  ❸ Obtains constraint
     ConstraintViolation<Book> violation =                    violations reported
       (ConstraintViolation<Book>) itr.next();

       bindingResult.rejectValue(                         ❹ Sets property
           violation.getPropertyPath().toString,             path and message
           violation.getMessage()
       );
   }
 }
 ...
}
```

The `LocalValidatorFactoryBean` is autowired ❶. The `validate` method of `javax`
`.validation.Validator` is invoked ❷, which refers to the `LocalValidatorFactory-`
`Bean` instance configured in the web application context XML file. The constraint vio-
lations (if any) reported during validation are obtained ❸. The property path and
validation error message are obtained ❹ from the `ConstraintViolation` object using
the `getPropertyPath` and `getMessage` methods respectively, and set in the `Binding-`
`Result` object.

Both the `javax.validation.Validator` and `org.springframework.validation`
`.Validator` interfaces define `validate` methods, but their signatures are different.
The `org.springframework.validation.Validator`'s `validate` method returns `void`,
and the `javax.validation.Validator`'s `validate` method returns a set of `Constraint-`
`Violations` (refer to listing 8.27) reported during validation. In listing 8.27, you can
see that the `@Valid` annotation wasn't specified for the `Book` argument in the `addBook`
handler method. That's because the `Book` object is being validated programmatically;
you're not asking Spring Framework to validate the `Book` object when the `addBook`
method is invoked.

> **NOTE**   The `@Valid` annotation should only be specified for a handler method
> argument if you want Spring Framework to do the validation. If you're validat-
> ing objects programmatically, you must not specify the `@Valid` annotation.

If you don't want to deal with the JSR 303 API directly when programmatically validating your application objects, you can use Spring's `Validator` interface, instead of JSR

303's `Validator` interface, to invoke the JSR 303 validation API. The following listing shows how the `AddBookController` can be rewritten so that Spring's `Validator` performs the JSR 303 validation.

Listing 8.28 Programmatic validation using the Spring `Validator`

```
import org.springframework.validation.Validator;
...
public class AddBookController {
  @Autowired
  private Validator validator;
  ...
  @ActionMapping(params="myaction=addBook")
  public void addBook(@ModelAttribute(value="book") Book book,
      BindingResult bindingResult, ActionResponse response,...) {
    validator.validate(book, bindingResult);
    ...
  }
  ...
}
```

❶ Autowires Spring's Validator implementation

❷ Validates Book command object

The `LocalValidatorFactoryBean` is autowired ❶. Because `LocalValidatorFactory-Bean` implements Spring's `Validator` interface, it's possible to store a reference to `LocalValidatorFactoryBean` in a variable of type `Validator`. The `addBook` method invokes the `LocalValidatorFactoryBean`'s `validate` method ❷, passing the `Book` command object and `BindingResult` object as method arguments.

The `addBook` method in listing 8.28 is much simpler than the version in listing 8.27. In listing 8.28, the `validate` method of Spring's `Validator` is responsible for validating the `Book` object, which makes use of JSR 303 constraints. During validation, the `BindingResult` object is populated with property paths and messages that were received as part of `ConstraintViolations` reported during validation. This saves the effort of iterating over `ConstraintViolations` and populating the `BindingResult` object, as was done in listing 8.27.

Hibernate Validator comes with many built-in constraints, like `@NotEmpty`, `@Size`, and so on, but you'll often need to create your own custom constraints, like the `@Unique` constraint that applies to the `isbnNumber` property of the `Book` domain object. Let's look at JSR 303's support for creating custom constraints.

JSR 303 CUSTOM CONSTRAINTS
You can create a custom constraint in two steps:

1 Create a constraint annotation. The annotation is used to annotate the properties, methods, and so on.
2 Create a validator class for the constraint. The validator class contains the actual validation logic.

The following listing shows how the `@Unique` annotation in the Book Catalog portlet is defined.

Listing 8.29   Defining the @Unique constraint annotation

```
import java.lang.annotation.*;
import javax.validation.*;

@Target({ElementType.FIELD})
@Retention(RetentionPolicy.RUNTIME)
@Constraint(validatedBy=
        ➥MyUniqueConstraintValidator.class)
public @interface Unique {
  String message() default
      ➥"{unique.constraint.failure}";
  Class<?>[] groups() default {};
  public abstract Class<? extends Payload>[] payload() default {};
}
```

❶ Link constraint annotation with validator

❷ Constraint violation error message

Listing 8.29 shows how you can create a constraint annotation. The `@Target` annotation specifies that only attributes of a class can be annotated with the `@Unique` annotation. The `@RetentionPolicy` indicates that the `@Unique` annotation has runtime semantics and that at runtime it can be accessed using reflection. You must specify `message`, `groups`, and `payload` attributes in your constraint definition. To learn more about `groups` and `payload` attributes, refer to the JSR 303 specification and Hibernate Validator reference documentation.

The `@Constraint` annotation **❶** links the constraint annotation with the validator responsible for implementing the actual validation logic. In this case, the `@Constraint` annotation specifies that if an attribute of a class is annotated with `@Unique`, the `MyUniqueConstraintValidator` class is responsible for validating that field.

The `default` attribute **❷** identifies the message's error code that will be used to resolve the error message if the constraint is violated. The error message corresponding to the error code must be defined in a `ValidationMessages.properties` file, which must be in your portlet's classpath.

> **NOTE** If you want to use a different properties file as the resource bundle for your messages, you'll have to create a custom `MessageInterpolator`. For more information on the `MessageInterpolator`, refer to the JSR 303 specification and API.

Once your constraint annotation is ready, the next step is to write the validator that's responsible for validating the constraint. The following listing shows the implementation of the `MyUniqueConstraintValidator` class, which is responsible for providing the actual validation logic behind the `@Unique` constraint.

Listing 8.30   The MyUniqueConstraintValidator validator

```
public class MyUniqueConstraintValidator implements
    ConstraintValidator<Unique, Long> {
  @Autowired
  @Qualifier("myBookService")
```

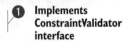

❶ Implements ConstraintValidator interface

```
    private BookService bookService;              ←──②  Autowires BookService by name

    public void initialize(Unique annotation) {   ←─┐
    }                                                │  ③  Initializes validator
    public boolean isValid(Long isbnNumber,
        ConstraintValidatorContext context) {          ④  Implements
      return bookService.isUniqueISBN(isbnNumber);          validation logic
    }
}
```

MyUniqueConstraintValidator ❶ implements JSR 303's ConstraintValidator interface. The ConstraintValidator specifies two parameters: the constraint's *annotation
type* (which is Unique in this case) and the *object type* to which the validator is applicable. In the case of MyUniqueConstraintValidator, the object type is Long because the
ISBN is defined as a Long in the Book Catalog portlet's Book domain object.

   MyUniqueConstraintValidator ❷ defines its dependency on the BookService
bean using Spring's @Autowired and @Qualifier annotations. This is one of the main
highlights of Spring's integration with the JSR 303 framework; you can inject dependencies into your ConstraintValidators just as you do in a typical Spring bean.

   The initialize method ❸ is responsible for initializing the MyUnique-
ConstraintValidator instance. Because there's nothing to initialize, the method
implementation is empty. In the initialize method you'll usually obtain the values
of attributes defined in the annotation and store them in the validator instance.

   The isValid method ❹ implements the validation logic for the constraint annotation. The isValid method can make use of the information that was stored in the validator instance during initialization.

   So far in this chapter, we've discussed annotations that can help you create annotated controllers and validate command or form-backing objects. Spring Portlet MVC
not only makes it easy to write controllers and provides features like dependency
injection, validation, and so on, but it also provides a *form* tag library, which makes it
easy for you to create your JSP pages and bind form fields to your command or form-
backing objects. In a typical situation, you'll use the portlet tag library (discussed in
chapter 6) along with Spring's form tag library to create your JSP pages. Let's look at
Spring's form tag library and see how the Book Catalog portlet makes use of it.

8.6   Spring's form tag library

Spring's form tag library is a set of tags that can help you create JSP pages. Spring's
form tag library defines tags for creating various input form elements (like text fields,
text areas, combo boxes, check boxes, radio buttons, and so on) on the JSP page and
for binding the input form elements on the JSP page to command or form-backing
objects. The benefit of using the form tag library instead of writing plain HTML in JSP
pages is the library's support for internationalization, data binding (to command and
form-backing objects), and showing error messages.

   The following listing shows how the addBookForm.jsp page of the Book Catalog
portlet makes use of Spring's form tag library tags.

Listing 8.31   The addBookForm.jsp page

```
<%@ taglib prefix="form"
    uri="http://www.springframework.org/tags/form"%>
...
<form:form name="addBookForm" commandName="book"
    method="post"
    action="${addBookActionUrl}">
    <table>
        <tr>
            <td>Title:<font style="color:
            ➥#C11B17;">*</font></td>
            <td><form:input path="name" /></td>
            <td>
                <font style="color: #C11B17;">
                    <form:errors path="name" />
                </font>
            </td>
        </tr>
        ...
    </table>
</form:form>
```

❶ Spring form tag library

❷ Spring <form> tag

The Spring form tag library is included ❶ by the @taglib directive.

The <form> tag of Spring's form tag library is used ❷ to create an HTML form that binds form fields to the book command object. The commandName attribute identifies the command object to which the form fields are bound; this object must be available as a model attribute to allow the WebDataBinder instance to control the binding of form fields to the command object. The action attribute specifies that the form is submitted to the addBookActionUrl, which is an action URL.

The Spring form tag library's <input> tag is used to create an HTML input field. The path attribute identifies the path to the property in the command object to which the value of this field is bound when the form is submitted. When the form is rendered, the path attribute is used to read the property value from the command object, so it can be displayed on the form.

The <errors> tag of the Spring form tag library is used to display binding or validation errors associated with the property identified by the path attribute.

Testing plays an important role in any application's development. Spring provides multiple ways in which you can test handlers. In the next section, we'll look at unit testing handlers using mock objects and Spring's TestContext framework.

8.7   *Unit testing with mock objects and TestContext*

A developer's job isn't over until the unit testing of handlers is complete. Spring Portlet MVC provides mock objects that you can use to test your portlet handlers. Mock objects mimic real objects like ActionRequest, ActionResponse, RenderRequest, Render-Response, PortletURL, and others, making it possible to unit test handlers outside the portlet container. In this section, we'll discuss unit testing using JUnit 4.5+ and Spring's TestContext framework.

Before we get started writing unit test classes, let's take a quick look at how to configure our Ant buildfile (discussed in chapter 1) to run JUnit tests.

8.7.1   *Ant buildfile to run unit tests*

Unit tests are executed immediately after the compilation of source files and before the WAR file for your portlet application is generated. The following listing shows JUnit Ant task for running *batch tests* for your portlet project.

Listing 8.32   The build.xml JUnit ant task

```
<target name="build" depends="clean,compile">
  <junit haltonfailure="true"                           Specifies JUnit task
          printsummary="withOutAndErr">                 to run JUnit tests
    <classpath>
      <pathelement path="${class.path}"/>               Sets classpath
      <pathelement path="${webinf.dir}"/>               for JUnit tests
    </classpath>
    <batchtest>
      <fileset dir="${src.dir}">
        <include name="**/*Test*.java"/>                Specifies running
      </fileset>                                        tests in batch
    </batchtest>
  </junit>
  ...
</target>
```

In listing 8.32, the `<junit>` element runs JUnit tests identified by the `<batchtest>` element. The `build` target depends upon `clean` and `compile`, which means that JUnit tests are executed after the `clean` and `compile` targets are complete.

The following listing shows the `AddBookController` handler of the Book Catalog portlet that we'll unit test using JUnit and the TestContext framework.

Listing 8.33   The `AddBookController` handler to be tested

```
@Controller("addBookController")
@RequestMapping(value="VIEW")
@SessionAttributes(types=Book.class)
public class AddBookController {
    @Autowired
    @Qualifier("mybookService")
    private BookService bookService;

    public void setBookService() {
        this.bookService = bookService;
    }

    @ModelAttribute("book")
    public Book getCommandObject() {
        return new Book();
    }

    @RenderMapping(params="myaction=addBook")
    public String showAddBookForm(RenderResponse response) {
```

```
      return "addBookForm";
  }

  @ActionMapping(params = "myaction=addBook")
  public void addBook(@Valid @ModelAttribute(value="book") Book book,
      BindingResult bindingResult, ActionResponse response,
      SessionStatus sessionStatus) {
    if (!bindingResult.hasErrors()) {
      bookService.addBook(book);
      response.setRenderParameter("myaction", "books");
      sessionStatus.setComplete();
    } else {
      response.setRenderParameter("myaction", "addBookForm");
    }
  }
}
```

8.7.2 Unit testing with mock objects

If you're directly using JUnit for unit testing, your tests will be responsible for
creating application objects and for dependency injection. For instance, to test Add-
BookController, shown in listing 8.33, you'll need to create an instance of AddBook-
Controller and a mock implementation of BookService that is explicitly set in
AddBookController.

The following listing shows how the Book Catalog portlet's AddBookController-
Test class uses mock objects to test the AddBookController handler.

Listing 8.34 A JUnit test for AddBookController

```
import static org.junit.Assert.*;
import org.junit.*;
import org.springframework.mock.web.portlet.*;
import org.springframework.web.bind.support.SimpleSessionStatus;

public class AddBookControllerTest {
  private AddBookController addBookController;
  private BookService bookService= new MockBookService();      ❶ Creates instance of MockBookService

  @Before
  public void setUp() {
    addBookController = new AddBookController();
    addBookController.setBookService(bookService);             ❷ Assigns MockBookService to handler
  }

  @Test
  public void testShowAddBookForm() {
    RenderResponse response =
        new MockRenderResponse();                              ❸ Creates MockRenderResponse object
    assertEquals("addBookForm",
            addBookController.showAddBookForm(response));
  }

  @Test
  public void testAddBook() {
    Book book = new Book("test book", "test author", 1234567890L);
```

```
    MockActionResponse response =
        new MockActionResponse();
    addBookController.addBook(book,
        new BindException(book, "book"), response,
        new SimpleSessionStatus());
    assertNotNull(bookService.getBook(1234567890L));
    assertEquals("books", response.getRenderParameter("myaction"));
  }
}
```

4 Creates MockActionResponse object

An instance of the `MockBookService` class **1** is created; it's a custom class for testing the `AddBookController` handler. `MockBookService` implements the `BookService` interface and provides mock implementations for the methods. For example, when you call the `MockBookService`'s `addBook` method, it simply stores the book information in an instance variable. The `@Before` annotation specifies that the `setUp` method is executed before any other method of the `AddBookControllerTest` class; `setUp` initializes the `AddBookControllerTest` instance with object instances that are used by the `@Test` methods of the class.

The `BookService` dependency of `AddBookController` **2** is fulfilled by `MockBookService`. The `@Test` annotation indicates that `testShowAddBookForm` is a JUnit test method.

Spring Portlet MVC's built-in `MockRenderResponse` object **3** is instantiated to pass the `MockRenderResponse` instance to the `showAddBookForm` method of `AddBookController`. Spring Portlet MVC's built-in `MockActionResponse` object **4** is instantiated to pass the `MockActionResponse` instance to the `AddBookController`'s `addBook` method. Because the `addBook` method accepts a `SessionStatus` object, Spring's built-in `SimpleSessionStatus` object (an implementation of the `SessionStatus` interface) is created and passed to the `addBook` method.

> **WARNING** JUnit invokes the `@Before` annotated method before each test method of the class is executed. If you want to perform a one-time initialization for all the tests, you should perform that initialization in a `public static void` method annotated with the `@BeforeClass` JUnit annotation.

8.7.3 *Unit testing with Spring's TestContext framework*

The test cases in listing 8.34 run outside the Spring container, requiring the test class to explicitly instantiate a controller and provide it with the dependencies it needs. But if your portlet makes use of complex object structures, it's cumbersome to create such structures programmatically. Spring's TestContext framework makes it easier to write unit and integration tests by providing you with a framework that resides on top of testing frameworks like JUnit and TestNG, and that lets you take advantage of Spring container features.

The following listing shows the Book Catalog portlet's `AddBookControllerTest-Context` class, which makes use of the TestContext framework to test the `AddBook-Controller` handler.

```
import org.junit.Test;
import org.junit.runner.RunWith;
import org.springframework.test.context.*;
import org.springframework.test.context.junit4.*;
import org.springframework.test.context.support.
    ➥DependencyInjectionTestExecutionListener;

@RunWith(SpringJUnit4ClassRunner.class)                    ❶ Runner for
                                                              the tests

@ContextConfiguration(                                     ❷ Application context
 locations="classpath:bookCatalogTest-portlet.xml"           configuration
)

@TestExecutionListeners(value =                            ❸ TestExecutionListeners
{ DependencyInjectionTestExecutionListener.class }            for the tests
)

public class AddBookControllerTestContext extends          ❹ Test class extends Abstract-
        AbstractJUnit4SpringContextTests {                    JUnit4SpringContextTests
 @Autowired
 @Qualifier("addBookController")
 private AddBookController addBookController;

 @Autowired                                                ❺ AddBookController
 @Qualifier("myBookService")                                  is autowired
 private BookService bookService;

 @Autowired
 private Validator validator;

 @Test
 public void testShowAddBookForm() {
  RenderResponse response = new MockRenderResponse();
  assertEquals("addBookForm",
    addBookController.showAddBookForm(response));
 }
 ...
 @Test
 public void testBook() {
  Set<ConstraintViolation<Book>> violations =
    validator.validate(new Book());
  int[] actual = {violations.size()};
  int[] expected = {4};
  assertArrayEquals(expected, actual);
 }
}
```

The @RunWith JUnit annotation ❶ instructs JUnit to use SpringJUnit4ClassRunner as
the runner for the test cases. SpringJUnit4ClassRunner is a JUnit 4.5+ compliant runner that supports JUnit 4.5+ annotations, like @Test, @Ignore, and so on.

The @ContextConfiguration annotation ❷ specifies the application context
that's used in running the tests. The locations attribute specifies the location of the
application context XML that will be used by the test cases in the class. If you're doing
integration testing, you can specify the actual web application context XML file of your

portlet. In the case of unit testing, you'll usually create a simplified application context XML with the bare minimum configuration expected by your tests. For instance, you won't be using your actual business services in unit testing, so they shouldn't be part of the application context XML that's provided to your unit test cases. This example uses the bookCatalogTest-portlet.xml file (shown in listing 8.36), which only contains bean definitions used by the test cases.

The @TestExecutionListeners that are configured for executing the test ❸ are specified. In unit testing, you'll mostly use DependencyInjectionTest-ExecutionListener, which provides support for dependency injection in your tests. TestExecutionListeners, like DependencyInjectionTestExecutionListener, TransactionalTestExecutionListener and DirtiesContextTestExecutionListener are invoked by the TestContext framework, giving these listeners an opportunity to respond to events that occur during test preparation or execution. It's because of the DependencyInjectionTestExecutionListener that AddBookControllerTest-Context in listing 8.35 can use the @Autowired and @Qualifier annotations to inject dependencies into the test class.

The test class ❹ extends Spring's AbstractJUnit4SpringContextTests class, which allows the integration of JUnit tests with the application context. This is a JUnit 4.5+ specific class.

The AddBookController, BookService, and JSR 303 validator beans ❺ are autowired into the tests from the application context. The JSR 303 validator is defined in the application context as shown in listing 8.36. The testBook method shows how the Book domain object is validated programmatically using the JSR 303 (Bean Validation) framework.

The following listing shows the bookCatalogTest-portlet.xml application context XML file that's used by the AddBookControllerTestContext class shown in listing 8.35.

Listing 8.36 Listing 8.36 The bookCatalogTest-portlet.xml application context XML file

```
<beans ...>
  <bean id="addBookController"
     class="chapter08.code.listing.domain.AddBookController"/>

  <bean id="myBookService"
     class="chapter08.code.listing.controller.test.MockBookService"/>

  <bean id="validator"
    class="org.springframework.validation.beanvalidation.
      ➥LocalValidatorFactoryBean" />
</beans>
```

Listing 8.36 defines the addBookController, myBookService, and validator beans only. The LocalValidatorFactoryBean class is configured as the validator because it does the bootstrapping of the JSR 303 Bean Validation framework, as discussed in section 8.5.2. The testBook method in listing 8.35 makes use of the validator bean configured in the bookCatalogTest-portlet.xml file to programmatically validate the Book domain object, saving the effort of explicitly bootstrapping the JSR 303 Bean Validation framework.

The unit testing described in this section sets the stage for doing both unit and integration testing using Spring's TestContext framework. Let's now look at some miscellaneous topics that you may need to know about when developing portlets using the Spring Portlet MVC framework.

8.8   *Localizing content, uploading files, and adding CSS and JavaScript*

In this section, we'll address the three most common requirements you'll come across in portlet applications: localizing content based on the user's locale, adding custom JavaScript and CSS to the portal page, and uploading files.

8.8.1   *Localizing content*

If you're using the Spring Portlet MVC framework, you can use Spring's Resource-BundleMessageSource implementation to access messages, labels, and texts stored in a resource bundle. If the properties defined in your resource bundles are expected to change after the portlet is deployed, you may prefer to use Spring's Reloadable-ResourceBundleMessageSource implementation of the resource bundle. If you want to programmatically access resource bundles in your controller classes, you can have your handler implement the MessageSourceAware interface or you can simply use the @Autowired annotation to autowire the MessageSource bean.

The MessageSourceAware interface defines a single setter method, setMessage-Source(MessageSource messageSource), that lets you set the messageSource property. If you define a bean of type MessageSource, with the name messageSource, in your web application context, any object that implements the MessageSource-Aware interface will be able to access the resource bundle. Because Resource-BundleMessageSource and ReloadableResourceBundleMessageSource are concrete implementations of the MessageSource interface, you can define a messageSource bean in the application context XML that makes use of either of these Message-Source implementations.

The following application context XML fragment shows how you can define a MessageSource bean in your portlet's web application context XML file:

```
<bean id="messageSource"
    class="org.springframework.context.support.ResourceBundleMessageSource">
  <property name="basenames">
    <list>
      <value>content.messages</value>
    </list>
  </property>
</bean>
```

Note that the name of the bean is messageSource in the preceding code fragment. The basenames property identifies the fully qualified name of the resource bundle.

For instance, in the preceding code content.messages refers to the resource bundle with the name messages that resides in the content package in the classpath.

The following listing shows how the SomeController handler can access a resource bundle using the MessageSourceAware interface. Alternatively, you can use the @Autowired annotation to inject the MessageSource bean into the Some-Controller instance.

Listing 8.37 The SomeController handler using the MessageSourceAware interface

```
public class SomeController                          1  Implements
    implements MessageSourceAware {                     MessageSourceAware
  private MessageSource messageSource;
                                                        Defines
  public void setMessageSource(MessageSource messageSource) {  messageSource
    this.messageSource = messageSource;              2  property
  }

  @RenderMapping
  public void showSomething(RenderRequest request,
    RenderResponse response, Model model)
      throws IOException, PortletException {
      response.setTitle(
      messageSource.getMessage("portlet.title.books",  3  Retrieves message
      null,request.getLocale())                          using messageSource
      );                                                 property
    ...
  }
}
```

SomeController implements the MessageSourceAware interface ❶ and provides the implementation of the setMessageSource method. SomeController defines a property named messageSource ❷ of type MessageSource. Spring Framework is responsible for setting the messageSource property using the SomeController class's setMessageSource method. SomeController uses the messageSource bean ❸ to retrieve the title for the portlet from the resource bundle referenced by message-Source. The getLocale method of PortletRequest returns the user's locale information, which is then used to retrieve a localized message for the user's locale.

As listing 8.37 shows, the MessageSource defined in the web application context isn't autowired. Instead, Spring Framework is responsible for calling the setMessage-Source method of SomeController and passing the messageSource bean defined in the web application context XML file.

Let's now look at how to add a JavaScript or CSS file to the portal page when using Spring Portlet MVC.

8.8.2 Adding external JavaScript and CSS files

To add custom JavaScript and CSS files to the head section of a portal page, you need to extend the DispatcherPortlet class (which extends the GenericPortlet class) and override the doHeaders method, as shown here:

```
public class MyDispatcherPortlet extends DispatcherPortlet {
  protected void doHeaders(RenderRequest request, RenderResponse response)
  {
    super.doHeaders(request, response);
    Element cssElement = ...
    ...
    response.addProperty(MimeResponse.MARKUP_HEAD_ELEMENT,...);
  }
}
```

In the preceding code, the doHeaders method of the MyDispatcherPortlet class includes a call to DispatcherPortlet's doHeaders method to ensure that if DispatcherPortlet adds any property or headers to the response, they aren't lost. As of Spring 3.0, DispatcherPortlet doesn't override the GenericPortlet class's doHeaders method to add additional properties or headers to the response, so it's fine if you don't invoke the doHeaders method of DispatcherPortlet from your subclass.

Let's now look at how Spring Portlet MVC simplifies uploading files.

8.8.3 *Uploading files using PortletMultipartResolver*

In chapter 4, you saw that you can use the PortletFileUpload class of the Apache Commons FileUpload library to upload files in portlets. Chapter 4 showed the complete code to check for multipart requests and convert the file input stream to a byte array, before writing it to a local filesystem folder. If you're using Spring Portlet MVC, implementing file upload feature in portlets is simplified. The Spring Portlet MVC framework provides a PortletMultipartResolver bean that you can use to resolve multipart portlet requests.

Like ViewResolver and ExceptionResolver, PortletMultipartResolver is an interface—you can implement it to create your own multipart resolver or you can use a built-in implementation provided by Spring. Spring provides a concrete implementation of PortletMultipartResolver, called CommonsPortletMultipartResolver, which makes use of Apache Commons FileUpload to upload files.

> NOTE If you're using Spring's PortletMultipartResolver to upload files, ensure that you're using Apache Commons FileUpload 1.2 or above.

You can configure PortletMultipartResolver in your application context XML file, like any other bean. As with ViewResolver and ExceptionResolver, you don't need to explicitly associate PortletMultipartResolver with handlers that define action methods to upload files. That is taken care by the Spring Framework itself.

The PortletMultipartResolver gets applied to the multipart portlet requests received by DispatcherPortlet. The PortletMultipartResolver transforms the incoming ActionRequest to MultipartActionRequest, which provides additional methods to deal with multipart content. The action methods that are responsible for handling file uploads in a handler can cast the ActionRequest to MultipartAction-Request to deal with the multipart content.

8.9 Summary

This chapter showed how annotation-driven development can save you the effort of maintaining the application configuration in separate configuration files. You saw how various Spring features can be accessed using annotations to simplify portlet development. For instance, the classpath-scanning feature can autoregister Spring components, JSR 303's @Valid annotation can validate objects, and other annotations can map portlet requests to handlers, store model attributes in the handler's conversational session, autowire objects by type or by name, and so on. The example Book Catalog portlet showed how these features can be combined together to build a multipage portlet. We also looked at how Spring's TestContext framework simplifies performing unit and integration testing of controllers.

In the next chapter, we'll look at how Spring simplifies interacting with a database.

Integrating portlets
with databases

9

This chapter covers

- Using the Spring JDBC module for data access
- Addressing cross-cutting concerns using aspect-oriented programming (AOP)
- Spring's support for transaction management
- Working with the Hibernate ORM framework

So far in this book, we've looked at portlets that store data in memory. In this chapter, we'll look at how you can create portlets that interact with databases to store and retrieve data. Because there are multiple mechanisms you can use to integrate a portlet with a database, we'll focus on widely used frameworks for data access: the Spring JDBC module and the Hibernate ORM (object-relational mapping) framework. Haven't heard of these or not quite sure how to use them? Keep reading.

In this chapter, we'll first enhance the non-Spring Book Catalog portlet that we developed in chapter 6 to use the Spring JDBC module, and then we'll look at how Spring simplifies integration with the Hibernate ORM framework—a Java Persistence API (JPA) provider. In the context of database interaction, we'll also look at Spring's support for aspect-oriented programming (AOP) and transaction management.

But let's first take a quick look at why it's important to develop portlets that interact with databases.

> **TIP** To get the most out of this chapter, refer to appendix B for details on how to install and configure MySQL with Liferay Portal. The rest of this chapter assumes that you've created a database named myportaldb in MySQL and that is used as Liferay Portal's internal database.

9.1 Combining portlets and databases

Suppose you've created a web portal for selling books. You can use the Book Catalog portlet, as described in previous chapters, to let your users view the book details, download the table of contents (TOC), and so on. The book information displayed by the Book Catalog portlet changes as new books are added and out-of-stock books are removed from the portlet, and someone, such as a web portal administrator, must update the information displayed by the portlet.

To make it easy for an administrator to change the content, you could develop the Book Catalog portlet to show static content that's updated by the portal administrator. The downside to this approach is that the book information can't be reused by other portlets in the portal. For instance, if you want to create a Recently Added Books portlet to show information about recently added books, the administrator would need to update the content displayed by both portlets every time a new book is added or removed.

If you choose to use a persistent store, like a flat file or a database, to store the book data, it's easy to modify the data using administration screens and to reuse the same data across different portlets or applications. Also, the Book Catalog portlet could generate content dynamically in response to user actions; that's not possible if the portlet shows static content.

Let's say that tomorrow a new technology arrives that's bound to give you an edge over your competitors. If your data is embedded in the portlet, that will prevent you from quickly moving to the new technology. Application data stored in a persistent store outlives the application itself; the applications that use it may change as new technologies and business opportunities come and go, but the data used by the applications remains.

Another thing to consider is that if the responsibility of persisting or retrieving data is outside the scope of the portlet, the portlet doesn't need to deal directly with the persistent store. In scenarios where the portlet is directly responsible for saving data to or retrieving it from the persistent store, you need to consider the design of your portlet's data access layer.

As mentioned in chapter 1, portal servers make use of an internally managed database to store configuration information, user roles, permissions, and so on. So far in this book, we've relied on Liferay Portal's default HSQLDB in-memory database to store this information. But information stored in the portal server's database is for internal use by the portal server; portlets shouldn't directly interact with database tables that are used internally by the portal server.

> **WARNING**   HSQLDB is meant only for development purposes and isn't recommended for use in production environments. Because we're developing portlets for the real world, databases like Oracle, MySQL, and DB2 should be used: they're capable of handling high-volume transactional data.

Let's now discuss the database tables that will hold data for the Book Catalog portlet.

9.2   *Exploring the Book Catalog portlet's database tables*

The Book Catalog portlet's requirements in this chapter are the same as those defined in chapter 6 (section 6.1). The only additional requirement is that each book record in the database should have a creation date and time and a modification date and time.

Figure 9.1 shows the two tables used by the Book Catalog portlet to store book information: BOOK_TBL and TOC_TBL. Let's look at what information is stored in each of these tables.

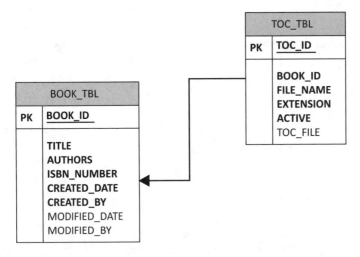

Figure 9.1   Database tables used by the Book Catalog portlet to store book data

9.2.1   *The BOOK_TBL table*

The BOOK_TBL table stores information about the book, excluding the TOC information. Table 9.1 describes the columns of BOOK_TBL.

Table 9.1   Columns defined in the BOOK_TBL table

Column name	Description
BOOK_ID	Primary key of the BOOK_TBL table. Its value is autogenerated by the MySQL database.
TITLE	Title of the book. The column accepts a non-null value.
AUTHORS	Authors of the book. The column accepts a non-null value.
ISBN_NUMBER	ISBN of the book. The column accepts a non-null value.
ACTIVE	Status of the book. If the record represents a deleted book, the value is 0. If the record represents a book that's available to users, the value is 1.
CREATED_DATE	Date and time when the book record was created in BOOK_TBL. The column accepts a non-null value.
CREATED_BY	Username of the logged-in user who created the book record. The column accepts a non-null value.
MODIFIED_DATE	Date and time when the book record was *last* modified. The column can accept a null value.
MODIFIED_BY	Username of the logged-in user who modified the book record. The column can accept a null value.

Now, let's look at the TOC_TBL table, which stores the book's TOC information.

9.2.2   *The TOC_TBL table*

The TOC_TBL table stores book's table of contents (TOC) information. It's not mandatory for a book to have a TOC at any given time, so it's possible for BOOK_TBL to contain book information but for TOC_TBL to not contain any corresponding TOC details.

Table 9.2 describes the columns of the TOC_TBL database table.

Table 9.2   Columns defined in the TOC_TBL table

Column name	Description
TOC_ID	Autogenerated primary key of TOC_TBL.
BOOK_ID	Foreign key, which identifies the book in the BOOK_TBL table with which this record is associated. The column accepts a not-null value.
FILE_NAME	Name of the TOC file that was uploaded by the user. The column accepts a not-null value.

Table 9.2 Columns defined in the TOC_TBL table *(continued)*

Column name	Description
EXTENSION	File extension associated with the uploaded TOC file. The column accepts a not-null value.
ACTIVE	Status of the TOC. If the record represents the latest TOC, the value is 1. If the record represents an old TOC that is now not available to users, the value is 0.
TOC_FILE	The actual TOC file of the book. The file can be in any format, such as MS Word, PDF, TXT, and so on.

As shown in figure 9.1, TOC_TBL and BOOK_TBL are linked to each other via the BOOK_ID column. The tables semantically have a one-to-one relationship because at any given time there are zero or one active TOC records in TOC_TBL for a book in BOOK_TBL. It's expected that when a book is removed by a user, the ACTIVE column for the book is set to 0 in the BOOK_TBL and TOC_TBL tables.

CODE REFERENCE In order to run the Book Catalog portlet project later in this chapter, you'll first need to create the tables defined here. The book's source code contains a sql folder that contains two SQL scripts, book_tbl.sql and toc_tbl.sql, for creating these tables. You can either create the tables in the myportaldb database used by Liferay Portal, or you can create your own database for these tables. In either case, you must configure the database in JNDI so that it's accessible to Spring's `JdbcTemplate` class, as described in section 9.3.2.

Now that you know what tables are involved, let's look at how the Spring JDBC module can simplify the development of a portlet that interacts with a database.

NOTE If you're new to Spring, you should make sure you understand the topics covered in sections 7.2, 7.6, 8.3.2, and 8.3.3 (fundamentals of Spring Framework and how the classpath-scanning, autodetection, and autowiring features work in Spring), because they will be used to develop the Book Catalog portlet with the Spring JDBC module.

9.3 *Spring's JDBC module for database interaction*

In this section, we'll look at how the Spring JDBC (Java Database Connectivity) module simplifies interaction with the database and use it to implement the data access layer of the Book Catalog portlet. In the context of the Book Catalog portlet, we'll look at how to configure the data source in a properties file or JNDI, how to access JNDI-bound data sources in Spring's application context XML, and how to create data access objects (DAOs) that use Spring JDBC classes for executing SQL statements. We'll wrap up this section by creating a Spring-based `BookService` service that uses DAOs to access the data source containing book catalog data.

> **NOTE** In section 9.4 we'll look at how non-Spring classes, like `Book-CatalogPortlet`, can access the Spring-based `BookService` to interact with the database.

In chapters 7 and 8, we discussed the Spring Portlet MVC framework—a Spring *module* that forms part of the Spring Framework. A module in Spring Framework represents a framework that can be used independently of other Spring modules in an application. The only dependency that modules, like Spring's JDBC module, have is on the core modules of Spring Framework, which provide dependency injection, IoC container features, and so on.

This modularity in Spring Framework allows you to choose the module that fits your application requirements without requiring the application to carry the baggage of other modules. For instance, in chapter 7, where you developed portlets using the Spring Portlet MVC framework, you only used the Spring Framework modules that address portlet development.

> **NOTE** For a detailed list of Spring modules and their functionality, see the Spring reference documentation at the SpringSource website (http://www .springsource.org/documentation).

Let's look at a scenario in which you decide to write the complete data access code for the Book Catalog portlet yourself. You'll be responsible for writing logic to do the following:

- Open and close the database connection
- Close the `Statement` and `ResultSet`
- Process exceptions thrown during database operation
- Handle database transactions and leaving the data in a consistent state

If you had to write code to perform all these functions, it would not only clutter your data access code but also introduce lots of potential for bugs in your code. If you using the Spring JDBC module, you don't need to worry about these concerns, as you'll see later in this section.

Let's now look at the steps you'd follow to create the Book Catalog portlet if you use Spring JDBC to assist you with writing the portlet's data access layer.

9.3.1 *Defining a data source*

The first step in developing a portlet that interacts with data sources is to define `javax.sql.DataSource` objects (representing data sources accessed by the portlet) that the portlet will use to create connections to data sources. Data sources can be defined in two ways:

- Define the data source in the portlet's application context XML file as a `javax .sql.DataSource` bean.
- Define a data source that's bound to a JNDI name in your application server.

Let's explore both options in detail.

DEFINING A DATA SOURCE IN THE APPLICATION CONTEXT XML

In chapter 7, you used the application context XML file to define controllers, handler mappings, interceptors, services, and so on. The concept of the application context is central to Spring-based applications, regardless of which Spring module you're using in your application.

The type of beans you define in your application context will vary depending upon which layer of your application uses Spring Framework. For instance, if you're using the Spring JDBC module, you'll define DAOs and data sources in Spring's application context XML file. If you're using Spring's Web module, the application context XML file will contain controller and handler mapping definitions.

> **NOTE** In a layered architecture, DAOs are accessed by business services that form part of the application; DAOs are never accessed directly. For the sake of simplicity, the examples in this chapter will use Spring to manage business services, which in turn interact with the data access layer.

This listing shows an application context XML file that reads data source properties from an external properties file to define a `DataSource` bean.

Listing 9.1 Defining a `DataSource` bean in the application context XML file

```
<beans ...>
  ...
  <bean id="propertyConfigurer"
      class="org.springframework.beans.factory.
      config.PropertyPlaceholderConfigurer">            ❶ Defines Property-
    <property name="locations">                            PlaceholderConfigurer
      <list>                                               bean
        <value>WEB-INF/jdbc.properties</value>          ❷ Specifies
      </list>                                              properties file
    </property>
  </bean>

  <bean id="dataSource" class="org.apache.commons.dbcp
      .BasicDataSource" destroy-method="close">
    <property name="url">                               ❸ Defines
      <value>${database.url}</value>                       DataSource bean
    </property>                                            and its properties
    <property name="driverClassName">
      <value>${database.driver}</value>
    </property>
    ...
  </bean>
  ...
</beans>
```

Spring's built-in `PropertyPlaceholderConfigurer` bean is defined ❶. It reads the properties files specified by the `locations` property ❷ and it makes the properties defined in those files available to the bean defined in the application context XML file. In this example, `PropertyPlaceholderConfigurer` reads the jdbc.properties file located in WEB-INF directory.

A `dataSource` bean of type `javax.sql.DataSource` is defined ❸, and its properties are assigned values retrieved from the jdbc.properties file. The implementation class can be any class that implements `javax.sql.DataSource`. The bean has the following attributes:

- The `class` attribute specifies `org.apache.commons.dbcp.BasicDataSource` as the class that implements the `javax.sql.DataSource` interface. `BasicDataSource` is an Apache Commons DBCP class that provides database connection pooling features (see http://commons.apache.org/dbcp/ for more details).
- The `destroy-method` attribute identifies which method of the `DataSource` implementation class should be called when the bean is destroyed. This ensures that the database connection is explicitly closed by Spring when you shut down your application. The `destroy-method` attribute is available to all the beans defined in the application context, and it can be used for cleanup purposes.

The `datasource` bean definition specifies values for the `BasicDataSource` class's `url`, `driverClass`, `username`, and `password` properties. The value of the `url` property is specified as `${database.url}`. The `${}` syntax is used to refer to properties loaded by `PropertyPlaceholderConfigurer`; for example, `${database.url}` refers to the value of the `database.url` property defined in the jdbc.properties file. Similarly, values are specified for the other properties of the `BasicDataSource` class.

The next listing shows the jdbc.properties file that was read by `PropertyPlaceholderConfigurer` in listing 9.1.

Listing 9.2 The `jdbc.properties` data source properties file

```
database.url=jdbc:mysql://localhost/myportaldb?useUnicode=true&
database.driver=com.mysql.jdbc.Driver
database.username=root
database.password=root
database.maxAction=5
database.maxIdle=2
```

If you're using only the Spring JDBC module to develop your portlet, you also need to figure out some way to load the application context XML shown in listing 9.1. If you're using Spring Portlet MVC, the application context XML file named *<portletName>*-portlet.xml is loaded by `DispatcherPortlet` (refer to section 7.5 for more details). But you aren't using Spring Portlet MVC in this example portlet, so the simplest way to load the application context is to define your beans in the root web application context XML file and configure `ContextLoaderListener` in your web.xml file, as described in section 7.6.2. The Book Catalog portlet makes use of the root web application context to register its services and DAOs, as you'll see later in this chapter.

In most application scenarios, the data source configuration isn't part of the application. Instead, the data source is bound to JNDI in the application server, and applications retrieve the data source from JNDI using the `javax.naming.InitialContext` object. Spring's `jee` schema has a `<jndi-lookup>` element that provides an abstraction around retrieving a JNDI-bound data source in the application context.

Spring comes with multiple XML schemas that provide tags that can help with configuring beans in the application context XML file. Let's look at how you can define a JNDI-bound data source and retrieve it in your application context XML using Spring's `jee` schema, which provides tags for looking up JNDI-bound objects and defining EJB references.

> **NOTE** The example Book Catalog portlet in this chapter uses a JNDI-bound data source instead of defining the data source directly in the application context XML file.

DEFINING A JNDI-BOUND DATA SOURCE AND RETRIEVING IT IN THE APPLICATION CONTEXT

In this section, we'll look at configuring a data source in JNDI for a Tomcat 6.x application server. The steps required for defining and binding a data source in JNDI vary from one application server to another, so if you aren't using the Liferay-Tomcat bundle, refer to your application server's documentation for details on how to create a JNDI-bound data source.

If you're using the Eclipse IDE to run your Tomcat server, ensure that the `<Resource>` and `<ResourceLink>` elements (defined later in this section) are added to the server.xml and context.xml files of the server configuration in Eclipse. You can find these files in the Servers Eclipse project that's created when you configure a new Tomcat server with the Eclipse IDE, as shown in figure 9.2.

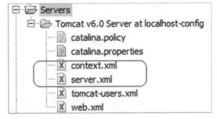

Figure 9.2   The context.xml and server.xml files in the Eclipse IDE's Server project

Once you have made changes to the context.xml and server.xml files, *publish* these changes using the Publish option to synchronize the changes with your Tomcat instance, as shown in figure 9.3.

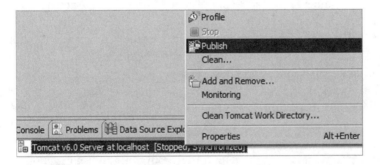

Figure 9.3   Right-clicking the server instance in the Servers view shows the Publish option.

To create a JNDI-bound data source in Tomcat 6.x, open the TOMCAT_HOME/conf/ server.xml file and define the data source as shown next.

Listing 9.3 The Tomcat server.xml file

```
<GlobalNamingResources>
   ...
  <Resource name="jdbc/myportalDB"                           ❶ JNDI name for
     auth="Container"                                             data source
     type="javax.sql.DataSource" username="root" password="root"
     driverClassName="com.mysql.jdbc.Driver"
     factory="org.apache.commons.dbcp.                       ❷ Data source
       ➥BasicDataSourceFactory"                                   factory used
                                                                   by Tomcat
     url="jdbc:mysql://localhost/myportaldb?useUnicode=true&amp;"
     maxActive="5"                                           ❸ Connection
     maxIdle="2"/>                                               settings
   ...
</GlobalNamingResources>
```

The <Resource> element ❶ defines the data source that you want to bind to JNDI. The name attribute specifies the name with which the data source is bound to JNDI.

The BasicDataSourceFactory ❷ represents the JNDI factory that creates Basic-DataSource. It implements the javax.naming.spi.ObjectFactory interface.

The maxActive attribute ❸ indicates the maximum number of connections that the connection pool can provide at any given time. The maxIdle attribute indicates the maximum number of connections that can remain idle in the pool.

NOTE The <Resource> element must be defined inside the <GlobalNaming-Resources> element in the server.xml file.

The <Resource> element in listing 9.3 binds a data source in the global JNDI context with the name jdbc/myportalDB.

WARNING This chapter uses Commons DBCP to configure a JNDI data source in Tomcat 6.x, so you must copy the commons-dbcp 1.3 (http://commons .apache.org/dbcp/) and commons-pool 1.5.5 (http://commons.apache.org/ pool/) JAR files to the TOMCAT_HOME/lib directory.

To make the JNDI-bound data source defined in listing 9.3 available to portlets, you need to configure a <ResourceLink> element in the TOMCAT_HOME/conf/context. xml file, as shown here:

```
<Context>
    ...
   <ResourceLink name="jdbc/myportalDB"
           global="jdbc/myportalDB"
           type="javax.sql.DataSource"/>
   ...
</Context>
```

In this element, the name attribute of `<ResourceLink>` is the JNDI name with which the `jdbc/myportalDB` data source in the global JNDI context is available to the portlet applications. The `global` attribute identifies the global JNDI-bound data source, defined in the server.xml file.

> **WARNING** To create an appropriate link to a global JNDI-bound data source, the value of the `global` attribute in `<ResourceLink>` must be same as the value of the `<Resource>` element's name attribute, defined in the server.xml file.

Now, that you've defined a data source in JNDI, let's look at how you can retrieve it in Spring's application context using the `jee` schema.

> **CODE REFERENCE** At this point, you should import the ch9_BookCatalog-SpringJdbc Eclipse project that accompanies this book in order to follow along with the code references in the rest of this discussion of the Spring JDBC module. The project contains a README.TXT file in the root directory that defines the steps you need to follow to deploy the Book Catalog portlet contained in the project.

Spring provides the `jee` schema, which helps in retrieving resources from JNDI. Listing 9.4 shows how you can use Spring's `jee` schema to retrieve a resource bound in JNDI and make it available as a Spring bean in your application context. In this case, the resource being retrieved is the JNDI-bound data source with the name `jdbc/myportalDB`.

Listing 9.4 The `jee` schema's `<jndi-lookup>` element

```
<beans ...                                                        ❶  Spring's jee
    xmlns:jee=http://www.springframework.org/schema/jee   ◁┘        schema
    xsi:schemaLocation="
    ...
    http://www.springframework.org/schema/jee
    http://www.springframework.org/schema/jee/spring-jee-3.0.xsd
    ">
    ...
    <jee:jndi-lookup                                              ❷  <jndi-lookup>
        jndi-name="java:comp/env/jdbc/myportalDB"                    element
        id="dataSource"/>
    ...
</beans>
```

Spring's `jee` schema is referenced ❶ by the application context XML file.

The `<jndi-lookup>` element is used ❷ to look up a JNDI resource (a JDBC resource in this case). The `jndi-name` attribute specifies the JNDI name of the resource to be retrieved. You can either specify jdbc/myportalDB or java:com/env/jdbc/myportalDB to retrieve the data source from JNDI. The java:com/env is prepended if you don't specify it as part of the `jndi-name` attribute value. The `id` attribute assigns a unique name to the data source retrieved from JNDI.

Listing 9.4 shows that the data source retrieved from JNDI is assigned a unique name, which can be used like any other bean's `id` in the application context. This means that if you want to inject a data source as a dependency in an object, you can use the standard Spring dependency injection techniques.

You now know how to define a data source in Spring's application context by either defining it explicitly or retrieving it from the JNDI. The next step is to create connections to the data source.

9.3.2 Creating database connections

As mentioned earlier, if you're using Spring's JDBC module, you don't need to worry about managing database connections. Spring's JDBC module provides many built-in classes that accept objects of type `javax.sql.DataSource` and relieve you of the responsibility of managing `Connection`, `Statement`, and `ResultSet` objects. Let's look at the most popularly used class of the Spring JDBC module: `JdbcTemplate`.

`JdbcTemplate` is one of the core classes in the Spring JDBC module; it provides the basic functionality of executing SQL queries, performing updates and inserts, catching exceptions, and so on. The `JdbcTemplate` obtains connections from the data source that's passed to its constructor or set using its `setDataSource` method. Additionally, `JdbcTemplate` provides callback interfaces, which help with creating `Prepared-Statement` objects and extracting results from `ResultSets`.

The following listing shows how you can create `JdbcTemplate` in the application context and set the `DataSource` it needs to use to obtain database connections and execute SQL statements.

Listing 9.5 A `JdbcTemplate` bean

```
<beans ...>
  ...
  <jee:jndi-lookup
    jndi-name="java:comp/env/jdbc/myportalDB"          ❶ Obtain data
    id="dataSource"/>                                      source from JNDI

  <bean id="jdbcTemplate"
      class="org.springframework.jdbc.core.JdbcTemplate">
    <property name="dataSource">                         ❷ Define JdbcTemplate
      <ref bean="dataSource" />                              object
    </property>
  </bean>
  ...
</beans>
```

Listing 9.5 shows the initial setup required to set up a `JdbcTemplate` to use a data source to create connections and execute SQL statements. The `<jndi-lookup>` element of Spring's `jee` schema ❶ retrieves the data source from JNDI and assigns dataSource as its name. The dataSource bean ❷ is set as the `JdbcTemplate`'s data-Source property.

In addition to the `JdbcTemplate` class, Spring defines a couple more template classes that you can use, depending upon the level of abstraction you want in your SQL code. Let's look at an example that uses the Spring JDBC module's `NamedParameter-JdbcTemplate` class.

If you're using `JdbcTemplate`, you need to specify placeholders in SQL statements using a question mark (?), as shown here:

```
jdbcTemplate.update("insert into book_tbl (title, isbn_number, authors, "
    + "created_date, created_by) values(?, ?, ?, ?, ?)", ...);
```

If you're using the `NamedParameterJdbcTemplate` class, you can replace the ? placeholders with named parameters, as shown here:

```
namedParameterJdbcTemplate.update("insert into book_tbl "
    + "(title, isbn_number, authors, "
    + "created_date, created_by) values(:title, :isbnNum, :authors, "
    + ":createdDate, :createdBy)", ...);
```

In the preceding SQL statement, the ? placeholders were replaced by named parameters, like `:title`, `:isbnNum`, and so on.

An application that interacts with a database usually has a separate data access layer that consists of data access objects (DAOs). A DAO contains methods that use SQL statements to retrieve information from and store it to a database. We'll now look at how you can create DAOs that use Spring's `JdbcTemplate` to interact with the database.

9.3.3 *Creating DAOs*

You can create DAOs in your application by using a factory for DAOs, or you can use Spring's classpath scanning along with annotation support to automatically create and register DAOs. As you saw in chapter 8, the classpath-scanning feature saves a lot of configuration overhead, so we'll use classpath scanning here to create and register services and DAOs in the Book Catalog portlet.

Because the services will depend upon an interface and not on the actual DAO implementation class, we'll create a DAO interface and its implementation class. The next listing shows the `BookDao` interface, which defines methods that are used by the Book Catalog portlet to read information from the BOOK_TBL table, update it, and remove it.

Listing 9.6 The `BookDao` interface

```
public interface BookDao {
    List<Book> getBooks();
    List<Book> searchBooks(String bookName,
        String authorName);
    void addBook(Book book);
    void removeBook(Long id);
    boolean isUniqueISBN(Long isbnNumber);
    Book getBook(Long id);
}
```

Listing 9.6 highlights the `getBooks`, `addBook`, and `removeBook` methods of the Book-Dao interface, which you'll see often in the rest of this chapter. The `getBooks` method returns currently *active* books from the BOOK_TBL table; those are books where the value of the ACTIVE column is 1. The `addBook` method is responsible for saving the book information in the BOOK_TBL table. The `removeBook` method deactivates a book and its associated TOC record by setting the ACTIVE column of the book record to 0 in BOOK_TBL. If there's an associated TOC, the ACTIVE column of the TOC record is also set to 0.

The `BookDao` interface is implemented by `JdbcBookDao`, which provides the necessary data access logic, as shown next.

Listing 9.7 The `JdbcBookDao` class

```
import org.springframework.jdbc.core.JdbcTemplate;
import org.springframework.jdbc.core.RowMapper;
import org.springframework.stereotype.Repository;

@Repository("bookDao")
public class JdbcBookDao implements BookDao {

 @Autowired
 @Qualifier("jdbcTemplate")
 private JdbcTemplate jdbcTemplate;

 public List<Book> getBooks() {
  List<Book> books = this.jdbcTemplate.
   query("select * from book_tbl where active = 1",
     new BookMapper());
  return books;
 }
 ...
 private static final class BookMapper implements RowMapper<Book> {
   public Book mapRow(ResultSet rs, int rowNumber)
       throws SQLException {
    Book book = new Book();
    book.setName(rs.getString("title"));
    book.setId(rs.getInt("book_id"));
    book.setIsbnNumber(rs.getLong("isbn_number"));
    ...
    return book;
   }
 }
}
```

❶ Specifies JdbcBookDao is a Spring component

❷ Autowires JdbcTemplate

❸ Executes SQL statement

The `@Repository("bookDao")` annotation ❶ specifies that the `JdbcBookDao` class is a Spring repository (or DAO) component (a specialized form of Spring component), and if the classpath-scanning feature is configured in the application context XML file, this class will be registered with the `bookDao` bean `id` in Spring's application context.

`JdbcTemplate` ❷ is autowired by name into the `JdbcBookDao` class. The `Jdbc-Template` class was defined in the application context XML file in listing 9.5. This shows that an object registered in the application context by the classpath-scanning feature can autowire a dependency that's defined in the application context XML. Similarly, an object defined in the application context XML can have a dependency on an object that was registered in the application context by the classpath-scanning feature.

The JdbcTemplate's query method ❸ is used to execute a SQL query. The query method accepts two arguments: a SQL query to execute, and a RowMapper callback implementation. RowMapper is a callback interface in the Spring JDBC module, and it maps each row in the returned ResultSet to a result object. The BookMapper is an implementation of the RowMapper interface, and in the mapRow method it maps each row in the returned ResultSet to a Book object.

Listing 9.7 shows that the RowMapper callback interface makes it easy to write a DAO method that retrieves data from the database. Similarly, you can use the Prepared-StatementSetter callback interface to set values on a PreparedStatement. Listing 9.8 shows how JdbcBookDao's addBook method makes use of the PreparedStatement-Setter callback interface.

Listing 9.8 Using the `PreparedStatementSetter` callback interface

```
import org.springframework.jdbc.core.PreparedStatementSetter;

@Repository("bookDao")
public class JdbcBookDao implements BookDao {
...
  public void addBook(final Book book) {
this.jdbcTemplate
  .update(                                                    ❶ JdbcTemplate's
    "insert into book_tbl (title, isbn_number,                  update method
    ➥authors, created_date, created_by)
    ➥values(?, ?, ?, ?, ?)",

    new PreparedStatementSetter() {                           ❷ PreparedStatementSetter
                                                                callback
      public void setValues(PreparedStatement ps)
        throws SQLException {
      ps.setString(1, book.getName());
      ps.setLong(2, book.getIsbnNumber());
      ps.setString(3, book.getAuthor());                      ❸ Placeholder
      ps.setDate(4, new                                         values
        java.sql.Date(book.getCreatedDate()
          ➥.getTime()));
      ps.setString(5, book.getCreatedBy());
      }
    }
  );
  }
}
```

The JdbcTemplate's update method ❶ is used by the addBook method to insert new book information into the BOOK_TBL table. The update method accepts the SQL statement and an instance of PreparedStatementSetter.

The `PreparedStatementSetter` callback ❷ is implemented to set values for the placeholders in the `PreparedStatement` corresponding to the specified SQL statement.

The `PreparedStatementSetter` defines a single method, `setValues`, that's used to set values for the placeholders in the `PreparedStatement`. The values for all the placeholders in the SQL statement ❸ are set using the relevant methods of `PreparedStatement`.

Listings 9.7 and 9.8 show that you no longer need to use `try-catch` blocks to catch `java.sql.SQLException`, as you had to do when you directly used the `java.sql` `.Statement` object to execute SQL statements. That's because Spring converts generic *checked* exceptions, like `SQLException`, into more specific runtime exceptions. For instance, `CannotGetJdbcConnectionException` is thrown when your DAO is unable to connect to the database. The other important thing to notice is the absence of code that closes the `Connection`, `Statement`, and `ResultSet` objects. `JdbcTemplate` handles this behind the scenes so that you don't need to explicitly do it in your code.

As mentioned in chapter 3, the Book Catalog portlet in this chapter makes use of user attributes (explained in chapter 3) to associate a book with the user responsible for adding it. If you refer to portlet.xml file of the Book Catalog portlet, you'll find that a `user.login.id` user attribute is defined, as shown here:

```
<user-attribute>
        <description>user id</description>
        <name>user.login.id</name>
</user-attribute>
```

The `user.login.id` user attribute provides the login ID of the logged-in user to the portlet. The `BookCatalogPortlet`'s `addBook` method retrieves `user.login.id` attribute from the portlet request and passes it to the DAO class, so that its value can be assigned to the `createdBy` attribute of the `Book` object.

Now that you know how to create DAOs, it's time to create the services used by the Book Catalog portlet—services that will use `JdbcBookDao` to store data in and retrieve it from the database.

9.3.4 *Creating service interface and implementation classes*

In a layered architecture, DAOs are accessed via business services, so the next step is to create a service layer in the Book Catalog portlet that uses `JdbcBookDao` and `JdbcTocDao` to interact with the database. You saw earlier that `JdbcBookDao` contains the data access logic for storing book data in and retrieving it from the BOOK_TBL table. `JdbcTocDao` is a DAO that contains data access logic corresponding to the TOC_TBL table.

The Book Catalog portlet should depend on the service interface and not on the actual service implementation class, so we'll create a service interface, `BookService`, and its implementation class, `BookServiceImpl`. The `BookService` interface defines service methods like `getBooks`, `addBook`, `removeBook`, `isUniqueISBN`, and so on, all of which are implemented by the `BookServiceImpl` class.

The next listing shows the `BookServiceImpl` implementation class that implements the `BookService` interface.

```
import org.springframework.stereotype.Service;

@Service("bookService")
public class BookServiceImpl implements BookService {          ❶ Specifies class is a
 @Autowired                                                        Spring component
 @Qualifier("bookDao")
 private BookDao bookDao;
                                                               ❷ Autowires
 @Autowired                                                       JdbcBookDao
 @Qualifier("tocDao")
 private ToCDao tocDao;
                                                               ❸ Autowires
 public List<Book> getBooks() {                                   JdbcTocDao
  return bookDao.getBooks();
 }

 public void addBook(Book book, String user)...{
  ...
  if(bookDao.isUniqueISBN(book.getIsbnNumber())) {
   book.setCreatedBy(user);
   bookDao.addBook(book);
  } else {
   ...
  }
 }

 public void removeBook(Long book_id) {
  bookDao.removeBook(book_id);
  tocDao.removeToc(book_id);
 }
 ...
}
```

The `@Service("bookService")` annotation ❶ specifies that the `BookServiceImpl` class is a Spring service component; if the classpath-scanning feature is configured in the application context XML file, this class will be registered with a bean id of `book-Service` in Spring's application context.

`JdbcBookDao` ❷ is autowired by name (refer to the `@Repository` annotation usage by the `JdbcBookDao` class in listing 9.7) into the `BookServiceImpl` class. `Jdbc-TocDao` ❸ is also autowired by name into `BookServiceImpl`.

Listing 9.9 shows that the `BookServiceImpl` class makes use of `JdbcBookDao` and `JdbcTocDao` to perform data access operations. In some methods, like `removeBook`, the service interacts with both `JdbcBookDao` and `JdbcTocDao`.

So far, you've seen how to retrieve a data source from JNDI using Spring's `jee` schema and how to register DAOs and services in Spring's application context using the classpath-scanning feature. The Book Catalog portlet's `BookCatalogPortlet` class provides the portlet's action and render methods. It's independent of the Spring Framework because we aren't using Spring Portlet MVC in the examples in this chapter, but it still must be able to interact with the `BookServiceImpl` class to retrieve data from or store it in the database. Let's look at how the `BookCatalog-Portlet` class (a non-Spring object) can access the `BookServiceImpl` class (a Spring bean) in Spring's application context.

9.4   *Accessing Spring beans from non-Spring objects*

Let's take a step back, look at the components that form the Book Catalog portlet, and see how they interact with each other. Figure 9.4 shows the various components and a typical request flow in the Book Catalog portlet.

In figure 9.4, a request is sent to the `BookCatalogPortlet` class ❶ which results in the invocation of a render, action, or resource method. The `BookCatalogPortlet` calls `BookService` ❷ to perform the requested operation, such as removing a book, adding a book, and so on. `BookService` makes use of `BookDao` and `TocDao` ❸ to access the BOOK_TBL and TOC_TBL tables, respectively.

Figure 9.4 shows that the non-Spring `BookCatalogPortlet` class must be able to access the `BookService` bean configured in Spring to perform its function. In chapter 7 you saw that Spring's root web application context is represented by the `Web-ApplicationContext` object, which is stored in the `ServletContext`. If you can access the `WebApplicationContext` object, you can access the beans that are registered with it. So the question is, how do you retrieve the root `WebApplicationContext` object from `ServletContext`, which was loaded by `ContextLoaderListener`? Spring provides the `PortletApplicationContextUtils` class, which does exactly what you need: it retrieves the root `WebApplicationContext` object.

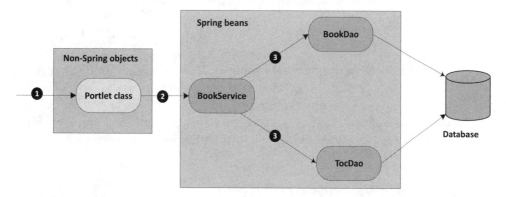

Figure 9.4   The Spring and non-Spring components that form the Book Catalog portlet. The `BookCatalogPortlet` class is a non-Spring object because it's not registered with Spring's web application context.

The next listing shows how the `BookCatalogPortlet` class makes use of `Portlet-ApplicationContextUtils`.

Listing 9.10 Retrieving beans from root `WebApplicationContext` object

```
import org.springframework.web.portlet.context.
➥PortletApplicationContextUtils;

public class BookCatalogPortlet extends GenericPortlet {
  private BookService bookService;

  public void init() {                                    ❶ Initializes portlet
   bookService = getBookService();                            instance
  }

  public BookService getBookService() {
    ApplicationContext springCtx =                        ❷ Obtains root
      PortletApplicationContextUtils.                        WebApplicationContext
        getWebApplicationContext(getPortletContext());
    return (BookService)springCtx.                        ❸ Retrieves
      getBean("bookService");                                BookService bean
  }
  ...
}
```

The `BookCatalogPortlet`'s init method overrides the `GenericPortlet` class's init method ❶ to obtain a reference to the `BookService` bean configured in Spring. The `PortletApplicationContextUtils` class is used ❷ to obtain the root `WebApplication-Context` object. The `getWebApplicationContext` method accepts a `PortletContext` object and returns a reference to the root `WebApplicationContext` object. The `Web-ApplicationContext`'s getBean method is used ❸ to retrieve the bean named book-Service. Because `BookServiceImpl` is registered in the root `WebApplicationContext` with the name bookService (refer to the `@Service` annotation in listing 9.9), a call to the getBean method will return a reference to the `BookService` bean.

Now that you have a reference to the `BookService` object, the `BookCatalog-Portlet` can invoke `BookService` methods to update, remove, and add book information in the database.

So far you've seen how to use some of the basic Spring JDBC features to create a Book Catalog portlet. But in real-world portlets you'll usually come across situations where using aspect-oriented programming (AOP) will make your code cleaner and more maintainable. Let's look at a scenario where you could consider using AOP in the Book Catalog portlet, and you'll see how Spring Framework's AOP support can be incorporated into the portlet.

9.5 *AOP support in Spring Framework*

Aspect-oriented programming (AOP) is a programming model in which the cross-cutting concerns are cut off from the core business logic and moved to a different class, called an *aspect*. The cross-cutting concerns that an aspect defines are referred to as *advices.* You can think of an advice as a method that provides an implementation for a cross-cutting concern. Because advice needs to be applied to a business method, a *pointcut expression* is used to identify the business methods to which a particular advice should be applied.

To put it into object-oriented terms, in AOP you create a class called an aspect, and inside it you define methods, called advices, that address cross-cutting concerns. These methods are associated with an expression, called a pointcut expression, that identifies business methods in the application to which the advice should be applied. At runtime, business methods that match the pointcut expression of an advice are intercepted, and the advice is executed.

In applications, cross-cutting concerns include transaction management, logging, security, and so on. For instance, if you're using programmatic transaction management in your application, you'll start the transaction at the beginning of the service method and commit it at the end of the service method. Transaction management isn't part of the main business logic of the application, so it's a candidate for AOP. In the Book Catalog portlet, transaction management is handled using Spring's transaction support, which internally makes use of AOP.

The Book Catalog portlet offers a few other scenarios where you can use AOP. For instance, you can use AOP to log messages at the entry and exit of every service method defined in `BookService`, or you can set audit fields in the `Book` domain object before a book record is inserted into the BOOK_TBL table using the `BookService`'s `addBook` method. Later in this section, we'll look at how to create a logging advice and an audit field advice for the Book Catalog portlet.

Figure 9.5 shows a simplified view of how the three different kinds of objects involved in AOP work. The target object represents an object to which you want to apply an advice. In the case of the Book Catalog portlet, the `BookService` object is the target object because you want to apply your logging and audit advices on the methods of the `BookService` object. The calling object represents the client of the target

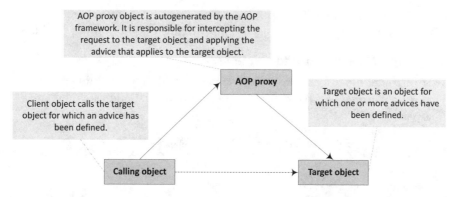

Figure 9.5   A high-level view of how AOP works. Calls to the target object are intercepted by an intermediate AOP proxy object, which is generated by the AOP framework.

object. In the Book Catalog portlet, the `BookCatalogPortlet` class is the calling object for the `BookService` target object.

If you're using AOP, instead of directly invoking the target object, the calling object invokes a proxy object (referred to as the AOP proxy) for the target object. The AOP proxy is responsible for applying the appropriate advice to the target object. In the case of the Book Catalog portlet, the AOP proxy is responsible for applying logging and audit field advices to the `BookService` object. The AOP proxy object is created by the AOP framework that you're using, so you aren't required to implement it in your application.

9.5.1 *Spring AOP and AspectJ annotations*

In Spring you can either use a *schema-based* or *AspectJ annotation* style to create aspects. In the schema-based approach, aspects, advices, and corresponding point-cuts are declared in the application context XML file. In the AspectJ annotation approach, an aspect is an annotated Java class that defines the advice and the associated pointcut.

> **NOTE**   AspectJ is a sophisticated AOP framework that provides a rich set of features for implementing AOP in your projects. To learn more about AspectJ, see the AspectJ home page (http://www.eclipse.org/aspectj/).

Spring has its own AOP framework that provides the most common AOP features you'll need in your projects. The Spring AOP framework allows you to use AspectJ annotation style to create aspects, but at runtime it's the Spring AOP framework that does the job of the AOP framework. You've already seen that objects in Spring are registered with application contexts; aspects are also registered with the application context. If you want to use the AspectJ AOP framework (instead of the Spring AOP framework) in your project, you would do well to refer to *AspectJ in Action, Second Edition*, by Ramnivas Laddad.

> **NOTE**   Like Spring JDBC, Spring AOP is a module of Spring Framework, which you can use in your project independently of other Spring modules.

9.5.2 *Using AspectJ annotations to create aspects*

In Spring AOP, aspects are simple Java classes. The following listing shows the `AuditAspect` class, which uses AspectJ's `@Aspect` annotation to indicate that `AuditAspect` is an aspect.

Listing 9.11   AspectJ annotations in the `AuditAspect` class

```
import org.aspectj.lang.annotation.*;
import chapter09.code.listing.domain.Book;

@Aspect
public class AuditAspect {
```

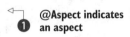 **1** **@Aspect indicates an aspect**

```
@Before
 ("execution(
  * chapter09.code.listing.service.
  ➥   BookService.addBook(..)) & args(book,..)")
public void before(Book book) {
 if(book.getCreatedDate() == null) {
  book.setCreatedDate(new Date());
 } else {
  book.setModifiedDate(new Date());
 }
 }
}
```

❷ **@Before indicates a Before advice**

❸ **Action to be taken on target object**

The @Aspect annotation ❶ indicates that AuditAspect is an aspect.

The @Before annotation ❷ specifies that the before method is an advice that must be executed *before* the invocation of the target object's method. The following expression represents the pointcut expression:

```
(execution(*chapter09.code.listing.service.
  ➥BookService.addBook(..)) && args(book,..))
```

The pointcut expression identifies the target object's methods to which the advice must be applied—this example identifies the BookService object's addBook method as the method to which the advice must be applied.

The before method ❸ defines the advice action, which is to set the created and modified date properties of the Book object.

In listing 9.11, the @Before annotation is used to instruct the Spring AOP framework to execute the advice before the target object's method is executed. An advice that's invoked *before* the execution of the target object's method is called a *before* advice. Similarly, you can use the following advice types in your application:

- *After returning*—An advice that's executed after the target object's method execution is complete, without exceptions. An after-returning advice is specified with the @AfterReturning annotation.
- *After throwing*—An advice that's executed when the target object's method throws an exception. An after-throwing advice is specified with the @After-Throwing annotation.
- *After*—An advice that's executed after the target object's method returns normally or it exits abruptly due to an exception. An after advice is specified using the @After annotation.
- *Around*—An advice that's executed before and after the target object's method is executed. An around advice is specified using the @Around annotation.

In listing 9.11, the @Before annotation is followed by the pointcut expression that identifies the methods of the target object to which the advice applies. The pointcut expression in listing 9.11 is a combination of two pointcut expressions combined using &&. The first pointcut expression,

```
*chapter09.code.listing.service.BookService. addBook(..)
```

specifies that the advice applies to the `addBook` method of `BookService`. The `add-Book(..)` part of the expression means that the advice will apply to *all* of the `addBook` methods of `BookService`, regardless of the arguments they accept.

The other pointcut expression,

```
args(book,..)
```

specifies that the target object's method must accept at least one parameter. You might be wondering how to specify the type of this parameter so that the pointcut expression identifies the `addBook` method of `BookService` that accepts a `Book` object as an argument. The `before` method in listing 9.11 shows that it accepts a single parameter named `book` which is of type `Book`. As the name of the parameter specified in the pointcut expression is same as the name of the argument passed to the advice method, it's implied that the type of the parameter is `Book`.

The use of the `args(book,..)` expression along with the `before` advice method that accepts a `book` argument of type `Book` has a dual advantage:

- It specifies that the target object's method must accept at least one parameter of type `Book`.
- The `Book` object that's available to the target object's method is now also available to the `before` advice method.

The next listing shows the `LoggingAspect` aspect, which makes use of the `@Around` advice to log messages at the entry and exit of methods defined in the `Book-Service` object.

Listing 9.12 The `LoggingAspect` aspect with an `@Around` advice

```
import org.apache.log4j.Logger;
import org.aspectj.lang.*;

@Aspect
public class LoggingAspect {

  @Around("execution(* chapter09.code.listing.          ❶ Specifies around advice
    ➥service.BookService.*(..))")                            using @Around
  public Object logMessage(ProceedingJoinPoint pjp)
    throws Throwable {
  Logger logger = Logger.getLogger
      (pjp.getTarget().getClass());
  logger.info("Entering " + pjp.getSignature());
                                                          ❷ Executes target
  Object returnValue = pjp.proceed();                         method

  logger.info("Exiting " + pjp.getSignature());
  return returnValue;
  }
}
```

The `@Around` advice annotation ❶ specifies that the `logMessage` method is executed before and after the execution of the target object's methods. The pointcut expression following the `@Around` advice annotation specifies that the advice applies to all the methods of the BookService object. The logMessage advice method accepts a ProceedingJoinPoint argument, which is mandatory for the @Around advice method. The ProceedingJoinPoint object lets the advice control the timing of the execution of the target object's method. The ProceedingJoinPoint object's getTarget method returns the target object on which the advice is currently being applied. The getClass method is used to get the class of the target object.

The ProceedingJoinPoint's proceed method ❷ is used to execute the target object's method. You may have noticed that before and after the proceed method is called, Logger is used to log the entry and exit from the target method. If you don't call the proceed method, the target object's method isn't executed at all.

The result value from the call to proceed is stored locally and is returned when the advice method completes. It's important to return the result value obtained from the proceed call so that the calling object can get the result value from the invocation of the target method.

Listing 9.12 shows that the @Around advice works in an interesting way. It controls when the target object's method is executed. An advice may not even invoke the target method. Because the advice can call the proceed method multiple times, the advice can actually invoke the target method multiple times. A more practical use of the @Around advice can be in programmatic transaction management, where a transaction is started before calling the proceed method, followed by a call to the proceed method, and finally the transaction is committed.

You have now created the aspects. It's time to register them in the root web application context and instruct Spring to create a proxy object for each of the aspects.

REGISTERING ASPECTS IN THE WEB APPLICATION CONTEXT

You can register an aspect in the web application context by defining it in the web application context XML file, as you do for other objects. This listing shows that aspects are defined like any other object in the application context XML file.

Listing 9.13 Defining aspects in the applicationContext.xml file

```
<beans ...
  xmlns:aop="http://www.springframework.org/schema/aop"      ◄┐  Includes reference to
  xsi:schemaLocation="                                         ❶  Spring's AOP schema
  http://www.springframework.org/schema/aop
  http://www.springframework.org/schema/aop/spring-aop-3.0.xsd
  ...">                                                              ❷  Enables
                                                                        AspectJ
  <context:component-scan base-package="chapter09.code.listing" />    annotation
  <aop:aspectj-autoproxy />      ◄┘                                    support
  ...
  <bean id="auditFieldAspect"                                    ❸  Defines
    class="chapter09.code.listing.base.AuditAspect" />               aspects
  <bean id="loggingAspect"
    class="chapter09.code.listing.base.LoggingAspect" />
</beans>
```

Spring's AOP schema is referenced ❶ by the application context XML file. The `<aspectj-autoproxy>` element instructs the Spring Framework ❷ to enable Spring AOP support for AspectJ annotation-based aspects and to autogenerate a proxy object for the target object (which is the `BookService` object in this example). The aspects that are used by the Book Catalog portlet are defined ❸ like any other object you define in the application context XML.

In listing 9.13, aspects are declared explicitly in the application context XML file because aspects can't be autodetected when using the classpath-scanning feature. Aspects aren't Spring components, so they aren't autodetected by Spring Framework.

> **INFORMATION** For more information on Spring AOP and AspectJ annotations, refer to the Spring reference documentation.

The use of aspects brings modularity to the application and removes cross-cutting concerns from the core business logic. This not only increases the maintainability of your code, but it also increases its testability. With the cross-cutting concerns moved to aspects, AOP results in a clear separation of concerns in an application.

Let's now look at how the Book Catalog portlet makes use of Spring's transaction support.

9.6   *Transaction management support in Spring Framework*

Spring provides both declarative and programmatic transaction management. In *declarative transaction management*, transactions are defined in external configuration files or are specified using Java annotations. The actual transaction management is taken care of by the Spring container. In *programmatic transaction management*, the developer is responsible for explicitly starting, ending, and committing the transactions. In this section, we'll focus on Spring's declarative transaction management facility, because it's the preferred way to handle transactions.

In the Book Catalog portlet, the `removeBook` and `uploadToc` service methods execute multiple update statements against the database. If you don't execute these statements within a transaction, it may leave the application's persistent state inconsistent. For instance, when you remove a book from the catalog, the book and TOC records in BOOK_TBL and TOC_TBL are made inactive by setting the value of the ACTIVE column to 0. If the portlet fails to update either the TOC_TBL or BOOK_TBL table for some reason, it leaves the catalog data inconsistent.

Let's look at how you can handle transactions using Spring's transaction support.

9.6.1   *Defining a transaction manager*

The first step towards using Spring's transaction management feature is to identify an appropriate Spring's transaction manager implementation for your application. The choice of transaction manager depends on whether your application uses single or multiple transactional resources:

- If transactions span multiple transaction-aware resources, you should use a Java Transaction API (JTA) transaction manager.
- If transactions are limited to a single transactional resource, the choice of transaction manager is driven by the data access technology used in the application, like JDBC, Hibernate, JPA, and so on. For instance, if you're using JDBC to access the data source, you should use `DataSourceTransactionManager`, and if you're interacting with a data source using the Hibernate ORM framework (discussed later in this chapter), you should use `HibernateTransactionManager`.

The Book Catalog portlet in this chapter uses JDBC to access the myportaldb database, so `DataSourceTransactionManager` should be used for managing transactions.

The following listing shows how `DataSourceTransactionManager` is configured in the root web application context XML file of the portlet application that contains the Book Catalog portlet.

Listing 9.14 Configuring `DataSourceTransactionManager` in applicationContext.xml

```
<beans xmlns="...">
  ...
  <jee:jndi-lookup
    jndi-name="java:comp/env/jdbc/myportalDB"     ❶ Obtains data
    id="dataSource" />                               source from JNDI
  ...
  <bean id="txManager"
    class="org.springframework.jdbc.datasource.      ❷ Defines transaction
    ➥DataSourceTransactionManager">                    manager
    <property name="dataSource" ref="dataSource" />
  </bean>
  ...
</beans>
```

The `DataSource` is obtained from JNDI ❶ using the `<jndi-lookup>` element of Spring's `jee` schema. The transaction manager that will be used to manage transactions is defined ❷. Because the Book Catalog portlet interacts with a single database, `DataSourceTransactionManager` is specified as the transaction manager. The `dataSource` property identifies the `DataSource` for which the transaction manager is used.

9.6.2 *Specifying transactional methods*

Listing 9.14 defined which transaction manager to use for managing transactions, but not which methods are transactional in nature. In Spring, you can define transactional methods using Spring's `@Transactional` annotation, as shown next.

Listing 9.15 Using the `@Transactional` annotation

```
import org.springframework.transaction.annotation.Transactional;

@Service("bookService")
public class BookServiceImpl implements BookService {
```

```
...
@Transactional
public void removeBook(Long book_id) {...}          ◁┐   @Transactional
                                                     │   annotation
@Transactional                                      ◁┘
public void uploadToc(ToC toc) {...}
}
```

In listing 9.15, the `removeBook` and `uploadToc` methods are annotated with the `@Transactional` annotation, which indicates that these methods are transactional.

9.6.3   *Configuring annotation-driven transaction management*

Registering a transaction manager with the application context and declaring `@Transactional` annotated methods isn't enough to use transaction management in Spring. You also need to activate transaction management with the `<annotation-driven>` element of Spring's transaction schema, as shown next.

> **Listing 9.16   Activating transaction management using `<annotation-driven>` element**

```
<beans ...
  xmlns:tx=http://www.springframework.org/schema/tx        ◁┐   Includes
  xsi:schemaLocation="...                                   │   reference to
  http://www.springframework.org/schema/tx                  │   Spring's
  http://www.springframework.org/schema/tx/spring-tx-3.0.xsd│   transaction
  ">                                                       ❶   schema
  ...
  <tx:annotation-driven transaction-manager="txManager"/>  ◁┐   Enables
                                                            │   annotation-driven
  <bean id="txManager"                                    ❷   transaction
    class="org.springframework.jdbc.datasource.
    ➥DataSourceTransactionManager">                  ❸   Defines
    <property name="dataSource" ref="dataSource" />        transaction
  </bean>                                                  manager
</beans>
```

Spring's transaction schema is referenced ❶ by the application context XML. The transaction schema's `<annotation-driven>` element instructs Spring Framework to apply transactions to the `@Transactional` annotated methods ❷. The `transaction-manager` attribute identifies the transaction manager to be used for managing transactions. The transaction manager used for managing transactions is defined ❸.

If you're using a single transactional resource, you can choose any one of the following built-in transaction managers in Spring: `DataSourceTransactionManager`, `JpaTransactionManager`, `HibernateTransactionManager`, and so on.

If you're using multiple transaction resources, you must use the JTA transaction manager provided by the Java EE server. Spring provides vendor-specific JTA transaction managers for a couple of application servers, along with a generic implementation of the JTA transaction manager. For example, `WebLogicJtaTransactionManager` and `WebSphereUowTransactionManager` are vendor-specific transaction managers in Spring that extend `JtaTransactionManager`—a generic JTA transaction manager.

> **NOTE** For more information about JTA transaction managers, refer to the Spring reference documentation.

You've seen how you can use Spring JDBC, Transaction, and AOP modules to create the Book Catalog portlet. Spring also provides an ORM module that helps in integrating with frameworks like Hibernate, JPA, JDO (Java Data Objects), and iBATIS SQL Maps.

> **CODE REFERENCE** At this point, you should try running the Book Catalog portlet in the ch9_BookCatalogSpringJdbc project. If you haven't yet created the two tables used by the portlet in this chapter, refer back to section 9.2 for information on creating them.

In this chapter, we'll limit our discussion to the Hibernate framework, which is the most widely used ORM framework. Let's look at what the Hibernate framework is and how Spring makes it easy to use Hibernate in the Book Catalog portlet.

9.7 Using Hibernate for database interaction

An application's persistent data is predominantly stored in a relational database, and we deal with the object representation of this data in our Java programs. For instance, a book is stored as a record in the BOOK_TBL table, but we deal with the `Book` object in our programs.

As we saw in the Book Catalog portlet example that uses Spring JDBC, SQL is used to bridge the representational gap between object and relational database tables. Methods in the `JdbcBookDao` class used SQL to access a book record in BOOK_TBL table and create a `Book` object from the returned `ResultSet`. Similarly, when storing the book information (retrieved from the `Book` object) into the database, SQL is used to insert the book information into the BOOK_TBL table. This representational gap between Java objects and relational database tables puts the responsibility on developers to write SQL (and supporting code) to convert an object into relational table rows and vice versa.

The Hibernate ORM framework defines a metadata-driven approach to mapping Java classes to relational database tables, and it provides a persistence API that manages persistence, relieving developers of the responsibility of writing SQL (and supporting code). The Hibernate framework is responsible for transparently converting Java objects to relational data and vice versa, using *user-defined* metadata as the reference for performing this conversion.

In the Hibernate world, you can think of a persistent Java class as a representation of a relational database table with attributes of the class representing the columns of the table, and each instance of the Java class representing a record in that

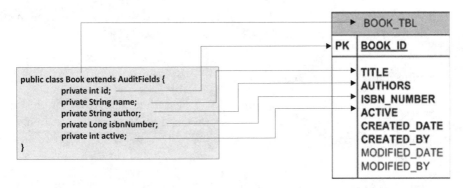

Figure 9.6 The Book class maps to the BOOK_TBL table in the database. Attributes of the Book class map to columns of the BOOK_TBL table.

table. Figure 9.6 shows how the Book persistent Java class maps to the BOOK_TBL in Hibernate terminology.

> **NOTE** Hibernate is a sophisticated framework that can handle all ORM scenarios that you'll come across in developing database-backed applications. For simplicity, we'll be discussing only a small subset of Hibernate's features. To learn more about Hibernate's capabilities and features, refer to the Hibernate reference documentation: http://www.hibernate.org/.

Figure 9.6 shows that the Book class and its attributes are mapped to BOOK_TBL and its columns, respectively. The Book class extends AuditFields, which adds to the complexity of mapping the Book class to the BOOK_TBL table. We'll see later in our discussion how Hibernate simplifies the mapping of persistent attributes defined in AuditFields to the BOOK_TBL table. For now, you can assume that Hibernate enables the mapping to work.

So how do you provide a mapping between the Book class and the BOOK_TBL table to the Hibernate framework? You can create an XML-based mapping file or you can use annotations.

Let's take a look at JPA (Java Persistence API) before going into the details of mapping persistent Java classes to database tables.

9.7.1 *Using the Java Persistence API (JPA)*

The Java Persistence API defines a standard ORM and persistence API for Java objects. It's inspired by ORM frameworks like Hibernate, TopLink, and JDO. If you have prior experience working with Hibernate, you'll find a lot of similarities between JPA and the Hibernate framework. There are multiple frameworks available on the market that implement JPA 2.0, such as Apache OpenJPA (http://openjpa.apache.org/) and EclipseLink (http://www.eclipse.org/eclipselink/).

Like the Hibernate framework, JPA doesn't require your Java objects to be running in a Java EE environment, so you can use JPA in the Java SE platform. Hibernate implements JPA, so you can use all of JPA's features when you're using the Hibernate framework, along with the additional features offered by Hibernate. Hibernate is a more mature framework and can be considered to be a superset of JPA.

> **NOTE**   Because the focus of this discussion is Hibernate, we'll limit the use of JPA in the Book Catalog portlet to mapping persistent Java classes to relational database tables. Hibernate's Persistence API will be used for retrieving or persisting the objects.

Let's now look at how you can map the persistent classes in the Book Catalog portlet to database tables.

9.7.2   *Mapping classes to relational database tables*

JPA defines a standard set of annotations that are used in mapping persistent Java classes to relational database tables. As Hibernate provides an implementation of JPA, it lets you use JPA annotations along with the annotations defined by Hibernate.

> **CODE REFERENCE**   You should now import the ch9_BookCatalogHibernate Eclipse project that accompanies this book in order to follow along with the code references in the rest of this Hibernate framework discussion. You'll find that the project shows a build error because it's not able to find the mysql.jar file. You need to edit this build entry to point to the {LIFERAY_HOME}\tomcat-6.0.26\lib\ext\mysql.jar file.

The following listing shows the persistent `Book` class that makes use of annotations to map itself to the BOOK_TBL table.

Listing 9.17   Annotation-driven object-relational mapping for the `Book` class

```
import javax.persistence.*;

@Entity(name="MyBook")                                    ❶ Persistent entity and
@Table(name="book_tbl")                                      corresponding table
public class Book extends AuditFields {
 @Id
 @Column(name="book_id")                                  ❷ Primary key
 @GeneratedValue(strategy=GenerationType.AUTO)
 private int id;

 @Column(name="isbn_number")
 private Long isbnNumber;
 ...
 private Book() {                                         ❸ Default
 }                                                           constructor
 ...
}
```

The @Entity annotation indicates that the Book class represents a persistent entity; the objects of the Book class are stored in a relational database ❶. The optional name element of the @Entity annotation assigns a unique name to the entity, which *must* be unique in the application. If the name element isn't specified, the name of the entity defaults to the *unqualified* name of the class. You'll see later in this chapter that the entity name is primarily used with Hibernate queries written in DAO.

The name element of the @Table annotation specifies the table into which the persistent attributes of the entity are stored.

The @Id annotation identifies the persistent attribute of the entity that acts as the primary key in the database table ❷. The @Column annotation specifies the BOOK_TBL column to which the id attribute of the Book entity maps. As the book_id column represents the primary key of the BOOK_TBL table, the id attribute is mapped to the book_id column. The @GeneratedValue annotation is used to define the strategy followed by the persistence provider, which is Hibernate in this case, to generate the value of the primary key. The strategy element identifies the strategy that the persistence provider must follow to generate the value of the primary key.

A default *private* constructor for the Book entity is defined ❸. The entity class must provide a default no-argument constructor, which can be private.

In listing 9.17, the @Entity annotation specifies the name of the Book entity as MyBook, which is the name it's registered with in the persistence provider. If you attempt to register more than one entity with the same name, you'll get an exception.

The @GeneratedValue annotation specifies the primary key generation strategy as GenerationType.AUTO, which means that the persistence provider is responsible for choosing an appropriate strategy to create the primary key values. If you want to use a database sequence or a table to generate unique primary keys, you can specify that instead.

NOTE   The Book entity class defines JavaBean-style attribute getter and setter methods, which isn't mandatory, but it's recommended.

The Book class extends the AuditFields class, which defines audit fields such as created-Date, modifiedDate, createdBy, and modifiedBy. In listing 9.17, the attributes of the Book entity are mapped to columns in the BOOK_TBL table, which brings us to the question of how attributes defined in AuditFields can be mapped to the same BOOK_TBL table. The following listing shows how that's done.

Listing 9.18 AuditFields superclass of Book entity

```
import javax.persistence.Column;
import javax.persistence.MappedSuperclass;

@MappedSuperclass                                        ◁⎯┐ Superclass of
public class AuditFields {                                   │ an entity
 @Column(name="created_date")
 private Date createdDate;
```

```
@Column(name="modified_date")
private Date modifiedDate;
...
}
```

As shown in listing 9.18, the `AuditFields` class isn't defined as an entity using the `@Entity` annotation, because it's not a persistent entity itself. Because the state defined by the attributes of `AuditFields` must be persisted in the BOOK_TBL table, the `AuditFields` class only provides the column mapping for each of the attributes using the `@Column` annotation. As you can see, the `AuditFields` class itself doesn't define the table to which its attributes are mapped. The table information associated with the `Book` entity, which inherits the `AuditFields` class, is applied to the attributes of the `AuditFields` subclass.

The `Book` entity is a simple entity; in real projects, entities are usually more complex than that. For instance, an entity may define attributes that are stored across multiple tables; the primary key value may be generated using a sequence; the entity may have relationships with other entities in the application, and so on. To address such requirements, JPA provides an extensive set of annotations, which you can read about in the JPA specification: http://jcp.org/en/jsr/detail?id=317.

Now that the persistent `Book` class is in place, with annotations that map the class and its attributes to the BOOK_TBL table, it's time to configure Hibernate to connect to the myportaldb database.

9.7.3 *Connecting to a database*

In Hibernate, you can configure database properties and entity classes using an XML file or properties file, or you can do it programmatically. We'll configure the Hibernate framework programmatically here so you can see some of the classes and methods that are used.

Listing 9.19 shows the `MyFirstHibernateExample` class, which demonstrates how you can configure Hibernate using the `AnnotationConfiguration` class.

CODE REFERENCE The ch9_BookCatalogHibernate Eclipse project contains MyFirstHibernateExample, which shows how to write a standalone Java application using Hibernate. Before running MyFirstHibernateExample, ensure that the Hibernate properties are set to values that apply in your environment.

Listing 9.19 Configuring Hibernate

```
import org.hibernate.*;
import org.hibernate.cfg.AnnotationConfiguration;
import chapter09.code.listing.domain.Book;

public class MyFirstHibernateExample {
  ...
  private static SessionFactory getSessionFactory(){
    SessionFactory sessionFactory =
```

```
    new AnnotationConfiguration()
    .addAnnotatedClass(Book.class)
    .setProperty("hibernate.connection.driver_class",
      "com.mysql.jdbc.Driver")
    .setProperty("hibernate.connection.url",
      "jdbc:mysql://localhost/myportaldb?
    useUnicode=true&")
    .setProperty("hibernate.connection.username",
      "root")
    .setProperty("hibernate.connection.password",
      "root"  )
    .buildSessionFactory();
  return sessionFactory;
  }
}
```

① Adds entity to configuration object

② Sets Hibernate properties

The `AnnotationConfiguration` class initializes Hibernate **①** using configuration information (such as the database to use, mapped entity classes, connection pool properties, and so on). The `AnnotationConfiguration` class extends Hibernate's `Configuration` class. If you define mappings between persistent classes and relational database tables in an XML format, Hibernate's `Configuration` class should be used for configuring Hibernate. The `addAnnotatedClass` method of `Annotation-Configuration` adds a persistent entity class that makes use of annotations to provide object-relational database mapping. `AnnotationConfiguration` reads object-relational database mapping information from the persistent entity class.

The properties required to configure Hibernate are set **②** using the `Annotation-Configuration`'s `setProperty` method. The `AnnotationConfiguration`'s `build-SessionFactory` method creates a `SessionFactory` object, which is used to create a Hibernate `Session`, which in turn provides applications with methods to save, update, and remove instances of persistent entities.

By using the `AnnotationConfiguration`'s `addAnnotatedClass` method, you inform Hibernate about the entities that are mapped to relational database tables. This information is necessary for Hibernate to figure out how to perform a delete, remove, or save operation on an instance of an entity. For example, if Hibernate doesn't know which table an instance of `Book` is saved to, and which columns the attributes of `Book` are saved in, it wouldn't be possible to transparently save an instance of the `Book` entity.

The next listing shows how `MyFirstHibernateExample`'s `main` method uses the `getSessionFactory` method shown in listing 9.19 to save an instance of the `Book` entity in the database.

> **Listing 9.20 Saving a Book entity instance**

```
import org.hibernate.*;
import org.hibernate.cfg.AnnotationConfiguration;

public class MyFirstHibernateExample {
    ...
```

```
public static void main(String args[]) {
  Session session = getSessionFactory().openSession();      ◁┐   Obtains session
  session.beginTransaction();                                   │   and begins
                                                              ❶   transaction
  Book book = new Book("Portlets in Action",
    "Ashish Sarin", 9781935182542L);          ┌─ ❷  Creates
  book.setCreatedBy("myuserid");              │      Book
  book.setCreatedDate(new java.util.Date());  │      instance

  session.save(book);                         ┌─ ❸  Saves Book and
  session.getTransaction().commit();          │      commits transaction
  session.close();                            │
}
  private static SessionFactory getSessionFactory(){...}
}
```

The `getSessionFactory` method that was defined in listing 9.19 is used to obtain the `SessionFactory` ❶. The `openSession` method returns the Hibernate `Session`, which provides methods to save, update, remove, and obtain database entities. The `beginTransaction` method demarcates the beginning of activities that need to be atomic in nature.

A `Book` entity instance is created ❷. The `Session`'s save method is used to save the newly created `Book` entity in database ❸. The transaction that was started at ❶ is committed, and the `Session` is closed, meaning that you're done with the task that you wanted to complete during the lifetime of the `Session`.

If you run the `MyFirstHibernateExample` Java program, you'll find that a new row is inserted in the BOOK_TBL table every time you run the program. All this happens without you having to write a single line of SQL. Hibernate made use of the mapping information that you provided in the `Book` entity class (and the `AuditFields` class) and it generated a SQL insert statement that saved the `Book` entity as a row in the BOOK_TBL table. You may also have noticed that you didn't tell Hibernate how a particular Java type like `String`, `Long`, `int`, and so on, mapped to the SQL type specific to the MySQL database. Hibernate took care of mapping Java types to appropriate SQL types for the database. This is one of the major strengths of Hibernate: you can write data access code without worrying about the target database, and Hibernate takes care of creating appropriate SQL.

So far we've looked at mapping persistent classes to database tables using annotations, and at saving entity instances using Hibernate. We'll now look at how you can use Hibernate instead of the Spring JDBC module at the DAO layer in the Book Catalog portlet.

9.7.4 *Using Spring with Hibernate*

If you look at listings 9.19 and 9.20, you'll find that there's still some boilerplate code, such as for configuring and building `SessionFactory` (see the `getSessionFactory` method in listing 9.19) and for starting and ending transactions (see listing 9.20). If you use Spring, you can configure a `SessionFactory` as a bean in Spring's application context and let Spring handle the transactions.

USING THE ANNOTATIONSESSIONFACTORYBEAN

Listing 9.20 suggests that you'll need access to `SessionFactory` to obtain a `Session` for performing database operations, so the DAO classes in the Book Catalog portlet must have access to `SessionFactory`. Spring provides an `AnnotationSession-FactoryBean` bean that you can use to create a `SessionFactory` and inject it into DAO classes using dependency injection. The DAO classes can then use the `Session-Factory` to obtain a `Session` and perform their database operations.

The next listing shows the application context XML file of the Book Catalog portlet, which defines the `AnnotationSessionFactoryBean` bean.

Listing 9.21   Defining the `AnnotationSessionFactoryBean` bean

```
<beans ...>
 ...
 <context:component-scan base-package="chapter09.code.listing" />
 <jee:jndi-lookup jndi-name="java:comp/env/jdbc/myportalDB"
     id="dataSource" />

 <bean id="sessionFactory"                                    ❶ Session factory
    class="org.springframework.orm.hibernate3.                   definition
    ➥annotation.AnnotationSessionFactoryBean">                ❷ DataSource
  <property name="dataSource" ref="dataSource"/>                  for factory
    <property name="annotatedClasses">                        ❸ Persistent
    <list>                                                       entities
      <value>chapter09.code.listing.domain.ToC</value>
      <value>chapter09.code.listing.domain.Book</value>
    </list>
  </property>
 </bean>
 ...
</beans>
```

The `AnnotationSessionFactoryBean` configuration ❶ is defined in the application context XML file, which is responsible for building the Hibernate `SessionFactory`. The data source information for `AnnotationSessionFactoryBean` ❷ is set using the `dataSource` property. In listing 9.19, the data source associated with the factory was specified using the `AnnotationConfiguration`'s `setProperty` methods. The `AnnotationSessionFactoryBean`'s `annotatedClasses` property ❸ specifies the persistent entities that are associated with the `SessionFactory`; in listing 9.19, persistent entities were specified using the `addAnnotatedClass` method of `Annotation-Configuration`.

If you compare listing 9.21 with listing 9.5, you'll find that the `jdbcTemplate` bean definition has been replaced with a `sessionFactory` bean definition in order to use Hibernate in the Book Catalog portlet. The following listing shows the `HibernateBookDao` class, which provides the data access logic using Hibernate's `SessionFactory`.

Listing 9.22   A DAO implementation using Hibernate's `SessionFactory`

```
import org.hibernate.SessionFactory;
import org.springframework.beans.factory.annotation.Autowired;
import org.springframework.stereotype.Repository;

@Repository("bookDao")
public class HibernateBookDao implements BookDao {        ❶ Specifies class is a
 @Autowired                                                  Spring component
 private SessionFactory sessionFactory;
                                                          ❷ Autowires Annotation-
 public List<Book> getBooks() {                             SessionFactoryBean
  return sessionFactory.getCurrentSession().
    createQuery("from MyBook as book where "              ❸ Executes SQL
    + " book.active=1").list();                             query using HQL
 }

 public void addBook(final Book book) {
  book.setActive(1);
  sessionFactory.getCurrentSession().save(book);          ❹ Saves Book
 }                                                           entity instance

 public Book getBook(Long book_id) {
  String hql = "from MyBook as book where "
   + "book.active=1 and book_id=" + book_id;
  return (Book) sessionFactory.getCurrentSession().       ❺ Gets unique
      createQuery(hql).uniqueResult();                       Book entity
 }
 ...
}
```

The `@Repository` annotation ❶ is used to specify that the `HibernateBookDao` class is a Spring component; it will be autoregistered in the web application context because you're using Spring's classpath-scanning feature (see listing 9.21).

The `AnnotationSessionFactoryBean` ❷ defined in the web application context (listing 9.21) is autowired into the `HibernateBookDao` object. Even though `Annotation-SessionFactoryBean` is a Spring class, it implements Hibernate's `SessionFactory` interface, which means it can be assigned to a variable of type `SessionFactory`.

The `Session`'s `createQuery` method ❸ is used to create a `Query` object using Hibernate Query Language (HQL). The `Query` object's `list` method executes the SQL corresponding to the specified HQL to return the list of books from the BOOK_TBL table. HQL is a Hibernate-specific query language suited for defining queries using persistent entities and their relationships. You can think of HQL has an object-oriented version of SQL. Hibernate converts queries specified in HQL into appropriate SQL.

The `Session`'s `save` method ❹ is used to save an instance of the `Book` entity. The `Book` entity instance corresponding to the passed `book_id` argument ❺ is retrieved from the database.

Listing 9.22 shows that in Hibernate you can create DAO objects that don't use SQL statements. These database queries are specified using HQL, and the save, update, and remove database operations are available as methods of the `Session` object.

> **NOTE**   Listing 9.22 shows that Spring integration with Hibernate is non-invasive; the Hibernate DAO isn't dependent on Spring-specific classes or interfaces. This is one of the key strengths of Spring Framework.

USING HIBERNATE QUERY LANGUAGE

HQL is a powerful but easy-to-understand query language because it's similar to SQL. In HQL you specify your query in an object-oriented style.

For instance, consider the following HQL query used by the `getBooks` methods from listing 9.22:

```
from MyBook as book where book.active=1
```

There are a couple of things to notice in the preceding HQL:

- `MyBook` is the name by which the `Book` persistent class is known to the `SessionFactory`. That's because in listing 9.17, you specified `@Entity(name="MyBook")`, which meant that the `Book` persistent class is available in the `SessionFactory` with the name `MyBook`. The HQL queries need to refer to a persistent entity by the name they used to register with the `SessionFactory`.
- To refer to an attribute of an entity, you can use the dot (`.`) Java bean style of property access.

> **NOTE** Hibernate also defines a Criteria API that provides a simplified API for retrieving objects without using HQL.

You may have noticed in listing 9.22 that instead of using the `SessionFactory`'s `openSession` method, we used `getCurrentSession`. Both methods return a `Session` object, so you might wonder what the difference between them is. The `openSession` method returns a *new* `Session`, whereas `getCurrentSession` returns the `Session` that's associated with the current *transaction* or *Java thread*. You saw in listing 9.20 that after a call to `openSession`, you had to explicitly begin a transaction; you're not required to do that in listing 9.22 because the transaction is managed by Spring.

The `getCurrentSession` method is useful if you want Spring to manage transactions, which is the case with the Book Catalog portlet. For example, the `removeBook` method of `BookService` (a Spring component) interacts with both `HibernateBookDao` and `HibernateTocDao`. To ensure that the remove book action is atomic in nature, the transaction must be managed by Spring Framework and not by the respective DAO classes.

The next listing shows the configuration for Spring-managed transactions in `applicationContext.xml` if you're using the Hibernate framework for data access.

Listing 9.23 Configuring Spring-managed transactions

```
<beans ...>
 <bean id="sessionFactory"                                    ❶ Defines session
  class="org.springframework.orm.hibernate3.                     factory bean
     ➥annotation.AnnotationSessionFactoryBean">              ❷ Enables
  ...                                                            annotation-
 </bean>                                                         driven
 <tx:annotation-driven transaction-manager="txManager" />  ◁──┘ transaction
 <bean id="txManager"
  class="org.springframework.orm.hibernate3.               ❸ Defines
     ➥HibernateTransactionManager">                            transaction
  <property name="sessionFactory" ref="sessionFactory" />      manager
 </bean>
 ...
</beans>
```

Spring's `AnnotationSessionFactoryBean` is defined ❶. The `<annotation-driven>` element of Spring's transaction schema specifies that the transaction is applied to methods that are annotated with the `@Transactional` annotation ❷. The `transaction-manager` attribute identifies the transaction manager to be used for managing transactions. The transaction manager used for managing transactions is defined ❸.

Listing 9.23 shows that Spring's `HibernateTransactionManager` is used to manage transactions because you're only dealing with a single transactional resource—the database. If you're using multiple transactional resources, you should use a JTA transaction manager.

This is how the transaction management works in the Book Catalog portlet:

1 When an `@Transactional` annotated `BookService` method is invoked, `HibernateTransactionManager` begins a new transaction.

2 `HibernateTransactionManager` uses Hibernate's `SessionFactory` (see listing 9.23) to create a new `Session` and bind it to the current Java thread.

3 When the `getCurrentSession` method is called in DAO objects, it returns the `Session` that `HibernateTransactionManager` had bound to the current Java thread.

4 When the `BookService` method completes, the transaction is committed and the `Session` object is removed from the Java thread.

This sequence of steps ensures that all of the DAO methods invoked during the execution of a transactional `BookService` method are in the same transaction.

9.8   Summary

In this chapter you saw some of the approaches you can follow to create portlets that interact with a database. We discussed how Spring JDBC and Hibernate can be used for data access when the portlet isn't based on Spring Portlet MVC.

If your portlet interacts with a transactional resource, you'll also need to decide how to handle transactions. We only covered examples using a single transactional resource, but in real-world projects you may need to handle transactions that span multiple transactional resources using JTA. Spring's JDBC, AOP, and Transaction modules are just some of the many modules offered by Spring, and you should refer to the Spring reference documentation for more information about these modules and others that we haven't covered in this book. We've only covered Spring's integration with Hibernate, but Spring can integrate with other data access frameworks like iBATIS SQL Maps, JDO, and so on.

In the next chapter, you'll see how you can personalize the content and behavior of a portlet using the Portlet API's personalization support.

Part 3

Advanced portlet development

Support for personalizing content and behavior and inter-portlet communication are key features of portlets. Also, it's important to be able to create highly responsive portlets in today's Web 2.0 world.

This part of the book begins by showing how Java portlet technology provides built-in support for personalization and inter-portlet communication. It then takes a deep dive into Ajax and shows how you can develop highly responsive portlets using jQuery, Dojo, and DWR. For those who want to use portlets to show real-time data, this part discusses Comet (or Reverse Ajax) support in DWR in the context of an example portlet.

The second half of this part shows how you can use portlet bridges to expose an existing web application as a portlet, and how to use Web Services for Remote Portlets (WSRP) to access remotely installed portlets. You'll also be introduced to portlet filters, which are similar to servlet filters.

Personalizing portlets

10

This chapter covers

- Personalizing portlet content and behavior
- Defining portlet preferences
- Validating portlet preferences
- Using the `portletPreferences` implicit variable

How many times have you Googled something, been directed to a website that you hope will provide the information you're looking for, and find a website that's so cluttered with information that it's useless and you close the browser out of frustration?

Often you'll find information on websites that isn't relevant or that doesn't pique your interest. For instance, if you're a Java developer interested only in Java books, you probably found yourself losing interest when the Book Portal in chapter 5 showed books from other categories, like .NET and software engineering. Or imagine looking at a website that provides stock quotes for *all* stocks, regardless of which stocks are in your portfolio. In this case, you're usually only interested in the prices or news related to your stocks.

The extraneous information on a portal or website not only has the potential to adversely affect the user experience, but it may also drive customers away to websites that provide personalized content.

It isn't necessary for a portlet to provide some level of personalization to its users. For instance, an announcement portlet in a B2E (business-to-employee) portal may not support any personalization options, because the business's announcements can't be personalized based on employee preference. Nevertheless, when you're determining the requirements for a portlet, it's important to focus on the personalization aspects, because incorporating them will have an impact on your portlet code. Implementing personalization features in web applications can be a huge pain. Fortunately, the inherent support for personalization in Java portlet technology makes it easier to develop portlets that enrich the user experience by providing relevant content and personalized behavior.

> **NOTE** Extra information is sometimes useful. Sometimes, when visiting a website, you'll stumble upon some useful information that you weren't looking for. The content of a website is generally designed around how best to serve its readers, based on usage patterns that have been observed over a period of time. For instance, when you look up a movie on IMDb (http://www.imdb.com/), it also displays recommended movies that you may be interested in.

In this chapter, we'll look at personalization support in Java's portlet technology and see how it can help you to quickly incorporate personalization features in your portlets. You'll see how the Book Catalog portlet can be personalized to show books belonging to a particular category, like Java or .NET, and to prominently display books preferred by the users of the portlet, and so on.

We'll begin this chapter with a quick introduction to personalization.

10.1 *Introducing portlet personalization*

Personalization of content plays an important role in enriching the user experience. It lets your application's users specify the content that they're interested in, and the application in turn honors each user's preferences. Application personalization isn't limited to personalizing content but can also apply to customizing the behavior of the application. For instance, the Gmail portlet in the iGoogle portal allows users to specify the number of emails they want to view in the portlet (personalization of content) and whether they want to open a selected email in the same or a new browser window (personalization of behavior), as shown in figure 10.1.

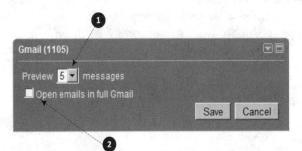

Figure 10.1 The Gmail portlet provides personalization options for portlet content and behavior.

The Gmail portlet ❶ allows the user to select the number of messages that should be displayed when the portlet is in a normal window state. The portlet ❷ lets the user specify whether it should open email in the original Gmail web application and not within the portlet window; the portlet has limited features compared to the full Gmail web application.

The Java servlet technology isn't designed to support the personalization of applications, so if a JSP- and servlet-based web application is required to support personalized content and behavior, it has to be taken care of in the design and implementation of the web application itself. For instance, a database designer will be responsible for creating a database structure for storing preferences; a developer will be responsible for writing code to save preferences in the database and read them again later.

If you're using Java portlet technology, the portal server database provides the necessary structure to store user preferences for each portlet in the web portal. The portal server shields you from the database details of saving and retrieving the user preferences. The portal server reads the user preferences of the logged-in user from the database and makes them available to your portlets in the portlet request. As a developer, you're only responsible for making use of the portlet API to retrieve user preferences and use them to personalize the content or behavior of the portlet.

> **CODE REFERENCE** The source code for the Book Catalog portlet discussed in this chapter is located in the ch10_BookCatalog folder. Before you build or deploy the portlet, make sure you change the value of the `uploadFolder` initialization parameter in the portlet deployment descriptor. Also set the `liferay.portal.home` property in the build.properties file to point to your Liferay Portal installation directory.

Now that you understand the basic concept of personalization, let's dive deeper. First, let's discuss the requirements of the Book Catalog portlet, which now include the personalization options. Once you understand the portlet's personalization options, we'll look at how they can be implemented in the portlet.

10.2 Personalization requirements for the Book Catalog portlet

The Book Catalog portlet's content and behavior is personalized according to the preferences set by the user. Figure 10.2 shows the preferences that users can set for this portlet.

The user can specify the category of books (like, Java and .NET) to view ❶ on the Book Catalog portlet's home page (see figure 10.3). The user can select multiple categories from the list; if no categories are selected, all are shown.

The user can specify whether the book search is case sensitive or case insensitive ❷. In previous chapters, the Book Catalog portlet searched books in a case-sensitive manner. If the user doesn't select the search type, it defaults to a case-sensitive search.

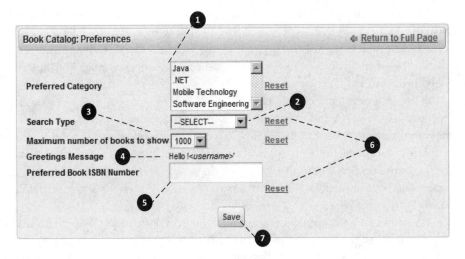

Figure 10.2   The Book Catalog portlet's Preferences page shows the options that can be personalized by users, including the preferred category, case-sensitive or case-insensitive search, preferred book, and so on.

The user can specify the maximum number of books that should be displayed ❸. The available options are 1000, 10, and 5. By default, a user will be shown all the books in the catalog.

The user can view a *read-only* option ❹ that says that the greeting message displayed on the home page of the Book Catalog has this format: "Hello! *<username>*", where *<username>* is the name of the logged in user.

The user can enter the ISBN ❺ of the book that should be highlighted in the catalog display (see figure 10.3). If there's no book in the catalog corresponding to the ISBN entered here, an appropriate error message is displayed.

Clicking one of the Reset links ❻ resets the corresponding option to its default value. The Greetings Message personalization option doesn't have a Reset link because it's a read-only option.

The user can click Save ❼ to save the selected preferences.

Figure 10.3 shows the home page of the Book Catalog portlet, which displays the books in the catalog.

The book category information is displayed ❶ for each book in the catalog. If a user has chosen to view books belonging to certain categories on the preferences page, only books in those categories will be shown to the user. Because every book must be associated with a category, the book category information must be entered when adding a book to the catalog.

The book search will be either case sensitive or case insensitive ❷ depending upon the preference chosen by the user.

If the user has specified certain books as preferred books, these books will be highlighted ❸ in yellow in the catalog.

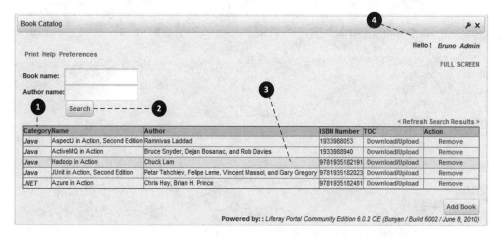

Figure 10.3   The Book Catalog portlet's home page shows personalized content to the user. Each book catalog entry shows the category to which the book belongs.

The greeting message format that was predefined for the Book Catalog portlet will be used ❹ to show the greeting message to the user.

CODE REFERENCE   The sample code for the Book Catalog portlet in this chapter is located in the ch10_BookCatalog folder of the book's source code.

If your portlet needs to support personalization, you'll typically follow these steps to implement personalization:

- Show personalization options in EDIT mode
- Save user preferences into a persistent store using the PortletPreferences object
- If required, validate preferences set by the user before persisting them
- Retrieve user preferences using the PortletPreferences object, and customize the content and behavior of the portlet based on the user preferences

In the following sections, we'll look at each of these steps in detail.

10.3   *Showing personalization options in EDIT mode*

To show the personalization options in EDIT mode, you need to do the following:

- Add support for EDIT portlet mode
- Write a render method for EDIT portlet mode

Let's look at how you can accomplish these tasks in the Book Catalog portlet.

10.3.1   *Adding support for EDIT portlet mode*

If you recall from chapter 2, the purpose of EDIT portlet mode is to show personalization options for the portlet. Figure 10.2 shows the personalization options applicable to the Book Catalog portlet; those options should be generated in EDIT portlet mode.

The first thing that you need to do is add support for EDIT portlet mode to the Book Catalog portlet. You can define support for EDIT mode in the portlet deployment descriptor:

```
<portlet>
  <portlet-name>bookCatalog</portlet-name>
   <portlet-class>
      chapter10.code.listing.base.BookCatalogPortlet
   </portlet-class>
   <supports>
     <mime-type>text/html</mime-type>
     <portlet-mode>view</portlet-mode>
     <portlet-mode>edit</portlet-mode>
   </supports>
</portlet>
```

The preceding portlet deployment descriptor defines support for EDIT portlet mode by using the <portlet-mode> subelement of the <supports> element. For more details on how to define support for portlet modes, refer to chapter 4.

> **CODE REFERENCE**   Refer to the portlet.xml file in the ch10_BookCatalog folder to see how the <portlet-mode> element is used to support EDIT portlet mode in the Book Catalog portlet.

Now that the portlet supports EDIT portlet mode, let's look at how you can show personalization options in EDIT mode.

10.3.2   *Writing a render method for EDIT portlet mode*

In chapter 2 (section 2.5.1), I mentioned that there's a render method for every portlet mode supported by a portlet. To display the personalization options, you need to write a render method in your portlet class corresponding to EDIT mode.

The following code snippet shows the render method for EDIT mode:

```
@RenderMode(name = "edit")
public void showPrefs(RenderRequest request, RenderResponse response)
   throws IOException, PortletException {
     PortletRequestDispatcher dispatcher =
       getPortletContext().getRequestDispatcher(
         response.encodeURL("/WEB-INF/jsp/preferences.jsp")
         );
   dispatcher.include(request, response);
}
```

The showPrefs method in the preceding snippet is a render method in EDIT mode (specified by the @RenderMode annotation) that makes use of PortletRequest-Dispatcher to dispatch portlet requests to the preferences.jsp page. The preferences.jsp page shows all the personalization options applicable for the Book Catalog portlet, as shown in figure 10.2. This means that generating content in EDIT (or HELP) portlet mode is no different than in VIEW mode; the purpose of the content varies but not *how* it's generated.

CODE REFERENCE Refer to the `BookCatalogPortlet` class's `showPrefs` method in the ch10_BookCatalog folder to see how the `@RenderMode` annotation is used to mark a method as a render method for `EDIT` portlet mode.

Listing 10.1 shows the portion of the preferences.jsp page that shows the Preferred Category and Search Type options to the user.

CODE REFERENCE Refer to the preferences.jsp page in the ch10_BookCatalog folder to see how other personalization options of the Book Catalog portlet are specified in the JSP page.

Listing 10.1 The preferences.jsp page

```
<tr>
    <td><b>Preferred Category</b></td>
 <td>
    <select name="<portlet:namespace/>prefCategory"
       multiple="multiple">
      <option value="java">Java</option>                    ❶ Preferred book
      <option value=".net">.NET</option>                       category list
      <option value="mobile">Mobile Technology</option>
      <option value="softwareEng">
             Software Engineering</option>
    </select>
  </td>
</tr>
<tr>
 <td><b>Search Type</b></td>
 <td>
    <select name="<portlet:namespace/>searchType">
      <option value="-1">--SELECT--</option>                 ❷ Book search
      <option value="sensitive">Case-Sensitive</option>         options
        <option value="insensitive">
             Case-Insensitive</option>
    </select>
  </td>
</tr>
```

The JSP page shows the preferred book category options (Java, .NET, Mobile Technology, and Software Engineering) in a multiselect list ❶. The book search options (case-sensitive or case-insensitive) are displayed in an HTML combo box ❷.

NOTE Some of the details have been removed from the preferences.jsp page in listing 10.1 in order to focus on how the preferences are displayed by a JSP page. Later in this chapter, you'll see a more refined preferences.jsp page that shows how preference values that have been set by a user are displayed by the page.

The next step is to capture the portlet preferences specified by the user and save them in a persistent store.

10.4   *Saving user preferences*

The process of saving portlet preferences selected by the user can be divided into two steps:

1   Retrieve portlet preferences selected by the user
2   Save preferences in the persistent store using the `PortletPreferences` object

Let's look at each of these steps in detail in the context of the Book Catalog portlet.

10.4.1   *Retrieving user preferences from the portlet request*

You can retrieve preferences selected by the user from the portlet request as request parameters. In the Book Catalog portlet, when the user clicks Save on the preferences page (see figure 10.2), an *action* request is dispatched to the portlet. The selected preference category and search type values are available to the portlet class like any other HTML form fields.

The next listing shows how the `BookCatalogPortlet` class's `savePreferences` action method retrieves the preferences selected by the user.

> **Listing 10.2   Retrieving user preferences from request in `savePreferences` method**

```
@ProcessAction(name="savePreferences")
public void savePreferences(...)
  throws PortletException, IOException {
String[] prefCategories =
  request.getParameterValues("prefCategory");
String searchTypePref =
  request.getParameterValue("searchType");
...
  }
```

❶ Retrieves selected book categories

❷ Retrieves selected search type

The `savePreferences` method retrieves the preferred categories chosen by the user ❶. The categories are represented as a multiselect list, so the `ActionRequest`'s `getParameterValues` method is used to retrieve all the selected categories. If you were to use the `getParameterValue` method instead of `getParameterValues`, it would return *only* the first value of the `prefCategory` request parameter.

> **NOTE**   If a request parameter in your portlet is expected to contain multiple values, you should use the `PortletRequest`'s `getParameterValues` method to retrieve it in the portlet class. You can use the `getParameterValue` method for single-valued request parameters.

The `savePreferences` method retrieves the search type (case-sensitive or case-insensitive) chosen by the user ❷. The search type is represented as an HTML combo box from which only one value can be selected, so the `ActionRequest`'s `getParameterValue` method is used to retrieve the selected search type.

CODE REFERENCE Refer to the `BookCatalogPortlet` class's `savePreferences` method in ch10_BookCatalog to see how other personalization options are retrieved from the request.

Now that you've retrieved the preferences selected by the user, it's time to save the preferences in a persistent store.

10.4.2 Saving portlet preferences to the persistent store

Preferences set for a portlet need to live longer than the user's session; they must be saved in a persistent store for future use. When the user comes back to your portal later, the portlets should show content based on the preferences that the user set earlier.

Does saving the preferences in a database or other persistent store mean that you have to create a database and table structure to store preferences? Does it mean that you have to write data access code to save and retrieve preferences from the database? If you're using Java portlet technology, you don't need to worry about databases, table structures, and data access layers. You only need to know the Portlet 2.0 API in order to save portlet preferences.

The following listing again shows the `savePreferences` action method of the Book Catalog portlet. It uses the Portlet 2.0 API to save preferences in a persistent store (such as a database, flat file, and so on).

Listing 10.3 Saving the user's preferences in the `savePreferences` method

```
@ProcessAction(name="savePreferences")
public void savePreferences(...)
    throws PortletException, IOException {                    ❶ Obtains
  String[] prefCategories = ...                                  PortletPreferences
  String searchTypePref = ...                                    object from
  PortletPreferences prefs = request.getPreferences();    ◁──┘   request
  if(prefCategories != null) {                            ❷ Sets preferred categories
    prefs.setValues("category", prefCategories);      ◁──    preference values
  }
  if(searchTypePref != null && !searchTypePref.equals("-1")) {
    prefs.setValue("searchType", searchTypePref);            ◁──┐  Sets search type
  }                                                          ❸    preference value
  ...
  prefs.store();              ◁──┐  Saves preferences in
}                             ❹     persistent store
```

The `savePreferences` method uses the `ActionRequest`'s `getPreferences` method ❶ to obtain the `PortletPreferences` object. We'll discuss this object later in the chapter, but for now you just need to know that it's the object provided by the portlet container to help portlets write and read preferences to and from a persistent store.

The `PortletPreferences` object's `setValues` method ❷ is used to set the values for the preferred book categories selected by the user.

You set the user's search type preference in the `PortletPreferences` object **3** using the `setValue` method. Note the use of the `setValue` method instead of `setValues`.

You call the `PortletPreferences` object's `store` method **4** to save the preferences that have been set so far into a persistent store.

> **CODE REFERENCE**   Refer to the `BookCatalogPortlet`'s `savePreferences` method in the ch10_BookCatalog folder to see how all the preferences are set in the `PortletPreferences` object, and how they're saved in the end.

Listing 10.3 shows how you'll usually save preferences in the persistent store. There's no need to write any data access code or create any table structures to persist user preferences. So where is the preference information getting saved? You saw in chapter 9 that portal servers are backed by a database (referred to as the *portal database*) that contains, among other things, information about the users of the portal server and the portlets deployed on the portal server. This database also contains table structures to store portlet preferences set by users. The `PortletPreferences` object, which is provided by the portal server to your portlets, knows how to save portlet preferences into the portal database or any other persistent store; it's responsible for calling appropriate data access objects on the portal server to save the preferences.

Let's look at the `PortletPreferences` object in detail to understand its purpose and methods.

10.5   *Saving preferences with PortletPreferences*

You saw in the previous section that the `PortletPreferences` object is used to save user preferences into a persistent store. The `PortletPreferences` object is obtained by the portlet request's `getPortletPreferences` method, and it defines methods to retrieve, set, and store preferences.

In most situations, portlet developers treat the portal database as a black box, not worrying about how preferences are stored to or retrieved from it. The Portlet API shields portlet developers from details of the portal database by providing the `Portlet-Preferences` object, which is implemented by portal server vendors and encapsulates the logic for retrieving and storing preferences from and to the portal database.

In this section, we'll focus on saving preferences to a persistent store using the `PortletPreferences` object. In section 10.7, we'll discuss how you can obtain saved preferences from the `PortletPreferences` object.

Table 10.1 shows some of the important methods in the `PortletPreferences` interface and describes them briefly.

You saw in the previous section how you can use the `setValue`, `setValues`, and `store` methods of the `PortletPreferences` object. Later in this chapter, we'll discuss the use of the `getValue` and `getValues` methods to retrieve preferences to either personalize portlet content (and behavior) or to display the preferences already set by

Table 10.1   `PortletPreferences` methods

Method	Description
`String getValue(String key, String default)`	Returns the first `String` value associated with the preference identified by `key`. If the preference isn't found, it returns `default` as the value of the preference.
`String[] getValues(String key, String[] defaults)`	Returns the `String` values (as an array) associated with the preference identified by `key`. If the preference isn't found, it returns `defaults` as the value of the preference.
`void setValue(String key, String value)`	Sets the preference identified by `key` with a value identified by the `value` argument in the `PortletPreferences` object.
`void setValues(String key, String[] values)`	Sets the preference identified by `key` with an array of values identified by the `value` argument in the `PortletPreferences` object.
`void store()`	Saves preferences set in the `PortletPreferences` object to a persistent store.
`void reset(String key)`	Resets the value of the preference identified by `key` to its default value.
`boolean isReadOnly(String key)`	Checks whether the preference identified by `key` is read-only or modifiable.

the user on a JSP page. For now, we'll discuss the two most interesting methods of `PortletPreferences`: the `store` and `reset` methods.

The `PortletPreferences` object's `store` method persists the preferences that you had *previously* set using the `setValue` and `setValues` methods. If you set preferences on the `PortletPreferences` object after calling the `store` method, those preferences won't be persisted. To make this point clear, the next listing shows an example in which preferences are set after calling the `store` method.

Listing 10.4   Setting preferences after invoking the `store` method

```
@ProcessAction(name="saveMyPreferences")
    public void setMyPreferences(...)
      throws PortletException, IOException {                    Obtains
    ...                                                         PortletPreferences
    PortletPreferences prefs = request.getPreferences();  ◁──┘ from request
    prefs.setValue("pref1", pref1);                       ┐ Sets pref1,
    prefs.setValue("pref2", pref2);                       ┘ pref2
    prefs.store();                                              ◁── Saves portlet
    prefs.setValue("pref3", pref3);   ┐ Sets pref3,                 preferences
    prefs.setValue("pref4", pref4);   ┘ pref4
  }
```

In listing 10.4, the `pref3` and `pref4` preferences are set after the `store` method is invoked; the `pref3` and `pref4` preferences aren't saved in the persistent store by the portal server.

> **WARNING**   If you don't call the `store` method after setting the preferences, the preferences aren't saved to the persistent store.

The `store` method has two key features: *atomicity* and *consistency*. Let's look at atomicity.

10.5.1 *Atomicity in saving preferences*

The `store` method doesn't return a success or failure flag to the calling portlet, but it's guaranteed to be *atomic*; the `store` method either successfully saves *all* the preferences in the persistent store or *none*.

The `store` method call can fail because the persistent store is unavailable, or the values of the preferences don't match the criteria set by the `Preferences-Validator` (discussed in section 10.6). The portal server or portlet container is responsible for ensuring that saving preferences with the `store` method is always an atomic operation.

10.5.2 *Concurrency issues in saving preferences*

If multiple threads attempt to concurrently write portlet preferences into the persistent store, this may result in data inconsistency. Concurrency issues are handled by the `store` method implementation provided by the portal server or portlet container.

> **NOTE**   I mentioned in chapter 2 that a portlet's `render` method (in any portlet mode) shouldn't be used to change the portlet state. The `PortletPrefer-ences` object's `store` method follows this rule strictly, and if you invoke the `store` method in a portlet's `render` method, in any portlet mode, it will result in an exception.

Let's now look at the `PortletPreferences` interface's `reset` method, which allows you to reset previously set preferences.

10.5.3 *Resetting preferences*

Figure 10.2 shows that the Book Catalog portlet includes Reset hyperlinks to allow users to reset the preferences to default values.

You can reset a preference by calling the `PortletPreferences` object's `reset` method, as shown here:

```
prefs.reset("category");
```

Here, `prefs` is the `PortletPreferences` object, and `category` identifies the preference that needs to be reset.

What happens when you call the `reset` method? If the preference that you're resetting has default values, the value of the preference is set to its default. If the preference doesn't have default values, the preference is simply removed from the `PortletPreferences` object.

> **NOTE** The portlet specification doesn't specify any mechanism to define default values for portlet preferences. What the default value for a preference is and where it needs to be retrieved from depends upon the portlet container implementation. If you define your portlet preferences with initial values in the portlet deployment descriptor (discussed later in this chapter), the `reset` method considers the values defined for the preference in the portlet deployment descriptor to be the default values.

The only way to remove a preference from the `PortletPreferences` object is to use the `reset` method (assuming that no default values exist for the preference). You might think that using the `setValue` or `setValues` methods could also remove a preference, but this isn't the case; even the value `null` is considered a valid value for a preference.

If a preference is removed from the `PortletPreferences` object, the `getValue` and `getValues` methods will return the default value specified in these methods. If the preference was set to `null` using the `setValue` or `setValues` method, the `getValue` and `getValues` methods will return `null` as the return value.

Let's look at the following code listing, which shows the effect of using the `reset` and `setValue` methods to remove a portlet preference.

Listing 10.5 Removing a preference using the `reset` and `setValue` methods

```
@ProcessAction(name="setMyPreferences")
public void setMyPreferences(...)
  throws PortletException, IOException {
  ...
  PortletPreferences prefs = request.getPreferences();
  prefs.setValue("pref1", null);                         ❶ Sets value of
  prefs.setValue("pref2", "someValue");                      pref1 to null
  prefs.reset("pref2");                                  ❷ Resets value
  prefs.getValue("pref1", "-1");                             of pref2
  prefs.getValue("pref2", "-1");          ❸ Gets values of
}                                           pref1 and pref2
```

The value of the `pref1` preference is set to `null` and `pref2` is set to `someValue` using the `setValue` method ❶. The value of the `pref2` preference is reset using the `reset` method ❷. The values of the `pref1` and `pref2` preferences are retrieved using the `getValue` method ❸.

> **CODE REFERENCE** Refer to the `BookCatalogPortlet`'s `resetPreference` method in the ch10_BookCatalog portlet to see the `PortletPreferences` object's `reset` method in use. The Reset links in the Book Catalog portlet send the name of the preference to be reset as a request parameter. The Book Catalog portlet's `resetPreference` method retrieves the name of the preference from the portlet request and resets the preference.

In listing 10.5, the returned value of pref1 is null because null is a valid value for a preference. The returned value of pref2 is -1 because the reset method removed the pref2 preference from the PortletPreferences object (there were no default values found for pref2).

> **TIP** To remove a preference, don't set its preference value to null by calling the setValue method. Instead, use the reset method to reset or remove the preference from the PortletPreferences object.

When you use the reset method, the change in the preference isn't persisted automatically; you still need to call the PortletPreferences object's store method to persist the changes.

Validating information entered by a user is an important aspect of any application design. Applications are designed on the assumption that the data available from the data store will be consistent and that the application will handle any known inconsistencies that may exist in the data. Because preferences are saved in the data store and are later used to customize portlet content or behavior, the preferences entered by the user may need to be validated before they're saved in the persistent store.

Let's look at how preferences entered by users can be validated.

10.6   *Validating preferences*

Earlier in this chapter, you saw how to retrieve preferences selected by the user from the request and set these preferences in the PortletPreferences object. The next logical step is to validate these preferences before saving them in the portal database (by calling the store method).

For instance, in the Book Catalog portlet, you need to confirm that the preferred ISBN entered by the user exists in the catalog before saving it. There are several benefits of validating the ISBN:

- Users can't enter just any number as a preferred ISBN, which guarantees that you won't end up storing unnecessary ISBNs in the persistent store.
- You don't need to write code in the Book Catalog portlet to handle scenarios where the preferred ISBN isn't found in the catalog.
- If users enter a wrong ISBN by mistake, they'll be notified before the preferences are saved. This will also avoid leaving the impression that the Book Catalog portlet has bugs.

In your portlet, you can validate the user preferences at two places during request processing:

- Before setting the preferences in the PortletPreferences object. This is achieved by writing validation logic in the portlet class.
- After setting the preferences in the PortletPreferences object and before invoking the store method. This is achieved by using the PreferencesValidator.

Let's look at both of these approaches.

10.6.1 Validating preferences before setting them in PortletPreferences

This approach for validating preferences requires that you write validation logic in your portlet class. The following listing shows the Book Catalog portlet's `save-Preferences` method, which validates the user's preferred ISBN before calling the `PortletPreferences` object's `store` method.

Listing 10.6 Validating preferences before calling the `store` method

```
@ProcessAction(name="savePreferences")
public void savePreferences(ActionRequest request,
  ActionResponse response)throws PortletException,
    IOException {

  Map<String,String> errorMap =              ❶ Defines java.util.Map to
   new HashMap<String,String>();                hold validation errors

  BookService bookService = ...              ❷ Obtains BookService
  String prefBookISBN =                        and ISBN
    request.getParameter("prefIsbnNumber");
  PortletPreferences prefs = request.getPreferences();

  if(!"".equals(prefBookISBN) &&             ❸ Checks if ISBN
    !bookService.isUniqueISBN                  already exists
      (NumberUtils.toLong(prefBookISBN, -1L)) {

      prefs.setValue("prefBook", prefBookISBN);
  } else {                                   ❹ Sets ISBN preference
    errorMap.put("prefBookIsbn.error",         or error message
      "ISBN number doesn't not exist in catalog");
  }
  ...
  if(errorMap.size() == 0)                   ❺ Saves preferences
    prefs.store();                             in portal database
}
```

First, you create a `java.util.Map` ❶ to store the error keys and error messages for validation errors. Then you obtain a reference to the `BookService` ❷ that's later used to verify whether the book corresponding to the user-entered ISBN exists in the catalog, and you also obtain the ISBN number from the action request.

You check to make sure that the ISBN number entered by the user isn't blank and that it exists in the catalog ❸. Then, if it exists in the catalog, you add the ISBN number to the `PortletPreferences` object with the `prefBook` key ❹. If the entered ISBN number isn't valid or if it doesn't exist in the catalog, you add an error key and message to the `errorMap`.

If there are no validation errors, you call the `PortletPreferences` object's `store` method ❺ to save the user preferences in a persistent store.

In listing 10.6, you can store `errorMap` as a request attribute and retrieve it in the render method of your portlet class (assuming that your portlet uses the `javax.portlet.actionScopedRequestAttributes` container-runtime option) to show the error messages on your JSP page. Alternatively, you can set a generic error message using the `ActionResponse`'s `setRenderParameter` method and use the render parameter value to show the error message on your JSP page.

This validation approach works well, but it clutters the code in your portlet class, which affects code readability. Most web frameworks provide abstract validation classes, or interfaces, that are implemented by the application code to keep validation logic outside of the request-processing logic. Similarly, the Portlet API provides the `PreferencesValidator` interface, which helps keep your preference-validation logic outside your portlet class.

Let's look at how to validate preferences using the `PreferencesValidator` interface.

10.6.2 *Validating preferences using PreferencesValidator*

The `PreferencesValidator` interface of the Portlet API offers the benefit of keeping your preference-validation logic outside of your portlet class.

> **NOTE** Preference validation is different from business validation. Business validation is done in the portlet class or in a class that extends or implements the class or interface of the portlet framework that you're using to create portlets. For instance, in chapter 8, the `MyValidator` class of the Book Catalog portlet implements Spring's `Validator` interface to perform business validations.

This listing shows the `BookCatalogPrefsValidator` class, which implements the `PreferencesValidator` interface and provides the preference-validation logic.

Listing 10.7 `BookCatalogPrefsValidator` validation logic for preferences

```
import javax.portlet.PreferencesValidator;
import javax.portlet.ValidatorException;

public class BookCatalogPrefsValidator                    ❶ Implements Preferences-
   implements PreferencesValidator {                         Validator interface

  public void validate(PortletPreferences prefs)          ❷ Provides implementation
     throws ValidatorException {                              of validate method
    BookService bookService = ...

    String prefBookISBN = prefs.                           ❸ Checks if ISBN
      ➥getValue("prefBookISBN","");                           exists in catalog
    if(bookService.isUniqueISBN
      (NumberUtils.toLong(prefBookISBN, -1L)) {
      List<String> failedKeys =
                new ArrayList<String>();
      failedKeys.add("prefBookISBN");

      throw new ValidatorException(                        ❹ Throws Validator-
         "ISBN number does not exist in catalog",             Exception if
         failedKeys);                                         validation fails
    }
    ...
  }
}
```

The `BookCatalogPrefsValidator` ❶ implements the Portlet API `Preferences-Validator` interface. `PreferencesValidator` defines the `validate` method, which is implemented by the `BookCatalogPrefsValidator` class ❷. The `validate` method ❸ retrieves the preferred book's ISBN from the `PortletPreferences` object and uses `BookService` to check whether a book exists in the catalog with that ISBN. If no book matching the ISBN is found in the catalog, the class throws a `ValidatorException` ❹.

> **CODE REFERENCE** See the `BookCatalogPrefsValidator` class in ch10_Book-Catalog for the complete implementation of the preferences validator used by the Book Catalog portlet.

We'll discuss how to configure `BookCatalogPrefsValidator` for the Book Catalog portlet later in this section. For now, you can assume that the `validate` method of `BookCatalogPrefsValidator` is called *internally* by the `PortletPreferences` object's `store` method. In listing 10.7, the `ValidatorException` is a Portlet API exception class that *must* be thrown by the `validate` method of your validator class if validation fails. `ValidatorException` acts as an indicator to the `store` method that the validation of one or more preferences has failed for some reason, and that it must not save the preferences in the persistent store.

> **NOTE** `BookCatalogPrefsValidator` makes use of the `BookService` class to invoke the `isUniqueISBN` method. If you're using the Spring Portlet MVC framework, a class like `BookService` is configured in the portlet application context XML file with a dependency on a data access object (DAO). In such cases, you can configure the preferences validator class in the portlet application context XML file (instead of portlet.xml), autowire dependencies, and programmatically validate preferences by invoking the `validate` method. Alternatively, you can use Spring's `@Configurable` annotation along with load- or compile-time weaving to autowire dependencies into the preferences validator instance that is not created by Spring.

The `ValidatorException` class defines multiple constructors, and the one used in listing 10.7 accepts two parameters:

- An exception message
- A collection of preference keys that identify preferences that failed validation

The collection of preference keys can be used by the portlet class to display an appropriate error message. In listing 10.7, the exception message is "ISBN number does not exist in catalog," and the collection of failed preferences keys contains a single entry: `prefBookISBN`.

> **TIP** It's recommended that, if a preference fails validation, you keep the name of the failed preference key the same as the name of the preference key in the `PortletPreferences` object. For instance, in listing 10.7, the name of the preference key in the `PortletPreferences` object is `prefBookISBN`; if the validation fails for this preference, the same name is added to the collection

of failed preferences keys that's passed as an argument to the Validator-Exception constructor.

In your validator class, you have the option to throw a ValidatorException as soon as validation fails for a preference, or you can keep adding keys of failed preferences to the collection and throw the ValidatorException at the end, as shown here:

```
List<String> failedKeys = new ArrayList<String>();
if(...) {
  failedKeys.add("pref1");
}
if(...) {
  failedKeys.add("pref2");
}
if(failedKeys.size() > 0) {
  throw new ValidatorException("Exception",failedKeys)
}
```

The preceding code continues adding keys of preferences that failed validation to the failedKeys list, and it throws a ValidatorException after all the preferences have been validated.

Later in this chapter, you'll see how BookCatalogPortlet makes use of this collection of keys of preferences that failed validation in order to show appropriate validation error messages to the user.

10.6.3 Configuring PreferencesValidator in the portlet deployment descriptor

The BookCatalogPrefsValidator class that you created earlier must be configured in the portlet deployment descriptor to instruct the portlet container to use it to validate portlet preferences. The following listing shows how BookCatalogPrefsValidator is configured in the portlet deployment descriptor.

Listing 10.8   The BookCatalogPrefsValidator configuration

```
<portlet-app ...>
   <portlet>
     <portlet-name>bookCatalog</portlet-name>
     <portlet-class>
        chapter10.code.listing.base.BookCatalogPortlet
     </portlet-class>
     ...
     <portlet-preferences>
       <preferences-validator>
          chapter10.code.listing.validators.
          ➥BookCatalogPrefsValidator
       </preferences-validator>
     </portlet-preferences>
   </portlet>
   ...
</portlet-app>
```

Portlet preferences element

Preferences validator element

In this listing, the <preferences-validator> subelement of the <portlet-preferences> element is used to define the custom PreferencesValidator class that will validate preferences for the bookCatalog portlet. It's important to note that you must specify the fully qualified class name of your custom PreferencesValidator class.

CODE REFERENCE Refer to the portlet.xml file in the ch10_BookCatalog folder to see the configuration of the preferences validator in the Book Catalog portlet.

Now that all the validation code is in BookCatalogPrefsValidator, the BookCatalog-Portlet's savePreferences method (shown earlier in listing 10.6) contains no preferences validation logic, as you can see here.

Listing 10.9   The BookCatalogPortlet's savePreferences method

```
@ProcessAction(name="savePreferences")
public void savePreferences(...)
    throws PortletException, IOException {
  String prefBookISBN =
    request.getParameter("prefIsbnNumber");
  PortletPreferences prefs = request.getPreferences();
  if(!"".equals(prefBookISBN)) {                          ❶ Sets preference if
    prefs.setValue("prefBook", prefBookISBN);                ISBN entered
  }
  ...
  try {                                                   ❷ Surrounds store method
   prefs.store();                                            call with try-catch
  } catch(ValidatorException ex) {
    Enumeration failedKey = ex.getFailedKeys();          ❸ Sets failed keys as
    request.setAttribute("failedPrefs",                     request attribute
      failedKeys);
  }
}
```

First you check whether the user has entered the ISBN for a preferred book or not; if so, you set it in the PortletPreferences object ❶. You surround the call to the store method with a try-catch block ❷. If you're using a custom PreferencesValidator to validate preferences, then it's important to catch any ValidatorException in your portlet class to show appropriate validation error messages to the user. You add the collection of failed preference keys as a request attribute ❸.

WARNING You must not call the PortletPreferences object's store method from inside the validate method of the PreferencesValidator class because the portlet container constrains the validate method to perform validation only.

In listing 10.9, there's a reason for checking the ISBN for a blank value before setting it in the PortletPreferences object. BookCatalogPrefsValidator is responsible for validating the preferences set in the PortletPreferences object, and should *not* be used to modify or change them in any way.

Let's see what `BookCatalogPrefsValidator` would look like if you set the ISBN directly in the `PortletPreferences` object without doing a check for a blank entry. The modified `BookCatalogPrefsValidator` is shown next.

Listing 10.10 `BookCatalogPrefsValidator` checking if ISBN was entered

```
public class BookCatalogPrefsValidator
   implements PreferencesValidator {

  public void validate(PortletPreferences prefs)
        throws ValidatorException {
    BookService bookService = ...

    String prefBookISBN = prefs.getValue("prefBookISBN","");      ❶ Checks if ISBN
    if("".equals(prefBookISBN)) {                                    was entered
      prefs.reset(prefBookISBN);                                  Removes prefBookISBN
    }                                                             ❷ preference
    else if(bookService.isUniqueISBN
       (NumberUtils.toLong(prefBookISBN, -1L)) {
      List<String> failedKeys =
                    new ArrayList<String>();
      failedKeys.add("prefBookISBN");

      throw new ValidatorException(
          "ISBN number does not exist in catalog",
          failedKeys);
    }
    ...
  }
}
```

`BookCatalogPrefsValidator` ❶ checks whether the `prefBookISBN` preference is empty or `null`. The validator ❷ attempts to remove the `prefBookISBN` preference from the `PortletPreferences` object using the `reset` method, because saving blank or `null` as the value of the preferred book's ISBN is invalid.

In listing 10.10, `BookCatalogPrefsValidator` isn't only validating preferences; it's also modifying the value of the `prefBookISBN` preference, which isn't recommended. This is similar to using validators in the Spring or Struts frameworks; validators shouldn't change the attributes of the object being validated.

> **TIP** If your portlet offers many personalization options, you may have multiple personalization pages, with each page showing a subset of options. In such cases, the validation code in `PreferencesValidator` can become cluttered. You can consider creating multiple `PreferencesValidator` classes and invoking them programmatically from your portlet class.

Figure 10.4 summarizes the role played by `PreferencesValidator` in portlet request processing.

The action request for the `BookCatalogPortlet` ❶ is triggered when the user clicks Save (shown in figure 10.2) to save the preferences.

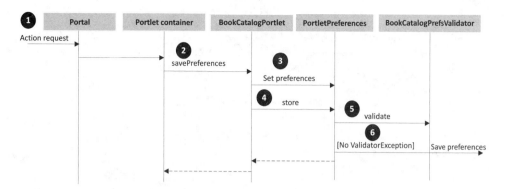

Figure 10.4 The PreferencesValidator's validate method is invoked when the store method of PortletPreferences is called by the portlet implementation class.

The BookCatalogPortlet class's savePreferences action method ❷ is invoked by the portlet container, which is responsible for saving preferences in the portal database. Then, the savePreferences method ❸ invokes the setValue or setValues method of PortletPreferences to set the preferences from the request parameters.

The savePreferences method ❹ calls the PortletPreferences object's store method. The store method ❺ internally calls the BookCatalogPrefsValidator's validate method, which in turn validates the preferences set in PortletPreferences. If the validate method doesn't throw a ValidateException or any other exception, the store method saves the preferences in a persistent store ❻. After this point, the normal portlet request-processing lifecycle continues.

Let's now take a look at how you can show a customized exception message when a preference fails validation.

10.6.4 Handling ValidatorException

You may recall that the PreferencesValidator throws a ValidatorException (see listing 10.7) which is then caught by the portlet class (see listing 10.9) to display a generic exception message to the user. ValidatorException is limited to providing a collection of preference names indicating which ones failed validation, but that isn't sufficient to show a user-friendly exception message in the portlet. In this section, we'll discuss an approach that will allow you to show a user-friendly exception message in the Book Catalog portlet.

Figure 10.5 shows a custom exception message displayed by the Book Catalog portlet when the prefBookISBN preference fails validation: "Please enter a valid value for the 'Preferred ISBN Number' preference".

A custom error message is shown to the user ❶ when the portlet fails to find a book with the ISBN entered by the user in the Preferred Book ISBN Number field. Let's see how the Book Catalog portlet manages to show a custom error message when validation fails for a preference.

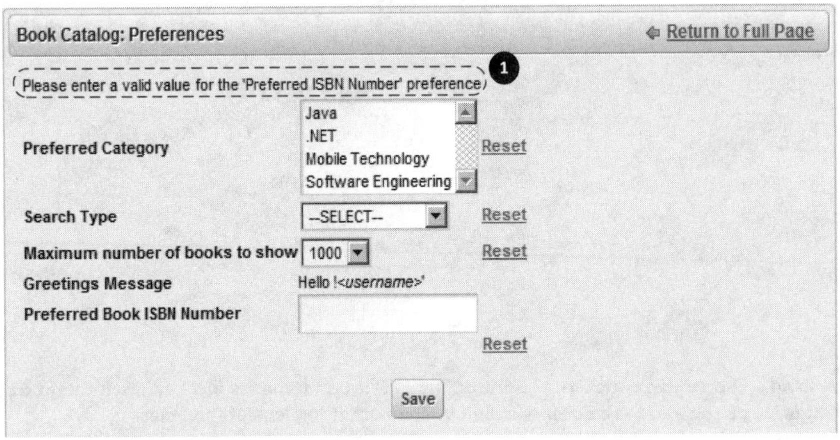

Figure 10.5   The Book Catalog portlet shows a custom error message when the validation of one or more preferences fails.

The next listing shows how the BookCatalogPortlet class makes use of the failed preferences names and keys, received with ValidatorException, to show a user-friendly message.

Listing 10.11   The BookCatalogPortlet class's savePreferences method

```
@ProcessAction(name = "savePreferences")
public void savePreferences(ActionRequest request, ActionResponse response)
   throws PortletException, IOException {
   List<String> errorMessages =                          ❶ Creates empty list
      new ArrayList<String>();                               for messages
   ...
   try {                                                 ❷ Invokes PortletPreferences's
     prefs.store();                                         store method
   } catch (ValidatorException e) {
    Enumeration<String> failedKeys = e.getFailedKeys();  ❸ Gets names of
    while(failedKeys.hasMoreElements()) {                   failed preferences
      String failedKey = failedKeys.nextElement();

     String errorMessage = getResourceBundle             ❹ Gets error
     (request.getLocale()).getString                        message
     (Constants.PREF_RESOURCE_IDENTIFIER_PREFIX
     + "." + failedKey + ".error");

     String prefName = getResourceBundle(request.
     getLocale()).getString(Constants.PREF_RESOURCE_
        IDENTIFIER_PREFIX + "." + failedKey +          ❺ Gets friendly
            ".name");                                     preference
     errorMessages.add(errorMessage.replace("{0}",        name
       prefName));
   }
   }
   request.setAttribute("errorMessages", errorMessages);
}
```

First, you create an empty list ❶ in which you can store validation error messages. The store method of PortletPreferences is invoked ❷. The preference name or key ❸ returned by ValidatorException is obtained using its getFailedKeys method.

The error message ❹ corresponding to a failed preference is obtained from the resource bundle. The name with which the error message is stored in the resource bundle follows this format:

```
javax.portlet.preference.<preference-name>.error
```

Here, *<preference-name>* is the name or key of the preference that failed validation. The error message in the resource bundle contains a placeholder for a user-friendly preference name or key, as shown here:

```
javax.portlet.preference.prefBookISBN.error =
    Please enter a valid value for the '{0}' preference
```

The placeholder for the preference name is identified by '{0}'.

Then you obtain the name of the preference ❺ from the resource bundle. The name of the preference follows this format:

```
javax.portlet.preference.<preference-name>.name
```

Here, *<preference-name>* is the name or key of the preference that failed validation. Then, with errorMessage.replace, you replace the preference name placeholder in the error message with its user-friendly name.

Finally, you add all the error messages to the request, which is then used by the JSP page to display the error messages.

Listing 10.11 shows one of the many possible ways you can display user-friendly validation error messages, and it's sufficient in most portlet development scenarios.

Phew! We've made it through adding personalization support, validating preferences, and saving portlet preferences. We've covered a lot of ground, but it wasn't too complicated. Stick with me for a few more pages and you'll learn how to retrieve saved preferences and use them to customize the content and behavior of your portlets.

10.7 Retrieving portlet preferences and personalizing the portlet

Here's the good news: you don't need to do anything in your portlet implementation class to retrieve preferences from the persistent store. Really!

Let's look at how you can access preferences in your portlet class and in the JSP pages included by the portlet. Later in this section, we'll look at how portlet preferences can be used to personalize content and behavior.

10.7.1 Obtaining preferences in the portlet class and JSP pages

The Book Catalog portlet's category preference attribute identifies the user's preferred book category, like .NET, Java, or Software Engineering. (Listing 10.3 shows that the category preference is set in the BookCatalogPortlet class's save-Preferences method.) If the user had earlier saved .NET and Java as their preferred book categories, the user's preference page (shown in figure 10.2) should show the Java and .NET values selected in the list box. That means you need to retrieve the preferences from the persistent store in order to display them.

Like when saving preferences, you don't need to know anything about the database or persistent store where saved preferences are kept. When your portlet's request-processing methods, like `render`, `serveResource`, `processAction`, and `processEvent`, are invoked, the portlet container is responsible for reading the current values of the portlet preferences from the persistent store and making them available in the `PortletPreferences` object.

The following code snippet shows how you can obtain a `PortletPreferences` object in a portlet's `render` method:

```
@RenderMode(name = "edit")
public void showPrefs(RenderRequest request, RenderResponse response)
  throws IOException, PortletException {
  PortletPreferences prefs = request.getPreferences();
  ...
}
```

In the preceding code snippet, the `PortletRequest`'s `getPreferences` method is used to obtain the `PortletPreferences` object. When you retrieve the `PortletPreferences` object with any of the request-processing methods, the portlet container guarantees it will provide saved preferences in the `PortletPreferences` object. If you had defined preferences with initial values in the portlet deployment descriptor, those preferences may also be available in the `PortletPreferences` object. Later in this chapter, we'll discuss how to define preferences in the portlet deployment descriptor, but for now you can assume that if a preference is defined in the portlet deployment descriptor for which no values exist in the persistent store, the `PortletPreferences` object picks the preference and its values from the portlet deployment descriptor.

For instance, consider the following code snippet, which retrieves the `pref1` preference:

```
@RenderMode(name = "edit")
public void showPrefs(RenderRequest request, RenderResponse response)
  throws IOException, PortletException {
  PortletPreferences prefs = request.getPreferences();
  String value = prefs.getValue("pref1", "-99");
  ...
}
```

In the preceding code, the value of the `pref1` preference attribute depends upon whether the preference was earlier saved in the persistent store, whether it's defined in the portlet deployment descriptor, and whether the persistent store is currently available. Let's look at the `pref1` preference attribute's value in those different situations:

- If the `pref1` preference was saved in the persistent store, the value of the `pref1` attribute in the preceding code is its current value in the persistent store.

- If the `pref1` preference was *not* saved in the persistent store *and* it was defined in the portlet deployment descriptor with an initial value, the value of the `pref1` attribute is its initial value specified in the portlet deployment descriptor.
- If the `pref1` preference was saved in the persistent store *and* it's defined in the portlet deployment descriptor with an initial value, but the persistent store isn't accessible for some reason, the value of the `pref1` attribute is its initial value specified in the portlet deployment descriptor.
- If the `pref1` preference was *not* saved in the persistent store, or if the persistent store isn't accessible and `pref1` wasn't defined in the portlet deployment descriptor, the value of the `pref1` attribute in the preceding code is `-99`.

Now that you know where the preference values come from, let's get back to our initial goal of showing a user's preferences on the preferences page. You can either retrieve preferences in the `render` method of `EDIT` mode, as described above, or directly in the JSP page by using the `portletPreferences` or `portletPreferences-Values` scripting variables introduced by the `defineObjects` tag of portlet tag library (portlet tag library tags were discussed in chapter 6). In most cases, directly retrieving portlet preferences in the JSP is sufficient for showing preferences.

The `portletPreferences` scripting variable represents a `PortletPreferences` object, and `portletPreferencesValues` represents a `Map<String, String[]>` object that contains a map of portlet preference names and values. You can use either of the two scripting variables in your JSP page to show preferences.

In listing 10.1, you saw how the preferences.jsp page of the Book Catalog portlet displays personalization options. Let's now modify the preferences.jsp page to highlight the preferences that were already saved in the persistent store. The modified page is shown here.

Listing 10.12 The preferences.jsp page, modified to show saved preferences

```
<portlet:definedObjects/>
...
<form ...>
<%
  java.util.List catList = java.util.Arrays.asList
     (portletPreferences.getValues("category",
      new String[] {"-1"}));
%>
...
  <td><b>Preferred Category</b></td>
  <td>
    <select name="<portlet:namespace/>category"
      multiple="multiple">
     <option value="java" <%=catList.contains("java")
      ? "selected" : ""%>>Java</option>
     <option value=".net" <%=catList.contains(".net")
      ? "selected" : ""%>>.NET</option>
...
  </td>
```

❶ Introduces scripting variables in JSP

❷ Retrieves category preference values

❸ Shows preferred book categories as selected

```
...
<td><b>Greetings Message</b></td>
<td>
  ${portletPreferencesValues.greetingMessage[0]}
  <i>&lt;username&gt;</i>'
</td>
...
</form>
```

④ Shows greetingMessage preference value

This listing makes use of scripting variables to show current preference values for the Preferred Category and Greetings Message preferences that apply to the user. First, you use the defineObjects tag **❶** in the JSP page to introduce scripting variables, which makes it easy to develop included and forwarded JSP pages in portlets. You retrieve values for the category preference using the portletPreferences scripting variable **❷**; then you show a book category as selected **❸** if it represents one of the values of the category preference. You show the value of the greetingMessage preference **❹** using the portletPreferencesValues scripting variable.

10.7.2 *Personalizing content and behavior*

So far in this chapter, you've learned about saving and retrieving preferences to and from the persistent store. The real value of the preferences shows up when you use them to customize the content and behavior of your portlet. In this section, we'll look at how the Book Catalog portlet makes use of preferences to customize its behavior and content.

Table 10.2 revisits the preferences defined at the beginning of this chapter and describes their effect on the content and behavior of the Book Catalog portlet.

Table 10.2 Book Catalog preferences

Preference	Effect on content and behavior
Preferred Category	Allows a user to personalize the Book Catalog portlet to show books from specified categories. For instance, if the user has chosen to view books in the Java and .NET categories, only books related to those categories are shown to the user when they visit the portal page.
Search Type	Allows a user to choose between case-insensitive and case-sensitive searches for books.
Maximum Number of Books to Show	Allows a user to specify the number of books that will be shown in the Book Catalog portlet. By default, the Book Catalog portlet shows up to 1000 books on the page.
Greetings Message	Represents the greetings message that's shown to the user on the portlet's home page. It can't be changed by the user and is shown as a read-only option.
Preferred Book ISBN Number	If the user specifies one or more preferred books, the books are shown highlighted, on a yellow background, on the home page of the Book Catalog portlet.

In this section, we'll look at how *content* is personalized based on the Preferred Category preference and how *behavior* is personalized based on the Search Type preference. The rest of the preferences in the Book Catalog portlet are implemented along similar lines.

NOTE The personalization of content affects what information is displayed by the portlet. The personalization of behavior deals with how the portlet behaves in response to user actions.

PERSONALIZING CONTENT BASED ON BOOK CATEGORY PREFERENCE

The Book Catalog portlet either displays books from user-selected categories or it shows books from all categories. The next listing shows how the showBooks method of the BookCatalogPortlet class personalizes catalog content based on the book category.

Listing 10.13 The showBooks method personalizes content by category.

```
@RenderMode(name = "VIEW")
public void showBooks(RenderRequest request, RenderResponse response)
  throws IOException, PortletException {
  ...
  PortletPreferences prefs = request.getPreferences();      ❶ Gets category
  String[] categories = prefs.getValues                         preference values
    ("category", new String[] {"-99"});
  if(categories != null && categories.length == 1
    && categories[0].equals("-99")) {              ❷ Retrieves all books from catalog
      books = bookService.getBooks();              ◁┘
  } else {                                         ❸ Retrieves books for
    books = bookService.getBooksByCategories(categories);  ◁┘ select categories
  }
  request.setAttribute(Constants.BOOKS_ATTR, books);  ◁┐ Sets matching books
  ...                                              ❹   as request attribute
}
```

The showBooks method ❶ retrieves the PortletPreferences object from the portlet request. Then you obtain the values of the category preference as a String[], because there can be multiple values associated with this preference. You check whether the category preference contains any values. If it contains a single value of -99, that means that there are no values associated with the category preference.

All the books are obtained from the catalog ❷ if no valid value is found for the category preference. The BookService class's getBooks method returns all books in the catalog, irrespective of the category to which they belong.

If valid category values exist ❸, you obtain books belonging to those categories using the BookService's getBooksByCategories method. You set the books that were obtained ❹, either by the getBooks or getBooksByCategories method, as a request attribute.

The home JSP page of the Book Catalog portlet is then responsible for using the books stored in the request attribute to display the list of books in the catalog. The list may represent all the books in the catalog or the set of books that belong to the user's preferred categories.

> **CODE REFERENCE**   Refer to the `BookCatalogPortlet` class's `showBooks` method in the ch10_BookCatalog folder to see how the Book Catalog portlet makes use of the `category` preference attribute to personalize content.

Listing 10.13 highlights some of the important decisions that you may have to make while writing code that uses preference information to customize portlet content or behavior. Here are two of these decisions:

- If there's a possibility that the preference may contain multiple values, you should use the `PortletPreferences`'s `getValues` method; otherwise use the `getValue` method.
- If a preference can't have a default value, the default value specified in the `get-Value` or `getValues` method should be a value that the preference will never have. Suppose you specify `.net` as the default value in the `getValues` method that returns the user's preferred book categories. If `.net` is also a valid value of the `category` preference, you won't be able to figure out whether the user chose `.net` as their preference, or if it was returned by the `getValues` method because the `category` preference wasn't found in the `PortletPreferences` object.

> **CODE REFERENCE**   The source code in the ch10_BookCatalog folder shows how the Book Catalog portlet customizes content. The home.jsp page shows how content is personalized based on the Maximum Number of Books to Show and Greetings Message options. The `<c:forEach>` tag used in home.jsp puts a limit on the number of books to display by using its `end` attribute. It also uses the `portletPreferencesValues` scripting variable to read the value of the `greetingMessage` preference from the portlet.xml file to show the greeting message. Later in this chapter, we'll discuss how you can define preferences in the portlet deployment descriptor.

PERSONALIZING BEHAVIOR BASED ON THE SEARCH TYPE PREFERENCE

You can personalize the behavior of a portlet in the same way that you personalize portlet content. The Search Type preference of the Book Catalog portlet lets a user choose between case-sensitive and case-insensitive book catalog searches; instead of affecting the content displayed by the portlet, it affects the portlet's behavior.

The following listing shows how the `searchBooks` method of the Book Catalog portlet personalizes search behavior based on the value of the Search Type preference.

Listing 10.14   The `BookCatalogPortlet` class's `searchBooks` method

```
@ProcessAction(name = "searchBookAction")
public void searchBooks(ActionRequest request, ActionResponse response)
    throws PortletException, IOException {
    ...
    PortletPreferences prefs = request.getPreferences();   ◄┘  ① Gets PortletPreferences
                                                                  object from request
```

```
    String searchTypePref = prefs.getValue("searchType",
        Constants.CASE_SENSITIVE);
    matchingBooks = bookService.searchBooks(request
     .getParameter("bookNameSearchField"), request
     .getParameter("authorNameSearchField"),
        searchTypePref);
    ...
}
```

2 Retrieves searchType preference value

3 Invokes BookService's searchBooks method

The implementation of the searchBooks method here is similar to the showBooks method in listing 10.13: both methods retrieve portlet preferences and personalize the content or behavior of the portlet. The BookCatalogPortlet class's searchBooks action method **1** obtains the PortletPreferences object from the request. You retrieve the value of the searchType preference **2**, which identifies the search type: case-sensitive or case-insensitive, with the default being case-sensitive. The BookService class's searchBooks method **3** is invoked, and it's passed the user's search type preference. The searchBooks method makes use of the search type preference to perform a case-sensitive or case-insensitive search.

So far in this chapter, you've seen examples in which portlet preferences are defined in the portlet class. Let's now look at how you can define preferences in the portlet deployment descriptor.

10.7.3 Defining portlet preferences in portlet.xml

Earlier in this chapter, you saw how you can define preferences on the fly, in the portlet code itself. Portlet preferences are similar to any other configuration option in the portlet.xml file—defining portlet preferences in portlet.xml informs the portlet deployer about the preferences supported by the portlet and their initial values.

You can define portlet preferences in the portlet deployment descriptor using the <preference> subelement of the <portlet-preferences> element. The following listing shows how the Book Catalog portlet defines the maxNumOfBooks and greeting-Message preferences in the portlet.xml file.

Listing 10.15 Portlet preferences defined in portlet.xml

```
<portlet>
    <portlet-name>bookCatalog</portlet-name>
    ...
    <portlet-preferences>
      <preference>
        <name>maxNumOfBooks</name>
        <value>1000</value>
      </preference>
      <preference>
        <name>greetingMessage</name>
        <value>Hello !</value>
        <read-only>true</read-only>
      </preference>
      ...
```

1 Defines preference

2 Specifies name of preference

3 Specifies initial value for preference

4 Marks preference as read-only

```
    </portlet-preferences>
</portlet>
```

First you define a preference using the `<preference>` element ❶. The `<name>` element is used to specify a name for the preference ❷, and `<value>` elements are used to define initial values for the preference ❸. The `<read-only>` element is used to mark a preference as read-only ❹.

If you define portlet preferences in the portlet.xml file, not only does this increase the maintainability of portlet preferences, but it also provides the following additional features:

- *Defines initial values for preferences*—The initial value of a preference is available to a portlet as long as the preference isn't saved in the portlet container's persistent store. Once preference values are saved, they're available to the portlet, but the initial values are not. The initial values of a preference can be useful in showing default personalization options to the user.

- *Defines read-only preferences*—A modifiable preference attribute can be modified by the `processAction`, `processEvent`, and `serveResource` methods. If you specify `true` as the value of a `<read-only>` element for a preference, you can't modify the value the preference using the `setValue`, `setValues`, or `reset` methods. Any attempt to modify a read-only preference will result in a `ReadOnlyException`.

Defining preferences in the portlet deployment descriptor has the added advantage that it informs portlet deployers about various personalization options available for the portlet. It's recommended that you define preferences in the portlet deployment descriptor, with initial values, to clearly indicate the preferences that are available for the portlet.

10.8   Summary

In this chapter, you saw just how easy it is to personalize portlets. You saw that the `PortletPreferences` object of Portlet 2.0 is at the heart of portlet personalization, because it lets you transparently save and retrieve user preferences.

If you liked the concept of preferences, you're going to love inter-portlet communication, which is one of the most exciting features of portlet technology. That's what the next chapter is about.

Communicating with other portlets

11

This chapter covers

- Inter-portlet communication using portlet sessions
- Public render parameters
- Portlet events
- Portlet event support in Spring Portlet MVC
- Pros and cons of different approaches to inter-portlet communication

In 2003, when Portlet 1.0 (JSR 168) was released, it didn't define support for communication between portlets. The only way to achieve inter-portlet communication in the Portlet 1.0 days was by using `PortletSession`, which required communicating portlets to reside in the same portlet application. If you wanted a third-party portlet to communicate with your custom portlet, you had to package them as part of a single portlet application.

The lack of inter-portlet communication support also led to using portal server–specific approaches to achieve communication between portlets, resulting in portability issues. This limitation in Portlet 1.0 made inter-portlet communication one of the highly anticipated features in Portlet 2.0.

There are many ways in which your portlets can communicate with each other; this chapter focuses on inter-portlet communication mechanisms that are primarily used in portals and that are supported by Portlet 2.0–compliant containers. We'll also look at how the inter-portlet communication approaches compare with each other, and the scenarios in which it makes sense to use one mechanism over another. We'll first look at how portlets can communicate using `PortletSession`, and then we'll move on to inter-portlet communication mechanisms available in Portlet 2.0–compliant containers.

Let's look at an example that demonstrates the importance of inter-portlet communication.

11.1   Why do you need inter-portlet communication?

Inter-portlet communication is a process in which an action taken on a portlet is communicated to other portlets in the web portal, giving them an opportunity to update their content if it's relevant in the context of the user action.

Inter-portlet communication is central to portlets for two reasons:

- It makes portlets reusable in different scenarios.
- It helps portlets that aren't the target of a particular user action provide relevant information based on the user action.

Imagine a portal page in a car manufacturing firm's web portal that consists of an Order portlet and an Inventory portlet. The Order portlet shows the current status of all the orders in the system, and the Inventory portlet shows the current inventory status for all the cars manufactured by the firm. The Order and Inventory portlets get their content from the order and inventory management systems, respectively. A user can log in to the web portal and can view an order in the Order portlet. When the user selects an order, the Inventory portlet should fetch the inventory of cars that are related to that order, to show their availability.

In this scenario, the Order portlet must communicate which cars are in the order so that the Inventory portlet can display information for those cars. Figure 11.1 shows how the Order and Inventory portlets communicate with each other and with their source systems.

The user selects an order ❶ from the Order portlet. The order details are fetched ❷ from the order management system, and ❸ the Order portlet communicates a list of cars to the Inventory portlet. The Inventory portlet fetches the inventory status ❹ for those cars from the inventory management system.

In figure 11.1, if it wasn't possible for the Order portlet to communicate with the Inventory portlet, the Order portlet would need to interact with the inventory management system to fetch the inventory status for the cars, making the portlet dependent upon the inventory management system for its content. If you then needed to display the price for each of the cars, based on information from a pricing management system, the Order portlet would become dependent upon yet another system.

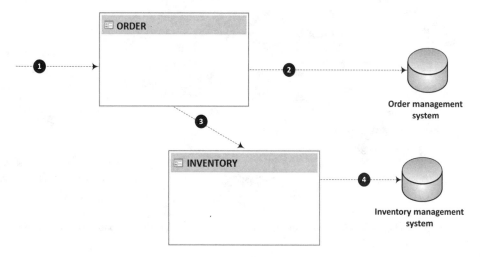

Figure 11.1   The Order and Inventory portlets communicate with their respective source systems and with each other.

Even though the pricing, order, and inventory management systems are distinct systems, the Order portlet would become dependent on all three to generate its content.

   This approach would defeat the main purpose of using portlets, because the Order portlet would be responsible for consolidating information from distinct sources. The Order portlet doesn't qualify to be called a *mashup* portlet (a portlet that provides a new service based on existing services) because it isn't providing any new service to the user. It's simply gathering data from distinct sources to generate its content.

   If the Order portlet is directly dependent on other sources of information, this dependency affects its reusability in different scenarios. For instance, if the Order portlet needs to be used in the web portal developed specifically for the manufacturing firm's marketing team to analyze demand for cars in different geographical regions, then it can't be reused because of its dependence on inventory and pricing management systems.

   To avoid these problems, we need some mechanism that allows portlets to coordinate with each other to break down the silo behavior. This will result in a dynamic web portal that presents content that's relevant based on user actions. The result will be an enriched user experience.

   Before we learn how to implement inter-portlet communication, let's take a look at the requirements of a web portal which will be used as the basis for implementing different inter-portlet communication mechanisms in this chapter.

11.2   *An inter-portlet communication example*

In previous chapters, you saw that the Book Catalog portlet is used to add books to and remove them from the catalog. Suppose you need to develop a new portlet

Book Catalog : Add Book   🔧 ✕

HOME
Category:* Java ▼
Name:* Griffon in Action
Author:* Andres Almiray, Danno Fe
ISBN:* 9781935182238
        Add Book

Powered by: *Liferay Portal Community Edition 6.0.2 CE (Bunyan / Build 6002 / June 8, 2010)*

Figure 11.2   The Add Book form of the Book Catalog portlet, for adding books to the catalog

named Recently Added Book that shows the book most recently added to the catalog. When a book is added to the catalog, the Recently Added Book portlet updates
its content to reflect the details of the recently added book. Let's see how this will
work when the Book Catalog and Recently Added Book portlets are deployed in a
web portal.

Figure 11.2 shows the Add Book form of the Book Catalog portlet, which allows
you to add a new book to the catalog.

When a book is successfully added to the catalog, the Recently Added Book portlet updates its content to show the details of the recently added book, as shown in
figure 11.3.

> **NOTE** It's expected that the Book Catalog and Recently Added Book port-
> lets are on the same portal page, but they could very well be on separate
> portal pages.

Looks pretty simple, right? The coordination between the Book Catalog and Recently
Added Book portlets can be achieved in a number of ways, such as by using a database, the portlet context, Ajax (discussed in chapter 12), and other techniques. In this
chapter we'll focus on the following mechanisms, which are predominantly used in
inter-portlet communication:

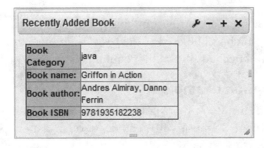

Recently Added Book	🔧 – + ✕
Book Category	java
Book name:	Griffon in Action
Book author:	Andres Almiray, Danno Ferrin
Book ISBN	9781935182238

Figure 11.3   The Recently Added Book portlet is updated every time a book is added to the catalog.

- Portlet session
- Public render parameters
- Portlet events

Table 11.1 identifies the scenarios best suited for using each of these approaches.

Table 11.1 Inter-portlet communication mechanisms and their preferred uses

Inter-portlet communication mechanism	When to use
Portlet session	If your portlets are part of the same portlet application, or if your portal server supports sharing session data between portlets in different portlet applications
Public render parameters	If your portlets communicate using simple string values and are in different portlet applications
Portlet events	If your portlets communicate with each other by sending or receiving complex objects and they're in different portlet applications

In the following sections, we'll look at each of these approaches in detail.

11.3 Inter-portlet communication using portlet sessions

Inter-portlet communication using `PortletSession` is one of the most commonly used techniques since Portlet 1.0. In this section, we'll explore `PortletSession`-based inter-portlet communication in the context of the Book Catalog and Recently Added Book portlets. We'll also look at how content caching can affect `Portlet-Session`-based communication and how you can make use of portal server–specific features to make inter-portlet communication possible between portlets in different portlet applications.

Let's see how the Book Catalog and Recently Added Book portlets can be set up to be part of the same portlet application so that they can communicate using portlet sessions. As we discussed in chapter 3, data stored in the `PortletSession`'s `APPLICATION_SCOPE` can be shared with servlets and portlets that form part of the same portlet application. All portlets belonging to a portlet application are defined in the same portlet deployment descriptor, so the first thing you need to do is to define the Book Catalog and Recently Added Book portlets in the same portlet.xml file. Portlets belonging to a portlet application *must* be packaged in the same WAR file, so you must create a single WAR containing the two portlets.

> **CODE REFERENCE** You should now import the ch11_ipc_session Eclipse project from the source code that accompanies this book, in order to view the code listings presented in this section.

11.3.1   *Defining multiple portlets in the portlet deployment descriptor*

You can define multiple portlets in portlet.xml by adding a `<portlet>` element for each portlet in the portlet application. The following listing shows the portlet.xml file from the ch11_ipc_session project, which defines the Book Catalog and Recently Added Book portlets.

Listing 11.1   Defining multiple portlets in the portlet deployment descriptor

```
<portlet-app...>
  <portlet>
    <portlet-name>recentBook</portlet-name>
    <portlet-class>
      chapter11.code.listing.base.
        ➥RecentlyAddedBookPortlet
    </portlet-class>
    <expiration-cache>0</expiration-cache>
    <cache-scope>private</cache-scope>
    ...
    <resource-bundle>
       content.Language-ext
    </resource-bundle>
    <portlet-info>
      <title>Recently Added Book</title>
    </portlet-info>
  </portlet>
  <portlet>
    <portlet-name>bookCatalog</portlet-name>
    <portlet-class>
        chapter11.code.listing.base.BookCatalogPortlet
    </portlet-class>
    ...
    <expiration-cache>60</expiration-cache>
    <cache-scope>private</cache-scope>
    ...
    <resource-bundle>
       content.Language-ext
    </resource-bundle>
    <portlet-info>
       <title>Book Catalog</title>
    </portlet-info>
    ...
  </portlet>
  ...
</portlet-app>
```

① Recently Added Book portlet

② Expiration cache set to 0

③ Resource bundle for portlet

④ Book Catalog portlet

⑤ Resource bundle for portlet

The name and fully qualified class name of the Recently Added Book portlet is specified **①**. `<expiration-cache>` specifies the expiration time for the cached content as 0 **②**, which means that the content generated by the Recently Added Book portlet is always considered expired by the portlet container. The `<resource-bundle>` element defines the resource bundle used by the Recently Added Book portlet **③**.

The name and fully qualified class name of the Book Catalog portlet is specified **④**, and the resource bundle is specified **⑤**.

NOTE   Listing 11.1 shows that the Book Catalog and Recently Added Book portlets use the same resource bundle for labels and messages, which isn't unusual.

In a portlet deployment descriptor, each <portlet> element contains configuration information specific to that portlet. The configuration information specified as a subelement of the <portlet-app> element applies to all the portlets in the portlet application. For instance, the <container-runtime-option> subelement of the <portlet-app> element applies to all of the portlets defined in the portlet deployment descriptor.

NOTE   Portlets packaged in the same portlet application are usually closely related to each other in their functionality and mostly share a common code base.

Now that you've defined the portlets in the portlet.xml file, let's look at how the Book Catalog portlet communicates with the Recently Added Book portlet using PortletSession.

11.3.2   *Storing and retrieving information from PortletSession*

When a user adds a new book with the Book Catalog portlet, the Recently Added Book portlet is supposed to display the information about the newly added book. Because the Recently Added Book portlet isn't the target of a user action, the Book Catalog portlet is responsible for informing the Recently Added Book portlet that a new book has been added, and that it needs to regenerate its content.

DETERMINING WHAT INFORMATION TO COMMUNICATE

You know *how* to pass information from the Book Catalog to the Recently Added Book portlet (by using PortletSession) but *what* information should you pass? While developing portlets, you need to carefully choose *what* information you want to pass, because that will affect the content generation logic of the target portlet.

NOTE   In the context of inter-portlet communication, we'll refer to the portlet responsible for initiating communication as the *sender portlet*, and the portlet at the receiving end of the communication will be the *receiver portlet*. Sender portlets are targets of user actions, and receiver portlets are the ones that should update their content based on the action taken by the user in the sender portlets. In our example, the Book Catalog is the sender portlet and Recently Added Book is the receiver portlet. In some inter-portlet communication scenarios, a sender may also act as a receiver, and vice versa.

Let's look at the possible information that could be sent to the Recently Added Book portlet:

- *Complete information about the newly added book*—The Recently Added Book portlet wouldn't need to hit the catalog data store because the complete information would be available in PortletSession.

- *ISBN of the newly added book*—The Recently Added Book portlet would retrieve book details from the catalog using the ISBN available in `PortletSession`.
- *A flag indicating that a new book was added to the catalog*—The Recently Added Book portlet would use this flag as an indicator that it needs to re-execute the logic to find the most recently added book.

You could send any of the preceding information to the Recently Added Book portlet, but there are trade-offs with each approach. If you send the complete information via `PortletSession`, you're overloading your session; if you send just the ISBN, there's a performance trade-off because the portlet will have to make a round trip to the catalog data store.

From the perspective of the receiver portlet, the communicated information can be classified as shown in table 11.2.

Table 11.2   Classification of information received by a portlet

Information received	Description
Complete	In this case, the receiver portlet doesn't need to do anything extra; the communicated information is sufficient for the receiver portlet to generate its content.
Partial	In this case, the receiver portlet processes the partial information received from the sender portlet to generate its content.
No information	In this case, the receiver portlet receives no information about the content that it needs to generate.

In most scenarios, the partial information approach is used; the receiver portlet usually needs to process the communicated information to generate its content.

> **NOTE**   As recommended in chapter 3, you should avoid putting information in `PortletSession` during the render phase. Only when an action method is invoked in response to a user action on the sender portlet should you set the session attributes. As mentioned in chapter 2, the sequence of render method invocations for portlets in a portal page is undefined; if you put information in a `PortletSession` in the render method, the other portlets may not be able to read it because their render methods will have already been invoked by the time the information was put in `PortletSession`.

In inter-portlet communication scenarios, it's also important to consider situations in which the communicated information isn't available to the receiver portlet or was not delivered—the no-information case in table 11.2. The receiver portlet should show meaningful content even if the information that should have been communicated wasn't delivered or is unavailable. For instance, if the Recently Added Book portlet is completely dependent on the ISBN stored in `PortletSession` for generating its content, it won't show any book details until a user adds a new book to the catalog. This gives the impression that no book has ever been added to the catalog and that the catalog is empty.

> **NOTE** Because we aren't using a database for the examples in this chapter, the book catalog is stored as a `ServletContext` attribute named `bookCatalog` by `BookCatalogContextListener` (a servlet context listener). Refer to the web.xml file and the `BookCatalogContextListener` class in the ch11_ipc_ session source folder that accompanies this book.

CACHING AND INTER-PORTLET COMMUNICATION

In inter-portlet communication scenarios, content caching in the receiver portlet can be a spoilsport. For example, if the receiver portlet caches content based on an expiration-based or validation-based caching strategy, the content of the receiver portlet isn't updated until the content expires or becomes invalid. Even if you pass information via `PortletSession` to the receiver portlet, the portlet's content won't be updated until the cached content expires and the render method of the receiver portlet is invoked.

In our example, the Book Catalog portlet communicates the ISBN of the newly added book to the Recently Added Book portlet via `PortletSession`. The Recently Added Book portlet's content generation logic is responsible for showing meaningful content if the ISBN of the newly added book isn't available in `PortletSession`.

This listing shows the `addBook` action method of the `BookCatalogPortlet` class, which adds the ISBN of the newly added book to `PortletSession`.

Listing 11.2 The `BookCatalogPortlet` class's `addBook` method

```
@ProcessAction(name = "addBookAction")           ❶ Defines addBook
public void addBook(ActionRequest request,          action method
    ActionResponse response)throws... {
 ...
 if (errorMap.isEmpty()) {
   bookService.addBook(new Book(category, name,
     author, Long.valueOf(isbnNumber)));         ❷ Adds ISBN of newly
   request.getPortletSession().setAttribute          added book to session
     ("recentBookIsbn", isbnNumber,
       PortletSession.APPLICATION_SCOPE);
   ...
 }
}
```

The `BookCatalogPortlet` class's `addBook` method ❶ is responsible for adding a book to the catalog. The `addBook` method ❷ checks whether `errorMap` is empty; `errorMap` is a `HashMap` that contains validation errors that occurred when the book information entered by the user was validated. If `errorMap` is empty (meaning that no validation errors occurred), the book information is saved in the catalog by calling the Book-Service's `addBook` method. The ISBN of the newly added book is then set in the APPLICATION_SCOPE of `PortletSession` with the name `recentBookIsbn`.

The ISBN stored in `PortletSession` is now accessible to the Recently Added Book portlet. The following listing shows how the `RecentlyAddedBookPortlet` class retrieves the ISBN from `PortletSession` and uses it to generate its content. If an ISBN is found in the session, the `RecentlyAddedBookPortlet` uses the `BookService` class to retrieve the recently added book.

Listing 11.3   The `RecentlyAddedBookPortlet` class

```
public class RecentlyAddedBookPortlet extends GenericPortlet {

 @RenderMode(name="view")
 public void showRecentBook(RenderRequest request,
    RenderResponse response)throws ...{
  String isbnNumber = (String)request.                      ❶ Retrieves ISBN from
   getPortletSession().getAttribute("recentBookIsbn",          PortletSession
   PortletSession.APPLICATION_SCOPE);
  ...
  if(isbnNumber != null) {
   if(bookService.isRecentBook
      (Long.valueOf(isbnNumber))) {
     book = bookService.getBook(Long.
       ➥valueOf(isbnNumber));
   } else {                                                 ❷ Retrieves recently
     book = bookService.getRecentBook();                      added book details
   }
  } else {
    book = bookService.getRecentBook();
  }
  request.setAttribute("book", book);                       ❸ Generates portlet
  getPortletContext().getRequestDispatcher(                   content using JSP page
    ➥response.encodeURL(Constants.PATH_TO_JSP_PAGE +
    ➥"recentPortletHome.jsp")).include(...);
 }
}
```

The `showRecentBook` method represents the render method for `VIEW` portlet mode. The `showRecentBook` method retrieves the `recentBookIsbn` session attribute ❶ from `APPLICATION_SCOPE`. The `recentBookIsbn` attribute contains the ISBN of the recently added book, set by the Book Catalog portlet (in listing 11.2).

If the ISBN stored in the `recentBookIsbn` session attribute represents a recently added book in the catalog, the `BookService`'s `getBook` method is called ❷ to retrieve the details of the book whose ISBN matches the value of `recentBookIsbn`. If the ISBN stored in the `recentBookIsbn` session attribute doesn't represent a recently added book in the catalog, or the `recentBookIsbn` session attribute isn't found, the `Book-Service`'s `getRecentBook` method is used to retrieve the most recently added book in the catalog.

The `Book` object returned by the `getBook` or `getRecentBook` method is set ❸ as a request attribute for use by the JSP page responsible for rendering content. The request is then dispatched to the recentPortletHome.jsp page of the Recently Added Book portlet to display the details of the recently added book.

Listing 11.3 shows that the `RecentlyAddedBookPortlet` class does a lot of work to ensure that the content is meaningful. For instance, if it doesn't find the `recentBookIsbn` session attribute, or if it finds that the ISBN referenced by the `recentBookIsbn` session attribute doesn't represent the most recently added book in the catalog, it executes some complex logic within the `BookService`'s `getRecentBook` method to fetch the most recently added book.

CODE REFERENCE The `BookService`'s `getRecentBook` method is responsible for fetching fresh catalog data and sorting it based on a sequence number assigned to each book in the catalog. The book with the highest sequence number is considered to be the most recently added book in the catalog. Refer to the `BookServiceImpl` class in the ch11_ipc_session source folder for more details.

You've seen in listings 11.2 and 11.3 how `PortletSession` is used to implement inter-portlet communication. Now it's time to look at how you can build, deploy, and test this inter-portlet communication between the Book Catalog and Recently Added Book portlets.

11.3.3 *Inter-portlet communication in action*

In the previous section, you saw how to write portlets that communicate using `PortletSession`. Now you'll see how the Book Catalog and Recently Added Book portlets communicate when deployed in a web portal.

Let's look at the steps that we need to take to test communication between our example portlets.

1 Build and deploy a portlet application WAR file.

The steps involved in building and deploying a portlet application containing multiple portlets are the same as for a portlet application containing a single portlet. Refer to chapter 1 for a discussion of how to build and deploy portlets in Liferay Portal.

2 Create portal pages.

Because you want to test inter-portlet communication in situations when the communicating portlets are located on different portal pages, you should create two portal pages named Book Catalog and Recent Book. Refer to chapter 1 for the steps required to create portal pages in Liferay Portal.

3 Test inter-portlet communication between portlets on the same portal page.

To test inter-portlet communication, add the Book Catalog and Recently Added Book portlets to the Book Catalog portal page, as shown in figure 11.4. Refer to chapter 1 for the steps required to add portlets to a portal page with Liferay Portal.

Figure 11.4 shows communicating portlets on the same portal page. To test communication between the portlets, add a new book to the catalog, as shown

Figure 11.4   The Book Catalog and Recently Added Book portlets are on the same portal page. The Recently Added Book portlet shows information when a new book is added using the Book Catalog portlet.

in figure 11.2. You'll find that the Recently Added Book portlet updates its content to reflect the new book, as shown in figure 11.3.

4 Test inter-portlet communication between portlets on different portal pages.

To test the communication between portlets when they're located on different portal pages, add the Book Catalog portlet to the Book Catalog portal page and the Recently Added Book portlet to the Recent Book page. Now add a new book to the catalog and check whether the Recently Added Book portlet's content reflects the details of the newly added book. You'll find that the Recently Added Book portlet does show the new information.

You've now seen how easy it is to get your portlets talking to each other, whether they're on the same portal page or different ones. Next, we'll look at the pros and cons of using `PortletSession` for inter-portlet communication.

11.3.4 *Advantages and disadvantages of using PortletSession*

`PortletSession` was the preferred way to achieve inter-portlet communication in the Portlet 1.0 days, and it still has many advantages in the Portlet 2.0 world. These are the advantages:

- The sender portlet can pass any object type to the receiver portlet.
- Portlets that are part of the same portlet application have access to the common `PortletSession`, so they can easily take up the role of sender or receiver portlet without needing any configuration changes.
- Portlets can communicate with each other using `PortletSession` even when they're on different portal pages.

And here are the disadvantages of using `PortletSession` for inter-portlet communication:

- Portlets must be packaged as part of the same portlet application to take advantage of `PortletSession` for communication. This means it isn't possible for a portlet to communicate with a third-party portlet.
- Web components that are part of the same portlet application can access and modify data stored in `PortletSession`, which can result in unpredictable outcomes.

You should consider these pros and cons before deciding on the approach you want to use for communication between portlets.

> **NOTE** Some portal servers provide additional features for sharing session attributes between portlets in different portlet applications. For instance, in Liferay Portal you can share `APPLICATION_SCOPE` session attributes with portlets in other portlet applications by using the `session.shared.attributes` property in the portal-ext.properties file (discussed in appendix B) and the `<private-session-attributes>` element of the liferay-portlet.xml file. Such features are portal-specific and will result in portability issues.

Let's now look at how public render parameters are used in inter-portlet communication.

11.4 *Inter-portlet communication using public render parameters*

Request parameters received in the portlet's render method are referred to as *render parameters*. Render parameters are meant to communicate information that's required by the portlet to generate appropriate content.

There are two types of render parameters:

- *Private render parameters*—These request parameters aren't visible to other portlets.
- *Public render parameters*—These request parameters are visible to other portlets on the same portal page.

So far in this book, you've seen that render parameters are received by a portlet in the following situations:

- When a form is submitted to a portlet's render URL, the form fields are sent as render parameters to the render method.
- When a hyperlink that references a portlet's render URL is clicked, the parameters set in the render URL are sent as render parameters to the render method.
- When a render parameter is set in the `ActionResponse` using the `setRenderParameter` method, the portlet container makes the render parameter available to the following render method call.

The render parameters used in these situations are *private* render parameters because they're not shared with other portlets. Each portlet has its own set of private render parameters that are made available to the portlet when its render method is invoked by the portlet container. *Public* render parameters, on the other hand, are available to all portlets in the same or different portlet applications.

> **WARNING** You should not submit a form to a portlet's render URL because form submissions are associated with updating system state, which isn't recommended in the render phase. For instance, in the Book Catalog portlet, you shouldn't submit the Add Book form to the render URL.

The primary purpose of both render parameter types is to provide information that portlets can use in generating their content. For instance, the render method of the Book Catalog portlet in chapter 6 uses the `myaction` private render parameter to decide on the JSP to be used for generating portlet content.

Let's look at how you can set or retrieve public render parameters in portlets.

11.4.1 Setting and retrieving public render parameters

If you take a quick look at the Portlet 2.0 API in chapters 3 and 4, you'll find that the `PortletResponse` interface and its subinterfaces don't define a setter method for public render parameters. So how do you set a public render parameter if there's no method available to set it? You can set public render parameters using the setter method for private render parameters. Sound misleading?

Public render parameters can be thought of as an extension to the concept of private render parameters. To create public render parameters, you just need to tell the portlet container to treat certain private render parameters as public render parameters. All you need to do is specify the names of the private render parameters that you want to be treated as public render parameters in the portlet.xml file.

The only thing that changes when a private render parameter is converted to a public render parameter is its *scope*. Like private render parameters, public render parameters are available to the portlet in the render method; additionally they're available in action, resource, and event methods. The *scope* of public render parameters goes beyond the current portlet, so they're also available in the lifecycle methods of other portlets in the same or different portlet applications.

Don't worry if you find the concept of private and public render parameters confusing; I'll come back to them later in this chapter to clarify the difference. For now, you can assume that they're mostly the same. Private render parameters are set in the action or event method and are available only in the render method. Public render parameters, unlike private render parameters, are also available to other portlets and in all lifecycle methods.

Let's look at how you can use public render parameters in the Book Catalog and Recently Added Book portlets we're discussing in this chapter.

PUBLIC RENDER PARAMETERS AND INTER-PORTLET COMMUNICATION

As discussed in section 11.3, the Book Catalog portlet should communicate the ISBN of the recently added book to the Recently Added Book portlet via the public

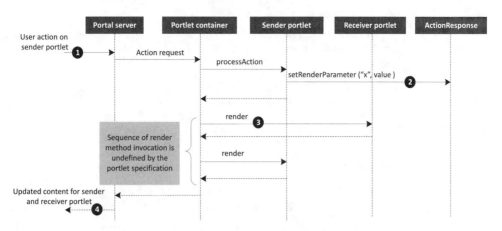

Figure 11.5 Public render parameters are set as if they were private render parameters. The portlet deployment descriptor is responsible for distinguishing public render parameters from private ones.

render parameter. Figure 11.5 shows how public render parameters are used by portlets for communication.

The user performs an action ❶ on the sender portlet. The sender portlet uses the `ActionResponse`'s `setRenderParameter` method ❷ to set a private render parameter named x. If this private render parameter is specified as a public render parameter in portlet.xml, it will be available to the receiver portlet ❸. The updated content of the receiver portlet ❹ is shown to the user.

> **CODE REFERENCE**   You should now import the ch11_BookCatalog_public and ch11_RecentBook_public Eclipse projects from the source code that accompanies this book, so you can view the code listings presented in this section. The ch11_BookCatalog_public project contains the Book Catalog portlet and ch11_RecentBook_public contains the Recently Added Book portlet.

SETTING PUBLIC RENDER PARAMETERS IN THE PORTLET DEPLOYMENT DESCRIPTOR

The distinction between public and private render parameters is made by the portlet deployment descriptor. Both the sender and receiver portlets must define the render parameters shared by the sender portlet. We'll revisit this concept after discussing the portlet deployment descriptors of the sender and receiver portlets.

The next listing shows the portlet deployment descriptor of the Book Catalog portlet—the sender portlet in our example.

Listing 11.4   The Book Catalog portlet's portlet.xml file

```
<portlet-app...>
  <portlet>
    <portlet-name>bookCatalog</portlet-name>
    <portlet-class>
      chapter11.code.listing.base.BookCatalogPortlet
    </portlet-class>
    ...
```

❶ **Book Catalog portlet**

```
    <supported-public-render-parameter>
          recentBookIsbn
    </supported-public-render-parameter>
  </portlet>
  <public-render-parameter>
    <identifier>recentBookIsbn</identifier>
    <qname xmlns:n="http://www.mynamespace.com/">
        n:myBookISBN
    </qname>
  </public-render-parameter>
  ...
</portlet-app>
```

2 Supported public
render parameter

3 Public render
parameter details

Listing 11.4 shows how the `<supported-public-render-parameter>` and `<public-render-parameter>` elements are used to transform the `recentBookIsbn` private render parameter into a public render parameter named `myBookISBN` in the namespace http://www.mynamespace.com/.

The Book Catalog portlet's name and class **1** are specified. The `<supported-public-render-parameter>` **2** specifies the render parameter name that the `bookCatalog` portlet retrieves or sets in its portlet class. Because it will be shared with other portlets, it's defined in the portlet deployment descriptor using the `<supported-public-render-parameter>` element. The `recentBookIsbn` render parameter name specified in the `<supported-public-render-parameter>` must uniquely identify a corresponding `<public-render-parameter>` element.

The `<public-render-parameter>` element **3** maps the render parameter used internally by the Book Catalog portlet to the qualified name by which it's known to other portlets in the portal. The value of the `<identifier>` element specifies the render parameter's internal name, `recentBookIsbn`, defined by the `<supported-public-render-parameter>` element. The `<qname>` element specifies the namespace-qualified name by which the render parameter is accessible to other portlets: the namespace is http://www.mynamespace.com/ and the local name is `myBookISBN`.

Now, other portlets can access the `recentBookIsbn` render parameter using the qualified name with which it was exposed.

The following listing shows the portlet deployment descriptor of the Recently Added Book portlet.

Listing 11.5   The Recently Added Book portlet's portlet.xml file

```
<portlet-app...>
  <portlet>
    <portlet-name>recentBook</portlet-name>
    <portlet-class>
      chapter11.code.listing.base.RecentlyAddedBookPortlet
    </portlet-class>
    ...
    <supported-public-render-parameter>
        myCustomRecentBookIsbnParamName
    </supported-public-render-parameter>
  </portlet>
```

1 Recently Added
Book portlet

2 Supported public
render parameter

```
  <public-render-parameter>
    <identifier>
      myCustomRecentBookIsbnParamName
    </identifier>
    <qname xmlns:n="http://www.mynamespace.com/">
        n:myBookISBN
    </qname>
  </public-render-parameter>
  ...
</portlet-app>
```

**❸ Public render
parameter details**

The Recently Added Book portlet's name and class are specified ❶. The <supported-public-render-parameter> element specifies the render parameter that the recentBook portlet retrieves ❷ or sets in its portlet class. The myCustomRecentBookIsbnParamName render parameter is mapped ❸ to the qualified name by which it's known to other portlets in the portal.

WARNING Up to Liferay Portal 5.2.3, the value of the <identifier> element must be the same in all portlets that communicate using public render parameters. To address this issue, the Recently Added Book portlet's portlet.xml file uses recentBookIsbn as the value of the identifier element instead of myCustomRecentBookIsbnParamName. If you're using Liferay Portal 6.x or GlassFish with OpenPortal Portlet Container 2.1.2, this warning doesn't apply.

If you compare listing 11.4 with listing 11.5, you can see that the qualified name for the recentBookIsbn render parameter is the same as for the myCustomRecentBookIsbnParamName parameter. This means that they are essentially the same render parameters; any change in the Book Catalog portlet's recentBookIsbn render parameter will be reflected in the Recently Added Book portlet's myCustomRecentBookIsbnParamName render parameter, and vice versa.

Figure 11.6 summarizes how the Book Catalog portlet communicates with the Recently Added Book portlet using public render parameters. This figure shows that public render parameters can be thought of as variables stored in a global namespace that's accessible to other portlets in the portal. You can define a namespace of your choice to qualify your public render parameter's local name. For

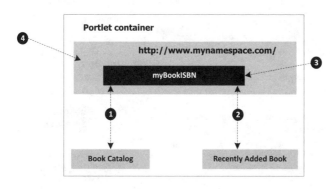

Figure 11.6 The Book Catalog and Recently Added Book portlets communicate with each other using a render parameter that maps to the myBookISBN name in the http://www.mynamespace.com/ namespace.

instance, the http://www.mynamespace.com/ namespace represents a fictitious namespace in this example.

The Book Catalog portlet ❶ exposes the recentBookIsbn render parameter as the myBookISBN variable in the http://www.mynamespace.com/ namespace. The Recently Added Book portlet ❷ exposes the myCustomRecentBookIsbnParamName render parameter as the myBookISBN variable in the http://www.mynamespace.com/ namespace. myBookISBN ❸ represents a global variable to which both the recent-BookIsbn and myCustomRecentBookIsbnParamName render parameters refer. At ❹, http://www.mynamespace.com/ represents a container for the myBookISBN variable.

> **WARNING**   Because we aren't using a database to demonstrate the examples in this chapter, there are some limitations on how the book catalog data is shared between the Book Catalog and Recently Added Book portlets. To keep things simple, the Recently Added Book portlet uses a ServletContext attribute to store some book catalog data, which contains books with the following ISBNs: 1, 2, 3, 4, and 5. When you add a book in the Book Catalog portlet, the ISBN of the newly added book is made available to the Recently Added Book portlet as a public render parameter. To see inter-portlet communication in action between the two portlets, you must add a book in the Book Catalog portlet with an ISBN of 1, 2, 3, 4, or 5.

If you want to avoid defining a namespace for each of the public render parameters, you can define a default namespace for all public render parameters defined in the portlet application by using the <default-namespace> element. The next listing shows the Book Catalog portlet's deployment descriptor from listing 11.4, rewritten using the <default-namespace> element.

Listing 11.6   A portlet.xml using the default-namespace element

```
<portlet-app...>
  <portlet>
    <portlet-name>bookCatalog</portlet-name>
    <portlet-class>
      chapter11.code.listing.base.BookCatalogPortlet
    </portlet-class>
    ...
    <supported-public-render-parameter>
          recentBookIsbn
    </supported-public-render-parameter>
  </portlet>
  <default-namespace>                              ❶ Default
        http://www.mynamespace.com                    namespace
  </default-namespace>
  <public-render-parameter>                        ❷ Public render
    <identifier>recentBookIsbn</identifier>           parameter
    <name>myBookISBN</name>
  </public-render-parameter>
  ...
</portlet-app>
```

The `<default-namespace>` element defines a default namespace ❶ for all the public render parameters defined using `<public-render-parameter>` elements. The `<name>` subelement of the `<public-render-parameter>` element is used ❷ to specify the local name of the public render parameter instead of using the `<qname>` subelement. In this case, the default namespace is implicitly associated with the unqualified local name of the public render parameter.

11.4.2 *Methods related to public render parameters*

As was mentioned earlier, the Portlet 2.0 API doesn't define any methods to explicitly set public render parameters; they're set the same way private render parameters are. But the API does provide methods to retrieve public render parameters explicitly from portlet requests.

You can retrieve a public render parameter by using any of the following `Portlet-Request` methods:

- `getPublicParameterMap()`—Returns public render parameters as a `java.util`
  `.Map` object. The name of the parameter is the key, and a `String[]` represents its value.
- `getParameter(String name)`—Returns the public render parameter's value. The public render parameter name is identified by the `name` argument.
- `getParameterValues(String name)`—Returns a `String[]` of the public render parameter's values. The public render parameter name is identified by the `name` argument.

NOTE You can use the `PortletConfig` object's `getPublicRenderParameter-Names` method to get the list of public render parameters supported by a portlet.

When it comes to removing a private render parameter, the Portlet API doesn't provide any methods to do this. But you can remove a private render parameter by setting its value to `null`. On the other hand, public render parameters can be removed using the `StateAwareResponse` interface's `removePublicRenderParameter` method. Because it's in the `StateAwareResponse` interface, this method only allows you to remove public render parameters in action and event methods.

The following code snippet shows how you can remove the `recentBookIsbn` public render parameter defined in listing 11.6 using the `removePublicRender-Parameter` method:

```
response.removePublicRenderParameter("recentBookIsbn");
```

Here, `response` represents the `ActionResponse` or `EventResponse` object.

The use of the `recentBookIsbn` name in the preceding method is consistent with using the internal name of a public render parameter in the portlet code, and not the name given in the global namespace.

NOTE Public render parameters don't have a well-defined lifecycle like private render parameters do. Private render parameters are available during the render phase, and then they're destroyed by the portlet container. Public render parameters are available until you explicitly remove them using the `removePublicRenderParameter` method of the `ActionResponse` or `EventResponse` object.

Now that you've seen how public render parameters are used in inter-portlet communication, let's discuss the advantages and disadvantages of using public render parameters.

11.4.3 Advantages and disadvantages of using public render parameters

As you saw, using public render parameters for inter-portlet communication is as simple as adding some configuration information to the portlet deployment descriptor. Here are some more benefits of using public render parameters:

- It's the simplest approach to achieve inter-portlet communication. This approach doesn't require code changes, and it gives you the flexibility to expose additional render parameters when required.
- The communicating portlets need not be in the same portlet application.
- If the portal server stores render parameters in the URL, it's easy to bookmark the URL to the portal page. When you visit the portal page, the portlets will use public render parameters to generate relevant content. Suppose a Flight Search web portal page contains Flight and Location portlets. When you select a city from the Location portlet, the Flight portlet displays inbound and outbound flights for that city, based on a `ZIPCode` public render parameter. If the portal server stores the `ZIPCode` public render parameter in the URL, the user can bookmark this URL, and when they use the bookmarked URL later, the Flight portlet will use the same `ZIPCode` public render parameter value to generate content for the same city. This saves the user the effort of reselecting the appropriate city from the Location portlet to view flights in the Flight portlet.
- Public render parameters don't impact the performance of the web portal. There's no extra processing required to pass public render parameters to other portlets, so there's no performance impact on the web portal. (In the next section, we'll discuss *event*-based inter-portlet communication, which does require extra processing on behalf of the portlet container.)

WARNING   Liferay Portal and Jetspeed portal servers don't store public render parameters in the URL, so you won't be able to take advantage of bookmarking URLs with public render parameters.

Public render parameters have their disadvantages too, which need to be considered before deciding to use them for inter-portlet communication:

- Render parameters (whether private or public) can only have `String` or `String[]` as their value type. If you're using `PortletSession` or event-based portlet communication, you can pass complex objects between communicating portlets. In the case of action and resource requests, public render parameters are merged with the action and resource parameters, respectively. If an action or resource parameter has the same name as the public render parameter, the public render parameter values appear towards the end of the parameter value array.

- Because public render parameters are available to all portlets in the portal page and to other web components, they can be removed or modified by other components.

- Public render parameters are available to portlets on the same portal page, but not to portlets on different portal pages. Some portal servers, like Web-Sphere Portal, allow portlets to access public render parameters on different portal pages.

- If the receiver portlet uses validation-based or expiration-based caching and it needs to update its content based on the values of a public render parameter, its content won't be updated until the cache expires. If you want to view the updated content immediately after the public render parameters are set by the sender portlet, you should set the <expiration-cache> to 0 in the receiver portlet's definition in portlet.xml.

Now that you know about the pros and cons, it's time to see public render parameters used in inter-portlet communication. Let's look at an example.

11.4.4 *Putting public render parameters to work*

The source code for the Book Catalog and Recently Added Book portlets is located in the ch11_BookCatalog_public and ch11_RecentBook_public source folders. The example portlets have been kept in separate portlet applications to show how public render parameters can be used for communication between portlets in different portlet applications.

Figure 11.7 shows how these two portlets communicate using public render parameters.

A book is added to the Book Catalog portlet ❶, with an ISBN value from 1 to 5. The book data is saved in the ServletContext of the portlet application that contains the Book Catalog portlet ❷. The ISBN of the newly added book is made available to the Recently Added Book portlet ❸ as a public render parameter. The ISBN public render parameter is retrieved by the Recently Added Book portlet ❹ to obtain the book information from the ServletContext of the portlet application that contains the Recently Added Book portlet.

Let's now look at how portlet events can be used to achieve inter-portlet communication.

11.5 *Inter-portlet communication using portlet events*

Portlet 2.0 introduced the concept of *portlet events* to allow a loosely coupled approach to inter-portlet communication that is tightly integrated with the portlet lifecycle. You can think of portlet events as being like emails. You send email using your favorite

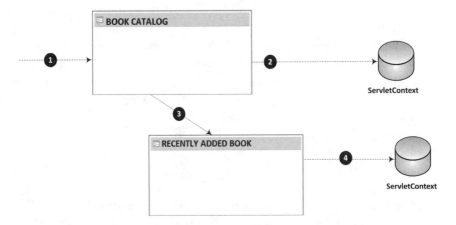

Figure 11.7   The Recently Added Book and Book Catalog portlets get book data from their respective `ServletContexts`. In a real-world situation, both portlets would obtain book data from a shared database.

email client, and the delivery is taken care of by a mail server. In the case of portlet events, the portlet sends the events, and the portlet container is responsible for making the event available to the receiver portlets.

In this section, we'll take an in-depth look at how portlet events are used for inter-portlet communication. You'll see how portlets can communicate with each other using portlet events, using the Book Catalog and Recently Added Book portlets as examples. Toward the end of this section, we'll also look at how Spring Portlet MVC controllers support the processing of portlet events.

When you use public render parameters or the portlet session for inter-portlet communication, it's your responsibility to retrieve the communicated information in the receiver portlet's render method (or in an appropriate lifecycle method) and to process the communicated information. When you use portlet events, the sender portlet uses events to communicate the information to the receiver portlets. The portlet container acts as the broker, delivering the events to the portlets that define an interest in receiving the event.

As mentioned in the previous sections, if you're using `PortletSession` or public render parameters for inter-portlet communication, you need to be aware of the following limitations:

- You shouldn't perform updates in the receiver portlet during the processing of the communicated information because application state shouldn't be updated during the render phase.
- If the receiver portlet caches its content, it won't generate fresh content until the cache is expired by the portlet container.

On the other hand, if you're using portlet events for inter-portlet communication, the receiver portlet can update application state, and the portlet container is responsible

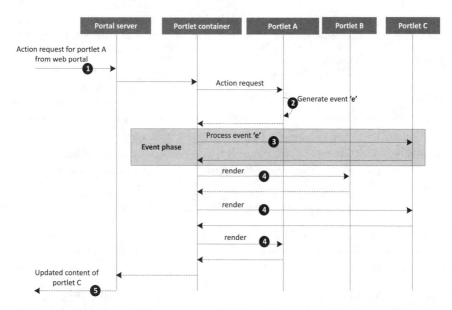

Figure 11.8 **Portlet C processes the event generated by portlet A in the event phase. The portlet container processes generated events before invoking the render method of the portlets on the portal page.**

for expiring the cached content of the portlet, giving it the opportunity to generate fresh content in response to event processing.

Figure 11.8 shows how the event lifecycle phase fits into the portlet's request-processing lifecycle.

The action request for portlet A **①** is received by the portal server. Portlet A generates an event named e **②** during action request processing. Portlet C processes the event e **③** generated by portlet A. The render methods of portlets A, B, and C are invoked **④** by the portlet container. The updated content of portlet C is shown to the web portal user **⑤**, because the portlet container expires the content of portlets that are the target of an event.

Let's now look at how events are sent and received by portlets.

11.5.1 *Sending portlet events*

To send events to other portlets, a portlet must do the following:

- Set the events that the portlet wants to publish to other portlets
- Define, in portlet.xml, the events that the portlet wants to publish

Let's look at both of these tasks in detail.

CODE REFERENCE You should now import the ch11_BookCatalog_event and ch11_RecentBook_event Eclipse projects from the source code that accompanies this book, so you can view the code listings presented in this section.

The ch11_BookCatalog_event project contains the Book Catalog portlet, and the ch11_RecentBook_event project contains the Recently Added Book portlet.

SETTING EVENTS FOR PUBLISHING

A portlet can set events that it wants to send to other portlets by using the following two methods of the `StateAwareResponse` interface:

- `setEvent(QName qname, Serializable value)`—The `qname` argument, of type `javax.xml.namespace.QName`, represents the namespace-qualified name of the event. The `value` argument, of type `java.io.Serializable`, represents the data (also referred as the *payload*) that's associated with the event.
- `setEvent(String name, Serializable value)`—The `name` argument represents the *local* name of the event. The `value` argument represents the event's payload.

Because the `setEvent` methods are defined in `StateAwareResponse`, which is the superinterface of the `ActionResponse` and `EventResponse` interfaces, you can only send events in the action or event phases.

> **NOTE**   You earlier saw how the `<qname>` subelement of the `public-render-parameter` element is used to specify the qualified name of the public render parameter in the portlet deployment descriptor. The `QName` class provides an object representation of a qualified name.

The next listing shows how the `BookCatalogPortlet` class sets the `bookAddedEvent` event when a new book is successfully added to the catalog.

Listing 11.7   The addBook method of the `BookCatalogPortlet` class

```
import javax.xml.namespace.QName;

public class BookCatalogPortlet extends GenericPortlet {

@ProcessAction(name = "addBookAction")
public void addBook(...)... {
  ...
  Book book = new Book(category, name, author, Long
    .valueOf(isbnNumber));
  bookService.addBook(book);
  QName eventName = new QName(                              ❶ Creates
    "http://www.mynamespace.com", "bookAddedEvent"            qualified name
    );                                                        for event
  response.setEvent(eventName, new BookAddedEvent(book);   ❷ Sets event for
  ...                                                         publishing by
}                                                             container
```

The `addBook` action method is responsible for adding a new book to the catalog. The `addBook` method ❶ creates a qualified name for the event that the portlet wants to publish to other portlets. This qualified name consists of two parts: the namespace (`http://www.mynamespace.com`) and the local name (`bookAddedEvent`).

The setEvent method ❷ sets the event for publishing by the portlet container. BookAddedEvent represents the payload or data associated with the event, which is a newly added book in this case.

In listing 11.7, the setEvent method sets the bookAddedEvent event that the Book Catalog portlet wants to publish to other portlets. The event is published to interested portlets by the portlet container after the addBook action method completes, but before the rendering of portlets begins.

The following listing shows the BookAddedEvent class, which is used as a payload for the bookAddedEvent event.

Listing 11.8 The BookAddedEvent event payload

```
import chapter11.code.listing.domain.Book;
import javax.xml.bind.annotation.XmlRootElement;

@XmlRootElement
public class BookAddedEvent implements Serializable {
  private static final long serialVersionUID = ...
  private String name;
  private String author;
  private Long isbnNumber;
  private String category;

  public BookAddedEvent() {
      //-- do nothing
  }
  public BookAddedEvent(Book book) {
      this.name = book.getName();
      this.author = book.getAuthor();
      this.category = book.getCategory();
      this.isbnNumber = book.getIsbnNumber();
  }
  ...
}
```

❶ @XmlRootElement class-level annotation

❷ Event payload defined as Serializable

❸ No-argument constructor

The @XmlRootElement class-level annotation of JAXB (Java Architecture for XML Binding) indicates that BookAddedEvent acts as the root element of the generated XML document ❶. The BookAddedEvent class implements the java.io.Serializable interface ❷. BookAddedEvent defines a no-argument constructor ❸.

> **NOTE** In the context of event-based inter-portlet communication, we'll refer to the event-publishing portlet as the *sender portlet* and the event-processing portlet as the *receiver portlet*.

You might be wondering why the BookAddedEvent event payload class implements the Serializable interface and defines a no-argument constructor. As I explained earlier, the portlet container plays the role of event broker and is responsible for delivering events to portlets. If a portlet wants to send events to a portlet located on a remote portlet container, the portlet container will need to serialize the event payload to send it across the network. The remote portlet container will then need to deserialize the event payload to make it available to the receiver portlets. To support inter-portlet communication with remote portlets, portlet containers use JAXB to serialize the event payload (a Java object) set by the sender portlet to XML, and then to deserialize the XML back to the event payload and to make it available to the receiver portlet. JAXB doesn't know how to instantiate the `BookAddedEvent` class, so you need to provide a no-argument constructor.

It's important to note that if sender and receiver portlets are located in the same Java runtime, the portlet container can use the Java serialization mechanism to pass the event payload or it can pass a reference to the event payload object to the receiver portlet. Your receiver portlet implementation should be independent of the mechanism (JAXB, Java serialization, or object reference) used by the portlet container.

> **NOTE**   The Book Catalog portlet in the current example sends the complete details of the newly added book as the event payload, to demonstrate that the event payload can be a complex object and not just a `String` object.

When `BookAddedEvent` is set by the Book Catalog portlet, it's serialized to an XML document by the portlet container, as shown here:

```
<?xml version="1.0" encoding="UTF-8" standalone="yes"?>
<bookAddedEvent>
    <author>Ramnivas Laddad</author>
    <category>Java</category>
    <isbnNumber>1933988053</isbnNumber>
    <name>AspectJ in Action, Second Edition</name>
</bookAddedEvent>
```

The preceding XML fragment shows that the properties of `BookAddedEvent` were converted to subelements of `bookAddedEvent`.

> **NOTE**   You don't need to learn JAXB in depth unless your portlet events represent a complex object structure consisting of custom Java objects, for which JAXB doesn't provide default bindings. For more details on JAXB, see the JAXB website (http://jaxb.dev.java.net).

CONFIGURING GLASSFISH WITH OPENPORTAL PORTLET CONTAINER

If you're using Java SE 6, you don't need to include the jaxb-api JAR file to compile the source code of the ch11_BookCatalog_event and ch11_RecentBook_event projects because JAXB is included with Java SE 6.

If you're using Java SE 5, you do need the jaxb-api JAR file to build the projects. If you're using Java SE 5 to run the examples, you must have jaxb-api, stax-api, and the stax implementation JAR files in the server classpath, as described in section 1.7.1 of chapter 1.

CONFIGURING LIFERAY PORTAL 5.2.3

If you're using Liferay Portal 5.2.3 (and not Liferay Portal 6.x), you need to add the JAR file containing your event class, and any classes that it depends on, to your server's classpath. The `BookAddedEvent` that's sent from the Book Catalog portlet to the Recently Added Book portlet depends on the `Book` class, so the `BookAddedEvent` and `Book` classes must be packaged in a JAR file and put in the server classpath.

You can create a JAR file from the source code of the ch11_BookCatalog_event or ch11_RecentBook_event projects by using the Eclipse IDE's JAR export utility. If you're using Liferay Portal bundled with Tomcat, you can add the generated JAR file to the TOMCAT_HOME/lib/ext folder and add it to the server classpath, as described in section 1.7.1 of chapter 1.

> **NOTE** A bookAddedEvent.jar JAR file is already provided in the event-jar subfolder of ch11_BookCatalog_event.

Setting events in the `ActionResponse` or `EventResponse` object is the necessary first step in sending events to other portlets. You also need to define, in the portlet deployment descriptor, the events that a portlet publishes.

DEFINING EVENTS IN THE PORTLET DEPLOYMENT DESCRIPTOR

To publish an event, you must do the following:

- Define the event at the portlet application level.
- Define support for the event in portlets that publish it.

The next listing shows how the Book Catalog portlet defines the `bookAddedEvent` in portlet.xml.

Listing 11.9 Defining an event in the Book Catalog portlet's portlet.xml file

```
<portlet-app...>
  <portlet>
    <portlet-name>bookCatalog</portlet-name>           ❶ Book Catalog portlet
    <portlet-class>                                        definition
      chapter11.code.listing.base.BookCatalogPortlet
    </portlet-class>
    ...
    <supported-publishing-event>
        <qname xmlns:n="http://www.mynamespace.com">   ❷ Supported
          n:bookAddedEvent</qname>                          publishing event
    </supported-publishing-event>
  </portlet>
  <event-definition>
    <qname xmlns:n="http://www.mynamespace.com">       ❸ Event
      n:bookAddedEvent</qname>                              definition
    <value-type>chapter11.code.listing.base.
      BookAddedEvent</value-type>
  </event-definition>
  ...
</portlet-app>
```

The Book Catalog portlet name and class are specified ❶. The `<event-definition>` subelement of the `<portlet-app>` element ❸ defines the event that one or more portlets in the portlet application can publish or process.

The <event-definition> element is specified as follows:

- The <qname> element specifies the qualified name of the event: bookAdded-Event is the local name, and http://www.mynamespace.com is the namespace.
- The <value-type> element specifies the fully qualified name of the class that acts as the event payload.

If you want to use a default namespace for the events defined in portlet.xml, you should use the <default-namespace> subelement of <portlet-app>. If you are using <default-namespace>, instead of <qname> you should use the <name> element to specify a local name for the event.

The <supported-publishing-event> subelement of the <portlet> element ❷ defines support for the bookAddedEvent event. In <supported-publishing-event>, you can identify an event using either a qualified name or a local name. The <qname> element has been used here because <event-definition> defines the bookAdded-Event event with a qualified name. Alternatively, you can use the <name> element to identify an event with a local name.

> **NOTE**   You can use the getPublishingEventQNames method of the Portlet-Config object to obtain the QNames of the events published by a portlet.

This is all you need to do to send portlet events. You may have gotten a déjà vu feeling while going through the event definition in portlet.xml, because events and public render parameters are defined similarly. Now let's look at how portlets can receive events published by other portlets.

11.5.2 *Receiving portlet events*

To receive portlet events, a portlet must do the following:

- The portlet must define in portlet.xml the events that it can process.
- The portlet implementation class must implement the EventPortlet interface.

DEFINING EVENTS THAT A PORTLET CAN PROCESS
In listing 11.7 you saw how the Book Catalog portlet sets the bookAddedEvent portlet event. Listing 11.9 showed how that event is exposed to other portlets by defining it in portlet.xml. As the Recently Added Book portlet is interested in bookAddedEvent, it defines support for processing the event, as shown next.

> **Listing 11.10   Defining support for processing an event in the portlet.xml file**

```
<portlet-app...>
  <portlet>
    <portlet-name>recentBook</portlet-name>
    <portlet-class>
      chapter11.code.listing.base.
        ➥RecentlyAddedBookPortlet
    </portlet-class>
    ...
```

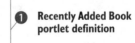

❶ Recently Added Book portlet definition

```
    <supported-processing-event>
        <qname xmlns:n="http://www.mynamespace.com">
            n:bookAddedEvent</qname>
    </supported-processing-event>
</portlet>
<event-definition>
    <qname xmlns:n="http://www.mynamespace.com">
        n:bookAddedEvent</qname>
    <value-type>chapter11.code.listing.base.
        BookAddedEvent</value-type>
</event-definition>
    ...
</portlet-app>
```

❷ **Supported processing event**

❸ **Event definition**

The Recently Added Book portlet name and class are specified ❶. The `<supported-processing-event>` element ❷ specifies that the Recently Added Book portlet supports processing for the `bookAddedEvent` event. `<event-definition>` specifies the `bookAddedEvent` event and its payload object ❸.

> **NOTE** Portlets that publish events use the `<supported-publishing-event>` element to specify the event that they publish, and portlets that consume or receive or process events use the `<supported-processing-event>` element to specify the events that they can process. A portlet can use both of these elements to specify events it publishes and consumes. You can obtain the QNames of the events that a portlet can process using the `PortletConfig` object's `get-ProcessingEventQNames` method.

Now that you've defined support for the `bookAddedEvent` event, let's see how the event is processed by the portlet.

IMPLEMENTING THE EVENTPORTLET INTERFACE

You saw in chapter 2 that the `Portlet` interface provides `render` and `processAction` lifecycle methods, which handle render and action requests respectively. Event processing is an optional feature for portlets, so it's defined in a separate interface, `EventPortlet`.

The `EventPortlet` interface defines a single method that has the following signature:

```
void processEvent(EventRequest request, EventResponse response)
  throws PortletException, java.io.IOException
```

If your portlet is to receive events from other portlets, your portlet class must implement the `EventPortlet` interface, directly or indirectly. The portlet's `processEvent` method is executed when events for the portlet are received by the portlet container.

> **NOTE** Events aren't delivered immediately to other portlets when you set them in your portlet class (see listing 11.7). The portlet container records all the events set by the sender portlets and delivers them to the receiver portlets before initiating the render phase for all the portlets on the portal page.

If your portlet class extends the `GenericPortlet` class, you don't need to worry about implementing the `EventPortlet` interface, because `GenericPortlet` already implements it. The default implementation of the `processEvent` method in `Generic-Portlet` attempts to invoke the `@ProcessEvent` annotated method defined for the received event. The following listing shows the `@ProcessEvent` annotated event for the Recently Added Book portlet.

Listing 11.11 The process event in the `RecentlyAddedBookPortlet` class

```
import javax.portlet.Event;
public class RecentlyAddedBookPortlet extends GenericPortlet {
  ...
  @ProcessEvent(qname=                                      ❶ Specifies @ProcessEvent
    "{http://www.mynamespace.com}bookAddedEvent")              annotation
  public void processAddedBookEvent(EventRequest
    request, EventResponse eventResponse) throws...{

    Event event = request.getEvent();                       ❷ Retrieves event and
    BookAddedEvent bookAddedEvent =                            its payload
      (BookAddedEvent)event.getValue();

    eventResponse.setRenderParameter("category",
      bookAddedEvent.getCategory());
    eventResponse.setRenderParameter("name",
      bookAddedEvent.getName());                            ❸ Sets render
    eventResponse.setRenderParameter("author",                parameters in
      bookAddedEvent.getAuthor());                            response
    eventResponse.setRenderParameter("isbnNumber",
      String.valueOf(bookAddedEvent.getIsbnNumber()));
  }
}
```

The `@ProcessEvent` annotation ❶ specifies that the `processAddedBookEvent` method processes the `bookAddedEvent`. You can specify the `qname` or `name` element in the `@ProcessEvent` annotation: the `qname` element is used to identify the event using its `QName` (see listing 11.7); the `name` element is used to identify the event using its local name. Listing 11.11 uses the `qname` element because `QName` was used to define the event, as shown in listings 11.7, 11.9, and 11.10. The value of the `qname` element has the following format:

```
{<namespace-uri>}<local-name>
```

Here, `namespace-uri` identifies the namespace URI associated with the event, and `local-name` identifies the local name of the event. The `processAddedEvent` is the event processing method, which accepts `EventRequest` and `EventResponse` objects as arguments.

The `getEvent` method of `EventRequest` ❷ returns the `Event` object associated with the incoming event. The `getValue` method of the `Event` object returns the payload object associated with the event, which is the `BookAddedEvent` object in this case.

The book details ❸ are retrieved from the `BookAddedEvent` object and are set as render parameters in `EventResponse`.

WARNING The order in which events are executed isn't necessarily the order in which they're set by the portlet. The portlet container may reorder the events before delivering them to the receiver portlets.

One of the interesting things to notice in listing 11.11 is the use of the `setRender-Parameter` method to set render parameters in `EventResponse`. You've seen in earlier chapters that render parameters are set in the action method and are available in the following render method. Similarly, render parameters set in the event method are available in the following render method. Because the event method is invoked after the action method, it's possible to replace or remove the render parameters set in the action method.

Let's now look at the pros and cons of using portlet events in inter-portlet communication.

11.5.3 Advantages and disadvantages of using portlet events

Portlet events offer a sophisticated form of event-driven portlet communication that's coupled with the portlet lifecycle.

These are the advantages of using portlet events for communication:

- Portlet events are associated with a payload object, which is useful in communicating complex information. Public render parameters can only send `String` values to receiver portlets.
- The portlet container removes (or expires) the cached content of the portlet that is the target of a portlet event. This feature isn't available for public render parameters. Content expiration guarantees that the render method of the receiver portlet is invoked and fresh content is generated.
- You can create event chains. If portlet *A* processes event *X*, then it can generate another event *Y* in the event method. Event *Y* is processed by portlet *B*, which generates event *Z* in its event method. This can go on and can be used to create an interconnected network of portlets that are affected by the single event *X*.

These are some disadvantages of using portlet events for communication:

- Portlet event processing puts an extra strain on the portlet container, impacting the performance of the web portal. For simple cases, it's preferable to use public render parameters.
- You can't make an existing portlet publish or process events, because it requires writing event processing code or setting portlet events. When using public render parameters, you can make portlets communicate with each other without writing any code.
- A portlet must be the target of action processing to generate an event in the first place, but if your web portal stores public render parameters in the URL, you can have all the portlets on the portal page show relevant content without any user actions.

- Portlet events aren't guaranteed to be delivered to the target portlets, so receiver portlets should behave appropriately even when the events aren't received.

So far in this chapter, we've discussed different approaches for implementing inter-portlet communication. Remember those tough chapters on Spring Portlet MVC? Let's take a quick look at how you can implement inter-portlet communication when using the Spring Portlet MVC framework.

11.5.4 Event support in Spring Portlet MVC

In chapter 7, you saw that you can create Spring controllers by implementing the `org.springframework.web.portlet.mvc.Controller` interface. The `Controller` interface doesn't define any methods for processing events because, as mentioned earlier, it's an optional feature in portlets. But the Spring Portlet MVC's `EventAware-Controller` provides event processing capabilities to controllers. It defines only one method with the following signature:

```
void handleEventRequest(javax.portlet.EventRequest request,
                        javax.portlet.EventResponse response)
                throws Exception
```

You can see that the `handleEventRequest` method is similar to the `processEvent` method defined in the `javax.portlet.EventPortlet` interface of the Portlet 2.0 API.

If you're using annotated controllers, you can annotate any method with the `@EventMapping` annotation to specify that the method is meant for processing events. That wasn't so hard, was it?

11.6 Summary

In this chapter, we discussed how portlets can use `PortletSession`, public render parameters, and portlet events to coordinate with other portlets in the web portal. It's hardly possible to create a web portal with portlets that work in silos, so it's important to carefully choose the inter-portlet mechanism that fits your web portal requirements. You can end up using all three inter-portlet communication approaches in your web portal, depending upon the communication needs of your portlets. One of the biggest advantages of having portlets that communicate with each other is that it enriches the user experience of the web portal; at any given time, the portlets reflect content that's relevant in the context of user actions.

As mentioned at the beginning of this chapter, there are multiple ways in which portlets can communicate with each other; in chapter 12 we'll look at how portlets can communicate using the Comet (or *Ajax Push*) mechanism.

So far in this book, you've seen examples in which you upload a book's TOC into a database or to a file folder. In the next chapter, we'll explore the `Resource-ServingPortlet` interface of Portlet 2.0 and see how it can be used to download resources in portlets.

Ajaxing portlets

12

This chapter covers

- Developing highly responsive portlets using Ajax
- Serving resources with the `ResourceServingPortlet` interface
- Sending resource requests with resource URLs
- Resource serving support in Spring Portlet MVC
- Pushing data with Comet (or Reverse Ajax)

Developing highly responsive portlets is crucial for an enriched user experience. In this chapter, we'll see how Ajax can be used to that end. This chapter provides a gentle introduction to Ajax, and it should be sufficient if you're new to Ajax. The chapter does, however, assume that you have a basic understanding of JavaScript, CSS, and DOM (the Document Object Model). If you're new to JavaScript, CSS, and DOM, please refer to resources that cover these topics.

We'll also look at how the `ResourceServingPortlet` interface provides Ajax support to portlets, and how you can secure Ajax requests in the portal world. The `ResourceServingPortlet` interface serves the dual purpose of handling Ajax requests and serving binary content, so we'll also look at how to download a binary file from a portlet that implements the `ResourceServingPortlet` interface.

Once you have a good grip on the basics of Ajax and how it can be used to develop portlets, we'll look at how Ajax can be used to develop rich user interfaces in the context of the Book Catalog portlet. We'll use the Ajax support available in the Dojo, jQuery, and DWR JavaScript frameworks—the three most popular frameworks for developing applications using Ajax.

At the end of the chapter, we'll also look at the emerging *Comet* (or Reverse Ajax) and the traditional *polling* approach to creating portlets that display real-time data. We'll look at how the Book Catalog portlet example uses Comet to notify users every time a book is added or removed from the catalog.

> **NOTE**   Downloading binary content isn't related to the concept of Ajax, but it's covered in this chapter because the `ResourceServingPortlet` interface's `serveResource` method isn't only responsible for handling Ajax requests, but also for serving binary content.

You may be wondering why Ajax is important in developing highly responsive portlets. Let's say that you create a portal page that consists of multiple portlets. Each portlet on this portal page retrieves its data from one or more databases during the render phase, so the load time of the portal page is high.

Now, imagine that one of the portlets on this portal page is the Book Catalog portlet. If a user clicks the Add Book button on the Book Catalog portlet's home page, an HTTP request is sent to the portal server, and the portal page may disappear momentarily from your computer screen as the whole portal page is submitted to the server. The portlet request corresponding to the Add Book button click is processed by the portlet container and additionally invokes the render methods of all the portlets on the portal page. This portlet request handling process results in a significant delay in displaying the Add Book form.

As you can see, sometimes even the simplest of user actions on the portal page results in significant overhead on the portal server. If the processing for the submitted portlet request takes a long time, the user can't do anything with the portal page during that time. We need some mechanism to address these issues with submitting and reloading the complete portal page. This is where Ajax comes into the picture.

Ajax is short for *Asynchronous JavaScript and XML*. It isn't a single technology but a set of technologies, like JavaScript, CSS, DOM, and so on, that allows you to create highly interactive portlets. When using Ajax, the entire portal page isn't submitted to the portal server. Instead, portlets send only the necessary request details over the HTTP protocol to the portal server. The response returned by the portal server represents data that's used by JavaScript embedded in the portal page to update the *dynamic content* of the portlet, and *not* the complete portal page.

NOTE When an HTML form of a portlet is submitted, only that form is submitted to the portal server, and not the entire portal page. Because the complete portal page disappears from the browser on submitting a form, I've mentioned that the entire portal page is submitted.

These are the benefits of using Ajax in portlets:

- *Reduced network traffic*—Requests contain only relevant request information, so the amount of request data sent to the server is less than submitting the complete portal page. Also, the portal server doesn't generate the complete portal page but sends only limited data to the client browser. As a result of this reduced network traffic, portals that use Ajax provide an enriched user experience even over slow networks.

- *Enriched user experience*—The user experience takes a hit in web portals if the portal page is reloaded every time the user interacts with a portlet. Because the entire portal page isn't reloaded to display updated content when using Ajax, the user experience is improved.

- *Asynchronous request processing*—A typical Ajax request is asynchronous; portal users need not wait for a request to be processed to initiate a new request. We'll see an example of this feature later in the chapter.

- *Highly interactive portlets*—You can use Ajax to create highly interactive portlets that deliver rich user interfaces. For instance, you can show information in a data grid (as in Microsoft Excel) that users can directly modify, and let Ajax take care of persisting changes in the background.

It's difficult to find a popular website these days that doesn't make use of Ajax. Gmail, Flickr, Facebook, and Twitter, among others, make use of Ajax to make web pages more responsive.

Let's now look at what makes Ajax ideal for developing highly responsive portlets.

12.1 Ajax basics

Building portlets using Ajax is a slightly more involved process than building conventional portlets, which is why I've waited until this chapter to go into it. In a typical Ajax-based portlet, a servlet or portlet component is responsible for processing the request and returning response data. JavaScript in the web browser is responsible for sending the request and processing the response data to update the portlet content.

Figure 12.1 shows how the various Ajax technologies work together to create dynamic portlets.

The user performs some action on the portlet ❶ by clicking a button or a hyperlink. The JavaScript that was loaded as part of the portal page ❷ initiates an *asynchronous* HTTP or HTTPS request in response to the user action. This request is referred to as an *Ajax request*. The servlet or portlet component that is the target of this request is responsible for processing the request and returning a response to the web browser.

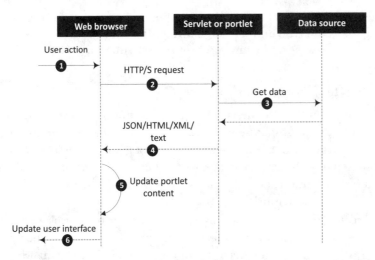

Figure 12.1 Ajax request handling. JavaScript in the portal page sends an asynchronous request to a servlet or portlet component, which processes the request and returns an HTML, XML, text, or JSON response to the browser. JavaScript in the portal page makes use of the response data to update a part of the portlet's content.

As part of the request processing, the portlet or servlet component ❸ retrieves data from a data store, and ❹ it returns the response to the Ajax request in one of the following formats: XML, HTML, plain text, or JSON (JavaScript Object Notation). The JavaScript that was loaded as part of the portal page ❺ processes the returned response to update the portlet content. The updated portlet content ❻ is made visible to the portal user.

You saw in earlier chapters that servlet and portlet components are used to return an HTML response. Figure 12.1 shows that when dealing with Ajax requests, servlet and portlet components can return HTML, XML, JSON, or plain text, depending upon the portlet or servlet developer's choice.

Figure 12.1 also shows a scenario in which response data is obtained from a data store. Ajax isn't limited to retrieving data from portlet or servlet components—you can also use Ajax to perform update operations in portlet or servlet components. For instance, you can use Ajax to submit an HTML form to a servlet or portlet that updates the data store with the user-entered values in the form.

Enough theory! Let's get started with writing a simple portlet using Ajax, and along the way you'll learn how Ajax can be used in web portals.

12.2 *Your first Ajax portlet*

In this section, we'll use Ajax to develop a Date/Time portlet that displays the server's current date and time. We'll first look at the requirements for the Date/Time portlet, and then we'll implement it step by step.

Refresh hyperlink

Server's current date and time

Figure 12.2   A Date/Time portlet that displays a "Hello World" message and the server's current date and time when the Refresh hyperlink is clicked

Figure 12.2 shows a Date/Time portlet that displays a "Hello World" message and the server date and time when a user clicks the Refresh hyperlink.

Suppose for a moment that we were building the Date/Time portlet in the same way we built the portlets in previous chapters. We would write a render method in the portlet class that generates content consisting of a Refresh hyperlink and the server's date and time, as shown in figure 12.2. The Refresh hyperlink would refer to the portlet's render URL, so when a user clicked the Refresh hyperlink, the render method of the portlet would be invoked to generate the Refresh hyperlink and the server date and time. This would achieve the functionality we expect from the Date/Time portlet—but at a cost. The render methods of all the portlets on the portal page would be invoked when the Refresh hyperlink was clicked, resulting in reduced portal performance. It would also adversely affect the user experience of the web portal, because the user would have to wait for the portal page to be reloaded by the browser to show the server date and time.

Instead, as you saw in figure 12.1, we need to do the following to develop an Ajax portlet:

- Create a portlet that displays the server's date and time.
- Write JavaScript that will send an asynchronous Ajax request to a servlet or to the portlet instance.
- Write a servlet that processes the Ajax request. You can also use the portlet instance itself to handle Ajax requests, as you'll see later in this chapter.
- Write Ajax request-handling logic in the servlet or portlet to process the Ajax request and return a response in one of the following formats: JSON, XML, HTML, or plain text.
- Write JavaScript that will process the response returned by the portlet or servlet and update the portlet content.

For the sake of simplicity, we'll develop a Date/Time portlet in which the Ajax request is handled by a servlet and that returns an HTML response. Let's see how each of the above-mentioned functions is realized in our example Date/Time portlet.

> **CODE REFERENCE**   You should now import the ch12_DateTime Eclipse project that accompanies this book in order to see how the code references in this section are used in the example portlet.

12.2.1   *Creating a portlet that displays date and time*

The first thing that you need to do is create a portlet that will show the server date and time.

DateTimePortlet in the ch12_DateTime project is a simple portlet that shows the home.jsp JSP page when a render request in VIEW portlet mode is received.

> **Listing 12.1   The DateTimePortlet class**

```
public class DateTimePortlet extends GenericPortlet {

 @RenderMode(name = "view")
 public void showHomePage(RenderRequest request,
    RenderResponse response)throws ...{

    ...
    getPortletContext().getRequestDispatcher(        Shows home.jsp
    response.encodeURL("/WEB-INF/jsp/home.jsp"))     page
    .include(request, response);
 }
}
```

As you can see, DateTimePortlet is like any regular portlet with no Ajax-specific request-handling code. You'll see later in this chapter how Ajax request-handling code can also be defined within the portlet class itself. In this example, though, we'll use a servlet component to do the Ajax request handling.

12.2.2   *Sending Ajax requests using the XMLHttpRequest object*

The XMLHttpRequest object is the backbone of Ajax—it's used for sending and receiving HTTP requests and responses. The XMLHttpRequest object is provided by the web browser, so if you're using a browser, you can access the XMLHttpRequest object via JavaScript. Most modern web browsers, like Internet Explorer, Firefox, Chrome, Safari, and so on, support the XMLHttpRequest object.

> **NOTE**   In this chapter, we'll refer to the HTTP request sent by the web browser's XMLHttpRequest object as the *Ajax request.*

The DateTimePortlet's home.jsp page, which contains a JavaScript function to send an Ajax request, is shown next.

> **Listing 12.2   Sending an Ajax request with the XMLHttpRequest object**

```
<%@include file="include.jsp"%>                            ❶ Defines
                                                             setCurrentDateTime
<script type='text/javascript'>                              function
 function <portlet:namespace/>setCurrentDateTime() {
    var xhr = new XMLHttpRequest();
    ...                                                    ❷ Creates
    var url =                                                XMLHttpRequest
     "<%=request.getContextPath()%>/DateTimeServlet"         object, sends request
    xhr.open("GET", url, true);
    xhr.send();
 }
```

```
</script>
<table>
 <tr>
  <td><b><a href="#"
    onclick="<portlet:namespace/>setCurrentDateTime();"
    style="color: black;">Refresh</a></b></td>
 </tr>
</table>
<br/>
<div id="<portlet:namespace/>messageText">
</div>
```

❸ Creates Refresh hyperlink

❹ Defines empty messageText div element

The `setCurrentDateTime` JavaScript function is defined ❶, which is responsible for sending an HTTP request to a servlet component.

A new instance of `XMLHttpRequest` is created ❷ and an Ajax request is sent to `Date-TimeServlet`. The `url` variable specifies the URL of the `DateTimeServlet` servlet that's responsible for handling the request sent by `XMLHttpRequest`. The `XMLHttpRequest`'s `open` method is used to initialize the `XMLHttpRequest` object instance with the HTTP request method, the URL to which the request is sent, and a flag to indicate whether the request is asynchronous or synchronous. For instance, the `xhr.open("GET", url, true)` method invocation indicates the following:

- The request uses the HTTP `GET` method.
- The `DateTimeServlet`, identified by the `url` argument, is responsible for handling the request.
- The request must be sent asynchronously, as specified by the `true` argument.

The `XMLHttpRequest`'s `send` method sends the request to the specified URL. Because the previous line has already specified that the request is sent asynchronously, the `send` method returns immediately. If the request is sent synchronously, the `send` method would return only after the response is received from the target servlet.

NOTE Some browsers may cache response generated by Ajax requests. Though it's not shown in listing 12.2, current date and time (obtained using the JavaScript `Date` object) is appended to the `DateTimeServlet` servlet URL so that the browser treats each Ajax request to `DateTimeServlet` as unique.

The Refresh hyperlink ❸ invokes the `setCurrentDateTime` JavaScript function when it's clicked; an Ajax request is dispatched to `DateTimeServlet` each time the user clicks the Refresh hyperlink.

An empty HTML `div` element ❹ is defined with an id of `<portlet:namespace/>messageText`, which is a placeholder to show the current server date and time. You'll see shortly how the current server date and time, received from `DateTimeServlet`, is placed inside this `div` element.

Because you can specify in the `XMLHttpRequest`'s `open` method that the request is synchronous, you can have both *synchronous* and *asynchronous* Ajax requests. In listing 12.2, the `GET` HTTP asynchronous request is sent to the `DateTimeServlet` to retrieve date and time information from the server. `XMLHttpRequest` also supports

sending POST, HEAD, PUT, DELETE, and OPTIONS HTTP requests to servlet and portlet components.

> **NOTE** When using Ajax, it's important to uniquely identify HTML elements
> and JavaScript functions that belong to the portlet, to avoid calling another
> portlet's function or updating another portlet's content. Listing 12.2 uses the
> <namespace> tag of the portlet tag library to uniquely identify HTML elements
> and JavaScript functions. For more information on the <namespace> tag, refer
> to chapter 6.

Now that you know how to send an asynchronous HTTP request using the XMLHttp-
Request object, you're ready to look at how DateTimeServlet handles the request
and returns a response.

12.2.3 *Handling Ajax requests using portlet or servlet components*

A portlet or a servlet component can handle the requests sent by the XMLHttpRequest
object. The DateTimeServlet servlet, which is responsible for processing the GET
HTTP request sent by the XMLHttpRequest object, is shown next.

Listing 12.3   Ajax request handling in the DateTimeServlet

```
import java.io.OutputStream;

public class DateTimeServlet extends HttpServlet {

  public void doGet(HttpServletRequest request,          ❶ Processes HTTP
    HttpServletResponse response) ... {                     GET requests
  SimpleDateFormat sdf =
    new SimpleDateFormat("dd-MMM-yyyy hh:mm:ss a");
  OutputStream outStream = response.getOutputStream();
  StringBuffer buffer = new StringBuffer();
  buffer.append("Hello World (<i> "                      ❷ Constructs string containing
    + sdf.format(new Date()) + " </i>)");                   server date and time
  outStream.write(buffer.toString().getBytes());         ❸ Writes server date
  }                                                          and time to response
}
```

In listing 12.3, DateTimeServlet returns an HTML fragment as a response in its doGet
method. The DateTimeServlet's doGet method ❶ handles GET HTTP requests
received from the XMLHttpRequest object. A string containing the "Hello World" message followed by the server date and time ❷ is created. The use of the <i> HTML tag,
which shows the server date and time in italics, reflects that it is indeed an HTML
response. This is the data that we need to send to the calling XMLHttpRequest object.
The response data ❸ is written out to the HttpServletResponse object.

> **NOTE** The only difference between a plain text response and an HTML
> response is that a plain text response doesn't contain HTML tags.

The DateTimeServlet in listing 12.3 returns an HTML response to XMLHttpRequest,
which you need to put in the <div> element identified by the messageText id in the

home.jsp page (refer to listing 12.2). The `XMLHttpRequest` object provides the means to obtain the response from the target servlet or portlet component.

Let's look at how the home.jsp page makes use of the response from the `Date-TimeServlet` to show the server date and time.

12.2.4 *Retrieving the servlet response to update portlet content*

The `XMLHttpRequest` object provides an event listener, `onreadystatechange`, that's invoked during asynchronous request processing. As the request passes through each phase, the JavaScript function identified by the `onreadystatechange` event listener is invoked, allowing you to perform custom actions.

For instance, in the following code fragment, the `showDateTime` method is invoked whenever a request enters a particular phase:

```
function <portlet:namespace/>refreshDateTime() {
  var xhr = new XMLHttpRequest();
  xhr.onreadystatechange = showDateTime;
  ...
}
```

You can use the `XMLHttpRequest` object's `readyState` attribute to determine the current phase of the request. The following code fragment shows how the `showDateTime` method can use the `readyState` attribute to find the current request phase and perform a specific action if the value of `readyState` is 4. (The possible values of the `readyState` attribute are outlined in table 12.1.)

```
function showDateTime() {
  if(this.readyState == 4) {
    ... do something
  }
}
```

In this code, `this` refers to the `XMLHttpRequest` object with which the JavaScript function is associated.

Instead of separately defining the `showDateTime` function, you can also define it as an inline JavaScript function, as shown here:

```
function <portlet:namespace/>refreshDateTime() {
  var xhr = new XMLHttpRequest();
  xhr.onreadystatechange = function() {
    if(this.readyState == 4) {
      ...do something
    }
  };
  ...
}
```

The various phases of an asynchronous request sent by `XMLHttpRequest` are described in table 12.1. In most scenarios, you'll be interested in performing an action only after the request processing is complete, when the `readyState` attribute value is 4.

Table 12.1 `XMLHttpRequest` phases

XMLHttpRequest phase	readyState attribute value	Description
Opened	1	Indicates that the `open()` method of `XMLHttpRequest` has been invoked
Sent	2	Indicates that the `send()` method of `XMLHttpRequest` has been invoked
Loading	3	Indicates that the response headers have been received and that the loading of the response data is about to start
Complete	4	Indicates that the request processing is complete and that the response data is now available

Once the request processing is complete, you need some way to access the response data. This data can be obtained using the following methods of the `XMLHttp-Request` object:

- `responseText`—Returns response data as plain text. You'll use this method to obtain HTML, plain text, or JSON response data.
- `responseXML`—Returns response data as a DOM `Document` object.

Because we're returning an HTML response from `DateTimeServlet`, we'll use the `responseText` method. The following listing shows how the `setCurrentDateTime` JavaScript function of the home.jsp page displays the server date and time received from `DateTimeServlet`.

Listing 12.4   Displaying the server date and time on the home.jsp page

```
<script type='text/javascript'>
 function <portlet:namespace/>setCurrentDateTime() {        ❶ Processes
   var xhr = new XMLHttpRequest();                             response data
   xhr.onreadystatechange = function() {                     ❷ Checks if request
     if(xhr.readyState == 4) {                                  is complete
       var messageText = document.
       getElementById("<portlet:namespace/>messageText");   ❸ Obtains and displays
       messageText.innerHTML = xhr.responseText;               response data
     }
   };
   var url =
   "<%=request.getContextPath()%>/DateTimeServlet";
   xhr.open("GET", url, true);
   xhr.send();
 }
</script>
```

The `onreadystatechange` event listener ❶ defines an inline JavaScript function that handles events generated as the request goes through different phases of processing.

If the request processing is complete—if the value of the `XMLHttpRequest` object's `readyState` property is 4—the response received from `DateTimeServlet` ❷ will be displayed. The `document` object's `getElementId` method ❸ is used to obtain a reference to the `messageText` element in the HTML. The `innerHTML` property of the `<div>` element with the `messageText` id is used to set the HTML fragment inside the `<div>` tag.

You've now created your first portlet using Ajax. If you deploy the example Date/Time portlet and click the Refresh hyperlink, you'll find that it fetches the server date and time without reloading the complete portal page. The Date/Time portlet demonstrates that by using Ajax you can create portlets that are dynamic but that don't need to reload your complete portal page, resulting in enriched user experience.

In this Date/Time portlet, you've used a servlet component to handle requests sent by the `XMLHttpRequest` object. The main drawback with using servlets to handle Ajax requests is *security*. A servlet component is outside the portal permission system, which only applies to portlets, making it accessible to anonymous users. For instance, if you enter the URL of the `DateTimeServlet` in your web browser, it will execute its `doGet` method and return the server date and time.

Let's now look at how you can deal with security issues related to Ajax in the portlet environment.

12.3 Securing Ajax requests

Security is an important aspect of applications, including portals, that use Ajax. A portal server provides a security framework for the web portal, and it's responsible for authenticating and authorizing portlet requests.

Servlets fall outside the portal security framework provided by the portal server, and it's up to the portal server to provide proprietary ways of securing servlets or to leave it to the portlet developer to implement a custom security framework for securing servlets. If the portlet developer is responsible for implementing servlet security, then the developer is responsible for creating portlets that can share authentication and authorization data with servlets using portlet sessions.

In the context of the Date/Time portlet, let's see how you can secure Ajax requests dispatched to a servlet.

12.3.1 Date/Time portlet's security requirements and possible solutions

Let's say that you want the server date and time to be visible in the Date/Time portlet only for *registered* users of the portal. By default, Liferay Portal assigns the User role to registered users, so you need to secure the `DateTimeServlet` from users who don't have the User role.

A simple way to achieve this is by storing the role of the logged-in user in the `PortletSession`'s `APPLICATION_SCOPE` scope in the `DateTimePortlet`, and then checking for the User role in the `DateTimeServlet`.

> **NOTE** Alternatively, you can restrict the portlet so it's displayed only to registered users. The Date/Time portlet shows an invented scenario in which we

want to secure only the Ajax requests that will be processed by a servlet component. In real-world portlets, only a portion of the portlet content is shown using Ajax requests, so hiding the portlet in such a scenario isn't an option.

It's possible that the servlet component responsible for processing Ajax requests is outside the portlet application. In such cases, you'll have to rely on a portal server–specific feature to share the `PortletSession` across different web applications. For instance, in Liferay Portal you can share `APPLICATION_SCOPE` session attributes with portlets in other portlet applications by setting the `session.shared.attributes` property in the portal-ext.properties file (discussed in appendix B) and the `<private-session-attributes>` element in the `liferay-portlet.xml` file. Note that such features are portal server–specific and will result in portability issues.

> **CODE REFERENCE** This is a good time to import the ch12_DateTimeSecured Eclipse project into your Eclipse IDE. To compile the project, add the portal-service.jar JAR file, located in the TOMCAT_HOME/lib/ext directory of your Liferay Portal installation, to the build path of the project, and also add it to the lib directory of the project.

Let's now look at how the Date/Time portlet is secured using Liferay Portal–specific APIs.

12.3.2 *Implementing security using portal server–specific APIs*

To secure the Date/Time portlet, you first need to obtain the role of the logged-in user in the `render` method of `DateTimePortlet`, and then store that user's role in the `PortletSession`'s `APPLICATION_SCOPE` scope so that it's available to `DateTimeServlet` when the servlet receives the Ajax request.

The next listing shows how the `DateTimePortlet` class obtains the role of the current user using Liferay Portal's `RoleLocalServiceUtil` class and stores it in the `PortletSession`'s `APPLICATION_SCOPE`.

Listing 12.5 Storing user roles in `PortletSession`

```
import com.liferay.portal.model.Role;
import com.liferay.portal.service.RoleLocalServiceUtil;

public class DateTimePortlet extends GenericPortlet {

  @RenderMode(name = "view")
  public void showHomePage(...)... {
    List<String> userRoles = new ArrayList<String>();         ❶ Creates placeholder
    try {                                                          for user roles
      List<Role> roles = RoleLocalServiceUtil.
        getUserRoles(Long.valueOf(request.getRemoteUser()));
      for(Role role : roles) {                                 ❷ Obtains and
        userRoles.add(role.getName());                            adds user roles
      }                                                           to session
      request.getPortletSession().setAttribute("userRoles",
        userRoles, PortletSession.APPLICATION_SCOPE);
```

```
  } catch (Exception e) {
    ...
  }
  getPortletContext().getRequestDispatcher(
    response.encodeURL("/WEB-INF/jsp/home.jsp")).
    include(request,response);
  }
}
```

❸ Dispatches request to JSP page

The empty userRoles list ❶ is defined to hold the different role names associated with the current web portal user.

The getUserRoles(long userId) method ❷ of Liferay Portal's RoleLocal-ServiceUtil class returns the roles that the current user is associated with. The PortletRequest's getRemoteUser method returns the login ID of the logged-in user or null for unauthenticated users. The login ID isn't the username that you enter during login but the userid that's assigned to the authenticated user on successful login. In the case of Liferay Portal, the userid is a long number, stored in its USER_ table (refer to appendix B). The list returned by RoleLocalServiceUtil is used to populate the userRoles list with the role names associated with the user. The userRoles list is then set in the PortletSession's APPLICATION_SCOPE so that it's accessible to Date-TimeServlet, which is responsible for handling Ajax requests.

The portlet request ❸ is dispatched to the home.jsp page so the portlet content can be rendered.

As you saw in chapter 4, Liferay Portal's *Util utility classes provide static methods for accessing Liferay Portal services. Listing 12.5 uses the RoleLocalServiceUtil class to obtain user roles based on the userid. Behind the scenes, RoleLocalServiceUtil looks into the _USER, _ROLE, and USERS_ROLES tables in Liferay Portal to find out which roles a logged-in user is associated with.

> **NOTE** Java EE doesn't provide any standard approach for obtaining role information for an authenticated user, so you're limited to using portal server–specific APIs or database tables to find that role information.

Now that you've stored the user's role information as a session attribute, it'll be accessible to DateTimeServlet while it's processing the Ajax request. The following listing shows how DateTimeServlet provides programmatic security based on the user's role.

Listing 12.6 Role-based programmatic security in DateTimeServlet

```
public class DateTimeServlet extends HttpServlet {

  public void doGet(...)... {
    List<String> userRoles = (List<String>)
      request.getSession(false).getAttribute("userRoles");

    OutputStream outStream = response.getOutputStream();
    StringBuffer buffer = new StringBuffer();

    if (userRoles != null && userRoles.contains("User")) {
      SimpleDateFormat sdf = new SimpleDateFormat(
```

❶ Obtains role info from session

❷ Checks if user is in User role

```
    "dd-MMM-yyyy hh:mm:ss a");
  buffer.append("Hello World (<i> "
    + sdf.format(new Date()) + " </i>)");
} else {
  buffer.append("<font color=\"red\">
    ⟿You are not authorized to view server date/time");
}
outStream.write(buffer.toString().getBytes());
 }
}
```

③ Writes
appropriate
content to
response

The role information for the authenticated user is obtained from the HttpSession object ❶. If the user isn't authenticated, no role information is available. A check is made to determine whether the incoming HTTP request is from an authenticated user who belongs to the User' role ❷. If the user meets the criteria in the preceding check, a response message containing the server date and time is created ❸; otherwise, a response message saying, "You are not authorized to view server date/time" is created. The response content is then written out to the HttpServletResponse.

Listing 12.6 demonstrates that you can achieve role-based security in portlets that use Ajax by embedding the security logic in the servlet component. Most portal servers offer sophisticated access-control features to control which actions a user can perform on a portlet. If you want to use the same access control to secure Ajax requests, it will involve additional overhead to retrieve access control data and use it in the servlet component.

Portlet 2.0 introduced a new lifecycle interface, ResourceServingPortlet, which allows an implementing portlet to handle Ajax requests. Let's look at the Ajax support in Portlet 2.0 and see how it simplifies the development of Ajax portlets.

12.4   *Ajax support in Portlet 2.0*

Portlet 1.0 didn't provide any support for serving resources, like binary content. For instance, if you wanted to download a PDF file or a GIF image from a portlet, you had to use a servlet to implement the download functionality. Similarly, if you wanted to use Ajax in your portlets, the only option was to use a servlet component to handle the Ajax requests. To address these limitations, Portlet 2.0 introduced the ResourceServingPortlet lifecycle interface, which portlets can implement to handle Ajax requests.

Let's look at this interface in detail.

12.4.1 *Serving resources using the ResourceServingPortlet interface*

ResourceServingPortlet is a lifecycle interface that your portlet *must* implement if it needs to serve binary content or use Ajax to create a highly interactive user interface. If your portlet implements the ResourceServingPortlet interface, then your portlets don't need to use a servlet to serve binary content or handle Ajax requests. Because the portlet itself handles Ajax requests, they are secured by the portal's security infrastructure.

Even though Portlet 2.0 provides support for using Ajax, you may still prefer to use servlets to handle Ajax requests in some scenarios. For instance, if multiple portlets in your web portal need access to common functionality delivered via Ajax, it may make sense to deliver it via a servlet. If your Ajax request-handling logic is inside a portlet, it can't be reused by other portlets (because portlets *can't* create URLs referring to other portlets). In contrast, if the Ajax request-handling logic is inside a servlet, multiple portlets can easily access the servlet and reuse the logic. Also, if you're using an Ajax framework, like DWR (Direct Web Remoting), which uses a servlet to process Ajax requests dispatched by portlets, you need to secure that servlet using the approach discussed in the previous section.

`ResourceServingPortlet`, like the `EventPortlet` interface, is an optional lifecycle interface. It defines a single method that has the following signature:

```
void serveResource(ResourceRequest request,
   ResourceResponse response)
      throws PortletException, IOException
```

As you can see, the `serveResource` method accepts `ResourceRequest` and `Resource-Response` objects as arguments. It's invoked when the portlet container receives a resource request for a portlet.

The `ResourceRequest` object provides information that the portlet requires to process a resource request, including the resource identifier, portlet mode, render parameters, and so on. The *resource identifier* is a `String` value that uniquely identifies the resource to be served by the portlet.

The `ResourceResponse` object is used by a portlet to render a resource, such as an image. Like other request and response objects in portlets, the `ResourceRequest` and `ResourceResponse` objects are created by the portlet container and are made available to the `serveResource` method.

In chapter 3 you saw that `ResourceResponse` and `RenderResponse` are subinterfaces of `MimeResponse`, which means you can't publish portlet events, issue a redirect, or change window state, portlet mode, or render parameters during a `serveResource` method invocation. As in the `render` method, you can use `PortletRequestDispatcher` in the `serveResource` method to render *markup* using JSPs or servlets. This also means you can render markup as well as serve binary content, like images and PDF documents, in the `serveResource` method, but you need to be careful about choosing when to return markup and when to return binary content. We'll discuss that shortly.

Let's look at how resource requests are handled by portal servers. Suppose you have a portal page with two portlets, Portlet A and Portlet B. Figure 12.3 shows how a resource request for Portlet A is processed by the portal server.

A user performs some action on Portlet A on a web portal ❶, which kicks off a resource request. The resource request results in the invocation of Portlet A's `serveResource` method ❷. The response is returned from Portlet A—this could be HTML markup, XML, JSON, plain text, or any binary content ❸. The resource is served via the web portal ❹.

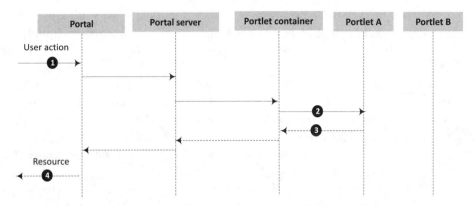

Figure 12.3   A sequence diagram of the resource request-processing lifecycle. The resource request doesn't result in the invocation of the `render` methods of other portlets on the portal page.

One of the interesting things to notice in figure 12.3 is that the portlet container completely ignores Portlet B and doesn't invoke its `render` method. It doesn't even invoke the `render` method of Portlet A. This means that whenever a resource request is dispatched to a portlet, neither the target portlet nor any other portlets on the portal page are rerendered by the portlet container.

You saw in chapter 2 that the portal server is responsible for combining the portlet content, putting window decoration around the content, composing the portal page, and so on. Because the portlet `render` methods aren't invoked and the window state, render parameters, and portlet mode can't be changed in the `serveResource` method, the portal page doesn't need to be updated by the portal server in response to the resource request. This means the role of portal server, in resource-request processing, is to simply dispatch the resource request to the portlet container and deliver the resource response *directly* to the web portal.

Because the resource response is delivered directly to the web portal, without any updates to the portal page, this makes it ideal for handling Ajax requests. The following advantages come with using the `serveResource` method to handle Ajax requests:

- *Security*—The portlet is within the portal's security infrastructure, so the call to `serveResource` is secured and can utilize the access controls defined by the portal's security framework.
- *Access to portlet state*—The `ResourceRequest` object provides portlet mode, window state, and render parameters, so the `serveResource` method can make use of this information while generating resource responses.
- *Access to* `PortletContext`—If you've defined any initialization parameters in your portlet, they're available in the `serveResource` method.
- *Access to* `PortletSession`—The portlet can make use of the `PortletSession` to obtain session data while processing Ajax requests in the `serveResource` method.

- *Access to* PortletPreferences—The portlet can access the PortletPreferences object associated with the portlet for the logged-in user, so the serveResource method can be used to customize responses based on preferences or to update user preferences.

The disadvantages of using the serveResource method to handle Ajax requests include these:

- *Performance*—Because the resource request is like any other portlet request and it's processed by multiple layers of the portal framework, it's slow compared to processing Ajax requests with a servlet.
- *Not reusable*—Because the Ajax request-processing logic is located within the portlet, it isn't reusable across multiple portlets. If you're using a servlet, it can be accessed by multiple portlets in the same or different portlet applications.

So far we've discussed how the ResourceServingPortlet interface can be used to address Ajax use cases and to download binary content, but how can you send a resource request to a portlet? Let's look at the self-referencing *resource URL* in portlets, which is used to send resource requests.

12.4.2 *Sending a resource request using a resource URL*

Like action and render URLs, a resource URL is a self-referencing URL that's used to send a resource request to a portlet. To create a resource URL, you can use the create-ResourceURL method of the RenderResponse or ResourceResponse object or you can use the portlet tag library's <resourceURL> tag. In either case, you should uniquely identify the resource that needs to be served by specifying a *resource ID*.

> **CODE REFERENCE** This is a good time to import the ch12_DateTime-SecuredResource Eclipse project into your Eclipse IDE. The code listings discussed in this section are used in that project's implementation of the Date/Time portlet.

Figure 12.2 showed that in the Date/Time portlet the Refresh hyperlink is responsible for retrieving the current server date and time. If you want to use the portlet's serveResource method to return the date and time information, the Refresh hyperlink must send an Ajax request to the resource URL of the portlet. Listing 12.7 shows how the DateTimePortlet class uses the RenderResponse object to create a resource URL, which is later used by the home.jsp page to send an Ajax request to the resource URL when the Refresh hyperlink is clicked.

Listing 12.7 Creating a resource URL in the DateTimePortlet class

```
import javax.portlet.ResourceURL;

public class DateTimePortlet extends GenericPortlet {

 @RenderMode(name = "view")
 public void showHomePage(...)... {
```

```
ResourceURL dateTimeResourceURL =                          ❶ Creates
    response.createResourceURL();                             resource URL
dateTimeResourceURL.setResourceID("dateTime");
request.setAttribute("dateTimeResourceURL",
    dateTimeResourceURL);                                  ❷ Sets resource
getPortletContext().getRequestDispatcher(                     URL in request
  response.encodeURL("/WEB-INF/jsp/home.jsp")).
    include(request, response);
 }
 ...
}
```

The RenderResponse's createResourceURL method ❶ creates a ResourceURL object, which represents a resource URL. The setResourceID method of ResourceURL is used to uniquely identify the resource to be served. The resource URL is set as a request attribute ❷, and the request is dispatched to the home.jsp page. The Refresh hyperlink in home.jsp sends an Ajax request to the resource URL set in the request.

If you compare the showHomePage render method shown in listing 12.7 with the showHomePage render method from listing 12.5, you'll see that we no longer need to worry about passing role information from the portlet to the servlet component. The security of the Ajax request is taken care of by the serveResource method itself, as you'll see shortly.

The DateTimePortlet's serveResource method processes the Ajax request that's received when the Refresh hyperlink is clicked, shown next.

Listing 12.8   The DateTimePortlet's serveResource method

```
public void serveResource(...)...{
  OutputStream outStream                                   ❶ Gets OutputStream
      = response.getPortletOutputStream();                   of portlet
  StringBuffer buffer = new StringBuffer();
                                                           ❷ Checks if user
  if (request.isUserInRole("User")) {                        has User role
   SimpleDateFormat sdf = new SimpleDateFormat(
     "dd-MMM-yyyy hh:mm:ss a");
   buffer.append("Hello World (<i> "
     + sdf.format(new Date())+ " </i>)");
  } else {
   buffer.append("<font color=\"red\">
     ⟹You are not authorized to view server date/time");
  }
  outStream.write(buffer.toString().getBytes());
}
```

The ResourceResponse's getPortletOutputStream method ❶ is used to obtain the OutputStream to which the serveResource method writes response data. The ResourceRequest's isUserInRole method ❷ is used to check whether the logged-in user belongs to the User role. The rest of the code listing is similar to the Date-TimeServlet's doGet method shown in listing 12.6.

> **NOTE** To get a better understanding of how programmatic security works in portal servers and how Liferay Portal maps a logical role name to a role available in the deployment environment, please refer to chapter 4.

Listings 12.7 and 12.8 show that using the portlet's `serveResource` method to handle Ajax requests simplifies development, because the security of the Ajax request is taken care of by the portal's security infrastructure.

Let's now look at how to serve resources using Spring Portlet MVC.

12.4.3 *Serving resources the Spring Portlet MVC way*

If you're using the Spring 3.0 Portlet MVC framework to develop portlets, you can serve resources from a handler method annotated with the `@ResourceMapping` annotation.

Here's what the handler method for serving resources will look like:

```
@ResourceMapping(value="myResourceId")
public void myServeResourceMethod(ResourceRequest request,...)...{
   ...
}
```

As you can see, the `@ResourceMapping` annotation accepts a single `value` element that identifies the resource ID associated with the incoming resource request. Like other annotated request-processing handler methods in Spring Portlet MVC, the `@Resource-Mapping` annotated method can have a flexible signature.

> **CODE REFERENCE** To see the `@ResourceMapping` annotation in use, import the ch12_SpringPortletDateTime Eclipse project into your Eclipse IDE. The Date/Time portlet in this project is created using Spring Portlet MVC's `@ResourceMapping` annotation.

If the `@ResourceMapping` annotation doesn't specify the resource ID to which it applies, then by default the handler method applies to all incoming resource requests that *map* to the handler.

So far, we've discussed how resource requests can be used to create portlets that use Ajax to show dynamic content. The Ajax response data is in HTML, XML, JSON, or plain text format. As mentioned earlier, the `ResourceServingPortlet` interface can also be used to serve binary content, such as images and PDF documents. Let's now look at how this interface is used to download binary content from a portlet.

12.5 *Downloading binary content using portlets*

You'll seldom come across real-world portlets that don't need to serve binary content. For instance, the Book Catalog portlet needs to serve the Table of Contents (TOC) of each book in the catalog, which could be in PDF or MS Word format. Similarly, a picture viewer portlet needs to serve images; an announcement portlet needs to provide announcement-related details in PDF or MS Word format.

To download binary content, you can either use a direct link to the resource or a resource URL pointing to the resource. Direct links are created by the portlet and encoded using the `encodeURL` method of the `PortletResponse` object. If the resource is located *within* the portlet application, you can access the resource using a direct link. In previous chapters, you used direct links to add portlet application resources, like CSS and JavaScript files, to the portal page. In the Book Catalog portlet, if the TOCs of all the books are located within the portlet application, direct links can be used to download them.

> **CODE REFERENCE**   To see how direct links are used to download TOCs, you should now import, build, and run the ch12_BookCatalogDirectLinks Eclipse project. The TOC files are located in the toc directory of the portlet application; their filenames are the ISBNs of the books.

There are downsides to using direct links for downloading resources:

- The resource must be located within the portlet application directory structure.
- No pre- or post-processing can be performed, before or after the resource is served.
- Direct links are outside portal security framework, so access to resources isn't secured.

If you're using resource URLs to download binary content, you can have resources that are outside the portlet application, you can perform pre- and post-processing in the `serveResource` method, and the resource is protected by the portal's access control features. The only downside of using resource URLs is that they affect the portal's performance. Because the resource URL has to pass through the portal infrastructure, resources are served more slowly than when you're serving resources using direct links.

The Book Catalog portlet in chapter 6 uploaded TOCs to the folder identified by the value of the `uploadFolder` portlet initialization parameter in the portlet.xml file. Let's now look at how these TOCs can be downloaded using resource URLs.

> **CODE REFERENCE**   You should now import the ch12_BookCatalogResourceURL Eclipse project so you can see how resource URLs are used to download TOCs. TOC files are located in the folder that you specified as the value of the `uploadFolder` initialization parameter.

The next listing shows how the TOC files can be served using the `BookCatalogPortlet`'s `serveResource` method.

Listing 12.9   Serving TOC files with the `serveResource` method

```
public void serveResource(...)...{
  File file = new File(getInitParameter("uploadFolder")        ❶ Identifies TOC file
    + File.separator + request.getResourceID());                  from resource request
  OutputStream outStream = response.getPortletOutputStream();
  if (!file.exists() || !file.canRead()) {                      ❷ Checks if file exists
   outStream.write("<i>Unable to find                              and readable
     ➥the specified file</i>".getBytes());
  } else {
```

```
FileInputStream inStream = new FileInputStream(file);
response.setProperty("Content-disposition",
    "attachment; filename=\"" +
    request.getResourceID() + "\"");
byte[] buffer = new byte[1024];
while (true) {
  int bytes = inStream.read(buffer);
  if (bytes <= 0) {
    break;
  }
  outStream.write(buffer, 0, bytes);
  }
}
outStream.flush();
outStream.close();
}
```

3 Instructs browser to save file to disk

4 Writes file content to response

The resource ID is obtained **1** from the resource request by using the `getResourceID` method. In our example portlet, the resource ID represents the name of the TOC file associated with the book. There's a check **2** to make sure the TOC file exists and is readable. If the TOC file doesn't exist or can't be read, an error message is sent to the portal user. If the file exists and is readable, the `Content-disposition` HTTP header is used **3** to instruct the web browser to prompt the user to save the TOC file to disk. The TOC file content **4** is written out to the response.

Listing 12.9 shows a scenario in which you may want to write HTML or binary content to the response. If the TOC file doesn't exist or is unreadable, the following HTML string is written to the response: `<i>Unable to find the specified file</i>`. If the TOC file exists and is readable, the content of the file is written to the response.

In the case of an Ajax resource request, the response is manipulated by JavaScript in the browser to update a portion of the portlet content. In the case of a non-Ajax resource request, the response is written directly to the web browser; when HTML is written to the resource response, it's the *only* HTML the user gets to see in the web browser. Figure 12.4 shows that when a TOC file isn't found or is unreadable, the only response received from the portal server is the HTML written out by the `serve-Resource` method.

Figure 12.4   In the case of a non-Ajax resource request, the only HTML displayed in the web browser is the HTML written to the `ResourceResponse`.

Let's now look at how you can improve the performance of your web portal by caching served resources.

12.6   *Resource URLs and caching*

Let's say that a portlet serves resources that are independent of the current state of the portal page or portlet. In that case, you don't need a portlet container to create resource URLs that contain the portal page or portlet state information. If the resource URL doesn't contain details about the portal page or portlet state, it increases the browser's ability to cache the response, because the response isn't dependent on the state of the portal page or portlet.

> **NOTE**   Resource caching is an optional feature for portlet containers. Please refer to your portal server's documentation to see if your portal server supports resource caching.

You can specify the portal page or portlet state information that should be made available to the `serveResource` method by using the `cacheability` attribute of the `resourceURL` tag or the `setCacheability` method of the `ResourceURL` object. Table 12.2 describes the valid `cacheability` values that you can specify for a resource URL.

Table 12.2   Resource cacheability description

Cacheability value	Description
`cacheLevelFull`	Instructs the portlet container to create a resource URL that doesn't include portal page and portlet state information. This means that you shouldn't access the portlet mode, window state, render parameters, or portal page state in the `serveResource` method triggered by this resource URL. Using the `cacheLevelFull` value for a resource URL means that the response generated by the corresponding `serveResource` method *must* contain resource URLs with cacheability set to `cacheLevelFull` and *must not* contain render and action URLs. If the portal page and portlet state remain unchanged, the resource will be served from the browser cache in response to a resource request.
`cacheLevelPortlet`	Instructs the portlet container to create a resource URL that only includes portlet state (window state, portlet mode, and render parameters) in the generated URL. Using the `cacheLevelPortlet` value for a resource URL means that the response generated by the corresponding `serveResource` method *must* contain resource URLs with cacheability set to `cacheLevelFull` or `cacheLevelPortlet` and *must not* contain render and action URLs. If the portlet state remains unchanged, the resource will be served from the browser cache in response to a resource request.

Table 12.2   Resource cacheability description *(continued)*

Cacheability value	Description
cacheLevelPage	Results in the creation of a resource URL that includes the state of the portal page in the generated URL. Using cacheLevelPage allows any type of portlet URL to be generated by the corresponding serveResource method. If the state of the portal page remains unchanged, the resource will be served from the browser cache in response to a resource request.

If the cacheability value is set to cacheLevelFull, the browser's ability to cache the resource is maximum because the cached resource is independent of the state of the portal page or portlet.

If no cacheability value is set for a resource URL, the default value depends upon the portlet lifecycle method in which the resource URL was created. For instance, if the resource URL is created in the render method of a portlet, cacheability is set to cacheLevelPage; if the resource URL is created in the serveResource method, the value of cacheability is set to the cacheability value of the resource URL that triggered the serveResource method.

You saw earlier how the Date/Time portlet makes use of Ajax to retrieve the current server date and time. That portlet demonstrates a simple use of Ajax in a portlet. The real benefit of Ajax is realized when it's used to create highly interactive user interfaces.

In section 12.7, we'll look at the Book Catalog portlet, which shows a rich user interface for displaying catalog data, uploading TOC files, and adding books to and removing them from the catalog. In section 12.8 you'll see how the Book Catalog portlet makes use of Dojo, DWR, and jQuery to create a highly responsive user interface. Section 12.9 explores how polling and Comet approaches can be used to show real-time data in portlets. We'll also look at how the Book Catalog portlet makes use of Comet to display notification messages to users when a book is added or removed from the catalog.

12.7 Creating a rich interface for the Book Catalog portlet

Rich user interfaces are like desktop applications—highly responsive and interactive. In this section, we'll redefine the Book Catalog portlet's user interface to use Ajax technologies to create a highly responsive user interface and display real-time data.

Figure 12.5 shows what the new initial page of the Book Catalog portlet looks like.

The Catalog and Add Book tabs ❶ are used to divide up the content displayed by the Book Catalog portlet. The Catalog tab shows catalog data, as shown in figure 12.5. The Add Book tab shows an HTML form for adding a new book to the catalog. The notification message ❷, "Book Catalog data has been modified" (followed by a Refresh hyperlink that will retrieve the latest catalog data from the data store) is displayed to inform the viewer that a book has been added to or removed from the catalog; the book could have been added or removed by the same user or

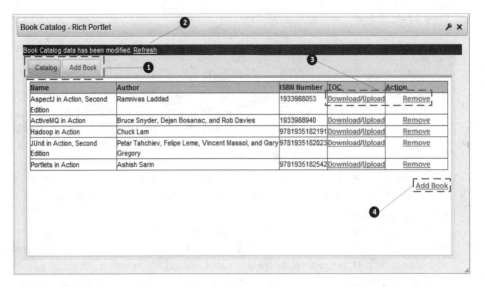

Figure 12.5   The Book Catalog portlet uses a tabbed pane to divide up content in the user interface. If a new book is added or removed from the catalog, a notification is displayed to the user.

by another user of the portlet. The Download link is used to download the TOC file associated with the book, the Upload link shows a file-upload form for uploading a TOC file, and the Remove link is used to remove a book from the catalog ❸. The Add Book link opens the Add Book tab, which displays an HTML form for adding a new book to the catalog ❹.

Figure 12.6 shows the HTML form that's displayed when the user clicks on the Upload link.

When a user selects the TOC file for uploading ❶, a GIF image is displayed to inform the user that the file upload process has been initiated. Once the file upload is complete, the GIF image is removed from the screen. The file upload process is asynchronous, so users don't need to wait for the upload to complete. Clicking the Let's Go Home link ❷ takes the user back to the catalog list shown in figure 12.5.

In figure 12.5, after the file upload process completes, a message is displayed at the top of the window to confirm that the TOC file was uploaded successfully. In the Book Catalog portlet, the name of the TOC file is the same as the book's ISBN. For instance, the ISBN of *Portlets in Action* is 9781935182542, so the TOC file for *Portlets in Action* is stored with the name 9781935182542.

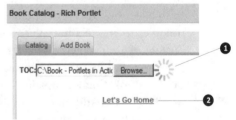

Figure 12.6   Form for uploading a book's TOC file. This form is displayed when the user clicks on the Upload link for a book (see figure 12.5).

Figure 12.7 shows the Add Book tab, which displays the form for adding a new book to the catalog.

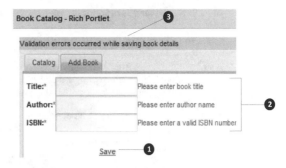

The Save link is used ❶ to asynchronously save the details of the new book. Validation errors that are reported while saving book details are displayed ❷. A notification message is displayed ❸ to inform the user that valida-tion errors occurred while saving book information.

Figure 12.7   Form for adding a new book to the catalog. The form is displayed when the user selects the Add Book tab or clicks the Add Book link shown on the catalog page (see figure 12.5).

The Book Catalog portlet in this chapter is highly interactive and makes use of Ajax technologies to create a rich user interface, resulting in an improved user experience. Figures 12.6 and 12.7 indicate one of the most important features of this version of the Book Cata-log portlet—it *asynchronously* executes user actions. For instance, in figure 12.6 you can enter new book details and click Save; then, while the book data is being saved, you can click the Catalog tab to view the book catalog. While you're viewing the cata-log data, the Book Catalog portlet informs you of whether your new book was success-fully added to the catalog or if any validation errors occurred while saving it. The asynchronous uploading of files and saving of book data improves the user experience by many notches.

> **NOTE**   For the sake of simplicity, the security of the Book Catalog portlet is not part of the requirements.

Now that we've seen the requirements, let's look at how the Book Catalog portlet can be implemented using Ajax technologies.

12.8   *Creating rich user interfaces using Ajax*

Using Ajax in developing portlets requires myriad skills, including a good understand-ing of JavaScript, CSS, HTML, DOM, the `XMLHttpRequest` object, and so on. As we go through the implementation details of the Book Catalog portlet in this section, we'll look at the JavaScript libraries that hide Ajax-related details from the developer and hence simplify the development of Ajax applications. We'll also look at some of the important concepts in various Ajax technologies that are involved in developing highly interactive portlets using Ajax.

Table 12.3 provides an overview of some of the libraries that enable you to build web applications and portlets with Ajax. Later in this section, we'll discuss how these libraries can be used to implement the Book Catalog portlet.

Table 12.3   Java and JavaScript libraries that enable Ajax development

JavaScript library	Description
Dojo Toolkit	The Dojo Toolkit is an open source cross-browser JavaScript library that provides rich UI widgets and Ajax support. For more information about the Dojo Toolkit, refer to its official website: http://dojotoolkit.org/.
jQuery	jQuery is an open source cross-browser JavaScript library that provides Ajax support. It also has a user interface library that provides widgets for developing interactive web pages. Refer to the official jQuery website for more information: http://jquery.com/.
DWR (Direct Web Remoting)	DWR is a servlet-based Java library that generates JavaScript code based on Java classes, making it easy for Java developers to use Ajax in Java-based web applications and Java portlets. Refer to the official DWR website for more information: http://directwebremoting.org/.

As you can see in table 12.3, jQuery, Dojo Toolkit, and DWR provide support for developing Ajax portlets. So what's the main distinction between these frameworks? The jQuery and Dojo Toolkit JavaScript libraries provide cross-browser support for sending Ajax requests and processing responses, but they're different from DWR, which provides features like *Comet* (or Reverse Ajax), exposing Java classes as JavaScript objects, handling conversions between JavaScript and Java objects, integrating with Spring and JSF beans, and so on.

Starting with Dojo, let's begin our discussion of how the Book Catalog portlet can be implemented using Dojo, DWR, and jQuery.

> **CODE REFERENCE**   You should now import the ch12_ResourceServing Eclipse project, which accompanies this book, to see how the code referenced in this section is used in the Book Catalog portlet. To use the Book Catalog portlet, you must change the location of the upload directory (specified in the project's dwr.properties file) for TOC files.

12.8.1 *Simplified Ajax with Dojo*

Dojo provides a multitude of features, including Ajax, a rich UI widget library, DOM utilities, animation effects, and so on. You can think of Dojo as consisting of three parts: a core Dojo library, Dijit (a UI widget library), and Dojox (an extensions library). For the purposes of this chapter, we'll focus only on Dijit and Ajax support (available in the core Dojo library).

The core Dojo library acts as the foundation for Dojo's Dijit library, which provides rich UI widgets, like the menu, tree, calendar, and so on. It also provides layout widgets that allow you to place UI widgets in different sections of the layout. For instance, the `BorderContainer` layout widget provides the layout for putting widgets in five different compartments (left, right, top, bottom, and center), and the `TabContainer` layout widget is useful for showing a tabbed pane. A portlet developer can make use of widgets available in the Dijit library to quickly add rich content to portlets.

The Book Catalog portlet requires a tabbed pane to display the catalog details and to add books, so we can use Dijit's `TabContainer` layout widget to show a tabbed pane.

INCLUDING NECESSARY JAVASCRIPT AND CSS IN A PORTAL PAGE

To use the Dijit `TabContainer` widget, you need to include the Dojo JavaScript library in your portal page along with the CSS file that identifies the theme to be used for styling Dijit widgets. Dijit provides four built-in themes: soria, tundra, nihilo, and a11y. You can use one of these built-in themes to give your Dijit widgets a consistent look and feel, or you can create your own custom theme.

The liferay-portlet.xml file, which shows the JavaScript and CSS files used by the Book Catalog portlet to render Dijit widgets, is shown next.

Listing 12.10   JavaScript and CSS files for using Dijit widgets in liferay-portlet.xml

```
<liferay-portlet-app>
 <portlet>
  <portlet-name>bookCatalog</portlet-name>
  <instanceable>true</instanceable>
  <header-portlet-css>
        /js/dijit/themes/soria/soria.css
  </header-portlet-css>
  <header-portlet-javascript>
        /js/dojo/dojo.js
  </header-portlet-javascript>
  ...
 </portlet>
</liferay-portlet-app>
```

❶ Soria theme CSS file

❷ Dojo core JavaScript library

The soria.css file from the Dijit library ❶ specifies that the Soria theme will be used to give the Dijit widgets used by the portal page a consistent look and feel. The dojo.js file ❷ is the core Dojo JavaScript library on top of which Dijit widgets are created.

> **NOTE**   The Book Catalog portlet makes use of version 1.4.2 of the Dojo Toolkit library. The Dojo Toolkit 1.4.2 download consists of three subdirectories: dojo, dijit, and dojox. The dojox directory contains extensions to dojo, which you can use based on your application's requirements. For instance, if your Ajax request returns data in JSON format, you can use the `JSONQuery` support available in dojox for parsing JSON data. To include a single copy of dojo.js by default on the portal pages, include dojo.js as part of your portal theme (refer to chapter 5 for portal themes).

ADDING WIDGETS TO A JSP PAGE

Now that you've included the necessary JavaScript and CSS files for using Dojo and Dijit, let's look at the JSP page that uses Dijit widgets to render a tabbed pane. The home.jsp page of the Book Catalog portlet, which uses the `TabContainer` layout widget to show a tabbed pane, is next.

```
<div class="soria" id="<portlet:namespace/>myPortletContent">                    ◁  ❶ soria CSS
    ...                                                                              class for
  <div dojoType="dijit.layout.BorderContainer"                                       widgets
    style="width: 700px; height: 300px"              ❷ BorderContainer
      id="<portlet:namespace/>borderContainer">         layout widget

    <div dojoType="dijit.layout.TabContainer"         ❸ TabContainer
      region="center"                                    layout widget
      id="<portlet:namespace/>tabContainer">

      <div dojoType="dijit.layout.ContentPane"
        title="Catalog"
        id="<portlet:namespace/>catalogData">         ❹ Catalog and Add
      </div>                                             Book tabbed panes
      <div dojoType="dijit.layout.ContentPane"
        title="Add Book"
        id="<portlet:namespace/>addBookData">
      </div>
    </div>
  </div>
</div>
```

Listing 12.11 shows that a Digit layout widget can be used in combination with other Digit layout widgets to create the layout of a portlet page. The `class` attribute's value of soria ❶ specifies the name of the theme that applies to the Dijit widgets inside the `div` tag. `BorderContainer` ❷ specifies a layout widget from the Dijit library. Then the `Tab-Container` layout widget ❸ is added to the `center` partition of the `BorderContainer` layout. Because no other components have been added to the `BorderContainer`, the `TabContainer` widget fills the complete area defined by the enclosing `Border-Container` widget. The `ContentPane` layout widget ❹ is used to add the Catalog and Add Book tabs inside the `TabContainer` layout.

The JSP page in listing 12.11 uses the `dojoType` and `region` attributes in the `<div>` tag, but the HTML `<div>` tag doesn't provide any `dojoType` or `region` attributes. So why use these attributes, and how are these attributes used to create a UI widget? It's evident from the value of the `dojoType` attribute that it identifies a widget, and the attributes specified along with `dojoType` provide additional information about the widget. For instance, the `region` attribute of the `TabContainer` widget specifies that it's positioned at the `center` of the enclosing `BorderLayout` container. When the home.jsp page is loaded in a web browser, Dojo reads the HTML page and interprets the `dojoType` attribute to create the user interface.

The JavaScript that you must have in your home.jsp page to allow Dojo to parse the HTML page and create the user interface is shown next.

```
<script type="text/javascript">
    dojo.require("dojo.parser");              ◁  ❶ Loads Dojo
                                                   parser
```

```
dojo.addOnLoad(function(){
    dojo.parser.parse();
    dojo.addOnLoad(<portlet:namespace/>getBooks);
});
dojo.require("dijit.layout.BorderContainer");
dojo.require("dijit.layout.TabContainer");
dojo.require("dijit.layout.ContentPane");
</script>
```

2 Runs Dojo parser **3** Executes getBooks function

4 Loads Dijit layout widgets

The `require` function **1** loads the Dojo parser. The `addOnLoad` function **2** is executed when all `require` function calls are complete, meaning that all the necessary dependencies have been loaded for parsing the HTML. It's immaterial whether the `require` function call is before or after the `addOnLoad` function call because `addOnLoad` is fired only after all the `require` function calls are complete. The `parse` function parses the HTML and creates the widgets using the `dojoType` information in the HTML DOM.

A nested `addOnLoad` method **3** is used to invoke the `getBooks` function. Later in this section, you'll see the purpose of the `getBooks` function and why it's called from inside the `addOnLoad` function. The `require` function **4** is used to load the `Border-Container`, `TabContainer`, and `ContentPane` widgets. These `require` function calls are executed before the `addOnLoad` function.

In listing 12.12, the `ContentPane` widget represents a basic widget that contains the actual content of a tab in the tabbed pane. Let's now look at how you can retrieve HTML content for `ContentPanes` by sending an Ajax request to the portlet's resource URL.

AJAX SUPPORT IN THE DOJO TOOLKIT

The Dojo Toolkit provides support for Ajax as part of its core library. The Book Catalog portlet makes use of Dojo's Ajax support to show the content of the Catalog and Add Book tabs, as described here:

- The Catalog tab shows a list of books from the catalog, which is obtained by sending an Ajax request to the portlet's resource URL.
- The Add Book tab shows an HTML form that's used to add a new book to the catalog. The HTML form is retrieved by sending an Ajax request to the portlet's resource URL.

The following listing shows home.jsp page's `getBooks` JavaScript function, which retrieves content for the Catalog tab. It uses Dojo's Ajax features.

Listing 12.13 Displaying catalog data with the `getBooks` JavaScript function

```
function <portlet:namespace/>getBooks() {
  var xhrArgs = {
   url: '<portlet:resourceURL id="books"/>',
   handleAs: 'text',
   preventCache: true,
```

1 Defines Ajax request properties

```
load: function(data) {
 var catalogDataContainer =
     dojo.byId("<portlet:namespace/>catalogData");
 catalogDataContainer.innerHTML = data;
},
error: function(error) {
 var msgContainer =
     dojo.byId("<portlet:namespace/>msg");
 msgContainer.innerHTML =
   "Exception occurred while loading catalog
    data. Cause : " + error;
 }
}
dojo.xhrGet(xhrArgs);
}
```

② **Defines callback function for response and error**

③ **Sends HTTP GET request**

The getBooks function is responsible for retrieving the content for the Catalog tab. It's invoked after Dojo parses the loaded HTML DOM, as shown in listing 12.12.

As you can see in listing 12.13 **③**, Dojo's xhrGet function is responsible for sending an HTTP GET request to the URL passed in the xhrArgs argument to the method. The getBooks function defines the xhrArgs object, which specifies the properties that the xhrGet function needs to send the Ajax request and process the response.

The mandatory url property **①** identifies the URL to which the Ajax request needs to be sent. The URL *must* point to the same server from which the page was downloaded, because browsers can send Ajax requests *only* to the server in the *same domain* from which the page was downloaded. The value of the url property is the resource URL of the Book Catalog portlet, which means that the Ajax request is dispatched to the serveResource method of the portlet class.

The mandatory handleAs property specifies how to handle the response data received from the Ajax call. The value text indicates that the response data is handled as text. If your serveResource method returns data in JSON or XML format, you can specify json or xml as the value of the handleAs property.

The optional preventCache property indicates that the browser should be prevented from caching the response. If the response data is cached, the browser will return the cached response data without hitting the request URL (identified by the url property). The value of true for the preventCache property indicates that browser caching should be prevented.

The load property identifies the callback function that's executed after the response data is received from the server **②**. The response data is passed to the function, and its format is driven by the value of the handleAs property.

The byId Dojo utility function returns an HTML element with a particular id attribute. The dojo.byId("<portlet:namespace/>catalogData") call returns the <div> element, which represents the Catalog tab of the Book Catalog portlet.

The innerHTML property of an HTML element is used to specify the HTML that exists inside the tag. The catalogDataContainer.innerHTML = data; statement means that the HTML response that was received from the call to the serveResource method is placed inside the <div> element representing the Catalog tab.

The error property identifies the function responsible for handling errors, like HTTP 404, that might occur during request processing. The error argument to the function provides information about the error that occurred during request processing.

> **NOTE** Listing 12.13 shows the basic Dojo properties and functions that you need for sending Ajax requests and for processing response data. You should refer to the Dojo reference documentation for more details on the Ajax features available in the Dojo Toolkit.

The Add Book tab is populated in the same way as the Catalog tab, the only difference being that the Ajax request for populating the Add Book tab is fired when the user clicks the Add Book hyperlink in the Catalog tab (see figure 12.5) or when the user selects the Add Book tab.

The implementation of the Book Catalog portlet's serveResource method, which handles the Ajax request fired by the getBooks JavaScript function, is shown next. It returns an HTML response containing the book catalog data.

Listing 12.14 Serving catalog data with the serveResource method

```
public class BookCatalogPortlet extends GenericPortlet {

 public void serveResource(...)...{
  String resourceID = request.getResourceID();      ❶ Retrieves resource
                                                        ID from request
  if ("books".equalsIgnoreCase(resourceID)) {       ❷ Checks value
   List<Book> books = bookService.getBooks();          of resource ID
   request.setAttribute("books", books);

   getPortletContext().getRequestDispatcher(        ❸ Dispatches request
     response.encodeURL(Constants.PATH_TO_JSP_PAGE     to JSP page
       + "bookList.jsp")).include(request, response);
  }
  ...
 }
}
```

The resource ID ❶ is retrieved from the resource request. A check is made ❷ to determine whether the request is for a resource with an ID of books. If the request is for a books resource, a list of books is obtained using the BookService's getBooks method, and it's stored as a request attribute. The resource request ❸ is dispatched to the bookList.jsp page, which displays the catalog.

Listing 12.14 shows that the serveResource method dispatches the resource request to a JSP page. If the resource request is sent by the XMLHttpRequest object, the HTML generated by the JSP page is sent as response data to the callback function of the XMLHttpRequest responsible for handling response data. The benefit of using a JSP page to generate a response for an Ajax request is realized when you have to show complex HTML in response to an Ajax request.

If JSP is used for generating the response, you can use portlet tag library tags, like resourceURL, renderURL, and actionURL, to create the response HTML that contains

HTML elements referring to portlet URLs. For instance, catalog data in the Catalog tab shows Download links for downloading TOC files (refer to figure 12.5), which must be resource URLs.

> **NOTE** If you're using the serveResource method to process Ajax requests, you can create portlet URLs programmatically or by using the portlet tag library, but if you're using a servlet component to handle Ajax requests, you can't easily create content containing portlet URLs.

Let's now move on to see how the Book Catalog portlet makes use of jQuery to send an Ajax request to the resource URL of the portlet.

12.8.2 Simplified Ajax with jQuery

The jQuery JavaScript library provides support for sending Ajax requests and for processing responses. To use jQuery in your portlet, you first need to include the jQuery JavaScript library in your portal page.

   You can download jQuery from the official jQuery website (http://jquery.com/) and include the jquery.js file in the head section of your portal page, as described in chapter 3. If multiple portlets on one or more portal pages need to make use of jQuery, it's best to add the jquery.js file as part of your portal theme.

> **NOTE** Liferay Portal 5.2.3 uses jQuery as its core JavaScript library for implementing its user interface, so it's included in portal pages by default. If you're using Liferay Portal server 6.x, you'll need to explicitly include jquery.js in the portal page. If you aren't using Liferay Portal server, please refer to chapter 3 to determine which approach to including JavaScript files fits your portal server.

jQuery can be used to send an Ajax request to the Book Catalog portlet's resource URL to remove a book from the catalog, shown here.

Listing 12.15   Removing a book with the home.jsp page's `removeBook` function

```
function <portlet:namespace/>removeBook(removeBookUrl) {           ◁─── removeBook
    if(confirm("Are you sure that you want to remove the book?")) {          function  ❶
        jQuery.ajax(                    ◁─── jQuery's ajax
            {                           ❷    function
                type: "POST",
                url: removeBookUrl,
                cache: false,                           ❸  Arguments to
                success: function( data ) {                 ajax function
                    jQuery( '#<portlet:namespace/>catalogData' )
                        ⇨.html( data );
                }
            }
        );
    }
}
```

When the Remove hyperlink for a book is clicked, the `removeBook` function is invoked. The `removeBook` function accepts a resource URL ❶ as an argument. The jQuery object's `ajax` method ❷ is invoked. The jQuery variable provides access to jQuery functionality. This variable is available by default when the portal page loads the jQuery JavaScript library.

The parameters that are passed to the `ajax` function ❸ are as follows:

- `type` identifies the HTTP request type (`GET`, `POST`, `PUT`, and so on).
- `url` specifies the URL to which the Ajax request is sent. Because you're going to use the `serveResource` method to handle the Ajax request, the value of the `url` parameter is the Book Catalog portlet's resource URL.
- `cache` is similar to the `preventCache` parameter in Dojo, and it's meant to prevent the browser from caching response data.
- `success` identifies the function that's invoked after the response data is received. In this example, the `data` argument to the function defined by the `success` parameter represents the response data, which is the updated HTML that shows the current state of the catalog.

Within the success parameter, `jQuery('#<portlet:namespace/>catalogData')` represents a jQuery *selector*, which selects elements that have the ID `#<portlet:namespace/>catalogData` from the HTML DOM. Listing 12.11 shows that this ID corresponds to the `<div>` element representing the Catalog tab, so the statement `jQuery('#<portlet:namespace/>catalogData').html(data)` means that jQuery's `html` method should be applied to elements returned by the jQuery selector.

The argument passed to the `html` method is set between the beginning and closing tags of the HTML element. This means that the behavior of jQuery's `html` method is similar to the behavior of the `innerHTML` property of the HTML element.

To summarize, the `jQuery('#<portlet:namespace/>catalogData').html(data)` statement first obtains the Catalog tab HTML element in the portal page and then sets the response data received from the `serveResource` method inside the Catalog tab HTML element.

Listing 12.15 shows that with jQuery you can quickly incorporate Ajax features in your portlet. Let's see how the various pieces of the Book Catalog portlet fit together to create the remove book functionality. When the Book Catalog portlet is loaded, Dojo loads the catalog data in the Catalog tab. Dojo sends a resource request to the Book Catalog portlet and receives the catalog HTML, showing each book in the catalog along with hyperlinks for downloading and uploading TOCs and for removing books from the catalog. The key point is that these hyperlinks are part of the HTML that was received in response to the Ajax request, which means that the JavaScript functions that these hyperlinks invoke must be *already* available in the downloaded portal page—this creates some performance overhead the first time the portal page is loaded by the web browser. The other critical point to notice is that the catalog HTML was served by a portlet, so it was possible to send the resource URL, which identifies the book it's associated with, as an argument to the `removeBook` JavaScript function call.

> **NOTE** Listing 12.15 shows the basic jQuery properties and methods that you require for sending Ajax requests and for processing response data. You should refer to the jQuery documentation for more details on the Ajax features available in the jQuery library.

The jQuery code for showing the upload TOC form is similar to the code shown in listing 12.15, except that the HTTP method used is GET, as shown here:

```
function <portlet:namespace/>showUploadToCForm( resourceUrl ) {
    jQuery.ajax(
    {
      type: "GET",
      url: resourceUrl,
      cache: false,
      success: function( data ) {
       jQuery( '#<portlet:namespace/>catalogData' ).html( data );
      }
    }
    );
}
```

The Book Catalog portlet also uses jQuery to create a fade-in and -out effect for the notification message that's displayed when a book is added to or removed from the catalog. jQuery provides easy-to-use functions that can quickly add animation to your portlets.

The next listing shows how jQuery displays the message, "Book Catalog data has been modified", followed by a Refresh hyperlink.

Listing 12.16   Displaying a message with the `showBookUpdateMsg` JavaScript function

```
...
<div id="<portlet:namespace/>bookUpdateMsg"                        ❶ Creates placeholder for
    style="background-color: blue; color: white;                      notification message
    ➥display: none;">
</div>
...
function showBookUpdateMsg() {
  document.getElementById("<portlet:namespace/>                    ❷ Sets notification
    ➥bookUpdateMsg").innerHTML =                                      message
    "Book Catalog data has been modified...;

  jQuery("#<portlet:namespace/>bookUpdateMsg").
    ➥fadeIn(2000, function() {                                     ❸ Fades in and out,
    jQuery("#<portlet:namespace/>bookUpdateMsg").                     removes notification
      ➥fadeOut(10000, function() {                                    message
      document.getElementById("<portlet:namespace/>
        ➥bookUpdateMsg").innerHTML = "";
      });
    });
}
```

The <div> element with a bookUpdateMsg ID ❶ is a placeholder for the message that's set when the showBookUpdateMsg function is invoked. You'll see how showBook-UpdateMsg is invoked in our discussion of Comet (or Reverse Ajax) in section 12.9.2.

The innerHTML property of the <div> element ❷ sets the notification message. Because the style attribute specifies display:none, the message is initially invisible.

The jQuery("#<portlet:namespace/>bookUpdateMsg") selector ❸ selects the <div> element and invokes jQuery's fadeIn function. This function accepts two arguments: the length of time in which the element should be made completely visible to the user, and the function that should be fired once the message is completely visible. In this case, the content of the <div> element containing the notification message is faded in over a period of 2000 milliseconds (2 seconds). Once the message is visible, the <div> element is again selected using the jQuery selector and the fadeOut jQuery function is invoked. The fadeOut function does the reverse of what fadeIn does—it makes the <div> element invisible. Like fadeIn, the fadeOut function accepts two arguments: the length of time in which the element should be made completely invisible, and the function that should be fired when the element is completely invisible. In this case, the <div> element is made completely invisible over a period of 10000 milliseconds (10 seconds). Once the <div> element is completely invisible, the notification message is removed from the <div> element to reclaim the space taken up by the message.

Listing 12.16 shows how quickly and easily you can add animation to your web page with the jQuery JavaScript library.

NOTE jQuery provides a vast number of plugins that are built on top of the jQuery core library and provide features related to Ajax, animation, drag and drop, UI widgets, and so on. Refer to the jQuery website for more information on the available plugins: http://jquery.com/.

Let's now look at DWR, which allows you to access server-side Java objects as JavaScript objects.

12.8.3 *Simplified Ajax with DWR*

Dojo and jQuery provide Ajax support, which simplifies adding Ajax capabilities to your portlets, but they don't provide any mechanism for transparently invoking methods of Java objects. DWR (Direct Web Remoting) is a framework that lets you expose a Java object as a JavaScript object to your portal page. The JavaScript object can then be used by portlets to asynchronously invoke methods of the Java object.

Let's say you define a ProfileBean Java object as part of your portlet application:

```
public class ProfileBean {
  private ProfileService profileService;

  public Profile searchProfile(SearchCriteria criteria) {
    return profileService.searchProfile();
  }
}
```

Now, assume that you want to invoke the `ProfileBean` object's `searchProfile` method using the `XMLHttpRequest` object. If you follow the raw approach for invoking methods of a server-side object using the `XMLHttpRequest` object, you'll need to send the object and method details to the servlet or portlet component that creates or retrieves an instance of the object, invokes the method by converting the request parameters to argument types expected by the method, and so on.

Figure 12.8 shows the sequence of steps required to invoke the `searchProfile` method of the `ProfileBean` object.

The Ajax request ❶ is sent to a servlet or portlet component. That component makes use of the information contained in the request to discover that the `search-Profile` method of `ProfileBean` needs to be invoked.

The servlet or portlet ❷ creates a `ProfileBean` object. Then ❸ the servlet or portlet creates an instance of `SearchCriteria`, which needs to be passed to the `search-Profile` method.

The `ProfileBean` object's `searchProfile` method ❹ is executed. Because it returns an object of type `Profile`, the servlet or portlet component converts the returned `Profile` object into XML or JSON format ❺, which is then sent back to the web browser. The callback JavaScript function of `XMLHttpRequest` ❻ is responsible for parsing the JSON or XML response data and updating the portal page.

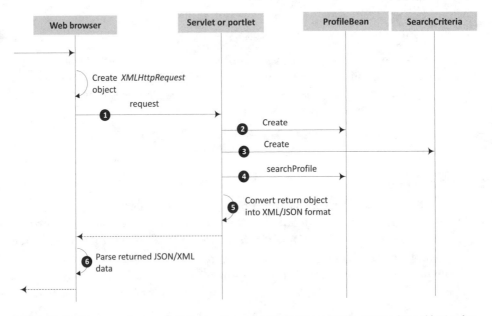

Figure 12.8   Sequence diagram that shows the steps required in calling a remote Java object using the `XMLHttpRequest` object and parsing the results to update the portal page. The web browser sends a request to a portlet or servlet component which creates the `SearchCriteria` object and passes it to the `searchProfile` method of the `ProfileBean` object.

Phew! That's a lot of work to do to invoke a method of a remote Java object. This is where DWR makes your life easy. DWR generates a JavaScript object that represents the server-side Java object.

For instance, if you want to access the `ProfileBean` object, DWR will generate a ProfileBean.js file that contains a `ProfileBean` JavaScript object, which in turn contains a JavaScript function named `searchProfile`. All you need to do is invoke the `ProfileBean` JavaScript object's `searchProfile` function and leave it up to DWR to invoke the `searchProfile` method of the remote `ProfileBean` Java object. You can say that DWR creates a *proxy* JavaScript object that hides the details of how methods of a remote Java object are invoked.

The Book Catalog portlet makes use of DWR in implementing the following features:

- *TOC file upload*—The Book Catalog portlet makes use of the DWR asynchronous file upload feature to upload TOC files.
- *Add book to catalog*—When a user clicks Save in the Add Book tab (refer to figure 12.7), DWR is used to save the book information in the data store.
- *Notification message*—When a book is added to or removed from the catalog, the notification message is displayed using the Comet (or Reverse Ajax) feature of DWR.

Let's explore how the Book Catalog portlet implements these features using DWR.

> **WARNING** The Book Catalog portlet uses the 3.0 RC1 version of DWR. If you're using an older version of DWR, please refer to the DWR website to find out which features are supported in that version: http://directwebremoting.org/.

CONFIGURING DWR

Before delving into the details of DWR configuration, let's first look at the Java object we'll invoke using Ajax.

The `BookCatalogAjaxBean` whose methods we'll invoke using the `XMLHttpRequest` object is shown next.

Listing 12.17 Invoking methods in a simple Java object—`BookCatalogAjaxBean`

```
import chapter12.code.listing.domain.Book;
import chapter12.code.listing.utils.Message;
import chapter12.code.listing.dwr;

public class BookCatalogAjaxBean implements Serializable {     ❶ Default
  public BookCatalogAjaxBean() {                                   constructor
    ...
  }
  public Message uploadToCFile(ToCFile tocFile,               ❷ Method to
      String isbnNumber, HttpServletRequest request)             upload file
      throws IOException, InterruptedException {
    ...
  }
  public Message addBook(Book book, HttpServletRequest       ❸ Method to
      request) throws InterruptedException {                     add book
```

```
  ...
 }
 public void startBookUpdateThread                         ❹  Method to
 ⇒(String portletNamespace, HttpServletRequest request) {      start thread
  ...
 }
}
```

The default constructor is defined ❶. The uploadTocFile method is defined ❷ to upload the TOC file, and ❸ the addBook method saves a new book in the catalog. The startBookUpdateThread method is used ❹ to start a Java thread that monitors catalog data and issues a notification message in case a book is added to or removed from the catalog.

Listing 12.17 shows that the BookCatalogAjaxBean's methods accept complex object types as arguments, such as Book and ToCFile, and they return complex types, such as Message. You'll see later in this section how DWR *converters* make it easy to transform JavaScript objects to Java objects, and vice versa.

Let's now look at how you can configure BookCatalogAjaxBean in DWR. The first step towards using DWR is to configure the Java objects that you want to expose to the web browser as JavaScript objects, and configure *converters* to convert the data exchanged between JavaScript and Java objects.

By default, DWR configuration information is stored in the dwr.xml file, which must be located in the portlet application's classpath. The following listing shows the contents of the dwr.xml file that configures the BookCatalogAjaxBean object.

Listing 12.18   The DWR configuration file—dwr.xml

```
<dwr>
 <allow>
  <create creator="new" javascript="MyAjaxBean">      ❶  DWR new
                                                           object creator
   <param name="class" value="chapter12.code.       ❷  Object type
         ⇒listing.dwr.BookCatalogAjaxBean" />            to create

   <include method="uploadToCFile" />                 ❸  Accessible
   <include method="addBook" />                           methods of object
   <include method="startBookUpdateThread" />
  </create>
  <convert match="chapter12.code.listing.
        ⇒dwr.ToCFile" converter="bean"></convert>
  <convert match="chapter12.code.listing.            ❹  DWR
        ⇒utils.Message" converter="bean"></convert>      converters
  <convert match="chapter12.code.listing.domain.Book"
        ⇒converter="bean"></convert>
 </allow>
</dwr>
```

In listing 12.18, the <dwr> element is the root element of the dwr.xml file. It contains an <allow> subelement that contains definitions of Java objects that are accessible remotely, and it may also define DWR *filters* that perform certain actions before and after the Java object's methods are invoked.

The `<create>` element is used ❶ to create an instance of a Java object and expose it as a JavaScript object. The `creator` attribute specifies how the Java object is created. For instance, if the value of the `creator` attribute is `new`, the Java object must be created using the *default* constructor of the object. The `javascript` attribute specifies the JavaScript object name by which the Java object is available in the web browser. For instance, if the value of the `javascript` attribute is `MyAjaxBean`, the Java object is accessed from the web browser using the `MyAjaxBean` JavaScript object.

The `<param>` element provides configuration information ❷ that's used by the DWR creator to create or retrieve the Java object. For instance, if you're using the `new` DWR `creator`, the `<param>` element specifies the fully qualified name of the class of the Java object that needs to be exposed as a JavaScript object. Because we want to access the `BookCatalogAjaxBean` Java object from the web browser, the `<param>` element specifies the fully qualified class name of the `BookCatalogAjaxBean`.

The `<include>` elements specify the methods ❸ that are available for remote access—these are the methods that can be invoked using the JavaScript object corresponding to the Java object. For instance, *only* the `uploadToCFile`, `addBook`, and `startBookUpdateThread` methods of `BookCatalogAjaxBean` can be invoked using the `MyAjaxBean` JavaScript object.

The `<convert>` elements specify DWR converters ❹ that apply to objects that are exchanged between the `MyAjaxBean` JavaScript and `BookCatalogAjaxBean` Java objects. As you can see, there's a converter for every complex data type that's exchanged between the `MyAjaxBean` JavaScript and the `BookCatalogAjaxBean` Java objects. The `match` attribute identifies the Java type to which the converter applies, and the `converter` attribute identifies the DWR converter that's responsible for performing the conversion. The `bean` converter is responsible for converting a JavaScript object to a Java bean object, and vice versa.

NOTE DWR also allows programmatic and annotation-driven configuration. For details on how to use them, refer to the DWR reference documentation.

The other thing you need to do before you can use DWR is to configure `DwrServlet`, which is responsible for receiving Ajax requests from the web browser and passing them to the appropriate Java object. Here we see the configuration of `DwrServlet` in the Book Catalog portlet application's web.xml file.

Listing 12.19 `DwrServlet` configuration in the web.xml file

```
<servlet>
  <servlet-name>DwrServlet</servlet-name>
  <servlet-class>org.directwebremoting.servlet.
  ➥DwrServlet</servlet-class>          ❶ Defines DWR's
                                            DwrServlet
  <init-param>
   <param-name>activeReverseAjaxEnabled</param-name>    ❷ Enables active
   <param-value>true</param-value>                         Reverse Ajax and
  </init-param>                                            debugging
```

```
    <init-param>
      <param-name>debug</param-name>
      <param-value>true</param-value>
    </init-param>
    ...
  </servlet>

  <servlet-mapping>
    <servlet-name>DwrServlet</servlet-name>
    <url-pattern>/dwr/*</url-pattern>
  </servlet-mapping>
```

2 **Enables active Reverse Ajax and debugging**

3 **Maps DwrServlet to /dwr/***

DWR's `DwrServlet` **1** is defined. Active Reverse Ajax **2** is enabled, as is DWR's debugging feature. You'll see later in this chapter what the active Reverse Ajax feature is and how it's used in the Book Catalog portlet. By enabling DWR debugging, you can view the debugging messages logged by DWR. `DwrServlet` **3** is mapped to the `/dwr/*` URL pattern.

> **WARNING** Because DWR uses a servlet component, Ajax requests sent using DWR are outside the portlet context and are not protected by the portal server's security infrastructure.

Now that you've defined the Java object that you want to access remotely and have configured the necessary DWR creator and converters in the dwr.xml file, it's time to see how you can invoke methods of the remote Java object using the JavaScript object generated by DWR.

INCLUDING NECESSARY JAVASCRIPT FILES

To use the `MyAjaxBean` JavaScript object, you need to include the following JavaScript files in your portal page:

- *engine.js*—JavaScript file provided by DWR that contains functions for handling communications between the local JavaScript object and the remote Java object. Including this JavaScript file in your portal page is *mandatory*.
- *util.js*—JavaScript file containing utility functions that you can use in your JavaScript code. Including this JavaScript file in your portal page is *optional*.
- *MyAjaxBean.js*—JavaScript file generated by DWR based on the configuration defined in the dwr.xml file. The MyAjaxBean.js file defines the `MyAjaxBean` JavaScript object, which is used by JSP pages to invoke methods of the `Book-CatalogAjaxBean` object.

The following XML fragment from the liferay-portlet.xml file shows how the preceding JavaScript files are included in the Book Catalog portlet application:

```
<liferay-portlet-app>
  <portlet>
    <portlet-name>bookCatalog</portlet-name>
    <header-portlet-javascript>/dwr/engine.js</header-portlet-javascript>
    <header-portlet-javascript>/dwr/util.js</header-portlet-javascript>
    <header-portlet-javascript>/dwr/interface/MyAjaxBean.js
      </header-portlet-javascript>
```

```
   ...
  </portlet>
</liferay-portlet-app>
```

As you can see, the built-in DWR JavaScript files, engine.js and util.js, are located inside the ${contextPath}/dwr directory, and the autogenerated JavaScript file, MyAjaxBean.js, is located inside the ${contextPath}/dwr/interface directory, where ${contextPath} represents the context path of the portlet application.

USING DWR

To start using DWR, you must understand how the *bean* converter works, and what the Message class does in the Book Catalog portlet application. A bean converter converts a Java bean to a JavaScript object and vice versa. The Message class defines the response message and data that's sent in response to the invocation of the uploadToC-File and addBook methods (refer to listing 12.17).

The next listing shows attributes and methods defined in the Message class.

Listing 12.20   The Message class

```
public class Message {                          ❶ Success or
 private String statusCode;                         failure code

 private String responseMessage;                    ❷ Success or failure
                                                        message
 private Map<String, String> responseData;
                                                    ❸ Response
 public String getStatusCode() {                        data
  return statusCode;
 }
 public void setStatusCode(String statusCode) {
  this.statusCode = statusCode;
 }
 ...
}
```

The statusCode ❶ indicates whether the request was processed successfully or not. The responseMessage ❷ is a text message, which could be a success or failure message. The responseData ❸ is the data that's sent with the Message object. The responseData can be used by the calling JavaScript object to update the portlet content.

Listing 12.20 shows that Message is a simple bean, which makes the Message class an ideal candidate to use a bean converter; it's converted to a JavaScript *associative array* when it's returned by methods of the BookCatalogAjaxBean object, and vice versa. Book and ToCFile are also simple beans, so they're also configured to make use of the bean converter.

> **NOTE**   If you're passing a custom object to a method argument or returning a custom object type from a method, you must configure an appropriate DWR converter in dwr.xml for the custom object. By default, DWR enables a couple of converters that you don't need to configure. For instance, converters for primitive types, String, Date, InputStream, and so on, are enabled by default.

If you want to create a custom converter, you can also do so. Refer to the DWR reference documentation for more details on DWR converters.

Let's now look at how DWR is used to add a book to the catalog, using the BookCatalog-AjaxBean's addBook method. The addBook JavaScript function in the home.jsp page, which makes use of the MyAjaxBean JavaScript object to invoke the addBook method of BookCatalogAjaxBean, is shown here.

Listing 12.21   addBook JavaScript function in home.jsp page

```
function <portlet:namespace/>addBook(titleFieldId,
  authorFieldId, isbnNumberFieldId, ...) {

  document.getElementById                                ❶ Shows loading
    ➥("<portlet:namespace/>imageId").                       GIF image
    ➥setAttribute("style", "visibility : visible");

  var book = {
    name : dwr.util.getValue(titleFieldId),              ❷ Creates book
    author : dwr.util.getValue(authorFieldId),              JavaScript object
    isbnNumber : dwr.util.getValue(isbnNumberFieldId)
  };                                                      ❸ Invokes
                                                             MyAjaxBean's
  MyAjaxBean.addBook(book, function(message) {              addBook function
    document.getElementById("<portlet:namespace/>msg").
      innerHTML = message.responseMessage;

    if(message.statusCode == "1") {
      ...
    }
    document.getElementById                               ❹ Handles
      ➥("<portlet:namespace/>imageId").                     response
      ➥setAttribute("style", "visibility : hidden");
    if(message.statusCode == "0") {
      <portlet:namespace/>showCatalogTab();
      <portlet:namespace/>getBooks();
    }
  });
}
```

The addBook function accepts HTML ids of form elements that are displayed inside the Add Book tab (shown in figure 12.7)—these include the book's title text field, author text field, ISBN text field, and so on. The addBook function is called when the user clicks Save in the Add Book tab.

The hidden "loading" GIF image inside the Add Book tab is made visible ❶ to suggest to the user that request processing has begun. The book JavaScript object is created ❷, which has the same properties as the corresponding Book Java object—this allows the book JavaScript object to be passed to the remote addBook method of Book-CatalogAjaxBean. The dwr.util.getValue function (defined in the DWR util.js file) is used to retrieve the values of elements from the HTML form.

The MyAjaxBean JavaScript object's addBook function is invoked ❸. Because MyAjaxBean represents a JavaScript proxy object for BookCatalogAjaxBean, invoking

MyAjaxBean's addBook function effectively means invoking the addBook method of BookCatalogAjaxBean. Notice that MyAjaxBean's addBook function accepts both a book JavaScript object and the callback function that's invoked when the response is received from the invocation of the remote BookCatalogAjaxBean's add-Book method.

When MyAjaxBean's addBook function is invoked, the request is sent to DwrServlet (see listing 12.19). DwrServlet is responsible for using the request details and the converter information in dwr.xml to create the Book Java object and for invoking BookCatalogAjaxBean's addBook method. The result of invoking the addBook method is a Message object, which is converted into a JavaScript associative array and made available to the callback function.

The callback function displays the responseMessage attribute value **❹** of the Message object (see listing 12.20). If a validation error occurs, the callback function shows an error message. Because the response has been received, the callback function hides the "loading" GIF image to indicate to the user that the request processing is complete. Finally, the Catalog tab is programmatically selected and the latest list of books is obtained from the book catalog.

Listing 12.21 shows that DWR simplifies using Ajax in portlets. You only need to use DWR's autogenerated JavaScript object to invoke remote object methods and let DWR handle the conversion of JavaScript objects to Java objects, and vice versa. If you compare the arguments passed to MyAjaxBean's addBook function and BookCatalogAjax-Bean's addBook method, you'll notice that the addBook method accepts an extra argument: HttpServletRequest. DWR is responsible for making servlet objects like HttpServletRequest, HttpSession, and so on, available to the target method without requiring you to explicitly code for it.

Another interesting thing to notice about the Message object is that even though it contains a responseData attribute of type Map<String,String>, there's no converter defined for it in the dwr.xml file. This is because DWR's map converter is enabled by default; it converts java.util.Map type objects into JavaScript associative arrays.

DWR 3.0 introduced a converter for InputStreams, which can be used for uploading files asynchronously. The Book Catalog portlet makes use of this feature to upload TOC files. The home.jsp page's uploadToCFile function, which uses DWR to upload TOC files, is shown here.

Listing 12.22   The home.jsp page's uploadToCFile function

```
function <portlet:namespace/>uploadToCFile
 (fileInputFieldId, isbnNumber) {
  ...
  var file = {
    fileName :
      ➥dwr.util.getValue(fileInputFieldId).value,        ❶ Defines file
    tocFile : dwr.util.getValue(fileInputFieldId)            JavaScript object
  };
};
```

```
MyAjaxBean.uploadToCFile(file,                              ❷  Uploads
    isbnNumber, function(message) {                            TOC file
    ...
});
}
```

The `file` JavaScript object is created ❶, and it needs to be passed to the `uploadToC-File` function of the `MyAjaxBean` JavaScript proxy object. The `fileName` property represents the name of the file selected by the user. The `tocFile` property represents the value of the `<input type="file"/>` element, which is meant for uploading files.

The `uploadToCFile` function of `MyAjaxBean` is invoked ❷, which in turn invokes the `BookCatalogAjaxBean`'s `uploadToCFile` method.

The `BookCatalogAjaxBean`'s `uploadToCFile` method accepts a `ToCFile` object and ISBN of the book for which the TOC file is being uploaded. The `ToCFile` object defines two properties: `fileName` (of type `String`) and `tocFile` (of type `Input-Stream`). The `file` JavaScript object in listing 12.22 is converted to a `ToCFile` Java object by the bean converter configured for the `ToCFile` object in the dwr.xml file (see listing 12.18). The converters for the `String` and `InputStream` types are enabled by default in DWR, so you don't need to configure them in the dwr.xml file.

Let's now look at Comet and see how you can use DWR's Comet feature to *push* data from the server to the web browser.

12.9   *Creating real-time portlets using Polling and Comet*

So far in this chapter, we've focused on using Ajax to *pull* data from the server in response to user actions. If the Ajax pull approach is used to show real-time information, this will require sending requests at frequent intervals to the server to retrieve the latest updates.

Let's say we wanted to create a Live Commentary portlet that shows live commentary for a sporting event. To provide the real-time commentary, the portal page would need to send an Ajax request to the server every few seconds to check for updates. This approach of sending requests to the server at regular intervals to check for updates is referred to as *polling*. If, at a given time, 1000 users are viewing the portal page containing the Live Commentary portlet, a few hundred concurrent requests would be received by the server.

The Comet approach, on the other, hand makes use of *long-lived* HTTP connections, which are kept open by the server for a considerable amount of time, and the browser receives the data written by the server to the HTTP connection. As soon as the response is received, the browser sends another request to the server to receive more data.

Let's take a deeper look into the polling approach, and then we'll focus on the Comet approach.

12.9.1 Polling—pulling data at regular intervals

When a request is received by a Java EE container (which could be either a portlet or servlet container), a thread is associated with the request for the *duration of the request processing*. Let's see how this thread-per-request approach limits the number of concurrent requests that can be handled by the container.

Most Java EE servers allow you to specify the maximum number of threads that can be created by the server instance to process incoming requests. For instance, in Tomcat 6.x, the HTTP connector configuration in the server.xml file specifies the maximum number of threads that can be created to handle concurrent requests. Suppose the maximum number of threads that can be reasonably created in our server instance, without making the server unstable, is 200. If we set the maximum number of threads as 200 and we receive 300 concurrent requests, the server will create 200 threads and store the remaining 100 requests in the server to be processed when threads become available. If processing of a request takes 2 seconds, a request in the waiting list will be processed in 4 seconds: the 2 seconds that it spends waiting for a thread to become available, and 2 more seconds in processing.

This example shows that Ajax requests sent to the server at frequent intervals will overload the server, resulting in reduced performance. One way to address this issue is by increasing the interval between Ajax requests, the downside of which is *high latency*. For instance, in the Live Commentary portlet mentioned earlier, if the commentary is updated every few seconds at the server and if the Ajax request is sent from the web browser every 30 seconds, the result will be unwanted delay in displaying updates.

There are also other issues associated with polling:

- *Increased network traffic*—Because the requests are sent to the server at regular intervals, network traffic increases.
- *Unnecessary requests*—Requests are sent to the server for processing even when the server doesn't have any fresh updates available. In such cases, the server returns nothing to the web browser.

Even though issues exist with the polling approach, it's useful in scenarios where high latency isn't a constraint in providing updated information to users.

Let's now look at how Comet simplifies the creation of portlets that show real-time data.

12.9.2 Comet or Reverse Ajax—pushing data when it's available

When you use Comet, data is *pushed* by the server to the web browser. In general, when an HTTP request is sent from a browser to a server, an HTTP connection is created, a response is written out, and the HTTP connection is closed. Comet makes use of *long-lived* connections, which are kept open by the server for a considerable amount of time. When the server needs to send updates to the web browser, it simply writes the response to the held-open connection. The browser processes the response, updates the portal page, and immediately sends another HTTP request to the server for more updates.

Let's say we were to develop a Live Commentary portlet using long-lived HTTP connections. When a portal page containing the Live Commentary portlet is loaded, a long-lived connection would be established with the server, which the server uses to send a response to the portal page as soon as updates are available. The JavaScript embedded in the portal page is responsible for updating the contents of the Live Commentary portlet to show the commentary in real time. Because the response is written to the connection as soon as the data becomes available, this Comet approach results in low latency in showing real-time data.

SCALABILITY—PROBLEM AND SOLUTION

An open connection on the server means that a dedicated server thread is associated with the connection until it's closed; the thread is *blocked* and unavailable for processing any other requests. If 10,000 users are viewing the Live Commentary portlet, the server must be able to maintain 10,000 active threads at a given time. This gives the impression that using Comet is even more resource intensive than the polling approach and can't scale to an increased load.

In classic Java I/O, a thread reads the stream from start to finish and is *locked* until the stream is completely exhausted and the connection is closed. Thanks to the Java NIO API (the java.nio package), it's possible to perform nonblocking I/O. A Java EE server that makes use of Java NIO reads the available data from the stream and releases the thread held by the open connection for serving other requests. Events are fired when data is again available for reading, and a thread is again associated with the open connection to read data. The process of releasing and associating threads to an open connection continues until the connection is closed by the server. This makes it possible for a few threads to serve a large number of requests. Because no standards exist for performing nonblocking I/O, the Comet approach relies on *server-specific* APIs for using nonblocking I/O to achieve high scalability.

> **NOTE**   Tomcat 6.x provides a CometProcessor interface (in the org.apache .catalina package), which you can implement to create your own servlet that performs asynchronous I/O. You'll also need to configure the org.apache .coyote.http11.Http11NioProtocol protocol instead of HTTP/1.1 in the <Connector> element of server.xml to instruct Tomcat to use Java NIO in processing streams. Similarly, Jetty 6 has the concept of Continuations, which use Java NIO to allow you to write scalable Comet applications. Servlet 3.0 has introduced the concept of asynchronous request processing, which standardizes how HTTP requests can be handled asynchronously, thus addressing the much-needed support for writing Comet applications without getting tied up with server-specific APIs like CometProcessor (in Tomcat 6.x) and Continuations (in Jetty 6).

12.9.3 *Comet support in DWR*

DWR provides support for building Comet applications using long-lived HTTP connections. In the case of the Book Catalog portlet, when a book is added to or removed from the catalog, the portal page makes use of DWR's Comet support to display a notification message to all users.

Let's first cover a few basic concepts that you'll need to be aware of when implementing Comet applications using DWR.

- *Script session*—A script session is similar to an `HttpSession`, but it's managed by the engine.js file included in the portal page. A script session is created when a user visits a portal page (that includes engine.js) for the first time, and it's uniquely identified with a *script session ID*. It's represented by a `ScriptSession` object on the server side, which is used to push JavaScript code from Java objects to a portal page and also for selectively sending updates.

- *Script session manager*—A script session manager is represented by a `Script-SessionManager` object, and it's responsible for managing the lifecycle of `ScriptSession` objects on the server side. The JavaScript in engine.js interacts with the `ScriptSessionManager` implementation to create, retrieve, and invalidate `ScriptSessions`.

- *Script session listener*—A script session listener provides notification when a `ScriptSession` is created or destroyed.

Figure 12.9 shows how DWR is used in the Book Catalog portlet to display the notification message when a book is added to or removed from the catalog.

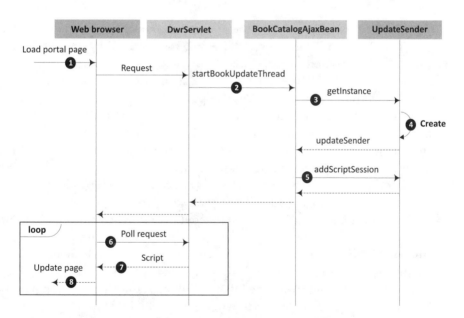

Figure 12.9   The Comet implementation in the Book Catalog portlet using DWR. The web browser creates a `ScriptSession` when the portal page containing the Book Catalog portlet is loaded. Every 60 seconds, a long-lived HTTP connection is created by sending a request containing the `ScriptSession` ID to the server. `UpdateSender` writes JavaScript code to `ScriptSession`, which is sent to the browser for execution.

The web browser ❶ loads the portal page containing the Book Catalog portlet. Because the portal page includes the DWR engine.js file, it sends a request to `DwrServlet` to create a `ScriptSession` on the server. You can think of `ScriptSession` as an object that represents a portal page on the server side. A `ScriptSession` is associated with a unique ID that's also available to the web browser as a JavaScript variable.

`BookCatalogAjaxBean`'s `startBookUpdateThread` method ❷ is invoked using DWR. The `startBookUpdateThread` is responsible for starting a thread, represented by the `UpdateSender` object, which continuously monitors changes in the number of books in the catalog.

The `UpdateSender` object's `getInstance` method ❸ is used to create (if required) an instance of the `UpdateSender` object and to start the `UpdateSender` thread. `UpdateSender` is a singleton, so `getInstance` creates a new `UpdateSender` instance ❹ if it doesn't exist.

`UpdateSender`'s `addScriptSession` method ❺ is used to add the portal page's `ScriptSession` object to the list of `ScriptSessions` maintained by the `UpdateSender` object. The `UpdateSender` thread iterates over the `ScriptSessions` it maintains internally, to send JavaScript to the portal page for execution.

The web browser ❻ sends a request to `DwrServlet` to check for updates to the `ScriptSession` associated with the portal page. The request contains the unique `ScriptSession` ID, which is used by `ScriptSessionManager` to return the corresponding `ScriptSession`.

If JavaScript has been added to the `ScriptSession` ❼, it's executed by the web browser. The JavaScript in the `ScriptSession` ❽ is executed by the web browser to update the portlet content. In the case of the Book Catalog portlet, `UpdateSender` sends the name of the JavaScript function that needs to be invoked to `ScriptSessions`. The browser executes the JavaScript function to show the notification message to all users who are currently viewing the Book Catalog portlet.

In this example, the web browser repeatedly sends requests to the server to retrieve updates via the `ScriptSession` object, but this doesn't mean that it's using the polling approach to retrieve updates. In this case, a request sent to retrieve updates opens a long-lived connection with the server, which is closed every 60 seconds or so, to check that the browser was not closed by the user. If the browser is closed, the `ScriptSession` is invalidated after a predefined timeout period. When the request returns, a fresh request is sent to the server to again open a long-lived connection. This process continues until the web browser is closed or the portal page is unloaded.

Let's now look at the source code of the Book Catalog portlet to see how the Comet approach is realized using DWR. The following listing shows the home.jsp page of the Book Catalog portlet, which defines the necessary JavaScript to initiate Reverse Ajax.

Listing 12.23   JavaScript in home.jsp that begins Reverse Ajax

```
<script type="JavaScript">
  dwr.engine.setNotifyServerOnPageUnload(true);
```

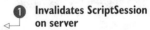 ❶ **Invalidates ScriptSession on server**

```
dwr.engine.setActiveReverseAjax(true);                    ⤺┐  Starts active
                                                          ② Reverse Ajax
MyAjaxBean.startBookUpdateThread      ┐ ③ Starts UpdateSender
      ➟('<portlet:namespace/>');      │      thread

function <portlet:namespace>showBookUpdateMsg() {       ┐
  document.getElementById                                │
  ➟("<portlet:namespace/>bookUpdateMsg").innerHTML =     │ ④ Shows notification
  ➟"Book Catalog data has been modified.                 │      message
  ➟<a style='color: white;' href='#'                     │
  ➟onclick='<portlet:namespace/>getBooks();'>            │
  ➟Refresh</a>";                                         ┘
  ...
}
</script>
```

When the portal page containing the Book Catalog portlet is loaded, engine.js is responsible for creating a `ScriptSession` on the server. The `setNotifyServerOn-PageUnload` function ❶ notifies the `ScriptSessionManager` to invalidate the corresponding `ScriptSession` when the portal page is unloaded.

The `setActiveReverseAjax` function ❷ creates a long-lived connection with the server that's closed every 60 seconds by the server. The `setActiveReverseAjax` method sends an Ajax request containing the script session ID (created earlier by engine.js), which is used by `ScriptSessionManager` to retrieve the corresponding `ScriptSession`. If JavaScript code is added to the `ScriptSession`, it's executed by the web browser.

MyAjaxBean's `startBookUpdateThread` function ❸ invokes the `BookCatalogAjax-Bean` object's `startBookUpdateThread` method on the server side. It starts an `Update-Sender` thread, which listens for modifications to book catalog data and adds a call to the `showBookUpdateMsg` function to `ScriptSession` if it finds that a book has been added to or removed from the catalog.

The `showBookUpdateMsg` function ❹ is invoked when a book has been added to or removed from the catalog.

Server-side configuration is also required for using Reverse Ajax, which includes adding the following initialization parameters to `DwrServlet` in the web.xml file:

- `activeReverseAjaxEnabled`—A `true` value enables Comet and the polling feature in DWR.
- `maxWaitAfterWrite`—A value of `-1` indicates that as soon as a response is written out, the connection is closed. If no response is written out, the connection is kept open for a maximum of 60 seconds.

`BookCatalogAjaxBean`'s `startBookUpdateThread` method, which is responsible for registering a `ScriptSession` with the `UpdateSender` thread, is shown next.

> **Listing 12.24 The `BookCatalogAjaxBean` class's `startBookUpdateThread` method**

```
import org.directwebremoting.WebContextFactory;
...
```

```
public void startBookUpdateThread(String portletNamespace,
        HttpServletRequest request) {
 ServletContext context = request.getSession(false).getServletContext();

 UpdateSender  updateSenderThread =
   UpdateSender.getInstance(context, portletNamespace);

 updateSenderThread.addScriptSession(
   WebContextFactory.get().getScriptSession());
}
...
```

1 Retrieves Update-Sender instance

2 Adds current ScriptSession

UpdateSender's getInstance method **1** is used to retrieve an instance of Update-Sender. The ScriptSession associated with the current request **2** is added to the list of ScriptSessions maintained by the UpdateSender thread.

The next listing shows the UpdateSender class, which is responsible for sending updates to web browsers using ScriptSession.

Listing 12.25   The UpdateSender class

```
import org.directwebremoting.ScriptBuffer;
import org.directwebremoting.ScriptSession;

public class UpdateSender implements Runnable {

 private static UpdateSender updateSender;
 private Set<ScriptSession> scriptSessions =
      new HashSet<ScriptSession>();

 private static int initialBookCount = 0;
 private String portletNamespace;

 public static UpdateSender getInstance(ServletContext
      context, String portletNamespace) {
  if(updateSender == null) {
   updateSender = new UpdateSender(context,
     portletNamespace);
   Thread updateSenderThread = new Thread(updateSender,
     "Book Catalog update sender thread");
   updateSenderThread.setDaemon(true);
   updateSenderThread.start( );
   initialBookCount = ...;
  }
  return updateSender;
 }

 public synchronized void addScriptSession
      (ScriptSession scriptSession) {
  Set<ScriptSession> scriptSessionsCopy =
    new HashSet<ScriptSession>(scriptSessions);
  scriptSessionsCopy.add(scriptSession);
  scriptSessions = scriptSessionsCopy;
 }

 public void run() {
  while(running) {
   int currentBookCount = ...;
```

1 Creates HashSet to store script sessions

2 Returns Update-Sender instance

3 Starts UpdateSender thread

4 Adds script session

```
if(currentBookCount != initialBookCount) {
  Iterator<ScriptSession> iterator =
  ➥scriptSessions.iterator();
  while(iterator.hasNext()) {
   ScriptSession scriptSession = iterator.next();
   if(!scriptSession.isInvalidated()) {
    ScriptBuffer scriptBuffer = new ScriptBuffer();
    scriptBuffer.appendScript(portletNamespace +
       "showBookUpdateMsg()");
    scriptSession.addScript(scriptBuffer);
   } else {
    synchronized(this) {
     iterator.remove();
    }
   }
  }
  initialBookCount = currentBookCount;
 }
...
```

⑤ Checks update to book catalog

⑥ Checks if Script-Session is valid

⑦ Adds JS function to be invoked

The scriptSessions variable ❶ stores the ScriptSession objects that are currently registered with the UpdateSender thread for receiving responses. The getInstance method ❷ returns the UpdateSender instance. Because UpdateSender represents a singleton, getInstance creates a new instance if an instance doesn't exist. Using a single thread to send notifications to all the portal pages is a more scalable approach than having a dedicated thread for each portal page. The UpdateSender thread ❸ is started as a daemon thread.

The addScriptSession method ❹ is used to add a ScriptSession to the internally managed ScriptSession list, scriptSessions.

The UpdateSender thread ❺ checks if there has been any change in the book count in the catalog. A ScriptSession in the scriptSessions variable ❻ is checked to see if it's still valid. A ScriptSession may be invalid because a user may have closed the web browser. The ScriptSession's addScript method ❼ is used to instruct the web browser to invoke the showBookUpdateMsg function of the JavaScript that was included as part of the portal page.

Listing 12.25 shows that all you need to do to send notifications to users is to send the name of the JavaScript function using the ScriptSession object. The Script-Buffer object is used to inform the web browser to invoke the showBookUpdateMsg function. You can also use ScriptBuffer's appendData method to send data to the JavaScript function. ScriptSession also has a provision to selectively send updates to users. For instance, you can send updates to particular users whose HttpSession contains a certain value for a particular attribute.

Another important point to notice in listing 12.25 is the presence of the portlet namespace. Because you send the name of the JavaScript function to the web browser for execution, you need to prefix the value of the portlet namespace to the JavaScript function. DWR is a servlet-based solution, so you need to explicitly send the portlet namespace to the UpdateSender thread.

> **WARNING**   Because the Book Catalog portlet doesn't use server-specific extensions (like `CometProcessor` or `Continuations`) to scale when server load increases, the Book Catalog portlet doesn't represent a scalable Comet application. If you're using Jetty 6, DWR transparently uses Jetty's `Continuations` to handle Reverse Ajax, making the Book Catalog portlet scale well when the load on the server increases.

12.9.4   *DWR integration with other frameworks*

DWR can easily be used along with frameworks like Spring, Hibernate, and JSF. For instance, you can use a DWR *creator*, which uses a Spring bean or a JSF bean. You can also return a Hibernate object using `HibernateBeanConverter`. You should refer to the DWR website to learn more about the various integration options available for the framework you're using (http://directwebremoting.org/).

Let's now take a brief look at *cross-domain* Ajax and the issues involved.

12.10   *Cross-domain Ajax*

Cross-domain Ajax refers to a scenario in which an Ajax request is sent from a web page or portal page, downloaded from domain X, to a server that is in domain Y.

Let's say your web portal's domain name is www.my-bookportal.com (domain X), and one of the portlets in your web portal needs to asynchronously access a servlet hosted by www.your-bookportal.com (domain Y). You might think that you could easily go ahead and create an `XMLHttpRequest` object and send an Ajax request to www.your-bookportal.com, but it isn't so simple. Web browsers limit Ajax requests from a web page or portal page to the server from which the web page or portal page was downloaded. So, in this scenario, you could only send Ajax requests to www.my-bookportal.com.

One approach to handling the cross-domain issue is to send an Ajax request to the server from which the portal page was downloaded, and then forward the request to a server in another domain, as shown in figure 12.10.

Sometimes you may still want to directly send a request to the other domain, without going through the same-domain server. In such cases, you can consider using JSONP (JSON with Padding), which contains JSON data wrapped inside a function call.

jQuery provides support for JSONP to send cross-domain Ajax requests, Dojo provides the iFrame proxy to perform cross-domain Ajax, and DWR provides the `ScriptTag`, which simplifies using cross-domain Ajax in your application. For more details on how to use cross-domain Ajax in your portal, refer to the jQuery, Dojo, and DWR websites.

Cross-domain issues are also faced when using Reverse Ajax (or Comet). If you're developing portlets that use Ajax or Comet, you should choose an Ajax toolkit that provides support for cross-domain Ajax or Comet.

Let's now look at how we can achieve inter-portlet communication when using Portlet 2.0's Ajax support.

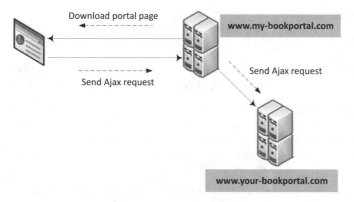

Figure 12.10 A cross-domain request can be proxied through the server from which the portal page was downloaded, in order to address security issues related to cross-domain requests.

12.11 *Ajax and inter-portlet communication*

You saw earlier in this chapter how the serveResource method of the Resource-ServingPortlet lifecycle interface is used to implement Ajax use cases in portlets. In many scenarios, you'd like to perform certain tasks in the serveResource method of a portlet and trigger other portlets on the portal page to update their content. For instance, you might want to use Ajax to add a book to the catalog using the Book Catalog portlet and then communicate the ISBN of the newly added book to the Recently Added Book portlet, so that it can show the most recently added book.

In the serveResource method, a portlet *can't* publish events, so it can't communicate with other portlets when responding to an Ajax request. This leaves us with no option but to implement custom approaches to perform inter-portlet communication.

To implement inter-portlet communication using Ajax, you need to do the following things:

- Inform the target portlet that it should update its content.
- Send data that the target portlet requires to update its content.
- Update the content of the target portlet.

In most scenarios, the approach followed by the target portlet to update its content determines how the target portlet is triggered to update its content and how the necessary information is passed. There are two approaches that can be employed by the target portlet to update its content:

- *Pushing* data via Comet
- *Pulling* data via a JavaScript function

Let's first look at how Comet can be used in inter-portlet communication.

12.11.1 Inter-portlet communication using Comet

Figure 12.11 shows one of the possible ways in which inter-portlet communication can be achieved between the Book Catalog and Recently Added Book portlets. In this case, Comet is used to push information about the most recently added book to the Recently Added Book portlet, and ActiveMQ (or any other messaging middleware) is used to communicate information from the Book Catalog portlet to the Recently Added Book portlet.

In this figure, the Book Catalog portlet's serveResource method adds a book to the catalog (represented by the database) **❶**. The serveResource method sends the ISBN number of the newly added book to a JMS destination configured in the in-memory ActiveMQ **❷**. The UpdateSender thread (similar to what you saw in listing 12.25) retrieves the ISBN from the JMS destination **❸**. The UpdateSender thread retrieves details of the book from the database **❹** based on the ISBN received from the JMS destination, and it pushes the book details to the web browser **❺** to let the Recently Added Book portlet show the details of the newly added book.

There could be multiple variants of the approach shown in figure 12.11:

- You may not use JMS at all if the UpdateSender thread is constantly checking the database to find out whether a new book has been added to the catalog.
- If the Book Catalog portlet's serveResource method sends the complete details of the newly added book as a JMS message, the UpdateSender thread won't need to hit the database to retrieve book details.

TIP   If you're using Spring, you can easily configure in-memory ActiveMQ and use Spring-JMS integration to send and receive messages.

The Comet approach to inter-portlet communication is quite involved compared to using JavaScript functions. The main advantage of the Comet approach is that the portlets don't need to be aware of other portlets in the portal, resulting in loose coupling between portlets.

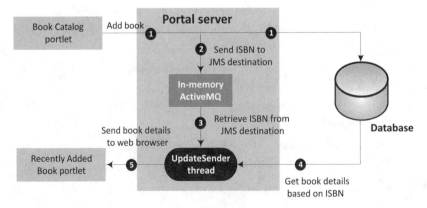

Figure 12.11   Inter-portlet communication using Comet. The UpdateSender thread retrieves communicated information from the in-memory ActiveMQ JMS destination.

12.11.2 Inter-portlet communication using a JavaScript function

The Comet approach to inter-portlet communication relies on the server-side pushing of data. Inter-portlet communication can also be achieved if a portlet defines a JavaScript function that updates the content of the portlet.

Figure 12.12 shows the Book Catalog portlet invoking a getRecentBook JavaScript function defined by the Recently Added Book portlet after a new book is added to the catalog. The getRecentBook JavaScript function retrieves the most recently added book information from the catalog and updates the content of the Recently Added Book portlet.

> **CODE REFERENCE** You should now import the ch12_ResourceServing_Ajax_ipc Eclipse project that accompanies this book in order to see how the code references in this section are used in the example portlets. The ch12_Resource-Serving_Ajax_ipc project contains a Book Catalog portlet and a Recently Added Book portlet. The Book Catalog portlet is almost the same as the Book Catalog portlet discussed in the ch12_ResourceServing project.

The Book Catalog portlet will invoke the Recently Added Book portlet's getRecent-Book JavaScript function, so the Recently Added Book portlet stores its *namespace* value in the PortletContext or in a central cache, ❶ so that it's accessible to the Book Catalog portlet. Then a new book is added to the catalog using DWR or the serve-Resource method of the portlet class ❷. Refer to chapter 6 for more information on portlet namespaces.

After the book is added, the Ajax callback function processes the response received from the server. If the response indicates that the book was successfully added to the catalog, another Ajax call is made by the Book Catalog portlet to retrieve the namespace value of the Recently Added Book portlet from the PortletContext or cache ❸. The Book Catalog portlet prepends the Recently Added Book portlet's namespace to the getRecentBook JavaScript function name and invokes it ❹,

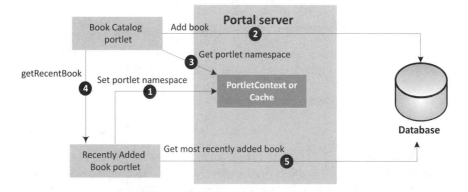

Figure 12.12 Inter-portlet communication using a JavaScript function. The Book Catalog portlet invokes the getRecentBook method of the Recently Added Book portlet, which updates the content.

which results in the invocation of the Recently Added Book portlet's getRecentBook function. Finally, the getRecentBook function updates the content of the Recently Added Book portlet by fetching the most recently added book information from the catalog ❺.

Let's now see how the Book Catalog and Recently Added Book portlets in the ch12_ResourceServing_Ajax_ipc project implement inter-portlet communication as defined in figure 12.12.

The following code shows the render method (in VIEW portlet mode) of the RecentlyAddedBookPortlet class, which shows how the namespace value for the Recently Added Book portlet is stored in PortletContext:

```
@RenderMode(name = "VIEW")
public void showRecentlyAddedBook(
    getPortletContext().
        setAttribute("recentlyAddedBookPortletNamespace",
            response.getNamespace());
    ...
}
```

The preceding code shows that the namespace value of the Recently Added Book portlet is stored as a PortletContext attribute with the name recentlyAddedBook-PortletNamespace. It's not necessary to use PortletContext for storing namespace information. If the portlets are located in different portlet applications, you'd need to store the information in a central cache that can be accessed by the communicating portlets. You should avoid storing namespace information in a database because the portlet's render method is invoked every time the portal page is refreshed, which would result in performance issues.

The following code shows the addBook JavaScript function defined in the Book Catalog portlet's home.jsp page, which adds a new book to the catalog:

```
function <portlet:namespace/>addBook(...) {
  ...
  MyAjaxBean.addBook(book, function(message) {
    ...
    if(message.statusCode == "0") {
      ...
      MyAjaxBean.getObserverPortlet(function(namespaceValue) {
        var fnName = namespaceValue + "getRecentBook";
        window[fnName]();
      });
    }
  });
}
```

In the preceding code, MyAjaxBean represents the JavaScript object corresponding to the BookCatalogAjaxBean object on the server side (see section 12.8.3 for the details of MyAjaxBean and BookCatalogAjaxBean). The addBook function of MyAjaxBean saves the new book information entered by the user. If the book is saved successfully (that is, if message.statusCode == "0"), the getObserverPortlet function of MyAjaxBean is invoked, which returns the namespace value of the Recently Added Book portlet. Once this namespace value is obtained, the `getRecentBook` JavaScript function is invoked using the `window[fnName]()` function; where `fnName` is the name of the JavaScript function to be invoked.

The following code shows the `getObserverPortlet` method of the `BookCatalog-AjaxBean` class, which is invoked when the `getObserverPortlet` function of `MyAjax-Bean` is invoked:

```
public String getObserverPortlet(HttpServletRequest request) {
  ServletContext ctx = request.getSession().getServletContext();
  String portlet = (String) ctx.getAttribute
    ("recentlyAddedBookPortletNamespace");
  return portlet;
}
```

An attribute stored in `PortletContext` can be accessed from `ServletContext`, so in the preceding code the `recentlyAddedBookPortletNamespace` attribute is obtained via the `ServletContext` object.

Inter-portlet communication using JavaScript functions results in tight coupling between communicating portlets. For instance, the Book Catalog portlet needs to know about the JavaScript function of the Recently Added Book portlet.

12.12 *Summary*

In this chapter you saw how portlets with rich user interfaces can be created using Ajax. Ajax adds complexity to portlet development, which can be accommodated by using frameworks like jQuery, Dojo, and DWR.

We took a deep dive into the DWR framework to show that it's a one-stop solution for your Ajax needs. You can use it to create Ajax or Comet portlets, and it also helps you take care of cross-domain Ajax issues. We focused only on the use of open source Ajax frameworks to create rich user interfaces, but you can also consider using commercial frameworks like Adobe Flex.

In the next chapter, we'll look at a new addition to Portlet 2.0—*portlet filters*, which are used to preprocess portlet requests and postprocess portlet responses.

Reusable logic with portlet filters

13

This chapter covers

- Types of portlet filters
- The portlet filter lifecycle
- Creating portlet filters
- Configuring portlet filters

In previous chapters you saw examples where the complete request-processing logic was contained within the lifecycle methods of the portlet. For instance, in the Book Catalog portlet, the logic that sets the title of the portlet window, based on the value of the `myaction` request parameter, is part of the request-processing logic. Similarly, you can have request-logging logic in lifecycle methods that log requests to a log file, which is later analyzed by a log-analyzer tool to generate important statistics. The logic inside a lifecycle method can't be used by other portlets, because it's tightly coupled with the portlet class, so you can't reuse the logic to programmatically set the portlet title and to log requests.

A *portlet filter* is a reusable component that allows you to write request- and response-processing logic that can be applied to multiple portlets and that can be reused in different portlet applications with just a few configuration steps. A portlet filter is similar to a servlet filter, and it's responsible for preprocessing requests *before* they're handled by the portlet and for postprocessing responses *before* they're sent to the portal server.

In this chapter, we'll look at different types of portlet filters, their lifecycles, implementation, configuration, and how they can be used individually or in combination with other portlet filter types. We'll also see how portlet filters can be used by the Book Catalog portlet to dynamically set the portlet title and to convert the title of a book into a hyperlink pointing to a Wikipedia page related to the subject covered in the book. By the end of this chapter, you'll understand how portlet filters are typically used to preprocess requests and postprocess responses, and how they can be used together to create a filter chain.

13.1　*Types of portlet filters*

In this section, we'll look at various types of filter interfaces that you can implement to create portlet filters. You saw in chapter 2 that different request and response object types are available to a portlet, depending upon the request-processing phase. Because portlets have multiple request-processing phases, and each phase uses different request and response objects, portlets have a different filter type for each phase.

The functionality of portlet filters is similar to that of Spring interceptors (discussed in chapter 8) and to AOP *before* and *after* advice combinations (see chapter 9) which preprocess portlet requests and postprocess portlet responses. You can correlate the functionality of a portlet filter to that of a security guard who records entry and exit times of the people entering or leaving a building.

Table 13.1 describes the interfaces provided by the Portlet 2.0 API for creating filters specific to a phase.

Table 13.1　Filter interfaces defined in Portlet 2.0

Filter interface	Description
`ActionFilter`	Filter for preprocessing *action* requests sent to the portlet (before the invocation of the `processAction` method) and for postprocessing the response received from the portlet (after `processAction` returns)
`RenderFilter`	Filter for preprocessing *render* requests sent to the portlet (before the invocation of the `render` method) and for postprocessing the response received from the portlet (after `render` returns)
`ResourceFilter`	Filter for preprocessing *resource* requests sent to the portlet (before the invocation of the `serveResource` method) and for postprocessing the response received from the portlet (after `serveResource` returns)
`EventFilter`	Filter for preprocessing *event* requests sent to the portlet (before the invocation of the `processEvent` method) and for postprocessing the response received from the portlet (after `processEvent` returns)

You'll choose the interface that's appropriate for creating a filter that meets your requirements. For instance, if you only need to preprocess render requests and post-process render responses, then you only need to create a filter that implements the `RenderFilter` interface.

> **NOTE** Your filter implementation class can implement multiple filter interfaces if your filter applies to multiple lifecycle phases of the portlet.

Let's now look at the methods defined in the portlet filter interfaces and their lifecycle.

13.2   *Portlet filter interface methods and lifecycle*

The `PortletFilter` interface defines methods for managing the lifecycle of a portlet filter. In this section, we'll look at the methods defined by filter interfaces and the `PortletFilter` interface, and at when these methods are invoked by the portlet container to manage the lifecycle of the portlet filter.

13.2.1 *Portlet filter interface methods*

Even though there are different filter interfaces, they define similar methods. Figure 13.1 shows that different filter interfaces inherit from the `PortletFilter` interface. This figure shows that the `PortletFilter` interface is the superinterface of the other filter interfaces. `PortletFilter` defines the `init` and `destroy` lifecycle methods, and the filter interfaces define a `doFilter` method that accepts request and response objects specific to the portlet lifecycle phase they apply to. Table 13.2 describes the purpose of each of the methods defined in the base `PortletFilter` interface and in the interfaces specific to the portlet lifecycle phases.

The signature of `init` method is as follows:

```
void init(FilterConfig filterConfig) throws PortletException
```

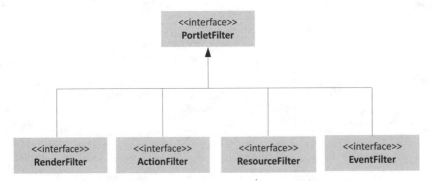

Figure 13.1   The filter interfaces that apply to the different lifecycle methods of a portlet. `PortletFilter` defines `init` and `destroy` methods, and each subinterface defines a `doFilter` method.

Table 13.2 Filter methods

Method	Description
`init(FilterConfig config)`	Invoked by the portlet container *before* the filter is made available for filtering requests and responses. In this method, the filter initializes the resources that it needs to filter requests and responses.
Destroy	Invoked by the portlet container to inform the filter that it is being removed from service. In this method, the filter releases the resources that are being held by the filter instance. If the filter holds any persistent information, that information is persisted in the `destroy` method.
doFilter	Invoked when the portlet request is passed to the filter. Each filter interface has a different `doFilter` method, depending upon the lifecycle phase to which the filter applies.

The `FilterConfig` object, passed to the `init` method, is used to access the filter initialization parameters and the `PortletContext` associated with the portlet application in which the filter is deployed. You'll see later in this chapter how the initialization parameters are specified for portlet filters in the portlet deployment descriptor.

The `doFilter` method signature varies from one filter interface to another because different request and response objects are available to a filter in different portlet lifecycle phases. For instance, `RenderFilter` defines the `doFilter` method like this:

```
void doFilter(RenderRequest request, RenderResponse response,
    FilterChain chain) throws IOException, PortletException
```

The `ActionFilter` interface defines the `doFilter` method as follows:

```
void doFilter(ActionRequest request, ActionResponse response,
    FilterChain chain) throws IOException, PortletException
```

As you can see, the `RenderFilter` interface's `doFilter` method accepts `RenderRequest` and `RenderResponse` objects, whereas the `ActionFilter` interface's `doFilter` method accepts `ActionRequest` and `ActionResponse` objects.

The `FilterChain` object is provided by the portlet container, and it represents the filter chain that applies to the portlet request. It's used to pass portlet requests to the next filter in the chain or to the target portlet lifecycle method.

Now that you know the methods that you need to implement to create a portlet filter, let's look at how the filter lifecycle is managed by the portlet container.

13.2.2 *Portlet filter lifecycle*

Figure 13.2 shows the portlet filter lifecycle, which begins with the call to the `init` method and ends with the `destroy` method.

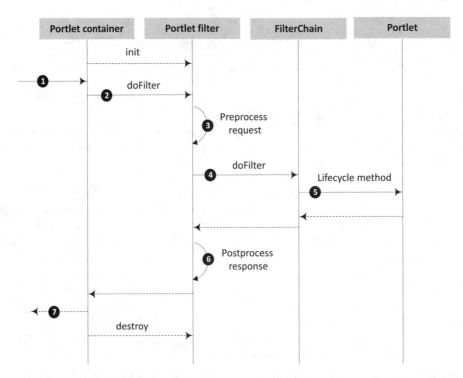

Figure 13.2   The portlet filter lifecycle. The portlet filter does the preprocessing of the request or the postprocessing of the response. `FilterChain` passes the request to the next filter in the chain, or to the target portlet if the filter is the last filter in the chain.

When a portlet application is deployed, the portlet container identifies the portlet filters that apply to the portlet and creates a `FilterChain` object. The portlet request **1** is received for the portlet. The portlet container invokes the `doFilter` method of the first filter in the `FilterChain` **2**, passing the request and response objects and the `FilterChain` object.

The portlet filter **3** preprocesses the portlet request, which may include creating wrapped request or response objects. For instance, in the case of `RenderFilter`, you may create a `RenderRequestWrapper` or `RenderResponseWrapper` object to be passed down the `FilterChain`.

The filter **4** invokes the `FilterChain`'s `doFilter` method, passing the original (or wrapped) request and response objects and the `FilterChain` object. `FilterChain` is responsible for invoking the `doFilter` method of the next filter in the chain, or the lifecycle method of the portlet if the filter is the last filter in the chain.

The lifecycle method of the portlet **5** is invoked after the last filter in the chain is invoked. The response generated by the portlet **6** is postprocessed. For instance, in the case of `RenderFilter`, you may set the title of the portlet window or write additional data to the response. A response **7** is sent by the portlet container to the portal server.

Figure 13.2 shows that a filter's `init` and `destroy` methods are invoked by the portlet container at appropriate times to indicate that the filter is being put into or taken out of service. A portlet request flows through the filter chain and finally invokes the lifecycle method of the target portlet.

It's important for a filter to invoke the `FilterChain`'s `doFilter` method to pass the request to the next filter in the chain, or to the target portlet in case the filter is the last filter in the chain; if it doesn't, that indicates that the filter no longer wants to continue processing the request, and that the filter itself is responsible for generating the response. For instance, an error filter may check for the existence of a request attribute that indicates whether the processing of a previous filter resulted in an error. If the request attribute is found, the error filter stops processing of the request—it doesn't invoke the `doFilter` method and instead generates the response itself.

Before we delve into the details of writing and configuring portlet filters, let's first look at the requirements of the Book Catalog portlet that you'll address in this chapter using portlet filters.

13.3   *Using portlet filters with the Book Catalog portlet*

You saw in chapter 4 that you can set the title of a portlet window using the `Render-Response` object's `setTitle` method. You used the portlet resource bundle, the Language-ext.properties file, to specify portlet titles and programmatically set the title based on the value of the `myaction` request parameter.

> **NOTE**   If you don't remember the details, you can refer to the ch3_Book-Catalog Eclipse project and see how the Book Catalog portlet made use of titles specified in the resource bundle, the Language-ext.properties file, to dynamically set the title of the portlet.

The logic that set the title of the Book Catalog portlet was inside the request-handling methods defined in the `BookCatalogPortlet` class, making it nonreusable. Dynamically setting the portlet title based on the value of a request parameter is a good candidate for filters because the same logic can be used by different portlets to set their window titles. This brings modularity to the request-processing logic—another advantage of using portlet filters.

You can also use portlet filters to perform checks on the portlet request and response. For instance, the Book Catalog portlet can use a filter to check whether an action request contains a parameter named `javax.portlet.action`, which identifies the action method of the portlet to be invoked. If no `javax.portlet.action` parameter is found, it means that the portlet doesn't make use of the `@ProcessAction` annotation to identify an action method to be invoked. In this case, a warning message can be displayed on the portlet, specifying that the recently invoked action request didn't contain the `javax.portlet.action` parameter. Another check that you can perform using filters is determining whether the action request uses an HTTP `POST` or HTTP `GET` method. You should use HTTP `POST` for action requests because they're meant to change state on the server.

Because you can use filters to modify responses generated by the portlet, you can use a filter to convert text in the response to hyperlinks. In the Book Catalog portlet, the titles of the books contain the name of the technology (or tool or framework) that the book discusses. You can use a filter to convert the name of the technology in the book title to a hyperlink that opens the official website or Wikipedia page for that technology. For instance, if the title of the book is *Portlets in Action*, the filter could convert the word "Portlets" in the book title to a hyperlink that refers to the Wikipedia page for portlet technology.

Let's now look at some examples that demonstrate how to create a portlet filter and configure it in the portlet.xml file.

13.4   *Setting the portlet title with the portlet filter*

Before you create a filter, you need to first identify the filter interface or interfaces that you must implement to create the filter class. The filter interfaces that you implement will depend on the portlet lifecycle phases to which your filter applies.

For instance, to set the title of a portlet dynamically, your filter must invoke the setTitle method on the RenderResponse object returned by the portlet's render method. This means your filter class must implement the RenderFilter interface. On the other hand, if you need to check for the existence of the javax.portlet.action request parameter in the action request and display a warning message if it's not present, you'll need to implement the ActionFilter interface (to check for the javax .portlet.action parameter) and also the RenderFilter interface (to write the warning message).

> **CODE REFERENCE**   At this point, you should import the ch13_BookCatalog_ Filter project into your Eclipse workspace so you can see how the code listings in the rest of this chapter are used in the Book Catalog portlet.

Listing 13.1 shows the PortletTitleFilter filter, which sets the title of the portlet window based on the value of the request parameter whose name is configured as an initialization parameter for the filter. The Book Catalog portlet uses Portlet-TitleFilter to set the title of the portlet based on the value of the myaction request parameter.

Listing 13.1   PortletTitleFilter dynamically sets the portlet window title.

```
import javax.portlet.*;

public class PortletTitleFilter implements RenderFilter {       ❶ Implements
  private String reqParamName;                                     RenderFilter
  private Properties props = new Properties();

  public void init(FilterConfig filterConfig) ... {
    reqParamName = filterConfig.                                  ❷ Retrieves
            ➥ getInitParameter("reqParamName");                     reqParamName
    InputStream inStream = this.getClass().getClassLoader()          init parameter
      .getResourceAsStream("title.properties");
```

```
  try {
   props.load(inStream);                          Loads titles from
  }                                           ❸ properties file
  ...
 }

 public void doFilter(RenderRequest request, RenderResponse response,
  FilterChain filterChain) ...{
  filterChain.doFilter(request, response);          Invokes doFilter
  String reqParamValue = request.getParameter(reqParamName); ❹ method
  if (request.getPortletMode() == PortletMode.VIEW) {
   String title = props.getProperty("portlet.title."
     + reqParamValue);
   if (title == null) {                           Obtains and sets
    response.setTitle(props.getProperty      ❺ portlet title
          ➥("portlet.title.default"));
   } else {
    response.setTitle(props.getProperty("portlet.title."
      + reqParamValue));
   }
  }
 }
 ...
 }
 ...
}
```

The `PortletTitleFilter` filter implements the `RenderFilter` interface ❶ because it's responsible for postprocessing responses generated by the Book Catalog portlet's render method.

The `FilterConfig` object's `getInitParameter` method obtains the value of the `reqParamName` filter initialization parameter ❷. This parameter specifies the name of the request parameter whose value is used to determine the title of the portlet window. In the case of the Book Catalog portlet, the `myaction` parameter is used as the value of the `reqParamName` initialization parameter. The `title.properties` file containing the titles of the portlet is loaded ❸.

The `FilterChain` object's `doFilter` method is invoked ❹, which passes the portlet request to the next filter or to the target portlet. If you need to do any preprocessing of the request, that preprocessing code must be executed before the call to `FilterChain`'s `doFilter` method. The portlet title is retrieved from the `title.properties` file ❺ based on the value of the request parameter specified by the `reqParamName` filter initialization parameter. The portlet title is set using the `RenderResponse` object's `setTitle` method.

To dynamically set the portlet title, `PortletTitleFilter` uses the following strategy to identify the portlet title in the title.properties file:

- The portlet title has the following format: portlet.title.*<value of reqParamName parameter>*, where *<value of reqParamName parameter>* refers to the value of the request parameter whose name is the value of the `reqParamName` filter initialization parameter. In the case of the Book Catalog portlet, the value of `reqParamName` is `myaction`, so the value of the `myaction` parameter is used to identify the portlet title in the title.properties file. For instance, if the name of the `myaction` parameter is addBookForm, the value of the `portlet.title.addBookForm` property in the title.properties file is set as the title of the Book Catalog portlet.

- If the portlet title isn't found in the title.properties file, the value of the `portlet.title.default` property is used as the portlet title. This situation will arise if the developer forgets to specify a portlet title in the title.properties file or if the request parameter isn't found in the request.
- The portlet title in `EDIT` and `HELP` portlet modes is identified by the values of the `portlet.title.preferences` and `portlet.title.help` properties, respectively.

If you follow this strategy in defining portlet titles in the title.properties file, the `PortletTitleFilter` filter can be reused by any portlet for setting the portlet title dynamically.

To use a filter, you must also configure it in the portlet.xml file. The next listing shows how you can configure `PortletTitleFilter` in portlet.xml and map it to the render phase of the Book Catalog portlet.

Listing 13.2   `PortletTitleFilter` configuration in the `portlet.xml` file

```
<portlet-app...>
 <portlet>
  <portlet-name>bookCatalog</portlet-name>                    ❶ Book Catalog
  <portlet-class>                                               portlet definition
   chapter11.code.listing.base.BookCatalogPortlet
  </portlet-class>
  ...
 </portlet>
 ...
 <filter>
  <filter-name>titleFilter</filter-name>                      ❷ PortletTitleFilter
  <filter-class>chapter11.code.listing.filters.               definition
       PortletTitleFilter</filter-class>
  <lifecycle>RENDER_PHASE</lifecycle>
  <init-param>                                                ❸ Filter initialization
   <name>reqParamName</name>                                    parameters
   <value>myaction</value>
  </init-param>
 </filter>
 <filter-mapping>
  <filter-name>titleFilter</filter-name>                      ❹ Filter mapping
  <portlet-name>bookCatalog</portlet-name>                      definition
 </filter-mapping>
 ...
</portlet-app>
```

The Book Catalog portlet ❶ is defined. The `PortletTitleFilter` filter ❷ is defined using the `<filter>` element. It has several subelements:

- `<filter-name>`—Specifies a *unique* name for the filter.
- `<filter-class>`—Specifies the fully qualified name of the filter class.

- `<lifecycle>`—Specifies the portlet lifecycle phase to which the filter applies. The value `RENDER_PHASE` indicates that the `PortletTitleFilter` is applied to the render phase of the portlet to which the filter maps. The value of the `<lifecycle>` element should be the lifecycle phase supported by the filter class. For instance, `PortletTitleFilter` doesn't implement the `ActionFilter` interface, so it shouldn't specify `ACTION_PHASE` as the value of the `<lifecycle>` element. If a filter applies to multiple lifecycle phases of a portlet, additional `<lifecycle>` elements are used to specify the lifecycle phases to which the filter applies.

- `<init-param>`—Specifies the initialization parameter for the filter ❸, which a filter can obtain using the `FilterConfig` object. The `reqParamName` initialization parameter identifies the request parameter that's used by `PortletTitleFilter` to dynamically set the portlet title. Because the Book Catalog portlet uses the `myaction` request parameter to determine the title of the window, `myaction` is specified as the value of the `reqParamName` parameter.

The `<filter-mapping>` element ❹ maps the portlet filter to one or more portlets in the same portlet application. It includes these subelements:

- `<filter-name>`—Identifies the filter for which this `<filter-mapping>` element is defined.

- `<portlet-name>`—Specifies the portlets to which the filter applies. The value of the `<portlet-name>` element must match a `<portlet-name>` subelement of the `<portlet>` element. You can also use the asterisk (*) wildcard character to map a filter to multiple portlets in the portlet application. For instance, if the value of the `<portlet-name>` element is specified as `book*`, the `PortletTitleFilter` would apply to all portlets whose name starts with `book`, like `bookCatalog`, `booking`, `bookShopper`, and so on.

> **WARNING**   If a filter definition specifies a value of `<lifecycle>` element that is not supported by the filter (meaning that the filter doesn't implement the corresponding filter interface), the portlet container may ignore that filter or throw an exception during deployment. In the case of Liferay Portal 6.0, the portlet container throws an exception at runtime.

Let's now look at `UtilityFilter`, which applies to both the render and action lifecycle phases of a portlet.

13.5   *Validating requests with portlet filters*

The `UtilityFilter` checks that a portlet's `action` method is invoked via the HTTP `POST` method and that the portlet class makes use of the `@ProcessAction` annotation to identify an action method. If a portlet uses the `@ProcessAction` annotation, the action request will contain a parameter named `javax.portlet.action`.

If `UtilityFilter` finds that the HTTP method is `GET`, it displays the following warning message: "WARNING: Action request makes use of GET HTTP method." If

Category	Name	Author
Java	ActiveMQ in Action	Bruce Snyder, Dejan Bosana
Java	Hadoop in Action	Chuck Lam
Java	JUnit in Action, Second Edition	Petar Tahchiev, Felipe Leme,
.NET	Azure in Action	Chris Hay, Brian H. Prince

WARNING: Action request makes use of GET HTTP method

Figure 13.3 `UtilityFilter` shows the message, "WARNING: Action request makes use of GET HTTP method" when the action request sent to the Book Catalog portlet uses the HTTP `GET` method. In the case of the Book Catalog portlet, an HTTP `GET` is used for the action request that's sent when a user clicks the Remove hyperlink.

`UtilityFilter` finds that the `javax.portlet.action` request parameter isn't present in the action request, it displays the following warning message: "WARNING: Action request doesn't contain javax.portlet.action parameter. Are you using annotations?"

Figure 13.3 shows that the warning message is displayed by the Book Catalog portlet when a user removes a book from the catalog.

The `UtilityFilter` checks the incoming `ActionRequest` and writes a warning message to the `RenderResponse` object, as shown next.

Listing 13.3   `UtilityFilter` checks the action request.

```
public class UtilityFilter
    implements ActionFilter, RenderFilter {                      ❶ Implements ActionFilter
  public void init(FilterConfig filterConfig)... {                  and RenderFilter
  }

  public void doFilter(ActionRequest request,
    ActionResponse response, FilterChain filterChain) ... {
    StringBuffer sb = new StringBuffer();
    String httpMethod = request.getMethod();

    if ("GET".equalsIgnoreCase(httpMethod)) {                    ❷ Checks HTTP
      sb.append("WARNING: Action request                            method
          makes use of GET HTTP method");
    }

    String actionName = request.
            getParameter(ActionRequest.ACTION_NAME);
    if (actionName == null || "".equals(actionName)) {           ❸ Checks request
      sb.append("WARNING: Action request doesn't contain            parameter
        'javax.portlet.action' parameter.
            Are you using annotations ?");
    }
    request.setAttribute("warningMsg", sb.toString());           ❹ Adds message to
    filterChain.doFilter(request, response);                        action request
  }

  public void doFilter(RenderRequest request, RenderResponse response,
    FilterChain filterChain) ... {
    String warningMsg = (String) request.
          getAttribute("warningMsg");
    if (warningMsg != null && !warningMsg.equals("")) {          ❺ Shows warning
      response.getWriter().append("<b>" +                          message
          warningMsg + "</b>");
    }
  }
```

```
    filterChain.doFilter(request, response);
  }

  public void destroy() {
  }
}
```

The UtilityFilter ❶ implements both the ActionFilter and RenderFilter interfaces. If the HTTP method associated with the action request is not POST, a warning message ❷ is created. If the request parameter javax.portlet.action doesn't exist in the action request, an appropriate warning message ❸ is created. The warning messages ❹ are set in the ActionRequest with an attribute named warningMsg. The warningMsg attribute that was set in the ActionRequest ❺ is retrieved and written to the portlet response using the PrintWriter object.

In listing 13.3, because the UtilityFilter needs to share the warningMsg action request attribute with the render request, you must set the actionScopedRequest-Attributes container-runtime option to true. Because UtilityFilter implements both the RenderFilter and ActionFilter interfaces and assumes that the doFilter method for the render request is invoked after the doFilter method for the action request, you must configure UtilityFilter to apply to both the RENDER_PHASE and the ACTION_PHASE of the portlet.

So far in this section, we've looked at examples where you use one or more filter interfaces and preprocessed portlet requests or postprocessed portlet responses. We'll now look at an example in which a response wrapper object is used to customize a response generated by the Book Catalog portlet.

13.6   *Converting text to hyperlinks with portlet filters*

Request and response objects received by a filter's doFilter method are passed to lower-order filters in the FilterChain and to the lifecycle method of the portlets to which the filter applies. This gives you an opportunity to use portlet request and response wrapper objects to customize the behavior of the request and response objects to perform filtering.

For instance, you can use RenderResponseWrapper and override the getWriter method to return a CharArrayWriter (a subclass of the java.io.Writer class, like the PrintWriter class), which is used by lower-order filters in the filter chain and the target portlet to write response data. Later, the filter can retrieve response data from CharArrayWriter and modify it.

Suppose we wanted the Book Catalog portlet to display the technology identified in the book title as a hyperlink to the official website or Wikipedia page for that technology. For example, figure 13.4 shows that the name of the technology, like AspectJ or ActiveMQ, is shown as a hyperlink; these links open the Wikipedia pages for the relevant technologies.

Category	Name	Author	ISBN Number	TOC	Action
Java	AspectJ in Action, Second Edition	Ramnivas Laddad	1933988053	Download/Upload	Remove
Java	ActiveMQ in Action	Bruce Snyder, Dejan Bosanac, and Rob Davies	1933988940	Download/Upload	Remove
Java	Hadoop in Action	Chuck Lam	9781935182191	Download/Upload	Remove
Java	JUnit in Action, Second Edition	Petar Tahchiev, Felipe Leme, Vincent Massol, and Gary Gregory	9781935182023	Download/Upload	Remove
.NET	Azure in Action	Chris Hay, Brian H. Prince	9781935182481	Download/Upload	Remove

Figure 13.4   The name of technology in the book title is displayed as a hyperlink. RenderResponseWrapper is used to convert the text to a hyperlink in the response.

NOTE   Figure 13.4 shows the Book Catalog portlet deployed on OpenPortal Portlet Container 2.1.2 with GlassFish Server v3.0.1, because Liferay Portal 6.0 doesn't allow the modification of response data.

To transform the text in the response to a hyperlink, you need to access the response generated by the portlet. Portlet response wrapper objects are used to customize the behavior of methods defined in portlet response objects. For instance, you can use `RenderResponseWrapper` to override the behavior of the `RenderResponse`'s get-Writer method.

The next listing shows how you can override `RenderResponse`'s `getWriter` method to store character data written by a portlet or filter for later use.

Listing 13.4   The `CharResponseWrapper` class

```
import java.io.*;
import javax.portlet.filter.RenderResponseWrapper;

public class CharResponseWrapper
   extends RenderResponseWrapper {
 private CharArrayWriter writer;            ①  Defines CharArrayWriter instance

 public String toString() {
  return writer.toString();
 }

 public CharResponseWrapper(RenderResponse response) {   ②  Defines Char-ResponseWrapper constructor
  super(response);
  writer = new CharArrayWriter();
 }

 public PrintWriter getWriter() throws IOException {   ③  Overrides getWriter method
  return new PrintWriter(writer);
 }
}
```

`CharResponseWrapper` represents a `RenderResponseWrapper` object. `CharResponse-Wrapper` ① defines an instance of a `java.io.CharArrayWriter` object. `CharArray-Writer` (a subclass of `java.io.Writer`) stores character data. The `CharResponseWrapper` constructor ❷ creates a new instance of CharArrayWriter. Then ❸ CharResponse-Wrapper overrides RenderResponseWrapper's getWriter method to return a Print-Writer object that writes the character stream to CharArrayWriter.

In listing 13.4, overriding the getWriter method has an important implication. A portlet calls the RenderResponse object's getWriter method to write character response data. If you pass CharResponseWrapper, instead of the RenderResponse object, to a portlet, the call to getWriter will return a PrintWriter object that writes the character stream to the CharArrayWriter instance. Because the response data is available in the CharArrayWriter instance variable of CharResponseWrapper, it can be obtained and modified by a portlet filter before sending it to the portal server.

The HyperlinkFilter configuration in the portlet.xml file defines initialization parameters specifying the names of technologies and the hyperlinks to which they should be converted when they're found in the response, as shown next.

Listing 13.5 HyperlinkFilter configuration in the `portlet.xml` file

```
<filter>
  <filter-name>hyperlinkFilter</filter-name>
  <filter-class>chapter11.code.listing.filters.
     HyperlinkFilter</filter-class>
  <lifecycle>RENDER_PHASE</lifecycle>
  <init-param>
   <name>AspectJ</name>                                    ◁── Text to convert
   <value>http://www.eclipse.org/aspectj/</value>              to hyperlink
  </init-param>                                            ◁─┐ URL of the
  <init-param>                                                │ hyperlink
   <name>ActiveMQ</name>
   <value>http://activemq.apache.org/</value>
  </init-param>
  ...
</filter>
```

HyperlinkFilter searches the response data for the initialization parameter names and replaces them with hyperlinks specified by the initialization parameter value. The following listing shows how HyperlinkFilter makes use of the CharResponseWrapper to convert names of technologies in book titles to hyperlinks.

Listing 13.6 The `HyperlinkFilter` class

```
public class HyperlinkFilter implements RenderFilter {
 private List<String> searchNames = new ArrayList<String>();
 private List<String> replacements = new ArrayList<String>();

 public void init(FilterConfig filterConfig) ... {
  Enumeration<String> initParamNames = filterConfig
    .getInitParameterNames();
  while (initParamNames.hasMoreElements()) {
   String name = initParamNames.nextElement();
   String value = filterConfig.getInitParameter(name);    ❶ Adds init param
                                                        ◁─    name to list
   searchNames.add(name);
```

```
    replacements.add("<a href='#'
      onclick='javascript:window.open("
      + "\"" + value + "\"" + ");'>" + name + "</a>");
  }
}

public void doFilter(RenderRequest request, RenderResponse response,
  FilterChain filterChain) throws IOException, PortletException {
CharResponseWrapper responseWrapper =
      new CharResponseWrapper(response);
filterChain.doFilter(request, responseWrapper);

String str = responseWrapper.toString();

String[] searchNamesArray = new String[searchNames.size()];
String[] replacementsArray = new String[replacements.size()];

str = StringUtils.replaceEach(str, searchNames
  .toArray(searchNamesArray), replacements
  .toArray(replacementsArray));
response.getWriter().write(str);
}

public void destroy() {
}
}
```

2 Adds init param value to list

3 Creates response wrapper

4 Retrieves response data

5 Replaces text with hyperlinks

The name of the filter initialization parameter **1** is added to the searchNames list; the value of the filter initialization parameter **2** is added as an HTML <a> element to the replacements list. We want to search the response data for names in the searchNames list and replace them with elements from the replacements list.

The CharResponseWrapper **3** is created during the preprocessing of the request and it's passed to the lower-order filters in the chain or to the portlet mapped to HyperlinkFilter. The response postprocessing **4** begins by first retrieving the response data from the CharResponseWrapper instance. All occurrences of search-Names elements in the response data **5** are replaced with the corresponding replacements elements. Because the replacements elements are HTML <a> elements, this effectively converts text matching searchNames elements in the response data to hyperlinks.

Now that you've seen examples of developing and configuring portlet filters, you're ready to see how you can create and configure filter chains.

13.7   *Filter chaining*

In previous examples, you saw how a single filter performs request and response processing. It's also possible to define a set of filters that preprocesses requests or postprocesses responses. When multiple filters apply to a request, they're referred to as a *filter chain*. Filters are applied to the request in the order in which the <filter-mapping> elements are defined in the portlet.xml file.

Consider the following sequence of <filter-mapping> declarations in the Book Catalog portlet's portlet.xml file:

```
<filter-mapping>
 <filter-name>hyperlinkFilter</filter-name>
 <portlet-name>bookCatalog</portlet-name>
</filter-mapping>

<filter-mapping>
 <filter-name>titleFilter</filter-name>
 <portlet-name>bookCatalog</portlet-name>
</filter-mapping>

<filter-mapping>
 <filter-name>utilityFilter</filter-name>
 <portlet-name>bookCatalog</portlet-name>
</filter-mapping>
```

Because filter mappings for the Book Catalog portlet are declared in the sequence `hyperlinkFilter`, then `titleFilter`, then `utilityFilter`, they're invoked in the same order when a portlet request is received for the Book Catalog portlet.

It's important to note that only those filters that apply to the lifecycle phase of the portlet are invoked. For instance, if an action request is received for a portlet, only the filters that apply to `ACTION_PHASE` are invoked.

NOTE The request and response objects passed by a filter to the `doFilter` method are available to the next filter in the chain. If you passed a request or response wrapper object to the `doFilter` method, it would be available to the next filter in the chain.

Filter chaining can be useful when you want the preprocessing of a request or post-processing of a response to occur in a particular sequence. For instance, you may have a request-logging filter that must be invoked after the security filter has verified that the request comes from an authenticated user.

13.8 Summary

In this chapter, you saw how filters can be created to preprocess different types of portlet requests and postprocess different types of portlet responses. We also looked at an example of how portlet response wrapper objects can be used to modify responses generated by portlet filters.

Filter logic is reusable, which makes *write-once-use-anywhere* possible. Portlet filters bring modularity to your portlet code, so their use is recommended if the processing logic needs to be reused across different portlets or portlet applications.

In the next chapter, we'll explore the concept of portlet bridges, which make it possible to expose your existing web applications as portlets.

Portlet bridges

14

So far in this book, we've focused on creating portlets using the Portlet 2.0 API, but in some, if not all, portal development projects you may also want to expose an existing web application as a portlet. Let's say that you have a Book Catalog web application for managing your book catalog, and it's developed using the JSF, or Struts, or Wicket web application framework. You have the choice of rewriting the Book Catalog web application as a portlet or exposing it as a portlet by using an appropriate *portlet bridge*.

Think of a portlet bridge as a wrapper around your existing web application that's responsible for converting portlet requests to something that your web application can understand and converting responses from the web application to something that your portlet environment can understand. Rewriting a web application as a portlet may be undesirable in many scenarios, mainly due to the learning curve associated with portlets, extra development and testing effort, and duplication of

510

business logic. Rewriting an existing web application as a portlet may only be desirable if an appropriate portlet bridge doesn't exist, or if the portlet bridge doesn't support important portlet features, like using portlet events and public render parameters for inter-portlet communication.

In this chapter, we'll first look at the concept of portlet bridges and how they expose a web application as a portlet. We'll then move on to look at some specific portlet bridges, like Liferay Portal's built-in iFrame portlet, PortletFaces Bridge for JavaServer Faces (JSF) web applications, and the Wicket framework's `WicketPortlet` class, which acts as a portlet bridge for Wicket web applications. We'll look at how a Book Catalog web application developed using JSF or Wicket is exposed using these portlet bridges. We'll also look at how you can use a standard directory structure to keep artifacts specific to web and portlet applications separate.

This chapter assumes that you already have a working knowledge of the JSF and Wicket frameworks. If you want to learn about these frameworks, refer to an introductory text on these frameworks.

NOTE The example JSF web application in this chapter makes use of JSF 2.0; the example Wicket web application uses Wicket 1.4.8.

Let's now take a deeper look at what portlet bridges are.

14.1 What is a portlet bridge?

A portlet bridge is a component that sits between the portlet environment and a web application. It's responsible for bridging the differences between the portlet environment and the environment in which the web application is designed to execute.

For instance, in the portlet world, a request has distinct lifecycle phases for processing user actions and rendering a response, whereas in the web application world, action processing and response generation are part of a single request lifecycle phase. Also, in the web application world, the response to a request is a complete web page, whereas in the portlet world, the response is a markup fragment that's handed over to the portal server, which renders the portal page.

A portlet bridge abstracts the web application environment from the portlet environment and vice versa, which makes it possible to develop web applications without knowledge of portlet technology. You can use an appropriate portlet bridge at a later date to expose it as a portlet.

Figure 14.1 shows the flow of a portlet request and response when a portlet bridge is used to adapt a web application to the portlet environment.

A portlet request ❶ is received by the portlet container, and ❷ the portlet container dispatches the request to the portlet instance for which the request is targeted. The portlet here acts as a wrapper around the portlet bridge, which in turn acts as a wrapper around the underlying web application.

The portlet dispatches a request ❸ to the portlet bridge for processing. The entry point into the bridge is generally through a bridge-specific class that extends the

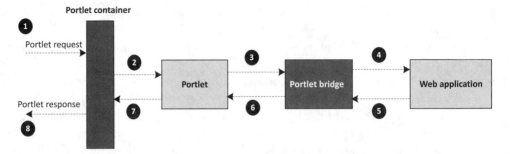

Figure 14.1   The Portlet bridge plays the mediatory role in adapting a web application to the portlet environment.

GenericPortlet class and is configured as the portlet class in the portlet.xml file. The portlet bridge translates the incoming portlet request to a request type that can be understood by the web application. For instance, if your web application is a Struts-based web application, the portlet bridge uses the portlet request information to find and invoke the appropriate Struts Action.

The portlet bridge ❹ sends the portlet request context information to the web application for processing of the request. For instance, in a Struts-based web application, the portlet bridge will send the portlet request context, request parameters, request attributes, session attributes, and other information that's required to process a Struts Action. Because servlet-based web applications don't have the concept of multiple request-processing phases, the portlet bridge is responsible for maintaining state, on behalf of the web application, across the multiple request phases of a request. For instance, in the case of a Struts application, the portlet bridge will split a portlet action request processing into a Struts Action invocation and the rendering of the view, making it look as if the web application also follows the portlet request-processing phases.

The portlet bridge ❺ receives a response from the web application. At this point, the bridge is responsible for translating the response for the portlet environment. The translated response is sent to the portlet, which acts as a wrapper around the web application ❻. Then the response from the portlet ❼ is sent to the portlet container. The portlet container ❽ sends the response to the portal server.

Portlet bridges for widely used web application frameworks exist, but there are situations in which you can't use a preexisting portlet bridge:

- If the web application is remotely located
- If the web application was developed using a web framework for which a portlet bridge isn't available
- If the web application doesn't use a standard web framework for developing the web application (which means a portlet bridge can't be developed)

If you have such a web application, you can still use a portlet that uses an HTML iFrame to provide access to it as a portlet.

NOTE Most portal servers come with built-in portlets to provide access to web applications without using a portlet bridge. For instance, WebSphere Portal Server provides a `WebClipping` portlet (an `iFrame`-based portlet), which also allows you to clip the HTML page of the web application served by the portlet.

Let's look at how a web application can become part of a web portal by using Liferay Portal's built-in iFrame portlet.

14.2 *iFrame portlets*

The HTML `<iframe>` element is used to embed an HTML page within another HTML page. It defines an `src` attribute, which identifies the URL of the HTML document to be served by the `<iframe>` element. You can create a simple `iFrame` portlet by writing an HTML `<iframe>` element as the response generated by the portlet.

Liferay Portal comes with a built-in `iFrame` portlet that can be used to serve a web-based application via your web portal with minimal effort. This built-in `iFrame` portlet provides a lot more features than if you were to show a web-based application in an `<iframe>` element, so using it is recommended over developing your own `iFrame` portlet. For instance, Liferay Portal provides configuration options to authenticate against the external web application and control the attributes of the `<iframe>` element used by the portlet to display the web application.

NOTE When a user interacts with the web application rendered by an `iFrame`-based portlet, the requests are sent directly to the web application; the `iFrame` portlet only plays the role of a proxy. Because of this, `iFrame`-based portlets are not considered to be portlet bridges in this chapter.

To use Liferay Portal's built-in `iFrame` portlet, go to the Sample category of the preinstalled portlets and select the `iFrame` portlet, as shown in figure 14.2.

After adding the `iFrame` portlet to a portal page, you must configure it to point to an external web application, as shown in figure 14.3.

The Source URL field specifies the web application URL ❶ that you want to show using the `iFrame` portlet. If the external web application is deployed in the same Liferay Portal server, you can specify the source URL

Figure 14.2   The `iFrame` portlet in the Sample category is used to display external web applications as portlets in a web portal.

relative to the context path and select the Relative to Context Path check box ❷. Select the check box labeled Authenticate ❸ if the external web application requires basic or form-based authentication. You can modify the attributes of the `<iframe>` HTML element ❹ that's rendered by the iFrame portlet to show the external web application.

Figure 14.3   Configuration options for the `iFrame` **portlet. You can specify the URL of the external web application, the authentication details, and the attributes of the HTML** `<iframe>` **element that's used by the** `iFrame` **portlet.**

Table 14.1 lists the benefits and drawbacks of using the built-in `iFrame`-based portlets available in most portal servers.

Table 14.1   Advantages and disadvantages of using the `iFrame` **portlet**

Advantages	Disadvantages
It provides the simplest way to bring your web applications to a portal platform.	This simplicity comes at the loss of web portal features that are available to portlets that use a portlet bridge. For instance, when the user interacts with the web application, the request doesn't pass through the web portal security infrastructure.
It allows you to authenticate against external web applications.	Authentication is limited to basic and form-based authentication mechanisms.
	The external web application's session timeout isn't synchronized with that of the web portal.
	A page refresh invokes the `render` method of the `iFrame` portlet, which redisplays the initial page of the web application; the state of the web page isn't maintained by the portlet.

Table 14.1 Advantages and disadvantages of using the `iFrame` portlet *(continued)*

Advantages	Disadvantages
	The look and feel of the web portal is generally poor because of the presence of menus and a header and footer in the external web application. Scrollbars in the `iFrame` portlet, allowing the user to see the complete content of the web page, further affect the user experience.

As evident is from table 14.1, the `iFrame` portlet is well suited for scenarios where you don't need most of the portal features, like inter-portlet communication, a consistent look and feel, portal security infrastructure, and so on.

Most portal servers provide portlet bridges for the standard frameworks, such as JSF, Struts, and Wicket. Let's take a look at how a JSF portlet bridge can be used to expose an existing web application, developed using JSF 2.0, as a portlet.

14.3 JSF portlets

JSF is a popular web MVC framework that's based on the concept of developing user interfaces as a tree of components. In JSF 2.0, the Facelets view technology is the preferred way to create JSF views.

In this section, we'll look at how to create a simplified Book Catalog JSF web application, which we'll expose as a portlet using PortletFaces Bridge. For more information about PortletFaces Bridge, see its official website (http://www.portletfaces.org/projects/portletfaces-bridge).

> ### Current state of JSF portlet bridges
>
> If you're using JSF 1.2 for developing new applications, or your existing web applications use JSF 1.2, there are two JSRs that define standard JSF portlet bridges: JSR-301 (JSF 1.2 portlet bridge for Portlet 1.0) and JSR-329 (JSF 1.2 portlet bridge for Portlet 2.0). The Apache MyFaces portlet bridge (http://myfaces.apache.org/portlet-bridge/index.html) project provides implementations for both JSRs. As I write this book, there's no JSR for developing a portlet bridge for JSF 2.0, but most portal server vendors provide a JSF 2.0 portlet bridge based on JSR-329.

CODE REFERENCE You should now import the ch14_portletfaces-example Eclipse project. Before you build the project, set the `liferay.portal.home` property in the build.properties file to point to your Liferay Portal installation directory. If you want to test the JSF web application, set the tomcat.home directory to point to your Tomcat installation.

Let's first look at the Book Catalog web application that we'll use to demonstrate the use of the PortletFaces Bridge.

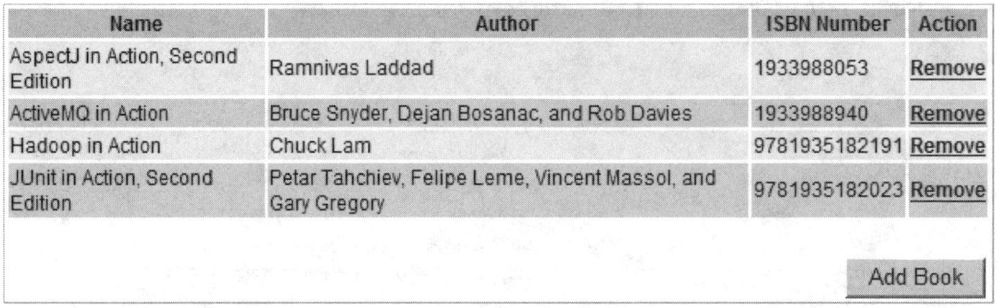

Name	Author	ISBN Number	Action
AspectJ in Action, Second Edition	Ramnivas Laddad	1933988053	Remove
ActiveMQ in Action	Bruce Snyder, Dejan Bosanac, and Rob Davies	1933988940	Remove
Hadoop in Action	Chuck Lam	9781935182191	Remove
JUnit in Action, Second Edition	Petar Tahchiev, Felipe Leme, Vincent Massol, and Gary Gregory	9781935182023	Remove
			Add Book

Figure 14.4   The Book Catalog web application home page. The Remove hyperlink lets a user remove a book from the catalog, and the Add Book button show a form for adding a new book to the catalog.

14.3.1   *Book Catalog JSF web application requirements*

Figure 14.4 shows the home page of the Book Catalog web application that we'll expose as a portlet using PortletFaces Bridge.

In figure 14.4, if a user clicks the Add Book button, a form is displayed in which the user can add a new book to the catalog, as shown in figure 14.5.

As shown in figure 14.5, the Title, Author, and ISBN Number fields of the Add Book form are mandatory. An input field is validated when the focus is removed from that field; JSF 2.0 Ajax support is used to validate the fields.

Let's now look at the directory structure used for developing the web and portlet applications. An important point to note here is that we're using the same code base to develop web and portlet applications.

14.3.2   *JSF web application project structure*

Figure 14.6 shows the directory structure of the project. The directory structure has been designed such that you can create a JSF web application and the corresponding portlet application using the same code base, as you'll see later in this section.

Figure 14.6 shows the important directories in the project structure for the Book Catalog JSF web application and portlet application. The directory structure is generic and can be reused in most JSF-based portlet projects.

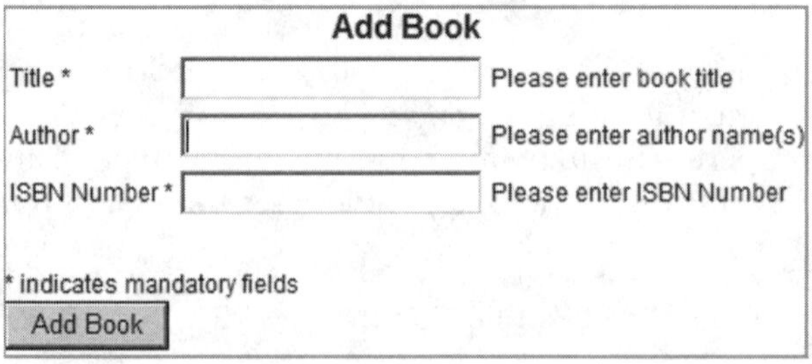

Add Book

Title *		Please enter book title
Author *		Please enter author name(s)
ISBN Number *		Please enter ISBN Number

* indicates mandatory fields

Add Book

Figure 14.5   The Add Book form is used to add a book to the catalog. This page makes use of JSF 2.0 Ajax support to validate the form.

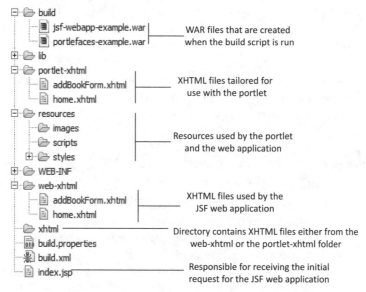

Figure 14.6 Directory structure for creating Book Catalog JSF web application and portlet application that uses PortletFaces Bridge

NOTE If you keep different code bases for web applications and the corresponding portlet applications, you'll end up with a duplication of code and you'll need to copy changes from one code base to the other. Using the same code base allows developers to test the web application before it's moved to the portal environment or to compare the behavior of the web application in portal and nonportal environments.

Let's look at each of the important directories shown in figure 14.6:

- *build*—Contains the web application and portlet application WAR files generated by the build process.
- *portlet-xhtml*—Contains the JSF web application's XHTML files that have been modified for use within the portlet environment. For instance, the XHTML files in the portlet-xhtml folder don't contain tags that generate <head>, <html>, and <body> HTML elements.
- *web-xhtml*—Contains the JSF web application XHTML files.
- *resources*—Contains resources used by the portlet application and the JSF web application, such as JavaScript, CSS, and images.
- *xhtml*—Used by the JSF web and portlet applications to serve views. This is an empty directory into which XHTML files are copied from the portlet-xhtml or web-xhtml folder during the build process. For instance, while creating a WAR file for the web application, the build process copies files from the web-xhtml folder to the xhtml folder; while creating a WAR file for the portlet application, the build process copies files from the portlet-xhtml folder to the xhtml folder.

Figure 14.6 shows the presence of an index.jsp file in the project. It's packaged in the JSF web application WAR file and is the first page that's accessed by the JSF web application user. The index.jsp page simply forwards the incoming request to the home page of the Book Catalog JSF web application.

Let's now go through the important files of the Book Catalog JSF web application. We'll look at how, with minimum modification to XHTML files and by adding portlet application–specific configuration files, you can expose the JSF web application with PortletFaces Bridge.

14.3.3 *Developing the Book Catalog web application using JSF*

A JSF web application consists of the following:

- *faces-config.xml*—This is a JSF-specific configuration XML file that contains managed beans declarations and page navigation information. As of JSF 2.0, a JSF application isn't required to provide managed beans declarations and navigation information in the faces-config.xml file.
- *XHTML files*—Because we're using the Facelets view technology, XHTML files represent JSF views that are responsible for generating the user interface of the web application. Alternatively, you can use JSP as the view technology, though Facelets is recommended. As of JSF 2.0, you don't need to do anything special to use Facelets because JSF 2.0 uses Facelets as its view technology by default.
- *Managed beans*—These are form-backing beans used by a JSF application to store application state. As of JSF 2.0, you can specify a class as a managed bean by using the `@ManagedBean` class-level annotation.
- `FacesServlet`—The `javax.faces.webapp.FacesServlet` servlet component is configured in the JSF web application's web.xml file, and it's used to resolve JSF views and to manage the request lifecycle in the application.
- *Resources*—Like any other web application, a JSF web application consists of images, JavaScript, and CSS files. JSF 2.0 provides special tags—`<outputScript>` and `<outputStylesheet>`—as part of its core HTML tag library to include JavaScript and CSS files in a web page.
- *Services and DAOs*—A real-world JSF application usually has service and DAO layers for providing business services and data access logic, respectively.

NOTE The Book Catalog JSF web application uses Mojarra JSF RI. For more information about Mojarra RI, refer to the official Project Mojarra website (http://javaserverfaces.java.net/). Alternatively, you can use Apache MyFaces RI to develop your JSF web application. For more information about Apache MyFaces RI, see the MyFaces project website (http://myfaces.apache.org/).

Now that you know what files and classes are involved in a JSF web application, let's look at the managed beans and XHTML files in the Book Catalog JSF web application.

MANAGED BEANS

The Book Catalog web application consists of two JSF-managed beans:

- BookCatalogBean—A session-scoped managed bean that defines validation and request-processing logic for the Book Catalog web application.
- BookService—An application-scoped managed bean that maintains catalog data and defines methods to retrieve books from the catalog, add a new book, and remove an existing book from the catalog.

The following listing shows some of the important properties and methods of the BookCatalogBean session-scoped managed bean.

Listing 14.1 The `BookCatalogBean` class

```
import javax.el.ELResolver;
import javax.faces.bean.ManagedBean;
import javax.faces.bean.SessionScoped;
import javax.faces.context.FacesContext;

@ManagedBean(name = "bookCatalogBean")          ❶ Session-scoped
@SessionScoped                                      managed bean
public class BookCatalogBean implements Serializable {
 private Book book = new Book();                 ❷ Properties of
 private Map<String, String> errorMap              managed bean
    = new HashMap<String, String>();

 public Book getBook() {
  return book;
 }
 ...
 public Map<String, String> getErrorMap() {
  return errorMap;
 }
 ...
 public String showAddBookForm() {
  return "addBookForm";
 }

 public List<Book> getBooks() {
  FacesContext fc = FacesContext.getCurrentInstance();
  ELResolver elResolver =
       fc.getApplication().getELResolver();
  BookService bookService =                       ❸ getBooks method
    (BookService) elResolver.getValue(fc              to obtain books
   .getELContext(), null, "bookService");
  return bookService.getBooks();
 }

 public String removeBook() {
  FacesContext fc = FacesContext.getCurrentInstance();
  String isbnNumber = fc.getExternalContext().    ❹ removeBook method
    getRequestParameterMap().get("isbnNumber");       to remove a book
  ...
 }
```

```
public void validateIsbn(ValueChangeEvent vce) {
  ...
}
  ...
}
```

The @ManagedBean annotation ❶ indicates that BookCatalogBean is a managed bean in the JSF application. The name element identifies the name with which Book-CatalogBean is registered in a scope. The @SessionScoped annotation specifies that the BookCatalogBean must be stored in session scope, which means it's available until the HttpSession is invalidated.

The book and errorMap properties ❷ are defined. The book property identifies an empty Book object that's populated when a user submits the Add Book form shown in figure 14.5. The errorMap property stores error messages corresponding to the input fields shown on the Add Book form.

The getBooks method ❸ is invoked by the JSF data table (see listing 14.2) to retrieve the list of books in the catalog. Internally, the getBooks method retrieves the BookService application-scoped managed bean and invokes its getBooks method to retrieve the list of books.

The removeBook method ❹ is invoked when a user clicks the Remove hyperlink shown in figure 14.4. Like the getBooks method, the removeBook method makes use of BookService to remove the selected book from the catalog.

NOTE   If your managed bean includes calls to ExternalContext's redirect method, you should remove such calls from your managed bean because it will attempt to redirect the portal user to somewhere outside the web portal. PortletFaces Bridge overrides the default behavior of the redirect method to do nothing, essentially ignoring calls to redirect.

XHTML FILES

The XHTML files in the Book Catalog web application represent JSF views. The next listing shows the home.xhtml file, which generates the list of books in the catalog, as shown in figure 14.4.

Listing 14.2   The home.xhtml file

```
<html xmlns:h=http://java.sun.com/jsf/html...>
  <h:head>
    <title>Book Catalog Web Application</title>
  </h:head>
  <h:body>
    <h:form>
      <h:outputStylesheet name="bookCatalog.css"
        library="styles" target="head"/>
      <h:dataTable border="0"
        headerClass="headerBgColor"
        value="#{bookCatalogBean.books}" ...>
        ...
      </h:dataTable>
```

❶ HTML, HEAD, and BODY elements

❷ CSS inserted inside HEAD element

```
        ...
      </h:form>
    </h:body>
</html>
```

The `<html>`, `<head>`, and `<body>` HTML elements ❶ are rendered in the generated markup by the JSF HTML tag library tags. The `<h:head>` and `<h:body>` tags are new additions to the HTML tag library, and they provide the *resource relocation* feature in JSF 2.0; you can specify the location, in the generated markup, where a particular resource must be inserted.

The `<h:outputStylesheet>` tag ❷ is used to insert a style sheet (a resource) into the web page. The `target` attribute of the `<h:outputStylesheet>` tag identifies the location in the generated markup where the style sheet needs to be inserted. In this example, the bookCatalog.css style sheet is inserted in the `<head>` element. Alternatively, you can specify the value of the `target` attribute as `body`, which means that the style sheet will be inserted inside the `<body>` element of the generated markup. The `library` attribute of `<h:outputStylesheet>` identifies the location of the bookCatalog.css file in the resources directory of the project. The bookCatalog.css file is located inside the resources/styles directory, so the value of the `library` attribute is specified as `styles`.

In section 3.3.5 of chapter 3, you saw that the use of `<html>`, `<head>`, `<title>`, and `<body>` elements is discouraged in the markup generated by the portlet because it can potentially break the portal page. The home.xhtml file contains these elements, so you must remove them to allow the Book Catalog JSF application to render correctly in the portal environment. This explains why there are separate sets of XHTML files for the JSF web application and for the portlet application.

If you remove the `<head>` and `<body>` elements from home.xhtml, the `<h:output-Stylesheet>` tag is rendered useless, because you can no longer specify the target location in the markup where you want to insert the bookCatalog.css file. This is perfectly fine, because portlets use a portal server–specific approach to add JavaScript and CSS files to the `head` section of the HTML, or they make use of the `Render-Response`'s `MARKUP_HEAD_ELEMENT` property, as described in section 3.3.5 of chapter 3. So you also need to remove the `<h:outputStylesheet>` tag from the home.xhtml file and use the liferay-portlet.xml configuration file to inject the bookCatalog.css file into the `head` section of the portal page.

> **NOTE** JSF 2.0 introduced the `<h:outputScript>` tag to insert JavaScript files into the generated markup. If your JSF view uses the `<h:outputScript>` tag, you must remove this tag from your JSF view and insert the JavaScript file using the mechanism supported by your portal server.

The Book Catalog JSF application also makes use of the JSF 2.0 Ajax feature to validate the fields in the Add Book form. The following listing shows the addBookForm.xhtml file which displays the Add Book form.

Listing 14.3   The addBookForm.xhtml file

```html
<html xmlns:h="http://java.sun.com/jsf/html"
      xmlns:f="http://java.sun.com/jsf/core"
 ...>
<h:head>
 <title>Book Catalog Web Application</title>
</h:head>
<h:body>
 <h:form>
   <h:inputText id="isbnNumber"
    value="#{bookCatalogBean.book.isbnNumber}"
    valueChangeListener="#{bookCatalogBean.
         ➥ validateIsbn}"
    converterMessage="Please enter a valid ISBN Number"
    required="true"
    requiredMessage="Please enter ISBN Number">

    <f:convertNumber type="number" />

    <f:ajax event="blur"
     render="isbnNumberErrorMsg
           ➥ isbnNumberValidationMsg" />
   </h:inputText>

   <h:message styleClass="plainText"
        id="isbnNumberErrorMsg" for="isbnNumber" />
   <h:outputText id="isbnNumberValidationMsg"
     value="#{bookCatalogBean.errorMap.isbnNumber}" />
   ...
</h:form>
</h:body>
</html>
```

❶ Input text field component

❷ `<f:ajax>` tag

❸ Message and text components

`<h:inputText>` is used ❶ to render an HTML text field in which the user enters the book's ISBN.

The `<f:ajax>` tag ❷ represents the Ajax tag of the JSF core tag library. Because it's specified inside the `<h:inputText>` tag, it associates an Ajax action with the text field rendered by the `<h:inputText>` tag. The event attribute identifies the event with which the Ajax action is associated. The value blur indicates that the Ajax action is fired when the cursor moves out of the ISBN Number text field. The Ajax request processes the ISBN Number text field component on the server, executes the validateIsbn method (refer to listing 14.1) corresponding to the valueChange-Listener attribute, and renders the components identified by the render attribute of the `<f:ajax>` tag. If the user enters an ISBN that already exists in the catalog, an error message is stored in the errorMap property (see listing 14.1) with isbnNumber as the key.

`<h:message>` ❸ represents a component that displays messages associated with the ISBN Number text field, and `<h:outputText>` represents a component that shows the value corresponding to the isbnNumber key in the errorMap property of the Book-CatalogBean managed bean.

In this section, you saw some important aspects of the Book Catalog JSF web application. Now the moment you've been waiting for—we're ready to expose this web application as a portlet.

14.3.4 *Developing the Book Catalog portlet using a JSF portlet bridge*

In the previous section, we discussed how the Book Catalog web application makes use of new JSF 2.0 features, like resource relocation and Ajax. In this section, we'll look at what you need to do to expose the Book Catalog web application as a portlet using PortletFaces Bridge.

You need to perform the following steps to expose the Book Catalog web application as a portlet:

1 Remove the `<html>`, `<h:head>`, `<h:body>`, `<h:outputScript>`, and `<h:outputStylesheet>` tags from all XHTML files in the web application.

2 Remove calls to the `ExternalContext`'s `redirect` method from the managed bean class. PortletFaces Bridge ignores calls to the `redirect` method, so this step can be considered optional.

3 Add the portlet.xml file to your web application to convert it into a portlet application. Later in this section, we'll look at the Book Catalog portlet application's portlet.xml file.

4 Add portal server–specific files to the portlet application. Because we're using Liferay Portal, this includes the liferay-portlet.xml and liferay-display.xml files.

5 Add references to any CSS and JavaScript files that are required by the web application to the liferay-portlet.xml file.

6 Add the PortletFaces Bridge JAR files (portletfaces-bridge-api and portletfaces-bridge-impl) and dependencies to your web application's WEB-INF/lib directory.

Let's look at the Book Catalog portlet application's portlet deployment descriptor (the portlet.xml file), which explains how PortletFaces Bridge is used in exposing a JSF web application.

PORTLET DEPLOYMENT DESCRIPTOR

The portlet deployment descriptor of a portlet that uses a portlet bridge relies on the portlet bridge to provide two things:

- The portlet implementation class
- The portlet initialization parameters to configure the portlet bridge for the portlet

The next listing shows how PortletFaces Bridge is configured for the Book Catalog portlet.

Listing 14.4 The Book Catalog portlet application's portlet.xml file

```
<portlet-app ...>
 <portlet>
  <portlet-name>bookCatalog</portlet-name>
```

```
<portlet-class>
    org.portletfaces.bridge.GenericFacesPortlet
</portlet-class>
<init-param>
 <name>javax.portlet.faces.defaultViewId.view</name>
 <value>/xhtml/home.xhtml</value>
</init-param>
<supports>
 <mime-type>text/html</mime-type>
 <portlet-mode>view</portlet-mode>
</supports>
<portlet-info>
 <title>Book Catalog</title>
</portlet-info>
</portlet>
</portlet-app>
```

❶ Portlet class

❷ Default JSF view in VIEW mode

`org.portletfaces.bridge.GenericFacesPortlet` ❶ is the portlet class that extends the Portlet API's `GenericPortlet` class. `GenericFacesPortlet` is the entry point into the bridge framework, and it's responsible for bridging the gap between the portlet and the JSF web application environments. The `javax.portlet.faces.default-ViewId.<portletMode>` initialization parameter ❷ identifies the default JSF view for the `<portletMode>` portlet mode. For instance, the `javax.portlet.faces.default-ViewId.view` initialization parameter identifies the default JSF view for the VIEW portlet mode, and `javax.portlet.faces.defaultViewId.edit` identifies the default JSF view for the EDIT portlet mode.

You've now seen the basics of using PortletFaces Bridge, but there's more to it than just exposing an existing JSF web application as a portlet. A couple of questions arise when you use a portlet bridge to expose a web application as a portlet to a web portal:

- How will the portlet interact with other portlets on the portal page?
- How will the portlet make use of the portlet preferences feature that's exclusively available to portlets?

JSR-329 did a pretty good job of defining JSF portlet bridge requirements to ensure seamless integration between JSF web applications and the portlet environment. And because it religiously follows JSR-329, PortletFaces Bridge helps you address inter-portlet communication and the personalization requirements of your portal-enabled JSF web application.

For instance, you can specify an event handler for your JSF portlet to process portlet events, as shown in the following portlet.xml file:

```
<portlet-app ...>
 <portlet>
  <portlet-name>bookCatalog</portlet-name>
  <portlet-class>
     org.portletfaces.bridge.GenericFacesPortlet
  </portlet-class>
```

```
  <init-param>
    <name>javax.portlet.faces.bridgeEventHandler</name>
    <value>ch11.code.listing.BookAddedEventHandler</value>
  </init-param>
  ...
</portlet-app>
```

In the preceding XML fragment, `BookAddedEventHandler` represents a portlet event handler for the Book Catalog portlet that receives an event when a book is added by some other portlet on the same portal page. The `BookAddedEventHandler` must implement the `org.portletfaces.bridge.BridgeEventHandler` interface.

Even though JSF applications aren't capable of handling portlet events, Portlet-Faces Bridge makes it possible for the JSF-based portlet to process portlet events generated by other portlets. Similarly, a JSF portlet can access public render parameters set by other portlets and bind them to JSF-managed bean properties or access `PortletPreferences` objects associated with a JSF portlet to access or update the preferences of the portlet. For more information on how you can personalize a JSF portlet or access public render parameters, refer to the official PortletFaces Bridge website (http://www.portletfaces.org/projects/portletfaces-bridge).

> **WARNING** At the time of writing, PortletFaces Bridge was in Beta2 release and the support for public render parameters was under development. Please refer to the PortletFaces Bridge website for the current state of the bridge.

We'll now look at a web application that's developed using the Wicket framework and that's exposed as a portlet using the portlet bridge provided by Wicket.

14.4 Wicket portlets

The Wicket web application framework is similar to JSF in the sense that it's also based on the concept of developing user interfaces as a tree of components. You can develop a Wicket web application and expose it as a portlet using the portlet bridge provided by the Wicket framework.

Let's first look at the requirements of the Book Catalog web application that we'll expose using the Wicket portlet bridge.

14.4.1 Book Catalog Wicket web application requirements

Figure 14.7 shows a simple Book Catalog web application that we'll create using the Wicket framework and expose as a portlet. This figure shows a page of the Book Catalog web application, which displays books in a tabular format, sorted by book title, and lets you page through the complete list of books using the data scroller provided at the top-right corner of the table. When a user clicks a link in the data scroller, an Ajax request is sent to the server to asynchronously retrieve more books to display to the user, and the table is updated without refreshing the web page.

Showing 1 to 5 of 7		<< < 1 2 > >>
Name	**Author**	**ISBN Number**
ActiveMQ in Action	Bruce Snyder, Dejan Bosanac, and Rob Davies	1933988940
AspectJ in Action, Second Edition	Ramnivas Laddad	1933988053
Griffon in Action	Andres Almiray and Danno Ferrin	9781935182238
Hadoop in Action	Chuck Lam	9781935182191
JUnit in Action, Second Edition	Petar Tahchiev, Felipe Leme, Vincent Massol, and Gary Gregory	9781935182023

Figure 14.7   The Book Catalog web application developed using the Wicket web framework. It shows the books in the catalog in a tabular format and lets you page through the list.

CODE REFERENCE   You should now import the ch14_wicket-example Eclipse project so you can follow along with the code examples. Before you build the project, set the `liferay.portal.home` property in the build.properties file to point to your Liferay Portal installation directory. If you want to test the Wicket web application, set the tomcat.home directory to point to your Tomcat installation.

Now, let's look at the directory structure for the Book Catalog web and portlet applications.

14.4.2   *Wicket web application project structure*

Figure 14.8 shows the directory structure of the project. The directory structure has been designed such that you can create a Wicket web application and the corresponding portlet application using the same code base, as you'll see later in this section.

Let's now look at each of the important directories shown in figure 14.8.

- *build*—Contains the web and portlet application WAR files generated by the build process.
- *html-portlet*—Contains the HTML files of the Wicket web application that have been modified for use within the portlet environment. For instance, the HTML files in the html-portlet folder don't contain tags that generate <head>, <html>, and <body> HTML elements.
- *html-web*—Contains HTML files for the Wicket web application.

Figure 14.8 shows an index.jsp file in the project, which is packaged in the Wicket web application WAR file. It's the first page that's accessed by the Wicket web application user, and it simply forwards the incoming request to the home page of the Book Catalog Wicket web application.

In Wicket applications, web pages are represented by HTML pages that specify placeholders for Wicket components (like HTML tables, text fields, and so on), and there's a WebPage class corresponding to *each* HTML page that's responsible for assigning Wicket components to the placeholders defined in the HTML page. By default, the Wicket framework expects that the HTML page and the corresponding WebPage class are in the same package.

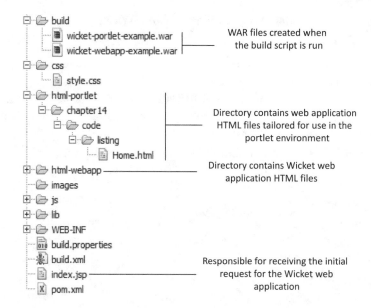

Figure 14.8   Directory structure for creating the Book Catalog Wicket web and portlet applications

If you need to develop a Wicket portlet and Wicket web application from the same code base, storing HTML pages in the same package as the corresponding `WebPage` class will limit you to using only a *single* HTML page for both the Wicket portlet and web application. You already know that HTML pages for the portlet shouldn't contain certain HTML elements, so you need to have different HTML pages for the Wicket portlet and web application.

To address the requirement of having a different set of HTML pages for the Wicket portlet and the Wicket web application, there are html-portlet and html-webapp folders that contain the HTML pages for the portlet and web application, respectively.

NOTE   In this project structure, you don't need to worry about putting an HTML page into the directory that contains the corresponding `WebPage` class because both the html-portlet and html-webapp directories mimic the package in which the corresponding `WebPage` class resides. For instance, in figure 14.8, the Home.html page is located in the chapter14/code/listing folder, which is the location of the corresponding `WebPage` class in the source folder. The build script in this example project simply copies the HTML pages to WEB-INF/classes directory, which ensures that each HTML page ends up in the same directory as the corresponding `WebPage` class.

Let's now look at how you can go about creating the Book Catalog web application using Wicket.

14.4.3 *Developing the Book Catalog web application using Wicket*

A Wicket web application typically consists of the following:

- HTML pages that contain references to Wicket components, like tables, text fields, and so on.

- WebPage classes corresponding to each HTML page in the web application. A WebPage class is responsible for binding Wicket components to the component references defined in the HTML pages.

- A WebApplication class that defines the Wicket application and provides application-wide settings. For instance, if you want to keep the HTML pages of your Wicket application in a different package than the one in which the corresponding WebPage class is located, you can override this default behavior by extending the WebApplication class. As you'll see shortly, you can also specify the home page of a Wicket application by overriding the getHomePage method of the WebApplication class.

- Services and DAOs.

Let's look at some of the important files in the Book Catalog web application.

HTML PAGE

As mentioned earlier, HTML pages in a Wicket application contain references to Wicket components. The Home.html page, which displays the data table shown in figure 14.7, is shown next.

Listing 14.5   The Home.html page

```
<?xml version="1.0" encoding="UTF-8"?>
<html ...>
  <body>
    <table class="dataview" cellspacing="0"          ❶ Wicket component
        wicket:id="table"/>                               with ID table
  </body>
</html>
```

The wicket:id attribute ❶ references a Wicket component. The value of this attribute is table, which means that the WebPage class corresponding to the Home.html page will be responsible for describing the Wicket component associated with table.

Let's now look at the Home class corresponding to the Home.html page, which sets the Wicket component identified with the wicket:id of table in the Home .html page.

WICKET WEBPAGE

The Home class corresponding to the Home.html page associates the components referenced by the Home.html page, as shown next.

Listing 14.6   The Home class

```
import org.apache.wicket...AjaxFallbackDefaultDataTable;
import org.apache.wicket...IColumn;
```

```
import org.apache.wicket...PropertyColumn;
import org.apache.wicket...SortableDataProvider;
public class Home extends WebPage {
 public Home() {
  List<IColumn<Book>> columns =
        new ArrayList<IColumn<Book>>();                    ❶ Creates columns
  ...                                                        of data table
  columns.add(new PropertyColumn<Book>(
    new Model<String>("Author"), "author"));

  SortableDataProvider<Book> sdp =
        new BookDataProvider();                            ❷ Creates Ajax data
  sdp.setSort("name", true);                                 table component
  add(new AjaxFallbackDefaultDataTable<Book>
     ➥ ("table", columns,sdp, 5));
 }
}
```

The columns of the data table are created ❶. The arguments to the Property-
Column<Book> class identify the header of the column and the name of the Book's
property whose value is displayed in the column.

SortableDataProvider acts as the provider of the data that will be displayed in the
data table ❷. AjaxFallbackDefaultDataTable is a Wicket component that renders an
Ajax-based data table. Once the AjaxFallbackDefaultDataTable is created, it's added
to the component hierarchy maintained by the Home class for the Home.html page.
The first argument to AjaxFallbackDefaultDataTable is a unique identifier of the
component, and it must match a wicket:id value in the corresponding HTML page. In
this example, the first argument to AjaxFallbackDefaultDataTable is table, which
means it's associated with the wicket:id="table" component reference defined in the
Home.html page.

Let's now look at the WebApplication object that defines the Wicket web application.

WICKET WEBAPPLICATION

The WebApplication object that defines the home page of the Book Catalog web
application is shown next.

Listing 14.7 The BookCatalogApp class

```
import org.apache.wicket.protocol.http.WebApplication;
public class BookCatalogApp extends WebApplication
{
    public Class<Home> getHomePage()
    {                                              ❶ Define home page
        return Home.class;                           of application
    }
}
```

BookCatalogApp overrides the getHomePage method of WebApplication ❶ to
return the WebPage class that corresponds to the home page of the Book Catalog
web application. Because it returns Home.class, the home page of the Book Catalog web application is the Home.html page.

This is all you need to know about this example Wicket web application. Let's now look at the steps involved in bringing this web application to a web portal.

14.4.4 Developing the Book Catalog portlet using a Wicket portlet bridge

You need to perform the following steps to expose the Book Catalog Wicket web application as a portlet:

1 Remove the <html>, <head>, and <body> elements from all HTML pages of the web application. The HTML pages tailored for the portlet environment are stored in the html-portlet directory.

2 Remove any calls to redirect requests outside of the Wicket application.

3 Set the WicketFilter's detectPortletContext initialization parameter to true. WicketFilter is a servlet filter that's configured in the web.xml file of the Wicket web application, and it's responsible for intercepting Wicket requests to set off request processing. Setting detectPortletContext to true instructs Wicket-Filter to check for the presence of the PortletContext and, if it's present, to override the default behavior of WicketFilter to suit the portlet environment.

4 Add the portlet.xml file to your web application to convert it into a portlet application.

5 Add the portal server–specific files to the portlet application. Because we're using Liferay Portal, this includes the liferay-portlet.xml and liferay-display. xml files.

6 Add a reference to the CSS and JavaScript files that were required by the web application to the liferay-portlet.xml file.

As you can see, you need to make some changes to your existing Wicket web application to expose it as a portlet. This is similar to what we did to expose a JSF web application as a portlet. The good thing is that the changes to the web application are limited to its views and configuration.

Let's now look at the Book Catalog portlet application's web.xml and portlet.xml files, which use the same code base as the Wicket web application.

WEB APPLICATION DEPLOYMENT DESCRIPTOR
The following listing shows the web.xml file of the Book Catalog web application.

Listing 14.8 The web.xml file

```
<web-app ...>
 <filter>
  <filter-name>BookCatalogApp</filter-name>
  <filter-class>org.apache.wicket.protocol.
     ➥http.WicketFilter</filter-class>
  <init-param>
   <param-name>detectPortletContext</param-name>
   <param-value>true</param-value>
  </init-param>
```

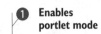 **Enables portlet mode**

```
 <init-param>
  <param-name>applicationClassName</param-name>
  <param-value>chapter14.code.listing.
        BookCatalogApp</param-value>
 </init-param>
 <init-param>
  <param-name>filterMappingUrlPattern</param-name>
  <param-value>/bookCatalogApp/*</param-value>
 </init-param>
</filter>

<filter-mapping>
 <filter-name>BookCatalogApp</filter-name>
 <url-pattern>/bookCatalogApp/*</url-pattern>
 ...
</filter-mapping>
</web-app>
```

② Specifies WebApplication class name

③ Specifies filter-mapping URL

detectPortletContext instructs the WicketFilter to run in a portlet mode **❶** if PortletContext is available. applicationClassName specifies the fully qualified class name of the WebApplication class **❷**. The filterMappingUrlPattern parameter informs WicketFilter about the URL to which WicketFilter is mapped **❸** using the <filter-mapping> element.

PORTLET DEPLOYMENT DESCRIPTOR

The next listing shows that the portlet.xml file configures the WicketPortlet class as the portlet class for the Book Catalog portlet. The WicketPortlet class acts as a portlet bridge.

Listing 14.9   The Book Catalog portlet application's portlet.xml file

```
<portlet-app ...>
 <portlet>
  <portlet-name>bookCatalogApp</portlet-name>
  <portlet-class>
     org.apache.wicket.protocol.http.portlet.
     ➥WicketPortlet</portlet-class>
  <init-param>
   <name>wicketFilterPath</name>
   <value>/bookCatalogApp</value>
  </init-param>
  ...
</portlet-app>
```

Built-in portlet class

The WicketPortlet class is responsible for bridging the gap between the portlet and Wicket environments. It accepts a wicketFilterPath initialization parameter, which points to the path of the WicketFilter, as defined in the web.xml file, except that it doesn't have a trailing /*.

Listing 14.9 shows how the Wicket framework's built-in WicketPortlet class allows you to use a Wicket web application as a portlet. Unlike PortletFaces Bridge, WicketPortlet doesn't restrict you from redirecting a Wicket request outside the Wicket web application, so you must remove all redirect calls that point outside of the web application.

NOTE As of Wicket 1.4.9, `WicketPortlet` doesn't support the use of public render parameters and portlet events, which are required for inter-portlet communication. If you want to use inter-portlet communication with your Wicket portlets, you may have to wait until Wicket 1.5 is released. See the official Wicket website (http://wicket.apache.org/) for the latest updates on its support for portlet events and public render parameters.

You've now seen all you need to do to convert your Wicket web applications into portlet applications. You can now deploy the Book Catalog portlet application in Liferay Portal and use it like any other portlet.

14.5   *Summary*

In this chapter, we looked at how you can develop web applications using your favorite framework and expose them as portlets using a portlet bridge. We looked at two sample web applications—a JSF and a Wicket web application—and saw how portlet bridges simplify the process of bringing existing applications to a web portal. You also saw how you can expose an existing web application using Liferay Portal's built-in iFrame portlet.

In most portal projects, you'll come across scenarios where developing an existing web application as a portlet isn't feasible, or the developers are well acquainted with a particular web framework but not with portlet technology. In such scenarios, using a portlet bridge can accelerate the development of portlets and bring existing web applications to web portals.

As you saw in the examples in this chapter, portlet bridges may not support all of the features that are available to portlets developed using Java portlet technology. It's recommended that before choosing a web framework for developing portlets, you should check out the portlet bridges that are available for that web framework and make sure that it supports the features you need in your portlets.

In the next and last chapter, we'll look at how you can access remotely deployed portlets using Web Services for Remote Portlets (WSRP).

Web Services for
Remote Portlets (WSRP)

This chapter covers

- WSRP concepts
- Publishing portlets as a service
- Consuming remote portlets as a service

Just as you'd expect, a *web service* is a service that's accessible over the web. HTTP and XML form the backbone of web services, which fact makes them platform and language independent. Web services provide the means to achieve SOA (service-oriented architecture)—an architectural approach in which systems are composed of loosely coupled services.

In the context of SOA, a *service* refers to a functionality of *value* to the consumer of the web service. Amazon's Fulfillment Web Service (Amazon FWS) is a good example of this concept. This feature allows merchants to request Amazon to physically fulfill customer orders on their behalf: Amazon does the work for a small fee, and you reap the benefits of not having to lug your stuff to the post office and fulfill orders on your own. Web services are *data-oriented* services—they process requests and return *data*. This puts the burden on web service consumers to provide presentation logic for the web service.

Web Services for Remote Portlets (WSRP) is an OASIS specification that defines *presentation-oriented* web services that not only provide data but also the presentation logic. This makes WSRP ideal for incorporating content from different data sources without writing a single line of code. Because WSRP is an extension of data-oriented web services, this chapter assumes that you're conversant with web service concepts.

What does all this have to do with portlets? Let's say that an online seller allows merchants to sell their products by publishing product details on the seller's website. This seller provides a Sales web service to its merchants that can be used to add, view, and modify product details. The merchant is responsible for creating a user interface to interact with the Sales web service, allowing its users to add, view, and modify the product details. Figure 15.1 shows the role played by a web service and its client in a scenario where the web service provides only the business logic, and the client is responsible for providing the user interface and presentation logic for interacting with the web service.

The downside of this approach is that the merchant is able to use the business logic provided by the Sales web service, but they need to write the presentation logic and user interface to present the data returned by the web service. Instead of providing a Sales web service, if the seller provides a WSRP-compliant portlet, the merchants would simply need to add these portlets, as they would any other locally developed portlet, to their web portal.

Figure 15.2 shows the scenario in which a WSRP-compliant Merchant portlet is provided by the seller. In this figure, the seller publishes a Merchant portlet via a *WSRP producer*, and the portlet is consumed by a *WSRP consumer* of the merchant's portal server. The merchant adds the Merchant portlet to their web portal as if it were locally deployed. The WSRP consumer retrieves *markup* and *data* for the Merchant portlet from seller's portal server by interacting with the WSRP producer. Also, when users interact with the Merchant portlet, the user interaction is dispatched to the WSRP producer by the WSRP consumer for processing. We'll discuss WSRP producers and consumers in detail in the next section.

You can think of WSRP as a standard that lets you publish a portlet as a *service*. In this chapter, we'll discuss WSRP and look at how portal servers' WSRP administration

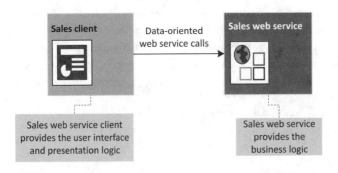

Figure 15.1 The web service provides the business logic, and the web service client provides the user interface and presentation logic.

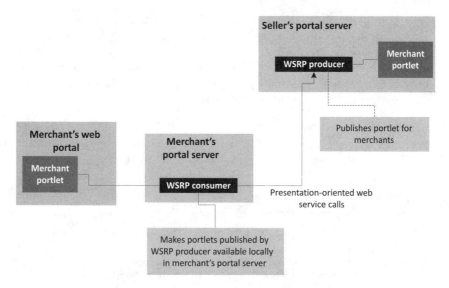

**Figure 15.2	The seller publishes a Merchant portlet that merchants add to their web portal. The WSRP producer and WSRP consumer act as publisher and consumer of the Merchant portlet, respectively.**

features simplify both publishing and consuming portlets. We'll also look at how you can use the WSRP administration features available in Liferay Portal to publish and consume some of the portlets that we developed in previous chapters. The OpenPortal WSRP implementation is also covered in the context of WSRP's registration and leasing concepts.

> **NOTE**	OASIS released two WSRP specifications: WSRP v1.0 and v2.0. WSRP v2.0 introduced features like inter-portlet communication, caching, and resource serving, which are aligned with the Portlet 2.0 specification. In this chapter, we'll focus on WSRP 2.0 because it complements the features supported by Portlet 2.0–compliant portlet containers.

Let's begin by looking at how WSRP works behind the scenes to *publish* a portlet installed in a portal server as a web service, and to *consume* this web service to access the portlet.

## 15.1	*What makes remote portlets a reality?*

WSRP defines two key actors—*producers* and *consumers*. A producer is part of the portal server that wants to publish its portlets to the external world as presentation-oriented web services. The portlets published by a producer are referred to as *remote portlets*. A consumer is part of a portal server that intends to use remote portlets (portlets published by producers). You can think of a producer as a web service *endpoint* and a consumer as a web service client. We'll shortly see that producers expose multiple web services, which are used by consumers to interact with remote portlets.

NOTE The intent of the Portlet specification is to build portlets that behave consistently across compliant portlet containers, and WSRP deals with publishing and consuming portlets, irrespective of the technology used to develop them. WSRP isn't specific to a particular technology; you can have a WSRP-compliant consumer written in Java for consuming portlets published by a WSRP-compliant producer written in .NET.

Figure 15.3 shows the role played by producers and consumers in WSRP. Obviously, there's a lot going on in this figure. Let's walk through it together. Portal server A aggregates content from portal servers B and C. Because portal server A *consumes* portlets from B and C, it hosts the consumer. Because portal servers B and C publish portlets for use by portal server A, they host the producers. The producers act as *containers* for portals B and C's portlets and are responsible for managing their lifecycles.

NOTE It's possible for a portal server to act both as a publisher and consumer of portlets, in which case, it contains both consumer and producer applications.

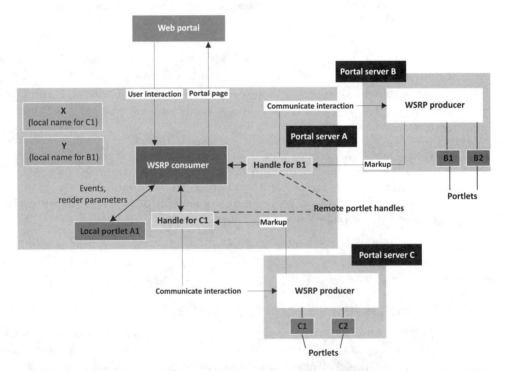

Figure 15.3   Producers and consumers communicate with each other to make remote portlets a reality. A consumer communicates with remote portlets using portlet handles.

In figure 15.3, the web portal (hosted by portal server A) shows remote portlets B1 (from portal server B) and C1 (from portal server C) and the local portlet A1. To use remote portlets, the consumer registers (if required) with the producers and holds references to the remote portlets, also referred to as *portlet handles*. Remote portlets C1 and B1 are registered with portal server A with local names X and Y, respectively. When the user interacts with portlet X or Y, the interaction is passed to remote portlet B1 or C1 via the portlet handle.

You can think of a producer as a bank, with portlets published by producers being bank accounts, portlet handles being ATM cards issued by the bank, consumers being ATM machines, web portals being the user interfaces presented by ATM machines, and web portal users being bank customers. In figure 15.3, the web portal user (bank customer) interacts with portlet X or Y displayed by the web portal (ATM machine's user interface). The consumer (ATM machine) makes use of the portlet handle (ATM card) to interact with the producer (bank) to invoke remote portlet B1 or C1 (bank account) for processing a user interaction.

Figure 15.3 also shows that portal server A has a local portlet A1 that communicates with the consumer. The consumer is responsible for mediating communication between the local portlet A1 and locally registered remote portlets B1 and C1, making it look like the remote portlets B1 and C1 are also local to portal server A. As in the case of local portlets, you can use portlet events or public render parameters for communicating between remote portlets and local portlets or between remote portlets from the same or different producers.

The WSRP specification defines multiple web service interfaces that a producer implements to allow consumers to interact with portlets published by the producer. Table 15.1 describes both the mandatory and optional web service interfaces that a WSRP producer implements.

Table 15.1 Web service interfaces implemented by WSRP producers

Web service interface	Description
Service Description	A *mandatory* interface that allows WSRP consumers to discover information about the portlets hosted by the producer. Additionally, it provides information on how consumers can register with the producer and interact with the portlets hosted by the producer.
Markup	A *mandatory* interface that allows WSRP consumers to interact with the portlets hosted by WSRP producers.
Registration	A WSRP producer may require WSRP consumers to register with it to interact with the portlets it contains. The Registration interface is an *optional* interface that allows WSRP consumers to register with WSRP producers that implement it.
Portlet Management	As the name suggests, this interface allows WSRP consumers to manage the lifecycles of portlets hosted by WSRP producers that implement the Portlet Management interface. This is an *optional* interface.

Let's now look at how WSRP is typically used in web portals and what setup we need to try out the WSRP features described in the rest of this chapter.

15.2   *Getting started with WSRP using Liferay Portal*

Portal servers simplify using WSRP by providing administration screens for managing producers and consumers. The typical process for publishing portlets consists of using the portal server's administration screens to do the following:

- Create a producer by specifying a unique name for it. At the same time, you can also provide information on how consumers can register with the producer to use the published portlets. You may want to create multiple producers if the producers' *registration* requirements vary or if they expose different sets of portlets. Successful creation of a producer generates a unique web service URL for accessing the producer's functionality.
- Add portlets to the producer that need to be published to the external world.

The process of consuming remote portlets involves using the portal server's administration screens to perform the following steps:

- Create a consumer by specifying both a unique name for it and the web service URL of the producer with which the consumer interacts. A consumer can't be associated with more than one producer at any given time.
- Register the consumer. If the producer requires consumers to register, the registration information must be supplied to the producer. If the registration information is found to be valid by the producer, the producer's published portlets are made available to the consumer. (Section 15.6 discusses the registration approaches defined in the WSRP specification.)
- Locally register any portlets that are published by the producer and associated with the consumer. You can locally register some or all of the portlets published by the producer—doing so makes the portlets published by the producer available to your portal server like any other portlet. During local registration, you specify a local name for the remote portlet—the title with which it's registered with the portal server.

> **WARNING**   Local registration of remote portlets means that a local portlet is created by the WSRP consumer to show the markup received from the remote portlet. Any interaction with the markup is forwarded by the WSRP consumer to the corresponding WSRP producer.

The preceding process is generic and is followed in almost all portal servers. In the rest of this chapter, we'll look at the producer and consumer administration portlets provided by OpenPortal Portlet Container and Liferay Portal to demonstrate this process. If you're using any other portal server that supports WSRP, like WebSphere Portal and GateIn Portal, you can refer to their documentation to find out how to create producers and consumers and how to publish and consume portlets.

NOTE The WSRP implementation has always been an integral part of Liferay Portal Enterprise Edition (EE) and it is supported in the Community Edition (CE) starting with Liferay Portal 6.x.

In real-world scenarios, WSRP consumers and producers are part of portal server instances installed on remotely located systems, and you only need to know the URL of the WSRP producer web service endpoint. For the purposes of this chapter, we'll install two different instances of Liferay portal server on the same machine to mimic a real-world situation.

To create two different instances of Liferay Portal on the same machine, you need to do the following:

1 Unzip the Liferay-Tomcat bundle into two different folders on your machine.

2 Modify the {TOMCAT_HOME}/conf/server.xml file on one of the instances to use different port numbers. A simple approach is to increase *all* port numbers for one of the Tomcat instances by 100. With this approach, the HTTP port number of one of the instances will become 8180, so you'll be able to access that Liferay Portal instance using the following URL: http://localhost:8180/.

In the rest of this chapter, we'll assume that the Liferay Portal instance using HTTP port 8080 is the WSRP producer (referred to as instance *P1* in the rest of the chapter) and the instance using HTTP port 8180 is the WSRP consumer (referred to as instance *C1* in the rest of the chapter).

WARNING You can have both the WSRP producer and the corresponding WSRP consumer on the same portal server instance. In such a scenario, the web portal accesses local portlets through the WSRP consumer. This approach will result in reduced web portal performance because of the overhead involved in accessing local portlets as remote portlets. For this reason, it's recommended that local portlets should *always* be accessed directly, and not through a WSRP consumer.

In the rest of this chapter, you'll learn how to do the following with Liferay Portal 6.x:

- Create a WSRP producer and add portlets to it
- Create a WSRP consumer
- Locally register remote portlets
- Register WSRP consumers with WSRP producers

15.3 *Creating a WSRP producer and adding portlets to it*

In Liferay Portal, a portal administrator can create a WSRP producer. In this section, we'll look at how to do that and then add portlets to it.

From the home page of your P1 Liferay Portal instance (http://localhost:8080/), select the Login as Bruno hyperlink to log in as the administrator of the Liferay Portal. Now you can go to the dockbar and select Manage > Control Panel to view a list of options reflecting the tasks that a Liferay Portal administrator can perform.

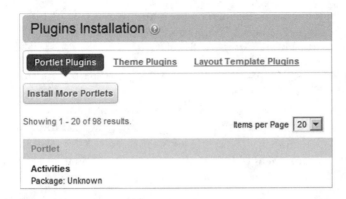

Figure 15.4 **Clicking the Install More Portlets button shows the list of portlets that aren't yet installed in the Liferay Portal instance. You can also search and install portlets.**

Click the Plugins Installation option under the Server category. This will show the list of portlets installed in your Liferay Portal instance. Click the Install More Portlets button, as shown in figure 15.4, to view and install portlets that are not yet installed.

Now, you can search for WSRP portlet, as shown in the figure 15.5.

The above figure shows that you need to enter wsrp in Keywords field and click the Search button. The search result consists of only a single entry – WSRP 6.0.5.1. This search result represents the WSRP plugin portlet of Liferay Portal that you need to install in your Liferay Portal instance to start using WSRP. Click the WSRP 6.0.5.1 hyperlink to view the details of the WSRP plugin portlet. It'll also show the option to install it, as shown in figure 15.6. This figure shows that WSRP plugin portlet is supported for Liferay Portal 6.0.5 and above versions. Click the Install button to install the WSRP plugin portlet. A successful installation will result in showing a WSRP option under the Portal Category in the Control Panel.

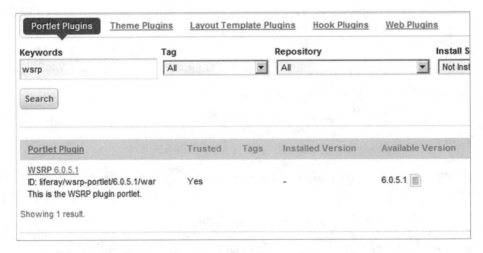

Figure 15.5 **Search for WSRP portlet by entering wsrp in Keywords field and click the Search button. Search result will show a WSRP plugin portlet.**

Plugin Installer

WSRP

Name:	(v6.0.5.1)
Author:	Liferay, Inc.
Types:	Portlet
Tags:	
Licenses:	(Open Source)
Liferay Versions:	6.0.5+
Repository:	http://plugins.liferay.com/official (Trusted)
Short Description:	This is the WSRP plugin portlet.
Change Log:	Adapted to the latest version of Liferay.

Install

Figure 15.6   Details of WSRP plugin portlet. Clicking the Install button installs the WSRP plugin portlet in Liferay Portal instance.

To add a WSRP producer or consumer, you first need to select the WSRP option (under the Portal category) from the list of available options, as shown in figure 15.7.

The WSRP option allows Liferay Portal administrators to view, add, edit, and remove WSRP producers and consumers configured for the Liferay Portal instance. As you're currently using the P1 Liferay Portal instance, you're only interested in adding a new WSRP producer to it. Click the Producers hyperlink from the screen that shows up after you select the WSRP option, as shown in figure 15.8.

Figure 15.8 shows two tabs, Consumers and Producers, which lets administrators manage WSRP consumers and producers. Figure 15.9 shows the screen that's displayed when the administrator selects the Producers option.

Figure 15.9 shows that the Producers tab displays a list of WSRP producers configured in the Liferay Portal instance. The Add Producer button lets you add new WSRP producers to the Liferay Portal instance. The Actions button corresponding to existing WSRP producers allows you to make changes to the producer, such as adding portlets to or removing them from the producer, or removing the producer from Liferay Portal.

Figure 15.7   The WSRP option allows the portal administrator to manage WSRP consumers and producers configured for the Liferay Portal instance.

Figure 15.8   Clicking the Producers option allows the Liferay Portal administrator to manage WSRP producers for the Liferay Portal instance.

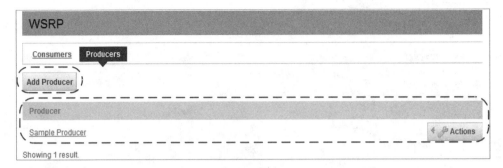

Figure 15.9   **The Producers tab displays a list of WSRP producers configured in Liferay Portal, and it allows the administrator to add new WSRP producers or make changes to existing WSRP producers.**

NOTE   At this point, you should build the ch2_UserRegistration, ch11_Book-Catalog_event, ch11_RecentBook_event, ch12_DateTime, ch12_SpringPortlet-DateTime, and ch12_ResourceServing projects and install the portlets in the P1 Liferay Portal instance. The portlets contained in these portlet applications will be added to the WSRP producer that we'll create in this section, for use by the WSRP consumer of the C1 Liferay Portal instance.

Let's now add a new WSRP producer to our P1 portal instance by clicking the Add Producer button. Figure 15.10 shows the form that's displayed for adding a new WSRP producer in Liferay Portal.

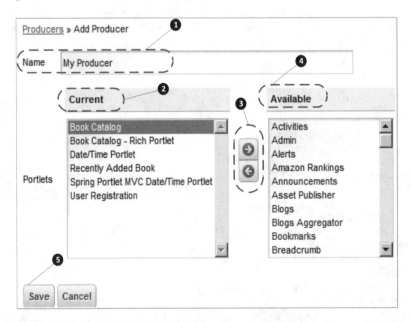

Figure 15.10   **The Add Producer form allows the administrator to add a new WSRP producer. It also allows one or more installed portlets to be added to the WSRP producer.**

WARNING   As of Liferay Portal 6.0, you *must* specify the value for the `<remote-able>` element in liferay-portlet.xml as `true` to expose a locally installed portlet through a WSRP producer.

The Name text field ❶ is for entering the name of the WSRP producer that you want to create. The Current list ❷ shows the portlets that are currently hosted by the WSRP producer, whereas the Available list shows portlets that are currently installed in the Liferay Portal instance ❹. The left and right arrows ❸ allow you to add portlets to and remove them from the list of portlets hosted by the WSRP producer. The Save button ❺ allows you to save the WSRP producer's details.

WARNING   In figure 15.10 you may have noticed that the Available portlet list only displays portlet titles, which may confuse you if you have multiple portlets installed with the same title. If you have multiple portlets (under different categories) with the same portlet title, it's recommended that you modify the titles to make them unique in the Liferay Portal instance before adding the portlets to a WSRP producer.

Figure 15.10 shows that you can add a WSRP producer along with the portlets that you want to be hosted by your WSRP producer. To set up a producer to match the examples that will follow in this chapter, enter My Producer as the name of the WSRP producer, add portlets to the producer from the Available list, and click Save. Select the following portlets from the Available portlet list:

- Book Catalog (from ch11_BookCatalog_event)
- Recently Added Book (from ch11_RecentlyBook_event)
- Date/Time Portlet (from ch12_DateTime)
- Book Catalog—Rich Portlet (from ch12_ResourceServing)
- Spring Portlet MVC Date/Time Portlet (from ch12_SpringPortletDateTime)
- User Registration (from ch2_UserRegistration)

Once the WSRP producer is successfully created, it's displayed in the list of WSRP producers configured for the Liferay Portal instance, as shown in figure 15.9.

You might wonder why we're adding multiple portlets to the My Producer WSRP producer when we could have tested the WSRP functionality by simply adding one portlet. The intent is to demonstrate that remote portlets behave just like local portlets; they can communicate using portlet events, respond to Ajax requests, and be developed using a portlet framework like Spring Portlet MVC.

TIP   The portlets that you've added to the My Producer provider will let you test inter-portlet communication between remote portlets using portlet events, the Ajax functionality of remote portlets, and that a portlet developed using the Spring Portlet MVC framework can also be published as a remote portlet. This book is accompanied by many example portlets that can help you test your portal server's WSRP implementation. For instance, if you want

Figure 15.11   The Edit option allows the administrator to modify the details of a WSRP producer, and it also displays the URL of the producer's web service endpoint.

to check whether inter-portlet communication is supported between remote portlets using `PortletSession` or public render parameters, you can try out the examples from chapter 11; if you want to test whether you can personalize a remote portlet or not, you can try out examples from chapter 10.

After successfully creating a WSRP producer, you need to find the WSRP producer's web service endpoint URL, which will be used by the WSRP consumer. The web service endpoint URL is autogenerated by Liferay Portal when you create a WSRP producer.

To obtain the web service endpoint of the newly created My Producer provider, select the Actions > Edit option corresponding to My Producer, as shown in figure 15.11. Figure 15.12 shows the information that's displayed when you select Edit.

Figure 15.12   The URL field shows the WSRP producer's web service endpoint URL. The WSRP consumer uses the producer's web service endpoint URL to interact with the portlets hosted by the producer.

Figure 15.12 shows that when you go about editing the details of the My Producer WSRP producer, the URL of the web service endpoint is also displayed. This is the URL a WSRP consumer needs to access the portlets hosted by My Producer. It's recommended that you copy the URL of My Producer so that it's accessible when you need to add a WSRP consumer in the C1 Liferay Portal instance, which uses portlets hosted by My Producer.

NOTE The web service endpoint URL of a producer is autogenerated by Liferay Portal and it can't be modified by the portal administrator.

You've now finished creating a WSRP producer. Next, we'll look at how to create a WSRP consumer that makes portlets hosted by My Producer available to the C1 Liferay Portal instance.

TIP To better understand the methods and interfaces exposed by the My Producer WSRP producer, you can use a web service tool like soapUI (http://www.eviware.com/) to investigate the My Producer WSRP producer's web service.

15.4 Creating a WSRP consumer

In Liferay Portal, a portal administrator can create a WSRP consumer. From the home page of your C1 Liferay Portal instance (http://localhost:8180/), click the Login as Bruno hyperlink to log in as the administrator of Liferay Portal.

Once you're signed in, you can go to the dockbar and select Manage > Control Panel to view a list of options reflecting the tasks that a Liferay Portal administrator can perform. To add a WSRP consumer, you first need to select the WSRP option (under the Portal category) from the list of available options, as shown earlier in figure 15.7. Next, click the Add Consumer button to add a new WSRP consumer to the C1 Liferay Portal instance, as shown in figure 15.13.

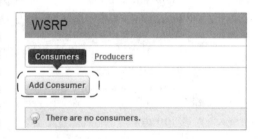

Figure 15.13   The Consumers tab displays a list of WSRP consumers configured for the Liferay Portal instance and also provides the option to add new WSRP consumers.

The Consumers tab shown in figure 15.13 displays a list of WSRP consumers that are configured for the Liferay Portal instance. Click the Add Consumer button to open the form for adding a new WSRP consumer to the C1 instance, as shown in figure 15.14.

Figure 15.14 shows that to add a WSRP consumer, you need to enter the WSRP producer's web service endpoint URL for which you're creating the consumer. Because you're creating a consumer for My Producer in this example, you need to enter the

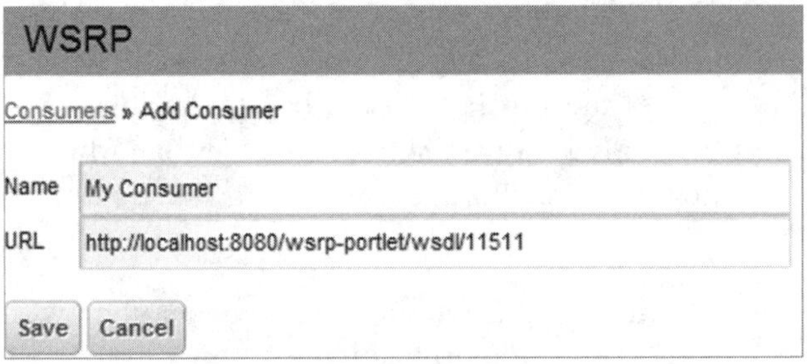

WSRP

Consumers » Add Consumer

| Name | My Consumer |
| URL | http://localhost:8080/wsrp-portlet/wsdl/11511 |

[Save] [Cancel]

Figure 15.14   Add a WSRP consumer by specifying a name for it and the URL of the WSRP producer web service endpoint for which it acts as a consumer.

URL of the My Producer web service. Enter My Consumer as the name of your WSRP consumer and the web service URL of My Producer, and click Save to create a new WSRP consumer corresponding to My Producer.

> **NOTE**   A WSRP consumer can only refer to a single WSRP producer. If you need to access portlets from multiple WSRP producers, from the same or different remote systems, you'll need to create a WSRP consumer for each WSRP producer.

Once the WSRP consumer is successfully created, it's displayed in the list of WSRP consumers configured for the Liferay Portal instance, as shown in figure 15.15. In this figure, the Consumers tab displays My Consumer as one of the WSRP consumers configured for the C1 Liferay Portal instance. The Actions button corresponding to each consumer shows additional options for editing and deleting the consumer and for managing remote portlets that the WSRP consumer makes available to the C1 Liferay Portal instance.

Table 15.2 describes the additional options that are displayed when you click the Actions button.

Now that you've successfully created the My Consumer WSRP consumer, let's look at how you can locally register remote portlets published by the My Producer WSRP producer.

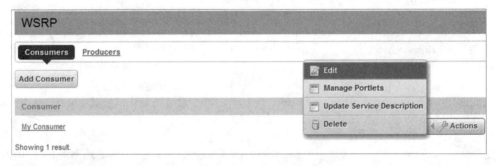

Figure 15.15   The Consumers tab shows the list of WSRP consumers. The Actions button allows you to manage remote portlets made available to the local Liferay Portal instance by each WSRP consumer.

Table 15.2 Options displayed when the Actions button is clicked

Option	Description
Edit	Allows you to modify WSRP consumer information, such as its name and the web service URL of the corresponding WSRP producer whose portlets it locally registers.
Manage Portlets	Allows you to manage remote portlets that are locally registered by the WSRP consumer.
Update Service Description	Retrieves updated service description information from the corresponding WSRP producer. These details include, among other things, the latest list of portlets published by the producer and any registration requirements.
Delete	Deletes the WSRP consumer from the Liferay Portal instance.
Edit Registration	This option is only displayed if the WSRP producer requires a WSRP consumer to register with the producer before locally registering portlets published by the producer.

15.5 *Locally registering remote portlets*

In the previous section, you saw how to create a WSRP consumer in Liferay Portal. When you created the My Consumer WSRP consumer in the C1 Liferay Portal instance, you simply associated it with the My Producer WSRP producer of the P1 Liferay Portal instance. To use a remote portlet in a web portal hosted by the C1 Liferay Portal instance, the My Consumer WSRP consumer *must* also specify the published portlets of My Producer that it wants to make available to the C1 Liferay Portal instance.

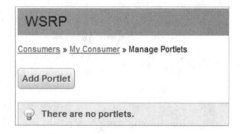

Figure 15.16 The Manage Portlets screen shows the list of portlets that have been locally registered by the WSRP consumer. The Add Portlet option allows the WSRP consumer to locally register remote portlets.

As mentioned in table 15.2, the Manage Portlets option allows you to manage the remote portlets that are locally registered by a WSRP consumer. As shown in figure 15.16, when you select the Manage Portlets option for My Consumer, the Add Portlet option for locally registering remote portlets is displayed, along with the list of locally registered portlets by My Consumer. Because the My Consumer WSRP consumer doesn't yet have any remote portlets locally registered, no portlets are listed in figure 15.16.

If you click the Add Portlet button in figure 15.16, you'll be able to select portlets that you want to register locally, as shown in figure 15.17.

In figure 15.17, the Remote Portlet combo box lists the portlets that are published by the corresponding WSRP producer. Because My Consumer is associated with My Producer, the combo box shows the portlets published by My Producer. The Name field allows you to assign a local name (or title) to the remote portlet for the local installation.

For this example, select the User Registration Portlet from the combo box, enter "Register Me !!" as the name for the portlet, and click Save. This will register the remote User Registration portlet locally with the name "Register Me !!". After locally registering a remote portlet, you can view it in the Manage Portlet screen shown in figure 15.16.

Now, how do you go about adding this locally registered remote portlet as a local portlet in a web portal? Like any other portlet, a locally registered remote portlet is available in the list of portlets

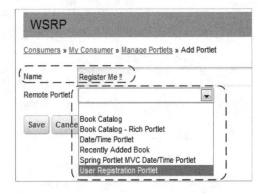

Figure 15.17   The Add Portlet screen allows you to locally register remote portlets.

displayed when you select the Add > More option from the dockbar, as shown in figure 15.18. As you can see, the User Registration portlet is registered locally with the title "Register Me !!" and is available under the WSRP category. You can go ahead and use the Register Me !! portlet like any other local portlet.

You can follow the same approach to locally register all the portlets published by My Producer and check out how they behave. Table 15.3 describes the behavior of each of the locally registered portlets published by the My Producer WSRP producer.

Table 15.3 suggests that if your WSRP producer and consumer are hosted by Liferay Portal instances, the following challenges with using remote portlets are automatically taken care of:

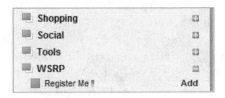

Figure 15.18   The User Registration portlet is displayed with the title "Register Me !!" under the WSRP category.

- CSS and JavaScript files defined in the liferay-portlet.xml file of the remote portlet are included. Because the liferay-portlet.xml file is specific to Liferay Portal, the CSS and JavaScript files won't be included if the WSRP consumer is configured in a different portal server.
- Ajax requests that are sent using the portlet's resource URL are transparently dispatched to the remote portlet for processing.
- Inter-portlet communication between locally registered remote portlets is mediated by the WSRP consumer via portlet events.

In table 15.3, you saw that Reverse Ajax didn't work when the remote Book Catalog–Rich Portlet was locally registered. The reason for this is that the URL that DWR generated for sending polling requests doesn't fit in the context of WSRP. Let's look at how a WSRP consumer in Liferay Portal generates URLs referring to the CSS and JavaScript files of the remote portlet.

Table 15.3 Behavior of locally registered remote portlets

Portlet	Observed behavior
Book Catalog (ch11_BookCatalog_event)	The action and render requests are handled correctly. The CSS and JS files are included from the remote portal server instance that hosts the My Producer WSRP producer. When a book is added, it's reflected in the Recently Added Book portlet.
Recently Added Book (ch11_RecentlyBook_event)	Works fine. The CSS file is included from the remote portal server instance that hosts the My Producer WSRP producer.
Book Catalog–Rich Portlet (ch12_ResourceServing)	Doesn't work. A little investigation will reveal that the issue is the use of Reverse Ajax. The polling request that's sent out every 60 seconds by DWR uses this URL: http://localhost:8180/ch12_ResourceServing/dwr/call/plaincall/ __System.pageLoaded.dwr It should instead use this URL: http://localhost:8180/wsrp-portlet/proxy?url=http://local-host:8080/ch12_ResourceServing/dwr/call/plaincall/ __System.pageLoaded.dwr. We'll soon discuss how the first URL is different from the second.
Date/Time Portlet (ch12_DateTime)	This portlet doesn't work because it sends an Ajax request to the `DateTimeServlet` servlet. If it had used the portlet's resource URL to address Ajax use cases, it would have worked.
Spring Portlet MVC Date/Time Portlet (ch12_SpringPortletDateTime)	When you click the Refresh button, the portlet displays the message "You are not authorized to view server date/time." This means that the Ajax request was successfully sent to the remote portlet, but it was not in the User role. The Ajax request was successful because the portlet made use of the portlet's resource URL to send the Ajax request. The failure to identify the correct role of the user suggests that if the remote portlet makes use of role-based security, you should configure your WSRP consumer (C1) and WSRP producer (P1) portal instances to use single sign-on.
User Registration Portlet (ch2_UserRegistration)	Works fine. The action and render requests are handled correctly.

URL FOR REMOTE CSS AND JAVASCRIPT FILES

If you view the source of the portal page that contains a locally registered remote portlet, you'll notice that the CSS and JavaScript references defined in the remote portlet's liferay-portlet.xml file are passed through a local `wsrp-portlet` servlet. For instance, consider the following liferay-portlet.xml file for the Book Catalog portlet defined in the ch11_BookCatalog_event portlet application project:

```
<liferay-portlet-app>
  <portlet>
    <portlet-name>bookCatalog</portlet-name>
      <instanceable>true</instanceable>
      <header-portlet-css>/css/bookCatalog.css</header-portlet-css>
```

```
        <header-portlet-javascript>
            /js/bookCatalog.js
        </header-portlet-javascript>
    </portlet>
</liferay-portlet-app>
```

The preceding liferay-portlet.xml file includes the bookCatalog.js and bookCatalog
.css files. If you add the Book Catalog portlet on a portal page of the P1 Liferay Portal
instance and view the source of the portal page in your browser, you'll find that the
URLs used by the <link> or <script> elements for including the CSS and JavaScript
files look like these:

```
/ch11_BookCatalog_event/css/bookCatalog.css
/ch11_BookCatalog_event/js/bookCatalog.js
```

Now, when you add the Book Catalog portlet on a portal page of the C1 Liferay Portal
instance and view the source of the portal page in your browser, you'll find that the
URLs used by the <link> or <script> elements look like these:

```
/wsrp-portlet/proxy?url=
http://localhost:8080/ch11_BookCatalog_event/css/bookCatalog.css

/wsrp-portlet/proxy?url=
http://localhost:8080/ch11_BookCatalog_event/js/bookCatalog.js
```

As you can guess from the generated URLs, the <link> and <script> tags make use of
a servlet mapped to a wsrp-portlet/proxy URL that accepts a url parameter identifying the location of the CSS or JavaScript file on the portal instance that hosts the
remote portlet.

　This means that if you specify references to CSS or JavaScript files in the liferay-
portlet.xml file, the WSRP consumer takes care of transforming these URLs to point to
the WSRP producer that published the portlet. But this is a Liferay Portal–specific feature, so how do we refer to CSS and JavaScript files when not using Liferay Portal? In
table 15.3, you saw that the portlet's resource URL can be successfully used to send
Ajax requests to a remote portlet. Similarly, you can use a portlet's resource URL to
refer to CSS and JavaScript files that are used by the portlet. For instance, you saw in
chapter 3 that Jetspeed 2.2 supports MARKUP_HEAD_ELEMENT, so you can use a portlet's
resource URL to add CSS and JavaScript files.

　Now back to why DWR generated a URL that doesn't refer to the wsrp-portlet/
proxy servlet. The DWR Java library generates a URL that identifies where the pooling request is to be sent. Because this URL wasn't defined in the liferay-portlet.xml
file, the URL isn't transformed by the WSRP consumer to refer to the wsrp-portlet/
proxy servlet.

　Let's now look at how the WSRP 2.0 registration feature works.

15.6　*Registering WSRP consumers with WSRP producers*

Registration is the process by which the consumer provides information about itself to
the producer. In this section, we'll look at the in-band and out-of-band registration

approaches that are followed by consumers to register with producers, and we'll also look at some examples. Toward the end of this section, we'll also look at the concept of *leasing* that was introduced in WSRP 2.0.

15.6.1   *Out-of-band registration*

In the out-of-band registration approach, the registration process isn't automated. You need to manually generate a *registration handle* using a WSRP producer and provide it to the businesses that want to access the published portlets. A registration handle uniquely identifies the consumer-producer relationship, and it's passed to the producer every time the consumer accesses the producer.

Suppose you create a Stock Watch portlet that you publish to the external world using WSRP. Only those businesses who have been granted access should be able to access your Stock Watch portlet. To gain access to the Stock Watch portlet, the businesses send an email request to you containing all the necessary information you require to register them. You manually enter the details and generate a unique *registration handle*—a string value that uniquely identifies the relationship between you and the business. You send the registration handle to the business, which is used by the business to create and register a WSRP consumer with your WSRP producer. The WSRP producer validates the registration handle and allows the business to access the Stock Watch portlet.

Let's now look at how in-band registration is different from out-of-band registration.

15.6.2   *In-band registration*

In in-band registration, the WSRP consumer is responsible for registering with the WSRP producer. The information that's required for registering with the WSRP producer is exposed using the Registration web service interface (see table 15.1), and it's entered using the WSRP consumer's user interface. The registration handle is generated during the registration process and is returned to the WSRP consumer.

The WSRP producer in Liferay Portal 6.x doesn't provide an option to enforce WSRP consumer registration, but Liferay Portal 6.x does let WSRP consumers register with a WSRP producer that supports in-band or out-of-band registration.

Let's now look at examples of using in-band and out-of-band registration.

15.6.3   *In-band and out-of-band registration examples*

As mentioned earlier in table 15.2, Liferay Portal's WSRP consumer displays the Edit Registration option only when the corresponding WSRP producer requires consumers to register. That means, to demonstrate registration, the first thing we need to do is find a WSRP producer that requires its consumers to register with the WSRP producer.

The OpenPortal WSRP producer does require consumers to register using either in-band or out-of-band registration. Figure 15.19 shows the WSRP producer from the OpenPortal WSRP implementation, which supports in-band registration.

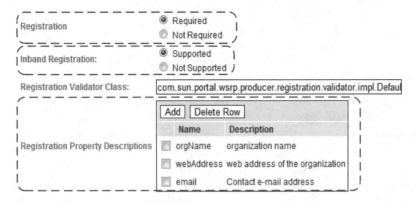

Figure 15.19   The OpenPortal WSRP producer portlet allows consumers to register using in-band or out-of-band registration. The Registration Property Descriptions section defines properties that are required for registering using the in-band approach.

In figure 15.19, the Registration option lets you chose whether you want WSRP consumers to register with the WSRP producer to use the published portlets or not. The Inband Registration option lets you chose whether you want to allow in-band registration or limit WSRP consumers to using out-of-band registration. The Registration Property Descriptions section defines the properties that *must* be supplied by the WSRP consumer during in-band registration.

Figure 15.20 shows that the Edit Registration option is available when a WSRP consumer is created in Liferay Portal, and it's associated with the WSRP producer in figure 15.19.

If you select the Edit Registration option shown in figure 15.20, it will display the screen in which you need to enter the registration information, as shown in figure 15.21.

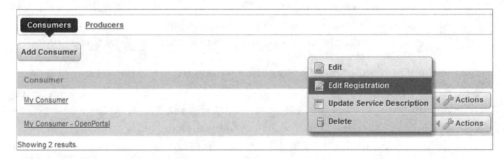

Figure 15.20   The Edit Registration option is available when the corresponding WSRP producer requires consumers to register.

Figure 15.21   The Registration screen allows you to enter the WSRP consumer's registration information so it can register with a WSRP producer. Registration can be in-band or out-of-band.

In figure 15.21, the Registration Type combo box shows Inband and Outband options. You might wonder why it shows Outband as an option, when we saw in figure 15.19 that the WSRP producer supports in-band registration. Just because a WSRP producer supports in-band registration doesn't mean that WSRP consumers can't register using the out-of-and approach. The out-of-band option is always available to WSRP consumers, irrespective of whether the WSRP producer supports in-band registration or not. The Registration Properties section shows the information that must be supplied to the WSRP producer to register the WSRP consumer.

If you select the Outband value from the Registration Type combo box, you only need to enter the registration handle that you received from the owner of the WSRP producer, as shown in figure 15.22. The registration properties aren't displayed; instead, the Registration Handle field is displayed.

Now that you know how to register a WSRP consumer with a WSRP producer, let's look at how the leasing feature in WSRP 2.0 works.

15.6.4   Leasing

The concept of registration in WSRP 2.0 was extended to include the concept of *leasing*, wherein registrations are valid only for a predefined amount of time. With leasing, the consumer specifies the time period for which the registration is valid. When the registration time period expires, the portlet and registration handles are destroyed.

Leasing is an optional feature that isn't supported by WSRP consumers in Liferay Portal 6.0, but the OpenPortal WSRP consumer supports leasing. Figure 15.23 shows the OpenPortal WSRP consumer creation screen that specifies the lifetime of the registration with the corresponding WSRP producer.

In figure 15.23, the WSRP consumer displays a check box labeled Lifetime Supplied, which lets you enter the time period for which the registration with the

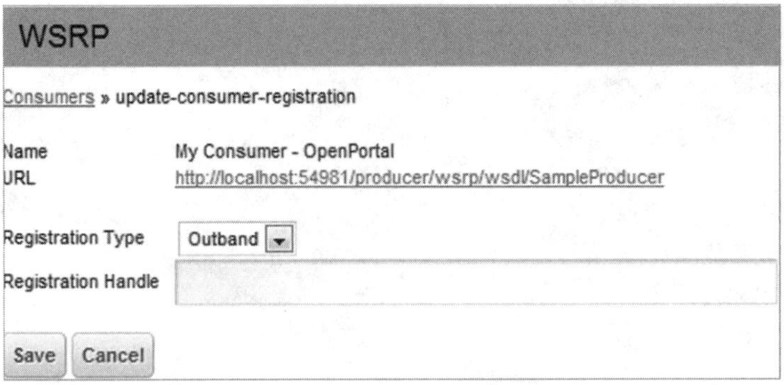

Figure 15.22   Out-of-band registration only requires you to enter the registration handle.

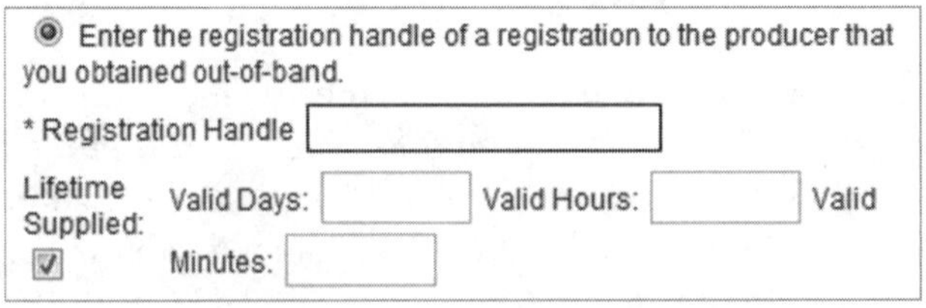

Figure 15.23   The Lifetime Supplied option allows you to enter a specified time period for the registration.

corresponding WSRP producer is valid. The feature is particularly useful when you want the remote portlet to be available only for a specified time period and for that connection to be destroyed once the registration time period expires. This saves the effort needed to manage locally registered remote portlets that aren't supposed to be used after a specified time period.

This is all you need to know about WSRP to start using it in your real-world portal projects.

15.7   Summary

In this chapter, we looked at the basics of WSRP and at how it simplifies using remote portlets. WSRP saves you the effort of deploying all your portlets on the same portal server, which results in optimal utilization of system resources.

We looked at how portlet examples from the previous chapters behave when they're used as remote portlets. The source code examples that accompany this book include loads of sample portlets that you can use to understand the behavior of your portal server's WSRP implementation.

By now you should know all that you need to know to create, manage, and experiment with portlets. Use this book as a reference when you need to fine-tune your skills and remind yourself about all that you've learned. But for now, the world of portlets awaits!

appendix A
Getting started with GateIn Portal

GateIn Portal is an open source portal server that merges the JBoss Portal and eXo Portal projects. In this appendix, we'll look at how to install GateIn Portal and create a web portal, the Book Portal. This example will demonstrate how to create a new web portal, create portal pages, add portlets to portal pages, programmatically secure portlet actions, create users and user groups, associate groups to roles, and define permissions for the web portal, its portlets, and portal pages. For more detailed documentation on GateIn Portal, please refer to the GateIn Portal website (http://www.jboss.org/gatein).

A.1 *Installing GateIn Portal*

To install GateIn Portal, all you need to do is download the bundle of your choice from the GateIn Portal website and unpackage it into an appropriate folder on your system. GateIn Portal comes prepackaged with JBoss AS and Tomcat. In this appendix, we'll use the GateIn-Tomcat bundle to demonstrate how to deploy portlets on GateIn Portal.

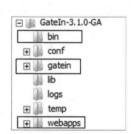

Figure A.1 shows the top-level directories that you'll see when you unpackage the GateIn-Tomcat bundle. In this figure, the bin directory contains batch files or shell scripts for starting GateIn Portal. The webapps directory is Tomcat's hot deploy directory where you need to copy your WAR files containing portlets. The gatein directory contains the data that's used internally by GateIn Portal.

Figure A.1   The GateIn-Tomcat bundle's directories. The gatein directory contains configuration and portal data used by GateIn Portal. The webapps directory is Tomcat's hot deploy directory, which contains the WAR files.

Figure A.2   The GateIn Portal home page. The Administrator option allows you to log in to the GateIn Portal as an administrator. The Sign In option allows you to provide your own login credentials to log in.

Before running the portal server, check that Java SE 5 or newer is installed on your system, and that the `JAVA_HOME` environment variable is set to the installation directory of Java SE 5. Verify that the installation is correct by executing `run` from the command prompt (on Windows) or the `run.sh` script in the bin directory (on UNIX). It may take some time for the server to start for the first time, as GateIn Portal creates its internal database and populates it with the setup data.

If the server starts up without errors, you can open your favorite web browser and point it to the home page of the GateIn Portal: http://localhost:8080/portal. If you see the home page of the GateIn Portal, you have successfully installed GateIn Portal on your system. Figure A.2 shows the GateIn Portal home page that you'll see if the server starts without errors.

To log in to the GateIn Portal, you can either choose the Sign In option at the top of the home page or you can log in as one of the predefined users in the system: Administrator, Manager, User, or Demo.

Let's now gain some familiarity with GateIn Portal before we get started creating a web portal.

A.2   *Getting familiar with the GateIn Portal user interface*

In this section, we'll look at the various options that are available to logged-in GateIn Portal users.

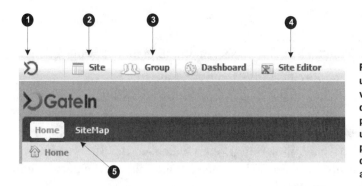

Figure A.3   A logged-in user sees a toolbar with various additional options determined by the access permissions defined for the user. Additional portal pages are also displayed, depending upon the user's access permissions.

First, click the Administrator link on the home page, or click the Sign In option and log in with a username of `root` and a password of `gtn`. The Administrator is the superuser in GateIn Portal and has full control over the portal server instance. When you log in to the GateIn Portal, you'll see a toolbar at the top of the window that shows the options available to the logged in user, along with the portal pages that the logged in user can view. Figure A.3 shows the home page that's displayed when you log in as Administrator.

The link ❶ provides options to change the language or skin of the portal and to sign out.

The Site option ❷ shows the various web portals available to the logged in user. An administrator can modify navigation hierarchy, add and remove web portals, change the skin and language of a web portal, and define permissions to restrict access to a web portal.

The Group option ❸ lets the user access special pages in the web portal, like Blog, Google, and Facebook. An administrator can additionally use the Application Registry option to import portlets from portlet applications that are deployed in the Tomcat webapps directory and to remove portlets that are registered with the GateIn Portal. Also, an administrator can use the Group option to manage pages, users, groups, and user-to-group relationships.

The Site Editor option ❹ is displayed only to portal administrators, and it's used for managing the portal pages and their layout.

The Home and SiteMap options ❺ represent the top-level portal pages that are accessible to every logged-in user.

Now that you know when to use the different toolbar options, let's look at how to create the Book Portal using GateIn Portal.

A.3   *Creating the Book Portal web portal*

In this section we'll develop a fully functional Book Portal web portal. To create a fully functional web portal in GateIn Portal, you first need to tell GateIn Portal about the web portal and then map the portal to the groups of users who should be able to access it. Additionally, you can define permissions for mapping portlets and portal pages to specific groups of users.

The Book Portal we'll create in this section will have the following features:

- It consists of two portal pages—Home and Catalog:
  - The Home page shows GateIn Portal's built-in calendar and calculator gadgets. The Home page will be accessible to everyone, including anonymous users.
  - The Catalog page shows the Book Catalog portlet (the appendixA_Book-Catalog Eclipse project). The Catalog page will only be accessible to users who are registered with the web portal and belong to a group named BookUser. Refer to the README.TXT file in the appendixA_BookCatalog project to copy GateIn Portal–specific JAR files in the project to remove build errors that show up when you import the project into Eclipse IDE for the first time.
- Only users belonging to the BookPortalAdmin group are allowed to add and remove books and to upload a TOC for a book. The users belonging to the BookPortalAdmin group are the overall administrators for the Book Portal and can perform all actions on the Book Portal.
- The web portal should support the French locale and show all the content in French if the user chooses to view the web portal in French.

Let's now look at the steps required to create the Book Portal.

A.3.1 *Setting up a new web portal*

In GateIn Portal, only administrators have permission to create a new web portal. As mentioned earlier, GateIn Portal comes with a predefined Administrator user who belongs to the administrator group. Log in as Administrator, as described in section A.2, and select the Site option from the toolbar to view the option for adding a new web portal.

> **NOTE** If you hover your mouse over the Site option, it will show the list of web portals that are currently configured in the GateIn Portal instance. As you haven't created any web portals so far, it shows a single web portal named Classic, which refers to the default web portal in GateIn Portal.

Clicking the Site option in the toolbar displays the web portals created in the GateIn Portal instance and the option to create a new web portal, as shown in figure A.4.

Figure A.4 shows that the Site option lets you manage the portals created in the GateIn Portal instance. The following options are available for existing web portals:

- *Edit Layout*—For editing the layout of the portal pages of a web portal
- *Edit Navigation*—For editing the overall navigational structure of a web portal
- *Edit Portal's Config*—For editing a web portal's name, skin, locale, and access permissions

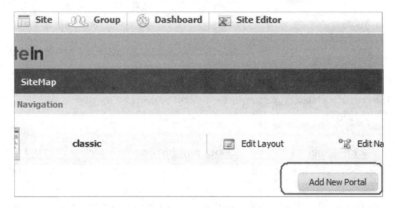

Figure A.4   The Site option is used to manage web portals created in the GateIn Portal instance. The Add New Portal option is used to add a new portal to the GateIn instance.

Apart from the preceding options, an Add New Portal button is also available for creating a new web portal in the GateIn Portal instance. Click the Add New Portal button to add the Book Portal details, as shown in figure A.5.

Figure A.5 shows the form in which you enter details about the web portal you want to create in the GateIn Portal instance. The three tabs display different categories of information that you can specify for the web portal at creation time:

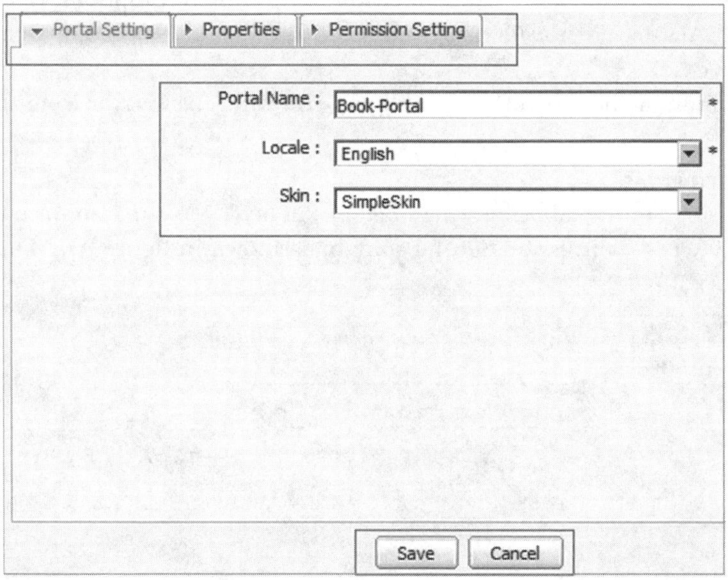

Figure A.5   The form for entering details to create a new web portal

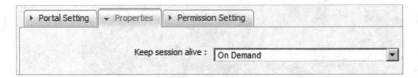

Figure A.6   The Properties tab lets you specify the timeout property for the user session.

- *Portal Setting*—Specify the name, skin, and locale of the web portal to be created
- *Properties*—Specify how the session timeout is handled for the web portal
- *Permission Setting*—Specify the user groups and roles of the users who can access the web portal and the groups and roles of the users who can make modifications to the web portal

Let's now look at what details you need to specify in each of the tabs to create the Book Portal.

THE PORTAL SETTING TAB
In the Portal Setting tab (shown in figure A.5), specify "Book-Portal" as the name of the web portal, and select the SimpleSkin portal skin. Because the content of the Book Portal will be displayed in English, keep English as the setting for the locale.

THE PROPERTIES TAB
In the Properties tab, you specify how GateIn Portal should handle the timeout of user sessions. It provides you with the following timeout options: Never, On Demand, and Always. For the Book Portal, keep the default value, On Demand, as shown in figure A.6.

If you don't want the session to ever expire, you can select Never from the drop-down list.

PERMISSION SETTING TAB
In the Permission Setting tab, check the Make It Public (Everyone Can Access) check box from the Access Permission Setting subtab, as shown in figure A.7. This means

Figure A.7   The Access Permission Setting subtab is used to specify access permissions for the web portal.

Figure A.8 Clicking the Select Permission button allows you to select the user groups and roles you wish to grant permission to make modifications to the web portal.

that, by default, all Book Portal pages and portlets will be accessible to *anonymous* users. We'll see later in this section how you can specify permissions for individual Book Portal pages and portlets to override these default permission settings.

The Edit Permission Setting subtab is used to specify the groups and roles of users who have permission to make changes to the web portal. The Book Portal requirements clearly mention that users belonging to the BookPortalAdmin group are responsible for performing administration tasks on the Book Portal, so we need to assign edit permission to users in the BookPortalAdmin user group. As we haven't yet created the BookPortalAdmin group, let's assign the edit permission to the Administrator user.

The Administrator user belongs to the Administrators subgroup of the Platform group, and it has the manager role. (In GateIn Portal terminology, *a role* is referred to as a *membership*.) To assign edit permission to the Administrator user, select the Edit Permission Setting subtab and click the Select Permission button.

In figure A.8, clicking the Select Permission button displays the Permission Selector form that lets you select groups and roles, as shown in figure A.9.

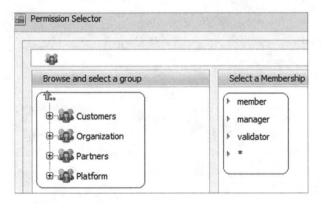

Figure A.9 The Permission Selector shows the user groups on the left side and the memberships (or roles) on the right side. Select the user groups on the left, and then the roles you want to assign to those groups on the right.

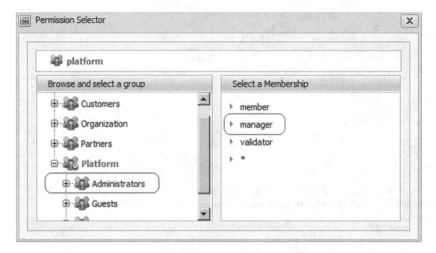

Figure A.10   Select Platform > Administrators as the user group and `manager` as the membership to assign edit permission to the Administrator user.

In figure A.9, the Browse and Select a Group pane on the left shows the user groups defined in the GateIn Portal, and the Select a Membership section on the right shows the roles or memberships that are defined. In this case, the figure shows the predefined groups and memberships in GateIn Portal.

Figure A.10 shows the selections that you need to make to assign edit permission to the Administrator user. This figure shows that to assign edit permission to the Administrator user, you expand the Platform group and select the Administrators group. The Administrator user has `manager` membership in the Administrators group, so to assign edit permission to the Administrator user you need to select `manager` as the membership. When you select the membership, the selected permission is displayed in the Edit Permission Setting tab, as shown in figure A.11.

Figure A.11   Selected permission settings are displayed in the Edit Permission Setting subtab.

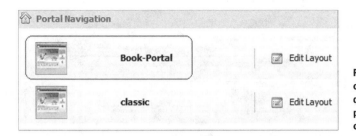

Figure A.12 The newly created Book Portal is displayed in the list of web portals that the Administrator can manage.

Now that you've provided appropriate values for creating the Book Portal, click the Save button (shown in figure A.5) to create the Book Portal. The newly created Book Portal will now show up in the list of web portals that the Administrator user can manage, as shown in figure A.12.

NOTE The newly added Book Portal is also visible when you hover your mouse over the Site option in the toolbar (see figure A.3).

This is all you need to do to set up a portal. Now let's create a user who belongs to the BookPortalAdmin group.

A.3.2 Creating a web portal user

In a web portal, some users are created automatically when users register with the web portal, and some are created manually, like the user responsible for administering the web portal. The registering users are usually associated with a group and role when they register, but manually created users need to be associated with an appropriate group and role by the portal administrator. In this section, we'll look at how you can create a user in GateIn Portal, and in section A.3.3 we'll look at how you can associate the newly created user with the BookPortalAdmin group and to an appropriate role.

To create a web portal user, select the Groups > Organization > New Staff option from the toolbar. The New Staff option displays the form shown in figure A.13, where you can enter user details.

Enter `portal.admin` in the User Name field, fill out the rest of the details for the user in both tabs, and click Save to create a new user in GateIn Portal.

NOTE By default, all users created by GateIn Portal belong to the Users subgroup of the Platform group and have `member` as their membership type.

Let's now look at how to create a new BookPortalAdmin group in GateIn Portal.

A.3.3 Creating a custom user group

GateIn Portal allows you to create custom user groups and custom memberships (or roles). Also, the groups created in GateIn Portal can be hierarchical; you can have a top-level group that contains subgroups, which can further contain subgroups, and so

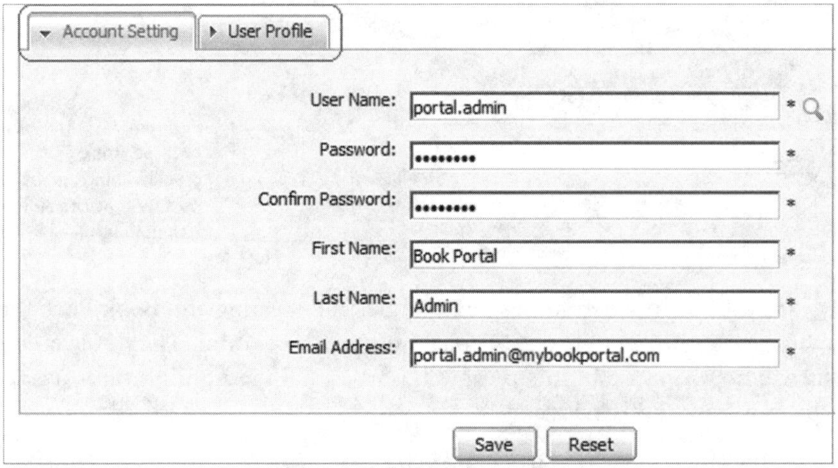

Figure A.13   The form for entering user details. The user's account details are entered on the Account Setting tab, and personal information about the user is entered on the User Profile tab.

on. In this section, we'll look at how to create a custom BookPortalAdmin group in GateIn Portal.

To manage groups and memberships, select the Groups > Organization > Users and Groups management option. Figure A.14 shows the various options that are available for managing groups and memberships.

Figure A.14 shows that an administrator can manage users, groups, and memberships that are defined in GateIn Portal:

- *User Management*—Allows administrators to modify or delete users. If you successfully created the portal.admin user in the previous section, it will now show up in the User Management page.

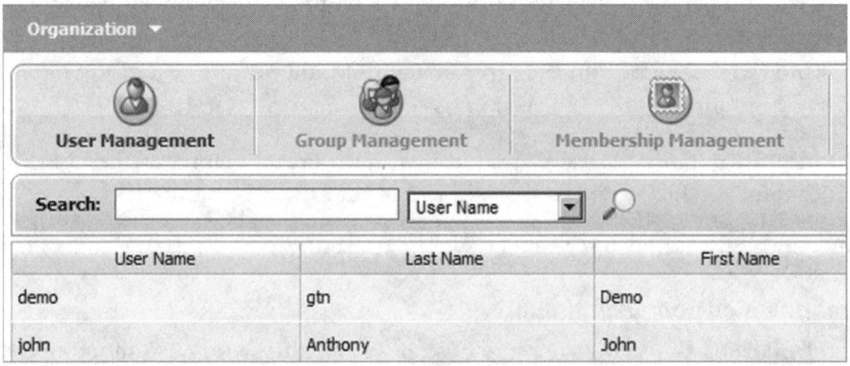

Figure A.14   User, group, and membership management options available to administrators

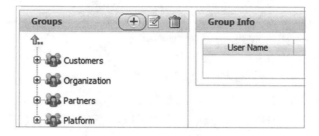

Figure A.15   **The + button in the Groups pane is for adding a new group or subgroup to GateIn Portal.**

- *Group Management*—Allows administrators to add, modify, or delete groups. As each group is usually associated with a set of users, this option is also used to view users in each group, remove users from a group, and associate users with a group.
- *Membership Management*—Allows administrators to manage memberships (or roles) defined in GateIn Portal. By default, GateIn Portal defines `manager`, `validator`, and `member` memberships. Administrators can create new memberships (or roles) and assign them to different users in the portal using the Group Management option.

To create the new BookPortalAdmin group, go to the Group Management tab and click the plus sign (+) button to add a new group, as shown in figure A.15.

Enter the new group's details in the Add New Group form, as shown in figure A.16.

Enter `BookPortalAdmin` in the Group Name field, `Book Portal Administrator` as the Description, and click Save to save the new group. If the BookPortalAdmin group is successfully created, it's displayed in the list of groups.

Repeat these steps to create the BookUser group, to which the registered users of the portal belong. Later in this appendix, you'll see how registered users are automatically mapped to the BookUser group.

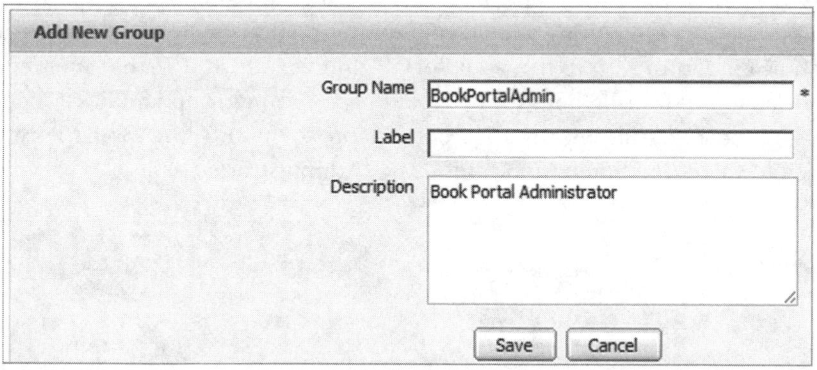

Add New Group

Group Name	BookPortalAdmin *
Label	
Description	Book Portal Administrator

Save   Cancel

Figure A.16   **The Add New Group form lets you add a new group or subgroup to GateIn Portal.**

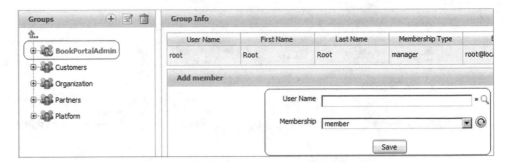

Figure A.17   Selecting a group shows the users that belong to that group, their memberships, and an option to search for and add users to the group.

Now that you've created the portal.admin user and the BookPortalAdmin group, let's look at how you can associate portal.admin with the BookPortalAdmin group.

A.3.4   *Associating users to groups*

To associate a user to a group, go to the Group Management tab shown in figure A.14 and select the BookPortalAdmin group.

Figure A.17 shows that when you select a group, the users associated with the group are displayed, along with the option to add more users to the group. Enter portal. admin as the user name, keep the membership option as member, and click Save to save the association between the BookPortalAdmin group and the portal.admin user.

Now you should modify the permissions for the BookPortalAdmin group in the Book Portal web portal. This is done on the Edit Permission Setting tab (discussed earlier in section A.3.1 and shown in figure A.8). Click the Site option in the toolbar, and click the Edit Portal's Config option corresponding to the Book Portal, as shown in figure A.18.

You should now see the dialog box shown earlier in figure A.5. All you have to do is go to Edit Permission Setting and assign edit permission (as described in section A.3.1 and shown in figure A.8) to the BookPortalAdmin group and member membership. As the portal.admin user belongs to the BookPortalAdmin group and has a membership setting of member, this means that permission to modify the Book Portal is now granted to the portal.admin user and *not* the Administrator user.

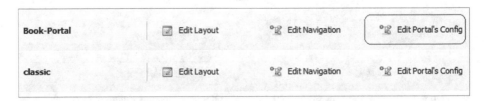

Figure A.18   The Edit Portal's Config option allows you to change the access and edit permission settings for a web portal.

NOTE Edit permission for a web portal in GateIn Portal can *only* be assigned to a single group and to a particular membership in that group. It *can't* span multiple groups and memberships.

To confirm the options that are now available to the portal.admin user, log in with the credentials of the portal.admin user and check out the toolbar options that are now available when you go to the Book Portal. You'll notice that the Book Portal already has a home page, and all the options like Site, Group, Dashboard, and Site Editor are available in the toolbar, but with limited functionality. For instance, portal.admin can't perform the following actions:

- Create a new web portal
- Create portal users, groups, or memberships, or associate existing users to existing groups
- Add or remove portlets from the predefined home page of the Book Portal

Let's now look at how the portal.admin user can remove Book Portal's default home page to create a new custom home page.

A.3.5 *Removing the portal's default home page*

When you login as portal.admin, you'll find that the Book Portal web portal already has a home page that shows general information about the GateIn Portal product. As the requirements of the Book Portal stated that the Book Portal home page should show GateIn Portal's built-in calendar and calculator gadgets, we need to edit the default home page of the Book Portal.

To remove portlets from the current portal page and add new portlets to it, GateIn Portal provides the Site Editor > Edit Page option. But if you look for the Edit Page option for the Book Portal home page, you won't find it because the Book Portal instance was created by the Administrator user, and Administrator is the *owner* of the home page. You first need to remove Book Portal's default home page and then create a new home page to meet the Book Portal requirements.

To remove the default home page, click the Site option in the toolbar and select the Edit Navigation option corresponding to the Book Portal. In the Navigation Management window, you can see and define the navigational structure of your web portal. The only navigation node that currently exists for Book Portal is Home, as shown in figure A.19. Right-click

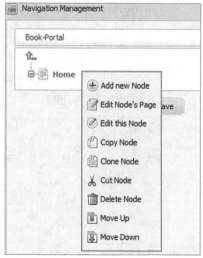

Figure A.19 The web portal's Navigation Management window allows you to modify the navigational structure of the web portal. Right-clicking a navigation node allows you to perform various actions on a node.

the Home navigation node and select Delete Node from the popup menu to delete that node and its associated portal pages.

Once you've deleted the Home node, save the changes to the navigation structure. Now if you go to the Book Portal, you'll find that the default home page has been removed.

It's now time to create the Home and Catalog portal pages and add the portlets.

A.3.6   *Creating portal pages and adding portlets*

To create a portal page, select Site Editor > Add New Page. This starts the Page Creation wizard, which allows you to enter page and node details for the new page.

As shown in figure A.20, enter the details for the navigation node and page and click Next. The next step is to select the layout for the portal page, which you don't need at this time. Click Next again to reach the last step of the wizard, where you can add containers for portlets, set portal page permissions, and add portlets.

Figure A.21 shows the Page Editor panel. You can set portal page permissions by clicking the View Page Properties button, add portlets and gadgets from the Applications tab, and organize portlets and gadgets on the portal page using containers via the Containers tab. You can also go back to the previous step in the Page Creation wizard, save changes to the portal page, or cancel the Page Creation wizard using the icons in the top-right corner of the panel.

To set up the Book Catalog portal's home page, drag and drop the calendar and calculator widgets from the Applications tab, and save the changes to the portal page. You don't need to set the permissions for the Home portal page because it's accessible to anonymous users by default.

Similarly, you can create the Catalog portal page using the Page Creation wizard and add portlets to it. But even though you can create the Catalog page, you can't add the Book Catalog portlet to it because you first need to make that portlet available to the Page Editor. For now, create an empty Catalog portal page and set permissions for it so that it's accessible only to the BookUser group. To set permissions for

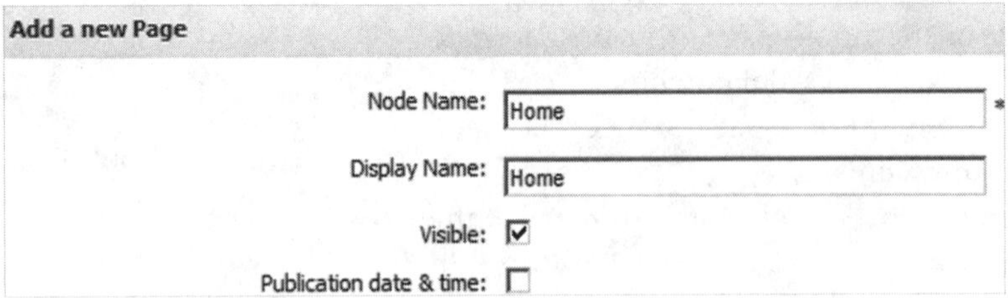

Figure A.20   The Page Creation wizard for entering navigation node and page details

the Catalog page, navigate to the Catalog page and select the Site Editor > Edit Page option from the toolbar. Selecting the Edit Page option displays the Page Editor panel (shown in figure A.21) for the Catalog portal page. Figure A.22 shows the dialog box that's displayed when you click the View Page Properties button on the Page Editor panel.

As shown in figure A.22, uncheck the Make It Public (Everyone Can Access) check box. This means the Catalog portal page won't be accessible to everyone. Then click the Add Permission button to set the access permission for users in the Book-User group having `member` as their membership in the group.

In this section, you created the Home and Catalog portal pages and made the Catalog portal page accessible only to the BookUser group. Now, we'll look at what changes need to be made to the Book Catalog portlet so that the add

Figure A.21 Page Editor shows portlets/gadgets that you can drag and drop on the portal page, view page properties, save changes to the portal page and add container(s) to the portal page to organize portlets/gadgets on the portal page.

and remove book and upload TOC functions are only available to users who belong to the BookPortalAdmin group and have `member` membership.

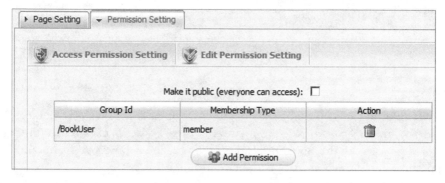

Figure A.22 The View Page Properties button opens this dialog box, which allows you to set permissions for the portal page.

CODE REFERENCE   You should now import the appendixA_BookCatalog project into your Eclipse IDE in order to follow along with how programmatic security is implemented using GateIn Portal–specific classes.

A.3.7   *Programmatically securing a custom portlet*

The Book Portal's requirements mention that the Book Catalog portlet should only allow add and remove book and upload TOC functions to be performed by users having a member role in the BookPortalAdmin group. GateIn Portal provides a UserACL class, which helps with implementing programmatic security in portlets. The UserACL object is at the center of implementing programmatic security in portlets. It provides methods, like hasPermission, which let you check whether a logged-in user belongs to a particular group and has a particular membership in that group.

The following listing shows the BookCatalogPortlet class's removeBook action method, which shows how programmatic security is implemented in GateIn Portal.

Listing A.1   The `BookCatalogPortlet` class's `removeBook` method

```
import org.exoplatform.container.ExoContainer;
import org.exoplatform.container.ExoContainerContext;
import org.exoplatform.portal.config.UserACL;

@ProcessAction(name = "removeBookAction")
 public void removeBook(ActionRequest request, ActionResponse response)
   throws PortletException, IOException {
   ExoContainer exoContainer =                                          ❶ Obtains UserACL
      ExoContainerContext.getCurrentContainer();                          reference
   UserACL userACL = (UserACL)exoContainer.
            getComponentInstanceOfType(UserACL.class);
   if(userACL.hasPermission                                             ❷ Checks if user belongs
 ➥ ("member:/BookPortalAdmin")) {                                         to BookPortalAdmin
    bookService
      .removeBook(Long.valueOf(request.getParameter("isbnNumber")));
    response.setRenderParameter(Constants.MYACTION_PARAM, "showCatalog");
   } else {
     ...
   }
 }
```

GateIn Portal's UserACL object is obtained from the ExoContainer object ❶. The UserACL object's hasPermission method is used ❷ to check whether the logged-in user is a member in the BookPortalAdmin group. The hasPermission method accepts a permission expression that takes the following format,

<membership>:*<group>*

where *<membership>* is the membership that the user has with a group, and *<group>* identifies the group to which the user belongs. While specifying the group, ensure that you specify the complete path to the group. For instance, if a user belongs to the administrators subgroup of the platform group, the path to the administrators group is /platform/administrators.

Now that you've seen how to use programmatic security in implementing portlets, let's look at how to install custom portlets in GateIn Portal.

A.3.8 *Importing custom portlets into GateIn Portal*

To add a custom portlet to a portal page, you first need to import the custom portlet into GateIn Portal. These are the steps for importing a portlet:

1 Deploy the portlet application WAR file. If you're using the GateIn-Tomcat bundle, copy the WAR file to the webapps directory, as described in section 3.1.

2 Log in as an Administrator user and go to Group > Administration > Application Registry to import the custom portlets that form part of the portlet application. The Application Registry shows all the portlets that have been imported into the GateIn portal.

3 Import the deployed portlets by clicking the Import Applications button shown in figure A.23.

4 Once the portlets are installed, they will appear in the Add Category panel.

To import the Book Catalog portlet, deploy the portlet application that contains the portlet and click the Import Applications button. Once it's imported, the Book Catalog portlet will appear in the Add Category panel and it'll also be available in the Page Editor panel when you go about creating or editing a portal page. Refer to section A.3.6 for more information on the Page Editor panel.

Now that the Book Catalog portlet has been imported, you can log in as portal.admin and select Site Editor > Edit Page to edit the Catalog portal page and add the Book Catalog portlet.

Let's now look at how you can associate the BookUser group and `member` membership with users who register with the GateIn web portal.

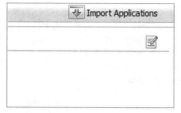

Figure A.23   The Add Category panel shows the portlets that are currently registered with GateIn Portal. Clicking the Import Applications option imports the portlets defined in the deployed portlet applications.

A.3.9   *Defining default groups and memberships for registered users*

GateIn Portal provides numerous configuration options to let you personalize its default behavior. In this section, we'll look at how you can configure the GateIn web portal so that users who register with the portal are automatically assigned the BookUser group and member membership in the group.

The GateIn portal's organization-configuration.xml XML file defines the group and membership with which newly created users are associated. In case of the GateIn-Tomcat bundle, the file is located in *<gatein-install-dir>*\webapps\portal\WEB-INF\conf\organization directory, where *<gatein-install-dir>* is the directory in which you extracted the GateIn-Tomcat bundle archive.

The next listing shows the <component-plugin> element, which is responsible for defining the default group and membership with which newly created users are associated.

Listing A.2   The organization-configuration.xml file

```
<configuration ...>
  <external-component-plugins>
    ...
    <component-plugin>
      <name>new.user.event.listener</name>              ❶ Plugin for setting group
        ...                                                 and membership
        <object type="org.exoplatform.services.
                      organization.impl.NewUserConfig">
        ...
          <object
              type="org.exoplatform.services.
                    organization.impl.NewUserConfig$JoinGroup">
            <field  name="groupId">
              <string>/platform/users</string>           ❷ Group and
            </field>                                         membership of
            <field  name="membership">                      new users
              <string>member</string>
              </field>
          </object>
        ...
    </component-plugin>
    ...
  </external-component-plugins>
</configuration>
```

The new.user.event.listener plugin component ❶ is responsible for assigning the default group and membership to newly created users. The <field> elements ❷ identify the default group and membership that are assigned to new users.

To change the default group and membership, all you need to do is to change the value of the `<field>` elements. The `<field>` elements in the following snippet indicate that newly created users will be associated with the BookUser group and with member membership.

```xml
<object type="org.exoplatform.services.organization.
    ➡impl.NewUserConfig$JoinGroup">
  <field  name="groupId"><string>/BookUser</string></field>
  <field  name="membership"><string>member</string></field>
</object>
```

appendix B
Configuring Liferay
Portal with
MySQL database

Liferay Portal comes with an embedded HSQLDB database, which isn't meant to be used in production. Liferay Portal provides support for many production-ready databases that you can configure easily. In this appendix, we'll look at how to configure Liferay Portal to use the MySQL database. If you want to use another database with Liferay Portal, refer to the Liferay Portal documentation.

Before you get started configuring MySQL with Liferay Portal, you need to install the following software on your machine:

- *MySQL database server*—Download the Community Edition of the database from http://dev.mysql.com/downloads/.
- *HeidiSQL client for MySQL*—The screenshots in this appendix use the HeidiSQL client, but you can use any other MySQL client to go through the tables described in this appendix. You can download the HeidiSQL client for free from http://www.heidisql.com/.

B.1 Installing MySQL database and HeidiSQL client

The first step toward integrating Liferay Portal with MySQL is to install the MySQL database server on your local machine. The most important step in the installation process is configuring the MySQL Server instance. This is where you specify the password for the root user, as shown in figure B.1.

The root user is a *superuser* in MySQL and it's created during installation. The Current Root Password input field in figure B.1 may confuse you if you choose to

Figure B.1 The MySQL Server Instance Configuration Wizard allows you to specify the root user's password.

configure the MySQL Server instance separately, instead of doing it during the installation process. By default, MySQL creates a root user with a blank password during the installation process. When you come across figure B.1, you don't need to try out obvious passwords like `admin`, `root`, and so on. Simply leave the Current Root Password field blank and enter the password you want to use in the New Root Password and Confirm fields.

If you have installed the MySQL database and the HeidiSQL client, you should first check whether the MySQL installation was successful. To do so, open the HeidiSQL client and connect to the MySQL Server instance you want to use with Liferay Portal. Figure B.2 shows the HeidiSQL client's Session Manager screen where you need to enter the MySQL information for the instance you want to connect to.

The HeidiSQL client's Session Manager window accepts the following input:

- *Session*—A name for the session that you are about to start.
- *Hostname/IP*—The hostname or IP address of the machine on which the MySQL database instance is running. If you have installed MySQL locally, you can specify `localhost` as the hostname or `127.0.0.1` as the IP address.
- *User*—The username you want to use to create the session with the MySQL instance. You can connect with the root username or any username that has permission to create a new database in the MySQL Server instance. The root user, being a superuser, has the permission to create a new database.

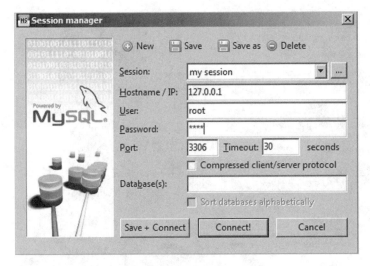

Figure B.2   The HeidiSQL client screen for connecting to a MySQL instance

- *Password*—The password corresponding to the username. If you're trying to log in using the root username, the password would be the one you set for the root user during the configuration of your MySQL Server instance.
- *Database(s)*—The database to which you want to connect. Because you're connecting for the first time, you don't need to specify the database name.

Once you're connected to the MySQL Server instance, you'll see a list of databases that currently exist in the instance, as shown in figure B.3. The databases that currently

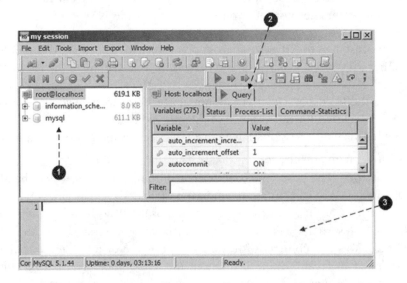

Figure B.3   The HeidiSQL client user interface lists databases in the MySQL Server instance, lets you run SQL queries, and offers many other features.

exist in the MySQL Server instance ❶ are displayed. You can select any database from the list to perform additional actions on the selected database. The Query tab displays an SQL editor ❷ where you can write SQL queries that you want to execute. The pane at ❸ is like the Console in the Eclipse IDE, which displays a log of activities you perform using the HeidiSQL client user interface.

Now that you are connected to the MySQL Server instance, you're ready to do something useful—create a database in the MySQL Server instance. The database that you'll create will be used by the Liferay Portal server to store information.

B.2   Getting started with your own portal database

To create a database using the HeidiSQL client, right-click in the pane that lists the databases (❶ in figure B.3). You'll see a popup menu, as shown in figure B.4, which gives you an option to create a new database.

As shown in figure B.4, the Create Database option is available to users who have permission to create new databases in the MySQL Server instance. When you select the Create Database option, you'll see the dialog box in figure B.5, which asks for the name of the database that you want to create.

As shown in figure B.5, enter `myportaldb` as the name of your new database and click OK. This will create a new database named myportaldb in the MySQL Server instance. The newly created database will immediately be added to the list of databases in the MySQL Server instance. The myportaldb database is currently empty but soon Liferay Portal will populate it with tables, triggers, and so on.

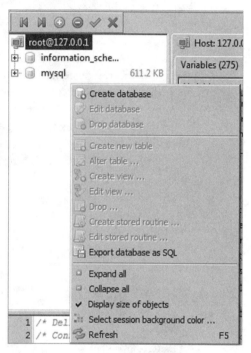

Figure B.4   The Create Database option is available when the user right-clicks inside the window pane listing databases in the MySQL Server instance.

Now that you have created myportaldb, you're ready to configure Liferay Portal to use this database, instead of HSQLDB.

B.2.1   Configuring Liferay Portal with MySQL

Liferay Portal provides a fairly simple approach to configuring the MySQL database as its primary database—you specify connection properties in the portal-ext.properties file and restart the Liferay Portal server. That's all you need to do.

Create database ...   ☒

Name: myportaldb

Character set: latin1   ▼

Collation: latin1_swedish_ci   ▼

                    [OK]   [Cancel]

SQL preview for CREATE DATABASE:

```
CREATE DATABASE `myportaldb` /*!40100
CHARACTER SET latin1 COLLATE
latin1_swedish_ci */
```

Figure B.5   The Create Database dialog box, where you enter the database name

Let's take a step back and understand the purpose of the portal-ext.properties file in Liferay Portal. Liferay Portal contains a portal.properties file in one of its JAR files, which defines properties that apply to the portal server and are meant to customize the behavior of the server. If you want to override the properties specified in portal. properties, you must create a portal-ext.properties file and specify the properties that you want to override. If you're using Liferay Portal bundled with Tomcat, the portal-ext.properties file must be located in the {TOMCAT_HOME}/webapps/ROOT/WEB-INF/classes directory.

The portal.properties file specifies HSQLDB as the database to be used by the Liferay Portal server. This means that if you want to use MySQL instead of HSQLDB, you have to override the database properties by redefining them in portal-ext.properties. Listing B.1 shows a portal-ext.properties file that instructs Liferay Portal to connect to the MySQL Server instance you created earlier.

Listing B.1   Overriding database properties in the portal-ext.properties file

```
jdbc.default.driverClassName=com.mysql.jdbc.Driver
jdbc.default.url=jdbc:mysql://localhost/myportaldb
➥?useUnicode=true&
➥characterEncoding=UTF-8&useFastDateParsing=false
jdbc.default.username=root
jdbc.default.password=asarin
```

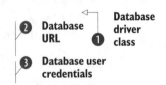

The jdbc.default.driverClassName property ❶ defines the fully qualified name of the driver class that's used by the portal server to connect to the database. Because you're using MySQL in this case, the name of the driver class is com.mysql. jdbc.Driver.

jdbc.default.url ❷ defines the database connection URL that'll be used for establishing a connection with the database. Because you want to use the myportaldb database, the connection URL points to that database. You don't need to worry at this point about the information that follows the question mark (?) in the connection URL.

The jdbc.default.username and jdbc.default.password properties ❸ define the credentials that will be used by Liferay Portal to connect to the MySQL Server instance. For simplicity, you can use MySQL's root superuser to connect with the myportaldb database. You can alternatively use any other user, as long as the user has permissions to create tables, indexes, and so on, in the database.

After you've entered the database properties in the portal-ext.properties file, you must restart the Liferay Portal server. During startup, Liferay Portal picks up the new database properties and creates the necessary database elements in the myportaldb database. If your Liferay Portal server starts without any errors, you can safely assume that Liferay Portal has been successfully configured to use myportaldb as the portal database.

Let's now look at some of the tables that Liferay Portal creates in the MySQL database.

B.2.2 *Exploring the Liferay Portal database tables*

When the Liferay Portal server starts up for the first time, it checks for the existence of Liferay Portal–specific tables that store configuration information, like the default portal administrator, in the database. If the database is empty, Liferay Portal creates the necessary tables and loads setup data into them. In this section, we'll look at some of the tables that Liferay Portal creates for internal use.

> **WARNING** The tables discussed in this section may be different for different versions of Liferay Portal. The tables discussed here are generic in nature and show what information a portal server usually saves in its internal database. The example tables shown in this appendix are from Liferay Portal 6.0.5.

PORTAL USER INFORMATION IN THE USER_ TABLE
A web portal stores information about the registered users in persistent storage. The USER_ table stores information about the users that are registered with Liferay Portal.

To view data inside a table using HeidiSQL, all you need to do is select the table in HeidiSQL and click on the Data tab, as shown in figure B.6. In this figure, you can see that the USER_ table contains user information such as first name, last name, active/inactive status, screen name, email address, greeting message, and so on.

PORTAL ROLE INFORMATION IN THE ROLE_ TABLE
To provide access to resources based on user roles, every user in the portal is assigned a role. The ROLE_ table in Liferay Portal stores the roles defined in Liferay Portal, as shown in figure B.7. In this figure, you can see that the ROLE_ table contains role information such as role name and description.

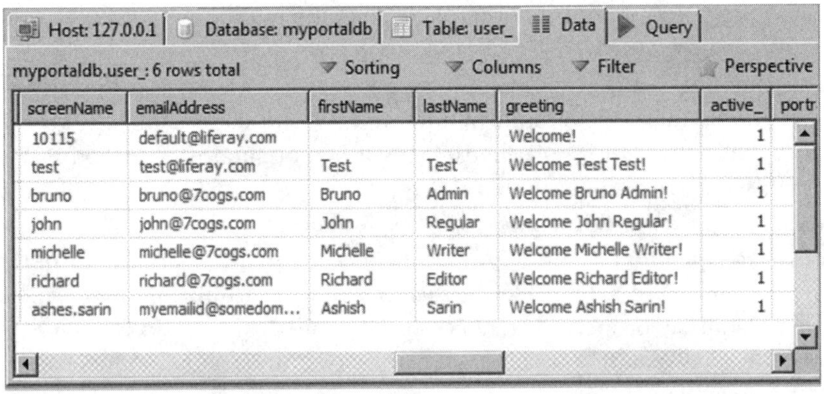

Host: 127.0.0.1 | Database: myportaldb | Table: user_ | Data | Query

myportaldb.user_: 6 rows total — Sorting — Columns — Filter — Perspective

screenName	emailAddress	firstName	lastName	greeting	active_	portr
10115	default@liferay.com			Welcome!	1	
test	test@liferay.com	Test	Test	Welcome Test Test!	1	
bruno	bruno@7cogs.com	Bruno	Admin	Welcome Bruno Admin!	1	
john	john@7cogs.com	John	Regular	Welcome John Regular!	1	
michelle	michelle@7cogs.com	Michelle	Writer	Welcome Michelle Writer!	1	
richard	richard@7cogs.com	Richard	Editor	Welcome Richard Editor!	1	
ashes.sarin	myemailid@somedom...	Ashish	Sarin	Welcome Ashish Sarin!	1	

Figure B.6 The _USER table lists the registered users in Liferay Portal.

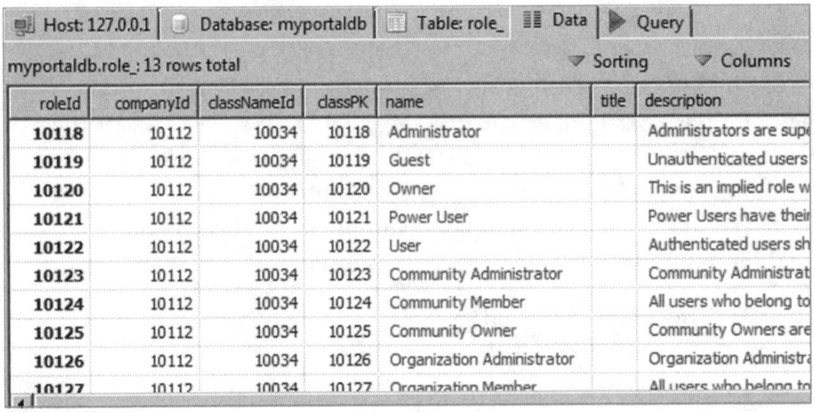

Host: 127.0.0.1 | Database: myportaldb | Table: role_ | Data | Query

myportaldb.role_: 13 rows total — Sorting — Columns

roleId	companyId	classNameId	classPK	name	title	description
10118	10112	10034	10118	Administrator		Administrators are sup
10119	10112	10034	10119	Guest		Unauthenticated users
10120	10112	10034	10120	Owner		This is an implied role w
10121	10112	10034	10121	Power User		Power Users have their
10122	10112	10034	10122	User		Authenticated users sh
10123	10112	10034	10123	Community Administrator		Community Administrat
10124	10112	10034	10124	Community Member		All users who belong to
10125	10112	10034	10125	Community Owner		Community Owners are
10126	10112	10034	10126	Organization Administrator		Organization Administr
10127	10112	10034	10127	Organization Member		All users who belong to

Figure B.7 The ROLE_ table stores the roles defined in Liferay Portal.

PERMISSIONS INFORMATION IN THE PERMISSION_ TABLE

Liferay Portal provides a fine-grained permissions system for managing permissions in the web portal. A portlet, for example, is a protected resource in a web portal, and by using the Liferay Portal permission system, you can control access to a particular portlet's functionality. For instance, you can define permissions to control access to the Add Book functionality of the Book Catalog portlet.

Figure B.8 shows the PERMISSION_ table, which defines the associations between actions and the resources protected by the portal. In this figure, the PERMISSION_ table contains permission definitions, which map user actions to the resource to which the action applies. For instance, the Add Discussion action applies to the Message Board portlet, which is a resource in the web portal.

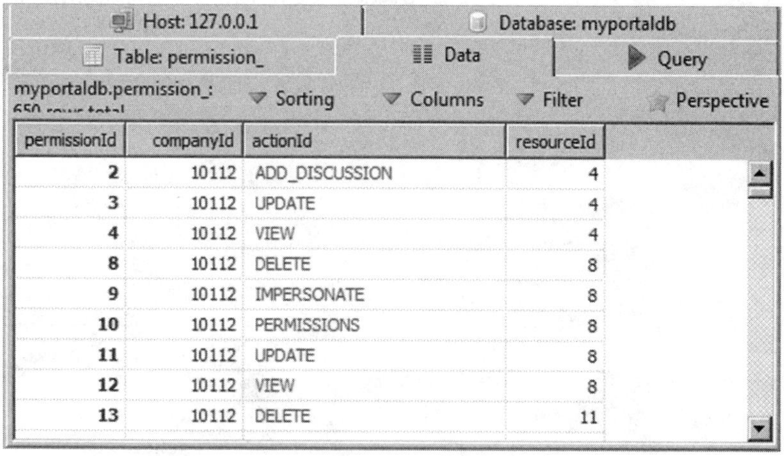

permissionId	companyId	actionId	resourceId
2	10112	ADD_DISCUSSION	4
3	10112	UPDATE	4
4	10112	VIEW	4
8	10112	DELETE	8
9	10112	IMPERSONATE	8
10	10112	PERMISSIONS	8
11	10112	UPDATE	8
12	10112	VIEW	8
13	10112	DELETE	11

Figure B.8   The PERMISSION_ table stores permission definitions for resources in Liferay Portal

WARNING   Even though it is possible to directly access Liferay Portal database tables to retrieve or store data, doing so may result in inconsistencies and security issues. For instance, when directly retrieving data from a Liferay Portal database table, Liferay Portal's permission system is completely bypassed. This poses a serious data security risk.

index